AIR FORCE BLUE

AND

TARGET TIRPITZ

PATRICK BISHOP

AIR FORCE BLUE

AND

TARGET TIRPITZ

**THE RAF'S EPIC ROLE DEFENDING BRITAIN
IN WORLD WAR TWO**

WILLIAM
COLLINS

William Collins
An imprint of HarperCollins*Publishers*
1 London Bridge Street
London SE1 9GF

www.WilliamCollinsBooks.com

This omnibus edition first published by William Collins in 2018

1

Air Force Blue: First published in Great Britain by William Collins in 2017
Copyright © Patrick Bishop 2017
Maps by John Gilkes

Target Tirpitz: First published in Great Britain by HarperPress in 2012
Copyright © Patrick Bishop 2012
Diagrams © Andrew Pinder 2012

Patrick Bishop asserts the moral right to
be identified as the author of this work

ISBN 978-0-00-797435-1

A catalogue record for this book is
available from the British Library

Printed and bound in Great Britain by
CPI Group (UK) Ltd, Croydon

MIX
Paper from
responsible sources
FSC C007454

This book is produced from independently certified FSC paper
to ensure responsible forest management.

For more information visit: www.harpercollins.co.uk/green

PATRICK BISHOP

AIR FORCE BLUE

THE RAF IN WORLD WAR TWO

WILLIAM
COLLINS

TO HEN

ANGEL GIRL IN CHIEF

Contents

Contents

Maps

Fighter Command's area
of operations 1940

Main Bomber Command
stations in the UK

North
Sea

0   10   20   30   40   50
miles

O Group HQ
• Airfield

• Croft

Leeming
•

• Thirsk
Skipton-on-   • Topcliffe   • Wombleton
Swale
Dishforth   • Dalton
• Tholthorpe
Linton-on-Ouse •   • East Moor   Carnaby •
Allerton O   Full Sutton •   Driffield •
Marston Moor •   Lissett •
Rufforth •   O YORK • Pocklington
Elvington •   • Leconfield
Riccall •   • Melbourne
Breighton   • Holme-on-Spalding-Moor
Burn •
Snaith •   • North Killingholme
Elsham Wolds
Sandtoft   • Kirmington
Lindholme •   SCUNTHORPE
Doncaster •   • Finningley   • Grimsby
Bircotes • O   • Blyton   • Binbrook
Bawtry   Sturgate   • Hemswell   • Kelstern
Worksop •   Faldingworth •   • Wickenby   • Strubby
Ingham •   • Dunholme Lodge   Ludford Magna
Gamston •   Scampton •   • Fiskerton
LINCOLN   • Bardney   • Spilsby
Ossington •   • Wigsley   Skellingthorpe •   • East Kirkby
Swinderby O   • Woodhall Spa
Winthorpe •   • Coningsby
Waddington •   Balderton • Fulbeck   Metheringham •
Syerston •
Newton •   • Bottesford   • North Creake
Langar   O Grantham   • Little Snoring
• Church Broughton   Sculthorpe •   • Oulton
O Eggington   Foulsham •   • Swannington
• Tatenhill   • Castle Donington • Saltby   Great Massingham •   • Attlebridge
Lichfield •   Wymeswold   • Cottesmore   West Raynham •   O Bylaugh   Horsham St Faith
• Woolfox Lodge   Swanton Morley •   Hall   •
North Luffenham •   Downham Market •   Marham •
• Watton
Nuneaton •   Methwold •   • Bodney
• Bramcote   Bruntingthorpe   Market   Polebrook •   Feltwell •   • East Wretham
Bitteswell •   Harborough   • Upwood   Mepal •   • Lakenheath
Husbands Bosworth •   Desborough •   Warboys •   • Witchford   Mildenhall •   • Honington
Harrington •   Alconbury •   Waterbeach •   • Tuddenham
• Honiley   Molesworth •   Huntington O   Wyton •   • Exning
Wellesbourne   Graveley •   Oakington •   Newmarket •
Mountford   Kimbolton •   Bourn •   • Chedburgh
• Gaydon   Little Staughton •   CAMBRIDGE   • Stradishall
• Stratford   • Chipping Warden   Tempsford •   Gransden Lodge •   • Wattisham
Edgehill •   Bassingbourn •   Wratting Common •   Woodbridge •
Hinton-in-the-Hedges •   • Silverstone   • Cranfield   Steeple Morden •   • Ridgewell
Croughton •   • Turweston
Barford St John •   • Little Horwood
Finmere •   O Winslow
Enstone •   • Bicester   • Wing
Upper Heyford •   • Westcott   • Cheddington
Weston-on-the-Green •   O Oakley

Mount Farm •   ⚑
Benson •
High Wycombe
Hampstead •   HQ Bomber Command
Norris

LONDON

N
W   E
S

Main targets in Europe

0   100   200   300
miles

Range circles are measured from Lincoln

⊙ ○   Bomb targets

N

Stockholm

Baltic Sea

EAST
PRUSSIA

• Minsk

SOVIET
UNION

gen

Sassnitz
Peenemünde
de   ⊙ Swinemünde
⊙ Stettin

Danzig ⊙

• Warsaw

POLAND

MANY
⊙

au

Dresden
⊙
nnitz

• Krakow

Prague •

⊙
Pilsen

CZECHOSLOVAKIA

erg
andorf
Regensburg

• Linz

Vienna •

• Bratislava

RUMANIA

nich
ntesgaden ⊙⊙

AUSTRIA

HUNGARY

• Budapest

Bucharest •

• Trieste

YUGOSLAVIA

Belgrade •

BULGARIA

ALY

Adriatic Sea

• Sophia

Rome

Naples

Bizerta
Sidi Omar
Tunis

Algiers
Sétif   Constantine

TUNISIA

Sfax

Mareth

ALGERIA

Sicily

MALTA

Mediterranea

Tripoli

Bengha

TRIPOLITANIA

LIBYA

Abu Sueir

Maiduguri ● ● Fort Lamy
● Kano
Geneina   Khartoum

● Lagos
Takoradi

Takoradi Route

The Mediterranean, Levant and Southern Europe

N
W E
S

100   200   300
miles

Black Sea

Athens

CRETE

CYPRUS   SYRIA

LEBANON
Beirut
Damascus

Sea

but   Bardia
Tobruk
El Adem
Sidi Rezegh
Sollum
Halfaya
Mersa Matruh
Sidi Haneish
Sidi Barrani
Ma'aten Bagush

Alexandria
Aboukir

Fuka
El Alamein

PALESTINE
Jerusalem

TRANS-
JORDAN

Abu Sueir
Port Tewfik

AICA

Cairo

EGYPT

to RAF Shaibah
(Basra)

Red
Sea

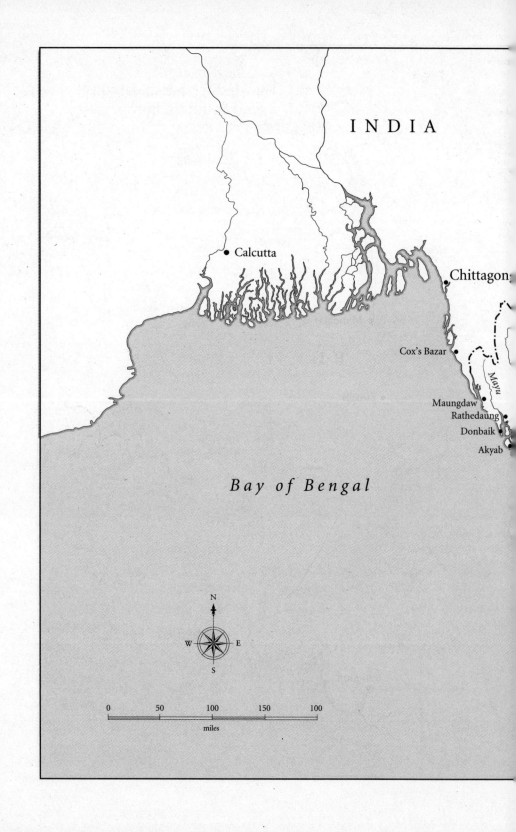

INDIA

• Calcutta

Chittagon

Cox's Bazar

Maungdaw
Rathedaung
Donbaik •
Akyab

Mayu

Bay of Bengal

N
W E
S

0   50   100   150   100

miles

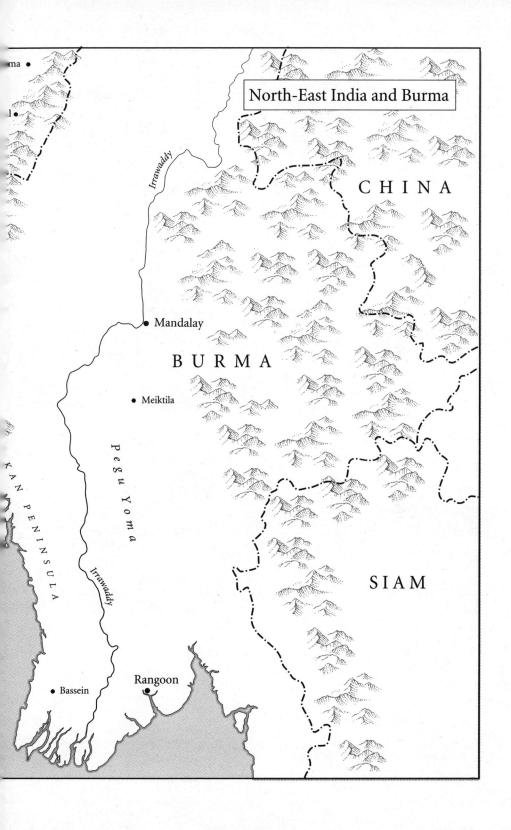

North-East India and Burma

CHINA

Irrawaddy

Mandalay

BURMA

Meiktila

P e g u   Y o m a

Irrawaddy

SIAM

KAN PENINSULA

Bassein

Rangoon

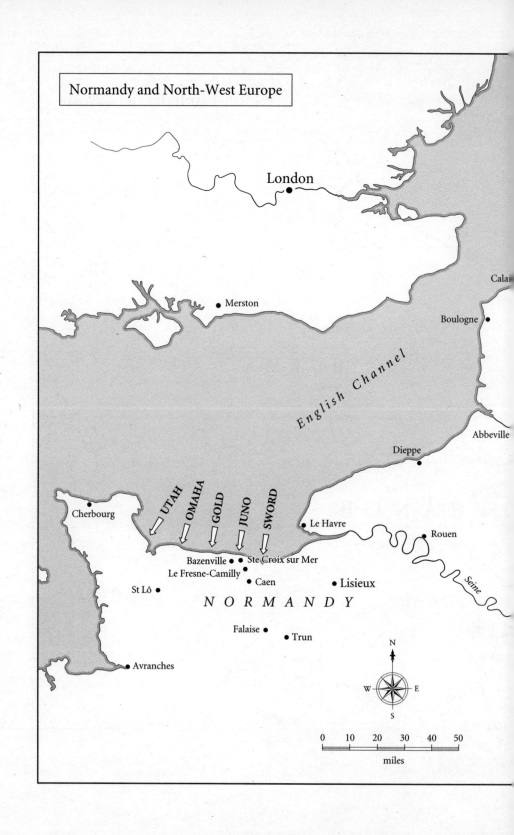

Normandy and North-West Europe

London

Merston

Cala

Boulogne

English Channel

Abbeville

Dieppe

Cherbourg

UTAH
OMAHA
GOLD
JUNO
SWORD

Le Havre

Rouen

Bazenville
Ste Croix sur Mer
Le Fresne-Camilly
Caen
Lisieux
St Lô

Seine

NORMANDY

Falaise
Trun

Avranches

N

W   E

S

0   10   20   30   40   50

miles

North
Sea

NETHERLANDS

Oosterbeek ●
Arnhem ●

Klundert ● Breda

Schelde

nkirk ●

✈ Grimbergen airbase

Brussels ● ✈ Evere airbase

Lille ●

BELGIUM

Meuse

GERMANY

FRANCE

Aisne

Paris ●

Seine

Prologue

Firstway

In the spring of 1944 the chief information officer with the Royal Air Force permanent delegation in Washington, DC, reported back to London on how the service was regarded on the other side of the Atlantic. 'We cannot hope to *enhance* the prestige of the RAF,' he wrote. 'Throughout the world it is a household word, and in the United States its reputation is so high that in some quarters it is almost regarded as something apart from, and superior to, Britain.'[1]

The Americans were not easily impressed. Since joining the war they had become the dominant partners in the alliance and the attitude of US commanders towards the British Army and Navy could be tinged with a condescension that was sometimes amused and often exasperated.

The information officer's report, smug though it sounded, was essentially accurate. The RAF *was* seen differently. Unlike the other services, it attracted quasi-automatic admiration and respect. American airmen regarded their British comrades as something like equals; energetic, efficient and providing an operational contribution that added real weight to the Allied war effort.

In March 1944 when the report was written, Britain and the US had settled on the command structure for the forthcoming great invasion of northern Europe, and Dwight D. Eisenhower was chosen as Supreme Allied Commander. Eisenhower knew who he wanted as his second-in-command: Arthur Tedder of the RAF, who he had got to know intimately during the Mediterranean and Italian campaigns. 'Ike' had been Tedder's best man when he married for the second time. Tedder was Eisenhower's 'warm personal friend'[2] and the man he most admired and trusted among the British high command.

The US military's assessment of the quality and worth of their allies was based initially on observation, then on direct experience. For the first ten months of the war the Army's record was one of debacle and defeat in Norway and France ending in the ignominy of Dunkirk. In North Africa, it floundered against a weaker enemy, and a golden chance for a quick ending was squandered when Churchill decided to switch forces to Greece in a hopeless attempt to stem the Nazi invasion. The eventual victory at El Alamein was the result of a marked numerical superiority in men, guns, tanks and aircraft. It was the first and last time that a British and Commonwealth force would beat the Germans on their own. Thereafter almost all of the Army's effort in the West would be in conjunction with, and ultimately subordinate to, the Americans.

At sea, the war disobligingly failed to develop along the lines that the Admiralty had planned for. There would be no major fleet show-down between the Royal Navy and the Kriegsmarine and the huge and expensive battleships the admirals set such store by absorbed commensurate resources and manpower, which had to be diverted from more productive activities in order to protect them. The Navy did, of course, secure at great cost and effort the sea lanes that kept Britain in the war, but the Battle of the Atlantic was a struggle for survival rather than an advance towards victory. Fighting it took all their time and British warships did not contribute anything to the US Navy's campaign in the Pacific until January 1945.

The information officer's belief that the Air Force was perceived as something 'apart from' and 'superior to' Britain was telling. The Americans did not do sentimentality. The notion that cultural and historical connections meant that Britain was owed deference had long ago vanished. Some in the British military and political establishment did not seem to have noticed that things had changed. Transatlantic visitors were used to being talked down to by their hosts, who drew on centuries of imperial wisdom to instruct and correct. Americans believed they had little to learn from a nation that was fast losing its world-power status and in the space of a generation had twice been forced to turn to them for salvation.

Their dealings with the RAF brought a pleasant surprise. In the early autumn of 1940, when America was still more than a year away from entering the war but already supplying Britain with materiel, a delegation toured Egypt. Colonel Harvey S. Burwell of the US Army Air Forces (USAAF) was greatly impressed by the spirit of the pilots and ground crews, praising their 'superb morale, extraordinary patience and wonderful courage'.[3] He met Tedder, then head of the RAF's Middle East Command, and some of his senior officers and was relieved to find that 'the [British] supercilious superiority so objectionable to Americans is rarely exhibited'. The impression persisted so that the information officer was able to state in his 1944 report from Washington that 'many people who dislike the British would not say a word against the RAF'.[4]

This image of unstuffiness was reinforced by a well-orchestrated stateside propaganda effort, promoting the RAF's achievements and personalities. Guy Gibson, hero of the May 1943 Dams Raid, was pressed into service as an ambassador. In September that year he swept across North America charming interviewers, reporters and radio audiences and receiving the sort of reception normally accorded to movie stars. Humility was not a quality readily associated with Gibson at home. Abroad, however, he was seen as a 'thoroughly nice, modest young man with a good sense of humour'.[5]

Above all, he was unmistakeably a great warrior. The Dams Raid was an epic feat of arms. It immediately attracted the attention of the Hollywood director Howard Hawks, who invited Gibson to stay with him in Los Angeles. Hawks commissioned a script from Flight Lieutenant Roald Dahl, a former fighter pilot then serving as a press attaché in Washington (though this version foundered on the objections of Barnes Wallis, the scientific brains behind the operation).

The Air Force projected confidence, aggression and efficiency. Whatever the Americans thought about Britain's contribution on land and sea, no one could deny that in the air it more than pulled its weight. The first American bombs fell on Europe in August 1942. In the twenty-nine months that followed, the USAAF never matched the tonnages showered down by the RAF. It was only in January 1945 that they began to pull ahead. The final balance showed that, in the bombing war in Europe, Bomber Command dropped 873,348 tons of ordnance and the United States Eighth Air Force 621,438.[6] In this field of the great Allied endeavour in the West, the British were seen to deliver more and suffer more than the US in both men and machines.[7]

At the business of strategic bombing, British aircraft were the best in the world. The Avro Lancaster and Handley Page Halifax were the same size as their American counterparts, the Boeing B-17 Flying Fortress and Consolidated B-24 Liberator. However, they carried much heavier bomb loads; 10,000lb against the Fortress's 5,000lb.[8]

So when Americans looked at the RAF they saw an organization that did not conform to their notions of Britishness but something more akin to themselves, matching them for ambition, efficiency and swagger. Military forces mirror the values of the society they spring from. The image of Britain that the RAF presented in the glass was not the same as that reflected by the Army and the Navy. The old services represented the past. The airmen were the incarnation of how new Britons viewed themselves: modern, competent, democratic and reluctant to give to those above them the automatic deference that had hitherto been expected.

This picture of the RAF was widely accepted both inside and outside its ranks. As a result of the great attention paid to it by the press, the radio and the newsreels, the Air Force came to be seen as a repository of a new set of national values. It was a development that suited the government's information strategy and it was soon endorsed as a recurrent trope of British propaganda. The approach carried hidden risks. In it was contained an implicit promise that the ethos the RAF enshrined would be given political expression and influence the future shape and direction of the country once the war was won.

As the conflict approached, the people of Britain absorbed the idea that the Air Force would play the dominant role in the coming struggle, as the guarantors of their survival and the agents of eventual victory. On 1 October 1938, the first issue of the weekly news magazine *Picture Post* appeared. It was lively, outspoken, thoroughly modern in outlook and almost immediately won a big circulation and considerable political influence. The second issue carried a long article entitled simply 'The RAF', part of a series intended to shed light on 'our great national institutions'.[9] It was written by Nigel Tangye, a young journalist-about-town who was also a pilot and officer in the RAF reserve. Tangye had good connections with the Air Ministry and it would have been surprising if he had not checked with them before making the momentous claim that 'the RAF holds today a position of importance higher than the Army or Royal Navy'. The duties of the Air Force of protecting the national territory, preserving vital sea trade routes, defending the empire and lending aid to allies amounted to 'everything which for hundreds of years has been the function of the Royal Navy'.

Publicity frequently stressed its 'democratic' nature, compared to the other services. 'Officers and men in the Royal Air Force share a common spirit which is unknown either in the Army or the Navy,' wrote Tangye. 'So much of the Navy's time is spent in scrubbing decks, so much of the Army's in massed drilling. But the Air Force Machines have to fly every day, and the crews of each are bent on keeping them in tip-top condition.'

It was never presented as a classless organization. That would have been too much to claim in a society which, though lines were blurring, was still strictly defined by birth, money, education, accent and manners. It did, however, seem something like a meritocracy in which the near-revolutionary notion that competence was more important than background had taken hold.

The Air Force needed a large cadre of expert tradesmen to keep it flying. They came, largely, from the lower-middle and upper-working classes, and the educational gap between other ranks and officers was consequently narrower than in the Army and Navy. The need for aircrew opened the door to the officers' mess to young men who would never have passed muster in the 1920s and 1930s.

The literary types sent in the early years of the war by the Air Ministry on fact-finding tours of bases to gather propaganda material were struck by the varied origins of the officers they encountered. The Oxford don Lord David Cecil noted after a visit to a bomber station in 1941 how 'compared with the Army or Navy the men of the RAF seem very diverse … very varied … drawing its members from every sort of rank and profession'.[10]

Sitting down to dinner in the mess he found on one side of him 'a boy fresh from a public school; on the other side a bank clerk; opposite, a New Zealander, next to him a garage worker, next to him a law student'.

The service was too young, he concluded, to have 'evolved a traditional type' to which all must conform: 'Their upper lips are not too stiff. On the whole their manners tend to be expansive. There is often a touch of jaunty flamboyance in the way they walk and speak and wear their uniforms, with an elegant identification bracelet glinting on the wrist.'

Air Force style was in bright contrast to the dowdiness of the other services. As a boy watching the build-up to D-Day around his home in the West Country the military historian John Keegan was disappointed that the British soldiers he saw 'wore khaki from top to toe ... so ill-cut, shapeless and hairy that I could find almost nothing in its wearers to admire'.[11] When the Americans arrived he and his school friends were amazed at 'how different they looked from our own jumble-sale champions, beautifully clothed in smooth khaki ...' They were even more impressed by the 'number, size and elegance of the vehicles in which they paraded about the countryside in stately convoy', so unlike the 'sad collection of underpowered makeshifts, whose dun paint flaked from their tin pot bodywork' that the Army had to make do with.

No one had to feel sorry for the RAF. The aircrew could equal their Yank counterparts in swank and dash and even the earthbound 'erk' had the edge over his 'brown job' and matelot comrades. Their uniform may have been of serge but they wore a collar and tie to go to work and their hair, curling from under their distinctive two-button side caps at a length that would have given a sergeant-major apoplexy, was as like as not gleaming with Brylcreem.

It was no longer the case that all the nice girls loved a sailor. In October 1939 'Just An Airman' wrote to Picture Post complaining that after joining the Air Force his girlfriend had dumped him and since then he had found that 'no decent girl seems to look at an airman'. He went on: 'I am five feet 10 inches tall, good at sports and reasonably good looking. Once I had girlfriends. Now the only place I seem welcome is at the public house.'[12]

His self-pitying and possibly self-serving missive produced an avalanche of positive responses, a selection of which was printed over a double-page spread. 'I, as a young lady of nineteen, was very surprised to read your correspondent's letter,' wrote Joyce Dickinson of London Road, Rainham, Gillingham, Kent.[13] 'Many young ladies, including myself, admire members of the Royal Air Force and feel especially proud when we read of their daring and brave exploits on the Western Front and over Germany. He may rest assured that although one girl has turned him down, many of us would like the opportunity to make his acquaintance.'

From Wallasey in Cheshire 'An Admirer' declared: 'I think many readers will agree with me when I say that the RAF is the finest of the three services. I am not saying anything against the Navy or the Army ... but I prefer the Air Force.'

It was little wonder that when conscription began more men exercised their right of choice in favour of the Air Force over the other services. The RAF seemed immune to the criticism that the Army in particular sometimes attracted. The war in the air got off to just as bad a start as it did on land and sea. Bomber Command's early record was one of continuous failure and heavy, pointless losses, and the pattern was maintained by all branches of the service in the campaigns in Norway and France. Government propaganda and a co-operative media skated over this truth.

Then, in the summer of 1940, in full view of the population, Fighter Command won the Battle of Britain, supercharging national morale and gilding the Air Force with an aura of success that never tarnished. 'The RAF are the darlings of the nation!' wrote John Thornley, a twenty-nine-year-old salesman from Preston, Lancashire, in his diary in July 1940.[14] 'What magnificent chaps the RAF pilots must be,' he declared a month later as the Battle approached its climax.

By the end of the summer its reputation seemed unassailable. Britain's city-dwellers proved remarkably willing to overlook Fighter Command's inability to protect them from the nightly Blitzes that devastated their homes in the winter of 1940–41, preferring to blame politicians for the lack of counter-measures. Major flaws in the Air Staff's thinking and preparations such as its blind faith in strategic bombing and the initial failures to co-operate effectively with the Army and Navy were never really exposed to public view. The RAF's numerous critics in the upper echelons of the other services complained that it appeared subject to different rules from the ones they had to obey. Often it seemed a law unto itself, holding, in the opinion of the soldier-historian Bernard Fergusson, 'an unwritten charter direct from the war Cabinet' that allowed it to direct bombing policy and decide on what types of aircraft were needed without having to consult with soldier and sailor colleagues.[15]

In two previous books, *Fighter Boys* (2003) and *Bomber Boys* (2008) I told the story of the RAF in the Battle of Britain and the Strategic Offensive against Germany, conveying events, emotions and attitudes as much as possible from the perspectives of the participants. In this final work in the trilogy, I hope to extend the field of vision to the whole of the Second World War. A comprehensive history is impossible in one volume. There was too much being done by too many people. Instead I have tried to examine essential aspects of the RAF wartime experience, both for those flying and those on the ground in selected battles and theatres, in the process, I hope, colouring in the RAF's distinct identity. So this is not a chronicle of the war in the air. It is about the spirit of the Air Force, its heart and soul.

Again, I have tried to see things through the eyes of the players, relying wherever possible on contemporary documents, diaries and letters and, where they are not available, memoirs and reminiscences. I was lucky enough to meet and interview many veterans during my earlier research and could draw on their memories of other parts of their service not covered in previous books. There is, I was pleased to discover, still much rich material lying undiscovered in the archives which provides new evidence and insights.

This book is about many things but a recurrent theme is the special relationship that the Air Force enjoyed with the nation at this uniquely testing time in its history. For much of the war the RAF was Britain and Britain was the RAF. The conflict arrived in the middle of a time of great transformation, when British characteristics and attitudes were undergoing profound changes.

Among the girls who responded to 'Just An Airman' was Joyce Robinson of Firstway, Raynes Park, London SW20. She, too, was an Air Force fan, admiring 'the spirit of adventure which prompts a man to join'.[16] The street is half a mile from where I grew up. It was built in the 1920s by an energetic master builder called George Blay who turned much of what was then countryside into suburbia. It is a tree-lined cul-de-sac of nice, three-bedroomed terraced houses, with bay windows, timberwork on the façades and ample back gardens. They cost £675 (with 85 per cent mortgages available) and were a few minutes' walk from Raynes Park station on the Southern Electric railway which ran straight in to Waterloo. Thousands of streets like Firstway were springing up around Britain's cities at the same time.

The families who lived in them were members of the most overlooked and underappreciated stratum of the social layer cake – the lower-middle class. The cautious patriarchs of these 'quadrants', 'crescents', 'drives' and 'walks' left each morning for their jobs as clerks, draughtsmen, shopkeepers and minor civil servants while Mum stayed home to clean and cook. Their children raised their eyes to broader horizons. I have not managed to discover anything about Joyce Robinson but I have imagined her: playing tennis at the club round the corner in Taunton Avenue, watching Clark Gable in *Gone With the Wind* at the Raynes Park Rialto, taking the District Line to Hammersmith to dance at the Palais, perhaps driving with a boyfriend to a roadhouse on the Kingston by-pass.

It was this emerging Britain which provided the wartime Air Force with much of its man- and womanpower as well as enriching its identity and ethos. There were fewer men and women in Air Force blue than there were in Navy blue or khaki. The Second World War was nonetheless in many ways an RAF show. From the beginning to the end it was the spearhead of almost every action and effort. Not only did it lead the way to victory, it shaped the contours of peace.

1

The Big One

The faint feeling of dread that was always there in the bad old days was absent this morning. Dawn was still several hours away and inside the chilly briefing room eighteen crews from 9 Squadron were gathered to hear their orders. They smoked and chatted, waiting for the CO to arrive to reveal the location of the target. Occasionally there was a burst of laughter. Today the hilarity sounded unforced and not just a cover for jangling nerves. The date was 25 April 1945 and Germany was in its death throes. One precious thought united the 126 men present: in twelve hours' time their war might be over and they would never have to do this again.

If so, it seemed likely they were going out with a bang. The previous evening the CO had toured the messes advising drinkers to take it easy as 'something special' was in the offing.[1] The word from Flights was that the fuel order was for 2,154 gallons per aircraft.[2] That meant an extra-long trip. And what was the BBC doing here? Next to the platform at the front of the room a reporter and technician were fiddling with microphone and disc recorder.

The large map of Europe on the wall behind the platform offered a clue. It was the first thing the crews looked at when they trooped in. The red tape that traced their route to the target 'started at Bardney, our base, ran down to the South Coast and across the Channel,' remembered Flight Sergeant Fred Whitfield, who, though 'tour expired' after completing thirty trips as a rear gunner, had volunteered to carry on.[3] 'At that point it diverted across France on a dog leg and ended up in Southern Germany.' Whitfield's first thought was that it 'looked like a daylight raid on Munich'.

The orderly officer called the crews to attention and with a scraping of chairs they got to their feet as Wing Commander Bazin walked down the aisle followed by his specialist officers, stepped onto the dais and began the briefing.

Jim Bazin, DFC and bar, seemed indestructible. Born in Imperial India, raised in a comfortable middle-class family in the North East of Britain, he served as a part-timer in an RAF auxiliary squadron for four years before the war and fought from the first day to what was now surely almost the last. By any reckoning of the odds he should have been dead several times over. Whatever terrors he had experienced had left no outward mark on him. When he spoke, it was in a cultured, amused accent, more like a university professor than a warrior.

'Well, Gentlemen,' he announced. 'This is the big one.'[4] He explained that at this late stage in the war they were being given a chance to land a blow on the man who had started it all. They were off to bomb Hitler's mountain retreat at Berchtesgaden. 'Your particular aiming point for this attack is the house where this gentleman is supposed to live,' he told them. 'Whether he's there is another matter.' He paused for a second before going on. 'But no doubt there will be plenty of people there to benefit from it.'[5] The room rocked with laughter.

They settled down as the met, navigation and intelligence officers delivered the weather forecast and took them through the technicalities of route, plan of attack and expected opposition. When they finally filed out into the Lincolnshire night, heavy with the muddy smell of the surrounding fields, everyone was talking excitedly. They had all heard of Berchtesgaden, of course. To the older ones who remembered it from pre-war newsreels, it brought back memories of Chamberlain and Munich and national humiliation. For the younger airmen it was a name from the news bulletins, one of the three main military headquarters from which Hitler directed his forces. None of those who planned Bomber Command operations had seen fit to attack it before. Now, for reasons that no one explained in the briefing, the time had finally come.

The sky was clear and the moon, one day away from fullness, silvered the ridges of the potato fields surrounding the base. The aerodrome stood just north of the village of Bardney on the plain which stretches north from the Lincolnshire fenlands to the rising hills of the Wolds. It was one of more than a hundred bomber stations built during the early years of the war, a standard pattern of three concrete runways and three hangars, interspersed with utilitarian huts and sheds where the airmen, ground crews and WAAFs ate, washed and slept.[6]

There were two hours to take-off and much to be done beforehand. Operations boiled down to a succession of routines which had to be followed to the letter if you wanted to succeed and survive. But first they would eat, a meal that had long ago become a cliché: bacon and eggs and wodges of bread and margarine, washed down with American canned orange juice and mahogany-coloured tea.

They cleared their plates and headed for the crew room to climb into multi-layered flying gear and pick up their parachutes. For those who needed it there was a detour to the latrines to empty their bowels before they all climbed into canvas-covered four-ton lorries that trundled them out to dispersal where the bombers loomed, casting long moon shadows on the tarmac. The ground crew had been there for hours, refuelling, bombing up, checking the control surfaces and undercarriage, fussing over the machine as if it was their own lives that were at stake.

Those flying were swaddled like Michelin men but it still felt cold. The metal tube of the fuselage carried its own special chill. They climbed the five rungs of the ladder, through the hatch behind the gun turret amidships, and struggled to their posts. Pilot, flight engineer, navigator, bomb aimer and wireless operator wriggled forward to the nose, clambering over the thick spar that pinned together the bomber's 102-foot wingspan. The gunners settled into their solitary nests behind them.

Each man began to run through the litany of checks and drills, second nature now from years of training and practice. For the gunners it took a few minutes. For the pilot and flight engineer it was more like half an hour. Then the pilot shouted down to the ground crew that he was 'ready for starting'. A mechanic jumped forward to work the Ki-Gas pump and prime the carburettor of the first engine. Someone swung a white torch to indicate which engine to fire up first. From his seat, squeezed in next to the pilot, the flight engineer flipped on booster coil and main ignition switches and opened the master fuel cock. The pilot thumbed the starter button and with an explosive thud and a volley of flame and smoke, one by one the Merlin engines burst into life, filling the rural silence with a deep-throated roar. In the farms and villages around the bomber bases the noise was now as familiar as birdsong.

More minutes passed before the dials showed every engine had reached the right temperature and pressure. It was a laborious business but there was no rushing it. The machine was what got you there and got you home. This day of all days, with the finishing line in sight, was no time to get careless.

A-Able was the first away. It was 5 a.m. and still pitch-black but the clear sky promised a fine day. The Lancaster moved off jerkily, stopping and starting as the pilot tested the flaps and brakes. It rolled onto the runway, waiting for the signal on the Aldis lamp mounted on the control van to flash from red to green. Lining the tarmac were the usual party of WAAFs and ground staff gathered to wave and smile and pray for a safe return. This morning there were others present. Standing among them were the BBC reporter and soundman who had been at the briefing. That evening the journalist's report, delivered in a bright, modern voice, very different from the plummy tones of the pre-war Corporation, would go out on the evening news:

'Hallo BBC. This is Brian Bliss with Bomber Command. It's Zero Hour, the attack is on and the first Lancaster's swinging into position at the head of the runway right opposite me now ... here she comes ... remember this is the squadron which sank the *Tirpitz* and now they're off to Berchtesgaden with twelve thousand pounders. *Twelve thousand pounders!* And they're taking the attack literally to Hitler's doorstep!'[7] Millions of listeners heard the engine note rising sharply as the revs climbed, then fading as Bliss, almost shouting now, announced that 'A-Able is off ... a marvellous sight as she races by!'

In Q-Queenie, rear gunner Fred Whitfield sat in his turret and waited with the rest of the crew for their turn. After thirty operations together they knew each other as well as they did their own families.

They were ordinary men from all over Britain. The pilot, Ron Adams, came from Wembley, London, Larry Brown the flight engineer was from Leeds, bomb aimer Phil Jackson from Nottingham, navigator Jim Lynam from Scunthorpe, wireless operator Jack Faucheux from Romford and the mid-upper gunner Frank Stebbings from Tunbridge Wells. Fred Whitfield was a Geordie, born in South Shields.

Starting operations in the aftermath of D-Day, they had bombed V weapons sites, marshalling yards, bridges and U-boat pens, before resuming the assault on German cities. They had been shot up by a night fighter and only made it home thanks to the skill and determination of 'Lucky' Adams who, though only twenty-one, was in Whitfield's eyes 'the best pilot in the RAF'. The gunners gave as good as they got. Whitfield and Stebbings had several kills to their credit, and the crew's 'press-on' spirit had earned them four Distinguished Flying Medals and one Distinguished Service Cross between them. It had needed courage, skill and the closest teamwork to come through these trials and their faith in each other was strong. The raid they were about to embark on seemed less hazardous than most. But everyone knew of a crew that had bought it on their last mission. While he waited Whitfield 'closed my eyes for a couple of minutes and had a few words with my God'.[8]

Then Q-Queenie was shuddering with the pent-up kinetic energy of four Merlin engines as Ron Adams jammed on the brakes and opened the throttle to maximum revs. He eased off and the Lancaster bounded forward. At about 50 knots (57mph) Whitfield 'felt the turret lift as the tail wheel left the ground. "90 knots, 100 knots, 120 knots," said the engineer, reading the speed. The skipper eased back on the control column. Queenie was airborne. We climbed, slowly gaining height.'

Once all aircraft were at 10,000 feet they formed a loose gaggle, and set course for Cap Gris Nez near their rendezvous with the squadron with whom they would be spearheading the raid. 617 Squadron were friends and rivals and their base was only a few miles from Bardney at Woodhall Spa. The two operated together often, specializing in missions requiring great skill and accuracy, and as Brian Bliss reminded his listeners six months before had finished off Hitler's last remaining battleship with a volley of 'earth-quake' bombs as she lay crippled in Tromsø fjord. The exploit had added extra lustre to the reputation of 617, already famous as the Dam Busters. However, as their sister squadron liked to point out, they were relative sprogs in the bombing game, having been created only two years earlier, whereas 9 Squadron dated back to 1914 and had been in continuous action from the very start of the war.

The sister squadrons made up just a small part of a huge force bearing down on Berchtesgaden. The pre-dawn sky of eastern England was thick with aircraft heading in the same direction. Three hundred and fifty-nine bombers were being thrown into the attack. Guiding them were sixteen Mosquitoes from Path Finder Force, equipped with special navigation aids to fix the target, tucked, safely until now, in the folds of the Bavarian Alps. Only five years before, an armada of this size was a distant fantasy. Yet this was not even the biggest raid of the day. An even larger formation was heading off to the North Sea island of Wangerooge, to smash up shore batteries that menaced Allied shipping delivering supplies to the port of Bremen for the armies encircling Berlin.

The RAF of April 1945 bore little resemblance to the organization Jim Bazin had joined eleven years before. In that time it had expanded enormously, evolving from a tight, professional elite drawn mainly from the top layers of society into a vast structure, more than a million strong. It had long ceased to be an overwhelm-ingly British enterprise. Scattered among the squadrons today were Poles, Australians, New Zealanders, Rhodesians, Americans, Canadians, Frenchmen and Dutchmen, Norwegians and Danes, only some of the sixty nationalities which had found a home in the Air Force.

The spirit of amateurism that still flickered in the pre-war service had long ago been snuffed out by the demands of war and replaced by a ruthless professionalism. Five years and eight months before, 9 Squadron had taken part in the first proper British air raid of the war. On 4 September 1939, together with 149 Squadron, they flew in appalling weather across the North Sea to attack German warships lying near Brunsbüttel. They had only dead reckoning to get them there and their twin-engine Wellingtons were loaded with primitive bombs. Against great odds, most of the raiders managed to find the target area but it was covered with cloud and fiercely defended by flak and fighters. Only one crew claimed to have hit anything. Two 9 Squadron aircraft were brought down and all ten on board killed. There would be hundreds of other futile sorties before the RAF began to function efficiently as a war machine. Now the process was complete. The days of wasted effort and useless sacrifice were long gone and the British and American air forces enjoyed almost total mastery of the skies of Europe.

The shoals of Lancasters cruised on, dark and ominous in the moonlight, pausing to circle at their rendezvous point above the towns of Arras, Valenciennes and Laon near the Franco-Belgian border. Then, with 9 Squadron and 617 Squadron in the lead, they set off south and east towards the Alps and Berchtesgaden.

The crews had been given their specific targets at early morning briefings at nineteen bases spread over the bomber counties of Yorkshire, Lincolnshire, Nottinghamshire and Norfolk. The lead squadrons had the most difficult task. Their objectives were, as Bazin warned his men, 'very, very small indeed'[9] and hidden in the pine-covered clefts of a tall mountain range. The first was the Eagle's Nest, a spectacular pavilion, built for Hitler as a retreat and diplomatic reception centre on top of a rocky spur called the Kehlstein, 6,000 feet above sea level. The second was Hitler's house, the Berghof, which sat, five miles down the mountain, on the shoulder of the humped ridge known as the Obersalzberg. The surrounding area was enclosed by fences and guard posts. Inside the security zone some of the leading figures of Hitler's court – Hermann Goering, Martin Bormann and Albert Speer – had built villas and the rock beneath it was honeycombed with bomb shelters and storerooms. The complex also housed a communications centre from where Hitler could keep in touch with his commanders.

The chances of a direct hit on either target were slight. With the armament 9 and 617 Squadrons were carrying, however, perfect accuracy was not essential. At the start of the war the biggest weapon in the RAF's armoury was the 500lb General Purpose bomb. It contained more metal than explosive and many of those produced were duds. Today the thirty-two aircraft of the lead squadrons were carrying 12,000lb 'Tallboys', aerodynamically optimized dart-like missiles devised by the engineering genius Barnes Wallis that plunged deep into the ground before exploding, creating an earthquake effect that devastated everything around.

Behind them came a stream of bombers from the Main Force, the workaday squadrons which had spent the last three years smashing Germany's cities, causing and suffering appalling casualties. They would attack in two waves. Their main objective was the most prominent feature on the Obersalzberg, the barracks which housed the SS troops who guarded Hitler and his entourage.

Was he there or wasn't he? It seemed unlikely, but it was left to squadron commanders to raise or lower the expectations of their men as they saw fit. Bazin had chosen to play down the possibility. Others decided it would be enjoyable to hint that Hitler might well be at home. Either way, this was an operation most were proud to be part of, something to tell the grandchildren they were beginning to allow themselves to believe they might one day have.

The Dam Busters were led by Squadron Leader John Brookes, who was also in overall charge of the operation. The honour should have gone to their CO, Wing Commander Johnny Fauquier but he had been told by his superiors that he had exceeded his permitted number of operations and would not be on the trip. The blunt-spoken Canadian did not bother to hide his annoyance when he spoke to Brookes at the briefing. 'I'd like to have this target in my log book,' he told him. 'In fact I would like to have this target tattooed on my arse, but you have got to lead it.'[10]

The route took the bombers southwards towards Paris. There they turned again, south and east cruising at a steady 145 knots and ninety minutes later saw the snow glowing pink as the sun broke over the ramparts of the Swiss Alps.

At points along the way they were joined by more than two hundred Mustangs from RAF Fighter Command and the US Eighth Air Force. For most of the war the bombers had gone forth alone with only their on-board guns to protect them from flak and fighters. Now long-range escorts shepherded Allied bombers to and from their raids. Today there scarcely seemed a need for them.

H-Hour had been set for 9 a.m. As the bombers droned closer, the people of Berchtesgaden blithely went about their morning routines. Hitler's presence had seemed like a blessing at first, bringing attention and excitement to the valley. The modest villa he had first rented in 1928 had been transformed over the years into something more suited to a man of destiny. The result was what one architectural historian described as 'a combination of *faux* rusticity and imposing grandeur akin to a Thurn und Taxis princess decked out in a haute-couture dirndl'.[11]

At the heart of the house was the Great Hall. It was the size of a hangar, furnished with elephantine armchairs and hung with tapestries and paintings by Italian masters. Set into the northern wall was a picture window, thirty yards square, which, thanks to an ingenious mechanism, wound down into a recess in the floor. It was, enthused Diana Mosley, wife of the Blackshirts' leader Oswald Mosley, 'the largest piece of glass ever made … through it one sees this huge chain of mountains and it looks more like an enormous cinema screen than like reality …'[12]

As well as being the closest thing that Hitler had to a home, the Berghof made useful propaganda. It was a backdrop against which he could demonstrate his more human side. He was pictured in

Uncle Adolf

trilby, loden jacket and flannels, feeding deer and smiling at flaxen-haired little girls. It was a place for relaxation where he breathed the mountain air and stood at the enormous window looking out at the Untersberg, where legend had it that the twelfth-century Holy Roman Emperor Frederick Barbarossa lay sleeping, awaiting the hour when he would rise again and build a German empire that would last for a thousand years.

It was also a place of business, an ideal setting in which to impress or intimidate the politicians who trooped there in the countdown to the war. Stamped in the memories of the older airmen were images of an infamous visit that had taken place six and a half years earlier. On the morning of 15 September 1938 the Prime Minister Neville Chamberlain arrived at Berchtesgaden to try and avert another European conflagration. Hitler was demanding that Czechoslovakia allow the ethnic Germans of the Sudetenland to unite with the fatherland or face invasion. By the end of the meeting, Chamberlain was persuaded it was worth sacrificing Czechoslovakia for the sake of a shameful peace. Twelve months later the Second World War began.

Allied bombers had since wrecked every major German city killing hundreds of thousands. Berchtesgaden had been left alone and was barely touched by the war. The local economy boomed, supplying the Nazi colony which expanded as the elite moved their families and wealth out of bomb-blasted Berlin. Hitler was a frequent visitor. Between 1939 and 1944 he spent more time at the Berghof than he did in the capital, but nine months ago he had left and not been seen again.

That Wednesday morning there was one very senior Nazi in residence, however. Hermann Goering had turned up at his villa to join his family a few days before. He left Berlin on 20 April, Hitler's birthday, and had tried to persuade the Führer to go with him to Berchtesgaden. The overture had been rejected contemptuously. As he drove out of the city and Allied air raids began, Goering and his entourage ducked into a public shelter. 'May I introduce myself,' he declared as the bombs rained down. 'My name is Meyer.' It was a bitter joke. Years before he had promised that if British bombers ever struck Germany 'you may call me Meyer' – a very common

German, and also Jewish, name. Astonishingly, the huddled crowd burst into laughter.[13]

His flight brought him no nearer to safety. On arrival at the villa, Goering had made an ill-judged attempt to take over leadership of the Reich, in accordance with an agreement struck with Hitler in June 1941 that he should assume the powers of the Führer should he be captured or incapacitated. The move was interpreted as an act of treachery, and that morning two senior SS officers had showed up, pistols in hand, to arrest him.

The drama was interrupted when, up and down the valley, the air raid sirens sounded. Despite interference from the mountains on the Pathfinders' 'Gee' electronic navigation systems, the lead aircraft arrived almost exactly on time, just before 9 a.m. Squadron Leader Brookes of 617 squadron was to bomb first. His target was the Eagle's Nest. It was extremely hard to spot from the bombing height of 15–16,000 feet. Neither Brookes nor his bomb aimer were able to identify anything that was worth wasting a Tallboy on. Three of the following aircraft did drop their bombs, but none scored a direct hit.

Then it was 9 Squadron's turn. As they approached the Berghof, the flak batteries set into the valley sides were banging away, pumping up streams of accurate flak at the bombers coming in at between 14,000 and 15,000 feet. Flight Lieutenant G. J. Campbell broadcast later on the BBC that he saw a ridge flash below him as his pilot Flying Officer J. Buckley brought him 'almost dead ahead of the house. I had a perfect run up and released my twelve-thousand pound bomb with the house dead in the sight.'[14]

Campbell's Tallboy was fuzed at twenty-five seconds.[15] From a Lancaster following close behind, rear gunner Flight Sergeant E. J. Cutting watched 'a twelve thousand pounder land about a hundred yards from Hitler's house'.[16] There was 'a terrific flash and though we were flying pretty high we could hear the explosion above the roar of our engines and the whole plane seemed to rock,' he told radio listeners. Then 'great piles of earth came shooting up, high into the sky. I thought to myself well, even if that's a bit short, it must have damaged the place. But just at that moment there was another flash, followed by a huge explosion. One of the other aircraft had planted its twelve thousand pounder bang on the target.'

By now the Main Force squadrons had arrived and the sky over the valley was dangerously crowded with huge aeroplanes. Cutting's pilot reported at the post-operation debrief that 'interference from other aircraft was so great' that he was unable to identify the target on the run-in and was ordered by the master bomber controlling the operation from another Lancaster not to bother making a second effort. Another pilot, Squadron Leader James Melrose, stated that 'just as the bomb aimer was preparing to drop the bomb, the aircraft was narrowly missed by a bomb from [an] aircraft above, and the target was accordingly overshot and it was impossible to bomb'.[17] Fred Whitfield's main concern was the anti-aircraft fire. The gunners had found their range and 'the sky was black with flak'.[18] The bomb aimer, Phil Jackson, seemed unaware of the shells rocking their kite as he talked Ron Adams in. Then Q-Queenie 'appeared to leap a thousand feet in grateful thanks for being relieved of five tons of metal'. Relief was brief. A few seconds later he heard a 'huge bang … we went into a steep dive. The port engine was on fire.' Then came 'another almighty bang' apparently caused by one of the giant bombs hitting the top of the mountain. This blast hurled Q-Queenie upwards, blowing out the flames licking around the engine in the process. Swinging his turret to port Whitfield looked back up the inside of the aircraft for damage and saw jagged holes in the fuselage but the Lancaster flew on unperturbed. As they turned away he had a grandstand view of the Main Force attack.

Their target was the SS barracks, about a hundred yards from the Berghof. From the bellies of the aircraft, 4,000lb, 1,000lb and 500lb bombs tumbled out. Some fell on a hotel next door to the Berghof used for housing visitors, others on the villa of Martin Bormann who had managed to secure a prime spot for his house right next to his master. Emmy Goering was in her bedroom when she heard the first explosion. Her first thought was for her daughter and she 'ran to Edda's room but the governess had already taken her to the shelter', in the cellar of the house.[19] Next, she sought her husband and found him shaving, apparently unconcerned. He told her to go to the shelter but said he would not be joining her. When she insisted on staying with him, he relented. Had he not, his story might have ended there. One bomb landed in the swimming pool a few yards from the window of his study. The blast brought down the roof of the villa and collapsed the main staircase.

The bombs fell on innocent and guilty alike. When the sirens sounded school children were ordered to return home. Ten-year-old Irmgard Hunt was hurrying back with her sister Ingrid and friends when they 'began to hear the droning of bombers overhead'.[20] They were given a lift by a passing SS driver who let them out near their house. As the car drove off the first explosions erupted. The noise of the bombs was 'hellish'. It was followed by 'an enormous storm-like wind that would have blown me off my feet had I not gripped the rough bark of the nearest spruce and pressed myself against it … We waited for a pause after each explosion to race to the next tree before the blast of air hit us'.

They reached home and crouched with their mother in the basement flinching from the 'horrendous noise that engulfed us, even in the cellar'. Next day Irmgard and Ingrid walked back to school. 'As the Obersalzberg came into view we saw the devastation. The plateau had become a chaotic brown-and-black mess of tree stumps that looked like charred matchsticks, dark craters and smoking ruins. "It's all gone", I said to myself.'

Half of the SS barracks was demolished. The villas of the elite were wrecked. Emmy Goering had left her jewellery in the house and was relieved when a servant found it among the wreckage. The Berghof had been gutted and the great picture window that had delighted pre-war guests was no more than a hole in the wall. The bombs had killed thirty-one in their usual indiscriminate fashion, with local civilians and foreign slave workers as well as SS troops among the casualties.

The raiders had suffered, too. Two Lancasters were brought down by flak. One crash-landed without casualties. Another, F-Freddie from 619 Squadron, provided a last story of heroism from the RAF's war. With the machine fatally damaged, the Canadian pilot Wilf DeMarco ordered the crew to jump while he held the aircraft steady. Three got out alive. The other three went down with their skipper.

The bombers landed at their home bases between noon and two o'clock. Because of the battering it had received, Q-Queenie was excused joining the queue of aircraft circling the base and given permission to land at once. Ron Adams made a smooth touchdown and taxied to dispersal where they were met by the ground crew eager to hear their adventures and dispensing cigarettes. After eight hours without a smoke, Fred Whitfield remembered, the first puff 'was pure nectar'.[21] When, in bomber bases up and down the east of England, the crews sat down to be debriefed by station intelligence officers, the same observation was repeated over and over. During the entire eight-hour trip they had not seen a single German aeroplane.

The exploit covered the front pages of the following day's newspapers. 'Hitler's Chalet Wrecked' was the headline in *The Times*. The *Daily Express* lead announced: 'Hitler Bombed Out – 5-tonners right on der Fuhrer's house', adding that 'Berchtesgaden was the target that every bomber pilot had longed to attack for nearly six years'.

Nobody asked why it had never been hit before now. Nor was the military usefulness of the exercise questioned. The truth was that the Berghof had been mentioned frequently when target lists were being drawn up but had always been rejected. Allied intelligence knew about the deep bomb shelters dug to protect the leadership and reckoned the negative publicity of a failed attempt to finish Hitler was not worth the effort. Later the calculation changed. The fear now was that the bombers might succeed, and the defence of Germany would pass to the hands of someone more competent and rational.

On 25 April 1945, with Hitler's empire reduced to a few square miles in the heart of a burning city, there was less reason than ever to attack Berchtesgaden with such extravagant force. None was offered. The raid on Hitler's mountain retreat was an overwhelmingly British operation, in conception and execution, with American aircraft playing only a secondary role. Its purpose was thus symbolic and the message was from Britain to the world. Hitler had started the war, and it was the British alone who had stood out against him. It had taken a great coalition to defeat him but without that initial defiance there might have been no victory. Smashing Berchtesgaden was a reminder of that truth. It was fitting that it was the Royal Air Force that delivered the blow.

2

A Cottage or a Castle?

One afternoon in the middle of the war Group Captain Arnold Wall sat down to tea and biscuits with Lord Trenchard, who was revered as the 'Father of the Royal Air Force'. Wall taught at the RAF Staff College and was preparing a lecture on the early history of the service. Among the questions he had for the great man were two that were 'pretty trivial', but which he 'felt personal curiosity about'.[1] The first was how it was that the RAF got its famous blue uniform.

There were 'two legends about this, both picturesque' in circulation, and he hoped Trenchard might be able to settle the matter once and for all. One claimed that in 1917 the textile mills of Bradford had received an order to weave a million yards or so of light blue cloth for the Tsar of Russia's cavalry. After the October Revolution, this was left on their hands. Thus, when the RAF officially came into being on 1 April 1918, there was a vast stock of surplus material going cheap that suited their requirements.

In the other version, the staff officer charged with choosing the colour was the beau of a musical comedy star named Lily Elsie, famous for starring in the London version of *The Merry Widow*. When samples were brought to him for a decision he decided to consult his girlfriend. 'This is it,' she is alleged to have replied, picking out the shade that the RAF has worn ever since, 'because it matches the colour of my eyes.' Trenchard was 'most apologetic' but could throw no light on the matter.

On the second subject – the origin of the RAF ensign – he was more helpful, saying 'Yes, yes. I can tell you something about that.' Trenchard recalled his staff coming to him with a sketch of the design. It featured the RAF red, white and blue roundel, originally devised to deter trigger-happy Tommies from blasting at friendly aircraft from their trenches, set on a sky-blue background. They warned him, however, that the Royal College of Heralds had ruled the roundels unacceptable as they were 'not heraldry'. Trenchard resolved to take the matter up with the King. On his next meeting with him he brought the design along and explained the difficulty. 'Well, Trenchard,' said George V, 'if it wasn't heraldry before, it will be from now on.' And he signed the drawing there and then.

Gilded Lily

The ensign anecdote sounds plausible enough. Trenchard was not the man to make up a tale about his sovereign. The truth of the origin of Air Force Blue remains obscure, though gossip certainly favoured the second version. John Slessor, who went on to be one of the outstanding figures of the wartime RAF, recalled being summoned one evening in October 1918 with other senior officers to a meeting in Salisbury to discuss sending reinforcements to France where the Germans were in full retreat. Before the main business began there was some light relief. Mark Kerr, a former senior naval officer who had switched to the Air Force, was to model the first uniform. As Kerr stepped forward into the light of a reading lamp in the new rig, the audience reacted with mirth and incredulity. '[It] was terrible,' Slessor recalled, 'a nasty pale blue with a lot of gold all over it, which brought irresistibly to mind the gentleman who stands outside the cinema.'[2] He reported that 'rumour had it that it was a joint design by Mark Kerr and Miss Lily Elsie, though I'm sure that this was a libel on a beautiful and talented lady who has far too good taste ever to have been party to such an atrocity. Fortunately, it was short lived ...'

These foundation stories say much about how the RAF saw itself – and how it wanted others to see it – in the first years of its existence. Unpicking the Russian story – the yarn about the yarn – reveals some enduring components of the RAF image. One is an aura of romance. The Air Force was being linked to what was traditionally the most dashing arm of the military. The message was that aviators were the aerial equivalent of the cavalry, bold, colourful and brimming with elan, éclat and all the other French words that go with sabre-wielding men on horseback. But there is also a suggestion that they were the target of some resentment from their dowdier colleagues. The implication was that the authorities had decided that, rather than weave a new cloth for the new service, they would have to make do with a quartermaster's windfall.

The second version reinforces the element of romance and introduces a raffish note. Lily Elsie was a big star of the day whose picture was plastered over mass-circulation illustrated papers. She was also married (as was Mark Kerr). Perhaps significantly, her playboy husband's fortune came from a family business that made textile machines. Here the RAF is presented as the sort of outfit that has in its upper ranks officers who hang out with beautiful celebrities. The tale gives the impression of modernity and a devil-may-care attitude to traditional proprieties.

Without stretching things too far, the ensign anecdote also carries a subtext. In this submerged narrative, the infant service, whose values are illustrated in an attractive and innovative design, runs up against the dreary forces of tradition in the form of the heralds. But where there's a will there's a way and help is at hand from an unusual quarter. Young and brash the newcomers may be, but the King recognizes them for the loyal liegemen that they are. At a stroke the hindrance is removed. There will be plenty more obstacles across their path in the journey ahead, the tale implies, but they will be approached and dealt with in the same undaunted manner.

The RAF's image developed naturally from the activities of the Royal Flying Corps in the First World War. The first task it was given was one that traditionally had been done by the cavalry – scouting the movements of the enemy. Once the front lines had solidified and trench warfare began, airmen mapped the battlefield, spotted for the artillery and clashed with enemy aviators trying to do the same thing.

At this stage they were a mere adjunct of the ground forces and did what the Army asked them to. But the nature of their activities meant they received a disproportionate amount of attention.

Aerial combat over the trenches seemed a clean, chivalrous business compared to the industrial carnage below. The isolated nature of much air fighting drew attention to individual warriors and the 'ace' was born. Both sides' propaganda boosted their own airmen heroes. In Britain William Leefe-Robinson, Mick Mannock, Albert Ball and James McCudden, all VC winners, were household names. The last three died flying. Aerial combat was clearly a very dangerous business but outwardly at least the airmen displayed a cheerful fatalism: 'Here's a toast to the dead already' ran a favourite song in the RFC's well-lubricated messes, 'three cheers for the next man to go.'

The airmen very quickly formed an identity that set them apart from soldiers and sailors. It was an attractive one, a blend of gallantry, individualism and insouciance in the face of death. The small-scale, tactical work they did was unsuited to the sort of regimented discipline that shaped the Army and Navy. They were old-fashioned warriors in modern fighting machines. These perceptions would persist long after this early 'heroic' age of air fighting was over.

Between 1917 and 1939 the Air Force would move from the periphery to the centre of British military thinking, planning and expenditure. The development was the result of two growth spurts, both of them brought about by fear of German air power. The Royal Air Force itself was conceived in the panicky atmosphere generated by continuing German air raids on Britain. Attacks by Zeppelins killed 500 civilians by the end of 1916 and diverted 17,000 servicemen from other duties. In the summer of 1917 long-range Gotha bombers struck London, killing and wounding nearly six hundred people in the initial raid. The fear felt on the streets spread upwards. 'One would have thought the world was coming to an end,' sniffed the Chief of the Imperial General Staff Sir William Robertson after attending an emergency cabinet meeting in July. 'I could not get a word in edgeways.'[3]

Something had to be done. The War Cabinet appointed the South African soldier-statesman Jan Smuts to investigate. His first, short recommendations arrived quickly and focused solely on improving the air defences of the London area.

His follow-up report, delivered only a month later, went much further. From the flimsy evidence of the air raids, Smuts drew a vision of the future. He was now convinced that there was 'absolutely no limit' to the use to which aeroplanes could be put. 'The day may not be far off,' he predicted, 'when aerial operations with their devastation of enemy lands and destruction of industrial and populous centres on a vast scale may become the principal operations of war, to which the older forms of military and naval operations may become secondary and subordinate.'[4]

This was quite a claim to advance on the basis of a few air raids. By making it, Smuts set a pattern for extravagant extrapolations, unsupported by serious data, of what air power might do that persisted through the years ahead and which profoundly shaped the development and condition of the Royal Air Force as it prepared for the next big war.

His prophecy was followed by an equally momentous proposal. He recommended that henceforth the RFC and its maritime equivalent, the Royal Naval Air Service, should no longer be tied strictly to the tactical needs of the Army and Navy and the two should be amalgamated in a single Air Force under the political control of a new Air Ministry. The Smuts plan was adopted and implemented with a speed that was remarkable even in wartime. The Royal Air Force came into being on 1 April 1918, the first – and for some years the only – independent air service in the world.

The original set-up was makeshift. The Air Ministry was initially sited in the Cecil Hotel, a second-class establishment in the Strand, before moving to a Portland stone block at No. 1 Kingsway, named Adastral House after the wonderful motto the RAF had inherited from the RFC – *Per Ardua ad Astra*. But the first great leap had been made and the airmen had their chance at reaching for the stars.

In less than four years the status of airmen had soared. Initially the lackeys of the traditional services they were now their nominal equals. The grant of independence had come out of nowhere. No one serving in the air had asked for it. Indeed, there were some in the RFC, including initially Trenchard himself, who were sceptical of the value of a third service, though it did not take him long to change his mind.

The airmen had been handed independence on a plate. They soon learned they would have to fight to keep it. The Army and Navy saw the measure as a temporary aberration. Once the flap was over and the war won, they set about trying to kill off the upstart and claw back control of their air assets.

The fight for survival that ensued had a profound effect on the fundamental character and outlook of the RAF. From birth it was forced to develop theories and practices that justified its existence and techniques for fending off a predatory Army and Navy, both operating from positions of massive institutional strength.

The Navy was particularly persistent. The Admiralty had a solid claim that as the Fleet was central to Britain's defences, anything connected to it should come under its control. The creation of the

Fleet Air Arm in 1924 still left naval aviation in the hands of the RAF and it was not until May 1939 that the Admiralty won it back. The Army felt that it had not been properly compensated for the loss of the RFC and senior officers complained constantly that the RAF showed no interest in providing for its legitimate needs. The belief that the Air Force was primarily out for itself ran deep in the traditional services. It was true that the RAF fought its corner hard in the early years of its existence, but self-interest was essential for self-preservation.

Mutual suspicion and misunderstanding, breaking occasionally into open bureaucratic warfare, placed a heavy strain on relations between the services that would last into the early years of the next war, hampering Britain's ability to fight it.

The RAF had to tread carefully in the post-war atmosphere of military cost-cutting that slashed budgets to the bone, a general loathing of war and a deep reluctance to contemplate the dreadful thought that Britain might one day have to fight another one. The newcomers were last in the queue for resources. Even getting kitted out in the new blue uniforms was a struggle. The Royal Army Clothing Department which dealt initially with supply, appeared unwilling to accept the change. 'Without presuming to criticize the decision of the Air Council, I venture to submit to you the following considerations,' wrote its director, General Sir Benjamin Johnson, in July 1918.[5] He went on to urge them to make sure they were happy with their choice as 'nothing could be worse for the prestige of the Air Service than the adoption of a colour which it might be found faded, went shabby or showed dirt and dust marks easily'. Eight years after the birth, the Treasury were still complaining that they had not been consulted about the clothing costs (which admittedly came to about £1.5 million).[6]

In the face of this resentment and a government which begrudged every shilling of military expenditure, the RAF needed outstanding leadership to keep it on its feet. It was provided by Hugh Trenchard who, as Chief of the Air Staff, was the professional head of the RAF for eleven of the first twelve years of its life. 'Boom' Trenchard dominates the story of the early days, simultaneously forbidding and benign, the patriarchal figure of the foundation myth. He claimed to dislike being referred to as the 'Father of the RAF' but had no difficulty accepting all the other accolades that would be heaped upon him over the years. Trenchard was a failure until he was forty. He was born in 1873, the son of a soldier turned failed West Country solicitor and a mother whose father had been a naval officer. He was supposed to join the Navy but flunked the entrance exam to Dartmouth then twice failed to pass muster for the Army academy at Woolwich. He finally scraped into the Royal Scots Fusiliers and spent the next nineteen years in India and Africa.

His career was going nowhere when in 1912, inspired by a letter from a brother officer describing ecstatically his experiences with the newly formed Royal Flying Corps at their aviation school on Salisbury Plain, he decided to try it for himself. He was immediately entranced – not with flying for he was too big and clumsy to be a good pilot – but with the opportunities it offered, for the military and for himself. Qualities the Army overlooked were appreciated in the RFC and promotions came rapidly. Three years later he was officer commanding in France.

Trenchard inspired something close to adulation among the generation of officers who led the RAF into the war and his thinking pervaded their outlook. Even after he was long gone from office, his protégé Arthur Tedder, who, as deputy to the Supreme Allied Commander in Europe, Dwight D. Eisenhower, was one of the busiest men in the world, still found time during the 1944 invasion to write to the old man asking for his advice.

He was seen to possess a quality that was not obvious in any other military figure of the time. 'There are some rare people in whose presence one instinctively and immediately feels: here is a really great man,' declared 'Jack' Slessor who first met him when a young RFC officer in France.[7] 'I felt it [then] … and I have felt the same about him ever since. It is difficult to define that quality of real greatness. Self-confidence without a trace of arrogance, a contemptuous yet not intolerant disregard for anything mean or petty; the capacity to shuffle aside non-essentials and put an unerring finger on the real core of a problem or the true quality of a man, a sort of instinct for the really important point; a selfless devotion to the cause of what he believed to be true or right.'

Those who served with him felt they had been gilded by the association. 'I'm one of the Boom boys,' boasted Air Marshal Sir Hugh Walmsley in later life. 'He put the fear of God into me but by God I loved him.'[8] He even managed to be a hero to his valet. The humorous, intelligent Maurice Baring, who as his adjutant saw him at very close quarters in the First World War, thought him 'one of the few big men of the world'.[9]

Trenchard had many failings. He could be bombastic, dogmatic and often got things badly wrong. He shamelessly interfered in Air Force matters long after leaving office, with the result that 'all his successors up to the end of the war had to cope with his promptings and criticisms'.[10] And despite his military disdain for civilian manoeuvrings, he could intrigue as enthusiastically as any grubby politician if he thought the cause was worth it.

In many ways, though, his reputation is deserved. He was a formidable operator in the corridors of Whitehall, forceful with officials but knowing when to bend, and showed a subtle understanding of political realities, tending to tell his masters what they wanted to hear. His methods intensified friction with the other services, but they worked. The historian Malcolm Smith, who took a sceptical view of the great man, nonetheless concluded that 'Trenchard's extraordinary personality was, without doubt, one of the greatest assets of the RAF in its fight for survival … when it was likely to have been wound up, if the other services had had their way'.[11]

His claims to greatness went further than that. He devised the institutions and established the traditions that enabled the Air Force to merge quickly into Britain's institutional landscape. He oversaw the development of the strategic theory that – rightly or wrongly – placed offensive air power at the centre of Britain's defence arrangements. Above all, he gave the RAF its identity, its self-belief and its credo, which was implanted in the DNA of the service in the years after the Great War by a cohort of disciples, suffusing the RAF 'with a vigour and aggression, a mixture of dogmatism and iconoclasm, characteristic of the Father of the Royal Air Force' himself.[12]

Trenchard initially stuck loyally to the Army chiefs' view that aeroplanes should be strictly subordinated to their own terrestrial needs. He began to change his mind after being given command of the 'Independent Force', which emerged from the deliberations of the Smuts inquiry. Its purpose was to give the Germans a taste of their own medicine by launching air raids into enemy territory to attack war industries. The campaign achieved little apart from killing German civilians but the notion of using aircraft to pursue strategic rather than simply tactical war aims was planted. Trenchard would end up the most energetic and effective preacher of the primacy of air power in future conflicts and the need to place an offensive air policy at the centre of all planning, organization and procurement.

Trenchard was a notoriously bad speaker but he had a physique and presence that more than made up for his inarticulacy. No one who met him forgot the experience. Many did meet him, for he clung to his baby long after his guardianship was ended, and he pops up often in memoirs and diaries, carrying out inspections and delivering pep talks, indulged by his old protégés who were reluctant to suggest his visitations might be inconvenient.

Arnold Wall, the officer who quizzed Trenchard about the origins of Air Force Blue, remembered a freezing day in December 1926 when he came to the RAF College at Cranwell to inspect the passing-out parade. Even at this early stage Trenchard's stature was immense. Wall, a young New Zealander in his first term as a cadet, noted every detail as he passed by. His first impression 'was of bigness. He was a tall man, heavily built, bearishly, this accentuated by his great-coat, his head seeming on the small side for a man of his size. Heavy eyebrows, shaggy; eyes deep set and rather close set, very keen in expression but friendly; greying moustache worn rather more heavily than was fashionable. His whole bearing was kindly and interested; an amiable Great Bear.'[13]

The parade trooped into the gymnasium for prize giving and speeches. All the cadets knew that Trenchard's nickname was 'Boom' on account of his penetrating voice. They 'were curious to discover whether he would speak to us in the voice of a howitzer, but in this he was a disappointment. He was gruff, certainly, and loud and clear but not a boomer ...'

Early in 1929 Wall went to RAF Uxbridge to hear Trenchard, who was stepping down as Chief of the Air Staff (CAS), deliver a farewell speech. 'I don't remember much of what he said, but one of the metaphors sticks in the mind,' he wrote. 'He stressed that all he and his contemporaries had been able to do since the RAF was formed was to lay "foundations (long pause), foundations for the future (pause). For you fellows to build on (pause). Could be a cottage, could be a castle. I don't know (pause). Nobody knows. Whichever it is, hope you'll find that the foundations are sound, strong ..."'

Laying a 'sound framework on which to build the service' had been one of Trenchard's main aims when he resumed the post of CAS in the spring of 1919 (a brief earlier stint had ended in his resignation after repeated clashes with the Air Minister, Lord Rothermere). The other was to find a role for the RAF that would justify its existence. Unlike his predecessor and rival Frederick Sykes, he understood the need for modesty and frugality. He came up with a proposal for how an Air Force, now pared down to a tenth of the size it had attained by the end of the war, could be employed in a way that projected military power effectively and cheaply.

The concept was called 'force substitution'. It meant simply that instead of relying on expensive ground forces to keep down rebellious natives in hot and dusty corners of the empire, the RAF could do the job by deploying a few aeroplanes. Inevitably, the idea raised Army hackles. The new boys were seeking to take over work that had previously been done by soldiers. Winston Churchill, who was both War and Air Minister, backed the idea, however, and henceforth the RAF would be engaged heavily in imperial policing.

The first success came early in 1920 when they crushed an uprising by the Dervish leader Mohammed Abdullah Hassan in Somaliland. The 'Mad Mullah' was defeated in a few weeks at a cost of £77,000 – 'the cheapest war in history' it was said.[14]

In one year, 1929, the RAF was in action in Iraq, Aden, Sudan, and the North-West Frontier. Its achievements were vaunted by the Air Minister Samuel Hoare in the House of Commons. In Iraq, it was 'the encroachment of certain tribes many miles over the Iraq frontier and the butchery of large numbers of men, women and children' that triggered operations. In Aden, it was 'the kidnapping of two sheikhs friendly to Britain'. In Sudan, it was 'the murder of a British Commissioner, a Greek trader and several natives'. The results were very satisfactory. 'The operations were carried out successfully with scarcely any casualties amongst either the Air Force or the native population,' Hoare reported. As a result of all this activity the RAF lost only one man. As for cost, the Aden mission came to £8,000, where 'under the older conditions of warfare the expenditure would have run into perhaps £6 millions'.[15]

These operations were of little use in preparing aircrews for modern warfare. Few of the tribesmen they subdued had ever seen an aeroplane, let alone had the means to shoot one down. Nor did they provide much practice in Army–Air Force co-operation. They did, however, have the beneficial effect from the airmen's point of view of keeping the RAF firmly in the public eye and in the minds of politicians.

At home Trenchard was anxious to establish and build up an institutional framework that would consolidate the Royal Air Force's independence forever. He set out to form a new generation of officers and airmen by training them from the outset in Air Force thought and method.[16] Cranwell – the first air academy in history – opened in February 1920. Alongside it was established the School of Technical Training to provide a pool of skilled ground crews.

The first Cranwell cadets were housed in a hutted camp formerly occupied by the RNAS planted on the windswept plain of south Lincolnshire. In time it would grow into a grand establishment that could hold its own with Sandhurst or Dartmouth. In October 1934, the Prince of Wales opened the new College Hall. The architect Sir James Wood had chosen the Royal Hospital in Chelsea, home to Army pensioners since 1692, for inspiration. The structure was a gigantic metaphor for Trenchard's approach. The brick and stone elevations and large dome looked as if they had been there for centuries. In fact, the classical exterior was all façade and the building was held up by thoroughly modern steel beams.

Cranwell graduates were, as the founder intended, a small and exclusive clique, 'the very heart and centre from which the RAF derives her vitality', as an inter-war Air Secretary Lord Londonderry described it.[17] This was the nucleus around which the service would grow. Trenchard made the ability to fly an aeroplane well a basic condition of entry to the RAF's future elite. As well as being a flying school, the college taught aviation technology and aeronautics alongside a basic academic curriculum. The course lasted two years and at the end the graduates passed out as 'General Duties Officers' ready to take their place wherever the service required them and in time to rise to the summit of the RAF.

There were two entries a year, and in the period between the wars the total number of annual entrants never exceeded seventy-one.[18] Entrance was by competitive examination, the same one sat by candidates for Dartmouth and Sandhurst, followed by interview. The college preferred candidates who came towards the top of the list (Sandhurst was prepared to consider anyone in the first hundred).[19] Before the college opened an Air Ministry Committee under Lord Hugh Cecil was set up to consider what sort of boy they were looking for. It concluded that RAF officers required a higher technical ability than was needed in the Army. As to character, they were seeking those with 'the quality of a gentleman'.[20] By this they did not mean 'a particular degree of wealth or a particular social position but a certain character'. This sounded egalitarian, a statement that the RAF was a modern service in tune with the democratic mood of the age. The problem was, as the Cecil report admitted, how to find candidates with the required education and qualities 'without excluding from the service men of small and humble means'.

Cranwell cost money – a hundred pounds a term, which was the same as the fees to a good public school. Parents also had to find another hundred pounds for uniform and books. This was far beyond the means of most British households. Six full scholarships worth £105 were awarded each year. But even if a grammar school boy's parents could scrape the funds together he was still at a disadvantage. Many public schools had separate, specialized curricula for boys trying for Sandhurst and Dartmouth and it was easy for them to extend the service to Cranwell aspirants.

In practice then, the selection process and entry requirements meant Cranwell was dominated by the sons of the affluent middle and upper classes and the products of the public school system. Of the 929 schoolboy entrants who passed through between 1920 and 1939, all but ninety-three went to fee-paying schools.[21] The public schools represented at Cranwell ranged from Eton, which sent twenty cadets, to small, long-vanished colleges for the sons of the shabby genteel, which sent one or two. The biggest block came from the Victorian foundations which sprang up in the nineteenth century to raise the soldiers, sailors and administrators needed to run Britain and its empire. Wellington, built as a national monument to the Iron Duke, provided the most with fifty. Other schools with strong military traditions were well represented. Cheltenham sent twenty-eight, Tonbridge and Imperial Service College twenty-two, and Marlborough and Haileybury twenty. Of military-minded schools, only Harrow, with five entrants, was under-represented.

The Cranwell course was rigorous and for much of the period the conditions were spartan. The cadets were marooned in the back of beyond. Sleaford, the nearest town, offered few temptations; one reason Trenchard had chosen the site was its distance from the fleshpots of London. After the rigours of boarding school, most of the entrants found it easy to cope. Peter Townsend, son of a colonial civil servant, arrived at Cranwell in 1933 from Haileybury where life at the outset at least was 'hard and sometimes cruel [and] there was no one to help us but ourselves … Survive your first two years at Haileybury and you could survive anything.'[22] At Cranwell he 'submitted, gladly for the most part, to the intensive and variegated process which was to mould me as a pilot, an officer and a gentleman'.

Brian Kingcome, another son of the empire, started in 1936 after leaving Bedford School, which had developed strong links with Cranwell. 'The college schedule was very civilised,' he remembered.[23] 'Each day, including Saturday, began with an early morning parade, and there was a church parade on Sunday. Parades were followed by classes, including an hour or so a day of flying instruction. Wednesday and Saturday afternoons were set aside for sport. We dined formally in mess each night from Monday to Friday. From Monday to Thursday we wore mess kit consisting of leg-hugging mess overalls strapped under half-Wellingtons, with black tie, blue waistcoat, stiff shirt and butterfly collar.' Dining in mess at weekends was optional when the dress code was slightly more relaxed – a suit on Saturdays and tweed jacket and flannels on Sunday.

Smartness was something of a fetish for the authorities. Tim Vigors, from a family of Anglo-Irish landowners, set off in January 1939 for his first term at Cranwell with hair cropped considerably shorter than he had worn it at his old school, Eton. On the train he bumped into an acquaintance, also Cranwell-bound, who advised him it was still too long, so he stopped off at a barber shop for another trim. On his first morning he lined up on the parade ground in regulation suit and bowler hat for inspection by a large and fierce warrant officer, who, after prowling up and down the line, stopped menacingly in front of him. He then 'bellowed at the top of his voice, for the whole of Cranwell to hear, "What do you think you are sir? A bloody woman! Go and have yer hair cut!" Vigors hurried off for his third visit to the barber in two days.[24]

The reverence for spit and polish, for parades and bull, was at odds with the reputation of the wartime RFC. On the 'dromes of the Western Front dress codes and discipline were relaxed and drilling and parading were not highly regarded. The emphasis on appearance was another instance of the determination of Trenchard and his followers to show that the RAF could match the other services in every department, down to the precision of their marching and the shine on their boots. The attitude rubbed off on some of the cadets, who, when the next war came, would frown on what they saw as the casual attitude of the greatly expanded service.

Soaked in the public school ethos, Cranwell offered a huge variety of sports and activities. There was rugby, football and cricket, of course, but also athletics, squash, tennis, badminton, fencing, hockey, swimming, boxing, basketball, rowing and water polo. The surrounding countryside offered shooting, fishing and above all riding to hounds. Lincolnshire was prime fox-hunting country and the Quorn and the Belvoir would sometimes meet at the college. Riding was voluntary but encouraged. The belief that a good horseman made a good pilot, dating from the first days of aviation, was still strong, 'the thinking being that the sensitive hands which could coax the best from a horse would be those most suited to the delicate controls of a flying machine'.[25] The same applied to yachtsmen, and a declared enthusiasm for sailing always went down well at interviews. The course included history, English, foreign languages, though as the college authorities admitted, in 1935 the officer responsible for organizing the academic programme faced a 'difficult and sometimes ungrateful task'.[26]

The cadets were attracted principally by the thrill of flying. There was certainly plenty of theory on offer from the course lectures on engineering and aerodynamics. The practice, though, was something else. Townsend reckoned that in his two years at Cranwell he clocked up only 157 hours of flying time, the same as a Luftwaffe trainee amassed in nine months.[27] One reason for not letting cadets get airborne too often was that flying, particularly for novices, was still a very dangerous business. They started off on the Avro Tutor, a small open-cockpit biplane with a 240hp engine which, according to Kingcome, was 'completely vice-free' and 'stood up to the cruellest abuse with a happy smile'.[28] Then in their second year they moved on to 'service type' aircraft. The Bristol Bulldog, which arrived in November 1933, was fine when flying straight and level, but, as Peter Townsend discovered, in a spin 'she was a bitch'.[29]

Putting an aeroplane into a deliberate spin then getting out of it was a regular exercise. One day Townsend was aloft with his instructor Flying Officer A. F. McKenna, a 'burly, smiling man with a rolling gait like a sailor'. They climbed to above 8,000 feet, which given the aircraft's proclivities was set as the minimum height at which the manoeuvre should be attempted, then McKenna in the rear cockpit told his pupil through the Gosport speaking tube to 'spin her to the left off a steep turn'. Townsend pushed the stick forward and the Bulldog spiralled briskly downwards. After three turns McKenna told him to 'bring her out'. Townsend followed the prescribed counter-intuitive drill of shoving the stick forward again and applying opposite rudder but nothing happened. He wrote:

> We were sinking rapidly and I was conscious of an eerie hush, of the clatter of the engine's poppet valves and the reek of burning castor oil … of the propeller, in a slow tick-over, brushing the air, of the air rushing past my ears and through the bracing wires, making them whine, while the aircraft pitched and tossed in a sickening, circular movement, totally, hopelessly, out of control. 'I've got her!' yelled McKenna, now far from

cheerful. Banging open the throttle lever, pumping the stick, kicking the rudder, he tried to rock the Bulldog back into flying position. In vain. 'Get ready to jump,' shouted McKenna and I moved my hand to the quick release of my ... harness, praying to God that I should not have to pull it. With throttle, stick and rudder McKenna kept fighting the Bulldog. We were down to 2,000 feet when at last he brought her back to an even keel with just enough height left to dive and pick up flying speed. His voice, now very quiet, came through the speaking tube: 'That was a near one. Now climb her up again and we'll do another.'

Others were not so lucky. During Townsend's time at Cranwell a mid-air collision killed two instructors and two cadets. Their dismembered bodies had to be collected from trees and fields for burial. The perils of flying training did not end there. Of the young men who passed through Cranwell between the wars, sixty-two were killed in flying accidents, many more than died in RAF operations in the same period.[30]

The Apprentice Schools were set up with the same devotion to excellence. Obviously, the RAF depended on a high level of mechanical expertise to function. Trenchard decided that the best way to create a dedicated workforce of career technicians was 'to enlist the bulk of our skilled ranks as boys and train them ourselves'.[31] The Apprentice Training Schemes started in April 1920. The Army and Navy tended to draw their recruits from the ranks of the young, poor and unskilled. The RAF, declared a 1934 article, was 'different from any other Service. The aircraftmen are the elite of their class. All, by comparison with former days, are educated. A great many of them are well-educated ... in no other Service is there closer association between all ranks.'[32]

Applicants had to have the School Certificate, an exam normally sat at the age of sixteen with papers in five subjects including English, mathematics, a foreign language and a science. Most British children left school at the first legal opportunity aged fourteen to find jobs and contribute to the family budget.

Candidates were nominated by local education authorities and sat a competitive exam which included papers in maths, experimental science and English. The intake was much bigger than Cranwell – upwards of three hundred a year. The great disparity in numbers reflected a basic fact about the nature of air forces. To function, the RAF needed a longer logistical and support tail than the Army or even the Navy and ground personnel greatly outnumbered fliers. By 1945, in an Air Force numbering more than a million, only 17.7 per cent flew aircraft. The function of the other 82.3 per cent was to project them into battle.[33] Even so, the Apprentice Schools could not fill all technical manpower needs and qualified tradesmen had to be recruited directly from civilian life to make up the shortfall.[34]

Successful applicants for apprenticeships were expected to serve at least ten years with two on the reserve. Clothing, food and lodging was free and boys under eighteen got one shilling, then one and sixpence a day, the older ones three shillings. Those destined for the larger trades – the fitters who serviced the engines and the riggers who looked after the airframes – were trained at Halton, a former Rothschild mansion in Buckinghamshire which had been bought by the War Office at a knock-down price. Those specializing in wireless technology were housed in a school on the Cranwell complex.

Trenchard's enthusiasm for the apprentice scheme was as great as his devotion to Cranwell. Those who passed through it would be known as 'Trenchard's Brats'. In some ways the Apprentice School mirrored the college. The boys lived a regimented life in which competition in everything was encouraged and smartness was enforced. Hubert Rawlinson, who arrived at Halton as a sixteen-year-old from Bolton in late August 1939, found himself plunged into an austere world where almost every minute was accounted for and rules governed virtually all human activity. After a bone-shaking ride from Wendover station in three-ton lorries with solid rubber tyres the new boys were set down at Bulback Barracks.

'We came to a halt by a huge parade ground and climbed down from the vehicles,' he wrote.[35] 'A roll call was made and we were then taken to three gigantic barrack blocks, each having six large rooms with rows of beds either side. Each bed had a wooden locker alongside, a wooden box which could be padlocked underneath the bed, and a steel locker fastened to the wall above. Underneath the wall locker were three clothes pegs fastened to a frame. The beds were made in two halves, the front sliding into the rear; no springs but thin metal slats ... upon the beds stood three square biscuit mattresses, five brown blankets, two calico sheets and a head bolster. Twenty of us were placed in each room ...' After this sobering beginning they were taken across to the dining hall for their first taste of service cuisine: rissole and chips followed by suet pudding and custard.

After three weeks of square bashing and PT they were assessed to determine which trade they would be trained in for the next three years. The order in which they were interviewed was set by their place in the entry exam results. The strong message the boys received was that they had entered a meritocracy and that success would be determined by talent and hard work. Rawlinson was selected as a metal rigger, the trade responsible for maintaining and repairing airframes. The archaic sounding term was justified in an era when many of the aircraft the RAF flew were still partly constructed of wood, canvas and wire and the pear-drop smell of the acetone used to 'dope' the canvas stretched over biplane wings permeated workshops and hangars.

The boys marched everywhere, back and forth every morning and evening to the workshops, twice a week to half a day of academic lessons in the school building, always to the tune of a band made up of older apprentices equipped with bagpipes, trumpets, fifes and drums. On Sundays, church parade was compulsory.

At weekends, after Saturday morning fatigues, the boys were allowed off the camp to visit Aylesbury, Tring and Wendover. They were on public display, representatives of the Royal Air Force, and correctness in behaviour and dress was essential. For these outings they had to wear 'best blues': breeches, puttees, boots and tunics with 'dog-neck' collars, set off with a swagger stick tucked under the arm. Only those over eighteen were allowed to smoke and then not in barracks.

After three years and several progress tests apprentices sat their passing-out examinations; one week for academic subjects and a second for their trade. Failures were re-mustered as aircraft hands, the dogsbodies of the RAF. The rest were then sent off to start their careers on a starting pay of twenty-six shillings and sixpence a week – good money for an eighteen-year-old in the 1930s.

Halton created something that had never been seen in the British armed forces: a body of educated NCOs and skilled technicians, confident in their abilities and well aware of their vital function in the organization. It showed in their attitude. T. E. Lawrence, writing to Air Vice Marshal Oliver Swann, noted that RAF officers 'were treated by the men off parade as rather humorous things to have to pay respect to'.[36] They tended to regard officers as ordinary humans, rather than, as Army and Navy other ranks were expected to, as more exalted and evolved members of the species. This relationship between commissioned and non-commissioned wearers of Air Force Blue was to be a defining characteristic of the new service, one that harmonized with the spirit of the times and the mood of the skilled lower classes on whom it would have to rely.

The gap between the two was slowly closing. Unlike the other services the RAF offered real opportunities for social mobility. When drawing up his strategy for the training of pilots who would be mostly officers, and ground crew who would be NCOs and other ranks, Trenchard had left a window open. It was decided that the best three apprentices from each entry would be awarded cadetships at Cranwell at the end of their time at Halton. The scheme also included Wireless School apprentices. Together they would send 124 boys to the college in the years between the wars, more than 10 per cent of the total intake.[37]

For Halton boys who had spent two years living twenty to a hut, Cranwell, where each cadet got a room of his own and had the services of a batman, must have seemed like luxury. The Brats, though, were unlikely to have been overawed by their surroundings or their classmates. They were already well versed in service ways and armoured with the confidence that came from hard-earned success. Two Halton boys won the Sword of Honour in the inter-war period, Patrick Coote in 1930 and John Badger in 1933. Both were killed in the war before they could achieve their full potential but, on the whole, apprentices who made it to Cranwell were destined for the top. The first Halton entrant, Walter Dawson, ended up an air chief marshal. Among the rest who passed through in the years between the wars were an air marshal, eleven air vice marshals, twenty air commodores and thirty group captains. Of the relatively small number who failed to make it beyond the rank of Flight Lieutenant, all but a handful attended at the end of the period and lost their lives in the war while still junior officers.[38]

The elite cadres that emerged from the college and training schools were far too small to satisfy even the limited manpower demands of the RAF in its shrunken post-war existence. Aviation was a young man's game and the active life of a pilot was relatively short. If everyone who flew an aeroplane had a permanent commission, the service would soon fill up with underemployed and expensive officers whose flying days were over.

Several solutions emerged. One scheme was to create a new class of airman pilots, drawn from the ranks. The preference was for men with 'a high standard of education and efficiency', showing the qualities of 'pluck, reliability, alertness, steadiness, keenness and energy'. Rather than lose their technical skills they would not receive commissions but were classed as sergeant pilots. They were expected to serve for five years then go back to their old trades.[39] In 1939, about a quarter of the pilots in RAF squadrons were NCOs, giving a core of toughness and skill to every unit. They had won their wings the hard way and would be regarded with slightly nervous respect by the younger newcomers who flooded in later.

Most of the flying personnel needs were supplied by the invention of the Short Service Commission (SSC). In 1924 the Air Ministry advertised for 400 young officers for flying duties. They were to be British-born and of pure European descent who would serve up to six years and then move onto the Reserve of Air Force Officers (RAFO). According to the official RAF account in the inter-war years these men 'formed the bulk of officers … the Air Force was essentially a short service force and its flyers were birds of passage'.[40]

In 1925 Trenchard backed a scheme suggested by some RFC veterans who studied engineering at Cambridge after the war to start a university air squadron. The idea spread to Oxford, then London, then elsewhere. He also got government backing for an Auxiliary Air Force of weekend fliers, the RAF's equivalent of the Army's territorial units. The pilots were amateurs who flew in their own time in aeroplanes supplied and maintained by the RAF and the squadrons would have a marked local character. The Auxiliary Air Force provided a home for men from affluent homes to meet up in a patriotic cause and enjoy each other's company. The atmosphere was clubby and exclusive and in some units the whiff of snobbery was strong.

These structures were bold and imaginative departures from contemporary military norms. The RAF's top officers, and those rising behind them, hardly seemed like radicals. They almost all came from conventional military backgrounds and on paper differed little from their Army and Navy counterparts. Trenchard was succeeded as CAS in 1930 by John Salmond, the son of a major general who, after Wellington and Sandhurst, had fought in the Boer War before taking up flying and transferring to the RFC. On 1 April 1933 he handed over to his brother Geoffrey who lasted only twenty-seven days in the job before dying. His replacement was Edward Ellington, a former gunner.

The rising generation of RAF officers, the men who would lead the RAF into the war, also came from the same strata of society in which the generals and admirals were traditionally nurtured. They were, on the whole, courteous (though there were some notable exceptions) and valued 'form'. They liked to hunt and shoot, fish and sail and their politics were conservative. Like their Army and Navy contemporaries who made it to the top, they could be vain, overbearing and unscrupulous in the pursuit of advancement and glory.

They differed from their peers in sharing a heightened sense of the possibilities of the new. It was this spirit that had led them into the air in the first place. All had been attracted by the excitement of aviation. They were risk-takers, hazarding not just their lives at a time when flying was a very dangerous game, but also their careers, for opting for the RFC was a gamble for anyone planning a long-term military future. And they were by and large an intelligent bunch: sharp, inquiring and well-educated, at a time when brain power was not regarded as a cardinal military virtue. Arthur Tedder read history at Cambridge and had just started in the Colonial Service when the Great War broke out. Trafford Leigh-Mallory was a Cambridge contemporary, planning a career as a barrister. Sholto Douglas, a professor's son, studied Classics at Oxford. Cleverness was prized and the cleverest, it was generally agreed, was Charles Portal, Winchester and Christ Church, Oxford, and 'the accepted star of the Air Force' as Churchill called him when appointing him Chief of the Air Staff in October 1940 at the young age of forty-seven (his Army and Navy opposite numbers were fifty-eight and sixty-four respectively).[41]

Not least, they looked different from their Army counterparts. The most senior, the best-known soldiers – Alan Brooke, Bernard Montgomery, Harold Alexander – sported Edwardian-era moustaches proclaiming their membership of a military caste. Portal and Tedder were clean-shaven. Tedder, with his fresh face and jutting pipe, cut a very unmartial figure, more like a liberal university professor than a man of action. Portal's hooked nose and hooded eyes did not look British at all, and he reminded Peter Townsend of 'an Arab sheikh'.[42]

Despite his relative youth, Portal would show himself the most detached and composed of the wartime chiefs of staff. He was as cool and hard as marble. High intelligence did not equate with an excess of human sympathy. This thoroughly modern warrior was as ruthless as any traditional commander and did not flinch from accepting or inflicting casualties. A spirit of restless aggression would pervade the direction of the wartime RAF, stimulated by a cadre of senior officers, most of whom had passed through Trenchard's kindergarten. The approach guaranteed a high casualty rate among those who flew. The question was whether the expenditure was matched by the results.

3

Smoke and Mirrors

In March 1934, Stanley Baldwin, the dominant figure in the National Government, announced in Parliament that henceforth it was official policy that 'in air strength and air power this country shall no longer be in a position inferior to any country within striking distance of its shores'.[1] That meant Germany. The great transformation in the RAF's fortunes had begun. It was now launched on a race to keep up with the Luftwaffe as German air power evolved from nothing to threaten domination of the skies over Europe.

Baldwin's words marked an end to wishful thinking. The physical and economic catastrophe of the last war had made a new one unbearable to contemplate, for government and people alike. Since 1919 defence spending had been governed by the 'Ten Year Rule' founded on the supposition that the country would not be engaged in a major conflict in the decade to come. Hard-headed Tories like Baldwin had become enthusiasts for Utopian formulas for world peace, embodied in the international disarmament talks which opened, attended by every major world power, in Geneva in February 1932.

The Ten Year Rule was scrapped in 1932 after service chiefs warned that the armed forces would soon be incapable of defending the empire. The Geneva talks effectively collapsed when Hitler pulled Germany out of both the conference and the League of Nations in October 1933.

With the Baldwin speech disarmament was all but buried. So too were the niggardly defence budgets that had starved the services of funds during the 1920s. When the purse strings were loosened it was the Air Force that benefited most. Once the poor relation of the forces, the Air Force was suddenly the Treasury's favourite son. In 1930 it received by far the smallest share of the military budget: £16.75 million compared with £55.75 million for the Navy and £40.15 million for the Army.[2] By 1939 it was getting the largest: £105.70 million against the Navy's £97.96 million and the Army's £88.29 million.

The money was emphatic proof that the Air Force was now at the heart of Britain's defence strategy. In the thirty years since the advent of heavier-than-air flight, air power had assumed the same vital significance as sea power in ensuring the defence of the nation.

Between 1934 and 1939 the government authorized a series of schemes to expand the RAF at a rate that would maintain numerical parity with the Luftwaffe in the hope that this would deter aggression. When it became clear that this was unrealistic the emphasis switched from quantity to quality. The aim became to shape a force that would be able to withstand an initial onslaught from the air, and in time strike back. Existing programmes were scrapped and new ones devised in a desperate effort to keep up with an ever-changing reality. Such was the pace of events that only one of the eight expansion plans – Scheme F – was completed.

The favoured status of the Air Force was the result of several intertwined developments. There was a general conviction, shared by amateur and expert alike, that air power would determine the outcome of future conflicts. It followed that a powerful Air Force was the best means of deterring potential enemies. It also offered the hope that, if war did come, it could be fought without the need to send British troops to the Continent, an awful prospect for a society in which the memory of the trenches was still raw. All these notions were promoted with arriviste confidence by air power lobbyists inside and outside the RAF.

Trenchard and the Air Staff did not support the more extreme doctrines circulating in international military and political circles, which held that aeroplanes could win wars on their own. They answered the question: 'what is the RAF really for?' with a theory of air power that has been described as 'strategic interception'.[3] This held that, until now, in wars between nations, one side had tried to beat the other by defeating its land and sea forces in battle. The coming of air power changed all that. Aeroplanes could reach out to undermine the enemy's capacity and will to fight. They would do so by smashing up war factories, power supplies and transport systems. As the targets were in populated areas, the onslaught would have a devastating effect on civilian morale. Trenchard was fond of quoting a maxim that had no basis in observable fact that 'the moral effect [of bombing] is to the material in the ratio of ten to one'.[4]

Sooner rather than later the pressure would become unbearable. Civilians would clamour for protection and soldiers would be withdrawn from the front to try and defend them. Public support to continue fighting would evaporate and the enemy's leaders would be forced to sue for peace. The prospect of mass civilian deaths and spectacular violence raised obvious ethical questions. They were to some extent answered by the claim that air power would put an end to the long agony of defensive terrestrial warfare as seen in the trenches of the Western Front. New wars would be short and sharp but less bloody in the long run than the old ones.

All this had profound implications for the futures of the Army and Navy. Trenchard was careful not to claim that the new reality would make the old services redundant. The Navy would have an important role undermining the enemy's war economy by exercising its traditional function of imposing a maritime blockade and securing Britain's supply lines. The Army would still have to defeat the enemy forces in the field – though these would be much weakened as a result of air action. If the Air Force claims were accepted, though, it would mean that in a time of crisis it would have a privileged call on resources and a dominant voice in war councils. It was a recipe for bad blood.

The supposedly scientific prognostications of the air professionals chimed with the instincts of the civilian amateurs. Politicians needed little persuasion about the menace posed by aerial warfare. Stanley Baldwin's doom-laden speech in the House of Commons on 10 November 1932 revealed how deeply the message had penetrated. Baldwin had twice been Prime Minister and was now the leader of the Conservative Party which dominated the National Government led by Ramsay MacDonald. He had been foremost in pressing for an international convention to outlaw, or at least limit,

the use of aircraft as weapons of war. Now, with the Geneva conference in its death throes, he had nothing to offer but despairing
prophecies.

The speech is remembered for his warning that 'the bomber will
always get through', a phrase that struck home immediately. It was
only one of a number of utterances that must have curdled the
blood of everyone reading the next morning's papers.[5] He had now
abandoned the hope that agreements to curb air power could ever
work. The stark conclusion was that 'the only defence is in offence,
which means that you have got to kill more women and children
more quickly than the enemy if you want to save yourselves'.

One of the many striking things about the speech is the sense of
dread that it sets out to create even though there was at that stage
no European war in prospect. Hitler and the Nazis were new on the
scene and were still presumed to be subject to the normal laws of
diplomacy and power politics.

As the decade progressed the spectre raised by Baldwin would
haunt the political landscape. The future arrived more rapidly than
he imagined and the distant nightmare began to feel like imminent
reality. Mass media stoked anxieties. The Alexander Korda film
Things to Come, based on H. G. Wells's novel, was released in 1936.
It painted a picture of a London-like metropolis being bombed
back into the Dark Ages by an unstoppable wave of enemy bombers. The movie was a critical and commercial success, the sixteenth
most popular at the box office that year.

It was to the RAF that everyone looked for protection from these
horrors and it was happy to offer reassurance. Adastral House had a
plan for dealing with the mounting threat from Germany. Almost
every senior officer who mattered was an adept of the cult of the
bomber. For John Slessor the paramountcy of bombing was 'an article of faith'.[6] Slessor was thoughtful and articulate, a Trenchard
protégé who had ghosted his writings and speeches and from 1937
was *de facto* head of the plans department that translated doctrine
into practice. He and his colleagues envisaged a scenario in which
deterrence broke down and the Luftwaffe launched a huge air
assault on Britain to land a 'knock-out blow' and deliver a swift
victory.

The RAF needed fighter aircraft that would 'provide a reasonable chance of parrying a knock-out blow'. But the real protection would be provided by a 'striking force' of bombers mounting a massive counter-offensive. Slessor admitted later that 'our belief in the bomber was intuitive' and that until war broke out 'we really did not know anything about air war on a major scale'.[7] The excuse was that there was a lack of hard evidence to work on. The RAF had little recent practical experience – bombing villages in Waziristan taught no lessons. There seems to have been no systematic military analysis of air operations in the wars in China, Abyssinia and Spain.[8]

'Jack' Slessor

The absence of data did nothing to undermine the Air Staff's confidence in the doctrine. It rested unsteadily on several untested propositions. One was that airspace was so vast that British bombers would be able to proceed directly to the task of destroying the enemy's war industry relatively unhindered. But what was true for British bombers would presumably be true of German ones. Surely, at some point, a battle would have to be fought to gain air supremacy in order to avoid an endless attritional cycle of attack and counter-attack?

Another was that bombing would have a devastating effect on enemy morale. Again if that was so – and some critics argued from the evidence of the Spanish Civil War, where the bombing of Barcelona by the Nationalists in March 1938 had galvanized Republican resistance, that if anything the opposite was the case – then British morale would be similarly affected. To the first the airmen had no answer. The second could only be dealt with by the assertion that innate racial superiority meant that, whereas Britons could 'take it', Germans couldn't.

Despite these obvious flaws the views of the Air Staff were generally accepted in Downing Street, Whitehall and Westminster. They harmonized with the mood of the times and the priorities of politicians. Everyone was desperate to avoid a war, especially one that meant sending troops to fight again on the Continent. Building up the Army and Navy could only provoke the Germans. Building up the Air Force might deter them. Expansion was seen as a defensive measure, popular with government and public alike. The decision to go ahead with it was essentially a *political* not a strategic choice. Once taken, the Air Force hogged both the public limelight and the Treasury's still limited largesse.

The Army and Navy boiled with exasperation at the favour bestowed on the new boys. It bubbles in the diaries of Henry Pownall, a sharp-eyed Army officer who watched the process from his seat on the secretariat of the Committee for Imperial Defence which brought together the professional service heads, cabinet ministers and senior officials. 'The public cry is all for the Air Force [first], Navy a distinct second, and the Army a very bad third,' he complained after a major report into how to repair the country's run-down defences that paved the way for rearmament was unveiled in February 1934.[9] 'The RAF have got too much,' he snapped a few months later as the details of how the budget would be carved emerged.[10] The Army's appeals for funds to build up a field force to send to France in time of war received a stony reception. 'Everyone will shout loud enough for the Army to practise as an Army when war comes but in peace it is the Cinderella of the Services,' wailed Pownall in 1938.[11]

It was not just about money. There was resentment at the tremendous strategic airs the Air Force had given itself. 'A constant bone of contention in our discussions was the role to be played by the Air Force,' wrote Major General Sir John Kennedy, the Army's Deputy Director of Plans on the eve of the war. 'Both the General Staff and the Naval Staff opposed the fanatical efforts of the Air Staff to press upon us their theory that the war would be decided by the action of air forces almost unaided by the other two services.'[12]

They were also aggrieved by the RAF's extreme reluctance to divert resources to meet their particular needs. The Army and Navy 'fought hard and unsuccessfully for the provision of adequate specialized air forces, properly trained and equipped for the support of naval and military operations'. The airmen's attitude was combative and defensive. Kennedy claimed that a senior officer at the Air Ministry had told him that the Air Staff regarded such co-operation as a 'prostitution of the Air Force'.

The fight for a share of air assets would go on far into the war. In the high-level meetings where defence priorities were decided the admirals and generals could only grind their teeth while the RAF got their way. 'The politicians were much attracted by the Air Force doctrine,' recalled Kennedy. 'The soldiers and sailors could never persuade the cabinet or the defence committee to settle the dispute in a way we thought right, either before or during the war.'[13]

For all their perceived cockiness, the newcomers showed respect towards political authority and voiced their arguments softly. Edward Ellington, CAS for the crucial 1933–7 period, was regarded by his own senior officers as being too deferential in the company of politicians. His successor, Cyril Newall, was more forceful but got on well with Lord Swinton and Sir Kingsley Wood, the air ministers who presided over the expansion period.

The Air Marshals' approach contrasted favourably with the high-handed ways of the soldiers and sailors. The Army brass barely bothered to disguise their contempt for Leslie Hore-Belisha, Secretary of State for War from 1937 to 1940. 'An obscure, shallow-brained, charlatan political Jewboy' was Pownall's verdict.[14] Their treatment of him is revealed in an episode recounted by Kennedy when he was taken on a tour of the front in northern France by Lord Gort, commander of the British Expeditionary Force, in November 1939.

> It was a cold, wet windy morning. We motored through the rain to the western side of the British salient ... on our way we crossed Vimy Ridge. Gort got us out of our cars ... he made Hore-Belisha climb a very muddy bank and kept him shivering in the howling gale while he explained the battle fought there in the 1914–18 war. In spite of his discomfort Hore-Belisha kept up a good appearance of polite interest. By this time his patent leather boots must have been giving him hell.[15]

There were further stops at other windswept battlefields. They paused at a château to meet the French commander and were taken to an attic window for yet another *tour d'horizon*. Gort deliberately 'opened a window and let in a piercing draught on Hore-Belisha; when we went out again into the rain he shouted jovially, "Isn't it a grand day!"'[16]

This schoolboyish bullying was all the more extraordinary given that Gort owed his appointment to Hore-Belisha's patronage. Nor would the War Minister be thanked for the great efforts he made in cabinet to obtain funds and equipment for the army Gort now commanded. Edmund Ironside, who Hore-Belisha appointed as Chief of the General Staff, was equally obnoxious towards his patron. Ironside, an outstanding linguist, gleefully recounted to Kennedy over lunch one day in his club how he had instructed his political master not to try and address French commanders in their own tongue: 'I told him that his French was Le Touquet French – good enough for talking to Mademoiselle X on the *plage* but no good for military conversations.'[17]

The hostile and surely anti-Semitic attitudes of Gort and Ironside were in sharp contrast to the warm relations between the RAF and Sir Philip Sassoon, Under Secretary of State for Air between 1931 and 1937. Sir Philip was rich, Jewish and unmistakeably gay.[18] He was famously generous and hospitable and every summer hosted the annual camp of the Auxiliaries of 601 (County of London) Squadron, of which he was honorary CO, at Port Lympne, his sumptuous country house on the Kent coast. In between flying, the young airmen lounged around the twin swimming pools in the grounds and there was a party every night. Sassoon's death aged only fifty in June 1939 caused the Air Force real sorrow. At a meeting of the Air Council ten days afterwards much of the discussion was taken up with whether or not to cancel the RAF garden party held each year at Trent Park, another Sassoon mansion in Hertfordshire, as 'the absence of Sir Philip would revive memories and cast a gloom over the proceedings'.[19]

Expansion piled enormous bulk on the organizational skeleton devised by Trenchard. In April 1934, on the eve of the great transformation, the RAF had 814 aeroplanes at home and abroad. When the war broke out it had 3,860.[20] The Air Force's new physique might look impressive but was there real muscle underneath? The speed of events in Europe had the Air Ministry perpetually scrambling to keep up. The Nazis' obfuscations about the extent of their own expansion programme meant there were no solid metrics on which to base the pursuit of parity. The result was that much of the budget was squandered on unsatisfactory aircraft which were ordered mainly to create the illusion of strength – an attempt at 'scaring Hitler by "window dressing"', as senior officers privately admitted to each other.[21]

The political imperative for numerical parity with the Luftwaffe had taken little account of the quality of the aircraft. In a time of fast-changing technology the policy was shockingly wasteful. The Air Ministry ordered new types in the knowledge that they would be out of date before they reached the squadrons. The Fairey Battle light bomber was known to be a dud from the outset, underpowered and short-ranged, yet more than 2,000 were bought before a halt was called, leaving their crews tethered to a lethally useless machine when the fighting began.

The RAF could argue that it was not their fault. Building a modern air force was hampered by the underdeveloped state of the domestic air industry and the government's laissez-faire economic policy. In Germany, the Nazis ensured that aircraft manufacturing was at the service of the state and the national airline Lufthansa was to a large extent the Luftwaffe in sheep's clothing. A senior Rolls-Royce executive, Willoughby Lappin, visited the Heinkel works on the Baltic coast in April 1936 and on his return reported his findings to British intelligence. Workers started their shifts at 6.15 a.m. and finished at 5.15 p.m., with two fifteen-minute meal breaks. 'The most significant thing,' he noted, 'is probably the fact that everyone young and old is disciplined and is thinking nationally, whether from fear or choice does not matter … the Government are solely responsible for the policy and working of all the aircraft factories and the directors thereof have no control except to provide the Air Ministry with what they require.'[22]

In Britain the state gave limited support to a range of smallish 'family firm' constructors, who had to pay the costs of developing new designs themselves and competed for orders when the Air Ministry issued specifications for a new type. Until late in the day, British governments avoided intervening, refusing to allow the international situation to interfere with the principle of 'non-interference with the flow of normal trade'.[23]

The result was a piecemeal approach to design producing a plethora of types. Multiplicity meant a lack of mass-production capacity and, though this was remedied when the government paid big motor manufacturers like Austin and Rootes to build 'shadow factories' for airframes and engines, there was a reluctance to mobilize industry on a war footing until it became absolutely necessary. Ultimately the failures and shortcomings were a consequence of Britain's political system – what happened when a free-market democracy tried to prepare for total war.

Each side used smoke and mirrors to try and persuade the other that there was no point in trying to outdo them in the air. They engaged in a pantomime of good fellowship which looks surreal at this distance in time. The fraternizing began at the instigation of the

RAF when in the spring of 1936 the Air Minister Lord Swinton invited General Erhard Milch to Britain.

General Milch was the man who could claim most of the credit for building up the Luftwaffe in the space of a few years from a puny collection of ill-assorted aircraft into the most feared air force in Europe. The Germans reciprocated and a party of senior RAF officers toured Luftwaffe facilities and aircraft factories the following January.

On 17 October 1937, Milch was back again, together with his chief of staff, Lieutenant General Hans-Jürgen Stumpff and Major General Ernst Udet, an internationally famous air ace and head of the Luftwaffe's technical division. Arriving at Croydon Airport Milch declared he had come to 'destroy mischievous rumours and create an atmosphere of comradeship and friendliness'.[24]

The programme that followed gave the impression that Britain was welcoming a trusted ally rather than a potential enemy. The day after arriving, Milch was taken to Buckingham Palace for an audience with King George VI. The itinerary covered almost every aspect of RAF operations, including visits to Cranwell and Halton and tours of the new shadow factories. Everything was done to make the Germans feel at home. At a cocktail party at the Carlton Hotel in the West End of London attended by everyone who was anyone in the British aviation world, the RAF band struck up the 'Badenweiler Marsch', which was always played at Hitler's public appearances, as well as 'Old Comrades' and 'Our Flag Flutters Before Us', a marching song of the Hitler Youth.[25]

On 19 October the Germans were given the run of the bomber station at Mildenhall in Suffolk. It was occupied by 99 and 149 Squadrons, both equipped with Handley Page Heyford biplane heavy bombers which lined up in facing ranks on the grass runway for the visitors to inspect. According to *The Times*, the German officers, who were dressed in Luftwaffe uniform, 'sat in the cockpits, waggled the controls, trained movable guns in their turrets, had bomb trapdoors opened for their inspections [and] asked questions which were readily answered …'[26] They were then treated to a mass flypast by an assortment of the bombers then in service: Vickers Wellesleys, Fairey Battles, Handley Page Harrows and Bristol

Blenheims. Lunch was served in the officers' mess. The table was decked out in the red, black and white Nazi colours.

The eagerness to please created moments of black farce. On 23 October Air Vice Marshal Victor Goddard, the RAF's deputy director of intelligence, took the Germans to Hornchurch in Essex which was home to two fighter squadrons. They were equipped with Gladiator biplanes which were swift and elegant but antediluvian compared to the sleek Messerschmitts now arriving at Luftwaffe fighter units. They did have one piece of equipment that was bang up to date – the latest optical reflector sights. Pilots had been told by the station commander Group Captain 'Bunty' Frew that 'if the Germans ask about the sight, keep mum'. So when General Milch peered into the cockpit of one of the Gladiators and inquired how the sight worked, the pilot, Bob Stanford Tuck of 65 Squadron, replied smartly: 'I'm sorry, General, it's so new, I've not yet found out.'[27] Tuck was 'quite appalled' when 'suddenly AVM Goddard interrupted and proceeded to give him the full details'. According to one version of the story, when Goddard had finished Tuck suggested: 'Sir, perhaps General Milch might like to take one home with him as a souvenir?'

The visit was presented by government and press as a hopeful sign that Hitler could be curbed. *Flight* magazine, the aviation bible, claimed that 'when the British mission visited German air force centres in January last, the members all felt that they knew, understood and respected their German hosts. It is permissible to hope and indeed to believe that the German party under the leadership of General Milch returned to Germany with the same feeling.'[28]

Others doubted that the Germans were fooled for a minute. Winston Churchill, the arch opponent of the government's policy of non-provocation, did not believe that the performance would have the slightest deterrent effect. It was, he wrote to the powerful Cabinet Secretary Maurice Hankey, 'a desperate effort ... to present a sham'. The truth was that at the Mildenhall display Bomber Command had struggled to 'put little more than a hundred bombers in the air – the great majority of which (as the Germans will readily see) can barely reach the coast of Germany with a bomb load'.[29]

Churchill's assessment of the RAF's power to intimidate was accurate enough. The Heyfords the Germans inspected had double-decker wings and fixed undercarriages and belonged to a bygone age. The machines in the flypast looked modern but were underwhelming in almost every department. The Battle was powered by a Rolls-Royce Merlin engine but carried only two single machine guns to defend itself and had a range of a sparse thousand miles. The Harrow, classified as a 'heavy', could manage a 1,250-mile round trip but was pathetically slow. The Wellesley 'medium' was capable of long distances but was also sluggish. The Blenheim, another medium, was the fastest of the lot, but was able to penetrate only to the fringes of German territory. These were the aircraft with which the RAF's bomber squadrons were currently equipped.

Better performing aircraft were emerging from the pipeline – the Whitleys, Wellingtons and Hampdens with which the RAF would fight in the first years of the war. But long-range aeroplanes capable of carrying a substantial bomb load were still in development. It would be twenty months before the Stirling, the first of the four-engine 'heavies', made its maiden flight. The Halifax did not start flying operationally until March 1941, the Lancaster a year later. In the meantime, the RAF would have to make do with machines which were plainly inadequate for the very ambitious role that had been claimed for them.

The Milch visit was merely a reminder of what the Air Staff already knew: that the service was utterly unprepared for war. Bomber Command – which had been created in a major structural reorganization of the Air Force in 1936 – had nothing in its armoury that was likely to cause Hitler to hesitate. Fighter Command, set up at the same time, was in better shape. It would be some time, though, before it had the machines and the system of detection, command and control needed to deploy them efficiently enough to withstand a mass attack. As things stood in the autumn of 1937, the Air Force was incapable of either deterring, defending or retaliating.

Slessor and the planning staff had already laid out the situation in stark terms in a paper to Newall a few days after he took over as Chief of the Air Staff on 1 September 1937. It stated that they would be 'failing in their duty were they not to express the considered opinion that the Metropolitan [i.e. home-based] Air Force in general and the Bomber Command in particular, are at present almost totally unfitted for war; that unless the production of new and up-to-date aircraft can be expedited, they will not be fit for war for at least two and a half years; and that even at the end of that time, there is not the slightest chance of their reaching equality with Germany in first line strength if the present German programmes are fulfilled'.[30]

The warning produced yet another scheme – J – but unlike its predecessors this was more than a mere exercise in upping the numbers. Quantity gave way to quality. The plan was based on what the Air Staff considered to be its minimum strategic requirements rather than on hoped-for deterrent effect, or some ill-defined numerical 'parity'. The goal was to have 3,031 front-line aircraft at home and abroad available by April 1941, that is 800 more than in Scheme F – the last one to get government approval.

As always, most of the new aircraft would be bombers, which would outnumber fighters by a factor of two to one. Nothing that had happened since the start of expansion had shaken the Air Staff's belief in the proposition that a big bomber force was the foundation for all air strategy. When submitting the new scheme for government approval, the Air Minister Lord Swinton made it clear 'there is no question of altering the ratio of fighter and bomber squadrons in the sense of reducing bomber squadrons to make fighter squadrons'.[31]

Faith in the offensive had blinded the Air Force professionals to the meaning of technological, military and political developments, the significance of which was dawning on amateur, civilian minds. Britain's defensive situation was improving fast. The domestic aircraft industry was at last producing fast, modern, low-wing monoplane fighters that could at least hold their own against the Luftwaffe. At the time Scheme J was proposed, 600 Hurricanes were on order from Hawker and the first small batch would start to arrive on squadrons at the beginning of 1938.[32] An order had been made for 310 Spitfires from Supermarine, though delays and complications meant production was stalled. Radar infrastructure was expanding rapidly. The first five stations in the Chain Home radar network covering the approaches to London became operational in 1938.

The Air Staff could take the credit for having identified and backed two world-beating fighters and for moving fast to exploit Radio Direction Finding. What they failed to grasp fully was the damage these developments had done to the premises on which their theory of air power rested. The combination of radar, the sophisticated command and control system that it made possible and fast, well-armed fighters seemed to provide a plausible shield against an attempted 'knock-out blow'.

The implications were spelled out by one senior officer who saw clearly the new reality. Hugh Dowding was appointed commander-in-chief of Fighter Command when it was created in July 1936, having been passed over for CAS in favour of Newall despite being his senior. He was regarded by his peers as humourless, earnest and aloof and well suited to his nickname, 'Stuffy'. Before his appointment he had been in charge of research and development at the Air Ministry and it was largely on his initiative that the Hurricane and Spitfire were ordered. He had no scientific training but was open to new ideas and soon grasped the significance of RDF. It was he who devised the finely tuned system of collating raw radar reports and sightings from ground observers, filtering them through control centres and translating the refined information into orders to the fighter squadrons.

Dowding's views ran head-on into the prevailing orthodoxy. He rejected the notion that counter-attack by bomber was the best form of defence in favour of a simpler idea. 'The best defence of this country is Fear of the Fighter,' he wrote. 'If we are strong in fighters we should probably never be attacked in force. If we are moderately strong we shall probably be attacked and the attacks will gradually be brought to a standstill … if we are weak in fighter strength, the attacks will not be brought to a standstill and the productive capacity of the country will be virtually destroyed.'[33] The overwhelming duty of the Air Force, he argued, was to secure the safety of the home base. Dowding's views were heresy to the bomber cult. It took courage to maintain his beliefs in contradiction to the overwhelming official wisdom but he did so tenaciously, in the words of the official historians choosing 'neither to understand other arguments, nor to compromise, nor even to accept with good grace the decisions that went against him'.[34]

On his own, Dowding was unable to deflect the Air Staff from the fixed notion that inspired all their strategic thinking. It needed an outsider to do that. The first major challenge to the primacy of the bomber arrived from an unexpected quarter. Sir Thomas Inskip came from a line of stolid West Country solicitors and parsons and was known, if at all, for his parliamentary objections to a new version of the Book of Common Prayer. The announcement early in 1936 that he was to be moved from his post as Attorney General to the newly created position of Minister for the Co-ordination of Defence was greeted with derision and incomprehension. The role had been created by the Prime Minister, Stanley Baldwin, in an attempt to harmonize the rearmament effort. It was a vitally important job and big names were bandied about to fill it, among them Winston Churchill's. Baldwin eventually decided Inskip was a safer bet, a decision that was approved by the Chancellor of the Exchequer Neville Chamberlain who noted in his diary that while he would 'excite no enthusiasm' he would 'involve us in no fresh perplexities'.[35] Inskip would confound the low expectations set for him.

When Scheme J arrived on his desk he coolly reassessed the *a priori* assumption contained within it that it was essential for Britain to possess a bomber strike force to match that of the Luftwaffe. To the quiet, God-fearing lawyer, it seemed that for the time being at least the emphasis should be on defence rather than offence and priority given to fighters. Admittedly, if war came that would mean that Britain would suffer more damage than it could inflict, but 'the result would not at once be critical'.[36] He believed that Germany did not have the resources to sustain a prolonged war and would therefore have to 'knock us out in a comparatively short time'. The best course was to concentrate on warding off the initial assaults while preserving military and economic strength for a long-drawn-out fight which Britain would win through its superior staying power. He was prepared to propose an increase of only £100 million on top of the existing allocation for the previous expansion scheme. If the money was to be used effectively, the Air Ministry should spend it on relatively cheap fighters rather than expensive bombers.

The airmen fought back vigorously against this impertinent rejection of the professional wisdom that suffused their thoughts and actions. Swinton reiterated the mantra that 'counter attack still remains the chief deterrent and defence' and warned that 'we must not exaggerate the possibilities' arising from radar and other developments. He also mounted a political defence, suggesting strongly that the change of direction would play badly with the public, making it seem as if the government was abandoning its public promises to keep up with the Germans in the air.

He had misread the changing mood. It was the here and now that mattered currently, not theories for the future. When the whole question of defence expenditure was considered in cabinet on 22 December 1937, it was Inskip's view that 'parity with Germany was more important in fighter aircraft resisting aggression, than in the offensive role of bombers' that prevailed.[37]

The Air Ministry was now compelled to work with him to draw up a new scheme – K – which reflected the reversal in policy. The bomber force was reduced from ninety squadrons to seventy-seven and allowance was made for only nine weeks of reserves, at the end of which, Newall observed bitterly, 'the war would have been lost'. The numbers of the front-line fighter force remained the same at thirty-eight squadrons and 532 aircraft but there would be more than half as many again in reserve.

The Inskip intervention was taken badly by the Air Staff who resented an amateur trespassing on their territory and, as they saw it, endangering Britain's security purely for the sake of financial expediency. The assault on the thinking that had sustained the Air Force for much of its short life was most resented by the chief evangelist. The fact that he was nine years retired did not stop Trenchard from publicly and privately denouncing the shift to fighters. 'The old man was obstinately unrelenting – not only at this time but even after the war broke out – about adherence in any circumstances to the bomber policy,' John Slessor remembered.[38] It would turn out that, in the short term at least, Inskip was right and the Air Staff were wrong. This realization did little to shake the faith of the bomber cult, an attitude that would have profound consequences when the time came for Britain to fight on land and sea.

4

Brylcreem Boys

The great lexicographer of slang Eric Partridge recorded that in 1937 soldiers and sailors began to refer to their Air Force colleagues as the 'Glamour Boys'.[1] The term was not necessarily admiring or affectionate. A little later on the RAF attracted another nickname. They were the 'Brylcreem Boys', a reference to their habit of slicking their hair with a best-selling pomade. The manufacturers, County Chemicals of Birmingham, were delighted with the association. In 1939, launching the 'handy active service tube' they chose to dress the model in Air Force forage cap and tunic and during the war a glossy-haired airman appeared regularly in their advertisements. It was only many years later that the man in the ads, one Tony Gibson, was revealed as a conscientious objector who did several stints in jail for his beliefs.[2]

Hair cream and the Air Force seemed to go together. The product had a practical use. Richard Passmore, a wireless operator/air gunner on Blenheims in the early part of the war, recalled how his 'side cap hung above my ear at angle which mocked gravity and was a mute testimony to the adhesiveness of Brylcreem'.[3] However, the main point of it was that it allowed you to look like an up-to-the-minute civilian male while wearing military uniform.

Like many of the trends adopted by the youth of Britain in the 1930s, the trend for sculpted men's hairdos was imported from America via Hollywood movies. The notion of glamour was a contemporary one. If any branch of the armed services had claim to it, it was the Air Force.

The RAF's modern image gave it a marked advantage over the other services in the competition for human resources. Expansion required men as well as machines, to fly them and to service them. In 1933 the RAF needed only one recruiting depot to fill its manpower needs, and took on less than a thousand extra men in addition to the regular Halton and Cranwell intakes. By the spring of 1938 there were eleven depots and thirty-one sub-depots which over the next eighteen months scooped up 43,795 recruits. With the introduction of conscription and the outbreak of war the numbers exploded. Between September 1939 and January 1942, 789,773 joined the ranks. By the time recruiting was halted in 1944, nearly 1.2 million men and women were wearing Air Force Blue.[4]

Trenchard had identified the need for manpower structures that were light and simple yet strong enough to support a rapid increase in numbers when needed. Initially, the system worked very well. In peacetime, in addition to the small core of regulars, the RAF could rely on a steady throughput of short service commission officers to supply most of its aircrew requirements. After doing their time they then passed into the Reserve of Air Force Officers (RAFO). The front-line squadrons were backed up by the amateurs of the Auxiliary Air Force and University Air Squadrons.

By early 1936, with the likelihood of war growing by the month, it was clear that these sources would soon dry up once the fighting began and a much bigger reservoir of aircrew would be needed. The

experience of the last war had taught that 'casualties in air warfare are high and the replacement of wastage is an even greater problem for a personnel than an equipment department'.[5] The need to make good the 'wastage' – the term must have struck some as inhumane even then – prompted the creation of a pool of airmen who had received at least a basic level of flying training. They would learn theory at evening classes in city schoolrooms and practise at civilian air schools at the weekend, in readiness to fill the gaps torn in the front line when hostilities commenced.

The RAF Volunteer Reserve (RAFVR) hastened the transformation of the Air Force from a tiny elite dominated by the comfortably off and privately educated into a mass organization drawn from every level of Britain's sharply stratified society.

From the outset it was presented as a democratic endeavour. 'The social and political setting of the time had considerable influence on [the] proposed scheme and there was strong popular feeling against any "caste" or "old school tie" attitude', the RAF internal narrative recorded.[6] It was 'visualized as a collection of young men drawn from the middle class in its widest sense and with no suggestion in its organization of a pre-determined social hierarchy'. In time it would be hailed as a great RAF innovation but the credit for the initial concept belongs as much to the imagination of an Air Ministry bureaucrat as it does to the progressive instincts of the Air Staff.

W. L. Scott was working for Air Commodore Arthur Tedder in the Air Ministry's training department when he was set the problem of finding pilot material from new sources. He had won a DSC with the Navy during the previous war and went on to be knighted for his labours in the Civil Service. Despite his conventional background, he seems to have had a sympathetic understanding of the contemporary mood. He realized that to get the numbers it needed the Air Force would have to reach beyond the social groups it felt comfortable with and embrace the young men growing up on the suburban streets of modern Britain.

Britain in the 1930s was changing shape. Towns that had not altered for centuries were being transformed by giant cinemas and blocks of flats. The surrounding fields filled up with new housing, arranged in 'crescents', 'avenues' and 'drives' lined with mock-Tudor houses. The people who lived in them often also owned them. They worked in modern jobs in offices and factories and when they wanted fun looked to America to entertain them. They watched American films at the Odeon and danced to American music at the local Palais, which they drove to in small cars mass-produced by Morris and Austin. They had little reason to regret the passing of old Britain. They were interested in the future, and determined to have a place in it, and not on terms of deference or inferiority.

It was to this generation that the RAF now turned, but with some caution.[7] Scott's initial memo warned that the sort of men they were looking for were unlikely to take kindly to strict military discipline. Instead, 'the desire to fly, patriotism, and retaining fees large enough to count in a young man's weekly budget will be the means of attracting our reservists'. In addition, he proposed, it was important that the whole experience was fun. 'Socially the reserves must be a great success,' he wrote. 'The young men must enjoy their evening meetings and their weekends.'[8]

This concept was a major departure from conventional military structures and a lot for the Air Staff to swallow. Its members had spent their lives inside an institutional cocoon where they kept company with each other and followed traditional leisure pursuits: riding, shooting, fishing and sailing by day, dining and playing bridge together by night. They knew those below them on the social scale only as servants or other ranks. They were unfamiliar with the new world emerging beyond the gates of the base and were not sure how much they liked it. To them the growth of mass consumerism was an affront in a time of crisis. 'If even a fraction of the energy, material and organizing capacity now being diverted to such non-essential channels as the production of unnecessary motor-cars, luxury cinemas and blocks of flats were directed … to the production of modern aircraft, we could overcome our present dangerous difficulties …' complained an Air Staff paper in November 1937.[9]

Nonetheless, after a few initial queries, the Director of Training Arthur Tedder backed the scheme. Tedder came from a conventional establishment background. He was the son of a senior civil servant, went to Whitgift School, then Magdalene College, Cambridge, where he studied history. He entered the Colonial Service but volunteered for the Army when war broke out. An accident resulted in a serious knee injury which seemed likely to keep him out of the fighting. Desperate to escape the tedium and ignominy of a cushy rear echelon job, Tedder harassed the authorities until he was finally accepted for pilot training with the RFC. In the summer of 1916, while the Somme offensive was raging, he was a flight commander with 25 Squadron which was carrying out constant bombing raids and reconnaissance missions and suffering heavy losses. On 17 July they were inspected by the RFC commander Hugh Trenchard, whose policy of all-out aggression was driving the high casualty rate. In a letter to his wife Rosalinde, Tedder reported that he 'had to go round with him while he looked at our machines. He asked a lot of questions, but made absolutely no comments, except "Yes."'[10] Trenchard had seen something he liked in the twenty-six-year-old officer. He would 'foster many careers during the next 30 years' among the men who served under him on the Western Front, wrote his biographer, Vincent Orange, but 'none more so than Tedder's'.[11]

With Tedder's support the basic format was adopted. Putting the scheme to the Treasury, the Air Council proposed 'to open the new force to the whole middle class in the widest sense of that term, namely the complete range of the output of the public and second-ary schools'.[12] Until now, anyone seeking entry to the RAF would have been initially graded as to whether or not they were officer material primarily on the grounds of their social class. In the new circumstances this was considered 'inappropriate'. Instead entry was to be 'on a common footing, airman pilot or observer and promo-tions to commissioned rank will be made at a later stage in accord-ance with the abilities actually displayed'.

It amounted to a near-revolutionary challenge to the assump-tions that governed the closed world of the British military. In the previous war, death and injury had cleared a path for lower-class men to receive the King's commission. In peacetime the old barriers were quickly re-erected. In principle at least, the RAFVR established a new universal criterion for officer selection: it meant that candi-dates would be chosen, not on the grounds of which school they went to and which accent they spoke with, but on the basis of whether they were any good or not.

Expansion also created a need for more short service officers. To attract the numbers needed, advertising campaigns were mounted and standards relaxed. The results were unwelcome to some career officers who preferred the old exclusivity.

The gentleman fliers of the Auxiliary Air Force had been similarly dismayed by the creation of the RAFVR which opened the club doors of weekend service aviation to Tom, Dick and Harry. All AAF Squadrons were exclusive to a certain extent, some ludicrously so. Outfits such as 601 (County of London) were founded in 1926 by Lord Edward Grosvenor who recruited the first members from the White's club bar. Originally the Auxiliaries were all bomber squadrons and in the words of the RAF narrative 'truth to tell, not very highly rated as such'.[13] However 'they had no inferiority complex: very much the opposite in fact. Indeed, some of the squadrons were inclined to look down on the regulars, as the cavalry in the army used to look down on the infantry.'

When planning for the RAFVR began it seemed that the AAF provided a natural nucleus around which to build an organization to train the newcomers. It resisted all pressure to do so, being 'reluctant to sacrifice its exclusive character to serve wider interests' as its 'standard of expenditure and social rigidity were incompatible with a democratic reserve'.[14] Frederick Bowhill, the Air Council member responsible for personnel, thought the Auxiliaries might be open to recruiting a reserve of accountant and stores officers 'who might have been thought socially acceptable'. Instead opposition 'was so violent that the suggestion was hastily dropped'.[15]

Some AAF members and some regular officers saw themselves as the paradigm of the upper-class warrior, bold and courageous but taciturn and emotionally restrained. These types populate the quasi-autobiographical stories of John Llewellyn Rhys, son of a Welsh rector who, after public school, in the early 1930s gave up a place at Oxford to join the RAF. He combined a love of flying with literary ambitions and began publishing short stories in 1936. In one, 'Too Young to Live', the narrator is in hospital recovering from an unspecified injury. In the neighbouring bed is a young pilot, dying slowly from the effects of a crash after only his second solo flight.

That afternoon he began to talk to me again, telling me about his people, who were in India, and how they hated him flying and how his mother had prophesied that his career as a pilot would end in disaster ... it seemed they had a place in England, a house in Suffolk in the lovely wooded country on the Norfolk border. There was a lot of game there and he wanted me to promise to come up for some shooting ... 'The riding's grand too; you could have Magpie, and there's bags of hunting and we'd go into market on Wednesday and drink with the farmers ...'[16]

England Is My Village, which appeared in 1940, describes the atmosphere in the officers' mess as the Wing Commander briefs his men on the eve of a big operation.

Robert heard his instructions and memorized them with an ease born of practice, but the words seemed meaningless, rattling like hail on the roof of his mind.

'Any questions?'

But they were all old hands and no naïve youngsters among them wanted to make themselves heard.

'Well ... good luck! I know you'll put up a good show,' his voice was suddenly shy, 'I wish they'd let me come with you.'

They went back to the ante-room, went on talking, reading ... Robert sat down by a friend. They had been together for years but were in different squadrons.

'If anything,' Robert's voice was quiet as he flipped the pages of a magazine, 'if anything were to happen to ... slip up ... tomorrow, would you attend to the odd detail?'

'Of course, old boy.' The other puffed his pipe alight, swung the match until it was extinguished.

'Tomorrow?'

'Yes.'

'Tough show?'

'Tough enough.'[17]

Robert does not return from the op. Rhys, a flight lieutenant in a bomber squadron, was killed on active service in August 1940.

This portrayal of an Air Force staffed by strong, silent men from good county families was more an expression of how some airmen liked to see themselves rather than a reflection of reality. The illusion was unsustainable. The social distinctions that marked the pre-war RAF soon became blurred when the fighting began. As the first clashes thinned their ranks and veterans were posted away, the AAF squadrons could no longer maintain their exclusivity and had to accept whoever they were sent as replacements. By the end of the Battle of Britain only five pilots remained from 601's pre-war strength. The sixty-one men who washed through the squadron in the months of the Battle made up what was by then a typical Fighter Command motley of RAFVR sergeants, former SSC pilots and Czech and Polish airmen rejoining the fight.[18]

Even so, some important aspects of the pre-war style survived to become embedded in the Air Force ethos and form a salient part of its image. British airmen, whatever their origins, disliked show-offs and insouciance and understatement were the form. Air Ministry officials who during the war organized morale-boosting visits by veterans to aviation factories had to urge them to speak vividly about their experiences. An official account noted that 'the reluctance of the aircrew personnel to "shoot a line" as they called it, had to be overcome'.[19] Above all, pre-war professionals, auxiliary amateurs and the citizen fliers of the wartime service were united in an all-but-unquestioned willingness to face any odds and accept any risk.

Scott and Tedder identified the desire to fly as the most powerful inducement in attracting aircrew candidates. Nowadays it is quite hard to appreciate the fascination with aviation that gripped young men – and women – growing up in the 1920s and 1930s. The jeremiads preached by politicians about the huge potential for evil created by the invention of the aeroplane had little effect on the young. In their minds, it was the magic of flying that prevailed.

In the 1920s and 1930s aviators, male and female, enjoyed the celebrity and sometimes the rewards of film idols. The British couple Amy Johnson and Jim Mollison were world-famous. Amy

was small, dark and gamine and looked as good in the severe fash-
ions of the day as she did in leather helmet and sheepskin flying
jacket – a paradigm of modern womanhood. She was born in Hull
in 1903, where her father was a prosperous businessman, and studied economics at Sheffield University only to end up as a secretary
in a solicitor's office in London.

She found her métier when she joined the London Aeroplane
Club, gaining a ground engineer's as well as a pilot's licence. Backed
by her father and wealthy air enthusiasts she made a record-break-
ing solo flight to Australia in 1930 inspiring a popular hit, 'Amy,
Wonderful Amy'. In 1932 she met and immediately married
Mollison, a Glasgow-born flier and former RAF short service
commission officer and instructor at the Central Flying School.
They competed as a team in air races and were fêted as 'the Flying
Sweethearts'. The marriage crumbled after four years, due it was said
to Mollison's drinking and inability to cope with his wife's fame.
When the war came she joined the RAF as an Air Transport Auxiliary
pilot delivering service aircraft around the country and died in
mysterious circumstances after baling out from an Airspeed Oxford
over the Thames Estuary in January 1941.

Aviation attracted the wealthy, fashionable and aristocratic but it
was also promoted as a marvel of the new democratic age that
should be open to everyone. No one pushed this message harder
than Alan Cobham. Even in an industry not lacking energetic
egotists, Cobham stood out. He flew with the RFC in the First World
War, then joined de Havilland as a test pilot before making a series
of flights to Australia and around Africa for which he was knighted
by King George V. He played himself – the starring role – in a 1927
silent movie, *The War Commander*. In 1929 he set out on an air tour
of Britain to encourage a trade-boosting programme of municipal
airport building under the slogan 'Make the Skyways Britain's
Highways'. His great achievement, though, was to get a generation
of British boys and girls airborne. Cobham believed that
'air-mindedness' was best started early. The airliner he flew around
the country was called 'Youth of Britain' and on the first tour of
Britain the Castrol oil magnate Lord Wakefield paid anonymously
for 10,000 children to get a first taste of 'going up' in it.

His proselytizing drive, as well as a keen business instinct, led him to dream up an event which he hoped would 'embed itself in the public consciousness as deeply as Pancake Tuesday or Fireworks Night', by persuading hundreds of towns around the country to host their own National Aviation Day.[20] Cobham provided the spectacle with a team of 'aces', dashingly kitted out in white flying overalls manning up to fourteen aircraft. They laid on exhilarating displays, putting the aircraft through rolls, inverted loops, and 'falling leaf' manoeuvres as well as clambering out of the cockpits for displays of wing-walking. In 1933 they visited 306 venues in the British Isles and 800,000 people paid to see them. Ticket prices were low – 1s. 3d. for an adult and 6d. for a child – but, to Cobham's exasperation, many others watched for free from what he called the 'Aberdeen Grandstand' – neighbouring high ground.[21]

Part of the huge appeal of Cobham's Flying Circus was the chance for punters to get airborne and about one in four of those who attended did so. This could be done sedately, in a multi-seat airliner or, more thrillingly, in the rear cockpit of one of the smaller planes. The tickets were priced for a wide range of pockets: a pound for a white-knuckle full aerobatic flight (about £60 today), 10s. for a seat in the opening Grand Formation Flight or 4s. for a four-minute flip.

For thousands of the young men who flew with the Royal Air Force in the Second World War, this was their initiation to the air and for many it was as powerful and unforgettable as a first sexual encounter. Charles Fenwick, son of a captain in the Royal Engineers, was in his early teens when Cobham's circus came to Rough Common just outside Canterbury. His aunt Edie took him to watch the show. Fenwick had never seen an aeroplane before. What followed was a *coup de foudre*. 'Soon after we arrived the first plane taxied out and flew off into the lovely clear morning sky,' he recalled, 'and sitting behind the pilot was a young boy.'[22]

Fenwick was 'green with envy'. Then Edie offered to treat him to a 'flip' and a few minutes later he was climbing into the rear cockpit of an elderly Avro 504. He had barely time to strap himself in 'before we were rumbling across the field. After a final frenzied race across the meadow the rumbling suddenly stopped and my heart followed suit as I left the earth for the first time.' Many years after the event he wrote: 'the thrill as we climbed up and away from the solid old Earth will never fade. I was dumbfounded ... we sailed over Hall Place and peered down into the rookery as the inmates squawked their way to safety ... there was our home, the Claverings, looking for all the world like a doll's house. On, on we flew. This was utterly stupendous ...' When he left school Fenwick went to the aircraft manufacturer Short Brothers as an apprentice, joined the Volunteer Reserve six months before the outbreak of war and flew Hurricanes in the Battle of Britain.

Boys who were not lucky enough to take a joy ride could fantasize about flying, their imaginations stimulated by a vast range of juvenile literature featuring aeroplanes and aviators. Lively mass circulation comics like *Modern Boy* were full of now-forgotten flying adventurers such as Jaggers of the RAF and Scotty of the Secret Squadron. The greatest of them all was James Bigglesworth. Biggles was the creation of W. E. Johns who had a brief but dramatic career as a bomber pilot with the RFC on the Western Front. Shot down in the last weeks of the war, he was captured but managed, briefly, to escape. He stayed on in the post-war RAF as a recruitment officer. On leaving he turned to editing, writing and illustrating on aviation themes. In 1928 he became editor of *Popular Flying* where Biggles appeared in the first of many short stories. In September 1932 a collection appeared called *The Camels Are Coming*. It was the start of a literary phenomenon. Johns was prolific and Biggles books flowed from his pen sometimes at the rate of four a year.

The characters were reasonably close to life and the detail and plots rang true. The young readers were not spared the realities of air fighting including the prospect of a ghastly death burning alive in a slow descent. But against this was set the camaraderie and gaiety of squadron life and the compelling figure of Biggles himself. Cool, technically competent and skilful yet understated, full of pluck and vitality, he was a hero made for his time.

Before long he would have a female counterpart. In 1941 Johns followed up with the first in the 'Worrals' series featuring the adventures of Joan Worralson of the Women's Auxiliary Air Force and her sidekick Betty 'Frecks' Lovell. Johns revealed that the character was based on two women fliers of his acquaintance, Amy Johnson and Pauline Gower. As well as setting up her own joy-riding and air taxi service in Kent, Gower wrote stories with air themes for the *Girl's Own Paper*. She would go on to head the Air Transport Auxiliary during the war.

The Air Ministry exploited the glamour of aviation to burnish the RAF's reputation and appeal. The annual Hendon Air Display and the Empire Air Days put on at RAF stations around the country from 1934 to 1939 emphasized the excitement of flying rather than the realities of aerial warfare with spectacular demonstrations of stunt and formation flying. Sometimes they included mock imperial policing operations in which aircraft dropped flour bombs on villages inhabited by rebellious 'Whatnot' tribesmen or on fake wooden battleships. The main purpose, though, was to impress and entertain.

In official publications the RAF naturally emphasized its defensive and deterrent role. The bomber force was designed for a *counter-offensive* not to launch aggressive war. This was a British version of air power framed by national characteristics of restraint and reserve, with rearmament presented, reasonably enough, as a reluctant necessity. A pre-war recruiting poster showed a young family picnicking on the cliffs on a sun-drenched summer day. Father and son are looking upwards at a flight of twin-engine bombers heading out to sea while mother and daughter prepare tea. The copy reads 'Air Defence is Home Defence'.[23]

When it came to attracting the specialist ground tradesmen needed to service the expanded squadrons, the RAF used a different approach, which ignored the prospect of war and made no appeal to duty and patriotism. The competition for skilled men was fierce, and there were plenty of well-paid jobs available in war industry factories. Advertising campaigns played up the prospect of travel and adventure and the attractions of outdoor life over a dreary works in the Midlands. A poster that appeared in 1939 showed a smart, confident figure in side cap and overalls, probing efficiently at an aero engine above the exhortation: 'Come on, skilled fitters! Your experience will earn you the finest job ever: and with it – security, good prospects and a grand outdoor life'.[24]

The inducements on offer were strong even in supposedly pros-perous parts of the country. Len Hayden was brought up in Henham-on-the-Hill in Essex, one of nine children who lived in a three-bedroom house without running water. He left school at four-teen and did a series of menial jobs in local haulage and engineer-ing companies which offered little pay and no security but where he picked up a knowledge of mechanics. One winter morning early in 1939 he arrived at work after pushing his bike for eight miles through thick snow only to be sent home for turning up late.[25]

It was then that he made up his mind to respond to a newspaper advert seeking air mechanics for the RAF. He decided against telling his parents. His father Billy had been a reasonably prosperous coal merchant and dairy farmer before the previous war. He volunteered for the Army in 1916 and served in the trenches where he was poisoned by mustard gas. His health, and his prosperity, never returned. 'Time after time he would return home [from hospital treatment] and try and rebuild his business, each time only to succumb to bouts of pneumonia and pleurisy caused by his wartime service,' Hayden remembered.[26] He scraped a living as a middleman buying cattle for local farmers and a 19s. 6d. weekly pension, squeezed out of the War Office after the intervention of the local MP. His son reflected that it was 'no wonder tears trickled down his cheeks' when he called home late in 1940 to say goodbye before following his squadron to North Africa. 'He must have been think-ing how a grateful nation would treat us when we returned from "our" war.'

The recruiting campaigns were almost too successful. In March 1939 Charles Portal, then in charge of personnel at the Air Ministry, reported that there was a shortfall of fitters, wireless and electrical mechanics, instrument makers and armourers. However, he concluded, 'basically the problem is not volunteers but the facilities in which to train them'.[27] The inability of the training machine at every level to keep pace with the increase in men and machines would contribute much to the RAF's multiple failures in the open-ing stages of the war.

Like their Army and Navy counterparts the men who ran the RAF regarded their service as a manifestation of British identity and a repository of British virtues. They were wary of outside attempts to portray it, no matter how great the resulting publicity might be. In July 1937 the weekly meeting of the Air Council which brought together the Air Minister Lord Swinton, his deputy and the top staff officers discussed a Hollywood proposal to make a movie with an RAF theme. British settings were popular with American audiences and Metro-Goldwyn-Mayer had recently set up a subsidiary, MGM-British, to develop co-productions.

One of the first projects was *Shadow of the Wing*. It had a screen-play by a Briton, Sidney Gilliat, but box office considerations demanded an American lead and Clark Gable, already a star, had been picked by Louis B. Mayer himself to play the hero. The minutes of the meeting record have Swinton stating that he was 'strongly in favour of films as valuable recruiting agents' – both the Navy (*Brown on Resolution*) and the Army (*OHMS*) had already co-operated with film makers in an effort to boost their appeal. However, he was 'in some doubt in this case as to whether we could or should acquiesce in an arrangement whereby the leading role – that of a Royal Air Force pilot – was to be taken by an American actor, Mr Clark Gable, who might prove to be possessed of a strong American accent'.[28]

He was followed by the CAS, Air Marshal Edward Ellington, who in a characteristic contribution affirmed that 'he too was opposed to such an arrangement but added that he did not know whether the actor in question had such an accent'. The senior civil servant at the Air Ministry, Sir Donald Banks, raised the possibility that MGM might be prepared to accept a British actor, though he warned that if they insisted on this point 'he feared that the company would abandon the project'. This prompted a discussion as to possible British stars. Leslie Banks (no relation to Sir Donald), a well-known character actor of domestic stage and screen but with no preten-sions to stardom, was 'generally felt to be the most suitable'. The item concluded with Swinton proposing that he sit down that evening with his deputy to study a Clark Gable film and decide whether or not his accent was acceptable.

In the event neither was able to make the screening. However, at the next meeting Ellington reported that he had since seen Gable play the English seaman Fletcher Christian in *Mutiny on the Bounty* and found him 'not offensive in any way'. The consensus remained that a Brit would be better. Seven months later there was still no progress. Sir Donald ventured that 'he rather suspected that our modest display of enthusiasm for Mr Clark Gable who had been Mr Mayer's selection might to some extent account for the film proposal to have hung fire …' (Clark Gable went on to fly several combat missions as an air gunner with the USAAF.)

Shadow of the Wing never made it to the screen but there were plenty of other air movies to keep audiences happy. Doom-mongering efforts like *Things to Come* were outnumbered by productions that showed military aviation in a heroic light. *The Dawn Patrol* was so popular it was made twice in the space of eight years. The second version starring Errol Flynn, Basil Rathbone and David Niven was a box office hit when it came out in 1938. It was an unsparing account of the life of Royal Flying Corps pilots operating on the Western Front in the summer of 1915 when German Fokker *eindecker* fighters were winning the battle for air superiority over the trenches. The men of 59 Squadron are a hard-drinking, fatalistic bunch. Among them are two friends, Dick Courtney and Douglas Scott, played by Flynn and Niven. They are at odds with their leader Major Brand (Rathbone) who has lost sixteen of his pilots in the previous fortnight, most of them greenhorns fresh from flying training school. The mental strain on a commander forced to send novices to almost certain death is convincingly depicted. But it also reinforces the propaganda message broadcast by both sides during the real war, which presented air fighting as a clean, almost chivalrous business in contrast to the industrial carnage going on in the mud below. Courtney is killed after shooting down the German ace von Richter. The film ends with an image of inescapable duty as Scott orders the remnants of the squadron off on another dawn patrol.

To many British boys who watched it, the film acted not as a dire warning about the perils of life in the Air Force but as a call to their spirit of courage, sacrifice and adventure. 'It may sound a bit odd and unlikely but this film really did have a tremendous influence on me,' remembered Charles Patterson.[29] 'It struck me that though casualties were very heavy it was much the most wonderful and exciting way to go to war ... some strange, but as it turned out accurate, instinct told me that if I was going to fight, this was about the only way that there was any chance of my doing it successfully.' As a Mosquito pilot with Path Finder Force, Patterson would take part in some of the most audacious daylight raids of the war, dropping his bombs and then filming the results of the operation for later analysis.

The multitudes who read aviation magazines and followed the air races and the fortunes of celebrity aviators had little chance of becoming pilots themselves. Flying instruction at most clubs and commercial schools during the 1930s cost two pounds an hour when a young man starting out in a clerical or factory job would be pleased to get two pounds a week. A course aimed at securing a basic 'A' licence cost anything from £15 to £35.

The RAFVR offered a passport to the enchanted domain. It was open to any male between the ages of eighteen and twenty-five with a reasonable level of secondary education. Those accepted would receive flying training gratis as well as an annual grant of £25. The educational requirements were a barrier to a large proportion of British males, most of whom left school at fourteen. Many who came forward were from the ranks of the comfortably off. But there were also large numbers of bank clerks, shop assistants, and minor civil servants eager to seize what seemed a God-given chance to break out of their dull existences and realize their fantasies.

Despite the obvious attractions of the offer, the Air Staff felt the mood of the country was tricky. They detected a hostility to 'militarism' and were alarmed by the prevalence of pacifist sentiments. At an Air Council meeting in May 1936 Frederick Bowhill complained that 'at present the Press give great prominence to pacifist manifestoes, particularly those from seats of learning, but make no attempt to inculcate a feeling among the youth of the country that service in its defence was a fine thing'. He proposed that 'we ought ... to aim at bringing about a change of heart in the Press'.[30]

Sensibly, the tone remained sotto voce, with publicity stressing adventure rather than patriotism, a wise approach given the mood of the times. In 1936 the Peace Pledge Union, inspired by a canon of St Paul's Cathedral, was in its heyday, attracting hundreds of thousands of supporters across the political spectrum, united in their renunciation of war and determination to work to remove its causes.

As the threat from Germany mounted attitudes hardened and the service chiefs' concerns about the willingness of the younger generation to fight would prove unfounded. When looking back, few would cite the worsening international situation or a sense of duty as a compelling motive for volunteering. 'I was walking down the Strand and there was an RAF recruiting office with a poster in the window and it said "London businessmen join the RAF and fly aeroplanes at the weekend",' said Maurice Leng who was just starting out in the advertising business. 'There were no patriotic reasons. I was interested in motor-racing but it was an expensive sport and I couldn't possibly afford the cost of a decent car ... here was this wonderful opportunity for flying these super aeroplanes provided by the government and that is exactly what I did.'[31] Brian Considine was a trainee at Unilever when he joined in January 1939. 'I was nineteen and I don't think I was bothered by [the political situation],' he recalled.[32] 'It was a way to learn to fly which was an expensive thing to do. In fact instead of paying out of one's own pocket one was actually going to be paid to do it.'

Some who went on to have gallant wartime careers enjoyed emphasizing the unheroic motives that had impelled them into the Air Force in the first place. Christopher Foxley-Norris, who flew Hurricanes in the Battle of Britain, liked to claim that his main reason for joining the Oxford University Air Squadron was the £25 signing-on fee. It enabled him to buy a car which his older brother had told him was essential if he was to have any chance of attracting a girlfriend.[33] But he also admitted that though life in the squadron was 'enormous fun, at the same time most of us realized there was going to be a bust up ... but at least some of us were doing something about it while the rest were just sitting around'.[34]

Tony Smyth, a graduate chemist working at the paint manufacturer Manders, did not 'join the RAFVR ... from patriotism, but only to increase my pay and show me the world'.[35] Like Foxley-Norris he soon learned that the fun came at a price. When in the spring of 1937 he began his basic training as part of the first intake of volunteers at Prestwick elementary flying school near Glasgow, the CO in his welcoming address left them in no doubt as to what it was they were being trained for. 'He told us … that the remilitarization of the Rhineland by Hitler had showed the world that German expansion as proposed in "Mein Kampf" was serious. An enlargement of the RAF was essential … to produce a reserve of civilian aircrew.' As time passed the truth that they were learning to fight as well as fly became increasingly apparent.

If war was coming, the Air Force seemed a good place in which to spend it. Almost everyone eligible to fight had someone close to them who had been killed or maimed in the previous war and most of the casualties had been suffered in the trenches of the Western Front. Reluctance to repeat the previous generation's experience was a powerful factor in choosing to serve in the relatively clean-seeming element of the air.

Tony Iveson's police inspector father had been 'shot on the first day of the Somme and very badly wounded. He had a huge scar on his chest … All my generation knew how horrible it had been.'[36] Growing up in York he heard his elders talk in ever more pessimistic terms about the crisis in Europe. 'I knew that there was going to be a war and I knew who it was going to be with so I came through my teens with that in my mind.' Early on he resolved that when it came 'I just wanted to fly'. Iveson joined the RAFVR and flew in the Battle of Britain before eventually joining 617 Squadron – the Dam Busters.

There was also the question of comfort. The RAF seemed to offer a cushier existence than you could expect in the Army or Navy. Sir Edwin Lutyens had been among those consulted on the design of the stations that sprang up in the 1930s. They were built to high specifications and airmen, or at least officers, were thought to live well. Charles Patterson was self-aware enough to know he could 'never have stood up to the rigours of fighting on land and in the dust and heat and dirt'. When later at a recruiting interview he was asked why he wanted to be a pilot he boldly replied, 'because the only way that I could consider it possible to fight was if one was provided with central heating and constant hot water'.[37] The group captain heading the panel 'gave me a broad smile and nodded approval and said: "Accepted. Recommended".'

The first RAFVR entrants began training in April 1937. Tedder saved money by using the network of flying clubs across the country to supply the infrastructure, with the instruction being supervised by the RAF's Central Flying School.[38] The reservists did basic training at an initial six- or eight-week course, at the end of which they were expected to go solo, then returned to their regular jobs and kept up training at weekends at local airfields operating under contract with the Air Ministry. The volunteers had only a semi-detached relationship with the RAF. They did not wear uniform and were part of a mass reserve rather than organized into squadrons like the Auxiliaries.

They started flying on Tiger Moths and similar easy-to-master aircraft and gradually progressed on to new types like the Avro Cadet before finally getting to grips with aircraft then in service in the squadrons. They also attended night classes in local towns to study basic aeronautics and navigation.

For those who had never flown the initial trip could come as an unpleasant surprise. Bob Doe, who, despite having left school at fourteen with no qualifications was accepted into the RAFVR, got his first taste of flying in June 1938. He worked as an office boy at the *News of the World* and took the train from Fleet Street to Hanworth aerodrome in south-west London for his first 'air experience'. The machine was a Blackburn B2 in which pilot and pupil sat side by side. His instructor, a former stunt pilot with the Cobham circus, was, like him, a big man and they had to 'sit a bit sideways' to make room for each other. 'I remember thinking how thin the sides of the airframe were and that it would not take much to fall out,' Doe remembered.[39] 'I was afraid of falling through it. When he banked the thing to turn round, looking down at the houses about four hundred feet below, it was a weird feeling. Quite frankly I was petrified ...'

When they first got their hands on the controls novices learned that simple aircraft were delicate creatures and the sensations of handling were both disturbing and thrilling. Edward Hearn, a trainee estate manager from Folkestone, 'was surprised to find the joystick extremely sensitive and even slight pressure had an effect on the machine'.[40] He felt he was 'handling something so delicate that even a slight touch would send us tumbling earthwards'. Repetition brought familiarity and then confidence until the day came to go solo, a great, never-to-be-forgotten moment in every pilot's life.

Hearn was a slow learner. The average time taken by pupils to go solo was ten hours. In his case, it was fourteen. Decades later he could still 'distinctly remember this first venture alone in the air … strapped in, propeller swung, goggles down, I opened up the throttle and it was the feeling of power as speed was gathered over the grass that gave me assurance and stability'. Hearn made three careful left-hand circuits without mishap. This was the easy part. Getting down was the problem. The training school canteens buzzed with stories of pupils who had come in to land fourteen or fifteen times before summoning the courage to put the aircraft down. Some finally had the decision made for them when they ran out of fuel. A rough landing did not qualify for 'that would mean a bounce and if the bounce was a real banger that would have meant opening up the throttle and going around again'. Hearn eventually brought the machine in smoothly, cutting the engine a few feet from the ground and drifting in to roll smoothly over to his relieved instructor.

The plan was to recruit 800 potential pilots a year but it soon became clear that the quota would easily be filled. The supply of pilot recruits, particularly in the London area, much exceeded the demand.[41] The problem was that everyone wanted to be a pilot. Few were interested in the less glamorous roles of observer – the contemporary term for navigators – and wireless operator/air gunner. The difficulty was solved when surplus pilots were diverted to fill the gaps in aircrew needs. By the time the war began there were 6,646 pilots in the ranks of the RAFVR; 1,623 had been trained as observers and 1,948 as wireless operators/air gunners.

The function of the RAFVR as a reserve did not last long. When the war started it became an administrative designation and the principal route for aircrew entry into the RAF. All those who applied for aircrew duties on their own initiative or chose the RAF when registering as required by the National Service (Armed Forces) Act which came into force in September 1939 joined its ranks. They were identified by a brass and cloth 'VR' worn on tunic lapels and shoulders. In 1943 the badges were phased out as they were considered divisive, though the surviving Auxiliaries were allowed to keep their distinguishing 'A'.

The airmen who went into battle with the Luftwaffe were a compound of professionals and amateurs and represented a broad social and geographical swathe of Britain. The fusion was remarkably successful. In the judgement of the internal narrative, borne out by and large by the testimony of the participants, 'so complete was the amalgamation that the distinctions of peacetime between the component parts ceased to be discernible and the memory of them failed to have any significance'.[42]

Those leading the force in the rush to war had managed to create a solid identity for a hugely expanded organization that would only get bigger with time. It was shared not only by the fliers but by the much larger number of men and women who kept them in the air.

5

'There's Something in the Air'

When the war broke out there was no repetition among the civilian population of Britain of the 'tragic enthusiasm' of August 1914. Most of those of fighting age fell in reluctantly, but quietly, with the demands that a succession of government decrees made of them, starting with the April 1939 Military Training Act. They accepted the need to serve, not because they wanted to, but because Hitler had given them no choice.

Full-scale conscription began on the first day of hostilities with the passing of the first National Service (Armed Services) Act and all males (with significant exemptions) between the ages of eighteen and forty-one were liable to call-up. The upper age limit for men was later increased to fifty-one, and from December 1941 single women and childless widows between the ages of twenty and thirty were required to report for war service.

On call-up, men had first to register, usually at their local Labour Exchange. There, they were asked to make a profoundly important choice. Which branch of the armed services would they prefer to spend their war in? Thus was created a popularity contest between the Army, Navy and Air Force. Initially, the RAF won it hands down. Of the 230,000 men aged twenty to twenty-two registering for the first conscription proclamation of 21 October 1939, nearly 30 per cent said they wanted to join the Air Force. The Navy was second with 17 per cent.[1] The rest appear to have taken the fatalistic decision to go where they were sent. In February 1941, when the conscription net was thrown wider to scoop up nineteen-year-olds, nearly 50 per cent opted for the RAF against 18 per cent for the Navy.[2]

Many decided not to wait to be summoned but reported to one of the Combined Recruiting Centres dotted around the country to volunteer for the Air Force. Indeed, enlistments by those outside the conscript age range outnumbered pressed men until well into 1940.

RAF recruiting staff could therefore afford to be choosy as they surveyed each new crop of sprogs. In the first five years of the war, of those who volunteered before waiting to be called up about one in six were rejected. Among those who waited to be summoned before plumping for the Air Force, the washout rate was brutal. Less than half of those interviewed by recruiting officers made the grade (463,773 out of 1,054,348), and many of them were shunted off to the Army.[3]

In the first sixteen months of the war, 203,239 volunteers were accepted into the RAF, together with another 140,462 who opted for the Air Force on being called up.[4] Having succeeded in joining their preferred service, each man had another crucial – and potentially fatal – choice to make. At an early stage they were asked whether they wanted to serve in the air or on the ground. Of the 343,701 who entered in that initial period only about one in ten – 35,267 – were assigned to aircrew duties.[5] Among younger men, a figure of 13 per cent of aircrew optants was normal until recruiting tailed off in 1944.[6]

Why was it that so many ended up earthbound? It was not a simple question of choice. One reason was that far more technical tradesmen were needed than aviators, and anyone with a relevant skill would be steered towards a ground job. Another major factor was the high standard of physical fitness and intelligence set for those who volunteered for flying duties. Flying required a higher degree of academic ability than most military activity and, initially, priority was given to those with more than the legal minimal level of secondary education.

In 1939 four out of five children left school at fourteen when free education more or less ceased.[7] The result was that the great majority of the first-wave applicants were automatically excluded from a flying career. Gloucestershire boy F. S. Reed had enjoyed a ten-shilling joy ride at the RAF aerodrome at South Cerney and was 'hooked on flying'. When the war came he decided to join the Air Force but 'having no academic qualifications I didn't have a hope of being accepted for pilot training'. Instead he 'applied to join the RAF ... as a flight mechanic. If I couldn't fly them then at least I could work on them.'[8] Fate determined that he would spend most of the war servicing aircraft in a flying training school in South Africa.

A job on the ground had many attractions. Working as a skilled tradesman brought greater standing and a higher level of satisfaction than an Army or Navy other rank could expect. This status was reflected in the uniform for, unlike his counterparts, from 1938 onwards the 'erk' wore a collar and tie (it was six years before the Army caught up). Initially at least, there seemed a diminished likelihood of being sent overseas. It was also evident that ground crew duties carried less risk than serving in the air, or indeed anywhere. The importance this factor played in the decision-making process is hard to calculate. Wing Commander Jimmy Lawson of the Air Ministry Personnel Department recorded in a memorandum that 'it is believed that a number of young men enlisted voluntarily or opted for the RAF on ground duties with the knowledge that such employment was the least dangerous in any of the services'.[9]

How Lawson, who elsewhere in the document shows himself to be sensible and humane, arrived at this conclusion was not made clear. It cannot have been his intention to portray aircraftmen as shirkers. Those who served on the ground anyway displayed their own brand of fortitude, enduring long hours in all weathers and often miserable conditions, and could show the same selfless disregard for their own lives when duty called, as an entry in the diary of 217 Squadron recording an air raid on their base at St Eval in Cornwall in May 1941 shows: 'A/Cs Collier and Ball put up a very good show by towing a bowser which was on fire away so that it could burn out in safety. One of them actually had to climb under the bowser to attach a cable to it. Their prompt and courageous action undoubtedly saved another aircraft from destruction.'[10]

There was a steady flow of non-flying personnel who, despite intimate knowledge of the dangers involved, gave up a safe billet to volunteer for operations. It was not as straightforward a process as the authorities made it appear and answering the call did not guarantee acceptance, even at times when the need appeared to be urgent. 'Chaps, driven by boredom, volunteer continually for Air Gunnery, but they aren't accepted,' wrote John Sommerfield to a colleague in November 1940. He was a former public schoolboy and a Communist who had fought with the International Brigades in Spain before joining up as a lowly aircraftman. 'In the meantime the RAF goes on inserting 11 inch double column ads [in newspapers and magazines] for men to be aircrew.'[11]

An initial insistence on education to School Certificate standard was eventually dropped on the grounds that it 'debarred many excellent candidates otherwise suitable'.[12] Nonetheless it is clear that many who wanted to fly could not because they had not been given the basic education that would prepare them for the rigorous classroom training that all aircrew roles required. Geoffrey Goodman was bright and ambitious but his war-invalid father had been unable to find steady work and he had left school early. He was seventeen when the war broke out, working as cub reporter for a small magazine in Camden Town, north London. His Jewish background and left-wing sympathies reinforced his determination to fight Fascism and he felt flying with the RAF – 'the most dramatic of the three services' – was the best way to do it.[13] When, having added a year to his age, he turned up at a recruiting office near Euston station, he found it was not as easy as that. 'I wanted to go straight into aircrew [but] I didn't have the required qualifications,' he said. 'I remember arguing with the recruiting sergeant who told me that once [I] was in I may be able to remuster.' At the reception centre at Cardington he was advised to volunteer to train as a radio mechanic as an entrée to aircrew. While training at Cranwell a flight lieutenant told him he would be better off specializing in photography – a tip he followed and which led to him eventually being commissioned as a reconnaissance pilot. Goodman found that 'about a third of the groundcrew lads wanted to get into aircrew – it didn't matter what it was. If it wasn't as a pilot then as a navigator or air gunner.' The stumbling block was education – or lack of it. They 'wished to do so but they were very much aware that they didn't have the ... qualifications to tackle the aircrew course'.

In the first five years of the war RAF numbers increased sixfold – from 175,692 in September 1939 to 1,185,833 in July 1944.[14] This stupendous growth spurt required production-line methods to manage and for many recruits the plunge into uniform was disorienting, often shocking. They were passing from the realm of the comfortable and familiar into a baffling new domain that seemed unconnected with the civilian universe, filled with noise, discomfort and a total absence of privacy. The first stop for all, whether you were destined to be a pilot, a fitter or a 'general duties' dogsbody was one of the reception centres like Uxbridge, on the fringes of west London, Cardington in Bedfordshire, or Padgate, Lancashire, where you swapped your civvies for a uniform and acquired a service number that would henceforth be welded to your name.

Padgate was a vast, ugly, hutted camp near Warrington. No one who passed through its gates retained any happy memory of the place. 'My main impression of Padgate is parading and waiting in biting cold and rain,' John Thornley, a twenty-nine-year-old printer's rep from Preston, confided to his diary after arriving there in December 1940. 'The camp is built on marshy ground and is open to all winds.'[15] Even young men who knew poverty and overcrowding felt the rawness of the place, and cringed at the constant state of exposure in which it seemed they would henceforth live. The nakedness was literal. Almost the first order an RAF entrant received was to drop his trousers and pants, prior to an inaugural 'FFI' (Freedom from Infection) inspection, one of many he would undergo in his career.

Nineteen-year-old Norman Lee, who had left his reserved occupation job with an engineering firm in Yorkshire to emulate his twin brother and volunteer for aircrew, arrived in Padgate in November 1941. For his first FFI he and his comrades 'were lined up in a hangar facing the open side with only a sheet of hessian as a very inadequate screen between us and a crowd of WAAFs who giggled and made faces through the window of a low building opposite.'[16] Then 'to complete our embarrassment, as soon as the inspection was over we were marched straight into that self-same building' where the female spectators served them plates of gristly brawn.

For gently brought-up young men like Sam Pritchard, the son of a Wesleyan minister who turned up in the spring of 1940 on his way to becoming a navigator, Padgate brought his first, rather dismaying, close encounter with the British proletariat. The thirty men in his barrack room 'contained what I suppose must have been a cross-section of British society; a few types with a reasonable education and the remainder representing rapidly dwindling standards [down to] a group of foul-mouthed objectionable young men'.[17] His first night was 'miserable and unforgettable ... lying in a bed with no sheets on; a mattress and a pillow filled with straw, looking round for a sympathetic or understanding face ...'

By this rough immersion, the RAF might have unintentionally been doing the new boys a favour. It was sink or swim. To survive you had to cling to the nearest kindred spirit, and the experience encouraged instant and often lasting friendships. There was sanctuary, too, in the humour that pervaded everything: strong, black and subversive. Surreal wit combated their surreal new circumstances. As everyone constantly told everyone else, 'if you can't take a joke, you shouldn't have joined'.[18]

Sam Pritchard and his comrades soon discovered ways to circumvent the obscenity-flecked rule of the NCOs who drilled them. A 'favourite stratagem was to start giggling or laughing on parade whilst punctiliously and smartly obeying all the orders barked at us. This would first puzzle the corporal and then drive him to foul-mouthed hysteria ... eventually when [he] finally accepted the impracticality of charging all of us under King's Regulations, he would lower his voice to offer an extra pass out of camp if we "stopped our bleeding laughing"'.

Any manoeuvre that thwarted authority or made it look ridiculous delighted men who were, on the whole, determined to hang on to their status as civilians in uniform. During his initial training my father Ernest Bishop was in a group being taught self-defence by an overbearing PT corporal instructor. One by one, the teacher invited each man to 'take a swing', then promptly knocked him flat when he obeyed. Come my father's turn, he warned the corporal that he had 'done a bit with the gloves', as indeed he had, fighting as 'Tiger' Bishop at the Blackfriars Ring in London. 'They all say that,' sneered the corporal, and waved him on. Moments later the instructor was stretched out cold on the gym floor and Ernie did not have to buy beer for a fortnight.

Places like Padgate were purgatorial rather than hellish and the suffering was temporary. Sam Pritchard's grim memories were soon blotted out in the summer of 1940 by the far more agreeable experience of No. 2 Initial Training Wing, based in Cambridge University. Pay parades took place on the lawn in front of King's College Chapel and in the evenings he and his fellow trainee pilots and navigators toured the pubs. They were a superior crowd to the reception centre clientele. The majority were grammar school boys like himself but there was also 'a goodly proportion from Public schools, and some even who had completed a university course', as well as Australians, New Zealanders and Canadians.[19] For the first time he 'met other young men in their early twenties who were smarter, richer, better-looking, better-educated and more amusing than I considered myself to be'.

In the RAF you tended not to linger anywhere for too long. Specialized requirements and constant technological advances meant long training periods at a variety of establishments. It took Ted Mace, who signed on as an aircraft electrician, a full year of more or less continuous instruction at various technical schools before he was posted to a squadron.[20]

Aircrew training was more intensive. Pilots went through nine phases of instruction before they flew their first operation, and when bottlenecks in the system developed early in the war, periods of 'deferred service' at home extended the process. Even training for a relatively uncomplicated trade such as air gunner was a protracted business. Norman Lee volunteered in November 1940 but did not take to the air with 428 Squadron until the summer of 1943.[21]

The RAF's geographical reach spread enormously in the course of the war. The empire had greatly helped its training needs by agreeing to flying training schools in the wide skies of Canada, Australia, Rhodesia, South Africa and elsewhere. With expansion, new bases sprang up all over each new theatre of war and old ones were enlarged. Air Force life could thus be amazingly peripatetic, with constant moves from training course to training course, from station to station, from one end of the country to the other and to every corner of the globe. An airman might find himself shivering in Iceland, hard up against the Arctic Circle, cursing the flies in the

Nile Delta, or sweating in the sultry humidity of Takoradi on the Gold Coast (Ghana) of Africa.

However grim your current circumstances there was always the prospect of change. 'It is like living in a cross between a public school and a concentration camp,' wrote John Sommerfield, in 1941 shortly after arriving at Silloth, a remote station in Cumberland.[22] 'The town of Silloth is hideous, small and unpleasant ... Cumberland has the highest average rainfall in Great Britain ...' Before long, though, he was writing notes on the nature of the Western Desert ('the sinister shadows of stones at sunrise, the purplish sunset shadows that dramatize sand ripples into mountain ranges ...') that he would put to good use when he resumed his career as a novelist and short story writer after the war.[23]

Wherever they went, the airmen carried with them a comforting, familiar ethos to sustain them. In its short life, the RAF had developed its own way of speech, some of it the legacy of its Army and Navy origins, much of it new. Like Sommerfield, Roderic Papineau was a writer who served in the ranks. Both acted as field reporters for Tom Harrisson, one of the founders of Mass Observation, set up in 1937 to study the lives of ordinary people and which continued its work into wartime. In May 1941, while with 256 Squadron in Blackpool, he compiled an 'Airman's Vocabulary' recording the usages he heard around him in workshop, NAAFI and pub.[24]

He and his comrades were 'erks', a term that applied to all other-ranks ground staff. Its origin would never be satisfactorily explained. Even Eric Partridge failed to nail it and his theory, proposed in his 1945 *Dictionary of RAF Slang*, that it was a corrupted abbreviation of 'air mechanic', does not convince.[25] 'Type' was a handy alternative to 'bloke'. Aeroplanes were 'kites' or 'crates'. The rumours that hung like ground mist over base and depot (as they did over all military establishments) could be graded for reliability as 'the real griff' – almost certainly true, through 'pukka gen' – quite possible – to 'duff' or 'shithouse gen' – almost certainly bollocks. An expression that seems unique to the RAF was 'by the centre!', usually with an expletive inserted, to indicate 'amazed and outraged disgust or surprise'. It does not appear to have lingered long in use after the war though Sam Pritchard chose it as the title for his memoir.

Some phrases had a different meaning for ground staff than for fliers. According to Papineau, when an erk was 'shooting a line' he was 'pretending to unwarranted expert knowledge'. When a pilot did the same he was making some exaggerated boast, usually in the bar, and his utterance might well be recorded in the squadron 'line book'. The 9 Squadron book reports Pilot Officer Arnold announcing loftily one night: 'No I'm not keeping a diary, but I have the press cuttings of my flights ...'[26] A 'shaky do' on the ground was a 'disappointing or unsatisfactory affair'. In the air, it meant a terrifying near-death experience, and was all the more eloquent for its understatement. A word that meant the same to all was 'wizard' – 'superb', according to Papineau.

Life in the RAF may not have been uniformly 'wizard' and, as in all branches of the military, the hours passed against a background buzz of moaning about the incompetence, laziness and stupidity of those in authority. Yet the overwhelming impression received from contemporaneous diaries and letters and subsequent fictional and factual accounts of the experience was that it was, by and large, positive, even enjoyable at times, and that if there had to be a war and you had to be in it, then the Royal Air Force was the place to be. The strong desire not to end up in the Army – still regarded as a stronghold of bovine generals and ovine troops – is often cited as a motivation, particularly in ground staff memoirs (which are far less numerous than those left behind by aircrew). But there was more to it than that. The RAF seemed modern, dashing and somehow less formal. Like the Navy, it also seemed to actually be doing something. According to Papineau, the Air Force nickname for sailors was affectionate and respectful – 'tars' or 'matelots'. The Army, however, were 'brown jobs' or 'the unemployed'. They themselves were 'The Firm', a term that indicates pride, purpose and efficiency.

Naturally this ebullience could easily be interpreted as cockiness and there were some, not just among their military peers, who found the high spirits of the junior service irritating. The avalanche of admiring mail published in the innovatory illustrated news magazine *Picture Post* in the early months of the war, following a letter from an anonymous erk complaining that 'no decent girl seems to look at an airman', contained a few caveats. 'I must say it's not true that no decent and respectable girls look at airmen,' wrote A. M. 'I know several … (I for one). But some of them are so sure of themselves, always talking about drink etc.'[27] 'I have come to the conclusion that foul manners are the badge of the Air Force,' wrote a middle-aged woman who had served with the Army in France in the First World War, after being subjected to rough or ribald comments from RAF men in Kensington Gardens on two occasions. The bulk of the postbag, though, was gushingly, blushingly positive. 'I was very surprised at your letter as I always imagined airmen were considered heroes' ran one from a nurse. 'I envied my girlfriend whose heart is in the sky and who is now knitting air-force blue socks! The fact that it's such a stiff test to get in always made me imagine that airmen are he-men!'

The RAF's appeal was felt everywhere. The Duke of Edinburgh confided in a BBC interview on his seventieth birthday that he would have volunteered for aircrew had he not been pressured by his uncle Louis Mountbatten to join the Navy.[28] It seemed to attract a disproportionate number of celebrities of one sort or another. Aircrew trainee Edwin Thomas was delighted to tell his mother that among his intake group at the Torquay reception centre was the England fast bowler Ken Farnes who was so tall that 'he has got to wait three months for a uniform because the RAF can't find one to fit him'.[29] Farnes was later killed when his aeroplane crashed on a night-flying exercise. His England colleague Bill Edrich flew with Bomber Command, won a DFC and finished the war as a squadron leader. Another famous cricketer Cyril Washbrook served as a PT instructor.

Tommy Farr, the Tonypandy ex-miner who had fought Joe Louis for the world heavyweight boxing title in 1937, volunteered the day after war broke out and 'wanted to be an air gunner or an observer'. During a routine medical while training he was found to have a defective ear and eye, probably the result of punishment in the ring, and given a medical discharge. 'I feel very miserable about it all,' he said when the news became known. 'I was very happy with food and conditions in the RAF and believe me I am terribly sorry to leave the force.'[30]

Actors flocked to the RAF. Richard Attenborough, Richard Burton, Denholm Elliott, Rex Harrison, Christopher Lee and Donald Pleasence all served. So too did the playwright Terence Rattigan whose *Flare Path* was an early example of the dramatic potency of the RAF experience. Not all showbiz aspirants were welcomed. David Niven made his way back from Hollywood in the autumn of 1939 but withdrew after a bruising first interview. On arrival at the Air Ministry he was besieged by secretaries asking for his autograph which got him off to a bad start with the group captain assessing him.

'The man restored order and eyed me with distaste,' Niven remembered.[31] 'He knew who I was. Unless he was blind he couldn't have avoided it. Nevertheless, he went through the motions of asking my name and occupation and what I wanted to do. When I told him, he pursed his lips, sucked in some breath with a whistling sound and shook his head.' He then asked him whether he knew Wilfred Lawson, a highly regarded theatre and screen player who had flown as a pilot in the last months of the First World War and had rejoined the colours. Niven replied that he was a 'wonderful actor'.

'He's also a heavy drinker,' said the officer. 'We took him on and we've had trouble with him ever since.' By now Niven was losing patience and told him: 'I've come seven thousand miles at my own expense and I'd like to join the RAF.'

'So I've read,' the officer replied. 'But we don't encourage actors to join *this* service.' At this point Niven stormed out, and ended up in the Rifle Brigade after a chance encounter in the Café de Paris nightclub.

Musicians were also drawn to the Air Force. The number of well-known artistes volunteering or choosing to join encouraged the authorities in 1940 to form the Royal Air Force Dance Orchestra. Among the fifteen members were several who had played in the Bert Ambrose Orchestra, the hottest act of the day, including saxophonist Harry Lewis who was married to the band's vocalist Vera Lynn. They became famous as The Squadronaires, by far the best known of the service dance bands, and played all over the country as well as being broadcast on the BBC and cutting records for Decca. They generated a lush, big-band sound, and their great hit 'There's Something in the Air' would ever after evoke for hundreds of thousands of servicemen and women memories of crowded dance halls, the smell of cigarette smoke, perfume and spilled beer and the last bus back to camp.

For aircrew, the progress to a squadron was long and jerky and there were many obstacles to overcome before you finally got into action. Edwin Thomas was eighteen and a half when the war started. Like many, probably most, who aspired to fight in the air, he wanted to be a pilot. He was summoned to the combined recruiting centre in Romford on 29 October 1940 for assessment for the RAFVR, by now the conduit for most wartime entrants. Edwin had the benefit of a secondary education at Canterbury Road Senior School and Snaresbrook College in east London but his reports marked him down as a plodder. 'He is a thoroughly honest and trustworthy lad,' declared his head teacher, T. H. Moore. 'He has shown earnestness and painstaking ability in his work. In manner he is quiet, serious

Band of brothers: The Squadronaires

and gentlemanly.'[32] Thomas's weekly letters home to the family's semi-detached mock-Tudor home in the east London suburb of Wanstead describing his life as a trainee provide a detailed account of the rigours and disappointments of the process, as well as a touching picture of youth, innocence and devotion to duty. The meeting with the selection board went well. A week later he was installed at the Babbacombe Hotel near Torquay, about to begin a fortnight's drilling with forty-nine other novices before being sent off to a two-month course at an Initial Training Wing (ITW).

They were starting on the lowest rung of the ladder, classified as Aircraftmen 2nd Class (Group V) and receiving 2s. a day pay. From the beginning cash, or the lack of it, looms large in the correspondence. 'It is amazing how much money is spent on necessities such as copying ink [and] the VR badges that aren't on the uniform and cost 6d a pair,' he wrote on 13 November. There were no complaints about the food, though. 'For breakfast yesterday we had porridge, fried egg and mashed potatoes, bread and butter, marmalade and a terrific mug or two of tea,' he reported. 'For dinner: a lovely stew with potatoes and veg: for sweet an apple conglomeration with custard and an apple: for tea plenty of liver and gravy, bread and butter, jam and a piece of fruit cake. Cake every day. Supper: jug of milk, liver between two crusts and a slice of cake.' In the evenings there were trips into town 'to play billiards snooker or table tennis and end up with a glass of Devonshire cider ... we are too broke to get tipsy.'

By mid-December he was at the Initial Training Wing at Pembroke College, Cambridge, one of five colleges requisitioned by the Air Ministry to house about a thousand trainees. The course was a mixture of gruelling classroom work – navigation, signalling by Morse and Aldis lamp, armaments, maths, law and administration, hygiene, ship and aircraft recognition – combined with large doses of PE. Like all the armed forces the RAF was keen on the noble art, believing it cultivated a fighting spirit. 'I put my name down for boxing,' he wrote, 'and in the afternoon had three rounds with a fellow of my own weight.' His partner 'had never boxed before and his defence was an opponent's dream'. Later the PE instructor, a corporal called Harry Mizler and a celebrated East End Jewish bantamweight who represented Britain in the 1932 Olympic Games in Los Angeles, 'bounced medicine balls on our stomachs to strengthen the muscles'. They then set off on a two-mile run.

Soon after arriving at the ITW Thomas suffered the first of a series of disappointments. He learned he had done badly in a grading test and his chances of selection for pilot training had taken a blow. To keep his hopes alive he would have to get more than 60 per cent in the maths exam. If he failed, he would have to re-muster as a wireless operator/air gunner. With characteristic stoicism he knuckled down to 'special maths swotting with friends after hours'. Like many others, he was learning that 'if you want to be a pilot you have to work like blazes'. However, he told his mother 'if I get through the maths test it will all have been worthwhile'. It was not to be. It is not difficult to imagine his mother Helen's feelings as her first-born child reported sheepishly in his next letter that he had some 'rather disappointing news to tell you. I did not pass the maths exam.' After learning of his failure he had been interviewed by a squadron leader who told him that he would be given another chance. It meant, however, that he would be assigned to another group of trainees: 'I shall not leave Cambridge but I shall lose all my friends.'

A few months later he was writing with the 'sad, sad news' that he had failed his navigation exam. His bid to become a pilot was over and he was offered the choice of being discharged from the service, re-mustering as a wireless operator/gunner or being assigned to a ground job. 'Naturally I said I would go for WOP/AG,' he told his mother. 'If I had my discharge I should only go into the army eventually – and I do want to make a go of it in the RAF.' His pride had been hurt. A postscript to the letter adds, 'Tell anyone who enquires that as I failed the exam for pilot I have *volunteered* for WOP/AG.'

Edwin spent the next two years moving around the country from training unit to training unit, until at last, at the end of March 1943, he was posted to 78 Squadron at Linton-on-Ouse near York. On 2/3 April he took part in his first operation, bombing the port area of Saint-Nazaire. The relief of getting the first trip out of the way and 'without a scratch on K for Kathleen [their Halifax]' shone out of the letter home. 'The whole business was little different from an ordinary cross-country flight,' he wrote. 'But what gave us all a thrill was when we crossed the French coast and knew we were well on our way to the target.' He finished by reporting that 'we have been searching for ideas for a name for our kite. Most names fellows have chosen for their kites are indelicate. Much to my crew's pleasure I hit upon the idea of "Happy Go Lucky." The decision was unanimous.'

Bad weather meant that it was two weeks until the next mission. On the night of 16/17 April 78 Squadron took part in a mass attack on the centre of Mannheim, a regular 'area' target at this stage of the war. Eighteen aircraft were lost. Edwin's was among them and all the crew were killed. A friend of the family called Lydia wrote a few days later offering what little comfort there was. 'It is some consolation to know that Edwin was so very keen on the Air Force and would not have wished to be in any other Service,' she wrote. She added: 'The RAF are marvellous boys and to hear them going over night after night does make one's heart ache.'

In the search for words to soften the blow of death it was often asserted that the victim had died doing what they wanted. In the case of Edwin Thomas it was obviously the truth. His letters brim with the pride of belonging and pleasure in the company of his fellow airmen. He never seems to have been lonely and made friends early who meant a lot to him. 'I am with a grand set of fellows,' he wrote after arriving in Blackpool for his wireless operators' course. On his twentieth birthday 'the whole gang went on a binge … Stanley, Stinker, Baxter (wee Scotsman, ex-Corporal Gordon Highlanders) and Ronnie Wells plus two girls who are holidaymaking and staying in Stanley's billet. I'm afraid we all had too much to drink.'

The arrivals and departures of wartime life meant friendships were often fleeting but no less real for that. Edwin's friend Malcolm, who he met at the Cambridge ITW course and was selected for pilot training, wrote to him in Blackpool months after they separated to say, 'I miss you like anything, you know, Edwin and I don't think I'll find a friend to replace you in this service.' He signed off: 'My best wishes to any of the lads up there and the same a hundred times over to yourself. See you soon, maybe over Berlin …'

Compulsory female war service only come into effect in early 1942. Until then, the Women's Auxiliary Air Force, which was created on 28 June 1939, was staffed by volunteers. Between September 1939 and December 1940 14,546 came forward. The following year the numbers jumped to 81,928. The increase was largely due to the introduction of a second National Service Act in the autumn that made it clear that conscription for women between the ages of twenty and thirty was in the offing. The result, the Air Ministry narrative noted, was that 'recruiting offices were inundated with applications ... just before Christmas in one week alone over 7,000 completed application forms were received'.[33] After January 1941 the WAAF started receiving conscripts. Over the course of the war, however, volunteers greatly outnumbered National Service recruits by 180,704 to 33,932.

For women, the attraction of the Air Force over the other services was not as obvious as it was for men. They would have little contact with aeroplanes, as at first they were not considered for ground trades and there was no question of them serving as aircrew. Later some women were used as delivery pilots in the Air Transport Auxiliary but these had already obtained pilot's licences for themselves and it was only in 1944 that seventeen WAAFs were trained to do the job.[34] At the outset, the Air Ministry's attitude was more restrictive than had been the case at the end of the First World War. The majority of the 32,000 women in the Women's Royal Air Force – the forerunner of the WAAF – had done traditional jobs as typists, clerks, cooks and cleaners, but some broke into fields that were hitherto the preserve of men, working as fitters and riggers.

According to the RAF's own account the early WAAF recruits were 'in the main patriotic women who were inspired by the spirit of adventure'. Sylvia Drake-Brockman was a well-educated forty-year-old spinster from a military family who was employed as private secretary to the Chairman of the Stock Exchange in the City of London when the war broke out. It was an 'easy job' and she had 'elegant hours and no Saturday work'.[35] As time passed she became 'increasingly restless and anxious to do something for the war effort'.

In July 1940, at the start of the Battle of Britain, she applied to join the WAAF. Turning up at the RAF's recruiting headquarters at

Victory House in Kingsway for processing she found the place awash with like-minded women. 'What a crowd was waiting with me,' she wrote. 'All sorts of conditions of girls and of all ages ...' The applicants had a first encounter with 'one RAF and four WAAF doctors to examine different parts of our anatomy'. There was a long wait for the result. Then a 'card was handed to me marked FIT. Great relief and joy.'

A fortnight later she arrived at the West Drayton reception centre to the west of London where recruits were rolling in at a rate of a hundred a day. She was feeling 'rather tired and depressed' when she got there, not helped by 'some small boys outside the camp calling out "turn back before it's too late!"'. The message was repeated that evening when the newcomers were 'addressed by a Flight Officer who spoke to us all sufficiently sternly about not joining if we were, any of us, under age, so that one little girl bobbed up and admitted the offence and was told she would be returned to her home the next day'. They were also given a final chance to 'get out of the WAAF if we felt we could not take the final plunge ... twenty-four hours to think things over before taking an irrevocable step'. This practice would continue until 1941, whereafter there was no allowance made for second thoughts.

Sylvia spent a restless first night in a quarter 'like a council house' with some other new girls. Almost every WAAF memoir makes unaffectionate mention of the 'biscuits' they had to sleep on, three thin three-foot by three-foot squares of straw-filled canvas, laid down on a slatted bedframe. Bedclothes consisted of two unbleached sheets and three hairy blankets in Air Force Blue and there was a straw-filled bolster for a pillow. The next day was taken up with 'waiting for enrolment, getting enrolled (which meant turning into a cipher – 896991), waiting to get kitted, getting kitted – waiting for meals, waiting again and more waiting'.

Sylvia's secretarial background meant she was selected as a 'clerk, general duties'. Her job meant that, somewhat to her regret, she was excused much of the initial drilling. Instead she attended endless lectures. 'It seemed to my somewhat confused mind that the system was; when in doubt, send the recruits to a lecture. In this way I heard lectures on service etiquette, office routine and correspondence, hygiene, sanitation, VD and again hygiene, sanitation and service etiquette.'

During the two-week initial training she was called to an interview by the female camp commandant and asked if she would like to put her name forward for a commission as an administrative officer. Sylvia was pleased to accept the offer as 'much as I was enjoying my experience in the ranks I knew that I would get very tired of the continual herding and lack of privacy before long'. There was also 'a better reason – I felt confident that I would do more good as an officer as I was and always [had] been very interested in my fellow human beings'.

Sylvia's name was duly submitted to the Air Ministry. Later she discovered that she had been recommended on the grounds of her 'education, personality and service connections'.

When a woman officer arrived to interview her 'the first question I was asked was "why I had joined the WAAF when I had so many relations in the Army". I replied that I liked the sound of the WAAF and thought it was a good idea to break fresh ground.' She did not confide 'another childish reason which influenced me: that I liked the uniform better than the khaki of the ATS!' The drily humorous and humane memoir that Sylvia Drake-Brockman left behind on her death in 1978 makes it clear that the next five and a half years were among the happiest in her life. She thrived on the responsibility denied to her in civilian life, was appreciated by her superiors and held several important command and staff jobs. She also found fulfilment in the camaraderie of service life and in acting as a stern but affectionate big sister to her charges.

Sylvia was born at the tail end of the Victorian era and came from the sort of family whose members made a profession of serving Britain and its empire and had been well rewarded for doing so. To a younger generation of women growing up in an era of expanding independence and diminishing deference, the pull of duty was felt in different ways. Marjorie Chaffe was twenty when the war began and working in a book-binding plant in Southwark. She did not volunteer for war service but when the Blitz began in September 1940 worked as a part-time firewatcher and member of Air Raid Precautions. For reasons she could not understand she was classed as doing essential war work in a 'reserved' occupation. Even if she had not been, as she explained in a frank memoir published twenty-five years after the end of the war, there were 'lots of reasons' why girls like her held back from rushing to the recruiting centres.[36] There was the 'obvious one of discipline and regimentation. Once you'd signed on the dotted line your life was no longer your own. What's more you didn't even know how long you would have to serve because you signed up for the duration of hostilities.'

But there were 'lots of other reasons too, petty no doubt, but all having to be taken into consideration when deciding just how far our patriotism was going to stretch'. One was uniform. 'Stockings must have lost more recruits than any other item,' she wrote. 'All the girls loathed them. They were thick, a ghastly blue and made the slimmest legs look twice their size.'

WAAF headgear did not suit the styles of the time. 'Rita Hayworth and Dorothy Lamour wore their hair cascading onto their shoulders … so civilian girls did the same. But on joining up, you either had to have your hair cut, or else dress it in such a way that it not only fitted under your cap but was also well above your collar.'

A bigger deterrent was family pressure. Almost all war work, be it in the services or employment in a war industry factory, meant moving away from home. Parents who had lost one or more sons to the forces were reluctant to see a daughter fly the nest to some possibly distant and inaccessible location.[37]

Boyfriends also presented a major difficulty. They 'didn't like their girls in uniform. They didn't mind who else's girl joined up, as long as theirs didn't.' Marjorie considered this 'natural enough … if he was a civilian himself he didn't want to walk down the road with the equivalent of an able seaman or an aircraftman who saluted every officer that came into sight, and if he was in the Forces he didn't want his girl running the gauntlet of hundreds of his own kind in camps all over the country.'

When conscription for young, single women came into force in January 1942, the matter was settled. When Marjorie was eventually summoned to do her National Service like everyone she could choose between the nursing services, the Land Army, the fire services, work in a war factory, or joining the WRNS, ATS or WAAF. She 'didn't like blood' and 'by no stretch of the imagination could conjure up a picture of myself mucking out a pigsty at five o clock in the morning'. She had had enough of factories and felt she had done her time firewatching, 'so it had to be the Forces'. Having lived through the Blitz she wanted to do something that had a direct impact on the enemy. 'The most aggressive jobs that a girl could do in the Army or Air Force was either to work on a gun site or the balloon barrage. So as I was feeling pretty aggressive after two years of air raids ... and preferring blue to khaki, I decided to go on the barrage.' Teaming up with two other Londoners, Rene and Dolly, who would be her best friends for the rest of her service, they set off to the reception centre at Gloucester, 'pleased at having gained the service we wanted' but with 'a few qualms about what sort of reception we would get as conscripts among a lot of volunteers'.

Marjorie's natural bolshiness made her impatient of the 'rules and regulations ... flung at us from all sides' which Sylvia accepted as the inescapable idiocies of service life. They were different ages, came from different backgrounds and had different expectations of what life could and should bring. Yet their years in the WAAF seem to have been among the most fulfilling in their lives, never to be regretted or forgotten.

6

'Tragic, Criminally Tragic'

Looking back at the first moments of the war, John Slessor recalled his feelings when, a few minutes after Neville Chamberlain's Sunday morning broadcast, the sirens sounded in London. He was in the Central War Room in Whitehall, talking to Lord Chatfield, until recently commander of the Navy, now Minister for Co-ordination of Defence. 'It was an odd sensation,' he wrote in a memoir published in 1956, 'standing there wondering whether this was in fact the "knock-out blow" to which we had given so much thought in the past two years.'[1]

The air raid warning was a false alarm, triggered by the appearance of a small aeroplane carrying Captain François de Brantes, the French assistant military attaché, on his way back from a visit to Paris. It would be another year before London suffered a serious attack from the air.

As the RAF's Director of Plans, Slessor had been deeply involved in the preparations for war. Now it was here he felt strangely relieved. As the all-clear sounded he was cheered by the thought that 'at least that awful period of indecision and uncertainty was over'.

Mobilization of the Air Force was already in full swing. Telegrams flew around the country ordering squadron members to break off their leave and return to bases now humming with activity. Guy Gibson rushed back from an idyllic Indian summer vacation swimming and sailing with his girlfriend on the Pembrokeshire coast to his bomber station at Scampton in Lincolnshire to see 'tractors driving around the perimeter roads in the sweltering heat, some with long bomb trailers bouncing behind; others pulling our Hampdens along cinder tracks far into the country to dispersal points fairly safe from enemy bombs. All around the airfield, sand-banked gun emplacements were being put up by aerodrome defence squads, but there were not many guns.'[2]

There was a lull on Sunday morning, when airmen stopped what they were doing to gather round wireless sets and hear Neville Chamberlain's announcement. Many accounts mention the 'heavy', 'solemn', 'defeated' tones of his voice. But there was also a message of defiance and hope, which inspired some of those listening, in which the character of the war was clearly defined. 'It is the evil things that we shall be fighting against,' the Prime Minister declared. 'Brute force, bad faith, injustice, oppression and persecution – and against them I am certain that the right will prevail.'

His words were followed by a burst of action. The staff of the RAF Flying Training School at Gravesend had orders to evacuate as soon as the declaration came, so as to clear the airspace around London for the coming battle. The chief instructor, Peter Johnson, had been given a sealed envelope giving the destination to which the school's aircraft were to be flown.

They took off immediately after the broadcast. Their wartime base would be Castle Bromwich near Birmingham and to reach it they were given a route that diverted them around London. 'It was a beautiful day with unlimited visibility,' he remembered. 'I had reached about two thousand feet when looking around to see all my flock were following, I was riveted, and I admit appalled, by an extraordinary sight. Over the southern suburbs, and behind them all over London, the balloon barrage was rising. The ungainly shapes, dozens of them, all fully inflated, were slowly rising to their operational height. Seen from the air it was a truly awesome spectacle, not least because of its implications. The only conclusion I could draw was that, even before the British declaration of war, a German air fleet had taken off almost certainly to raid London.'[3] When they landed to refuel at Hullavington in Wiltshire he was told that the balloons had been launched in response to the false alarm.

The fighter pilots of 43 Squadron, based at Tangmere at the foot of the West Sussex Downs, were waiting beside their Hurricanes at five minutes' readiness to take off when they were told the Prime

Minister was about to speak. They listened to Chamberlain's words in their stylish mess while bar stewards served them beer in pewter mugs. The mood, recalled Peter Townsend, was 'grim and solemn'.[4] Yet once the announcement came 'the tension broke. The fatal step had been taken ...' Caesar Hull, a South African, 'was the first to rejoice. "Wizard!" he kept repeating ...'

They went back to their aircraft 'waiting for the English sky to blacken, as Goering had promised it would, with hordes of his bombers. But only flaky white clouds sailed across England's sky ...'

There was a similar reaction at Cranwell. Tim Vigors was one of about fifty cadets gathered in the college ante-room. When the fatal words were spoken 'as one man we jumped to our feet cheering with excitement. There was not one amongst us who would not have been bitterly disappointed had the declaration of war not been made.'[5]

Every fighter pilot and bomber crew member believed that he would be at the forefront of a battle that would in all probability start immediately. In the words of the historian John Terraine they were holding what in medieval times was called 'the right of the line', that is 'the vanguard' and 'the place of greatest danger'.[6] Britain's long-term security still depended on the Royal Navy. The immediate danger, though, was from the air and the 'knock-out-blow' that had immediately flashed into Slessor's mind when he heard the sirens wail.

That thought had been followed by another: 'I wondered [he wrote years later] how my Service was going to come through this ordeal – wondered even whether it was going to be safe to be seen about in an RAF uniform after the next few days.'[7] He remembered an episode he witnessed as a young officer in the Royal Flying Corps based at Sutton's Farm in Essex, close to London. It was the early autumn of 1915 and the capital had been under repeated bombardments by Zeppelin airships. British aircraft and artillery seemed incapable of stopping the attacks and people were frightened and angry. Having failed to shoot down a raider the previous night, Slessor was driving through the East End in a lorry towing a trailer laden with aircraft components when he ran into trouble. 'As we entered the Mile End Road with our headlights on [he wrote] there were angry cries, and we were mobbed till we had to pull up and get a policeman to stand on the step on either side of the driver's seat of the tender, to get us through at all.'

In fact, Britain's air defences were in a much better state than they had been a quarter of a century previously. Of the three operational commands, Fighter Command was by far the best equipped and organized to carry out its task. Thanks to the political decision taken by civilian amateurs in 1938 to overrule the Air Force professionals and switch the focus of the rearmament programme away from bombers, the fighter squadrons were in reasonable shape to face an onslaught. An efficient defence system was coalescing. Through the summer of 1939 fighter squadrons traded in their biplanes for Hurricanes and Spitfires, future supplies of which looked secure. Having lagged behind for five years, Britain was about to overtake the Germans in aircraft manufacture and would outproduce them by 47 per cent in 1940.[8] The opening of a new Rolls-Royce shadow factory at Crewe to supplement the works at Derby ensured there would be no shortage of the Merlin engines that powered the fighters. The airfield building programme begun in 1935 provided a line of fighter bases strategically placed from Wick in the far north of Scotland to Exeter in the south of England which shielded all possible enemy approaches.

By the summer of 1939 there were twenty Chain Home radar stations covering the upper airspace which could identify aircraft at a distance of between fifty and 120 miles, stretching from Portsmouth to Scapa Flow. The coverage was soon to be improved by the addition of Chain Home Low stations which picked up low-altitude raiders. There were enough pilots to fly the fighters, though events had moved too quickly for there to be a comfortable manpower reserve. The main deficiency was in the quality of training.

Flying training never managed to keep pace with the great increase in manpower. In 1934 the RAF trained about 300 new pilots. In 1941 it trained 22,000 from all over the empire.[9] To give proper instruction that would keep them abreast of rapidly changing aviation technology required schools, instructors, practice aircraft and instructional aids. A scheme to provide all this was drawn up by Arthur Tedder during his 1934–6 stint as Director of Training. The programme involved capital investment and big ongoing costs which successive governments rejected. Rearmament was, after all, conceived as a temporary measure, an essentially political policy aimed at deterring Germany. There was no intention to build up and maintain an outsized Air Force in perpetuity. The result was that, in order to produce the numbers required within the budget allowed, course times were repeatedly cut and vital aspects of air warfare were inadequately taught.

Fighter Command was probably the least affected by the flaws in the training programme. Unlike Bomber Command it needed only one trained man to operate most of its aircraft. Nonetheless, its pilots were still ill prepared for the sort of war they would have to fight. They received no instruction in tactics at flying school. Instead they learned them from more experienced comrades in exercises when they arrived on their operational squadron. In the absence of real experience instruction was based on conjecture. The drills that were taught would turn out to have little connection with the reality of air fighting. There was an obsession with formation flying which turned out to be of limited military use. Once in action, pilots were supposed to respond to different situations by following different styles of attack, 'Number One', 'Number Two', etc., which relied on their target flying straight and level and taking no evasive action.

Contact with the enemy quickly revealed the chaos of combat which made nonsense of the air-display precision of the training manuals. Remarkably little trouble was taken in teaching pilots how to shoot. Gunnery played a small part in the curriculum and in the early part of the war pilots could arrive on front-line squadrons without having fired their guns while in flight, and most had only minimal experience of night flying.[10]

It would be nine months before Fighter Command was in heavy action. Despite all the foreboding about the 'knock-out blow', the Germans were in no hurry to try and land one. Hitler's offensive plans did not involve Britain at present and he was still hopeful of avoiding a clash if possible. This created a blessed hiatus that allowed pilots to bond with their aeroplanes and fit into the squadron team.

It was Bomber Command that suffered most from the weakness of the training set-up. Its failures further undermined the squadrons' ability to carry out the vital role that had been decreed for them. They started the war with stopgap aircraft that were incapable of launching the mass, long-range raids that were envisaged in the Air Staff's counter-offensive strategy. Even if the Stirling, Halifax and Lancaster had been available at this stage, the crews would not have been able to fly them efficiently.

The training they got for their existing aircraft was inadequate. The Wellington, Hampden, Blenheim and Whitley monoplanes were considerably more complicated than the biplanes they replaced and needed a high level of skill and teamwork from those who operated them. In 1934 it was unusual for an aircraft to carry more than one man in addition to the pilot.[11] By 1942 crews of four, five, six or seven were common. The aircrew instruction in place in the transition period from peace to war did not come close to creating the level of ability required.

Pilots were fledged at flying training schools which were supposed to transform them from absolute beginners into fully formed military aviators ready to take their place in the front line. The optimum course time was originally set at a year, then, when this proved unrealistic, reduced to nine months. When in 1937 it was decided that larger bombers would need two pilots to cope with long-range missions, the extra demand cut the training time to six months.[12] Adjustments were made, such as farming out 'ab initio' training to civilian flying schools under contract to the Air Ministry. However, the need to churn out pilots meant the standard reached was, in the words of the RAF's internal account, 'barely essential'.[13] Things began to change in May 1940 with the introduction of Operational Training Units (OTUs) that were supposed to fill in the gaps in training so that crews arrived on their squadrons properly prepared for action. But it was not until 1942 and the so-called 'New Deal' that aircrews finally received the time and attention they needed to reach efficiency.

In the meantime, in the RAF's own judgement the need to produce the maximum output meant that in the run-up to war 'practically none of the increased training requirements which

[new] technical developments called into existence were met by schools during the years of expansion'.[14] Cockpits came with a plethora of instruments and controls. Although 'advanced trainers for efficient instruction' were needed, 'the supply of these aircraft was slow and scanty'. Night flying, and flying on instruments only were now vital skills yet 'only rudimentary instruction ... could be given for lack of facilities and time'. The conclusion was that a pilot emerging from flying training school in 1939 had learned little more than a pilot graduating in 1934 when Hitler was still a curiosity.

The debate about how many pilots were needed to fly a long-range aircraft was not resolved until 1942 when it was finally settled that one was enough. The indecision was symptomatic of the confusion about aircrew roles. Long flights clearly required expert navigation. Yet until 1942, when the specialist aircrew category of 'navigator' was introduced, the job was allotted to the second pilot in a large aircraft or the observer in a smaller one.

Neither would have had any advanced training in navigation. Despite its centrality to the prevailing orthodoxy of bombing primacy, the subject was badly neglected. Before the war wireless-equipped aircraft depended on position-fixing signals from ground stations to find their way. These were useless over enemy territory and navigators had to use dead reckoning: following a course by means of sextant sightings of the sun or stars or landmarks below and setting them against speed and wind strength. Over a blacked-out landscape in skies that were frequently thick with cloud the margin of error was enormous. Four months before the war began a daytime practice exercise led a senior Bomber Command officer to report that 'dead reckoning navigation by day when above cloud could be expected to bring an aircraft only to within about fifty miles of its target'.[15] Poor navigation rendered useless much of the bomber effort in the first years of the war but senior officers never seemed to give the problem the urgent attention it deserved. 'Dilatory discussions about the need for technical aids such as radar and the Air Position Indicator did take place from time to time,' wrote the authorized historians of the strategic air campaign against Germany, Sir Charles Webster and Noble

Frankland, 'but a general inertia overcame all significant progress.'[16] It was only in the autumn of 1941, when Winston Churchill demanded action after seeing photographic analysis that revealed the shocking inaccuracy of much bombing, that things changed.[17]

An important, but untested, theory that had taken root at the Air Ministry maintained that on sorties over enemy territory, bombers flying in formation would be able to defend themselves with their on-board guns. If true, this would seem to demand a high level of competence in the airmen manning them. Before the war, the job was done by ground crew members for whom flying was a second-ary duty and who returned to their regular trades when not in the air. The category became full-time in 1939 and from May 1940 air gunners along with wireless operators were upgraded to the rank of sergeant.[18] However, as the RAF narrative records, 'during the first two years of the war, none of the non-pilot aircrew training was particularly satisfactory. Navigation training was hampered by war-time conditions, as well as lack of equipment: gunnery training suffered from lack of suitable aircraft and equipment: and in neither case were the instructors well suited to the work they had to do.' It was left to the OTUs to try and repair the deficiencies.

Shooting school

All these weaknesses were well known to those at the top of the Air Force. They had been pointed out with undiplomatic persistence by Edgar Ludlow-Hewitt, who took over Bomber Command in 1937. Ludlow-Hewitt was another member of the Air Force's upper-echelon awkward squad, 'far and away the most brilliant officer I have met in any of the three Services', according to Arthur Harris, his temperamental antithesis and not a man given to gushing compliments.[19] He was the son of a clergyman who left the Army to join the RFC, fought bravely on the Western Front and rose quickly in the post-war service. He was one of the few officers in the upper ranks who felt the need to maintain their flying skills.

Ludlow-Hewitt saw expansion as a trap. Numbers might grow but quality would inevitably plunge. He argued persistently that a smaller but war-capable force was much better than the larger but unprepared one that was in the making. As war approached his warnings became increasingly unwelcome. The attitude of the Air Council – the supreme body of the RAF which brought together the Secretary of State and senior officers and officials – was that it was an unfortunate inevitability that expansion would bring a reduction in efficiency. Like the head of the other commands, Ludlow-Hewitt would just have to play the hand he had been dealt.

His frequent warnings seem to have been dealt with piecemeal, or in some cases ignored. At a meeting of the Air Council on 18 July 1939 the Secretary of State, Kingsley Wood, insisted that a letter from Ludlow-Hewitt that had been lying around unanswered for two months be dealt with forthwith as it amounted to 'an indictment of the Air Council and Air Staff.[20] The reaction of the CAS Cyril Newall was brusque. In his view, the document was a back-covering exercise, 'written with the object of putting on record certain unavoidable shortcomings due to expansion'. Ludlow-Hewitt was 'trying to clear himself in the event of catastrophe'.

The exchange of letters that followed failed to pacify Ludlow-Hewitt. A fortnight later Newall told the Council that the latest communication from him 'contained a very serious statement which might even be taken as meaning that in the event of war [he] would not be prepared to fight with his present equipment'.

Ludlow-Hewitt was summoned to air his concerns at a special meeting, at which he told the Council that he was worried about the poor level of gunnery, the lack of adequate training the flying schools were providing before crews reached squadrons and the absence of proper bombing ranges. All of these complaints were wearily familiar. Only a fortnight before he had written to the Air Ministry that 'as things stand at present the gunners have no real confidence in their ability to use [their] equipment efficiently in war, and Captains and crews have, I fear, little confidence in the ability of the gunners to defend them against destruction by enemy aircraft'.[21] His insistence that operational squadrons should be removed from the first line to train flying school graduates up to combat standards was already causing serious friction. The need for proper bombing facilities was a hardy perennial of staff meetings (the lack of action was blamed on the strength of local opposition and the fact that non-populous areas tended to be full of mountains and bogs, though, as the Air Ministry mandarin Sir Maurice Dean later pointed out, there was no shortage of empty desert in the empire in which to place experimental facilities).[22]

What is most striking is the last item on Ludlow-Hewitt's list. According to the minutes of the meeting he 'stated that the question he wished to raise here was a very big one; the question of what type of bombing was most effective. It could not be decided of course around a table. Extensive experiments would be necessary and it was the importance of initiating these without delay which he wanted to stress.'[23] He went on to give an elementary tutorial on the relative merits of high-level and low-level bombing.

The discussion about which approach was best had been going on continuously since January 1934 when the Air Ministry had set up a bombing committee. Yet now, five and a half years later and with the outbreak of war a month away, the argument had got no further and no practical work had been done to decide an operational issue of fundamental importance.

It is possible to sympathize with the Air Council's argument that the hectic pace of expansion meant the unavoidable cutting of many corners. What is less easy to understand is why, in the light of the mass of negative evidence, they persisted in overestimating

Bomber Command's capabilities and exaggerating what it could achieve. It was perhaps a matter of self-preservation: facing reality would have resulted in a devastating loss of face and undermined the commanding position the RAF had staked out for itself in the political and military landscape.

The Air Staff entered the war with a list of objectives that had no possibility of being achieved. Their 'Western European War Plans' was a fantastical document establishing a schedule of action to bring Germany to its knees. The first step in the bombing campaign was a bid to pre-empt the 'knock-out blow' by attacks on 'the German Air Striking Force and its maintenance organisation (including aircraft industry)'.[24] Next would come military road, rail and canal communications. After that the effort would concentrate on obliterating Germany's war industry in its heartlands in the Ruhr, Rhineland and Saar and knocking out oil installations.

It was fortunate that events conspired to prevent any attempt to carry them out. Instead, offensive operations focused almost entirely on German warships lying in or near their North Sea bases, an objective that came twelfth in the War Plans list of priorities. There were several reasons for this restraint. At the declaration of war President Roosevelt had appealed to the main belligerents to undertake not to bomb cities or launch any air operations that endangered civilian lives. Britain and France agreed immediately, Germany two weeks later. The Chamberlain government was anxious to comply. The French if anything outdid their allies in their dread of doing anything to provoke the Germans into doing to Paris what they had done to Warsaw.

Slessor wrote after the war that, even before the fighting began, recognition of the true position had dawned on the Air Force high command: 'It became more and more obvious as war came nearer that the force likely to be at our disposal in the next few years … was sadly inadequate to our needs, whether in technical performance, hitting power, training or ability to sustain operations in the face of war wastage of aircraft and crews. The expression "conservation of the bomber force" began to take its place in our thinking, and by the outbreak of war had become a determining factor in policy …'[25]

That cannot have been how it felt to the crews operating in the opening days of the air war. The first proper sortie provided a tragic illustration of many of Bomber Command's weaknesses. At lunchtime on 4 September, Flight Lieutenant Ken Doran was waiting by his Blenheim at Ipswich civil airport with four other crews of 110 Squadron. They had moved there from their base at Wattisham in the expectation of action. Doran was an adventurous twenty-six-year-old who after leaving St Albans School had done a stint as a private in the Army before quitting to join the RAF on a short service commission. The tension of waiting was broken by the arrival of some 'gen'. Units of the German fleet had been sighted 'but weather in the Heligoland Bight, it appeared was bloody, and the only attack possible would be a low level one'.[26] A reconnaissance flight had spotted warships lying near Wilhelmshaven and further north off Brunsbüttel at the mouth of the Kiel Canal. Fifteen Blenheims and fourteen Wellingtons from a variety of squadrons were ordered off to attack.

The Blenheims of 110 Squadron had been carrying 500lb Semi-Armour Piercing bombs but for some reason a decision was made to replace them with General Purpose bombs with an eleven-second-delay fuse. Then 'at last everything was ready and the final briefing had been given by the Station Commander, who finished up with these words to the rear gunners: "Don't shoot till you see the whites of their eyes."'

Each squadron was to make its own way to the target area. There would be no fighter escort to protect them. Ludlow-Hewitt had suggested their desirability in August 1938 but the Air Ministry was unenthusiastic. They stuck to the view that existing fighters did not have the range to cover long-range missions and, even if they did, when they broke off to do battle with attacking fighters the bomber force would anyway be left undefended. Nor could they take comfort in armour if they came under fire. The Air Staff had opposed installing steel plating as it 'reduced the weight of the bomb load'.[27]

They took off at teatime. Navigators got a fix on their position from the last ground station they passed before crossing the coast. Then they were on their own, out over the North Sea with their maps and compasses and calculations of wind speed, operating on a system known in the service as 'by guess and by God'.

It was not long before they hit the weather. 'The Met forecast was only too accurate,' remembered Doran who led the attack.[28] 'A solid wall of cloud seemed to extend from sea level to about 17,000 feet. We obviously had to keep down below it to have any chance of finding our target so we went down to sea level and flew in and out of cloud between 50 and 100 feet.' In the disorientating greyness where sea and sky merged indistinguishably the great danger was of ploughing into the waves. There was nothing on which the observers could get a bearing. Then 'suddenly a couple of barges appeared out of the murk and vanished. At the same time we got our first sight of the German coast.' After 'a bit of feverish map reading' they realized that they were on the approach to the Schillig Roads that led into Wilhelmshaven. 'By an incredible combination of luck and judgement we were bang on our track.' The gods were smiling. The cloud lifted to 500 feet and they saw a large merchant ship. Just behind it lay the *Admiral Scheer*, one of the Kriegsmarine's pocket battleships, as well as a cruiser used as a training ship, the *Emden*. It was anchored in shallow water near the bank and protected on the landward side by a balloon barrage.

Before taking off they had decided that the five aircraft would attack in two sections of three and two, arriving from different angles, and pass over the target within the eleven seconds before the bombs exploded. Doran 'decided to make our attack slightly across the fore and aft line of the ship and make our getaway by a sharp turn to port to avoid the balloon barrage'.

They climbed to 500 feet and swooped in a shallow dive. As they approached they saw 'the matelots' washing hanging out around the stern and the crew idly standing about on deck. It seemed as though we had caught them literally with their pants down.' At first the sailors seemed to think the aircraft were friendlies, but 'when they realized our intention was hostile started running like mad'.

Doran led the first section into the attack. His Blenheim 'dropped its bombs bang amidships'. The crew were now working the anti-air-craft guns and the barrage was supplemented by onshore flak batteries which 'kept us pretty busy carrying out evasive measures'. The bombs from the second aircraft undershot by ten yards and exploded in shallow water under the ship. The pilot of the third aircraft reckoned he would not be able to get over the *Scheer* before his bombs exploded and dropped them on 'another target'. The second section of two aircraft was led by Flying Officer Henry Emden. He apparently decided to switch targets and go for the cruiser which shared his name. On the approach his aircraft was hit by flak and crashed into the *Emden*, killing nine sailors as well as all four of the Blenheim crew. This was the only damage inflicted on the Germans. The two bombs landed on the *Scheer* bounced off the armoured deck and then failed to explode.

The operation would prove shockingly expensive. Five Blenheims from 107 Squadron managed to locate the cruiser *Admiral Hipper*. In the ensuing attack, four of them were shot down. At Brunsbüttel, Wellingtons from 9 and 149 Squadrons arrived to find warships in the water but fierce anti-aircraft fire and bad weather meant that only one crew claimed a possible hit and two of the attackers were shot down. The tally for the day was seven aircraft lost, nearly a quarter of the force. Twenty-four men were killed, and two survived to be taken prisoner.

Ten aircraft in the force turned back after getting lost. Due to navigational error two Wellingtons missed Germany altogether and flew on to the Danish town of Esbjerg 150 miles to the north of the target area, dropping bombs that killed two people.

Despite the poor beginning, Bomber Command stuck with the same methods for the rest of the year. Senior officers were reluctant to abandon the idea that the bombers' on-board guns should be able to pump out enough defensive fire to see off attacking fighters. There was plenty of evidence from gunnery training school to make it clear that this was not the case. The standard of shooting accuracy was abysmal – not due so much to the incompetence of the gunners as to the fact that it was extremely difficult to connect with a fast and manoeuvrable aeroplane. Even in 1942, when air gunner Eric Banks was doing his training at Barrow-in-Furness he was surprised to find that when it came to the air-to-air firing at slow-moving towed drogues a hit rate of 'anything above four per cent or five per cent was regarded as a good score'.[29] A year later Norman Lee passed out successfully from the Elementary Air Gunnery School at Bridlington with an average score of 2.4 per cent.[30]

To acknowledge this fatal deficiency would have meant abandoning daylight operations, and with it any chance of hitting targets with any accuracy. The truth was exposed on two disastrous operations in December. On 14 December five out of twelve Wellingtons from 99 Squadron on a search for shipping off Wilhelmshaven were destroyed by flak and fighters. Four days later, while on a similar mission, twelve Wellingtons out of a force of twenty-two which reached the target area were shot down, most if not all of them by fighters. The notion of the self-defending bomber formation was now dead and from then on most operations would be conducted at night.

In this period, Bomber Command lost sixty-three aircraft and 171 men in operations over enemy territory. Even more aircraft had been destroyed in training exercises – sixty-nine with the loss of eighty crew. Most of the aircraft, including the training losses, were the most modern in service – Hampdens, Whitleys, Wellingtons and Blenheims.

This hardly seemed in line with a policy of 'conservation of the bomber force'. Crews were sent off on risky missions in the knowledge that likely results were pathetically small. The Blenheims that attacked the *Scheer* had no chance of sinking her. They had a payload of only 1,000lb. The bombs they carried were ineffective and underpowered with high explosive making up only 34 per cent of the overall weight.[31] They were unlikely to do much more than scratch a heavily armoured capital ship, even if they managed to explode. A significant proportion did not. Of the medium-capacity bombs dropped on south-west Germany in 1940–41, about 40 per cent were duds.[32] Clearing away the rubble of Cologne after the war, more than 10,000 unexploded Allied bombs were discovered.[33]

A proper bomber offensive would not be possible until the arrival of the big four-engine heavies and that was still at least two years away. Despite the costly debacles of December, attempts to hit German shipping continued intermittently until April 1940. Crews were ordered to stay away from the German coast and use cloud cover where possible, but no vessels were sunk. Most Bomber

Command sorties were night-time excursions to drop anti-Nazi leaflets over German cities, an activity which rated only fourteenth in priority in the Western War Plans. Six million leaflets were dropped in the first operation alone, declaring that 'this war is as repulsive to us as it is to you' but warning Germans 'not to forget that England, once forced into war, will wage it unwaveringly to the end'.[34] Neither this, nor the many millions more which fluttered down in the years to come, produced any discernible results. Nonetheless the operations, which often doubled as reconnaissance missions, were useful. New distance records were set and crews got vital experience of night flying and navigation. They were rarely troubled by flak or fighters, an encouraging but surely temporary state of affairs, which weighed in the decision to switch the main bombing effort from day to night.

The main enemy in the brutal winter of 1939–40 was the weather. On the night of 27 October 1939, a force of Whitleys was sent off to drop leaflets over Munich, Frankfurt and Stuttgart. None of them was equipped with de-icing equipment or cabin heating and the electrically heated flying suit had yet to come into service. As they climbed into cloud, they slowly became encased in ice. A post-operational report recounted how on one aircraft 'crystalline ice formed on the leading edges of the wings, over the gun turrets and on the cabin windows. The front gun was frozen up and rendered useless. The aircraft's trimming tabs were jammed by ice and the dustbin turret stuck about a third of the way down its travel ... after two and a quarter hours in the air the oxygen supply in the cabin was exhausted. Some of the crew occasionally banged their heads on the floor or navigation table as a relief from the feeling of frost-bite and [lack of] oxygen.'[35] On the return journey 'the icing became worse and the rear guns now also froze, lumps of ice flew off the airscrews, striking the sides and nose of the aircraft'. The Whitley nonetheless managed to struggle back and land at a base in France.

When opaque ice blotted out the windscreen and instruments of another Whitley the captain gave the order to bale out. The rear gunner, whose intercom had failed, stayed on board unaware that he was alone. The pilotless bomber duly crashed with the gunner still inside. In a quirk of fate that would bear endless repetition in pub and canteen, he staggered out of the wreckage having suffered only a few burns and bruises, convinced that his crewmates had been incinerated in the flaming debris.

The relative inactivity of Bomber Command during the Phoney War was a relief to its chief. Ludlow-Hewitt had seen nothing to change his gloomy view of its immediate prospects, and opinion that as much time as possible was needed to build up strength and competence. His caution, candour and pessimism made his continued tenure impossible. His replacement was Charles Portal, the dominant figure in the RAF story for most of the rest of the war.

'Peter' Portal, as he was known to his peers, would lead the Air Force until victory, making him the longest serving of the wartime chiefs. According to a contemporary, Hugh Walmsley, he was 'a brilliant pilot, a brilliant staff officer and a brilliant commander'.[36] He was short with a large head, bright, appraising eyes and a prominent nose. He went to Winchester, a brainy boy at a brainy school, and was studying at Christ Church, Oxford, when the war broke out. He ended up in the RFC and was taken under Trenchard's wing. After the war he was sent to the RAF Staff College established at Andover to hone the minds of the brightest young officers then given command of 7 Squadron, a bomber unit, based at Worthy Down. Portal was quiet, in a service that tended to be boisterous, and disapproved of self-publicity. He was nonetheless obsessively competitive. He acted as bomb aimer in the annual Lawrence Minot bombing trophy and won it twice. A contemporary, William Yool, remembered how when the squadron was assigned to one side in army manoeuvres on Salisbury Plain, Portal flew as observer with one of his pilots. 'On a night of blinding rain and poor visibility they effectively ruined the manoeuvres by flying around the area at a low height in a Virginia, pinpointing the "enemy" units so accurately with the aid of an Aldis lamp that Portal's side had a complete picture of the enemy's dispositions. Some of the soldiers were not amused and complained that it was not war.'[37] He liked to win at everything. When commanding RAF forces in Aden in the middle 1930s he took up sailing. On Wednesday afternoons, the wife of a colleague remembered, he would race dinghies with the senior naval officer, and beat him every time. The pair would then swap boats and Portal would beat him all over again.[38] His real passion was hawking. The fascination began when he was a young boy and lasted until work prevented him from pursuing it with the intensity that he felt it required. Nobody failed to notice that Portal, with his keen, dark eyes, deep-scored cheeks and great, beak-like nose looked remarkably like the birds he loved.

While serving as Chief Flying Instructor at Cranwell in the early 1920s he kept twenty-four merlin and peregrine falcons, training them, fussing over their diets and nursing them when they became ill. Between mid-July 1921 and the beginning of February 1922 he took them out on 127 occasions, noting every detail of the hawks' performances in obsessive detail. One of his favourites was Rattle, 'a beautiful hawk to look at and a fine flier. Did not take to partridges at once. Kills pigeons well.'[39] Each success was celebrated. The total bag for the season was 187 larks, 162 partridges and ten 'various'.

Falconry requires an unemotional acceptance of the beauties and cruelties of nature. The pleasure comes in watching a bird you have raised from young doing what it is supposed to do supremely well, that is, spotting its prey and driving it upwards in ever-widening circles until it has gained the height advantage. Portal described vividly in the college magazine what happened next: 'After a few more mighty strokes his wings shut close and he hurls himself with truly appalling speed, down through the sunlit air … "Whack!" The sound of the blow is carried back to you. Leaving a little puff of feathers hanging in the sun, that luckless partridge drops to earth like a stone …'[40] For all his urbanity Portal had an air of the hunter about him and always accepted the atavistic realities of existence. The quiet manner hid a broad streak of ruthlessness. He shared this outlook and disposition with Arthur Harris, his successor at Bomber Command, ensuring that it would maintain its posture of all-out aggression until the last days of the war.

On 9 April 1940 the Germans made their long-awaited next move. For the Air Force, the invasion of Denmark and Norway brought more losses with no significant results. RAF aircraft were sent off to try and bomb the ships ferrying men and supplies and to attack Luftwaffe bases covering the invasion. The bombers were operating beyond the range of fighter cover and were extremely vulnerable to the attentions of the Messerschmitt 109s and 110s. Pilot Officer Tony Smyth had moved with 214 Squadron up to Lossiemouth in the north of Scotland a few days before the invasion and had already seen fighters shoot down two Wellingtons from his sub-flight while on a shipping search off Denmark. At last light on 11 April he flew as second pilot to Flight Sergeant 'Darky' Powell, a pre-war regular, to attack Stavanger airfield from where transport planes were ferrying German troops forward. 'It was quite fine when we came to the first islands off the coast with their white light-houses and farms turning pink in the light of the setting sun,' he recalled.[41] 'It was very beautiful and I longed to revisit it in more peaceful times.'

These thoughts were interrupted when 'suddenly the air gunner in the astrodome called out "fighters one mile to port beam!"' The ribbons of red incendiary fell away harmlessly and after overshooting the airfield the first time they turned back to try again and flew into 'a real fireworks display with streams of tracer bullets flying in all directions ...' Two more attempts were thwarted by intense anti-aircraft fire and the presence of radio masts. Before they could try again Smyth looked over to see a Wellington piloted by Pilot Officer F. E. Barber engulfed in a sheet of flame. He had time to remember that the wireless operator was a leading aircraftman called Westcott whose father was a policeman in Worcestershire near Smyth's home, to whom he gave a lift to and from the base when the flight was granted leave. Then there was 'an almighty explosion in the cockpit with a flash of light that left us temporarily blinded and the plane leapt upward and then dived towards the harbour'. A 20mm shell, from a fighter or anti-aircraft gun, had exploded on the side of the cockpit, and two more hit amidships and in the rear turret. Powell was wounded in his left side but still capable of flying and the rear gunner was bleeding heavily from his thighs. Smyth, who had been saved from serious injury by the parachute buckle on his shoulder, bandaged the gunner and administered morphine while Powell jettisoned the bombs, announcing, 'I've had enough. I'm going home.'

They flew back into the sunset, with Smyth on the lower deck, pushing back on the control column to ease the weight on the pilot's arms. The pilot's compass had been smashed and they had only a small compass from the dinghy emergency pack to guide them. Somehow they made it to Kinloss 'with Darky still flying magnificently', a feat for which he later received the Distinguished Flying Medal. After seeing the crew into hospital Smyth collapsed, reflecting that 'in three weeks, of the eighteen aircrew in my sub-flight, twelve were dead, five were in hospital and I alone was on my feet'.

The cost to Bomber Command of the Scandinavian foray was nearly forty aircraft lost, 132 aircrew dead and twenty taken prisoner. The results were negligible. Fighter Command did not fare any better. After Allied troops were landed in central Norway in a doomed attempt to hold the Germans, fighter squadrons flew off from Royal Navy carriers and set up makeshift bases on frozen lakes from where they launched heroic attempts to provide the ground forces with some protection. The odds were hopeless and the squadrons lacked supplies, spares, communications and even shelter. Sergeant Richard Earp, an ex-Halton boy, flew Hurricanes with 46 Squadron from a makeshift airstrip of 'coconut matting and wire netting' alongside a fjord at Skaanland.[42] He slept in a tent on the ice with six others. 'All I had was a groundsheet and two blankets,' he remembered. 'You couldn't sleep ... It was terribly bloody cold.' In the week he was there he 'never saw anything or hit anything'. When the inevitable withdrawal was ordered, Skaanland was ablaze with crippled aircraft and fuel dumps, set on fire to deny them to the enemy.

Earp left Norway on a trawler. Ten of his comrades managed to land their Hurricanes on the carrier *Glorious*, a feat which was supposed to be impossible for a heavy monoplane. Lighter Gladiator biplanes from 263 Squadron were already embarked. The following afternoon the German battlecruisers *Scharnhorst* and *Gneisenau* intercepted *Glorious* and two destroyer escorts as they sailed for home. Two hours later, all three Royal Navy ships were sunk with the loss of 1,519 lives. Only two of the Air Force men aboard survived. So ended a costly ordeal that brought little in the way of compensatory knowledge or experience. It was, however, only the prelude to another passage of painful failure.

The German attack on the Low Countries and France on 10 May was to reveal yet more weaknesses in the Air Force's preparations. In the years between the wars little time had been spent on working out how aeroplanes could work in effective co-operation with troops on the ground. Air Staff officers, notably John Slessor, understood the importance of integrating air and land power. However, the primacy of the bomber doctrine and the scarcity of resources meant that little progress was made. Overseas, the Air Force and Army had worked together in small policing operations against primitive rebels. Back at home relations were often strained as airmen resisted what they saw as the soldiers' unreasonable demands to divert resources their way.

The tactical and strategic relationship between Air Force and Army faced its first big test in modern warfare conditions when, a few days after the start of the war, the RAF accompanied the British Expeditionary Force (BEF) across the Channel.

The British Air Forces in France (BAFF) were divided into two formations. The Air Component of the BEF, based in the Nord and Pas de Calais, was made up of five squadrons of Westland Lysanders, robust but slow, high-wing monoplanes with fixed undercarriages, and a single rear-mounted machine gun, which were tasked with tactical reconnaissance and artillery spotting. Four squadrons of Blenheims would carry out strategic reconnaissance up to the Rhine. Four Hurricane squadrons were assigned to protect the troops and the Lysanders, which could be reinforced from Britain when the balloon went up.

The Advanced Air Striking Force (AASF), based at Reims, had ten squadrons of Battles and Blenheims, charged with supporting the ground troops by attacking the German advance, preferably at choke points like bridges and road junctions. They were to be covered by two squadrons of Hurricanes, which again would be reinforced when hostilities began.

Blenheims carried a small bomb load but were at least reasonably fast. Battles were now recognized by aircrews and commanders alike as practically useless, slow and poorly defended and 'absolute death traps' even to the eyes of a very junior pilot like Tony Smyth.

Their utter helplessness against fighter attack was established in the first weeks of the war when five Battles of 150 Squadron were sent on a reconnaissance mission twenty miles the other side of the Franco-German border. Four were shot down by Me 109s and the fifth damaged beyond repair.[43]

Neither aircraft was designed for ground support work. The Luftwaffe had Junkers 87 Stuka dive bombers, which were used as aerial artillery to pound enemy defences as the Wehrmacht's tanks thrust forward. The RAF's focus on strategic bombing had left no room for the development of a British dive bomber. Existing aircraft were thought to be technically incapable of dropping bombs from a steep angle. There was talk of fitting aircraft with air brakes which might make dive bombing feasible or developing shallow dive bombing tactics but neither option was properly investigated or pursued.[44]

Thus, the choices were high- or low-level bombing, both of which brought considerable disadvantages. At heights of 15,000 feet and above the chances of hitting a small target like an advancing column, bridge or train were very small. Going in at a few hundred feet greatly increased accuracy but also vulnerability to flak. All this was understood by the Air Force chiefs. In January 1940 the operational instructions issued to commanders in France and presumably based on observation of the Polish campaign stated, 'Bomber aircraft have proved extremely useful in *support* of an advancing army, especially against weak anti-aircraft resistance, but it is not clear that a bomber force against an advancing army, well supported by all forms of anti-aircraft defence and a large force of fighter aircraft, will be economically effective.'[45] The events that followed the arrival of *Blitzkrieg* in the West proved the accuracy of this euphemistic assessment.

On 10 May, the massacre of the bombers began. The BAFF commander, Arthur Barratt, ordered the first aircraft off at noon to try and stem the German columns pouring across the Belgian border. By evening twenty-four Battles had either been shot down by fighters or the mobile artillery batteries that trundled alongside the advancing troops or otherwise destroyed on the ground. Another twenty-four light bombers were lost the following day. By 12 May the

Germans were across the River Meuse near Maastricht and had secured bridges across the Albert Canal to the west of the city at Veldwezelt and Vroenhoven through which they could channel forces on to Brussels. The bridges were strongly protected by flak batteries and machine guns and fighters were on hand to deal with any interference. That morning at the grass airfield at Amifontaine near Laon that they had occupied since the previous December, a call was made to the crews of 12 Squadron for volunteers to attack the bridges. By now everyone knew the likely outcome but every man stepped forward. In the end the first six on the duty roster were chosen. The raid was led by a twenty-one-year-old Flying Officer Donald Garland. He had been born in County Wicklow in the Irish Republic. His parents moved to London and he went to Cardinal Vaughan Memorial School, a Catholic direct grant college in Holland Park. He left at seventeen, working for a while in an insurance office before signing up for a short service commission. He was one of four brothers to join the RAF, none of whom would survive the war.

In the end five Battles took off from Amifontaine as one was held back with wireless trouble, a development the crew must have been profoundly thankful for when they learned what happened next. Garland led one section, Flying Officer N. M. Thomas the other. Before setting off they had a 'rather heated discussion' about tactics.[46] 'Garland was determined to carry out a low-level attack thinking it not only the best form, but the safest,' wrote Thomas who preferred a high approach and tried to persuade him to do likewise. 'My parting words were "it will be interesting to see the result, and may we both be lucky enough to return."'

As the formation approached the bridges they were met with a blizzard of flak and machine-gun fire and set upon by fighters. Garland hurled the Battle through it all, swooping down to deliver a bomb which damaged but did not demolish the Veldwezelt bridge. His aircraft was destroyed in the effort. Ablaze from stem to stern and trailing a great banner of black smoke, it smashed into the ground near the village of Lanaken killing him, his observer Sergeant Thomas Gray and the wireless operator/gunner, Leading Aircraftman L. R. Reynolds. Garland and Gray were both awarded the Victoria Cross, the first RAF men of the war to win it. The manifestly unjust criteria that the Air Force applied to determine gallantry awards meant that Reynolds was not. As a mere WOP/AG he was deemed not to have been in a 'decision-taking' position and could not share the credit. Only one of the five Battles made it back to base, the others falling to flak and fighters.

Another twenty-nine bombers were destroyed that day but the orders remained the same and the appalling losses seemed to do nothing to dent the resolve of commanders to order further attacks or the crews to carry them out. At mid-afternoon on 14 May Leading Aircraftman Len Clarke, a WOP/AG, flew off with his crewmates to attack bridges over the Meuse near Sedan with four other Battles from 12 Squadron. His pilot was Sergeant Reg Winkler an ex-apprentice. The observer Sergeant Maurice 'Bish' Smalley and he had joined the RAF as part of the expansion programme two years before. Amifontaine, where the airmen lived in tents and a single Nissen hut, had so far escaped attack but as they climbed to 6,000 feet there were signs everywhere of the Luftwaffe's power. Clarke saw 'bombed trains, burning buildings, halted road convoys meeting streams of refugees ...'[47]

As they approached Sedan they ran into concentrated flak and from his position behind his single Vickers machine gun he spotted Messerschmitt 109s closing up from behind. Almost at once one of the bombers faltered and started to smoke, victim of the ground flak, then fell away, jettisoning its bombs as it dived. He later learned that it managed to limp back to base, the only one to survive the trip. Soon, Clarke's aircraft 'began suffering damage. Several holes [appeared] in the wing upper surfaces although luckily the fuel tanks seemed to escape. One shell passed through the starboard wing between the bombs and the flare racks exploding above.'

The target was an old stone bridge on the edge of Sedan. 'On reaching the target we followed the leader into a dive, Reg pushing the nose down steeply, so much so that I queried over the intercom whether he was all right.' When the pilot levelled out he could 'see dust and smoke straddling the river. Houses were already burning on one side of the river by the old bridge.'

They were coming in at about 2,000 feet behind the lead aircraft when it took a direct hit from an anti-aircraft shell and it plunged to the ground showering debris. Astonishingly, one of the crew, the wireless operator AC1 J. D. Wright, survived. Then it was their turn. A shell struck the nose, destroying the Battle's sole engine. Clarke felt 'a heavy thud which threw the aircraft upwards. Smoke, oil and glycol [engine cooling fluid] poured back and flames swept upwards into Reg's cockpit.' The aircraft was still just controllable but they were losing height rapidly. I asked Reg whether he could get it down but at once he gave the order to bale out.' Clarke 'went out first, Bish giving me a final push over the side and I experienced that unique sensation of falling into a bottomless pit before being jerked into silent downward flight'. Looking around he saw their Battle slant into a final doomed dive and in the distance his two crewmates floating safely down. He landed heavily, just avoiding a ducking in a channel that fed the Meuse. As if to rub in their dominance, as he 'gathered myself together, a dozen Bf 109s [Messerschmitts] flew overhead'. Clarke, Winkler and Smalley were taken prisoner and spent the rest of the war in prisoner-of-war camps. Six of their 12 Squadron comrades died in the attack. Forty-seven bombers were destroyed that day in attacks on the Sedan bridges. Thirty-three of them were Battles. The seventy-three men who were killed died in vain for their sacrifice had no appreciable effect on the German advance. In twelve days of fighting, from 10 to 21 May, the AASF was all but wiped out.

The France-based fighter squadrons and those that flew across the Channel to help them struggled heroically to blunt the Luftwaffe's attacks but even having had nearly nine months in which to prepare they were still fighting under great disadvantages. Command and control was minimal with little or no radar cover to warn of enemy movements. Briefings were non-existent and fighters usually encountered the Luftwaffe by chance. Operating in threes and sixes they were almost always outnumbered. 'Well another day is gone, and with it a lot of grand blokes,' wrote Flight Lieutenant Ronnie Wight of 213 Squadron to his mother on the evening of 31 May.[48] 'Got another brace of 109s today, but the whole Luftwaffe seems to leap on us – we were hopelessly outnumbered. I was caught napping by a 109 in the middle of a dog fight, and got a couple of holes in the aircraft ...'

Despite the crippling handicaps they acquitted themselves magnificently, managing to destroy or badly damage 364 German aircraft. Of the 452 Hurricanes sent to France only sixty-six returned to England. Of the 386 lost, 178 were left behind in the retreat, most having first been set on fire. The figure would have been yet higher had it not been for Dowding's courage in opposing Churchill over French demands for reinforcements and reluctance to allow any more of his precious fighters to be sacrificed in a cause that was so obviously lost.

The sedate Lysanders of the Army Co-operation Squadrons never had a chance to do their job. 'Their performance ... was inadequate and the tasks they were set were impossible,' wrote Christopher Foxley-Norris of 13 Squadron.[49] 'After quite a short period of fighting, my own squadron had lost all its serviceable aircraft and those of us who survived joined the pathetic rabble of refugees fleeing westwards ...'

Fighter Command's attempts to cover the Dunkirk evacuation brought more serious losses. Much of the air fighting took place out of sight of the troops and the legend sprang up among them that the RAF had let them down. It was a lie. 'I believe the BEF troops were booing the RAF in Dover the other day,' wrote Ronnie Wight to his mother. 'If anyone says anything to you in the future about the inefficiency of the RAF ... tell them from me we only wish we could do more. But without aircraft we can do no more than we have done – that is our best ... I know of no RAF pilot who has refused combat yet – and that sometimes means odds of more than fifty to one.'

The RAF operated in France in an atmosphere of unreality and wishful thinking. An echo of it is heard in an anecdote told by the New Zealand officer Arnold Wall, who, after losing an eye, was no longer fit for flying duties and was commanding a component depot near Amiens. One day he was told to expect a visit from Trenchard who was touring RAF facilities. He found him 'a bit hard of hearing, but only slightly so – extremely affable'.[50]

After lunch in the mess, Wall recorded, the great man 'drew me over to a map of North West Europe that we had pinned up on the wall. During the morning I had been skiting a bit about our mobility – we had proved we could get the show on its wheels and away within an hour of a movement order, and Boom led off with this.

'"You say you can be on the move at an hour's notice. That's good. Now tell me where you'll be moving *to*?"

'Who the hell knew that? But one had to say something, and the best I could think of was "wherever Component HQ tell us to move, sir."

'"That's not what I hoped you'd say." He sounded very serious, and all I could think of was to ask, "what should I have said, sir?"

'"I hoped you'd say 'Forward! Forward into Germany!'"

'I was disappointed in the dear old man for I thought this was a damned silly thing to say.'

The RAF's record for the first nine months of the war was largely a story of failure. The experience did not produce any fundamental re-examination of overall strategy. A committee was set up to report on the debacle in France. It was chaired by sixty-one-year-old Air Chief Marshal Sir Robert Brooke-Popham, an old-school officer who stated at the outset that it was not his intention to 'allot blame or spread whitewash'.[51] The RAF's overall performance and the appalling losses sustained in men and machines were never analysed. The tone was relentlessly positive. 'With very few exceptions the whole of the personnel interviewed were cheerful, confident and ready to do anything,' he wrote. 'Where any signs of depression existed it appeared to be mainly due to the failure to obtain any obvious results.' He was full of praise for the airmen's initiative and disregard for the 'pernicious [peacetime] doctrine of "safety first"'. In all it was 'very gratifying to see the refreshing breeze of living dangerously once more ventilating men's minds'. He could even find something nice to say about the Battles, which he believed would 'still be able to do good work' in the event of an invasion.

Years after the war senior officers were reluctant to accept that there might have been alternatives to the course of their actions in this first phase or that less costly methods might have been used to determine what was feasible and what was not, in the largely unexplored sphere of modern aerial warfare. The willingness to endure heavy losses in the knowledge that they brought negligible results was sustained in the night-bombing campaign that began in earnest later that year. 'We had to feel our way towards the development of tactics and technique that we felt sure would in the end produce results,' explained John Slessor, who took over 5 Group of Bomber Command in May 1941.[52] 'The lessons we learnt could, I am afraid, have been learnt only in the grim school of actual war experience.'

Unsurprisingly, some of the guinea pigs saw things differently. Many of those who died in the opening passage were pre-war professionals, part of the core around which the civilian air force would have to be built. 'They were proving and disproving the basic doctrines by which air warfare had to be fought, but far too few of them lived through those first few months to practice themselves the lessons they had learned,' wrote Christopher Foxley-Norris, who, having survived the French disaster and the war, ended up an air chief marshal.[53] 'The manner in which the RAF's professional manpower ... was frittered away before the war had even started for most of the participants was tragic, criminally tragic. But nobody seems to have admitted responsibility for the mistakes made or been penalized in any way for them. Reputations survived, even when aircrews did not.'

7

The Battle

On 10 September 1940, Pilot Officer George Barclay of 249 Squadron described to his parents ('darling Mummie and Far') a patrol he had flown over the Thames Estuary in his Hurricane a few days before. 'It was a grand day and from 15,000 feet the view was so delightful that one was tempted to sit there and admire it instead of searching for the Hun,' he wrote.[1] Barclay knew the landscape beneath his wings very well. He had grown up in Great Holland on the Essex coast where his father was vicar. He picked out Westgate-on-Sea which brought back memories of his old prep school, Hawtrey's, and 'flying model aeroplanes on the cliff'.

> Then there was Burnham-on-Crouch, where Norman, Eddy and I became 'photographer's assistants' for a day … and there was Rochester and I thought of Aunt Chris's former home (and 'Tuppence!') and the Archdeaconry. Then right on the horizon I could just see Clacton and in the haze I could just make out where Great Holland ought to be, though I couldn't see it.

He was hauled back to reality by the sight of the balloon barrage below and the great sprawl of London which he was there to defend. He 'spent the next several minutes searching the sky for Huns and checking over the cockpit instruments' when 'over the wireless came a shout: "Hullo leader, Messerschmitt 109s behind us in the sun …"' In the 'scrap' that followed Barclay managed to shoot down one Me 109. He then climbed to attack a formation of bombers and 'did a head-on attack on the leader. As I broke away my ammunition gave out, but I saw one of the leader's engines smoking. Now I couldn't see anything as oil was pouring out of the engine onto the wind-screen and ... gave signs of packing up altogether.' Deciding he would not make it to his base at North Weald he 'made a successful crash landing in a field about five miles away ... quite OK and the Hurricane not much damaged'. He waited for some soldiers to arrive to guard the machine and arrange a lift back to his squadron. In the meantime, 'the whole local population had turned out to have a look'.

He got back just as the 249 pilots were taking off to intercept another raid but there was no serviceable Hurricane for him to fly so he 'sat in an air raid shelter and listened to two waves of Hun bombers go over after dropping bombs on London'. Signing off the letter he apologized for the central role he had given himself in the account: 'I'm afraid it's all about me but of course the rest of the squadron did their stuff and went off again after rearming.'

Barclay's account brings home vividly the intimate nature of the Battle of Britain. The pilots were looking down on the places and people they were fighting for. Looking up, the population had a grandstand view of the exploits of their champions. It was the first time in English history that a clash of almost incalculable impor-tance had taken place under the eyes of the nation. Fighter Command's victory was a turning point in the war. It was also a defining passage in the RAF's own history.

The Battle of Britain had been given a name and invested with a significance several weeks before events began to unfold. The name was supplied by Winston Churchill in his speech to the House of Commons on 18 June 1940, in which he also set out what was at stake – no less than 'the survival of Christian civilization ... our own British way of life and the long continuity of our institutions and our Empire'.

As an attritional struggle it lacked a clear-cut beginning, climax or end. The shape that it took on was imposed retrospectively. The official opening and closing dates were set, after some deliberation, by Fighter Command's C-in-C Hugh Dowding in his despatch, submitted in August 1941. He decided that the Battle began on 10 July and ended on 31 October. The timeline was, he admitted, a matter of opinion as 'operations of various kinds merged into one another almost insensibly'.[2] The Air Ministry's own account, published by the Stationery Office at the end of 1940, chose 8 August as the beginning.

For the airmen and the civilian onlookers, the event had no neat contours. Some pilots maintained that it was only subsequently that they thought of themselves as having taken part in the Battle of Britain.

When Churchill announced its debut, he assured his audience that it would end in victory. In the fighting of May and June the RAF had 'proved itself far superior in quality both in men and in many types of machine to what we have met so far'. Despite the disadvantages of operating from foreign soil the Air Force 'had still routinely managed to inflict losses of two-and-a-half to one'. The results were even better over Dunkirk, where, he claimed, 'we undoubtedly beat the German air force which gave us mastery locally in the air and we inflicted losses of three or four to one'.

In the next round of the contest, the RAF would enjoy all the benefits of operating from their home ground. In addition, he told the House, 'our fighter air strength is stronger at the present time, relatively to the Germans who have suffered terrible losses, than it has ever been'. He now looked 'forward confidently to the exploits of our fighter pilots who will have the glory of saving their native land, their island home and all they love from the most deadly of attacks'.

The factual claims in the speech were for inspiration not information. The true loss rate for the Battle of France was more like one-to-one. His account of the air war over Dunkirk was similarly exaggerated. He also misled the country about the favourable balance of fighters. The waste of men and machines in France had been prodigious. At the start of July, the Luftwaffe had at least 760 Me 109s against Fighter Command's 591 Hurricanes and Spitfires. On the other hand, aircraft production was at last running smoothly, there was a reservoir of pilots waiting to fill the gaps in the ranks, albeit only partly trained, and a radar-directed early warning system that on paper at least looked effective.

His reference to the psychological advantage of operating from the home base seemed justified. It made a difference that the pilots were fighting to defend British rather than French families and homes. There was also the significant practical benefit that pilots who were shot down and survived would live to fight again, sometimes only a matter of hours after they baled out or crash-landed.

A clinical assessment – the sort employed by revisionist accounts written decades after the event – might rightly conclude that the RAF had no excuse for not winning the Battle of Britain. But the issue would not be decided simply by numbers and equipment. The Battle of France had proved that. The French had strong fixed defences, an enormous army and a sizeable air force, albeit equipped with second-rate aircraft, and they too were fighting for their freedom, honour and loved ones. Yet they had collapsed with astonishing speed. Morale had played an important part in the story, and, as the airmen who lived through the catastrophe observed with pity and sometimes contempt, backbone was in short supply among French soldiers and airmen in May.

The RAF had outperformed the Armée de l'Air, in combat and in resolve. In defending France, it sustained great physical damage. The battles in the skies over Flanders bore some similarities with those the airmen's fathers and uncles had fought on the ground below, only twenty-odd years before. Like them, they had been thrown, again and again, into sacrificial assaults that brought no results, by men who seemed devoid of imagination and lacked the moral courage to call a halt.

Even with all the advantages of defence, would those who had survived one holocaust be willing to face another? And how long could those who had yet to be tested be able to endure an onslaught from a Luftwaffe which, whatever Churchill said, was still immensely strong and roaring drunk on victory? Morale was a vital factor in the Battle of Britain, not just for the Fighter Boys, as the pilots soon became known, but for the British people. At the end of a summer of shared dangers, the two had been fused together in mutual affection and admiration and the RAF was fixed at the front and centre of the British war effort.

Despite the complacent tone of Brooke-Popham's analysis of the air battles of May over France and Belgium there was good reason to worry about the possible effect of the debacle on Fighter

Command's pilots. The squadrons returning from France brought back some grim tales of chaos, incompetence and pointless losses of men and machines. The hardest hit unit was 85 Squadron, which got through twenty-five Hurricanes in a matter of days. It was the physical losses that mattered more: seven pilots killed, five wounded and one taken prisoner (the standard squadron strength averaged around twenty pilots). Next hardest hit were 3 and 87 Squadrons, each of which had six pilots killed, with a further six wounded between them. It was not just a matter of filling the gaps. The trauma had the potential to undermine each unit's identity and fighting spirit.

Concern about aircrew 'waverers' began to surface in the lull between the fall of France and the start of the Battle of Britain. The subject was first aired at the Air Council meeting of 10 July when the Air Member for Personnel described the arrangements in place for dealing with 'officers who had lost the confidence of their COs in their resolution and courage in operational flying'.[3] Air Marshal Edward Gossage reported that the current practice was for them to be posted to non-operational units where they worked as ferry pilots or towing targets for air gunnery practice. By September the mood had hardened and the Council decided there would be 'no rehabilitation or continued employment on flying duties' for waverers.[4] By November they had become official pariahs. Henceforth they were to be stripped of their pilot's, observer's and air gunner's badges and reduced to the ranks and their documents stamped with the letter 'W'. A new designation of their condition made an appearance. The Council noted that 'the delinquency was not cowardice but lack of moral fibre' – soon to be abbreviated to the notorious 'LMF'.

The tough line taken by the Air Staff seems more revealing of a rather ignoble lack of confidence in their own men than of any serious problem with morale. There is little evidence, official or unofficial, that 'waverer' cases were widespread. If anything, the opposite was the case. The men who went into battle with the Luftwaffe that summer seem to have been remarkably unaffected by the precedents set in Norway and France and the doubts that sometimes surfaced about the competence of their superiors failed to dent their devotion to duty.

It was not as if they did not know what to expect. Of the twenty-five Hurricane and Spitfire squadrons in 11 Group (which covered the approaches to London and where the fighting would be fiercest) at the start of the Battle, nineteen had been in action in France or over Dunkirk. Twelve had experience of both.

Trying to analyse the elements that made up the strength of the pilots' resolve is difficult, partly because of the absence of contemporaneous data. Most participants' accounts were produced after the event and are inevitably coloured by hindsight and the narratives and attitudes that prevailed at the time of writing. The Fighter Boys left little behind in the way of letters and diaries. Either they were out of the firing line and had nothing much of significance to record, or they were in the middle of it and too busy or exhausted to pick up pen or pencil at the end of a day's fighting. However, enough of this historiographical gold dust has drifted down to us, usually brief lines favouring fact over feeling, set out in Letts wash-leather diaries or on pale blue writing paper headed with the RAF crest, to give a glimpse of the way it was in those crowded months.

One striking aspect is the almost total absence of comment about significant political and military events that take place beyond the writer's horizon. George Barclay's diary was unusual in mentioning 'all sorts of discussions' involving the 'Station Commander, the CO, "Jersey" (a Pole) and the pilots' on 'the war, the Air Force etc'. Their main concerns were about the complacency shown by politicians and the public about the task ahead. The conclusion was 'that we shall eventually win this war, but it will be the hell of a job and more so unless we pull ourselves together'.[5] Barclay was at the sophisticated end of the Fighter Boy spectrum, coming from a long line of well-educated and distinguished soldiers and churchmen and joining the RAF from the Cambridge University Air Squadron.

In almost all the other testimonies, the historical landmarks by which we gauge the progress of the war do not seem to have been much noticed by the pilots. For all the titanic importance that Winston Churchill has assumed in our understanding of the story, he did not loom large in the Fighter Boys' thoughts, for no one in these documents mentions him. Nor did the causes of the war or the underlying ideologies.

When the bombing of London began in earnest on 7 September Denis Wissler, a nineteen-year-old pilot with 17 Squadron, was moved to write in his diary: 'What complete swine these Jerries are.' Six days later, as the Blitz continued, the entry reads 'God damn and blast Hitler'.[6] Wissler was intelligent but uncomplicated, a product of Bedford School, which provided the RAF with many officers, and had joined on a short service commission a few weeks before the war started. George Barclay, who knew Nazi Germany from two trips there during school holidays and studied the language, made only one reference to the nature of the enemy when he recorded the verdict of one of the squadron's discussions: 'one German is nice, two Germans are swine'.[7]

Their emotions were focused inward, on family and friends, spreading wider to embrace service chums, the squadron and the RAF. If there is any higher sentiment on display it is a mild patriotism, not overt or noisy, rather a barely articulated assumption that Britain is a good place with values that are worth fighting and dying for.

By the summer of 1940 the dilution of the old pre-war RAF elite was well advanced. Rapid expansion meant squadrons were manned by men drawn from a wide swathe of backgrounds and from the length and breadth not just of Britain but its Dominions. As such the Air Force could, and frequently did, claim to be a representative social and geographical distillation of the nation and empire. Of the 2,340 pilots and 594 other aircrew who flew in the Battle of Britain, 1,129 joined as regulars, the biggest category (665) serving on short service commissions. Reservists made up 1,436 of the total, the great majority of them being the 1,199 men from all walks of life who joined via the RAFVR. There was also a significant contribution from the Dominions (127 New Zealanders, 97 Canadians, 29 Australians) and defeated European nations, led by Poland and Czechoslovakia, as well as adventurers and idealists from America and Ireland. It was therefore the 'citizen' element of the Air Force that made up the largest component.

The great stream of manpower that poured into the RAF at the start of the war arrived from a dozen different directions. It sounded like a recipe for turbulence. At the smaller, more manageable level of a fighter squadron, the channelling process was quite smooth. The organization proved efficient at taking the variegated human material, blending from it a powerful institutional identity and giving it a strong *esprit de corps*.

Fighter squadrons were small, about the size of an Army company, with about fifteen to twenty pilots supported by eighty or so ground and administrative staff. The scale allowed a sense of belonging, creating an emotional tug that could rival that of family. 'I returned from ten days leave today,' wrote George Barclay in his diary in the autumn of 1940. 'I've had a grand time and an excellent change … But all the same, it's very good to be back with the squadron.'[8] A few weeks later he remarked again after a shorter break that 'even after forty-eight hours it's good to be back …'

Denys Mileham was heartbroken to be posted away from 41 Squadron four months after joining it in September 1940. 'Pretty sick about being here,' he wrote to his parents from Grangemouth where he was now an instructor.[9] 'This is a lousy station after Hornchurch.' Things had not improved a few weeks later. 'I hate this place more every day … I wish I could get back to my old squadron.' Among his personal effects collected after his death in action shortly afterwards was a card from his old CO Don Finlay, well known as an Olympic hurdler before the war, who trusts he is 'still showing the squadron spirit'.

Barclay had been at Stowe and Mileham at Berkhamsted, both public schools. For the many pilots with similar backgrounds squadron life must have felt familiar. There were the same close friendships, occasional rivalries, and emphasis on boisterous, communal fun that they had known in the classrooms, dormitories and playing fields of their boyhood. This was the atmosphere that prevailed in the officers' mess and, even though one third of the airmen who took part in the Battle of Britain were sergeants, the outlook that coloured the fighter squadron identity.

In the world evoked by the letters and diaries drink plays a multiple role: as a lubricant for jollity, a salve for frayed nerves and, in dark moments, the water of oblivion. But mostly alcohol was associated with fun. Drinking sessions on the station often ended with impromptu games of rugby and the forceful removal of trousers. 'A

Denys Mileham

bit of a party in the mess,' wrote Denis Wissler on 2 July. 'Everyone in sight was debagged, me included.' He had been up since three that morning so decided to call it a night at 10.30 as he had 'the prospect of getting up again at 3'.

It was sometimes said after the war in the pilots' defence that their boozy image was misleading and that the beer that was their drink of choice had been so reduced in strength by wartime regulations as to be barely intoxicating. Whatever it was Wissler drank seemed to do the job – or perhaps he had a weak head. 'Went out on the piss tonight but [I am] more or less OK tonight [sic] as I write this' is the diary entry for 13 March when he was finishing his training at Sutton Bridge. Three days later he 'had a drinking party with some of the instructors and really they are all damn good chaps and of course I couldn't hold the pace and I got a bit pissed'.

Unsurprisingly, his intake increased at particularly stressful times such as the latter part of April 1940 when his then unit, 43 Squadron, was standing by to be sent to France. Having survived a fortnight of hard fighting in conditions of utter chaos, he made a perilous journey back to the squadron base at Debden. There he 'got a shock' when he was summoned by the CO and told he was being transferred immediately to 17 Squadron, based at Kenley, south of London. Some friends went with him part of the way to have a farewell drink.

'We managed to get two hours in town and I had dinner alone at the Troc,' he wrote on 8 June. 'I really got completely plastered and was put to bed at Kenley by the Wing Commander there.' This saintly figure – probably the station commander Tom Prickman – then 'woke me up at 3.30 with some Alka-Seltzer, brought me his bath robe and had already run my bath'. The reason for the early start was that he was due for his first operation at dawn, flying back to France and Le Mans aerodrome with another 17 Squadron pilot, Count Manfred Czernin, to help cover the last stage of the withdrawal. Wissler was in the thick of the Battle of Britain from the end of July when drinking references fade away to be replaced by accounts of the relentless fighting.

But even the strain of being in action daily did not deter the pilots from enjoying themselves whenever the opportunity arose, and a restorative whiff of oxygen to take away the hangover did not always do the job. In an undated entry in his diary George Barclay described being scrambled one morning and trying 'to take an intelligent interest but my mouth was like the bottom of a birdcage as the result of last night's party ...'

Fighter Boys loved the 'flicks' and would watch any movie the local fleapits had to offer, even if they had seen them before. The prospect of a dance was always welcome, especially if there was a healthy ratio of women to men. 'Our squadron dance took place in the village hall at Steeple Bumpstead and it was a grand success,' 73 Squadron's unofficial diarist Pilot Officer Charlie McGaw recorded on 24 September.[10] 'Fifty WAAFs from Debden arrived by devious routes. The bar was so popular during the evening that it soon ran out of refreshments.' The presence of danger added a frisson for 'as the dance finished at 22.30 hours our friend the enemy passed over-head and loosed a salvo of bombs some miles away but close enough to cause a certain amount of twittering in the feminine ranks'.

The dances were segregated with officers and other ranks holding their own events. There was, though, a certain amount of social overlapping. At Debden, the sergeant pilots of 17 Squadron held a regular Sunday night dance at which the station band, all pre-war professionals, played. It was by invitation only and officers were gratified to be asked along.

On the whole, though, at this stage of the war it was still the officers, almost all of whom were steeped in the hearty traditions of the British public school, who set the tone. It did not matter that some of the sergeant pilots came from similar backgrounds. Possession of a commission created a distinction. It is revealed unconsciously in these letters and diaries where officers are usually referred to with Christian names or nicknames attached, NCOs only by their surnames. Officialdom recognized that, in an all-out war, some credit had to be given across the board. Nonetheless the achievements of the NCOs did not get the same attention as that devoted to the feats of the officers. When Cuthbert Orde, an artist who had flown with the RFC in the First World War, was commis-sioned by the Air Ministry to draw the portraits of some celebrated Fighter Boys, only ten of the 163 who were selected to sit for him were sergeants. The exercise resulted in a book. All but three of the sixty-four rather pedestrian portraits printed were of officers.

Perhaps too much can be made of these details and it may be that conventional formalities of expression of the time disguise the degree of fraternization. In the 72 Squadron diary, the sergeant pilots listed at the back have nicknames ('Duffy' Douthwaite, 'Snowy' Winter, etc.) while 73 Squadron's shows socializing together was unremarkable. The entry for 21 September records how, on hearing that Sergeant Maurice Leng had been invited to an Army officers' dance in Saffron Walden, 'Pilot Officers Langham-Hobart, Rutter, Hoole (the engineer officer) … decided that [he] needed support'. They set off with Leng and two other sergeants, Herbert Webster and Robert Plenderleith, and 'in spite of the fact that immaculate army types eyed their polo-neck sweaters askance, a good time was had by all'. Leng maintained after the war that 'there was no sort of officers vs sergeants ballyhoo. We were all in the same boat and there was marvellous camaraderie.'[11] The distinction was anyway usually a temporary one. Leng was commissioned in April the following year and virtually every Battle of Britain sergeant pilot ended up an officer.

Whether you wore stripes on your arm or pips on your shoulder there were governing codes and attitudes that bound the squadron together. The pervading mood was a studied cheerfulness and an *a priori* determination to make light of bad situations by understatement and attempts, no matter how feeble, at humour. Form dictated that brushes with death were to be treated as a joke. Denys Mileham passed on the news that James MacPhail, a boy he had trained with and who had come to lunch at the family home in Boxmoor, Herts, 'was shot up three days ago and had to leap out. He landed, by parachute, in a thorn bush, and is suffering from a sore bottom.' He must also have been badly burned for the records show he received plastic surgery treatment at the Queen Victoria Hospital, East Grinstead, and was one of Archibald McIndoe's 'guinea pigs'.

Barclay recorded how 'Butch Barton had to bale out when the squadron attacked some [Dorniers]. He landed quite OK and was brought back in an army car. The army couldn't make out why everyone just stood and laughed when Butch arrived, taunting him with the jibe, "shot down by a bomber!"'

If this insouciance was an act, it was remarkably well maintained. On 7 September Pilot Officer Bob Rutter of 73 Squadron wrote from St Andrew's Hospital in Billericay, Essex, to his CO Squadron Leader Maurice Robinson. Rutter was recovering from a bullet wound to his ankle, after being forced to bale out while flying alongside Robinson two days before. The letter is worth quoting in full.

> Although only slightly damaged, it appears that I shall be out of the show for some little time ... I followed you into the first attack, went into echelon and tackled the bomber to your right 'à la No 5 attack'! Smoke poured from his starboard engine and

as I broke away the engine was well ablaze. Turning for an attempt on the second one I noticed several 109s below. Next there was a sharp cracking as several bullets came through the floor from underneath and in front, presumably fired by the latter. I dived sharply out of trouble, as oil came spurting from the engine and covered the dashboard. The engine seemed to be running fairly well, so having wiped some of the oil from my eyes and the altimeter I noted that I was down to 5000 feet and looked round for a likely forced landing field.

The next minute there was a loud explosion from the engine followed by smoke and as I couldn't by then see anything much, baling out seemed the best course.

The machine crashed in a field and I touched down in a beet field, reached the road and was picked up some five minutes later by an ARP Warden who took me to his house. An Army Major and MO [Medical Officer] soon arrived and applied field dressings, whilst I knocked back a treble brandy, afterwards driving me here.

After an X-ray and a shot of gas I awoke to find a foot swaddled in bandages, a splint and the 'verdict.' One bullet was extracted, another went in and came out again and a bone was splintered. The wounds ought to heal in around a fortnight when the foot goes into plaster for a month so that's that.

I'm wondering how the squadron came through and whether you've had any further joy. Should you be too busy to drop me a line, will you please ask one of the boys to do so …

After asking for some personal items to be sent on he finished: 'Everybody here is thoroughly spoiling me, which is very unfair considering the Squadron is roughing it and carrying on, especially as it's due to my stupidity in getting shot down.' He signed off 'wishing you all the best of luck and good hunting and hoping to hear of your future successes'.[12]

The letter illustrates many of the virtues and qualities of the Fighter Boys: good-humoured, modest, polite but also cool, factual and competent. The apologetic and duly deferential tone towards his CO, while correct, was at odds with the facts. Rutter celebrated his twenty-first birthday two days before being shot down. However, he was far more experienced than Squadron Leader Robinson. He had fought throughout the Battle of France and was one of the last pilots to leave, flying from Nantes on 18 June. He had since been in the line with the squadron throughout the Battle of Britain. Robinson, a thirty-year-old Cranwell graduate, had done no operational flying until he took command a few weeks before.

Death's frequent appearances in these contemporary accounts are treated with routine solemnity that gets more perfunctory as time passes. On 29 September Barclay told the story of how Sergeant Edward Bayley, who flew as his number two in Red Section, 'vanished and apparently running short of oxygen ... lost consciousness and dived straight into the ground, knocking down two cottages and unfortunately three people were killed ... in peacetime it would have been a major tragedy. In war it is nothing. *C'est la guerre* ...'[13] Three weeks later, writing to his sister Mary he could not resist telling her to date he has '4½ Huns to my account as "destroyed" ... added to this I have three "probably destroyed" and six "damaged"'.

He went on: 'I suppose it sounds as if we are having a grand time – well I suppose we are really – I'm realizing an ambition, but it's a bit tough to see fellows wiped off one by one. There are only four officers in the squadron, myself included, who have come through September absolutely unscathed.' Four of his fellow pilots had been on the same course with him at Cranwell, which was turned into an OTU at the start of the war. 'I am the only survivor,' he wrote. 'Two ... are dead and two wounded. But it's remarkable how hardened one gets to people not coming back.'

Death was democratic, reaching out to claim the best pilots with the same even-handedness as it did the mediocre. Richard Lee was one of the dominant figures of 85 Squadron, bold, lively and handsome. As a Cranwell graduate he was destined for the top of the service. Denis Wissler came across him in France where Lee's reputation was made. 'Dickey Lee returned today after having crashed in German occupied Belgium and escaped in civilian clothes,' he wrote on 13 May. Six weeks later back at Debden he noted that 'Dickey Lee came down today with [his newly awarded] DSO and DFC which looked very nice. He is off flying at the moment recovering from a wound in the leg but he looks very cheerful.' Then, on 18 August, a day of huge battles, a simple entry: 'Dickey Lee ... was lost this afternoon.' Lee's end befitted his warrior spirit, shot down in the late afternoon while charging into a formation of Me 109s thirty miles off the coast of Essex.

Characters who were the life and soul of the squadron jollifications were one day no longer there. Oswald Pigg, a pre-war short service officer from Newcastle upon Tyne, features regularly in the unofficial history of 72 Squadron, based on the diaries of one of its pilots, Robert Deacon Elliot. 'That night [3 June] the whole Squadron was entertained by the Chief Constable of Gravesend in the Police Club,' reads one entry.[14] 'Transportation was a problem quickly resolved by the Gravesend Fire Chief who provided us with one of his fire engines. We swarmed onto this huge red brute – with Oswald Pigg as officer i/c Fire Bell – which he rang continuously all the way home, and in doing so brought the whole camp to a state of readiness ... the rest is a blank.'

Then, on 1 September, when the squadron was operating from Croydon: 'At 0955 we were scrambled – Squadron strength – and soon in the thick of it again. Enemy aircraft were everywhere it seemed. A terrific scrap with Me109s and once more we suffered a setback. F/O Oswald Pigg missing – and many days later confirmed killed. He was found buried under his Spitfire in some remote wood in Kent. A most cheerful fellow and an aggressive fighter in the air. He had a sister in the WAAF ...'

There was little time and no purpose in dwelling on these things. Occasionally, though, melancholy thoughts intruded. On 6 August Denis Wissler recorded matter-of-factly the death of Pilot Officer Henry Britton who 'returned to Debden after circling this 'drome [Martlesham] after taking off on patrol and later while testing he stalled in a turn and crashed and was killed'. Four days later, though, he was forced to reflect on the event. 'Had the day off,' he wrote. 'I attended P/O Britton's funeral and it was the most harrowing affair I have ever come upon.' The lesson was that life was too short to cry.

'I had a good time in the evening when I went to Cambridge to see a flick and then went to an Indian restaurant and had a fine curry, getting back to Debden at 12.30 approx.'

The airmen were sustained by the same thought that every soldier and sailor carried into battle with them since warfare began. The man standing next to you might be killed. But you, somehow, would survive. 'I feel invincible in the air,' wrote George Barclay. 'Probably experienced and older people would call it gross overconfidence, but I'm sure the average pilot is invincible in his own mind until he gets beaten up.'

They were also driven by a desire to succeed, for themselves, the squadron and the nation. Churchill had established the burden of responsibility resting on their young shoulders. The message was reinforced early in June by a letter from Dowding addressed to 'My Dear Fighter Boys'. After telling them how proud he was of their performance in northern France he spelled out the task ahead: 'I want you to know that my thoughts are always with you and that it is you and your fighting spirit which will crack the morale of the German Air Force and preserve our Country through the trials which yet lie ahead.'[15]

Fighting spirit on its own was not enough. A very specific sort of skill was needed in aerial combat. To shoot down an enemy aircraft a pilot had to manoeuvre into position, hold the target in his sights or calculate the angle at which he needed to deflect his bullets for the victim to fly into them, then keep the fire hosing into the fabric of the aircraft long enough to kill the captain or hit a vital part. It required a certain ruthlessness and detachment as well as outstanding dexterity and physical toughness. Attacks on bomber formations were usually followed by dogfights as the escorting fighters intervened. The dives and tight turns of these combats had alarming physical results. Steep turns caused the pilot to black out. The centrifugal forces made the blood feel as heavy as molten metal and gravitational pull of seven 'g' meant a man normally weighing 180lb now weighed 1,260lb.[16]

To succeed required not just flying ability but exceptional determination. Denis Wissler did not regard himself as a particularly good pilot and his diary is touching in its frank depiction of his shortcomings, disappointments and frustrations as he struggled to get off the mark. Mechanical problems with his aircraft or the vagaries of the duty roster meant that for one reason or another he never seemed to be flying when the squadron had a good day. Much of July was spent operating out of Debden and Martlesham Heath carrying out routine shipping patrols over the Channel and responding to 'flaps' which produced no action. Days went by without an enemy aircraft being sighted. His first combat of the Battle of Britain was an unsatisfactory affair. On 27 July while patrolling with his flight commander Alf Bayne and Harold 'Birdy' Bird-Wilson they encountered a Heinkel 111 being 'half-heartedly attacked by Spitfires'. They joined in, making 'a head-on attack and then an astern attack, pieces and oil coming out in all directions. The enemy aircraft slowly went down to the water. I thought it was trying to get away low down and made another head-on attack. This time it went into the water.' He watched as three crewmen climbed out into a dinghy then 'called up over the R/T for a boat to be put out'.

Wissler's flat account does not suggest he regarded this as a glorious encounter. It was not until 25 August, when the squadron was operating out of Tangmere and the Luftwaffe's assault on Fighter Command airfields was raging, that his doubts about himself seem to drop away and the tone changes to that of a competent and confident young warrior. 'This was a hard day being at 15 minutes and readiness the day long,' he wrote. 'At about half-past seven we had a hell of a scrap over Portland in which about 100 [aircraft] were engaged. Flt Lt Bayne made an attack below and astern quarter, the Me110 whipped up in a stall turn and I gave him a long burst while he was in a stalled condition. It fell over and went down. I then went on my own and made a Me110 break formation. I gave it another burst and it went down towards the sea.' Success tasted good. Five days later a rumour went around that the squadron was to be taken out of the line and posted to Northern Ireland. 'I hope not', reads the scrawled diary entry.

George Barclay's eagerness can be measured in his frustration and annoyance on the occasions when he checked on the 'state board' which listed the pilots who would be operating that day and the level of readiness (an hour, fifteen minutes etc.). 'I was off the state in the morning and was very angry ... because of it,' he wrote on 2 September. Three days later he was 'off the state again today worst luck'.

Barclay was an excellent pilot who loved flying. He had absorbed his father's creed and was a committed Christian. His beliefs did not blunt the unwavering hostility towards the would-be invaders whom he despatched with satisfied efficiency. In September, he destroyed at least two Messerschmitt 109s and Dornier 17 and Junkers 88 bombers as well as sharing a Dornier 215. His descriptions of the battles are unemotional. 'There was a good scrap over the Channel about eight miles off Folkestone,' he wrote on 15 October. 'I got a "probable" 109. He flew straight across my bows – I gave him a long burst and he went over on his back and went down seemingly out of control. I continued to fire at various deflections and he streamed glycol.' He had to break off when he was set upon by seven 109s but 'they were quite easy to evade so low down (5,000 feet)'. It must have been a hectic few minutes but he nonetheless enjoyed the flight back to base: 'It was fun skimming ... over Kent at 800 feet below cloud. Had a wonderful view of Canterbury Cathedral ...'

Barclay did not disguise his aggressive instincts and delight in victory. 'I saw five 109s at about 2000 feet streaking for home and pulling the plug gave chase,' he wrote on 7 November. 'I caught them and had a dogfight with one. Eventually he went into a climb and I saw that his engine had stopped. Whoopee!'

Contemporaneous accounts like this confirm the pilots' subsequent assertion that they felt they were attacking machines rather than men. One November afternoon curiosity took Barclay to view a Dornier 17 that had been shot down nearby. It was a curiously unaffecting experience. 'There were bits of German everywhere, but so mangled that it wasn't as gruesome as one would have thought – the toes of one foot rather put me off, but in the failing light it didn't look too human.'

Success was regarded as collective as much as individual, a cause for celebration by the entire squadron as well as the victorious pilot. Barclay recorded how when a batch of decorations were announced to four squadron members 'great jubilations and a most monumental party was the result', starting at an Epping pub, the Thatched House, which was only two miles from the base, before moving on to the mess. Boasting and line-shooting on the other hand were distinctly bad form. Denis Wissler recounted the reaction to a press interview given by a 17 Squadron pilot, Count Manfred Czernin, who, though born in Berlin, the son of an Austrian diplomat, had an English mother and had been educated at Oundle public school. 'Czernin has been shooting a grand line in the Daily Sketch about his dog and the number of enemy he has shot down,' he wrote on 2 August. 'It is treated with derision up here.' The temptation to mock led some of the pilots to write to the paper claiming the Count had been too modest and his true score was not eight enemy aircraft but eighteen.

The cult of understatement was so strong that pilots could not even admit in the privacy of their own diaries to any satisfaction when their efforts were recognized. On 12 November Barclay recorded: 'I was awarded the DFC – this morning the Wing Commander announced it. I don't feel I deserve a medal and I feel still less like the dashing type one imagines wins medals!' He spent the following morning at work on his tunics, 'sewing, sewing, sewing', not just the purple and white DFC ribbon but the stripes to mark moving up a rank to flying officer.

Collective pride was matched by an unwillingness to advertise failure. Not every pilot was a hero, but one has to look hard for evidence of dereliction of duty. 'The squadron ran into some 270 E/A [enemy aircraft],' Denis Wissler wrote on 19 August, 'P/O Solomon being shot down. FO X led his section back as soon as he saw the enemy and Sgt Y broke away and came home from the CO's section.' Underlying the reticence, perhaps, is the understanding that only another fighter pilot could have of how much resolve it needed to persevere, and the sympathy for those who faltered that went with it.

Congratulating Paul Richey after the publication of *Fighter Pilot*, a brilliant first-hand account of the fighting in France, his old 1 Squadron comrade Mark 'Hilly' Brown wrote: 'I like the way you have been so kind about the whole thing, Paul. Anyone who turned out dead-beat was left completely out and everyone's faults or shortcomings completely ignored. The squadron's history is now written as it should be.'[17]

There seems to have been little feeling among the pilots that they were operating inside a much bigger and steeply hierarchical structure. Identity and loyalty was focused on the squadron but extended to the other fighter units they fought alongside. Senior figures made appearances from time to time. Trenchard invited himself on a tour of fighter bases in June and gave the young pilots the benefit of his First World War wisdom, assuring 72 Squadron that 'there was no doubt in his mind that we would win through again'.[18] The 12 Group Commander Trafford Leigh-Mallory and 11 Group's C-in-C Keith Park visited frequently. Even 'Stuffy' Dowding took time from his crushing responsibilities to go to 249 Squadron to buck them up with the welcome news that new Mark II Hurricanes with improved Merlin engines and 20mm cannon instead of .303 Brownings for armament were on the way. These events merited only fleeting mentions. Denis Wissler recorded the arrival of the Duke of Kent to Tangmere in the middle of the desperate battles of late August for which the pilots had to line up for inspection at their dispersal huts just as they were ready to take off: 'He however only shook hands with us and asked how long we had been in the service and the squadron.'

The battlefield the pilots was fighting in was enormous – the whole realm of the skies – and the experience was essentially a lonely one. Once in combat, fighter pilots were on their own for it was impossible for a commander to control the actions of his men. Each had to respond to events, usually at lightning speed, with his own instincts and judgements. By contrast on the ground life was intensely collegiate, focused on the squadron and the base with little sense of a connection to the vast Air Force organization beyond the camp gates.

In these circumstances, the role of leaders took on a particular importance and their faults and qualities could have a considerable effect on levels of efficiency and morale. A popular and respected CO boosted spirits. Ronny Lees, the thirty-year-old Australian-born commander of 72 Squadron and a pre-war RAF professional, was a genial, fatherly figure to his men, making Robert Deacon Elliot 'feel very much at home' when he turned up as a raw RAFVR acting pilot officer at a snowbound Drem in Scotland in December 1939. He was also efficient, spotting fatal gaps in his pilots' training and trying to fill them. In the spring of 1940, while many squadrons were still pursuing the pre-war obsession with tight formation flying, he concentrated on night flying and air-to-air live firing practice, both hideously neglected in the pre-squadron training curriculum.

In the Dunkirk fighting, the squadron was based at Gravesend and Lees led from the front, destroying a Junkers 87 on 2 June. Then, wrote Deacon Elliot on 21 July, came 'a very sad day for the Squadron. News of the CO's posting to 13 Group Headquarters as Wing Commander operations came as a shock to us all … it was difficult to envisage the squadron under any other's command … his dynamic leadership, both on the air and on the ground, his deep understanding and the fine example he always set endeared him to officers and men alike.'

Lees was given a true Fighter Boy send-off, debagged after a scrum in the Schooner pub at Alnmouth, near the base at Acklington. The choice of replacement was one that, once again, caused wonderment at the mental processes of the Air Ministry personnel department. Squadron Leader Anthony Collins was another pre-war regular, whose last experience of operations had been against tribesmen in northern Iraq in the early 1930s. According to Deacon Elliot, 'he was a photographic expert and … came straight to the Squadron from his office in the Air Ministry, having not flown Spitfires before'. Elsewhere his previous appointment is listed as 'Officer i/c Photography at Coastal Command, Lee-on-Solent'.[19] Either way, 'we all thought this was not a very prudent move by higher authority nor was it fair on either the individual or the squadron'.

On 31 August, the squadron moved to Biggin Hill and were in action later that day. It was Collins's first operational mission and he was shot down, crash-landing near Hawkhurst. Although 'very shaken he came back for more'. A few days later he was in trouble again after a combat with Messerschmitt 110s over Herne Bay. He was wounded in the knee and hand and did not return to the squadron after treatment. Meanwhile, Ronny Lees had chosen to spend a week's leave flying with his old comrades. The fact that he too was shot down on the same day in combat south of Dungeness was evidence of the truth that experience only provided limited protection in the kaleidoscopic violence of air combat.

Some commanders managed to create a family atmosphere in the unit. Having a wife helped. At 73 Squadron, the diary notes, 'Mrs Robinson, the CO's better half, has got us adopted by a knitting circle'. She also 'collected all our "smalls" and took them off to launder them', and the following day 'brought our laundry back, beautifully done'. Station commanders like Victor Beamish at North Weald and Dick Grice at Biggin Hill imposed their big personalities on those they led, inspiring, cheering and sympathizing with pilots, ground crew, WAAFs and administrators alike.

Some leaders, though, seem to have made little impression. Denis Wissler barely mentions his first CO, Ralph MacDougall. When he was posted away to be a fighter controller on 17 July, he decided 'first impressions' of his replacement Cedric Williams 'are not good'. Williams was thirty years old, a Cranwell graduate who later returned to the college staff and seems to have moved to his new command from a post in the Air Ministry Directorate of Intelligence without any direct experience of the air war to date.

Wissler noted a few days later following a session of 'practice attacks' that 'the CO had never done them'. A few weeks later he records grumpily that after a day involving several patrols and 'flaps' 'the CO had the bright idea of doing attacks at 9.15 [p.m.]'. 'They were a failure and the CO lost us, what with darkness and mist. We did not get back until 10.15 [7 August].' On 25 August comes the laconic entry: 'SL Williams lost. Wing shot off.' He went down in the sea after launching a head-on attack on a Messerschmitt 110. By then his determination and keenness had brought some reward. Before he died he claimed a Dornier 17 and a Junkers 88 destroyed.

The upper levels of Fighter Command seem wisely to have made little attempt to interfere with the raw tactical conduct of the battle and left it to the pilots themselves to devise a methodology based on reality instead of theory. Carefully constructed pre-war drills, though, continued to be practised almost to the end of the summer. In the meantime, the pilots worked out their own tactics. In late

September, as fighters began to operate in wing formations, George Barclay described getting together with 46 Squadron to devise a system where one squadron was flanked by two sections of the other weaving protectively alongside. A few weeks later they agreed on a drill to 'work in sections of four and break away in pairs if attacked by 109s'.

The pilots, though, had no control over how, when and where they went into battle. Their daily lives were completely ruled by the decisions made by the officers who directed the squadrons' response to raids from the sector ops rooms. The relationship between controllers and pilots was tense. The contemporaneous accounts brim with exasperation. In mid-September, the 73 Squadron diary announced that 'faith in the ops room which continues to give "scramble" orders while still calling the squadron to "readiness" is dwindling. Soon we will be getting "scrambles" when we are on leave! That is if we ever get any leave!!'

The overcautious ordering of alerts meant that a pilot's day could stretch from 3 a.m. to 10 p.m., hours that were spent sitting around dispersal where the aircraft were parked and doing little or no flying but nonetheless simmering in a state of anticipation that did not allow the real rest that they all desperately needed.

By 4 July Denis Wissler was complaining that he had been 'up at 3 again this morning. I am getting a bit tired of seeing the dawn break ... we are now sleeping at the dispersal hut in order to get a little more sleep.' A month later things were no better: 'We went over to Martlesham today and did quite a bit of flying,' he wrote on 6 August. 'We did not see any Jerries though we chased some invisible ones. We were at readiness again until well after dark. Blast operations.'

Worse was when the instructions given by control either failed to put the squadron in a good attacking position or left them danger-ously exposed to the enemy. On 23 September 73 Squadron's day got off to a bad start when they were served an inedible mess of 'mince' for breakfast. They were then ordered to take off from Debden and join up with 257 Squadron at nearby Castle Camps to intercept a raid. They were to be covered by 17 Squadron, also at Debden, but they 'failed badly in their necessary task, and aided by what can only be described as crass stupidity on the part of Ops, the squadrons were broken up by Me 109s'.

The debacle – 'for debacle it was' – began when, while patrolling at 20,000 feet, the squadrons were ordered to come down to 10,000 feet, thereby losing the advantage of height. James Smith, the Canadian pilot officer who was leading the patrol, 'promptly and wisely questioned this but the order was confirmed, so being left no option he began to go down'.

> Disaster then came among us. At 17,000 feet when 17 Squadron had left the tail completely uncovered, Me 109s … hurtled down from the sun and the formations went over like ninepins. The first news the ground staff had … was the arrival of Sgt Webster, seething with rage and with machine well bullet-marked. One bullet had struck an ammo tank in the port gun bay and exploded a belt of rounds and weakened the wing struts … of the twelve machines which had taken off only eight returned …

Miraculously, all the pilots survived, two ditching into the sea, one crash-landing and one baling out, though two were severely burned. The incident served to further reduce the squadron's already diminishing reserves of enthusiasm and energy.

The diary reveals a pattern of initial eagerness gradually being eroded by the endless grind of action. At the beginning of September 73 Squadron was based at Church Fenton, out of the front line of the battle and chafing at the bit. 'Nothing ever seems to happen to us these days,' lamented Hugh Eliot, who was by then the squadron 'Venerable Bede' charged with chronicling their story. 'There are still rumours and hopes of a move towards the South but the days pass and it never comes'. The following day 'everyone's spirits rose a mile today when the news came to stand by for a temporary move to Duxford'. It was not to be but two days later they were installed at Debden and in action within a few hours. 'The Hun came over at 1300 hrs and we were after him like a shot,' reads the entry for 5 September. This first encounter was a painful one. The diary claims one enemy aircraft damaged and one 'probable' but the likelihood is only one Heinkel 111 was hit and managed to make it back to its base in France. Four of the squadron's aircraft were shot down, including that of the CO, Maurice Robinson, and Sergeant Alexander McNay was killed, though his death was not confirmed for several days. However, the following day the diary's cheerful note was maintained: 'Another bright day and everyone looking forward to more hunting.' The upbeat commentary continued as the squadron's performance improved 'with everyone ... elated by our success'.

The mood started to change on 14 September, 'our blackest day', when four aircraft were shot down, one of them in a friendly-fire clash with a Spitfire, and a pilot killed. Clear skies and good visibility became much less welcome. It was cloud and mist that they were now longing for. 'Glorious "pilots weather" today', reads the entry for 19 September, 'raining like blazes and blowing half a gale'. But the following day 'our luck did not hold ... and the morning turned out bright if somewhat windy.' Eight days later comes the complaint that 'this weather will persist in being cold and sunny. No rest for the wicked.' By 2 October there is no pretence at enthusiasm. 'As the day dawned windy and misty our hearts cheered as we said, "Ah, real pilots weather at last" but it was spoken too soon and the sky cleared by 11.' The sentiment was shared by Denis Wissler on 13 October: 'The weather again today was clear and bright,' he wrote. 'Oh for some clouds and rain.'

The diminishing appetite for danger does not seem to have been primarily the result of mounting fear or fraying nerves. Pilots would say after the Battle that they were frequently terrified but this is not particularly apparent in what was written at the time. Wissler's diary is candid but there is only one reference to feeling fear in the air; and that was when he flew into flak while patrolling over France on 12 June ('most terrifying') rather than during a dogfight. He had another 'most terrifying' experience on 11 September, this time during a visit to London where he was caught in the nightly Blitz.

George Barclay wrote that 'the worst part of the job is the few minutes before we actually get scrambled – when we know we are going off shortly. Once we are in the air, everything is OK.' He was on the ground at North Weald on 3 September when the tannoy warned of approaching hostile aircraft and ordered everyone to take cover. He 'hopped into the shelter and almost immediately hell was let loose. 250 bombs were dropped – the noise quite unbelievable and it seemed as if we were bound to get hit by at least one. The noise was utterly terrifying whilst it lasted …' He emerged 'to see the aerodrome enveloped in a vast cloud of smoke and dust'. He concluded 'if bombs are going to be dropped – give me an aeroplane every time'.

The Luftwaffe assault was directed at civilians and airmen alike and the pilots were well aware that the danger was shared by everyone. Two of Barclay's uncles, one an Anglican missionary, were killed when a bomb struck Church House in Westminster on 14 October, close to where Wissler's parents lived in Dolphin Square.

Barclay had been impressed by the sang-froid of the base personnel when the Luftwaffe struck, noting that 'the WAAFs took the bombing as staunchly as did the men'. The stoicism and devotion to duty the pilots saw around them and on their trips up to town left them in no doubt that they did not have a monopoly on courage and resolution.

The most insidious enemy of morale was fatigue. The references to exhaustion become a trope of Wissler's diary as the days pass and the Germans keep on coming: 'We are all awfully tired tonight' (5 July); 'I shall sleep very well tonight given half a chance' (23 July); 'God were we tired this evening' (25 July). Once while flying a patrol he 'felt very tired going round and round and only just managed to stop myself dozing off'.

George Barclay described in an undated, barely punctuated entry written in a scrawl that gives it a pungent immediacy of being woken at 4.30 a.m. in the dispersal hut, climbing into his Irvin fur-lined flying suit and taking down the blackout on the window to see a lovely autumn morning with a duck-egg-blue sky half covered with high cloud. 'John came and looked over my shoulder: "Another bloody fine day," he said with disgust … now a fine sunny day meant flying, flying, flying and terrific tension all day gazing endlessly into the burning sun to see what wily Hun was lurking there …'

He walked out 'almost asleep' to his Hurricane and went through his checks: tanks full, trail trimming wheel neutral, airscrew fine pitch, directional gyro set, gloves in their compartments, helmet with oxygen and R/T leads connected: 'in fact as I liked it, everything set for a quick getaway'. He went back into the hut to find his friend Tom Neil fully dressed but 'fast asleep in a deckchair, his head lolling on his yellow Mae West'. He lay down on a bunk and 'immediately became unconscious as if doped ...' He woke 'with a terrific start to see everyone pouring out of the hut, putting on Mae Wests, silk gloves ... I could hear the telephone orderly repeating "Dover – 20,000. Fifty plus bandits approaching from South East." Percy shouted scramble George, [you] lazy bastard and automatically I ran out parachute on, pulled into cockpit by crew who had already started up the engine, straps, helmet, gloves, check the knobs, taxi out, get into right position in my section and take off. I put the R/T on and only then do I wake up and realise l am in the air flying No 2 in Yellow section.'

In these hectic conditions there was no time to brood. It was in the slack time that the doubts surfaced and the glooms descended. Denys Mileham strayed from the habitually optimistic tone of his letters home to admit, shortly after his return from France in June: 'The strain of everything is almost unbearable at times. I have lost so many friends ...' At about the same time Denis Wissler confided to his diary: 'Oh God I do wish this war would end.' It was another three months, though, before he admitted to feeling 'very depressed tonight. I don't know why, just a passing mood.'

Aided by the entries in his diary, Robert Deacon Elliot later tried to analyse the emotional journey the Battle had taken him on. 'Looking back over the past weeks of intensive activity in the South I vividly recall that my reactions went through three most distinctive phases,' he wrote. 'The first being one of exhilaration; the intense excitement of mixing with the enemy and the determination to shoot something down. Then oneself having been shot down a time or two, and shot at on countless occasions, became a little more wary with more emphasis on trying to stay alive ... Finally, towards the end and during the days before we moved North again, every mission was the same to me. I did not really mind or care whether or not I survived. Perhaps in this I was not alone. I'm not being smug in thinking these reactions were unique. I'm sure they were not.'[20]

Survive he did, both the Battle and the war, remaining in the RAF and retiring an air vice marshal. Denis Wissler did not. He was shot down off the Essex coast while attacking Junkers 87s on 11 November, just after getting engaged to Edith Heap, a WAAF he met at Debden and with whom he fell immediately in love. George Barclay made it through but only just. On Friday 29 November, during a routine patrol over Kent:

> Suddenly four explosions down my right-hand side. I realized they were cannon shells and as I whipped into a left hand turn … two more explosions and something hit me hard in the right leg but it didn't hurt. I felt waves of hot air and the Hurricane went into a spin from which I couldn't recover so I decided to bale out. All this of course in a couple of seconds. Back with the roof, straps undone and lean out and push with feet on dashboard – no result – back into cockpit, undo oxygen bayonet connection and try again. This time I'm out straightaway and fell forward over the leading edge missing the propeller by inches![21]

As he tumbled out, he was face upwards and noted the presence of one of his boots falling above him. '[I] began to spin to the left as I lay on my back, ever faster until it became unpleasant. Meanwhile I felt for the rip-cord with both hands.' As soon as he found it he was 'quite happy and settled down to the novel sensation of dropping through space, but the spin had become unpleasantly fast to the left so I put out my right arm and gradually slowed up'. He tried to turn onto his front but 'was quite helpless … I eventually succeeded by drawing up my legs and I slowly rolled over but couldn't see the ground owing to the wind in my eyes.'

Looking up he could see his Hurricane 'spinning furiously directly above me and as I watched a large puff of white smoke shot out of it as if there had been an explosion inside. But I was so enjoying myself, nothing seemed to matter in the least.' Feeling he had delayed the drop quite long enough, he pulled the cord and 'the parachute streamed out between my feet and there was a small jerk followed immediately by a pretty severe jerk which … caused me to do a complete somersault and my second boot came off, and there I was, dangling in complete silence at about 2,000 feet.'

He was lucky not to be obliterated by his Hurricane which hurtled past and 'spun in', bursting into flames. He made a good landing in an apple orchard and was soon surrounded by locals who put him in a car which took him to Pembury Hospital in Tunbridge Wells. He calculated he had fallen about 18,000 feet before his parachute opened – pilots were told to delay pulling the cord for as long as possible to reduce the risk of colliding with friendly aircraft or being shot up by the Germans, an occasional additional hazard.[22] The descent was witnessed by Miss Christina Barclay, an elderly relation who lived near the hospital. A week later he visited her to celebrate his twenty-first birthday.[23]

By then, all chronologies agreed, the Battle was over. The great armadas of bombers were no longer seen in daylight and the Luftwaffe effort had switched to the night-time Blitz that would persist until late the following spring. It was an ordeal, but it did not feel like the prelude to invasion.

In no time at all the victory was mythologized. The legend was built while the fighting was still raging. The Air Ministry promoted vigorously Fighter Command's achievements. Pilots made evening broadcasts on the BBC during the Battle and continued to recount their exploits on the airwaves for months afterwards, reading out scripts written for them by Air Ministry hacks in a curious Hollywood-tinged style. Some of the propaganda effort was directed across the Atlantic, in keeping with Churchill's strategy of trying to persuade the United States that Britain was a worthwhile ally. On 13 July, pilots at Debden were ordered to carry out aerobatics for the benefit of a visiting team from *Life*, the American photo magazine with a circulation of nearly twenty million. The material arrived too late for a long article in the issue of 15 July which announced that 'the preliminaries of the Battle of Britain have already begun' and declared 'above all ... the 300,000 men of the Royal Air Force are the real shield of England'.

On the stout foundations of the Battle, the Air Ministry publicists built an image and a story that would endure when press cuttings were forgotten. A team of writers, artists and photographers was sent out to tour the bases gathering material for books.

In 1941 Cecil Beaton produced a record of all aspects of the RAF which came with a written commentary, but in the preface it was Fighter Command that moved him to rapture. 'Never before have battles been fought six miles above the surface of the earth at a speed of over three hundred miles an hour,' he wrote. 'Never before has it happened that the English hero, who, having shot down a German, has in turn immediately afterwards himself been shot down to return home by Tube, feeling, as he says, "rather depressed."' He concluded: 'A new model of men has been cast. The feats of their bravery haunt us, they baffle us, and satisfy completely the spirit of romantic daring inherent in our island race ... part of the sailing tradition and feeling of freedom and adventure that is the heritage from Drake ... and the Englishman who enjoyed drifting along with the breezes in his boat at four knots an hour is the father of the boy who now wishes to beat the winds in his Hurricane.'[24]

The war had already produced one RAF film, *The Lion Has Wings*, rushed out in the first months to reassure the public that the Air Force was well able to protect the nation from aerial attack. It was a mixture of documentary and with filmed reconstructions (some of it footage from MGM's abandoned *Shadow of the Wing*) and skilfully edited actuality. It was 'a hodgepodge' according to Michael Powell who worked on it, and looked distinctly dated by the time it appeared, as well as inaccurate.[25]

The Battle provided a wonderful basis for something more lasting and worthwhile. The British film industry rose to the occasion with *The First of the Few*, a much more subtle affair which approached the saga through the parable of R. J. Mitchell and the Spitfire. The plot, which did not handicap itself with too close an association with hard fact, presented the designer as a lone genius who overcame characteristic British indifference and sloth to provide the nation with the means of salvation. The Spitfire is a symbol of a more positive manifestation of Britishness – small, perhaps, but beautiful and powerful, and determined and deadly when its freedom is threatened. The photography of Mitchell's masterpiece in flight is accompanied by music by Vaughan Williams to add to the impression of airy joyfulness. Leslie Howard, an established romantic star in Britain and Hollywood, drove the enterprise, producing and directing and taking the starring role. It also featured David Niven who had generously overlooked the slights he had received at the hands of the RAF to appear as a station commander. Combat footage was cut in with staged take-offs and landings and ground scenes using Battle of Britain pilots and a staged dogfight between Spitfires and a captured Heinkel 111. *The First of the Few* did not appear until the summer of 1942 and was loved by the public and critics alike ('a tribute and a record true', according to the *Daily Herald*).[26]

By then the Battle of Britain was officially embedded in the national story. In September that year King George VI led a service of thanksgiving in Westminster Abbey, starting a tradition that lasts to this day, and plans were announced for the construction of a memorial chapel there, the first of many monuments to the pilots.

Nothing like the Battle would ever happen again. Soon after its end changes at the top of Fighter Command ensured that henceforth the Fighter Boys would be fighting a very different war. In an impressive display of ruthlessness, the new Chief of the Air Staff, Charles Portal, shunted Dowding aside, though he had made it clear he was eager to stay on. He was replaced by Sholto Douglas, Deputy Chief of the Air Staff, who was heavy-set, self-regarding and ambitious. He had made Dowding's life difficult during the toughest weeks of the fighting by supporting the 12 Group commander Trafford Leigh-Mallory's advocacy of massed 'Big Wing' formations over the smaller numbers and defensive approach favoured by Dowding and the 11 Group commander, Keith Park.

The Battle of Britain was a defining moment in the history of the RAF, as it was for the nation. Success brought the service its own cherished victory, one that rang with the same historic resonance as Trafalgar and Waterloo. Those battles came with the names of Nelson and Wellington attached to them. Uniquely in British history, this one belonged not to an individual but a group. The country owed its salvation to the Air Force and in particular the young men of Fighter Command. There was little time to savour the victory. One challenge was immediately replaced by another, in which the prospects of success were far less promising.

8

Fighting the Night

One night in the early summer of 1941, the men of 151 Squadron crowded into the guardroom of their base at Wittering to examine a German airman who was the sole survivor from a bomber that had just been shot down. 'We all gathered round to have a look at him,' wrote Pilot Officer Harry Bodien to his sister Vina.[1]

'He was a dirty looking bugger with close cropped hair and only stood five feet nothing. The CO is not friendly with Huns and made the interpreter ask if he got his two Iron Crosses for bombing women and children. That rather shook him but he was shaken a lot more when he was told we were going to shoot him at 5 o' clock in the morning.'

The letter was written when nightly raids on British cities were fresh in everyone's memories. The harsh tone fitted the grim struggle that the RAF had been waging all winter.

The aftermath of the Battle of Britain brought no sense of euphoria. Its ending was scarcely perceptible, for as one threat faded another arrived. It would take different skills, qualities and technologies to confront the new danger. Even before 15 September, the climax of the daytime battle, the Luftwaffe had opened a new front. On 7 September, the systematic bombing of London began. The capital was attacked on fifty-six out of the following fifty-seven days, from October mostly after dark. In November, the Blitz was extended to industrial cities in the Midlands, then, as German strategy focused on cutting Britain's transatlantic lifeline, on major ports. The Blitz hit civilians in a way that the Battle of Britain had not. More than 40,000 men, women and children were killed and a million houses destroyed. The suffering was felt in virtually every big population centre. Before it ended, the inhabitants of Belfast, Bristol, Birmingham, Cardiff, Coventry, Glasgow, Hull, Liverpool, Manchester, Newcastle, Portsmouth, Plymouth, Sheffield and Swansea had heard the wail of the sirens, run for shelter and cellar, felt the thud of falling bombs and emerged to see their old familiar streets, shattered and smoking.

The pre-war neglect of night-flying training and lack of research into the question of how to intercept raiders in the dark were laid bare by the Luftwaffe's switch to a night offensive. Initially, the heroes of Fighter Command were mostly powerless to stop the continuous incursions and the bomber fleets had the run of the skies.

Radar offered a solution. However, in the run-up to the war, Britain's first priority was a warning system to alert defending fighters to attacks from the sea, which the Chain Home radar stations did with great success. There had not been time to build a network that looked inland so that once a raider crossed the coast it could only be tracked by the eyes and ears of the Observer Corps, a situation that Churchill described as 'a transition from the middle of the Twentieth Century to the early Stone Age'.[2] Work was underway to create an all-round terrestrial radar network, as well as developing miniature sets that could be carried in aircraft, but it had not got far when the German focus shifted.

Only eight squadrons specialized in night fighting. They flew in Blenheims which were too slow to catch the bombers they were supposed to destroy and whose Mark I Air Interception (AI) radar had a range of only two miles. From October, regular Fighter Command squadrons were told to concentrate on night flying. However, their main function at first seems to have been to try and reassure those on the ground that something was being done to protect them. Any impression of security was, as the Air Ministry well knew, illusory. In the first ten weeks of the Blitz the Luftwaffe flew 12,000 night sorties, mostly against London. Eighty-one enemy aircraft were destroyed, most by guns and only eight by fighters. This equated to a very light loss rate of less than 1 per cent, placing no strain on replacement of men or machines and allowing the Luftwaffe to carry on indefinitely.[3]

The first the men of 264 Squadron heard about their new role was when they received a visit from the commander of 12 Group, Trafford Leigh-Mallory. The squadron had been badly mauled in the hectic fighting of late August while operating out of Hornchurch. They flew the Boulton Paul Defiant, a hybrid fighter which was reasonably fast and manoeuvrable and had a four-gun turret mounted behind the cockpit. It achieved some success shooting down bombers but the turret's field of fire was severely restricted. Against Messerschmitt 109s it was extremely vulnerable, and defenceless when attacked head-on. After losing eight aircraft within three days at the end of August, 264 were withdrawn to lick their wounds at Kirton-in-Lindsey in Lincolnshire. Such was the weight of casualties that the most senior pilot left alive and uninjured was a twenty-year-old pilot officer, Sam 'Tommy' Thomas.

The crews were not very impressed by their VIP visitor. One of the pilots, Desmond Hughes, recalled a 'somewhat pompous and over-weight' figure who sat in a deckchair in the warm sunshine with the pilots and gunners at his feet and delivered a pep talk.[4] He finished by ordering them to be ready for night operations by the time the next full moon period arrived. The instruction confirmed that, henceforth, the main fighter effort would be conducted in darkness not in daylight. The reference to moonlight was acknowledgement that, in confronting the night raiders, the crews would have no electronic aids to guide them and would have to rely on their eyes.

It was a situation they had been given virtually no preparation for. 'It was a new way of life altogether,' wrote Hughes. 'Gone were the endless days of fluctuating states of readiness; gone the frenetic scrambles ... gone the dog-fighting.' but also 'gone the constant peril of being jumped by 109s'. The main enemies were the darkness and the weather which would 'kill more night fighter crews than the Luftwaffe air gunners ever did ...'.

Flying in darkness was counter-intuitive. It meant placing utter reliance in what your instruments said, rather than on what your senses told you. Learning this rule was essential to survival. Shortly after dusk on a moonless night Hughes watched 'one Defiant take off and instead of climbing straight ahead, go into a slow turn to port. It got no higher than 150 feet before it began to lose height again and flew into the ground, exploding into a ball of flame.' The pilot, Derek O'Malley, and New Zealand-born air gunner, Lauritz Rasmussen, were killed. O'Malley was a lawyer who joined the RAFVR before the war and at twenty-nine was a comparatively old man by Fighter Command standards. He was nonetheless inexperienced and the episode taught Hughes that you 'just had to establish a sustained rate of climb on your instrument panel before going into a turn of any sort'.

To the crews of 264 Squadron it seemed that the extra hazards involved in their new work were not appreciated by their superiors. Early in October they moved south to Luton and there was another visit from the brass. It was a dark evening and the sky was completely covered by low cloud. Taking off was relatively straightforward and once above the clag they could operate as normal. But with no radio link to the ground, no electronic beacons and only feeble runway 'glim lamps' to guide them in, there would be almost no chance of putting down again safely. 'Tommy' Thomas, now promoted to flight lieutenant, was still leading the squadron. He had told the local ground controller the situation and Desmond Hughes and his air gunner, Fred Gash, who were one of the duty crews, settled down expecting a quiet night. Then,

a couple of hours after dark and without any advance warning, a car drew up outside our dispersal hut and a tall, brooding figure emerged. He asked a passing airman who was in charge and was told 'Flt Lt Thomas, sir.'

'Tell him that the C-in-C is here and wants to talk to him.'

Off ran the airman and soon 'Tommy' was out at the car saluting smartly.

'This is a fine airfield,' said Air Chief Marshal Dowding, gazing out towards our glim-lamps. 'How many aircraft have you got in the air, Thomas?'

'None sir! Until this low cloud lifts, we would lose any aircraft we scrambled. We can take off OK but there's nowhere to land afterwards – we would have to bale out.'

'But Thomas ... there are some Huns airborne. We should be after them. Why can't you land somewhere?'

The incarnation of the Air Force ethos. Guy Gibson and crew at Scampton in July 1943, two months after the Dams Raid. It was the zenith of Gibson's career and the threatening Lincolnshire sky seems to hint at trouble ahead.

Hugh Trenchard inspects men of the RAF Regiment. Though long-retired, the 'Father of the Royal Air Force' continued to exert strong influence, directly and through former protegés.

When war came, it was the RAF that recruits flocked to.

While the WAAF offered women the prospect of fulfilment and adventure. These are camera gun technicians.

Hugh Dowding with some of his Fighter Boys (Douglas Bader at right) at the war's end. The Battle of Britain fixed the RAF permanently in the nation's affections.

Much more than a wonderful fighter. The Spitfire would become an eternal symbol of graceful defiance.

Some of the Few. George Barclay (second from right) with 249 Squadron comrades.

'The beau ideal of the Fighter Boy.' Like many survivors of the battle, Paddy Finucane would be sacrificed by Douglas and Leigh-Mallory's policy of cross-Channel raiding.

'Sawn-off Lockie.' Eric Lock, one of the highest-scoring aces of the battle, drawn here by Cuthbert Orde, was another victim.

The youngest of the wartime service chiefs, 'Peter' Portal was also the most impressive: brilliant, driven and extraordinarily self-possessed.

Bomber Command's stout overlord. Arthur Harris looking unusually reflective.

The supreme instrument of the bombing cult. With the AVRO Lancaster, the RAF could finally deliver on its promises.

Flying in a bomber was the aerial equivalent of fighting in the trenches. In the spring of 1942 aircrew prepare to board a Short Stirling. More than 55,000 would die.

The Vickers Wellington served from the first day of the war to the last over land and sea. Nearly 11,500 were built – more than any other British bomber.

Architects of victory. In North Africa and Italy, Arthur Tedder (top) and Arthur 'Mary' Coningham (bottom) would forge the tactics that put air power at the centre of Allied success.

According to Hughes, Thomas then 'gave the C-in-C a detailed account of the problems: single channel short-range RT [radio-telephony], no direct link between scrambled aircraft and Luton; inaccurate sector fixing [direction from the controller]; quite inadequate weather conditions of one mile visibility and low cloud; no RT homer on the airfield, hills in the vicinity with cloud right down on them etc. etc.'

Dowding 'listened in silence, his expression growing grimmer all the time. When "Tommy" had finished, he growled: "I didn't come here to listen to a list of complaints, Thomas" and stumped off to his car.'[5]

Hughes was an upstanding man, modest and patently honest, who rose to the rank of air vice marshal and commanded the Cranwell cadet college, and there is no reason to doubt the story. Another officer left an account of how pilots were sent off in hopeless conditions with no chance of success and every possibility of disaster in order to build the fiction that air cover extended throughout the hours of darkness. Flying Officer Trevor Wade of 92 Squadron recalled patrols that were essentially 'a case of showing the flag to the locals, who no doubt got some satisfaction out of hearing a couple of Spitfires screaming overhead, even if the screams were brought about by our endeavours to get out of our own searchlights and subsequent AA fire'.[6]

It did not pay to be too frank about the difficulties. Hughes claimed that as a result of his youthful candour, Thomas received an adverse report from Dowding which 'stayed on his personal file and badly affected his promotion prospects for some two years after'.[7] Dowding's impromptu visit 'did nothing to cheer up 264's aircrew, frustrated as they already were by their inability to get at the German raiders'.

On 15 October 1940, Hughes and Gash did something to raise their spirits. It was a cold night but there was very little cloud and the moon was full. The pair scrambled just after nightfall and were given a patrol line just inside the Essex coastline on the Thames Estuary. They were flying at 17,000 feet when Hughes spotted a condensation trail, silvery in the moonlight, and set off in excited pursuit. It was only after three circuits without sighting the enemy that he realized he was chasing himself. He returned to base 'in disgust and embarrassment' but a few hours later was sent off again, patrolling the same area. The night was brilliantly clear now and they could see ominous whitish patches covering parts of London: smoke from another Blitz. He was 'just about to think, "Ah well! Another hour of watching the bombs fall and not being able to do a damn thing about it" when I saw something move across the stars and turned gently towards where I had seen the movement.'

He noticed a 'dark shapeless blob' which 'slowly grew into a long black line and then I picked up the incandescent glow of an exhaust. Shouting "Tally Ho!" on the RT, I turned gently back to starboard, throttled back a little and slid into wide formation on what was clearly a twin-engine aircraft. As I dropped down a little below it, some fifty yards on its beam, the unmistakeable wing-plan of a Heinkel 111 was revealed. I told Fred to open fire and he made no mistake. A long burst with the de Wilde [incendiary bullets] twin-kling brilliantly on its starboard engine and the Heinkel was a mass of flame. It slowly turned over to port and went down in a steep dive, trailing a plume of fire as it went. I started to follow it but it was obviously finished and I eased out of my dive. It crashed in open country with a mighty explosion ...'

These sorties were very different from the daytime operations of the summer. In the Battle of Britain squadrons operated as units. On being scrambled pilots ran to their machines and took to the air together, lining up in loose formation behind a commander who led them into combat as a group. The order did not survive more than a few seconds once the fight was joined, breaking down to a mêlée of individual actions. Nonetheless, these operations started as team efforts, and the feeling of camaraderie boosted confidence and the desire to be seen to do well. Night fighters were mostly lone wolves. In 264 Squadron, virtually all patrols were by single aircraft, except occasionally at dusk when a pair might operate together, separating when the light failed.

The accounts that the participants left seem rather cold and clin-ical compared with the testimony from the Battle of Britain. There was no talk of chivalry now and, for some at least, it was the man as much as the machine that was in their sights. Harry Bodien was a Halton apprentice who trained as a pilot and flew with Coastal Command before wangling a transfer to fighters at the end of 1940. In early 1941, aged twenty-five, he was flying Defiants with 151 Squadron. He explained his reasons in one of his remarkably frank letters to his married older sister, Vina, in which he discussed everything from his bowel movements to his sex life. 'There have been several things that have happened in the last two years or so that make it imperative that I get right at those Huns,' he wrote.[8] 'It's not hate but a combination of little things that have affected me.'

Like many airmen, Bodien appears to have taken the Blitz as a personal affront. It produced a double sense of outrage; both at the violation of the cities and the RAF's inability to prevent it. He approached his work with a cold fury, itching to get into action whenever possible and recording his successes with unapologetic pride. There were quite a few: eight kills and one probable by the summer of 1941, which were recognized with the award of a DFC. The citation states that 'on one occasion, despite having trouble with his own aircraft, [he] kept up a series of attacks on an enemy aircraft for some forty-five minutes and finally destroyed it'.

Bodien described the episode in detail to Vina. He came across his victim while patrolling north of Wittering. In his account the Heinkel 111 takes on a human identity. 'We opened fire and knocked some good lumps out of his belly but as he had dropped all of his bombs he didn't explode,' he wrote. The enemy gunners returned fire vigorously, hitting the Defiant's turret, destroying one gun and putting two of the other three out of action.

Bodien had to break off while the gunner struggled to get the damaged Brownings working again. The slow progress made him lose his temper and he 'yelled at the gunner if he didn't get his guns firing I'd kill him and after a while he said they were OK'. Then he went in again and 'got in a good squirt that killed the bottom gunner ...' The duel continued until they crossed the coast. The Germans appeared to have given up, for the Heinkel turned back towards land with its navigation lights switched on. It made no difference and Bodien moved in for the *coup de grâce*. 'I slid up in front of his port wing and told the gunner to kill the pilot from about five yard's range. He did this and the Heinkel dived straight into the sea where she burnt for a bit …'

Bodien's passion for the fight was matched by his detachment when considering the results. A few months earlier he and his gunner shot down a Dornier which crashed ten miles from the base. The following morning, he 'went out and had a look at what was left. There was a lot of meat strewn around, and five people were in it because nine feet were found. I took a gun, a quick release from one of the parachutes and a few scraps from the wireless operator's log, including a photo of the bloke in his identity card showing him to be nineteen years old and a photo of his girl. Not bad either, tho' I don't expect she would like me very much.'

Bodien was a pre-war professional, who prided himself on his skill and toughness and could be scathing about the influx of novices. While at the Sutton Bridge OTU he complained to Vina about the 'sprog pilots straight from flying school' who were 'new to blood' and 'get on my nerves with their nattering' about the crashes, deaths and injuries that were part of the training experience.

For those without hundreds of hours of flying time logged, the darkness produced bewildering sensations which were not there in daylight. Roderick 'Rory' Chisholm's account of his first operational flight with 604 Squadron, a specialist night-fighter unit equipped with Blenheims based at Middle Wallop in Hampshire in August 1940, reveals the huge mental effort involved in simply trying to keep the aeroplane in the air. He had orders to patrol along a line near Bristol that would be marked out by flares on the ground.

The patrol was a mixture of nervous tension and great exhilaration. Bristol was being Blitzed 15,000 feet below me. I saw bombs explode and anti-aircraft fire and plenty of fires, but since I was never sure of myself, or of the attitude of the aircraft or my own position, this patrol was of no potential value to our night defence. The situation as far as I was concerned was never under control, and when I was told that a 'bandit' was reported at 'angels ten' passing Point Four of my patrol line and asked whether I could see anything I had to say that I could see nothing. I was unable to take much notice of what was going on outside because all my attention was concentrated on trying to keep [the] aircraft on an even keel. My nervous grip on the controls always tended to unsteady it by making over-corrections, and when I could relax temporarily having won the advantage over gravity (the dreaded Isaac) for a moment, I would be looking down for the flares which marked the patrol line. Gravity would then get the upper hand and I would again have to pore over the instruments until they danced before my eyes. And so it went on until I was told to come home.[9]

In this world of solitude and disengagement the chemistry of the crew became a vital factor in morale and success. Desmond Hughes was first paired with a New Zealander who, though a 'sound enough gunner … was stolid to the extent of being monosyllabic and devoid of any sense of humour'. Then, when crews were switched around, he received Sergeant Fred Gash in his place. They hit it off immedi-ately and the partnership would endure for eighteen months. They were both unpretentious, good-natured and conscientious with a quiet but strong sense of duty and patriotism. Hughes was from a prosperous, well-connected Ulster family. He was studying law at Cambridge, where he was a member of the University Air Squadron, when the war broke out. Gash was brought up in Manchester, son of a textile factory manager, and went to the prestigious Manchester Grammar School, leaving at seventeen for a job in a printing works. Both had fallen in love with flying following a ten-minute flip at an air show. Gash joined the Lancashire Aero Club and gained his pilot's licence but such was the rush of volunteers that when he turned up at Manchester Town Hall on the first day of the war to apply for the RAF he was told that the only vacancies left were for air gunners.

Each had complete faith in the other. Many years later Gash recalled how the fact that he had such 'confidence in my pilot' was one reason why, though the squadron suffered dreadful losses, 'the thought never crossed my mind that I was not going to come back'.[10] They made a winning team, accounting for at least five enemy aircraft between them. Gash believed they could have shot down many more. He remained a staunch defender of the Defiant's battered reputation and felt that it was poor tactics rather than design deficiencies that were responsible for the heavy losses. 'We should have been used to attack the German bombers solely while the Spitfires and Hurricanes took care of the German fighters,' he argued. 'It was the fighters that knocked the hell out of us, not the bombers.'

Through the winter of 1940–41 great ingenuity went into bluffing and confusing the raiders. Colonel John Turner, late of the Air Ministry's works and buildings department, was brought out of retirement to lead a brilliant deception campaign, building scores of dummy airfields code-named 'Starfish', complete with flare paths and landing lights which tricked hundreds of raiders into dropping their bombs on empty countryside. Electronics experts were soon at work interfering with the German 'X-Gerät' radio beaming system so that attacks were directed away from their targets. These stratagems were surprisingly effective. But a really effective counter-offensive needed the same combination of technology, married to a command and control system, that had brought victory in the Battle of Britain. It began to take shape with the arrival of improved on-board radar and ground tracking stations. The stations were equipped with revolving radar arrays which gave 360-degree cover and the system that evolved from them was known as GCI (ground-controlled interception). Once an incoming aircraft was detected, a night fighter equipped with an airborne interception (AI) set was given a course to home in on it, and with luck to shoot it down. Success did not come easily. The first AI sets were crude and it needed much practice for the operator to gain the skill to use it effectively.

The process was slow and frustrating but by the beginning of 1941 it was clear that the potential existed to tilt the course of the battle. A remarkable air warrior was at the forefront of the fight. John Cunningham combined a deep theoretical and practical knowledge of aeronautics with extraordinary piloting skills. After Whitgift School in the outer suburbs of south London he was taken on as an engineering trainee by de Havilland's, the great pioneers of British aviation and still under the energetic control of its founder, Captain Geoffrey de Havilland. Cunningham not only designed aircraft but tested them. The company base was at Hatfield, just north of London, and he flew at weekends with 604 Squadron, an Auxiliary unit based not far away at Hendon. In July 1940, 604 was moved to Middle Wallop to concentrate exclusively on night oper-ations. GCI was being developed in the sector but by the autumn no one had managed to shoot down a bandit.

With the arrival of Beaufighters at the end of September, the squadron's fortunes began to change. The 'Beau' lived up to its name. It was big, powerful, streamlined and handsome and its twin Merlin engines could push it along at 335mph. On the night of 19/20 November, Cunningham took off on patrol with Sergeant John Phillipson who had been a ground radar operator before volunteering for aircrew. To reach targets in the Midlands, the raid-ers had taken to approaching from the south-west across a broad stretch of the Channel and the Beaufighters of Middle Wallop were well placed to interdict them as they came in from the sea. When the first blips blossomed on the cathode ray tube in the GCI station controlling operations at Sopley, near Bournemouth, Cunningham was vectored on to one of the intruders.

His natural distaste for drama meant he left behind only a sparse account of what was a historic moment. Seeing a concentration of searchlights glowing on the underside of clouds, he headed towards it. Then Phillipson announced that he had got a solid contact. It was now his job to steer his pilot towards it, watching the screen and calling out the adjustments. Eventually, as Cunningham told his biographer, he saw 'a cluster of stars which seemed to be moving in a different direction from the others and as he did a dark shape formed around them, only to fragment as [I] looked directly at it. Climbing a little closer, a silhouette took shape.'[11] He manoeuvred the Beau underneath the aircraft and identified the bulbous, glazed nose and broad, tapered wings of a Junkers 88. The Beaufighter carried four 20mm Hispano cannon in the nose, enormously destructive if brought to bear accurately. Cunningham got in close before opening up. The Ju 88 tipped over and dived straight to earth, exploding spectacularly on impact.

His feat was emulated a few nights later by the squadron CO Mike Anderson and thereafter the pattern was of gradual success, accelerated by the arrival of improved Mark IV AI radar. In April 1942 night fighters shot down forty-eight raiders, while anti-aircraft fire brought down thirty-nine. In May, the figures climbed to ninety-six by fighters and thirty-one by guns.[12]

Even with the change of fortunes, night fighters could not claim the credit for beating back the German night Blitz. In May 1941, the Luftwaffe's losses were still a sustainable 3.5 per cent of sorties. It was external events that brought the offensive to an end. In June, Hitler invaded Russia and the Luftwaffe was needed elsewhere.

By then the nocturnal aces were well established in the public mind as a new cast of Air Force heroes, with John Cunningham and his regular AI operator Sergeant Jimmy Rawnsley its stars. One night they were called on to perform for the King when he turned up at Middle Wallop just before the first patrol set off. In the course of chatting to Rawnsley, His Majesty asked how many aircraft he had downed. When he replied 'nine', the King requested that he get another one for him that night. The royal party began by watching events unfold on the screens of the Sopley GCI Station, a primitive establishment comprising a caravan and cluster of huts, over which a large antenna swept in 360-degree rotation. It was driven by a pair of airmen, hidden in a shack, pedalling a contraption like a tandem bicycle.

As the action moved closer it was suggested that the King move outside for the finale. By now Rawnsley had brought Cunningham into an ideal attacking position. The raider was still unaware of his presence when the cannons opened up. According to the account Cunningham gave his biographer, 'the crescendo of the guns opened the final act as [I] pulled away to avoid hurtling wreckage. A flickering glow lit the inside of the Heinkel ... and its wheels dropped down, the hydraulics shot through. Flying alongside [we] watched the glow expand through the skin as engulfing flames took over. Mortally wounded, the He III shuddered, and curved over into a steepening dive, flames streaming behind.'[13]

These feats were seized upon by the RAF's publicity machine which was anxious to continue promoting the Air Force as protectors and defenders, as well as to provide some evidence that the Luftwaffe were not able to attack with impunity. There were

'Cat's Eyes' meets the King

difficulties about how much could be said because of government reluctance to reveal the existence of the still secret AI technology. Cunningham, whose virtues included extreme modesty, had no choice but to accept the absurd role that the publicists cast him in. He became famous as 'Cat's Eyes Cunningham' whose amazing prowess at shooting down Germans in the dark was the result of phenomenal eyesight, enhanced by a diet of carrots.

Despite the battering they were receiving at the hands of the Luftwaffe, the public's fascination with and admiration for the Air Force seemed unaffected. The government kept a close watch on the state of civilian spirits. The Home Intelligence division of the Ministry of Information was charged with monitoring national morale and produced weekly reports based on data from a variety of sources including the Mass Observation network. From the outset, the public seemed to accept bombing as an ugly new fact of wartime life 'which if it cannot be cured must be endured'.[14] The bulletin for the week 11–18 December 1940 stated that 'in the Southern region, people are reported to be getting a little tired of the slogan "Britain can take it"'.[15] However, nowhere during the Blitz period is there any direct criticism of the men of the RAF. One respondent in a Mass Observation survey – 'the inhabitant of a Southern port, much blitzed' – remarked sourly: 'we hear a lot about their activities, but I have never seen an RAF fighter about when the air over our city has been thick with German bombers'.[16] But people seemed, rather, to blame pre-war politicians for not giving the Air Force the right equipment to face the threat than the airmen themselves, and to accept that an antidote might take time to arrive.[17]

The Battle of Britain effect, which raised the reputation of the whole service to stratospheric heights, would carry the Air Force through many setbacks and persist to the end of the war. The Air Ministry's Public Relations Directorate understood the need to keep the memory fresh. Shooting of *The First of the Few*, the first film version of the epic, began early in 1941. The film's producer, director and star Leslie Howard, internationally famous after playing Ashley Wilkes, the upstanding Southern gentleman who lost out to Clark Gable's caddish Rhett Butler in the competition for Vivien Leigh's Scarlett O'Hara in the great box office hit of 1939, *Gone With the Wind*, decided to lend authenticity to the flying scenes by using half a dozen real pilots including Brian Kingcome of 92 Squadron. The Fighter Boys were treated like kings. Kingcome recalled that the work itself was undemanding, calling for 'little more than lolling about in flying clothes in a fake dispersal hut, going outside to look sombrely skywards from time to time, and delivering such daft lines as, "Good luck – they'll need it," to cue in stock shots of Spitfires and German bombers flying overhead'.[18] One image of a pilot's gloved thumb jabbing at the control column gun button would be used in countless documentaries thereafter, cutting away to footage of an enemy aircraft going down in flames. It was Kingcome's proud boast that the 'thumb on the firing button, which must have been seen by more people than any thumb in history' belonged to him (it can still be seen in the video display accompanying the Spitfire suspended in the main hall of London's Imperial War Museum).

After their day's labours, they returned to the Savoy Hotel where Howard had put them up. For Kingcome the whole experience was 'a joyous interlude and a marvellous break from airfield routine. I hardly remember when I enjoyed myself more.' At the end of each day's shooting the pilots were taken on a round of 'London's best clubs and pubs, no expense spared ...'

Word soon got around the London area fighter stations and the actor-aviators noted the remarkable number of comrades who '"just happened" to be passing the Savoy as we were setting forth on our nightly expeditions'. They frequented the old Fighter Boy favourites, clubs like the 400 in Leicester Square, 'whose dimly lit dance floor and seductive music were excellent backdrops for young men in uniform trying their luck with the "I'm off to war tomorrow and may never come back" routine'. Then it was on to the Bag O'Nails in Kingly Street, Soho, a 'far more raucous affair where serious boozing took priority'. They finished with a nightcap or two at the hotel while Leslie Carroll and his Savoy Orpheans played the evening out.

Howard further demonstrated his gratitude by providing some illicit entertainment which he thought the young pilots might appreciate. Kingcome recalled that 'after much sly nudge-nudging and wink-winking and many taps to the nose, we were informed that a special treat had been laid on for us – one of "those" films. It required to be shown in great secrecy after the studio had finished the day's work and everyone else had gone home.' At the appointed hour, they sidled embarrassedly into the private projection room led by Howard himself and the fun began. It was called *A Walk in the Woods* and looked as if it had been shot in the 1920s. The action began 'with a car being driven along a woodland track by two pretty young women, who very soon decided to stop and take a walk in the woods – so justifying the title though from this point on, justifying the title ceased to be of any central concern. The young women pointed upwards at the sun and, with suitably histrionic gestures, indicated how hot it was today. This gave them the cue to begin to take off their clothes ...'

Meanwhile, 'visible to the audience but unbeknown to the girls, a shady-looking young bounder lurked amid the trees. One glance at his waxed moustachios and sleekly oiled hair had been enough to make us suspect that he was not there just to study botany ...' From then on 'it was all go, but projected as it was, with a jerky speeded-up action to match wildly exaggerated gestures and expressions which passed for acting in early movies, the effect was achingly funny'. As they split their sides, the pilots could only hope that they had not caused offence to their well-meaning host.

In the lonely period between the fall of France and the fundamental changes to the strategic game brought about by Operation Barbarossa and Pearl Harbor, the maintenance of national morale was of profound importance. Any sign of progress, any glimmer of hope, was to be magnified to maximum proportions, even if the picture that resulted bore little resemblance to reality.

The Prime Minister's tone shifted in the autumn of 1940 from ringing defiance to the promise of retribution and ultimate victory. On the first anniversary of the war he declared in a memo to the Cabinet: 'The Navy can lose us the war but only the Air Force can win it ... the Fighters are our salvation ... but the Bombers alone provide the means of victory.' The public was soon being assured that, although bombs were falling around them, over the horizon even worse things were happening to Germany. In a speech in the House of Commons he asserted that 'night after night, month after month, our bomber squadrons travel far into Germany, find their targets in the darkness by the highest navigational skill, aim their attacks ... with deliberate, careful precision, and inflict shattering blows upon the whole technical and war-making structure of the Nazi power'.

By now the conceptual underpinnings of the pre-war plans for the bomber offensive were trembling under the weight of operational realities and the difficulties of striking effectively were all too apparent. The Air Staff still clung to the belief that performance would eventually catch up with the montage that was being concocted. The real situation was too painful to divulge. After the failures and crises of 1940, neither politicians, nor the public, nor the Air Force itself were in a mood to confront the truth. Instead, illusions were fostered in the cause of maintaining morale. Bomber Command told Group Headquarters that 'full publicity should be given to our bomber operations in the fullest and most attractive light'.[19]

Everyone played along. Newspaper and magazine reports, BBC broadcasts and official announcements all presented the bombing effort as a story of continuous and growing achievement in this period, a narrative that was diametrically opposite to the truth. Initially at least, the fiction was relatively easy to maintain. Unlike the Battle of Britain, all the action took place out of public view. Official bulletins were backed up by accounts by participants. A typical one 'by a flying officer of a heavy bomber squadron' described a raid on Berlin in September 1940, one of a series ordered in retaliation for the bombardment of London.

'We found our targets without difficulty. It was a gas generating plant only a few miles from the centre of Berlin ... when the bombs burst, there were four huge explosions across the works ... it reminded me of a scene on the films ... two huge fires started and huge tongues of flame leapt up, then dense smoke ... the bombs had fallen about fifty yards apart. Almost immediately the fires and the explosions seemed to link up and for a distance of 200 yards through the works there was this great mass of flames ... we circled round and watched the fires blazing up. The rear gunner I remember, shouted: "Oh Boy, it's terrific."'[20]

In tandem with these accounts came reassurance that what the public was being told about the Air Force's activities was actually true. At the same time as the report above was made, Macdonald Hastings asked Picture Post's millions of readers: 'Can we believe the claims of the RAF? Are our bombers any more successful in raids over Germany than the German bombers over Britain?' The comforting answer was that the official version was accurate. He based the conclusion not on the word of the authorities but what he said was the rigorously checked testimony of the airmen themselves.

'Our bomber crews who night after night fly over Germany, say that the official communiques claim only a fraction of the destruction which the RAF heavy bombers are working on Germany's war economy,' he wrote.[21] 'When they come back from a raid, the Bomber crews are interrogated by Intelligence Officers who wouldn't believe we'd won the war unless they saw the Armistice signed with their own eyes ...' He described the process by which the debrief material was passed up to the Bomber Group headquarters 'which suspects even Intelligence Officers' reports. Group Headquarters pass on a revised account to Bomber Command, who are careful to modify any claim which might imply a tendency to boast. Bomber Command in their turn send a report to the Air Ministry ...'

The report was an early exercise in explaining to a mass audience the character, purpose and methods of Bomber Command. It was spread over seven pages and illustrated by sixteen excellent black and white photographs. Hastings was not an Air Ministry stooge. Nonetheless, the article must have pleased its readers in Adastral House. It presented bombing operations as they would like everyone from the Prime Minister down to see them.

The piece was based on a visit to 214 Squadron, equipped with Wellingtons and based at Stradishall in Suffolk, and appeared just as the Blitz began. Hastings described a routine that would soon become implanted in the minds of the British public; the initial briefing revealing the target and setting the number of aircraft on the trip, then the first preparations; plotting courses, testing engines, loading fuel and bombing up. In the afternoon came the final briefing with specialists giving the weather forecast and latest intelligence on enemy defences. There was a break for supper before the crew climbed into their flying gear and headed out to the aircraft. The report underlines approvingly the collective and unhierarchical spirit of the enterprise: 'Each aircraft has a crew of six men,' Hastings wrote, 'two pilots, navigator, air observer, wireless operator and rear gunner. There is no rule as to which are officers and which are not. Sergeant pilots are sometimes captains of aircraft in which officers are rear gunners. The ranks mix together on terms which are among the most pleasant features of Air Force life.'

It is made clear that Bomber Boys and Fighter Boys are different sorts of heroes, for 'the men who fly night bombers are quieter and more serious than the fighter pilots. Their responsibility is heavier; the technological knowledge required of them is more complicated and the physical strain is more prolonged. The fighters are in the air, at most, for a few hours ... the bombers are out all night, steering their course with cold deliberation, through the blackness, studying their maps, puzzling out the direction of their target, and taking everything that the enemy likes to throw at them.'

Back at base the staff grab what rest they can before awaiting the return. There are anxious moments when an aircraft is arriving, but 'more often than not … all our aircraft return safely'. The piece dwells on the rigours of the debriefing process which, he claimed, 'the crews will tell you [is] the worst part of the trip'. The intelligence officers inquire carelessly if they've had a good trip. 'The crew, true to the Air Force tradition of modesty, reply in an off-hand way that it was "very nice" or "not so nice"'.

Then 'they get down to brass tacks. What time were you over your target? How did you know it was the target? Did your bombs hit the target? What height were you? If you were as high as that, how did you identify the target?' The description of the night's work ends with a detail that would stick forever in the mind of civilians suffering the privations of rationing: a plate of bacon and eggs.

The impression given by the article is of calm, resolute efficiency producing solid results. 'If the bombers have done their job – and they usually have – they have brought back evidence that a specific object has been raided.'

He continued: 'that's the difference between German bombing methods and ours. The Germans pin their hopes on mass destruction; we count any bomb which fails to hit a predetermined military objective a wasted bomb. It is not merely a matter of the rules of warfare. It is sound common sense. Killing civilians and blowing up their homes won't win the war. But the systematic destruction of the enemy's internal economy will, in time, paralyse his armies.'

Hastings went on to claim that the RAF was superior to the Luftwaffe in navigational skill and the quality of its aircraft, bombs and bomb sights. The truth was that 'both the Luftwaffe and the RAF know that one side is claiming too much and the other too little. The Luftwaffe must think that the RAF is mad.'

Coming as it did as Londoners were feeling the full weight of the Luftwaffe's nightly bombardments, the article was obviously intended to promote the idea that Germany was suffering, too, though the RAF's campaign was aimed strictly at legitimate military targets. Woven into the text is the Air Ministry credo that it is the work of the bomber squadrons that will prepare the ground for victory.

As a reflection of what was going on at the time, the piece is wrong in almost every respect. To what extent was the propaganda believed? Ministry of Information-commissioned surveys reported scepticism. 'Many ... particularly inhabitants of the blitzed cities, doubt whether our bombing is as effective as it might be,' concluded one in mid-March 1941.[22] The effort to claim the high moral ground with claims that British bombs were aimed only at 'pre-determined military targets' appeared to be wasted on a population comfortable with the idea of retaliation in kind. 'Public feeling in favour of reprisals continues to be strong,' declared the Home Intelligence report for the last week in March 1941.[23] 'The moral aspects of the problem are now almost entirely discounted. Personal experience has made the inhabitants of blitzed towns believe that attacks on the centres of population is "a paying military proposition" and they demand that we should apply the lesson to Hamburg and Berlin.'

The men directing the bombing campaign had come to the same conclusion some months before. Shortly after the *Picture Post* article appeared, the Air Staff accepted that the precision attacks on strategic targets it had promised were unattainable with its current resources, and other means would have to be used if air raids were to have any effect at all.

A directive issued to Charles Portal, briefly chief of Bomber Command between April and October 1940, on 21 September reaffirmed that war industry targets and particularly oil storage plants remained the 'basis of our longer term offensive strategy'. However, in the meantime, Portal was told to broaden the scope of attacks to include Berlin, even though it contained no priority targets. The aim was to cause 'the greatest possible disturbance and dislocation both to the industrial population and to the civil population generally in the area'.[24] Portal needed no encouragement. He had already proposed raids in retaliation for the London Blitz on industrial towns like Essen in the Ruhr, 'the whole of which can for practical purposes be regarded as a military objective'.[25] In the next few weeks the pretence that Germany could be fatally undermined by pinpoint attacks on high-value industrial targets would be abandoned, to be replaced by the belief that it was more realistic to attack whole towns and with it the morale of the German people. At the end of October, Portal's successor, Richard Peirse, received precise instructions from the Air Staff directing him to carry on aiming at oil targets but in adverse weather conditions to switch to attacks on Berlin or towns in central and western Germany. He was urged to adopt the tactics that the Luftwaffe was using so effectively in Britain and open the raid with an incendiary bombardment, then bombing on the fires 'with a view to preventing the firefighting services from dealing with them and giving the fires every opportunity to spread'. So it was, wrote the authorized historians of the strategic bombing campaign, that 'the fiction that the bombers were attacking "military objectives" in the towns was officially abandoned. This was the technique which was to become known as area bombing.'[26]

This fundamental change in the direction of the bombing campaign coincided with an important reshuffle at the summit. On 24 October 1940 the Chief of the Air Staff Cyril Newall was defenestrated and Portal installed in his place. Newall had been a marked man for some months. His appointment to succeed Edward Ellington in September 1937 had come as a surprise, particularly to Dowding and Ludlow-Hewitt, who both fancied their chances. As the man overseeing the frantic preparations for war with Germany he inevitably took the blame for the major weaknesses revealed by the shock of combat. By the time the Battle of Britain was over he had lost the confidence of Churchill and gained the enmity of Lord Beaverbrook whose dynamic work as Minister for Aircraft Production still left him plenty of time for intrigue. Trenchard, fearing that Newall had abandoned faith in the bomber doctrine, joined the conspiracy against him and, at the age of fifty-four, Newall was despatched to the side lines as Governor General of New Zealand.

In truth it was time for him to go. He was worn out and by 1940 'an absolute bag of nerves' according to his then assistant Sholto Douglas, incapable of imposing grip and vision when the RAF desperately needed both.[27] He did not shrink from wielding the axe when he thought it was necessary, getting rid of Ludlow-Hewitt earlier in the year and making an unsuccessful bid to remove Dowding. Portal's appointment came as no surprise. He was the obvious choice and his tenure remained secure until the end. Under Portal, the primacy of strategic bombing was assured, even if the methodology changed. He did not think it necessary to spell out the new emphasis on 'area bombing' to either the public or the crews.

The men of Bomber Command carried on as before, buoyed up with the belief that they were engaged in a quasi-scientific process of dismantling the German war machine. Teddy Fry was a sergeant pilot, a trainee estate agent in Sittingbourne, Kent, before the war who joined the RAFVR in July 1938. He was one of the men Hastings observed on his visit to 214 Squadron for *Picture Post*. His letters reveal a pride in what he and his comrades were doing and apparent enjoyment of his work.

In the summer of 1940 he made several sorties to the Ruhr as well as taking part in a short-lived and unsuccessful effort to turn large German forests into blazing infernos by showering them with incendiaries. Fry was eager to hit Germany where it mattered. 'I've at last done a real trip,' he reported in a letter sent on 2 September to his widowed mother Eva and sister Elizabeth at their semi in Sidcup.[28] 'Nothing worth the DFM or anything … But it was my first trip there – Berlin. There and back 8 hours 20 mins flying … really good trip. Made the other trips to the Ruhr [seem] like a practice flight.' Two weeks later the night Blitz was underway and Sidcup lay under the flight path of the raiders. Fry offered the reassuring thought that Hitler would not have it all his own way: 'Two can play his game and we are as good at it as him.' The tempo of operations had picked up and he was in a routine of 'work all night, sleep all day. You must do it – sleep and lounge about *absolutely* as much as possible. The more you rest, the more racket you can stand, and the more racket you can stand the shorter will be the war.'

In November, he wrote proudly to his sister to alert her to his part in a raid three nights before. 'Boy! did we have fun and games that night over Berlin.' He enclosed a cutting from the *Daily Telegraph* for 25 November. Citing an Air Ministry communiqué, it reported that the attack 'began shortly before eight o clock when the Putlitzerstrasse and Lehrter railway goods yards right in the middle of the city were bombed. Ten very large fires were started … at the same time 1,000 incendiaries were dropped on the yards between the Potsdamer and the Anhalter railway stations.' An unnamed pilot described how, after an interval of a few seconds of his bombs being dropped, 'up went a whole lot of fires in the most amazing way ... we were flying at a good height but the inside of our machine was lit up as though we had the electric light on inside'. He recognized the account as his own, 'word for word the report that I gave after the trip ... I'm sending it because mother or yourself might like to hear about *some* of our exploits.'

By Christmas he had thirty-one trips under his belt. 'Just about time I got off,' he wrote. 'Still, with another four trips I get the record for the squadron. Rather tempting you know – should just be able to do it.' He fell just short for after two more trips he was moved to No. 12 OTU at Benson in Oxfordshire, presumably as an instructor. His efforts had won him a DFM. On 20 February, he wrote home to break the news and invite them to the investiture: 'Stand by you two for the 18th March at 10.15 at the Palace. Please don't say that you have nothing to wear or any other nonsense because you don't have to be a duchess or a glamour girl to be mother and sister to a DFM ...' Teddy Fry never kept the appointment at the Palace. He was killed in a flying accident eight days later.

Despite the move away from futile attempts at precision to unfocused attacks on cities, the Air Ministry continued to foster the illusion that bombing was both effective and a relatively clean business. The Air Staff used the cinema to promote a rosy account of Bomber Command's achievements. *Target for Tonight* was released in August 1941. Every facility had been granted to the director and writer, Harry Watt, one of a new breed of British documentary film makers. The film mixed drama with actuality, using RAF air and ground crew, aeroplanes and bases to tell the story of a single night raid over Germany. The action focuses on a Wellington bomber, F for Freddie, and its pilot and crew drawn from all over Britain. The captain was played by Squadron Leader Percy 'Pick' Pickard, a pre-war regular with dozens of operations to his credit and filmed at Mildenhall. Such was the enthusiasm for the project that Richard Peirse, then Bomber Command's C-in-C, agreed to play himself.

Once again great emphasis is placed on methodical preparations and the dispassionate professionalism of all involved. The target is an oil storage complex in the Black Forest. The raiders take off at dusk and find the target without difficulty. Despite fierce flak they drop their bombs, but F for Freddie is hit and its wireless operator wounded. Somehow it staggers most of the way home, but seemingly on its last legs the pilot gives the crew the choice of baling out or remaining while he attempts a crash landing. They elect to stay and the captain gets them all down safely. At the post-op debrief the crew report that the first bombs fell short but that 'the last one started a major fire' producing 'black smoke, dullish red flames'. That is enough for the intelligence officer: 'Sounds like oil all right.' The raid has been a success.

The fictional nature of the story was disguised by the patina of documentary authenticity. *Target for Tonight* successfully competed with escapist feature films at the box office and even did well in America. According to Watt its success was due to its upbeat underlying message. 'Away back in many people's minds there had arisen the doubt that we could ever win,' he said.[29] 'Then came this film, actually showing how we were taking the war into the heart of the enemy and doing it in a very British, casual, brave way. It was a glimmer of hope and the public rose to it.'

The impulse to move onto the offensive was strong, even when it made little strategic sense. It was displayed in the use to which the fighter squadrons were put, once the Battle of Britain was over. Fear of an invasion persisted well into 1941. Then, in June, Hitler launched Barbarossa and the hinge of the war swung eastwards. The danger to Britain fell away, and with it the need to concentrate Fighter Command's resources at home. There were several obvious places in the vulnerable territories which acted as stepping stones between Britain and its eastern dominions where Spitfires and Hurricanes and seasoned pilots were badly needed. At the top of the list stood the Mediterranean theatre and Egypt where, following Mussolini's decision in June 1940 to jump into the war, the Army and Navy were now fighting the Italians. As we shall see in Chapter Ten, the RAF's Middle East Command initially had nothing like the numbers or equipment it needed to offer adequate support on land or sea. Fighters and men began to flow eastwards at the end of 1940, but with Hurricanes rather than Spitfires, and then early models. Weakness in the air undermined the chances of early success in the

Middle East and compounded the muddle and hesitation that marked the British effort in the first phase of the war.

The demand for modern aircraft was even more acute in the Far East. Following the fall of France, the Chiefs of Staff had decided that, with Britain now isolated and the Fleet badly needed elsewhere, the RAF would have to take prime responsibility for defending Malaya and Singapore, the citadel on which the security of Britain's Far Eastern territories and trade depended. Yet, when, seventeen months later, the Japanese erupted westwards, the Air Force that faced them was pitifully unfitted to offer any serious resistance. The Australian and New Zealand squadrons that made up the fighter force went into battle against the 'Navy Type 0' – known ever after as the 'Zero' – with the Brewster Buffalo. The American-made machine was as lumbering as its name suggested, taking 6.1 minutes to climb to 13,000 feet against the Zero's 4.3 minutes, and with a top speed more than forty miles an hour slower. Spitfire squadrons may not have saved Singapore – there were too many other factors conspiring in its downfall – but they might have bought time and reduced the dimensions of the catastrophe.

But none were sent. Instead, most of the fighters were kept at home and put on the offensive, mounting continuous cross-Channel operations over northern France. The decision is one that was questioned at the time, and nearly eighty years on the rationale for it has become no easier to understand.

The ostensible reason for going over to the attack was that it would keep the Germans off balance and teach them that the occupation of France would be challenged every day. It also reinforced the propaganda theme of 'hitting back'. There was a further supposed benefit in that the Germans would be compelled to keep fighters, anti-aircraft guns and radar in France for force protection instead of using them in their campaigns in Greece and Yugoslavia.[30] This was a dubious proposition and the risks involved were high. The new campaign meant that Fighter Command was effectively assuming the disadvantages of mounting operations over enemy territory that the Luftwaffe suffered in the Battle of Britain, without any likely compensating strategic reward. The German defences were as good as Britain's, and with the arrival of the Focke-Wulf 190 in 1942 the defenders had a machine that outperformed the attackers. Losses were bound to be high. And the lucky pilots who survived being knocked down knew that for them the war was over.

The switch to the attack was led by the new men at the top of Fighter Command. Sholto Douglas, by then deputy CAS, replaced Dowding at the end of November 1940 as C-in-C. At 11 Group, Keith Park made way for his old enemy Trafford Leigh-Mallory. The hasty departure of Dowding and Park so soon after victory would come to be seen as an act of ingratitude bordering on betrayal by Churchill. Douglas and Leigh-Mallory have been regarded as accessories to the crime. Leigh-Mallory was already tainted with accusations of disloyalty for his part in the 'Big Wing' controversy. But it is hard to see what would have been gained by keeping the old team in harness. Dowding had already had his tenure extended once and was exhausted. Park had been long in the job and was due another posting. Both were garlanded for their achievements and progressed to other, important jobs.

The charge that can be made against the newcomers is that they were proud and ambitious. They wanted to make an impact and the methods they chose with which to make their mark killed many good men and brought few results.

Douglas later claimed that the initial impetus for the policy came from Portal. He in turn had been influenced by an intervention from Trenchard, still energetically offering his counsel whether it was asked for or not. According to Douglas, Trenchard 'thought that we should now "lean towards France," and he advocated a system of offensive sweeps of fighters across the Channel which was along much the same lines as that used by us in our operations over the Western Front in the First World War'.[31] The enterprise was certainly stamped with the Trenchardian notion that it was essential to maintain a spirit of aggression, and that, as the official historians of the war wrote, 'powerful moral advantages would accrue as our pilots grew accustomed to exercising the initiative ...'[32] As with the bombing campaign, displaying the offensive spirit seemed to be regarded as an end in itself, almost regardless of the ratio between cost and effectiveness.

Operations broadly consisted of two main types. 'Rhubarbs' involved smallish fighter formations roaming over the French coast in the hope, as the Luftwaffe had hoped in the summer of 1940, that the defenders would come up to meet them and a battle of attrition would be joined. 'Circuses' were small bombing raids sometimes with very large fighter escorts, with a similar intention. The Germans were reluctant to play along. Between 20 December 1940 and 13 June 1941, cross-Channel operations resulted in fifty RAF pilots being shot down for a gain of fifty-eight enemy aircraft destroyed. These paltry results might have brought the unfortunate experiment to a close. But the German invasion of Russia intervened to give an ostensible strategic value to the exercise. The raids could be presented as a British contribution to the Russian war effort, by forcing the Germans to divert air assets away from the Eastern Front. In fact the effect was negligible. In the second half of the year, activity mounted, and so did losses. The scale of operations increased sharply, and this time the Germans felt compelled to respond. Official figures claimed that in the six weeks from the middle of June, 322 enemy aircraft were destroyed for British losses of 123 pilots. As the official history noted, however, 'the German day fighter force in Northern France was only some two hundred strong, and losses of the order claimed would have meant either its complete extinction, or its renewal from top to bottom'.[33] It turned out later that the true German losses were eighty-four. Whatever minor successes the campaign achieved were heavily offset by the human cost. More pilots were lost in 1941 on these exercises than in the Battle of Britain, and many of the dead were survivors of that struggle. Douglas and Leigh-Mallory's policy meant that seventy-five fighter squadrons were kept in the UK that would have been far better employed filling desperate needs in the Middle and Far East.

By going on the offensive, the Fighter Boys no longer had the comfort of fighting over their own territory to sustain them, and the terrors of combat were reinforced by anxiety about the journey home. Flight Lieutenant Stanley Meares of 611 Squadron, twenty-four years old and a pre-war SSC officer who nonetheless had little combat experience, described one adrenaline-soaked encounter in a letter to his parents on 29 June 1941. The squadron was escorting bombers on a Circus when he got caught up in a dogfight which he emerged from to find, as was often the case, the skies miraculously empty of aircraft.

'Being ... about fifty miles inside France, all by myself, I felt a little lonely and headed for home, but on the way back I passed right over the middle of St Omer aerodrome, which had two Me 109s patrolling it. I thought to myself that this was no place to start looking for trouble, and continued on my way.'[34] The Messerschmitts spotted him and Meares dropped to below tree-top level to shake them off. It did not work. He made a tight turn preparing to fight, but was horrified to see the 'Hun' turning inside him, gaining the firing advantage. He 'began to perspire a bit'. He could not climb away because the Messerschmitt would outperform him, nor dive as he was already flat on the deck.

'It struck me [he wrote] that I was fighting for my life which is the strangest of sensations. I knew with terrific clearness that unless I did something within the next split second I would be one of those who did not get home.' He pulled the stick back until it would go no further, blacking out for what seemed like minutes. When he came to again, 'I was flying about 20 feet behind the Hun, and he was obviously wondering where I had got to.'

In the dogfight that followed Meares gradually won the advantage and with the bit between his teeth pursued his opponent back to the aerodrome where he 'chased him down his hangars, in between them, over the flying field and back again. He was trying to get his ground defences to shoot me down, then in desperation he turned on his back at about fifty feet and I gave him a long burst and in he went ...' With his magazines empty he turned for home only to be bounced by another Messerschmitt. After another sweat-drenched tussle he threw him off and raced at ground level for the Channel. He crossed at Dungeness. 'I never knew how well I loved England until I saw her shores again,' he wrote. 'I had learned more about tactics and flying in twenty minutes than in all my flying years.'

Meares had been lucky, although his good fortune did not last. He was killed later that year in a mid-air collision in home skies.

Hundreds of others joined the ranks of 'those who did not get home'. From mid-June 1941 to the end of the year alone, Fighter Command lost 411 fighters over the Channel and the Continent.[35]

Among the victims of the new policy were several pilots who had been pushed into the limelight by the Air Force's PR men. Eric Lock was one of the most successful of the Battle of Britain pilots. He was born in Shropshire in 1919, into a family of farmers and quarry-men, attended a local private school and left at sixteen to work for his father. He joined the RAFVR in February 1939. He was posted to 41 Squadron just before the Battle began, without having ever flown a Spitfire. He opened his account with the Luftwaffe on 15 August, shooting down a Messerschmitt 110 and a Junkers 88. He ended the Battle with possibly twenty-six victories, making him the highest scoring Allied pilot of the campaign.

In late autumn, his fortunes began to change. He was shot down twice in November. The second time he had managed to destroy one Messerschmitt 109 before being hit by cannon shells from another. He was badly wounded in both legs and his right arm and the throttle lever of his Spitfire was severed, sending his aircraft racing away at 400mph. He left the attackers behind but was now too badly hurt to bale out. He brought the aircraft screaming down to 2,000 feet then switched off the engine and somehow managed to glide in to make a wheels-down landing in a field near Martlesham Heath in Suffolk. According to Cuthbert Orde, who heard the story from Lock when he did his portrait in 1941, 'for two hours he sat in his cockpit, bleeding from his three frightful wounds before rescue arrived in the shape of a couple of soldiers. He told them how to make a stretcher out of two rifles and an overcoat, and then was carried two miles, being dropped three times on the way, once into a dyke of water.'[36] He spent six months in hospitals and was oper-ated on fifteen times before going back on operations with 611 Squadron in June 1941. On 3 August, he was returning from a Rhubarb over the Pas-de-Calais when he spotted a German column and his wingman saw him dive to attack. After that he disappeared. No trace of him or his Spitfire was found.

Looking at the few photographs and the sketched portrait by Orde, which are all that is left behind, 'Sawn-off Lucky' is a dim figure to modern eyes. The few contemporary references shed little light on him. Orde remembered that while he sat to him he 'never stopped talking and he never stopped laughing – everything was a joke'.

Six days after Lock's downfall another famous name was brought down. The story of Douglas Bader, the legless veteran of Dunkirk and the Battle of Britain who overcame every obstacle, physical and bureaucratic, to get back in the air, made him ideal hero material, projecting an image of bulldog resolve that matched the face Britain wished to show to the world. His personality hardly fitted the prevailing Fighter Boy ethos; he was boastful and enjoyed the lime-light, though the charge of line-shooting did not stick for his achievements were real enough. He lorded it over inferiors and cultivated those who could advance his cause. Fellow pilots tended to keep their thoughts about him to themselves. It was bad form to criticize and invited the charge of jealousy.

Bader revelled in combat. Having not been in the front line for much of the Battle, he seemed determined to make the most of the opportunities offered by the new campaign. In the spring of 1941 he was given command of a wing based at Tangmere at the foot of the Sussex Downs. From 24 March Bader flew sixty-two fighter sweeps over France. For Bader, war was a competition and he was always seeking to increase his score, which in the late summer stood at twenty, and inscribe his name in the record books. By then his squadrons were exhausted and his egotism provoked a near-mutiny. But with the backing of Leigh-Mallory, his patron and ally in the Big Wing controversy, Bader carried on. He finally came to grief on 9 August when he was shot up over northern France in disputed circumstances, baled out and was captured, to start a new phase of his wartime career as a spectacularly troublesome POW.

Of all the campaigns fought by the RAF in the Second World War, the fighter campaign over France was the most ill-conceived. It failed because there was nothing to win. It was obvious early on that gains were not worth the effort and losses and it settled down into a Trenchardian exercise in nurturing the offensive spirit in the mistaken belief that it would keep pilots up to the mark and sustain their morale. When the campaign was finally abandoned at the end of 1943 it had cost five aircraft destroyed for every German machine shot down.[37]

The sense of tragic waste hangs over this aspect of the air war as it does over the strategic bombing campaign. It is summed up by the brief story of Brendan 'Paddy' Finucane, born in Dublin to a father who fought in the 1916 uprising, who joined the RAF on a short service commission just before the war, and took part in the Battle of Britain. He was good-looking, clean-living, attending Mass each Sunday, and charming and easy with people high and low. His success in the air made him a natural for promotion by the RAF publicity machine. He was also singled out for his leadership qualities and in the summer of 1941, at the age of twenty-one, was the youngest wing leader in Fighter Command, operating over France from Kenley in Surrey. On 15 July, he led a 'Ramrod', a fighter attack with cannon and machine guns, on a German army camp near Étaples on the Channel coast in the Pas-de-Calais. The raid was timed for when German troops would be queuing for their midday meal. They crossed the Sussex coast at Pevensey Bay at 12.10 p.m. Finucane's wingman was Alan 'Butch' Aikman, a twenty-three-year-old Canadian, charged with eyeballing the airspace for German fighters.

At 12.22 p.m., as they whipped in at what seemed like wave-top height over the beach at Le Touquet, a light machine gun opened fire from a sand ridge, hitting Finucane's starboard wing. 'Immediately a wisp of white vapour streamed back from the damaged radiator,' wrote Anthony Cooper, Finucane's biographer. 'It was an extraordinary shot because the chances of a small calibre machine gun hitting a low flying Spitfire going at over 300 knots were minimal ...'[38] Aikman broke radio silence to report the damage to the radiator. Finucane acknowledged with a thumbs up and turned back to sea, apparently hoping to ditch. Aikman stayed with him. He watched as Finucane jettisoned the cockpit canopy. Before removing his helmet, he radioed a last message: 'This is it, Butch.' Trailing a stream of white coolant, the Spitfire ploughed into the sea and quickly sank. His end released a flood of heartfelt eulogies. 'We shall miss him greatly,' ran one. 'He was the beau ideal of the "fighter boy."' Another judged that 'as well as being a brilliant fighter pilot

... he had the true spirit of a crusader and a high purpose in all he did ... I anticipated that he would turn out to be one of the greatest leaders we have ever had.' The first tribute came from Douglas, the second from Leigh-Mallory, architects of the very policy that had sent him to his death.

9

Ten Million Miles of Sea

Squadron Leader Tony Spooner, a much-decorated pilot and veteran of numerous perilous flights over the Atlantic and Mediterranean, wrote a poem that reflected the feelings of many of his comrades who served in Coastal Command.

> Fighters or Bombers? his friends used to say
> But when he said 'Coastal' they turned half away ...[1]

The lines were often read at veterans' funerals, and the title – 'No Spotlight for Coastal' – seemed to sum up the unconsidered place they occupied in the war years; in the RAF's order of priorities, in the minds of the government and in the imagination of the British public.

It was Coastal Command's fate to be third in line for everything – resources, money, glory and attention. It operated far away from the public gaze and the nature of the work was repetitive and unglamorous and therefore harder for the propaganda factory to package. Yet its role in Britain's survival was at least as important as that played by Fighter Command, and its contribution to victory as significant as that of Bomber Command.

Unlike the others, it started the war lacking a clear role and simple, agreed objectives. It would take several years and much trial and error before its proper function became obvious and its squadrons were equipped with the right machines and technology to carry out their duties. The delay did not mean there was any slackening in the work rate. 'Constant Endeavour' was the motto given to Coastal Command, and it could not have been more appropriate.

The confusion over role and identity was partly the result of the Air Force's fractious and complicated relationship with the Navy. The Admiralty had never accepted the arrangement arrived at in 1924 by which aircraft and crews operating on Navy ships belonged to the RAF. In 1937 a compromise was reached in which control of all carrier-borne aircraft was returned to the Navy under the aegis of the Fleet Air Arm.

The deal did nothing to remove the fundamental incompatibility in the outlook of the services. At heart, the Admiralty continued to believe that logic and justice demanded that they should exercise full control over all air resources that directly affected the Navy's operations. The RAF, meanwhile, feared that ceding the principle would undermine, perhaps fatally, its hard-won status as an independent service.

The picture was made cloudier by prevailing strategic assumptions about how the war at sea would play out. The old charge that soldiers were always fighting the last war did not apply to the Admirals. Their plans and hypotheses suggested they had entirely forgotten it. Much of the naval effort in 1914–18 had gone into protecting the transatlantic sea lanes on which Britain relied for its survival. The main threat had come not from the powerful German surface fleet, which was neutralized after the Battle of Jutland, but from U-boats which in 1917 sank 6.6 million tons of Allied shipping, seriously weakening the country's ability to continue the war.

The danger had been overcome by a system of merchant convoys, protected by escorts armed with guns, depth charges and torpedoes. By then aircraft, too, were playing an important part and in November 1918 the Air Force had 285 flying boats and 272 land-based aircraft engaged in hunting U-boats. They managed to sink only seven enemy submarines but the deterrent effect was strong. The Naval Staff came to believe that 'the ideal was that a convoy should be escorted by at least two aircraft, one keeping close and one cruising wide to prevent a submarine on the surface from getting into a position to attack'.[2]

By the time the war started the wisdom had changed. Thanks to the development of 'Asdic', anti-submarine underwater detection, the Navy believed it could handle the threat without any need for heavy air support. Its main concern at the beginning was not the U-boats but the Kriegsmarine's squadrons of fast, heavily armed and long-ranging capital ships and pocket battleships which, once at large in the Atlantic, could savage Britain's supply lines.

So it was that in the joint discussions to design a co-operative air and sea organization, held between the Admiralty and Coastal Command, the emphasis was on defensive and passive tasks. The prime duty was to be reconnaissance: 'to assist the Home Fleet in the detection and prevention of enemy vessels escaping from the North Sea to the Atlantic', that is, the dreaded breakout of the surface fleet.[3] Next came the provision of air patrols to spot submarines and convoy escorts to scare them off in British coastal waters. Offensive operations were last on the list, the 'provision of an air striking force' and then 'mainly on the east coast'.

Despite the history of institutional wrangling, at the outset personal relations between Coastal and the Navy were good. Its chief, Frederick Bowhill, was a former sailor with 'sea water in his veins' who joined the RN in 1904, transferred to the RNAS in 1913 and started the First World War commanding the Navy's first aircraft carrier, HMS *Empress*, a converted cross-Channel ferry. He was no one's idea of a seadog, nor indeed of an aviator, with a bald pate, bulging eyes and shaggy red eyebrows that swept upwards across his forehead as if about to take flight. According to his successor Philip Joubert, the fierce impression they gave belied a 'puckish humour that solved awkward problems of prestige and smoothed ruffled sensitivities' – useful qualities in the circumstances.[4]

Joubert believed that Bowhill's 'wide knowledge of seafaring matters and his long experience in the flying service made him very well fitted to the control of the sea communications in war'. As a result he commanded the respect of the Navy. His successors, including Joubert himself, 'were not so fortunate. All of them had Army origins and as such were suspect ...' Nonetheless, though they might lobby persistently for greater air resources, the Admirals did not exploit wartime crises to pursue old claims. When, in the autumn of 1940, Lord Beaverbrook saw an opportunity to stir trouble with a dramatic proposal for Coastal Command to be handed over wholesale to the Navy, it was the opposition of the First Sea Lord, Dudley Pound, that effectively sunk the idea.

Joubert's one – inaccurate – criticism of Bowhill was that he harboured 'a grave suspicion of all scientists, and their works'. Service chiefs got used in wartime to being assailed by experts lobbying for a new gizmo that would supposedly win the war. Most of the innovations were useless but some did indeed turn out to have transformational powers. The breakthrough in the development of British radar, after all, emerged from initial research to test the validity of a 'death ray' that would kill the crews of hostile aircraft.

Joubert prided himself on understanding the crucial part that science would play in the war at sea, a struggle that Coastal Command would be in the thick of. Despite the Navy's initial breezy confidence, it would turn out to be just as much a life and death affair as the Battle of Britain, yet it would go on for years rather than months. The Battle of the Atlantic was waged in various forms from the first day of the war. Though a discernible turning point was reached in the middle of 1943, the U-boat menace persisted and the effort to protect the Allied oceanic supply lines by sea and air continued right until the very end. Everyone who mattered understood the immensity of the stakes. Yet there was never a systematic policy emanating from the government, or even from the Air Ministry, to give Coastal what it needed.

The struggle to keep the sea lanes open had many ups and downs. At the break of each false dawn there was a tendency to scale back the resources of the maritime air effort and divert them to other theatres. There was a perpetual clamour for men and machines from all branches of the service, but, with the bomber credo so deeply entrenched in the minds of the Air Marshals, it was Bomber Command's claims that carried the most weight.

At the start of the war the aircraft, armament and technical equipment with which Coastal Command was equipped were all pathetically inadequate for the tasks it was set. The situation would only get worse as the range of their duties grew ever wider. It was just as well that, at the beginning, its main responsibility was reconnaissance rather than offensive operations.

The Air Ministry issued specifications for a twin-engine recon-
naissance/bomber in 1935. Two types were approved but one, the
Blackburn Botha, turned out to be all but useless. At the outbreak
of hostilities, Coastal's striking power rested on the frail shoulders
of the Vickers Vildebeest, a lumbering, antediluvian biplane.
Seaplanes were an essential element in the armoury, extending
operational capacity to geographically difficult parts of the world
and greatly reducing infrastructure needs. The excellent Sunderland,
which carried a crew of thirteen, bristled with ten machine guns,
had a range of nearly 3,000 miles and could stay airborne for more
than thirteen hours, was due to be phased out and replaced with the
Lerwick, another Short Brothers design. Like the Botha it proved to
be a dud but when, in the spring of 1940, the Air Ministry turned
again to the Sunderland, Short's Belfast factory was at full capacity
churning out Stirlings for Bomber Command. Thus, Coastal's flying
boat fleet in 1939 was supplemented by antique-looking Saro
Londons and Supermarine Stranraers.

The unpreparedness of Coastal Command seems reprehensible
now but it is easy to forget the enormous hurry in which the RAF
went to war and the vast array of problems all services – but particularly the Air Force and Navy – faced with only limited resources
from which to contrive solutions. There was not just a nation but
an empire to defend and not one potential enemy but three, as Italy
and Japan hovered opportunistically on the side lines. What is
harder to justify was the later reluctance at the top of the Air Force
to make a more intelligent use of available assets when it was clear
that the Battle of the Atlantic was as crucial a struggle as the Battle
of Britain had been.

New machines were on their way in the shape of Bristol Beaufort
torpedo bombers, a happier result of the Air Ministry's 1935 specification, and 200 Lockheed Hudsons, ordered from the US in 1938,
largely on the initiative of Arthur Harris against the furious opposition of the domestic aviation industry lobby. Until then, Coastal's
backbone consisted of the ten squadrons equipped with Avro
Ansons, a converted six-seater civilian passenger plane. The aircraft's
reliability was reflected in its nickname, 'Faithful Annie'. Tony
Spooner thought the 'dear, safe, wallowing Anson ... possibly the

most viceless aircraft ever designed', but there were several crucial downsides.[5] It was slow, dangerous in violent manoeuvres and so short ranged that it could not get to the Norwegian coast – a vital area in the maritime war – and back. Guy Bolland, who in 1940 commanded Coastal's 217 Squadron, felt they were 'quite useless in any wartime role except a limited anti-submarine patrol to protect shipping'.[6]

At this stage, the mere sight or sound of any aeroplane was enough to cause any U-boat which had surfaced in order to vent the stale air from its hull and recharge batteries to make an immediate dive to safety. Tiger Moths, the game little biplane trainers that every RAF pilot knew from his basic training, were pressed into service on these 'scarecrow' patrols. The disruption they caused was valuable, but the German submarines had little to fear. According to Bolland, the Anson was 'both too slow and too fragile. The engines had to be started up by using a starting handle … Its undercarriage was retractable but only after the use of another (collapsible) handle which took many turns to retract it after take-off and to lower it for landing. For waddling along from A to B it was fine, but the performance, bomb load and armament were totally inadequate and it was soon to be taken off front line duties.'

Bolland joined the RAF on a short service commission in 1930 after a career at sea as a junior officer in the Royal Mail Steam Packet Company. He transferred to Coastal on its creation and commanded the station at Pembroke Dock before taking over 217 Squadron in August 1940 and was by all accounts a popular and efficient commander.[7] The story of his time in charge gives a taste of the demands and hardships common to many of the command's squadrons in the first phase of the war.

217 was based at St Eval, a hurriedly constructed station on the north-west Cornwall coast, and was mainly involved in flying anti-submarine patrols over the Western Approaches to the Channel. The unit was in the middle of re-equipping with the Bristol Beaufort, a much more impressive aeroplane. Its twin Taurus engines made it the fastest torpedo bomber of the day and it was reasonably well defended with a machine gun in the wing and two mounted in a dorsal turret. The transition was difficult. Beauforts were much

harder to fly than the placid Annie. In the meantime, operations with Ansons continued.

With the arrival of German U-boats, followed by large surface warships, in the French Atlantic ports the scope of the squadron's work had widened. The Kriegsmarine now had direct access to the Atlantic sea lanes and the Admiralty inundated the RAF with demands for bombing raids on the ports of Brest, Lorient, La Pallice and Bordeaux. Bowhill responded willingly and Coastal squadrons were diverted into pinprick raids aimed at stalling the gathering threat.

Bolland's predecessor, Wing Commander L. H. Anderson, who had arrived on the squadron on 1 July 1940, was dismayed at the new orders. The Ansons with their fixed, forward-firing .303-in.-calibre machine guns, were laughably easy targets for the four squadrons of Me 109s defending the port. Their payload of four 100lb bombs would do little significant damage if by any chance they managed to deliver them. When, in mid-July, Anderson was told to launch a daylight raid on Brest, he refused to sacrifice his men in what he saw as a pointless exercise. He was removed from his command and, at a court martial in October, reduced to the rank of squadron leader.[8]

If Bolland's superiors believed that he would be more biddable they were soon disappointed. One of his first acts was to fit Vickers 'K' machine guns in the waist of the Ansons to provide them with a little added protection. However, when this reached the ears of Group Headquarters in Plymouth he was told that the modification was unauthorized and the guns would have to be removed. 'This was an order which I did not obey,' he recorded.

Bolland found that 'squadron morale was very low'. One of the factors determining a unit's state of mind was the degree to which its members felt that their actions made some contribution, no matter how small, to the war effort. The business of going back and forth over vast grey wastes of water, while struggling to keep fatigue and boredom at bay, often to return having seen nothing, did not bring any sense of achievement. Bolland wrote that after the war U-boat commanders 'made it plain in their memoirs how much they feared the mere sound of an aircraft and just the possibility of being seen', causing them to dive and disrupting their pursuit of their victims. However, 'those facts were not known to us at the time and it [was] impossible to persuade many of those who flew thousands of miles without a sight of the enemy that they were doing [anything] to win the war'.

Life on the ground that winter was unsettling with constant air raid warnings and occasional bombs landing on and around the base from raiders on their way back from plastering Merseyside. On 21 January 1941 a parachute mine landed on an air raid shelter, killing twenty-one of the base ground staff.

While the Beauforts were bedding in, Ansons kept up attacks on the Atlantic ports. When operating in darkness the fighters left them alone and they escaped relatively unscathed by flak so that in 200 sorties not a single aeroplane was lost. The crews noticed that the shells always seemed to burst some way ahead of them and concluded that they owed their survival to the fact that German gunners did not realize that the attacking aircraft were so slow and made a correspondingly exaggerated guess at the degree of deflection needed to hit them. Better aircraft only brought heavier casualties. In December 1940, the first month of night operations by the Beauforts, six machines and eighteen crew members were lost; this out of a squadron with a nominal strength of eighteen aircraft.

Admiralty pressure on the Air Force intensified with the appearance of the German battlecruisers *Scharnhorst* and *Gneisenau* in Brest in the early spring of 1941. They had joined the U-boats and the long-range Focke-Wulf 200 'Condor' maritime patrol and bomber aircraft in ravaging the Atlantic traffic, sinking 115,622 tons of shipping during their voyage south. They were constrained by the fact that they did not have the guns to tackle convoys which sailed with a battleship escort. That deficiency would be remedied with the arrival of their own battleship, *Bismarck*, which had finished its final sea trials and was due to dart through the northern seas to join them. The worsening situation brought a new call to arms from Downing Street. On 6 March 1941 Churchill issued his Battle of the Atlantic directive which ordered all available resources to 'take the offensive against the U-boat and the Focke-Wulf wherever we can and whenever we can'. When the German cruisers were confirmed as having docked at Brest on 22 March, an all-out air assault by Bomber and Coastal Commands began.

217 Squadron had already been involved in the effort to sink the cruiser *Admiral Hipper* which arrived at Brest in mid-February after two successful Atlantic sorties. The order to attack the port would trigger the premature departure of a second CO. Guy Bolland recorded how 'one day in March … I had orders to send available aircraft to raid [Brest] in daylight. I was only too well aware how well-defended that was by guns and fighters. There was no possible chance of any of my machines getting anywhere near Brest, and if they were lucky enough to hit the ships, the damage they inflicted on the enemy would be negligible.' The chances of disaster were further increased by the fact that there would be no fighter escort to offer any protection over the target. He decided to take the drastic step of declaring that all his aircraft were unserviceable. Group Headquarters in Plymouth were immediately suspicious and queried the signal. Bolland recalled that 'as the day wore on C-in-C Coastal Command [Bowhill] came onto the phone demanding that I got some aircraft serviceable. The station commander at St Eval was not supporting me and I was out on a limb.'

Such was the pressure that he relented enough to make three Beauforts available, bypassing the station commander to warn Plymouth that 'this was a suicide order and I was dead against it as it would serve no useful purpose except to pander to the Navy's demand for action'. He told the Air Officer Commanding 19 Group, Air Commodore Geoffrey Bromet, 'that I did not expect to ever see any of my crews again and if this turned out to be true, to expect to see me in Plymouth that night'.

All three Beauforts were lost with only one of the twelve crew members surviving. Bolland kept his promise, turning up at the headquarters at Mount Wise that evening where he bearded Bromet and an unnamed senior naval officer. 'I told them as clearly as I could that the order to send young men to their deaths on useless missions was not on, and I did not think they could possibly understand what the defences of Brest were like.' He signed off with a suggestion that must have burned like acid: 'Perhaps it would be better if I could discuss this with someone on their staff who had fought in the war.'

For this insubordination Bolland was duly sacked. Unlike Anderson he was not subjected to court martial, and somewhat to his surprise found himself posted to the staff of the Commander of the Home Fleet, Jack Tovey, as Fleet Aviation Officer, handling liaison between the admiral and Bowhill.

The diversion of attacking ports did bring some results, in one case spectacular success. Bomber Command led the assault on the *Scharnhorst* and *Gneisenau* at Brest but it was a Beaufort of Coastal's 22 Squadron that did the most significant damage. On the morning of 6 April 1941, *Gneisenau* lay in the port's inner harbour having been moved there from dry dock the previous day due to the presence of an unexploded bomb delivered in an earlier RAF attack. The new position was spotted by a Spitfire from the Photographic Reconnaissance Unit and a strike ordered for first light.

Of the four Beauforts in the attacking force, only the one piloted by Flying Officer Kenneth Campbell managed to locate the target in the morning haze. Coming in low from seaward he would have seen before him, first, three flak ships bristling with anti-aircraft guns, then behind them a low stone mole that ran in from the west to curve protectively around the dock and five hundred yards beyond that the low bulk of the battlecruiser, hard up against the north wall of the harbour. More guns were clustered on the slopes behind the town, and other batteries sat on the two arms of land encircling the outer harbour. Within seconds of the Beaufort appearing every gun – a thousand weapons of all calibres – was in action. To hit the ship, Campbell had to drop his single torpedo just the other side of the mole. According to the official report 'coming in at almost sea level, he passed the anti-aircraft ships at less than mast height in the very mouths of their guns, and skimming over the mole, landed a torpedo at point blank range'.[9]

At that height and speed, he had no chance of clearing the high ground ahead and hauled the aircraft into a tight turn, thus presenting an unmissable target. The Beaufort plunged into the harbour in flames, but the torpedo ran straight and true, exploding beneath the *Gneisenau*'s waterline. The attack was followed by another Bomber

Command raid five days later, which killed many of the crew, and it would be eight months before the battlecruiser was seaworthy.

Campbell, of course, was dead, along with his crew, Sergeants J. P. Scott, the Canadian navigator, R. W. Hillman, the wireless operator, and W. C. Mullins, the air gunner. As the pilot and captain, Campbell was awarded the Victoria Cross. The others, in keeping with the practice of the time, were deemed to have played no part in the decision to press home the attack and got nothing. Campbell was a twenty-three-year-old Scot, born in Saltcoats, Ayrshire,

Campbell VC

educated at Sedburgh public school and Cambridge where he read chemistry and joined the University Air Squadron. What drove his extraordinary determination, what armoured him from the paralysing fear that the eruption of gunfire that met them must have provoked, we shall never know. In the photograph, from beneath his Air Force Blue side cap his steady eyes meet ours and tell us nothing.

The great Atlantic rendezvous of German surface ships never happened. In May, the attempted breakout by *Bismarck* came to a spectacular end when, after being battered by the shells and torpedoes of a combined naval task force, she went down 500 miles off Brest, with all flags flying. The episode provided some much-needed good news but also demonstrated that, used intelligently, combined air and sea operations could be devastatingly effective. Coastal played a crucial part in the battleship's demise. It was a Spitfire from the command's No. 1 Photographic Reconnaissance Unit, which on 21 May took the pictures from which *Bismarck* and its consort, *Prinz Eugen*, were positively identified as they steamed towards Bergen.

The following day a Fleet Air Arm Maryland dipped below the clouds blanketing the Bergen fjords to establish that they had now departed. Both Coastal and FAA reconnaissance aircraft dogged the battleship's steps as it passed through the Denmark Strait between Greenland and Iceland, and carried on the pursuit following the action of 24 May in which HMS *Hood* was sunk. When *Bismarck* shook off its shadowers on 26 May, it was a bold stroke by Frederick Bowhill that put them back on the trail. He ordered a patrol further south than the Admiralty reckoned the quarry to be. Coastal Command Catalina flying boats intercepted the battleship nearly 800 miles north-west of the haven of Brest and set in train the FAA Swordfish attack that slowed, and ultimately doomed, the battleship.

By now it was clear that the role allotted to Coastal Command at the outset was not ambitious enough. Its aircraft and crews would be better employed not just in reconnaissance and deterrent patrols but in an offensive role, hunting U-boats and destroying them.

The arrival of more and better aircraft and upgraded radar meant they were in a reasonable position to combine with the Navy to provide improved protection for the convoys and take the fight to the Germans.

Bowhill left in June 1941 to take over Ferry Command. On his watch, Coastal had undergone a quantitative and qualitative transformation. The nineteen squadrons it had started the war with had grown to forty. New aircraft like the US-manufactured PBY-5 Catalina seaplanes were almost as big as the Sunderlands and could operate 800 miles from base and stay in the air for seventeen hours. The flying boats were relatively spacious compared with most military aircraft but there was 'still less room in which to move than is to be found in a small fishing smack'.[10]

The Lockheed Hudson could be projected 500 miles with a time over the target area of two hours. Wellingtons and Whitleys ceded by Bomber Command could also spend two hours on station at that distance. The basing of a wing in Iceland in the late summer of 1940 opened the air umbrella wider, though a gap in mid-ocean still remained which could not be covered from either side of the Atlantic. There were some, though still not enough, long-range fighters to offer a degree of protection from the Condors and long-range Heinkels that reinforced the air offensive.

The men who flew the patrols had an identity which set them slightly apart. A disciplinary report noted that Coastal was 'a more stable command. The captains have earned their rank by long experience, and the crews as a whole are a more reliable and responsible type'.[11] Tony Spooner fitted the approving stereotype. In 1937 he had decided to try and become an airline pilot. The attraction was the pay and career prospects rather than any romantic attraction to flying. He had been an instructor before joining Coastal and had a strictly methodical approach to operations.

Steady types were needed in this unglamorous front of the air war. The report noted 'the isolated nature of many of the stations', far from the bright lights. Early in 1941 Spooner was based at Limavady, in Northern Ireland. The station was next to Lough Foyle, and he was able to vouch for the truth of the local saying that 'if you *can* see across the lough it's a sign that it's about to rain. If you can't, then it's raining already'.[12]

The work was tedious. As an official publication of the time put it, 'the chief enemy is not the German Luftwaffe or the German Navy, but boredom, which may provoke first inattention, then indifference. [The pilot] must spend hundreds of hours with nothing to look on but the expanse of sea and sky. "Wave, on wave, on wave, to West" stretches the vast monotony of the Atlantic Ocean. It may glitter in the noonday or lie devoid of light and colour in the hour after sunset; it may seem to crawl like the wrinkled skin of a beast or stretch in ridged and uneven furrows under the breath of strong winds; but it will be empty for hours.'[13] Protracted staring at the sea could prove fatal, sending the pilot into a trance and blinding him to the line between sky and water.

When disaster struck, as it all too often did, it was most likely to be caused by accident or error. It was hard to know, as the end came out of sight of ship or aircraft, witnessed only by the seabirds. On beginning his tour of operations with 221 Squadron flying Wellingtons over the North Atlantic, Tony Spooner noted how 'most of the losses remained unexplained ... crews went out and simply "failed to return." Perhaps an engine failed? Perhaps they got lost? Perhaps they flew into the sea deceived by their altimeters? Perhaps they got iced up, or ran out of petrol fighting engine ice?'[14]

The latter was a major hazard, 'our great enemy'. Whenever possible they tried to fly below the cloud base where icing was less likely, but when the weather made this too dangerous, they were forced to climb into the colder upper air. A chemical de-icing agent could offer protection to the wing and tail surfaces but rain soon washed it off. Propellers collected ice easily, as did the carburettor intakes of the engines. The drill in the case of the former was 'to make violent alteration in the revs per minute hoping to dislodge [it] by vibration and centrifugal forces'. In the latter it was to 'either try a full-power climb through the cloud to the clearer air on top or, as a last desperate remedy ... switch the ignition off – then on; the monumental back fire which resulted would with luck, clear the carburettor throat'. There was nothing they could do, though, to prevent ice encrusting the aerials which festooned their Wellingtons, emitting an eerie singing noise as they vibrated.

It seemed to Spooner that enemy action was the least likely explanation for disappearances, partly because it was obligatory to send an immediate 'ops flash' signal as soon as a hostile aircraft or vessel was sighted. A more dispiriting reason was 'the sad fact ... that neither 221 nor 502 Squadrons, [the sister unit] were finding the enemy, except on very rare occasions ...' Even if they did spot a U-boat, 'it usually was able to dive under the waves before the crew could drop their load of depth charges'. The figures bore out this judgement. In the first twenty-two months of the war, Coastal Command aircraft spotted 161 U-boats and attacked 125 of them. They managed to sink only two, and then with assistance from Navy craft.[15]

Philip Joubert took over command from Bowhill in June 1941 and, according to the official historian, made it his first task to 'develop the most effective operational technique for ASV aircraft, and in so doing to make the aeroplane at last a "U-boat killer"'.[16] ASV stood for air-to-surface-vessel radar, supposedly capable of locating U-boats on the surface and with a forward scan of twelve miles and a side scan of twenty. In its early forms, however, it was mainly of use as a navigational device, rather than as a means of pinpointing enemy submarines, and when the government's chief scientific adviser Sir Henry Tizard visited Limavady and asked the crews how many U-boats they had detected with it the answer came back 'none, or possibly one'.[17]

Fighting submarines was a mechanical, methodical business. The battlefield was vast, ten and a half million square miles of sea. The northern boundary lay inside the Arctic Circle and the southern on the Equator. It stretched in the east to the coasts of western Europe and West Africa, and in the west to the eastern seaboards of Canada, Newfoundland, the USA and Central America.[18] Finding U-boats in this wilderness meant catching them while they were leaving or returning from a hunting sortie, or as they tracked, or lay in wait, for a convoy. German cryptanalysts had partly penetrated the Navy's codes before the war began and also cracked those used by merchant shipping, which greatly helped the Kriegsmarine's commander Admiral Dönitz deploy his forces to maximum effect.[19] Much of Coastal's effort went into flying patrols in likely areas. This involved criss-crossing a designated grid for as long as the weather and fuel allowed until the 'Prudent Limit of Endurance' was reached.

If sighted, the patrolling aircraft had to get its attack in quickly for an alert commander could dive his boat in thirty seconds. On board the aircraft, a klaxon sounded action stations and bombs and depth charges were primed. There was often little to show for a successful operation except some mysterious debris. One report of an attack by a Sunderland 210 miles off Finisterre described how 'bombs were dropped within twenty feet when the submarine was at periscope depth and a large oil patch with air bubbles was observed. Later more bubbles appeared in the centre of the patch. After twenty minutes the oil patch extended with bubbles continuing to rise. The aircraft remained in the vicinity for three and a half hours ...'[20]

The crew of a Hudson, sent out from Iceland on 27 August 1941 after a patrolling aircraft from the same squadron attacked but failed to sink a U-boat, had the satisfaction of catching it just as it surfaced again. After it dropped depth charges 'the U-boat was completely enveloped by the explosions and shortly afterwards submerged completely'.[21] Two minutes later it reappeared and 'ten or twelve of its crew wearing yellow life jackets appeared on the conning tower and came down on deck'. The Hudson dived, 'firing all its guns it could bring to bear as it swept in tight turns around the submarine'. The crew then scrambled for the conning tower, re-emerging seven minutes later waving a white cloth, subsequently discovered to be the captain's dress shirt. Relays of aircraft then kept watch for eleven and a half hours until a naval trawler arrived to capture the prize.

The increasing success of the campaign was due to the greater number of better machines available, the improved quality of radar and the greater efficiency of depth charges, bombs and rockets. None of these were obtained without a struggle. Once again, the peculiar relationship that Coastal Command stood in, not just with the Navy but with the RAF itself, created special difficulties when it pressed for its fair share of resources.

Quite early in the war the Air Staff had accepted that the Admiralty should have overall control of joint air operations connected to the

Battle of the Atlantic. That meant Coastal Command was held in joint custody, with the RAF supplying men, machines and land bases while the Navy put them to work. It was a common-sense arrangement and the cogs, large and small, of the two services locked smoothly enough where they met in each of the command's operational areas.

The friction came at the top from the endless clashes between Admiralty and Air Ministry over resources. By the summer of 1941, Coastal Command had extended the protection it could provide to transatlantic convoys but a wide gap still remained in mid-ocean that was beyond the range of aircraft operating either from Britain and Iceland on one side and Newfoundland on the other. Aggressive patrolling to locate and sink U-boats was starting to have some success, but more machines and crews were needed to change the course of the battle decisively. The Admiralty naturally made repeated requests for very long-range aircraft to expand the air umbrella and maintain pressure on the submarines.

As Commander-in-Chief of Coastal, Philip Joubert supported the Navy 'with all my power', only to find that his own superiors were against him.[22] Requests for some of the new four-engine Halifaxes which began arriving on Bomber Command squadrons at the end of 1940 were ignored by the Air Ministry. In June 1941, a single squadron, No. 120, which was based in Iceland, was equipped with Consolidated B-24 Liberators supplied by America, which had the long legs to close the Atlantic gap. According to Joubert, Bomber Command only spared the aircraft from its 'private war with Germany' because 'their engines showed too much flame from the exhausts, and thus helped the enemy night fighters'. As detection technology improved very long-range aircraft like the Liberators turned out to be very effective hunters and killers of submarines, yet in February 1943 there were still only eighteen operating in the North Atlantic.

Coastal's bargaining power was diminished after the battle seemed to take a turn for the better in the middle of 1941. In 1942, another crisis developed. In March, more than 800,000 tons of Allied shipping was sent to the bottom, two-thirds by U-boats. There were similar losses in June and November. It seemed obvious to Joubert that some of Bomber Command's growing resources, in particular the Stirlings, Halifaxes and Lancasters arriving on the squadrons, would have to be switched to face the desperate threat looming in the Atlantic. His representations provoked more irritation than sympathy among those who were directing the larger shape of the war.

The reluctance to divert resources takes some explaining. No one could be in any doubt about the crucial nature of the struggle and the importance of Coastal Command's part in it. Dudley Pound, the head of the Navy, declared in March 1942: 'If we lose the war at sea, we lose the war.'[23] Churchill agreed with him, recording after it was over that 'the Battle of the Atlantic was the dominating factor throughout the war ... [everything] ultimately depended on its outcome'.

Why, then, the grudging responses, delivered with what felt like hostile relish by the likes of Arthur Harris, to Coastal Command's modest requests for the tools to do its job? The Air Marshals gave the outward impression of treating the Navy's needs sympathetically. Early in 1942 the First Lord of the Admiralty A. V. Alexander drew up a wish list for six and a half squadrons of Wellingtons, which were now being superseded by the 'heavies', to deal with increasing U-boat activity in the Atlantic. There was a further demand for two more bomber squadrons to be sent to Ceylon to help with the extension of the naval war into the Indian Ocean.

More memos fluttered across from the Admiralty carrying more requests. The response from the Air Staff seemed positive. The Secretary of State for Air, Archibald Sinclair, declared that it was the Air Ministry's duty to 'meet Admiralty requirements as quickly as possible', while Portal, the CAS, assured the Defence Committee that he and his colleagues shared the sailors' view 'that the present situation at sea calls for substantial assistance from the Royal Air Force'.[24] By this the airmen did not mean that they were in favour of any long-term transfer of resources away from the bombing campaign against Germany and towards the fight at sea. Sinclair was quick to point out that bomber squadrons would have to be re-equipped with ASV before they could carry out long-range reconnaissance duties, and by the time that happened aircraft that Coastal

Command had on order would have arrived and the deficiency made good. He added that the effort would anyway be 'largely wasted' as enemy targets were 'uncertain, fleeting and difficult to hit'.

The real motive behind the reluctance to give Coastal a higher priority was a determination not to allow the Air Force to be distracted from what it still passionately believed to be its true purpose: a strategic air offensive against Germany that would destroy its ability to wage war. The logic was that the Coastal Command effort was essentially defensive aimed only at preventing Britain from losing the war.[25] Only offence could bring victory, and that was the job of Bomber Command. It therefore followed that Coastal should get only the minimum resources necessary to avoid defeat.

The plethora of demands came at a particularly tense time for Bomber Command. A long period of heavy losses and consistent failure had forced it into a policy of conservation while it awaited better days. It was preparing to launch a new offensive, armed with bigger and better aircraft and a potentially game-changing navigational device called 'Gee', which raised hopes that the squadrons might at last be able to find their targets. By now Churchill and the government were losing faith in the Air Staff's claims for what bombing could achieve and the whole doctrine of the strategic air offensive was in danger of collapsing. Under a new commander, Arthur Harris, the bombers were being allowed another chance – quite possibly a last one – to live up to the role the airmen had claimed for themselves. Failure would mean humiliation, and the demolition of the RAF's arguments for its own independent existence. Most importantly, it would demonstrate that what it had presented as a broad thoroughfare to victory was in fact a dead end, thereby wrecking a fundamental premise of Britain's war planning. A breakthrough was imperative, but for the renewed campaign to have any prospect of success required the concentration of all Bomber Command's resources.

Thus, the reasonable tone that the Air Staff adopted when confronted with calls for assistance from the Navy and appeals for largesse from Coastal Command was not entirely sincere. Their minds were set on proving the truth of the Trenchard doctrine. If that meant inflicting a degree of hardship and raising the level of risk on other fronts, then so be it. They were convinced they were at last capable of bombing Germany effectively. By devastating the cities which supplied the Kriegsmarine with the wherewithal to sustain their war at sea, they would do more to win the Battle of the Atlantic than diverting effort to a defensive maritime role in which they had little expectation of success.

No one believed this more fervently than Bomber Command's new chief. Arthur Harris took over from Richard Peirse in February 1942. It was Peirse's bad luck to have held the job during a depressing period of international isolation and dismal results. Harris arrived just after the planets had undergone a momentous realignment. Thanks to Barbarossa and Pearl Harbor, Britain now had mighty allies and the technical and material difficulties that had crippled the bombing effort were coming to an end.

Ruthlessness, energy, ambition and a near-fanatical faith in the power of bombing made Harris the Air Force's most aggressive wartime leader. He had a laser intelligence and razor-edged powers of expression which he used to slash at anyone who dared to challenge his arguments and appreciations. Joubert learned straightaway that he could expect no help from Bomber Command's stout overlord. Within a few months of arriving Harris had created a buzz of success. Raids on the strategically unimportant but highly flammable old Hanseatic cities of Lübeck and Rostock gave substance to the claim that the Air Force was causing Germany real pain. At the end of May he launched the first Thousand Bomber Raid on Cologne. These were propaganda successes rather than serious blows to the German war economy but they reinforced Harris's faith that 'victory, speedy and complete, awaits the side which first employs air power as it should be employed'.[26] That meant throwing aircraft against German cities, not using them as a 'subsidiary weapon' in support of the Army and Navy.

Harris's hectoring voice echoed through Whitehall and Downing Street where Churchill's door seemed always open to him. In June, he called for the immediate return to Bomber Command of all the aircraft it had loaned to Coastal, for their absence from his order of battle was 'an obstacle to victory'. A few months later Churchill supported a move to prise two bomber squadrons seconded to Atlantic duties and send them back to Harris.[27] Harris also demanded the return of all bombers from the Middle East once the situation stabilized and the recall of all suitable aircraft and crews from Army Co-operation Command. According to one of the statistics, vivid but obscure of origin that he was apt to flourish, it took '7,000 hours of flying to destroy one submarine at sea ... approximately the amount of flying necessary to destroy one third of Cologne ...'

Would the Battle of the Atlantic have been won quicker if Bomber Command's men and machines had been thrown into the fray? The question burned fiercely from the beginning, spreading well beyond expert military and political circles, and was publicly aired in the House of Commons.[28] It has flared up frequently in the decades since. The debate is unresolvable. The truth is that the inter-war theories, policies and personalities of the RAF landed it in a place where there was little room for manoeuvre. Men, machines, training and doctrine all pointed in one direction, and that was to Europe and Germany. To change course so dramatically once the conflict was launched required a root-and-branch reorganization that needed to be both physical and conceptual. The timetable of war made the feat impossible. To construct an Air Force adequate to face all the challenges that Hitler threw up would have meant putting the clock back a dozen years.

To succeed, then, Coastal Command would have to adapt, to improvise, to analyse. Joubert sought solutions in science. Despite his disparaging remarks about Bowhill's alleged hostility to boffins, he inherited from him the brilliant brain of Professor Patrick Blackett who Bowhill had appointed as his Scientific Adviser in March 1941. Blackett, who went on to win the Nobel Prize in Physics, was sceptical about the value of strategic bombing and believed that priority should be given to winning the Battle of the Atlantic. He set up an operational research unit and recruited a star team to examine all aspects of the command's work. It was supplemented by scrupulous analysis of the pattern of U-boat activities overseen by the senior naval staff officer at Coastal, Captain Dudley Peyton-Ward, who valued every scrap of intelligence gleaned from crew reports, often debriefing the airmen in person.[29] The research resulted in the issue of precise tactical drills which offered the best chance of killing submarines.

Everything hinged on spotting and surprise. To stand any chance of damaging a submarine the hunter had to catch it unawares on the surface, for the window within which an attack might succeed was tiny. It took half a minute for a U-boat to disappear into the deep, where it was all but invulnerable, no matter how many depth charges were showered on the immediate area. Even the most fractional extension of the margins increased the possibility of success. Experiments showed that camouflaging the under-surface and sides of aircraft with white paint enhanced their invisibility against the pale skies of the North Atlantic, making the German lookout's job harder. From summer 1941, the livery of the Coastal Command aircraft operating in those latitudes earned them the nickname 'the White Crows'.[30]

Tony Spooner left Northern Ireland for a hair-raising spell in Malta, before eventually joining 53 Squadron to return to U-boat hunting. He was delighted by the improvements that had taken place in his absence. The 'greatest joy ... was to be given really effective radar. No longer were we to battle with the limited ASV Mark II. Now we had a circular screen which depicted the area around as a map orientated about our aircraft ...'[31] He was now flying a Liberator which 'could fly with one or possibly two engines inoperative', fitted with anti-icing devices and a radio altimeter which reduced the old danger of flying into the sea.

U-boats tended to remain submerged during the day when within aircraft range, surfacing at night to proceed more rapidly under cover of darkness. The arrival of enhanced ASV radar gave a little more point to night-time patrolling. Even if a conning tower showed up on the screen, the target needed to be lit up for a successful attack. Bowhill had backed an initiative by Squadron Leader Humphrey de Vere Leigh, labouring in a dull personnel job at Command Headquarters, to pursue the prospect of an ASV-directed searchlight mounted in the under-turret of a Wellington. Leigh was in his mid-forties and had served as an aviator in the RNAS in the First World War. He had no technical expertise but had developed his idea after chatting with returning aircrew about their operational frustrations.[32]

Experiments in May 1941 were encouraging and Bowhill referred the project to the Air Ministry. The dossier landed on the desk of Joubert, then an assistant to the CAS with responsibility for radio. But Joubert was pursuing his own night-illumination project, the 'Turbinlite', devised by Group Captain William Helmore to guide night fighters onto bombers. The aircraft carrying the Turbinlite had to work in tandem with another which would carry out the attack. The Leigh Light seemed more promising and, after taking over at Coastal, Joubert backed it. It still took a year before five Wellingtons from 172 Squadron were fitted with the new device. By the end of the war, Leigh Light-fitted aircraft had attacked 218 U-boats by night and sunk twenty-seven of them. The beam not only made the night day but tended to blind the German gunners as the attacker moved in for the kill. 'It was no wonder that nothing very dangerous ever came our way during this vital stage of the attack,' wrote Spooner. 'We were never hit once.'[33]

These improvements heaped yet more operational difficulties on the U-boats, forcing them to remain submerged as they made their way from the safety of their massively reinforced pens on the French coast to their hunting grounds. As was the way in the most technology dependent fronts of the war, dangerous innovation by one side stimulated counter-measures by the other. German boffins fought back with the Metox radar warning receiver necessitating a further refinement that tilted the odds back in the attackers' favour.

There was no great clash of arms that brought a decision in the Atlantic. Instead it was a story of huge and unflagging effort, both physical and mental, that brought only incremental advantages. Eventually the cumulative pressure told and by the middle of 1943 the joint operations of the Navy and Air Force had turned the tide. The continuing threat did not allow any relaxation of effort and Coastal Command was in continuous action not only in the Atlantic but across the world in every theatre where British troops were present. By the end of the war, by their own efforts, they had sunk 169 enemy submarines and seriously damaged another 111.[34]

For most of the time the crews on the air and the ground carried on their duties outside the glare of the propaganda limelight which played on their fighter and bomber comrades. The names and feats of outstanding warriors like Terry Bulloch, who sighted and attacked more U-boats than any other pilot, sinking four of them, and the New Zealand ace 'Mick' Ensor, are little known outside the ranks of the survivors. As John Slessor, who succeeded Joubert, remarked eleven years after the war, they 'certainly did not get their meed of public recognition at the time; nor have they since ...'[35]

10

The Blue

On breaks from the desert, Sam Pritchard and his friends had a well-established programme of rest and recreation. They would 'collect four to six weeks' pay, then spend it within two to three days on good food, good drink and the best ... accommodation available'.[1] Arriving in Cairo from his base at Gambut in Libya, the sergeant navigator from 216 Squadron would check into his hotel and 'luxuriate in the bath for about two hours from 9.30 am onwards, during which a hotel servant brought me a succession of cold Stella beers'. Then, 'dressed in my smartest bush jacket, immaculate slacks and "brothel creepers" I rendezvoused with friends at Groppi's or the Exmorandi Bar'. They lunched on 'wonderful fresh sea-foods, covered in sliced tomatoes, cucumber and other salads' washed down with more drinks. He then repaired to the hotel for a siesta before a servant awoke him by prior arrangement with a heart-starter of a raw egg mixed with brandy which rendered him 'suitably refreshed and full of beans for another rendezvous with friends and another night on the town'.

Three days of this was enough to empty his wallet and sap his strength to the point where he was 'sufficiently shattered and flat broke to return contentedly to my tent in the desert'. He found the sharp contrast between the dangers and hardships of life at the front and the fleshpots of Cairo strangely satisfying. The return to action 'felt like a 'period of spiritual atonement and asceticism. Never again in our lives would we relish the ambrosia nor taste the nectar in quite the same way once the "desert" component had been taken out of the equation.'

Pritchard was a nonconformist minister's son from North Wales. As for many of the British and Commonwealth and Allied refugee airmen who passed through the Middle East it was his first experience of 'abroad' and he was determined to make the most of it. Although he was only dimly aware of it at the time, as well as having a great adventure he was making history. The war in the desert would turn out to be a major evolutionary advance in the life of the RAF, in which its individual capacities and strengths were bundled into a powerful, coherent whole. Pritchard and his comrades were the instruments of a great achievement, albeit one that was a long time coming. In the Middle East, the Air Force became the essential element in the Allied war effort. In the campaigns in the Mediterranean and North African desert of 1940–43 air power came of age. It was the fulfilment of a long-proclaimed prophecy, though not at all in the way that Trenchard and his followers had envisaged.

The air war in the desert had its own particular feel. It was fought in a unique environment. Navigation was easy. There was bright blue sea on one side and sand and rock on the other. The battlefield was largely empty. Apart from bands of nomads and the inhabitants of coastal towns and villages, compared to northern Europe there were hardly any civilians to worry about. The landscape and environment had little meaning. When you landed, there were no family or friends on hand to give you moral strength, nor familiar streets, cinemas and pubs to remind you what it was you were fighting for. Nor was it the homeland of your enemies, just a way station on the long journey to the end of the war.

For the airmen, the fighting never stopped. In their role supporting the Army and Navy, there was always work to do. Later, some tried to romanticize the desert air war as something clean and chivalrous, an ennobling experience. The camaraderie that was forged between the Allied forces, whether airborne or earthbound, was real enough. So, too, were exhaustion, hardship and what the Australian fighter ace Bobby Gibbes called 'violent, terrible fear'. He was 'not afraid to confess to being frightened. I was almost always terrified.'[2] Nor did he shy away from admitting to feeling its awkward corollary; the joy of survival, revealed in a passage describing his mood immediately after a combat: 'The enemy has completely disappeared. You then collect the remnants of your squadron, count them hastily, then the fires burning below. Some of the fires … contain the mutilated bodies of your friends. But as you look down you have no real feeling other than … probably terrific relief that it is them and not you … as you fly back to your base, now safe at last, a feeling of light-hearted exuberance comes over you. It is wonderful to be alive …'

Britain needed desperately to hold on to the Middle East. If Egypt fell the Suez Canal would go with it. There would no longer be a direct route to the East and the resources of the empire, and the path to the oil fields of Arabia and Persia, on which it depended for a twelfth of its needs, would be blocked. As long as Italy stayed out of the military equation, Egypt was reasonably safe. On 10 June 1940, with France staggering towards collapse and Britain looking isolated and vulnerable, Mussolini declared Italy's entry into the war on the side of what he was confident were the sure-fire winners.

At a stroke, the strategic picture for Britain changed in a way that was every bit as dismaying as Germany's lightning conquest of Norway, Denmark, the Low Countries and France. A large Italian force was parked next door to Egypt in Libya. Deprived of the resources of the French navy, the British fleet now faced the sizeable and modern Regia Marina, alone. In the air, the Regia Aeronautica was equipped with machines that were as good as those the British could muster. The threat came from the south as well as the north. Large Italian forces were concentrated in the recently conquered territories of Abyssinia and Somaliland. The British garrison had also to contend with unfriendly neighbours in the Levant, in the shape of the pro-Vichy French forces in Lebanon and Syria. To complete the strategic horror show, Britain faced the prospect of the Balkans and Turkey falling to the Axis, thus completing their conquest of the entire northern shore of the Mediterranean.

Against this, the British could dispose only forces that, in the wry words of Denis Richards, were 'exiguous even by our own standards of military preparation'.[3] Reinforcing them and supplying them would present huge difficulties. There were yet more factors that further reduced the chances of success. In the early days, the theatre commanders of Army, Navy and Air Force were subjected to constantly changing orders from London as Churchill and the service chiefs struggled to meet new menaces which always arrived much more quickly than anticipated. The atmosphere of the solitary and desperate year from June 1940 to June 1941 seemed to incubate miscalculations. Chief among them was the decision at the end of 1940 to divert major resources away from North Africa to shore up Greece in its battle against first, Italy, then Germany. At the time, the top echelon of decision-makers agreed it was the sensible and proper thing to do. It soon became clear they had blundered, ensuring a debacle that set back victory in the Middle East by years.

The RAF's Middle Eastern Command bore great responsibilities and disposed minimal assets. It covered an area of four and a half million square miles including Egypt, Sudan, Palestine and Trans-Jordan, East Africa, Aden and Somaliland, Iraq and neighbouring territories, Cyprus, Turkey, the Balkans as well as the Mediterranean, Red Sea and Persian Gulf.[4] In June 1940, its commander-in-chief, Arthur Longmore, had twenty-nine squadrons to work with, equipped with an array of inter-war-period museum pieces. The bomber force had a single squadron of the latest Mark IV Blenheims. The rest was made up of Mark Is, supplemented by Vickers Wellesleys and Bristol Bombays. The fighters were all Hawker and Gloster biplanes. In time, aircraft numbers would expand vastly. In October 1941, the Western Desert Air Force (WDAF) which supported the Eighth Army in its back and forth battles across Egypt, Libya and Tunisia had sixteen squadrons (nine fighter, six medium bomber and one tactical reconnaissance) and fielded about 1,000 combat machines. A year later, there were twenty-nine squadrons and more than 1,500 aircraft, almost all new or newish types, more than twice the number the Axis could put in the air.

To stay in the war, Britain needed the resources of its overseas territories. The manpower of the Commonwealth would be a vital source of strength. The RAF was a particular beneficiary and, of the 340,000 men who served as aircrew in the course of the war, 134,000 came from abroad. The WDAF included squadrons from the South African Air Force, the Royal Australian Air Force, the Royal Canadian Air Force as well as exile units made up of Poles, Free

French and many other nationalities. Sons of the empire were well represented at the top. Arthur Longmore was born in New South Wales. Raymond Collishaw, the Desert Air Force's aggressive chief in 1940, and according to Arthur Tedder 'the very epitome of the offensive spirit', was born on Vancouver Island to Welsh parents who came to the RAF from the RNAS where he had ended the previous war as the service's highest scoring pilot. His successor, Arthur Coningham, left a rackety family background in New Zealand to join the RFC where he became known as 'Mary'. His father was a Test cricketer and also a con man who was forced to shift the family from Australia after he was exposed trying to blackmail a Catholic priest. The nickname, according to his biographer Vincent Orange, was 'worn down from the original Maori (then thought suitable for any New Zealander)'.[5] It stayed with him, with his blessing, for the rest of his life. He is a rather intangible figure now, dying soon after the war aged fifty-three when the airliner he was in disappeared in the Bermuda Triangle. 'Mary' would be as upright as his father was louche, a near-teetotaller who disapproved of swearing, in what was a boozy, expletive-rich milieu.

Australians in particular seemed at home in the desert. Philip Guedalla, a popular historian who travelled the region at the behest of the Air Ministry, put his finger on it after a visit to No. 3 Squadron. Meeting the pilots, equipped only with out-of-date Gladiators, he was struck by their air of 'reckless willingness and capacity to do something very soon'.[6]

The war in the Middle East got off to a good start. The Italians held most of the advantages. In Libya, a 210,000-strong army, operating within easy reach of home, stood ready under Marshal Graziani for the order to cross the border. Facing them were only 36,000 British and Commonwealth troops under the Middle East Commander-in-Chief, Archibald Wavell. At sea, the Mediterranean Fleet under Andrew Cunningham now had to contend with the Italian navy without the French, whose ships were either impounded or sunk following the British attack at Mers-el-Kébir in July 1940. The Italian air force had 329 aircraft in the immediate area against the RAF's 205. In the south, British land and air assets facing the Italians in Abyssinia and Somaliland were even thinner.

Despite the imbalance in forces, it was the British and the RAF who struck first. On the morning of 11 June, eight Blenheims of 45 Squadron came in low over the Italians' main airbase in eastern Libya at El Adem, south of Tobruk, and caught them utterly unprepared. The raiders were able to drop their bombs and incendiaries with little interference. The raid was followed by another in the afternoon. Eighteen aircraft were destroyed or damaged on the ground, and a pattern had been set of British aggression in defiance of the odds that kept the Italians on the defensive.

On 9 September Graziani's army finally attacked, crossing the border and covering fifty miles in two days to halt at Sidi Barrani on the coast. The British screening force withdrew in good order to Mersa Matruh, sixty miles to the east. From their base at Ma'aten Bagush, a few miles away, the RAF for the next few months kept the Italians off balance, bombing and strafing and never attacking the same target twice in succession.

Then, in early December, the British went on the attack in an operation that, for the first time since the war began, showed the Army and Air Force acting harmoniously and effectively in unison. Operation Compass was a complete success. On 9 December 30,000 British and Commonwealth troops under the vigorous leadership of Lieutenant General Richard O'Connor swept west in two columns, cutting through the Italian defences. Two months later Graziani's army was routed and the whole of Cyrenaica was in British hands. The ground forces were supported all the way by a steadily strengthening RAF (between September and the end of the year forty-one Wellingtons, eighty-seven Hurricanes and eighty-five Blenheim IVs arrived in theatre) which kept up a constant rhythm of operations.

All elements of air power were on display, strategic and tactical. In keeping with the precepts of the Air Ministry sages, the bombers undermined the Italian ability to wage war, bombing dumps and harbours. But they also attacked shipping, airfields and anything else that seemed likely to cause the enemy pain. The fighters provided reconnaissance and air cover as well as mounting a British version of *blitzkrieg*, shooting up the enemy in the path of the advancing troops. On the ground, soldiers and airmen worked together to plan joint operations that would apply violence as purposefully as possible. The result was a triumphant display of aggression when one was badly needed, and victory came cheap with fewer than 2,000 men dead and wounded. By the end, Egypt was out of danger and the acquisition of hundreds of miles of the south-east Mediterranean shoreline greatly extended the reach of the Air Force.

Things turned out equally well in the south. Once again, on paper the situation looked bleak. The Italians had 350,000 ground troops and an all-up total of 325 aircraft. The British forces amounted to about 19,000 men and 163 old-fashioned aeroplanes, widely dispersed around Kenya, Somaliland and Sudan. But most of the enemy soldiers were Africans whose loyalty was doubtful, their air force was plagued by maintenance problems and Ultra penetration of the Italian ciphers meant every hostile move was known. The Italian advances into British territory were pushed back by a pincer movement launched from Sudan and Kenya. On 6 April, Addis Ababa fell. Five weeks later the Italians surrendered.

Once again, the key to success was close co-operation between air and ground. At the spearhead of the Kenya force was the C-in-C of the RAF in East Africa, Air Commodore Bill Sowrey, and a flight of South African Air Force biplane fighters and light bombers which provided air support as needed 'on tap'. The aircraft belonged to the past but the service they provided was a vision of the future: a joined-up application of air and terrestrial power that would eventually sweep through North Africa, Italy and north-west Europe to deliver Allied victory.

The burden of operating at such long range and with sparse resources weighed on all the service chiefs. To get anywhere they would have to show a spirit of tolerance that had often been absent from the history of their dealings to date. Longmore and Wavell worked efficiently together from the outset, prompting the Foreign Secretary, Anthony Eden, to report back approvingly from a Middle East trip in October 1940 that 'liaison between the Army and the Air Force is excellent and the RAF are giving support for which no praise can be too high, given their limited resources'.[7]

The early success, compounded by the Fleet's victories against the Italians at sea, brought great strategic advantages and laid the basis for future success. The foundation was never to be built on. Early in 1941 aircraft and armour were switched away from Cyrenaica to Greece to protect against a German attack. In February, Rommel landed in Tripoli with the first elements of the Afrika Korps. The thin holding force was no match for his rapid and unexpected advance.

All that had been won would soon be lost and the ground would have to be clawed back slowly and painfully, this time from Germans not Italians. If different decisions had been made at the top the Italians might have been cleared from all of Libya, making a German intervention much more difficult. There would have been no need for a Battle of Alamein and victory in North Africa could have been wrapped up in months rather than years.

By no rational calculation did the Greek campaign seem winnable. Yet a decision that now looks senseless at the time seemed unavoidable. There were factors in play that outweighed strictly military calculations. Britain had pledged to go to the aid of Greece, following Italy's invasion of Albania in 1939, and the war leadership felt honour-bound to keep the promise. Churchill's entire strategy depended on luring America into the war, and he feared the negative response in Washington were Britain to break its word. Until that day came, America's material support was vital to build up the Middle East air fleet.

From January 1941 onwards, Longmore was forced to send one squadron after another to mostly inadequate and inaccessible Greek airfields. At the same time, he had to scrape together aircraft to defend Malta which, from the beginning of the new year, was under attack from Luftwaffe bombers based in Sicily.

By something like a miracle, Malta survived. Nothing that the Air Force could do was likely to tip the balance in Greece. The Nazi invasion was launched on 6 April. Twenty-one days later the Germans were in Athens. There was another disaster to come. In May, after ten days of desperate fighting, British forces evacuated Crete.

The token holding force left in Cyrenaica soon crumbled when Rommel immediately went on the attack confounding British expectations that there would be no offensive before May. By the middle of June, the British line was back where it started. For the next two years, the opposing forces pursued each other back and forth across a front that stretched from El Alamein in the east to Tunis in the west. For the Germans, the campaign was a distraction, a diversion from the titanic struggle on the Eastern Front. For the Allies, it was a precursor battle that had to be won before the reconquest of Europe could proceed. A great chance had been missed, but there was something to be salvaged from the wreckage of lost opportunities. North Africa was to provide the laboratory conditions in which the formula for eventual success was worked out.

As so often in the British war, it took the shock of failure to stimulate real action. Longmore's period of command was coming to an end. He had made enemies in London as a result of a steady flow of messages lamenting his lack of resources. In the early days, there was never enough of anything – machines, men or equipment. The climate seemed benign after the uncertain British summer and fog, mist, rain, sleet and snow of the long winter but the blue skies and sunshine brought their own problems. Perspex canopies buckled in the heat and the air that the engines sucked in was often laden with sand and dust, making maintenance schedules a Sisyphean nightmare. The air filters on Blenheims had to be serviced after five hours' flying time, an operation that took three hours. The grit penetrated everywhere, creeping into instruments and jamming the hinges of variable pitch propellers so they could not move from 'fine' to 'coarse' after take-off.

Longmore appeared to be a good man to handle a daunting situation. He understood the naval perspective from his days flying with the RNAS in the previous war, and was intelligent and cunning, shifting his aircraft around to create a false impression of strength; what Philip Guedalla called his 'happy gift for "bluffing a full house with a couple of pairs"'.[8] His grasp of the political side of command, though, was weak. He assumed that London would welcome his frank appreciations of his difficulties and be anxious to do what they could to help. This was naïve. The most important recipient of his reports soon became irritated with their importuning tone. Churchill seemed unable, or unwilling, to grasp the difficulties the

Air Force faced in maintaining aircraft and claimed not to understand the gap between Middle East Command's paper strength and its operational capabilities.

Even though aircraft began to arrive in numbers in the autumn of 1940, getting them battleworthy took time and there were always a large number of machines that were unserviceable due to the difficulty of local conditions. 'I was astonished to find that you have nearly 1,000 aircraft and 1,000 pilots and 16,000 air personnel in the Middle East,' Churchill wrote to Longmore on 12 November. 'I am most anxious to re-equip you with modern machines at the earliest moment; but surely out of all this establishment you ought to be able ... to produce a substantially larger number of modern aircraft operationally fit?'[9] Churchill's testiness seems particularly ungracious given that the Middle East was the only place where there was a patch of light in an otherwise gloomy sky.

Nonetheless, he had a point. When, in the spring of 1941, Air Commodore Cyril Cooke arrived to take over as Chief Maintenance Officer he found the whole repair organization 'in a deplorable state. Accumulations of damaged aircraft were dotted about the vast Command, and there were practically no reserve machines complete in all respects.'[10] He pushed for the creation of a Maintenance Command like the one in the UK, which was eventually set up that summer under Air Vice Marshal Graham Dawson, a boyish dynamo with a domineering personality and a hatred of red tape. The existing repair and salvage unit in the desert was expanded and two more created, all fully mobile, a necessity in a constantly shifting war. At the main bases, Egyptians were hired to expand repair capacity, including recruits from the engineering faculty of Cairo University. Dawson found uses for everything. The limestone hills of al-Mokattam, on the south-eastern edge of Cairo, were honeycombed with caves excavated to supply stones for the Pyramids. Dawson had them cleaned up, floors cemented, walls whitewashed and power laid on to provide workshops for the overhaul of aero-engines as well as secure storage for 'everything from bombs to photo-paper'.[11]

Longmore's lamentations finally got him the sack. In May 1941, he was called back to London for discussions and never returned to

Egypt. If he had got the backing of the CAS he might have survived longer, but Portal, too, had turned against him. His place was taken by his deputy, Tedder, a far more subtle political operator who had warned his chief against testing patience in London.[12] Unlike Longmore, Tedder nurtured his relationship with Portal, sending him (at the request of the CAS) regular telegrams for his eyes only, giving unvarnished assessments of events, not only concerning the Air Force but all three services.

Longmore had got on well enough with the Army and Navy – indeed, his repeated assertions that they shared his dire view of the supply situation was one reason for his recall, encouraging the suspicion in the Air Ministry that he had gone native. Tedder was brilliant at managing the egos and sensitivities of his fellow chiefs, while at the same time quietly imposing the Air Force perspective on the conduct of the war.

The success of Operation Compass seemed to augur well for inter-service relations in the Middle East. The debacles in Greece and Crete and the setback in Cyrenaica ensured a resumption of the familiar crossfire of blame and recrimination. With the aircraft and aerodromes available to them and the Luftwaffe's overwhelming strength in numbers and bases it was unreasonable to expect the RAF to give anything like comprehensive protection to ships or ground troops. Nonetheless, according to Tedder, Cunningham, who enjoyed living up to his irascible sea-dog reputation, was 'prone to sending explosive messages to London about the alleged lack of air support to the Royal Navy'.[13] He also anticipated a repetition from the Army of the charges that had been levelled at the RAF following Dunkirk. While the fighting in Crete was still raging he confided to his diary: 'I am quite sure the Army will say we lost Crete because the RAF let them down. Actually, we have been put out of commission because the Army have lost all our bases for us and without bases one cannot do much ... Our fellows have been doing some incredible things over Crete these last few days, but they will never get the credit for doing the impossible.'[14]

Lord Louis Mountbatten, fresh from having his destroyer HMS *Kelly* sunk under him by Junkers 87 Stukas during the evacuation of Crete, confirmed this prediction. Tedder recounted how after being

232 · PATRICK BISHOP

buttonholed by Mountbatten in Cairo, he 'heckled me extensively on the ability of the Hun to move forward quickly and establish, and operate from, forward bases'. Tedder explained patiently that German resources in the area dwarfed those of the RAF but Mountbatten's high connections and voluble opinions threatened potential trouble.

Later, when a good working relationship was eventually established, the Middle East would be cited as a paradigm of inter-service co-operation. At the beginning, though, Tedder was often exasperated by his colleagues, particularly the soldiers. 'The Army direction here makes me shudder,' he wrote on 11 April as the Afrika Korps pressed forward in Cyrenaica. 'We have got all our reorganisation to meet a new situation practically complete and working but they are still dithering as to ... whether General So-and-so is not too junior to take command because George So-and-so is in the offing. 'Orrible!'[15] The Army's (to Tedder's mind) dismal hesitancy was on display when yet another crisis erupted in May after pro-German rebels launched a coup in Iraq. Wavell was reluctant to send a small emergency force, fearing it would be insufficient to crush the revolt, and preferred to wait until things had quietened on another front, freeing up troops for a proper expedition. Tedder recorded in his diary that 'two men and a boy could do *today* what it would require a division to do in a month's time'.[16]

These frustrations, he confided to his diary, meant that 'there are times when I nearly lose my temper with the Army'.[17] But he did not. A positive outlook, reinforced by a wryly humorous view of the world, steely self-control and a willingness to rehearse his arguments ad nauseam served him better. There was a lot to contend with. The recriminations over Crete inevitably raised the old question of whether it be better for the Air Force to be split up so that the Army and Navy could control their own air support. Eventually, sailors and soldiers would accept his argument that it was a choice between 'the feeble single stick and the bundle of faggots'.[18] Crete had proved beyond doubt 'the central fact of the war', that 'air superiority was the pre-requisite to all winning operations, whether at sea, on land or in the air'.[19] Victory required machines and men and a command and control operation that was closely meshed with the needs of the soldiers and sailors. Above all, it needed bases from which to operate at maximum effectiveness. 'This campaign,' Tedder had concluded in the early summer of 1941, 'is primarily a battle for aerodromes'.[20]

Tedder's prescriptions were given substance by a heartening improvement in RAF resources. Portal secured approval for a major Middle East reinforcement that would boost strength to fifty squadrons. In mid-May the 'Tiger' convoy docked, virtually intact, at Alexandria carrying 238 tanks and forty-three Hurricanes. At the same time, aircraft were being flown in from West Africa via the 'Takoradi Route'.

The 4,000-mile supply line across the waist of Africa was a heartening example of official foresight. Envisaging a day when Mussolini might act on his assertion that the Mediterranean was 'Mare Nostrum', an alternative route to Egypt had been mapped out before the war began. It was based on the infrastructure put in place by Imperial Airways to open a weekly civil passenger and mail air service between Lagos and Khartoum which began to operate in 1936. The RAF extended the chain to the port of Takoradi on the British Gold Coast, where ships delivered crated aircraft which were reassembled and flown in convoy, staging at Lagos, Kano, Maiduguri, Fort Lamy (in the hands of the Free French), Geneina and Khartoum, finishing at Abu Sueir, seventy miles north-east of Cairo. The first flight of reinforcements, one Blenheim and six Hurricanes, took off on 20 September 1940.

Operating the Takoradi Route soaked up nearly 7,000 men but the investment was worth it.[21] During the war it would feed more than 5,000 aeroplanes into theatre. With America's greater involvement and eventual entry as a belligerent the crates swinging off the cargo ships increasingly contained US machines – Curtiss Tomahawk, then Kittyhawk fighters, not as good as a Spitfire perhaps but the performance equivalent of a Hurricane. After reassembly, they had to be test-flown, often by pilots who had no previous experience of the type. James Pickering, a ferry pilot with No. 1 Aircraft Delivery Unit, remembered how his first briefing before climbing into a 'Tommy' was 'more of a warning than a source of useful information'. Their reputation 'had not been enhanced when the chief test pilot at Takoradi had been killed testing the first one re-erected from its crate'.[22]

All aircraft had their foibles. The Tomahawk's was a unit in the airscrew that leaked oil: 'Sand stuck to this. It covered the windscreen and quarter panels and blanked forward visibility when landing.' It also had a tendency to swing on touching down, which novices tried to correct by stabbing at the brakes, tipping the aircraft on its nose or collapsing the undercarriage.

Single-engine, single-seat aircraft made the journey in groups of six, led by a light bomber carrying a navigator and wireless operator who obtained bearings from the next staging post. The pilots were an eclectic bunch including Poles deemed too old for operational flying (among them a former commander of the Polish Air Force, Ludomil Rayski), Rhodesians and greenhorns arriving from England with only twenty hours on Hurricanes behind them. In a break with pre-war service practice the convoy leader, whose authority was absolute, was chosen on experience not seniority so a sergeant pilot could find himself commanding a flight of officers.

The five-day journey was testing, flying over hundreds of miles of thick forest or great patches of emptiness with only the faint trace of a wadi or an outcrop of rock for landmarks, where engine trouble or a navigational mistake could end in a lonely death. Sandstorms blew in from the Sahara blotting out landing grounds and electric tempests arrived suddenly out of cloudless skies, creating what Sam Pritchard, who flew the route often in a Bombay, described as 'a noisy pyrotechnic display with blood-orange haloes in front and blue flames sparking along the wings'.[23] The journey was also exciting and exotic. At Fort Lamy, giraffe-necked native women stooped over crops in the fields around the airfield. For the regular ferry pilots, there were also opportunities for illegal private enterprise. Early on it was discovered that gold purchased in West Africa fetched a much higher price in Khartoum and Cairo. All you had to do was dodge the customs and resist the temptation to be too greedy. A story did the rounds of a fighter pilot who was rumbled when his machine failed to get airborne due to the weight of gold hidden under his seat.

As Sam Pritchard discovered, snake and lizard skins involved no such difficulty. 'We found that python skins could be bought in

Kano for an average of £1 each and sold in Khartoum for an average of £2,' he wrote. This 'marvellous loot presented no weight problem when carried by air ... a bag of 100 python skins weighed so little it could be carried easily in one hand'. He and his crewmates took the precaution of arranging for a friendly wireless operator on the ground at Khartoum to deliver a coded tip-off as they approached if there was a customs van present, giving them time to jettison the loot. They never had to. He was soon accumulating £100 a trip as his share of the enterprise, but the profits evaporated rapidly in the bars and nightclubs of the city which provided 'a refuge for wealthy Arabs, Jews, Greeks [and] some fleet-footed Anglo-Saxons, as well as the most alluring prostitutes from many Middle Eastern territories'.

The Takoradi Route was only one trans-African pipeline for aircraft and supplies. The Americans set up a base at Accra which received long-range Liberators, Flying Fortresses and Marauders arriving from across the South Atlantic and fighters flown in from carriers for onward transmission as far as the Pacific theatre. From the autumn of 1941, the RAF base alongside the deep-water dock at Port Sudan in the Red Sea began assembling sea-delivered British and American fighters and American Boston and Baltimore medium bombers. They were then flown from the steamy seaside to the relative cool of the depot at Summit, in the hills sixty miles to the west, for modification to desert conditions before delivery to the squadrons.

At RAF Shaibah, near Basra at the head of the Persian Gulf, crated Bostons and Baltimores were put together for the benefit of the Russian air force. The British and Americans received no thanks for this largesse. The Russian aircrews James Pickering encountered were 'taciturn and suspicious. On arrival in Shaibah on a transport aircraft they checked the aircraft inventories and would not take the aircraft unless everything was accounted for. They wore uniform with buttoned up collar, regardless of the heat and humidity ...'[24] The RAF's encounters with their Soviet allies seldom left fond memories. Aircraft delivering supplies to Teheran after Iran was jointly occupied by British and the Soviet forces were routinely shot at by Russian flak batteries. After surviving this experience one crew were then ordered to help unload the cargo by a Russian officer.

For almost everyone, aircrew and ground crew alike, the journey into theatre was a formative part of their Middle East experience and left a strong impression. The transition from monochrome Britain to the dazzle of the Orient could be abrupt. Despite the risk from the Luftwaffe and Italians, the urgent need for aircraft meant that bombers with the endurance for the journey continued to fly in via the Mediterranean. For the ground crews the change was leisurely, a six-week voyage south through the Atlantic round the Cape of Good Hope, then through the Red Sea and Suez Canal into Egypt.

Neither route was easy. Flying meant an initial, dicey 1,200-mile hop from a southern England airfield to Gibraltar. Sam Pritchard was serving as a navigator with 105 bomber squadron when, in July 1942, the crew were summoned and told they were to deliver a new Blenheim Mark IV to Egypt. They took off from Portreath in Cornwall, the most westerly base in Britain, for the first leg. The flying time was estimated at seven hours, and the maximum fuel load they carried was for seven and a half. It was the longest trip Pritchard had ever done but he nonetheless ignored the briefing officer's advice to follow a course well out to sea, preferring to stay within sight of the coast even if it increased the risk of interception by Luftwaffe patrols. His boldness probably saved them. They struggled with a strong headwind and his pilot, Ben, 'went in straight over the harbour onto the runway with all fuel gauges registering zero'.[25] A Blenheim following immediately behind ran out of fuel just short of the runway and crash-landed in neutral Spain. The day before another went down into the sea off Cadiz with the same problem.

The sea voyage brought its own anxieties. In May 1943 Brian Kingcome was posted to Malta to lead 244 Wing. It was decided he would travel by boat rather than aeroplane, which would allow him to recuperate after a long period on ops. He travelled to Durban aboard the SS Orion, a luxurious P&O passenger liner in peacetime, now stripped of its refinements and serving as a troop carrier. The first part of the cruise was delightful: 'The weather was superb, the seas were calm [he wrote]. The flying fish flew and the tropical heat was tempered by the breeze created by our cruising speed of between fifteen and twenty knots. We were in a dream world and the grey clouds, rationed food and general shortages of war torn Britain hardly seemed to be real any longer.'[26] Then suddenly 'the dream was shattered'. Somewhere off the Canaries the on-board atmosphere changed abruptly. It took Kingcome some time to realize that the engines had stopped. 'The silence was paralysing, almost palpable ... we stood and waited wherever we happened to be on the ship, nerves on edge and sensing danger but blind to what it could be or from the direction it might come at us. Then, over the klaxon, sounded the duty officer's abrasive orders: "Boat stations!"' As they scrambled to their mustering points they heard the explanation: U-boats had been reported in the area.

These alarms were frequent in the first half of the voyage, but the threat reduced with the journey south. At Durban there was a run ashore where the local whites opened their homes to the troops. Then the fun was over as the sea miles passed and the mood of seriousness deepened as all on board prepared for whatever it was that lay ahead.

Their destination was exotic, a place that most of the passengers knew only from the *Children's Encyclopedia*, never imagining that they might see it themselves. Many were grateful for the opportunity for adventure that the war had handed to them, no matter that it came with risks attached. To young men who had never known anything but the muted backdrop of Britain's towns and countryside, and the essential order of everyday life, Egypt came as a shock. Ernest Bishop, a twenty-one-year-old fitter on his way to the main RAF base at Aboukir, was eager to get ashore when his troopship docked at Port Tewfik at the head of the Suez Canal. During the five-week voyage from Durban he and his comrades had 'seen only the sea' and their 'eyes were greedy for something new'.[27] After disembarking and being processed at a nearby transit camp, he and some friends headed off to explore the port. 'A native village lay between us and the town,' he wrote later. 'As we passed through it we were appalled by the squalor. There seemed to be no sanitation at all and the smell of the place was overpowering.' However, the men they saw lounging about 'in long white gowns were not at all perturbed by their unpleasant surroundings'. The black-gowned, heavily veiled women they passed took no notice of them. One was carrying an enormous bundle of melons and Bishop marvelled at her strength. Later, 'learning that women do most of the heavy work, I was more able to understand the Egyptian male's contentment'.

Sam Pritchard was repelled by the contemptuous attitude of the pre-war RAF towards the 'wogs' and 'sought to give them every benefit of the doubt'.[28] However, he found 'they were difficult to like and seemed to lack those qualities that I had been brought up to admire – if not always to practice – such as steadfastness, trustworthiness, loyalty, industry and courage'. The wealthier and better-educated seemed closer to the British ideal, 'but even they seemed unattractive because of their indifference to the vast majority who had nothing ...'

There was 'no great bond of affection between us and the Egyptians', and Pritchard was honest enough to understand why. Once, when walking through central Cairo he saw a teenage boy carrying a tray packed with trinkets approach a large, drunken soldier who had just emerged from the New Zealand Services Club. The Kiwi 'brought his great boot up under the tray producing a nuclear-like mushroom of combs, brushes, and other paraphernalia ...' The British passers-by, even some Egyptians, 'thought it was screamingly funny'. He concluded that 'in retrospect it was small wonder that the local populace disliked the foreigners in their midst'.

Ernest Bishop (far right) and pals

The British presence in Egypt had always been uneasy and its long history of military, political and financial interference had done much in the late nineteenth century to nurture the growth of Arab nationalism. The country had been declared a British protectorate in 1914 after the Ottoman Empire, of which Egypt was nominally a part, sided with the Germans. The British deposed the Khedive and replaced him with Fuad, a member of the same family. He was succeeded in 1936 by his son, Farouk, 'a rather fat youth in blue suiting and a gaudy tie', as Tedder described him after their first encounter, who felt bitterly the frequent humiliations he suffered at the hands of his protectors.[29] To the British he was sly and ungrateful, the epitome of wog delinquency. According to Pritchard, when at the end of June 1942 Rommel's advance had taken him to within striking distance of Cairo, his transport squadron's Bombays were fitted with bomb racks and given provisional orders to attack Farouk's palace if he decided to abandon Egypt's neutrality and declare for the Axis. Somewhat to his disappointment, the order never came.

Farouk's resentment of the British seemed to be reserved for the governing class. My father was canoeing with some friends off a beach near Alexandria one afternoon when Farouk's yacht appeared. A boat was despatched and the airmen, none above the rank of corporal, brought aboard for drinks. 'He was gracious, funny and not at all how we expected him to be,' he remembered years later.[30]

There was another culture shock in store for some of the new arrivals. The Treasury's notorious stinginess in the inter-war years seems not to have affected the living standards of the overseas Air Force. Sam Pritchard was delighted by luxurious conditions at Abu Sueir in the Canal Zone east of Cairo which opened in 1917 and had been successively a flying training school and a maintenance base. It had a cinema, a church and the accommodation for all ranks was spacious and cool. The sergeants' mess was 'what we imagined the Savoy would be like' with 'a club like atmosphere ... a spacious bar, sumptuous ante-rooms and veranda and a billiard room with two full-sized tables'.[31] The members were another matter. Pritchard and his crewmates found the peacetime NCOs 'boorish and unfriendly', apparently resenting the fact that 'it had taken them many years of service to earn the privileges of rank whereas it took the new breed of aircrew only a matter of months'. With a tour on bombers under their belts, not to mention a hazardous journey out east, they decided that 'no pot-bellied old sweat from the Trenchard era was going to deprive us of our rightful inheritance'.

The interlude was brief. For those at the sharp end of the Middle East air war, the campaign was mainly lived in the wastes of sand and rock they called 'the blue'. Control of the airspace above it was the essential pre-condition of victory. Whoever won it would be able to interdict the enemy's supply lines by sea and land, destroy his stores, attack his airfields, harass his movements and kill his troops. To carry out these operations a flexible force was needed of light bombers, fighters and tactical battlefield machines capable of destroying armour. From its establishment in October 1941 the WDAF gradually accumulated the aircraft it needed to fulfil all these roles, while engaging in daily battles with the Luftwaffe and Regia Aeronautica for air supremacy.

By the autumn, the Eighth Army was ready to try and push the Germans out of Cyrenaica and relieve Tobruk, which had been under siege since May. Everyone engaged in Operation Crusader understood the central importance of air power, not least the New Zealand Prime Minister Peter Fraser who demanded assurances from Churchill that Kiwi troops would not have to undergo the ordeal they had endured in Greece and Crete of going into battle without adequate protection from the air. Tedder's cautious assessment of the numbers of available aircraft ignited Churchill's ire. Impatient as always for action and results, he interpreted this as an indication of defeatism and was all set to give Tedder the sack.[32]

His alliance with Portal saved him. He went forward to control the whole air operation which began well before the battle proper commenced. In the five weeks before the offensive opened on 18 November, the Air Force flew about three thousand sorties. The prelude gave Tedder 'the opportunity to show what air power could do when directed from one centre in accordance with a coherent plan'. Aircraft flying out of Malta bombed Naples, Palermo, Tripoli and

Benghazi, the enemy ports of departure and arrival, and attacked convoys on the high seas. The dumps where the goods that made it ashore were stored were subjected to a continuous hammering and the supply columns to the front areas regularly harassed. These attacks on the Axis logistics kept its fighters preoccupied, reducing their capacity to interfere with the Allied build-up. Tedder was confident that, overall, the Air Force would continue to give a very good account of itself. But as he wrote to his wife, success, and his continuation in post, depended on 'whether the soldiers do their stuff'. If they 'made a mess of it again there is no question at all but that I shall be made the scapegoat'.

By the middle of January 1942 Operation Crusader had succeeded in pushing the Germans out of Cyrenaica and relieving Tobruk, but it was clear that steam was running out and there would be no onward drive to the Axis headquarters at Tripoli. It was an all too predictable performance. Despite the Army's superior strength (680 tanks with 500 in reserve against Axis figures of less than 400) and the Allies' domination of the air, success had been laborious. Tedder found that the ground-force commander General Alan Cunningham, brother of the admiral, was easily dispirited and 'fluctuated between wishful optimism and the depths of pessimism'.[33] He also seemed obsessed with his opponent, telling Tedder during a visit to the front: 'I wish I knew what Rommel was going to do.' This struck him as 'a strange outlook for the commander of a superior force'. Auchinleck, who had succeeded Wavell as C-in-C, agreed and Cunningham was soon removed.

The air battle continued reasonably well. The WDAF had the advantage of numbers, with 1,000 aircraft facing a combined German and Italian force of 320. Bad weather and the reluctance of the Axis air to gamble with limited resources meant that opportunities for attrition were reduced. When combats did occur, the newly arrived Me 109Fs and Italian Macchi C202s proved superior to the Warhawks, Tomahawks, Kittyhawks and Hurricane IIs facing them. As Tedder ruefully remarked, a 'squadron of Spitfire Vs would have been worth a lot'. Policy in London was still to reserve the latest machines for the home front and it would not be until well into 1942 that the first Spits appeared.

One of Tedder's biggest frustrations was difficulty of providing effective close support to the advancing forces. There were plenty of medium bombers available to bomb the Germans on the ground, but poor communications and the problems of identifying friend from foe meant they were never put to full use. The battle 'showed only too clearly that we had not yet learned the secrets of bombing in the battle area'.

The initial success of Crusader was short-lived. Before January 1942 was out, Rommel was attacking once again and on the 29th he recaptured Benghazi. Huge air attacks on Malta made reinforcement easier and the reinvigorated Afrika Korps swept east once again. By the end of June, Tobruk had fallen and the Germans had reached El Alamein. The battle would ebb and flow throughout the summer until the new partnership of Alexander and Montgomery finally turned the tide in October.

For the airmen, life in the blue was exhausting, uncomfortable and dangerous. The ground troops were able to benefit from occasional lulls in the fighting. For the Air Force, the action was continuous. Neville Duke arrived in the desert just in time for the start of Crusader. He was not yet twenty, tall, lean, a natural pilot and not at all happy to be there. In the autumn of 1941 he had been ensconced with 92 Squadron at Biggin Hill, flying sweeps over France by day and hitting the London bars and clubs by night, when he was told he was being posted to Egypt. The bad news came with an assurance that the stint would only be for about six weeks. He arrived at Fayoum airport, south of Cairo, on 9 November with thirteen other fighter pilots, three of whom were killed within a few weeks of arriving.

His first glimpses of the blue were not encouraging. 'Arrived at Air Headquarters Western Desert at Sidi Hannish at 4 o'clock this afternoon,' he wrote in his laconic but revealing diary two days later. 'Not very impressed with the desert at all.'[34] The following day the newcomers were briefed by 'Mary' Coningham who informed them that their job was to 'knock down the thirty-odd Me109s the Huns possess and cover the army from bombing'. Duke was joining 112 Squadron as a flight commander, together with his 92 Squadron pal Peter 'Hunk' Humphreys. The CO came to pick him up in a car but

Duke noticed he was as 'tight as an owl and I was most put off and quite unhappy'. The following day he was introduced to the Tomahawk. He found it a poor substitute for his Spitfire. After being shown 'all the knobs and buttons' he took it up for a first flight 'and promptly crashed when I landed but only got a few bruises'. By now he was feeling sorry for himself. 'If only I could get home again,' he wrote. However, when he informed his fellow 112 Squadrons that he and 'Hunk' would be returning to the UK in six weeks 'everybody laughs and it rather hurts'.

It would be three days short of three years before Duke made it back. By then he was the top-scoring fighter pilot in the Mediterranean theatre, shooting down at least twenty-four enemy aircraft in Libya, Tunisia and Italy. His first German victim was flying one of the new Me 109Fs that were generally held to be superior to the Tomahawks. 'Squadron went ground strafing along the El Adem–Acroma road,' he recorded on 22 November. 'Whizzing along at telephone wire height – some fun. Wing sweep in the afternoon. Engaged by 15–20 Me109Fs. I got on the tail of one and followed him up. Got in a burst from stern quarter and its hood and pieces of fuselage disintegrated. Machine went into a vertical dive and he baled out. Flew round and round the pilot until he landed, then went down to look at him. I waved to him and he waved back. Poor devil thought I was going to strafe him as he initially dived behind a bush and lay flat.'

Duke was a Fighter Boy paradigm: cool, efficient, outwardly light-hearted and always game for fun. But a seam of sardonic melancholy runs through his observations. The war often seems a fatal game in which you kill and expect to be killed and none of it has a higher purpose or meaning. He felt no particular animus towards the enemy. The day before he downed the 109 he was on patrol near Tobruk when two Fiat CR42 biplanes appeared. 'Attacked same with P/O X and Sgt Y,' he recorded. 'Did three attacks on one which was flying at about 500 ft. He did a few turns and then went in to land. Turned over, after running a few yards, onto its back and the pilot was out like a shot. X and Y started to shoot the poor devil but I couldn't do it, so I set his machine on fire. Went down to look at the pilot who was running with his hands up. His face was full of fear and the next time I saw him he was lying on the ground. There was no need to murder the poor devil as our troops were coming up ...' This sort of air fighting produced contradictory emotions. Duke candidly admitted that 'it is a terrific thrill to come pelting out of the sun to let rip at the Huns with the .5s. To see your bullets making little spurts in the sand in front of a truck and then pull the nose up a bit until the spurts no longer rise and your bullets are hitting home.' But he could not 'help feeling sorry for the Jerry soldier ... they run, poor little pitiful figures, trying to dodge the spurts of dust racing towards them'.

The pace of operations never slackened. On Monday 24 November, the squadron escorted Maryland light bombers on a raid near El Adem returning to their base, Landing Ground 110, to find it swamped with troops and aircraft falling back from an enemy breakout. The following day he shot up tanks and transport near Sidi Omar and took part in a wing sweep in the afternoon which ended in a fight with seventy enemy machines. There were further sweeps on three successive days. Then, on Sunday 30 November, the squadron ran into a 'circus of 30–40 enemy aircraft'. Duke managed to shoot down a Fiat G50 monoplane fighter, before he was jumped by an Me 109. He 'dodged 4–5 attacks and got in a few shots at him but he was too fast'.

'Finally he hit me in the port wing, and I think, the petrol tank. Machine turned on its back at about 500ft, out of control. Saw the ground rushing up and then I kicked the rudder and pushed the stick and prayed. Got control just in time and the machine hit the ground on its belly. Hopped out jolly quick and then darted behind some scrub and lay on my belly about 20 yards from the crash. The Hun came down and shot up my machine, which was already smoking and set it on fire. Horrible crack and whistle of bullets near me and I thought I was going to be strafed but the Hun cleared off. Started to walk across home but saw a lorry coming my way. Lay down behind another bush thinking they were Huns but as they went past I recognised the uniforms and popped up and gave 'em a yell.'

Five days later he was shot down again, and once more it was a 109 that had got the better of him and his Tomahawk. Though

wounded in the leg by shell splinters he managed to crash-land at
Tobruk, where he was patched up and sent back to Cairo in a
Blenheim for a few days' rest.

Duke never learned to love the desert. The occasional trip to a
beach, where the emerald inshore water shaded into an infinite
expanse of electric blue, or the diamond-studded brilliance of the
night skies, failed to compensate for the general misery of the
climate. It rained in winter and baked in summer. The heat of the
day was matched by the cold of the nights. And then there was the
sand which 'gets in your eyes, ears, nose, mouth, hair, food, clothes,
in fact sand everywhere …'

In the blue, things never stayed still long enough for any degree
of comfort to be established. Sam Pritchard arrived at Fuka, a satellite near the main 202 Group Ma'aten Bagush airbase in the autumn
of 1941 to join 45 Squadron. It was equipped with Blenheims and
had been given the joint task of tactical support for the Army
combined with bombing attacks on ports like Bardia along the
coast to the west where supplies for the Axis forward units came in.
'We settled down … to "life in the blue" – sleeping in tents, eating
in tents and relaxing in a sergeants' mess consisting of a wooden hut
with a few wooden or cane armchairs, collapsible card tables and its
essential bar,' he wrote.[35]

There were no camp beds. Instead he kipped down each night in
'a flattened bit of sand which we tried to shape so as to accommodate the hip and shoulder with a small amount of sand at the top
for a pillow. This sculptured shape was then covered with a water-
proof ground sheet and a doubled blanket – grey service issue of the
coarsest quality – upon which one lay with one, two or three blankets on top' depending on the coldness of the night. Pritchard
would have found the discomfort more bearable if everyone had
been in the same boat. The knowledge that officers received a 'hard
lying allowance' was 'an unnecessary and stupid source of
disgruntlement'.

They ate the same field rations they would have been given
anywhere where British forces found themselves in the world and
which made no concession to climate or geography. When Norman
Poole arrived at a forward base in Sétif in Algeria early in 1943 he

found the 'food fairly dismal ... we saw a good deal of Maconochie's meat and vegetable stew and other delights of wartime cuisine'.[36] Everything came in tins, even the bacon, and the drinking water tasted of chlorine. They supplemented the fare with eggs, bartered from locals in exchange for cigarettes. Player's – the airmen's favourite – and other well-known brands were not always available in the NAAFI. There was never any problem getting the officially issued 'V for Victory' which tasted, it was said, of camel dung and were smoked only as a last resort. The Arabs soon came to learn the difference, though they were sometimes conned into accepting them when they came disguised in a regular NAAFI pack.

On top of the other privations the sanitary arrangements were primitive. Water was always scarce. Baths, showers and hot water to shave with were a luxury. A trip to the latrines was not for the faint-hearted. The set-up in Sétif was typical. 'The screens were some distance down wind, in accordance with the field training manual,' wrote Poole. The pits 'consisted of a long but stout tree-trunk suspended in a tree fork at an appropriate height'. The spoil from the excavated hole lay at the side to be kicked in when the job was done. The airmen thought it better not to face the ordeal alone and 'rather than make a solitary trip it was customary to make up a small party or at least a pair ...'

On top of all this there was little off-duty amusement to be had. To alleviate boredom they sunbathed, played cards and bet on fights between captured scorpions. The mess – usually a stifling bell or ridge tent – lost much of its appeal when the supply of drink was unreliable. Beer – the Cairo-brewed Stella or hangover-inducing Canadian Black Label – and spirits would arrive on resupply convoys, or was sometimes flown in by enterprising crews. The South Africans benefited from a flow of Cape brandy, provided by their government. As the war moved west towards the vineyards of Algeria, rough red wine and sweet muscatel became available. The uncertainty of the flow meant that when alcohol arrived it was sometimes rationed, a few bottles of beer or tots of spirits a night. In times of abundance it did not sit around for long. Those in authority tried sometimes to dispel the reputation for booziness that hung about the Air Force but the truth was that airmen in general were a thirsty lot. Getting 'hoggers', getting 'amongst the beer' at 'pissys' and 'binges' feature with cheerful regularity in Neville Duke's diaries.

Drinking was therapy, a way of escaping the tensions, frustrations and privations. Jimmy Corbin, a Battle of Britain veteran, arrived at the Maison Blanche aerodrome in Algiers in November 1942 shortly after the US–Allied invasion. His nickname was 'Binder' due to a perceived disposition to grumble. In Algeria that winter there was much to bind about. His fighter squadron, 72, slept first on concrete floors, then under canvas at dispersal. The Luftwaffe bombed regularly and the weather was dreadful. Red wine was a rare solace. 'Got drunk on vin rouge with Chas Pryth Forde in the evening,' he recorded in his diary on 9 December.[37] Overnight it 'rained like hell again' and in the morning German bombers hit the town. 'Brassed off with moving about,' he wrote. 'Bags of mud that sticks like glue. Pushing kites for one and a half hours to make way for Beaus. Bloody tired. Covered in mud. A little wine relieves no end.'

The only real escape was a spot of leave, though a few days in Cairo was rarely restful. Off-duty airmen would dutifully visit the Pyramids and Sphinx and have their photographs taken aboard a camel. Then it was on to the city's multiple cinemas, restaurants, ice-cream parlours and, of course, bars and nightclubs. The egalitarian conditions of the blue, where officers and NCOs, aircrew and ground crew more or less endured the same conditions, did not apply in Cairo. The best hotels like the Continental and Shepheard's as well as the top restaurants and nightclubs were 'officers-only', as were most of the facilities of the sumptuous Gezira Sporting Club on the island of Zamalek. Sergeant Sam Pritchard felt the injustice keenly. As at least 50 per cent of those who flew were NCOs it 'meant that more than half of all aircrew were denied entry into decent hotels and restaurants'.[38] Such distinctions, he came to believe, could 'partly explain why Mr Churchill lost the post war election'.

He and his friend Jock got around the ban by sewing flight lieutenants' shoulder insignia on their bush jackets before they arrived in town. One evening in the Bardia, famous for its belly dancers, they 'got plastered in company with a very smart Wing Commander who was exceedingly friendly. At the maudlin stage we became buddies for life, planning to run an airline together after the war.' At this point Jock thought it safe to reveal that they were in fact sergeants in disguise. 'The Wing Commander roared with laughter and said "don't worry about that chaps – I'm only a f—— corporal!"'

There was no discrimination at Groppi's, the famous café-restaurant opened by a Swiss chocolatier in the Sharia Soliman Pasha in 1909. According to Pritchard, the founder's son Achille 'successfully resisted any attempts by the authorities to designate his establishment "for officers only" so it became a favourite haunt for RAF aircrew on leave'. He and his friends would start their day with an iced coffee in the café before moving on to the bar. They passed the evening in a 'largish room containing cocktail bars and a dancehall with a small stage for the band which could be opened out on dry balmy evenings'. For Pritchard, who had left a much-loved wife in England, the fun ended there and he stood at the bar 'watching the HQ wallahs and the Egyptians dancing with their bints'.

The city's 'Berka' district was stuffed with brothels for those who wanted them. Respectable female company was harder to find. At home the women of the WAAF were everywhere, in sizeable numbers on every RAF station, depot and facility. For the airmen they were the natural and obvious first source of friendship, sex and love. There were no WAAFs in the desert and very few in Egypt. By the end of 1942, about 200 were in theatre, all officers.[39] Local Palestinians, Greeks and other Allied nationals were hired for clerical and other trades, later reinforced by 2,000 airwomen sent out from Britain to serve all over Middle East Command.

For almost every Air Force member, as for almost every serviceman, life in the Middle East was intensely masculine. There is a sense in the diaries and memoirs that it was better that way. In Jimmy Corbin's surviving diaries covering the winter of 1942–3 there are occasional references to 'dames', 'females' and 'frippet' but his attempts to connect with them seem more dutiful than urgent. Arriving for a few days' leave with the rest of the pilots in Constantine, Algeria, at the beginning of February they soon identified the American Bar of the Casino as their watering hole of choice and noted the presence of 'loads of lush dames', but when they 'tried to get the form in the way of frippet' there was 'no joy'.[40] The following morning he 'went on a frippet hunt with Judd but no joy'. They consoled themselves with 'a hell of a session in [the] American Bar on egg flips'.

That night, at the Casino once more, Jimmy 'gazed with open mouth and a peculiar feeling in certain parts of the body at the beautiful dames'. However, looking was all he could do as 'the army seem to have the form wrapped', and the evening ended with another 'hell of a session' back in the requisitioned school where they were billeted.

The impression is of much talk but little action. One of the few recorded encounters turned out a rather melancholy business. A Beaufighter pilot described an evening spent in Naples in late 1943 in a flat in the city which the squadron officers had rented as a rest and recreation facility. 'Naples had always been well-provided with "hostesses" who were able to do a quick conversion course from German to English and the tenancy agreement seemed to include their hospitality', he wrote. On his first visit with half a dozen others, including the CO, 'a couple of the girls joined us. This was quite a novel event and we were happy to share our wine with them and help them to improve their English.' When it 'got late enough to think of bed ... the general view was that as I was the youngest – still only nineteen – I ought to entertain the youngest girl and the oldest girl was allocated to the oldest of our navigators'.

When they repaired to the bedroom the girl 'unbuttoned her dress and stepped out of it to reveal she was wearing a complicated arrangement of underwear ... a foundation garment with suspenders holding up silk stockings'. His 'limited experience' to date 'was confined to passion killer WAAF knickers and lisle stockings'. The night was not a success. In the morning before the girl left 'she showed me her family photographs. I suppose they were calculated to increase her reward – and they did – but I was not proud of myself even though my reputation on the squadron advanced considerably.'

The airmen reinforced each other's spirits through an ethos of ragging, black humour and good-natured moaning. It needed a fair amount of maintenance, and sometimes the jolly façade crumbled.

Returning from a week's leave in Cairo on 15 December 1941, Neville Duke found 'the squadron is in a very poor state of morale. Everybody has had enough of the war.'[41] The following day the CO called him in to tell him that he was sending two of the pilots who had arrived with him home 'as he thinks they have "had" it'. Duke wrote that night that he 'could have cried on the spot when I heard that, as I know I have "had" this war good and proper. Got good and drunk ...'

This frank admission from an outstandingly brave man surely reflected a wider mood. It remained hidden to the men at the top, who were perhaps not looking very hard for signs of war-weariness. At about the same time as Duke was recording his despair, Tedder visited some fighter squadrons in the blue and found 'the atmosphere among them was quite splendid ... the whole tone amongst pilots and men was grand. I felt they were a much finer body of men than those of the First World War.'[42]

Retrospective contemplation of the place of the North Africa campaigns in the overall history of the war has bathed them in a kindly light, the 'end of the beginning' where the tide was turned and victory began to feel as if it was inevitable. That was not how it seemed at the time. For those who fought in the air, as for those in the sand and rock below, the desert war was an ordeal in which progress was almost always followed by a check or setback.

The airmen spent little time discussing the wider picture or questioning the competence of the personalities directing the war. In Sam Pritchard's account, what anger they might have felt was directed at civilians. 'We were satisfied from the information available to us that the British Army and its commanders were at a disadvantage simply because their equipment was inferior to that of the Germans and to a certain extent we felt the same about our equipment,' he wrote.[43] They were convinced that 'this inferiority was due to the stupidities of politicians and pacifists between the wars'.

Whether it was immediately discernible or not, victory at El Alamein in October 1942 was a pivotal point and from then on, no matter how difficult Rommel made it for the Allies, their eventual success was assured. A few weeks afterwards, US troops landed in Morocco and Algeria. Henceforth the RAF would always be working in alliance with the American air forces. The arrangement was cemented at the top by the partnership forged between Eisenhower and Tedder. Thanks to the hard-won knowledge acquired in the desert, they took forward a methodology of combined air–ground warfare that carried them unstoppably onwards through the landings in Sicily, Italy and Normandy to victory in the West.

11

'Eat, Drink and Be Merry ...'

Arthur Harris – 'Bomber' Harris as he became known to the world, but 'Butch' to the men who carried out his orders – liked shocking people. He presented himself as a leader for times of crisis, willing to confront hard decisions that weaker men would flinch from and to face uncomfortable truths with brutal frankness.

Even those accustomed to his ways were shaken by his reaction to a drama which blew up early in 1943. A comment scrawled on the bumf that flew back and forth between the departments involved in trying to sort the matter out, summed it up: 'This seems an incredible story!' wrote Reginald Maudling, the young private secretary to the Air Minister, Archibald Sinclair.[1]

The flap over an outbreak of venereal disease (VD) among Harris's men does not merit even a footnote in the official histories, whose authors, if they knew about it, perhaps regarded it as a small and rather sordid episode in the great saga of the strategic bombing campaign. But the tale has a larger significance. The small flashbulb lights up a big picture. At the centre is the bulky figure of Harris, who loomed over the wartime RAF, blustering and intimidating. Behind him stand the men he led, engaged in the most dangerous job of the British war. The after-image that lingers is stark, a chiaroscuro revealing the grim outlines of the bomber battle. One impression endures: far from sparing a new generation from the horrors of trench warfare as its advocates claimed, strategic bombing invented an aerial version of it, and flying bombers to Germany was to the Second World War what fighting on the Western Front was to the First.

The story began late in 1942 when the Air Ministry noted a sharp rise in the incidence of VD among RAF personnel. This was a serious matter. Treatment was with Sulfonamide antibiotics (penicillin had not yet come into widespread use) and infection could put a man on the sick list for several weeks.[2] The increase was highest in Bomber Command and particularly affected aircrew members. The situation prompted Sir Bertine Sutton, the officer in charge of personnel at the Air Ministry, to alert the chiefs of the various commands and ask for comments and possible remedies. As C-in-C of the command most effected, Harris's response had particular significance. He generally took an indulgent view when attempts were made from time to time to restrain the off-duty high-jinks of the Bomber Boys. This time, his reaction was savage.

On 9 January 1943, without consulting the Air Ministry, he wrote to his group commanders pointing out that the incidence of VD among aircrews was 35 per thousand per annum, 'four times that of all other RAF personnel in the Command'.[3] He went on:

> The consequences of this are far too serious for it to be regarded with tolerance as the natural result of war. At best, it shows criminal carelessness, but I am strongly inclined to believe that this is not the whole truth and that a substantial amount of deliberate malingering is involved ... Every member of a crew who contracts Venereal Disease incapacitates not merely himself but breaks up his entire crew and I will not have the efficiency of the Command to carry on the war impaired by individual irresponsibility in this way. Still less do I propose to allow anyone who may hope to do so to gain advantage from deliberately exposing himself to infection.

He concluded with a terrible warning to anyone henceforth unlucky enough to fall victim to the 'clap'. 'In future ... it will be the rule that anyone contracting Venereal Disease, irrespective of the stage he has reached in his operational tour, will be required to start afresh and complete his 30 sorties, as soon as he is in a fit state of health so to do.'

Without any evidence, Harris was accusing airmen of deliberately setting out to get infected in order to shirk their duty. More shockingly, in order to enforce sexual discipline, he was prepared to threaten his men with what might well be a sentence of death. In 1943 the chances of surviving a standard tour of thirty operations was about one in five.[4] To condemn a man who was nearing the end of his tour to start all over again for the crime of 'copping a dose' would be seen by many as amounting to a writ of execution.

Harris sent Sutton a copy of the letter claiming that his tough policy had the approval of the Chief of the Air Staff, Portal, himself. Perhaps for this reason, Sutton's criticisms of Harris's approach were mild. As an Air Marshal, Sutton was outranked by Harris and the tone of his correspondence with him is deferential, prompted no doubt by a wish to avoid provoking the Air Chief Marshal's fury.

It took him three weeks to make contact, offering the rather lame-sounding excuse that he 'wanted to wait until I could tell you that an [American-made] film' on VD was available for showing to RAF personnel. When he finally got down to business the approach was placatory. 'I was very glad to see that you were telling all your groups to tackle the subject of prevention of the disease with vigour,' he wrote.

However, he was 'surprised to note the particular action you suggested they should take'. With a reserve bordering on timidity, he listed his reasons: 'That one ought not to make the extension of operational tours a punishment in any way … secondly that if people unfit [sic] are sent on them they will not be able to do their best in action against the enemy, and thirdly it may lead to conceal-ment and that in turn leads to the spreading of the disease.'

There is no mention of the probable fatal consequences of the policy, nor of the charge of malingering. The soft approach did not work. Two days later, on 5 February, Harris wrote back that he was 'absolutely satisfied that no other form of deterrent will have the desired effect which is essential and urgent, and moreover, that this warning, which will not be made retrospective in action, will have the effect which is intended'.

It was left to the RAF's Director General of Medical Services, Sir Harold Whittingham, to fire a shot across Harris's bow. Harris had decided that the best method of delivering the threat of a repeat tour was via station or squadron medical officers. When

Whittingham heard of the order he was concerned by what he saw as a breach of medical ethics and condemned the idea of imposing 'a punishment for contracting disease'. On 25 February, a letter was sent from the Air Ministry stating that the 'present procedure lays us open to attack both in the House [of Commons] and in the Press'. It finished with a firm order: 'If any such instructions have been given they must be cancelled at once.'

Sutton assumed that Harris had backed off and the official focus now was on tackling VD through a programme of lectures by medical officers, more explicit than hitherto, on 'the physiology of sex … including the use of condoms' and screenings on stations of a US Army film on sexual hygiene.

The flap subsided. Then, in June 1943, news of the Harris order reached the ears of Archibald Sinclair. He learned about it only after a respected Labour MP, George Strauss, began making inquiries. Sinclair was annoyed at having been kept in the dark. He seems to have shared the view of his private secretary that the story was barely credible. 'Clearly, the methods of the Commander in Chief are objectionable,' he wrote to Sutton in July 1943. Harris, it seemed, had not rescinded his letter to the group commanders. Sinclair thundered that 'it should be made clear to him that it must be withdrawn at once'.

The intervention of the political brass generated action on all fronts. Philip Joubert, now an RAF Inspector General, was ordered to come up with a plan for combating what had become officially a 'scourge'. If Harris's draconian solution was ever applied – and there is no evidence I can find, documentary or anecdotal, either way – then it made no difference. The VD rate among bomber crews continued to climb in 1943, reaching a peak in August.

Joubert's inquiry took him to fifty-three stations across the operational commands in the company of Lord Amulree, a medical doctor. The report appeared on 17 September 1943 and its central conclusion was that 'indiscipline and idleness breed infection'. Joubert's tour seems to have left him with a poor impression of the conduct of airmen in general and bomber crews in particular. His solution was to make them more like soldiers, recommending that 'all RAF personnel including aircrew, must be trained to fight under their own officers and NCOs' – advice, which like most of that proffered in the report, was ignored by the Air Council.

What is most striking about the report is the absence of serious interest in the – surely relevant and certainly fascinating – questions of *why* the rate had risen and *why* it was so marked among the bomber crews?

The obvious explanation had been hinted at by Harris in a long letter to Sutton in which he set out justifications for his harsh approach – an important document that we will return to later. Repeating a tenaciously held but totally unsupported assertion, he wrote that 'there is not the least doubt that even after giving the fullest possible rein to the spirit of "Eat, Drink and be Merry" there is the very strongest possibility of deliberate malingering'.

The phrase, which would crop up regularly thereafter, of course continues: 'for tomorrow we die'. In the summer of 1943, there was every possibility that as a member of a Bomber Command aircrew you would die, if not tomorrow then at some point before the end of your operational tour. By the early months of 1943, only about seventeen out of a hundred men were likely to be alive after thirty operations. The survival rate for a second tour was a minuscule 2.5 per cent.[5] Senior commanders did their best to keep the information secret. 'I am extremely anxious that statistical information relating to the chances of survival of aircrews in certain types of operational employment should be confined to the smallest number of people,' Portal wrote to the Air Member for Training, at the end of 1942. 'The information can be so easily distorted and is then so dangerous to morale that all possible steps must be taken to safeguard it.'[6]

Though it might take a little time to sink in, the Bomber Boys knew soon enough what they had got themselves into. For a young man, fit and adventurous, the prospect of imminent extinction provided a plausible enough motive for wanting to live whatever remained of life to the full.

In the brief space he devoted to the subject, Joubert rejected the notion that the VD surge was a reflection of the fatalism felt by young warriors who assumed they were heading to their doom. As with Harris and his charge of malingering, he trusted to instinct and does not seem to have spoken to any airmen actually involved in operations, on the ground or in the air. He concluded that 'a large number' of infections were contracted in the last phase of training, at the end of courses at Operational Training Units (OTUs) and Heavy Conversion Units (HCUs) before crews joined their squadrons.

'The natural feeling of elation' that resulted, he wrote, 'leads to excess during the period of relaxation before the serious business of war has to be undertaken.' He went on: 'I do not believe that there is much of the "Let us eat, drink and be merry ..." feeling but rather a perfectly natural desire to show off. I should have expected to find a very high rate in the operational units if the former had been the case but the facts are against it.'

It was true that Lindholme, the station with the highest incidence of VD, housed two HCUs. Medical records put the infection rate at 85 per thousand per annum. According to Joubert, 'in many cases ... there is a record of a visit to Doncaster [the nearest town], a condition of drunkenness and a return to camp without taking any

precautions. In practically no case is the name of the woman known to the infected aircrew.'

The statistics confirmed that conversion units were the worst affected with a rate of 72.2 per thousand. But the rate in operational squadrons was still considerable, at 44.6. And a salient fact was, as Whittingham pointed out, that 'the incidence of venereal disease in air crews is about four times greater than in ground personnel in the command'. Ground crews worked hard but they had fixed hours, got time off, and were just as keen on beer and skittles as the aircrews. The big difference between the two groups was that one was facing imminent extinction and the other was not.

Joubert seemed reluctant to entertain this obvious explanation for the reckless encounters which his report described. At the Air Ministry, Sutton, too, tried to treat the issue as a problem that could be resolved in a tidy, bureaucratic manner. Like Joubert, he believed that more discipline, combined with greater pastoral care and 'welfare activities and discussion groups' were the way to keep the crews on the straight and narrow.

The men around Harris at Bomber Command headquarters in High Wycombe took a worldlier view. Responding to Sutton's proposals for a programme of 'useful diversions', Harris's chief administration officer, Arthur Sanders, gently pointed out some hard realities. After consulting with the command's medical authorities, his findings were that there was 'no evidence that one station is better than another because of a higher standard of welfare or of ethical counteraction'. The fact was that 'all station commanders are trying to do everything within their powers to provide compensatory attractions in the way of welfare activities, recreation and healthy diversions so that the personnel may be induced voluntarily to stay "in camp"'. Even so, despite 'all counter attractions [being] promoted *ad nauseam*, one is forced to the conclusion that these efforts at dissuasion ... give no positive results'.

Nor was a ban on excursions to local towns a practical proposition. 'No doubt if we were to put places known to be sources of infection out of bounds, or at least put a ban on the pubs, cheap dance halls and night clubs etc., and if we controlled personal freedom and increased surveillance of promiscuity in public parks, back alleys etc., we could reduce the disease to almost pre-war level. But with what reactions!'

Young men were 'not normally very receptive of the teachings of self-control, restraint and abstinence in any form'. With aircrews, there were other powerful factors. They basked in the 'enhanced "hero-worship"' they encountered in pub, shop and cinema. But there was also the 'uncertainty of the span of life' and the 'strain arising out of the nature of [their] war occupation'. Sanders concluded that examination of the figures and taking the human factors into account '[forced] one to regard the hazard of operations as being a supreme factor in the incidence'. As far as Bomber Command HQ were concerned, then, 'eat, drink and be merry ...' explained almost everything.

One small detail from the story seems particularly poignant. The VD rate at Leeming, in Yorkshire was one of the highest but Joubert's inquiries led him to believe that the figure could well be an underestimate. He warned that '[the] figures may not be by any means the total of actual infections since it is reported that a large number of M and B tabloids [tablets] ... have been found in missing aircrews' kit,' he reported. May and Baker tablets were antibiotics used for everything from urinary-tract infections to pneumonia. The implication is that VD sufferers were not reporting sick but somehow getting hold of the necessary medication. Why they were unwilling to follow correct procedures and how they got hold of the tablets is open to conjecture. One possibility is that, having learned of Harris's directive, they sought the help of sympathetic medical officers who were willing to provide treatment off the books. In any case those few words paint a sad picture: a young airman treating himself in secret, going to his death with the vague memory of a shop-door grapple as his last, and perhaps only, experience of sex.

The founders of the RAF claimed to have invented a new form of warfare. Technology would speed things up and cut down casualties, both for the victorious and the defeated. Death was supposed to be a by-product of military action, not the primary purpose. The fatalism implicit in the VD episode, however, seems to belong to an earlier, but not that far-distant, era: it feels like the spirit of the trenches.

By the summer of 1943, the aircrews of Bomber Command were enmeshed in a terrible slogging match that, despite being fought in the air, had some of the characteristics of the struggle their fathers and uncles had endured in the front lines of Flanders a generation earlier. Their work was repetitive. Their losses, proportionately, were huge and seemingly without purpose. There was no progress that they could measure and they were forced to return to the same targets over and over again. The men who sent them there, they seldom saw.

This was not how the bomber war had been conceived but this is where it had ended up. It had arrived there largely because of the triumph of the Air Ministry doctrines that dominated the military thinking of the previous decade and the long-term planning decisions that had resulted. The fantasy of the 'knock-out blow' had been exposed almost immediately. The realization that Bomber Command was incapable of delivering the results it had promised took a little longer. As the war progressed there were constant calls for a reordering of priorities and a reallocation of air assets – to Coastal Command, as we have seen, and to meet the ever-growing needs of the Middle and Far Eastern theatres. But the bombing lobby prevailed and the investment that had been made in strategic bombing; in huge four-engine machines that could deliver the payloads to cripple German industry and fulfil the prophecies of Trenchard and his followers; and the physical and human resources to operate them, could not be unspent.

Everything about bombing was expensive; in money for the machines and bases and in time for the training of the aircrews. The Ford Motor Company in Manchester, which began producing the Rolls-Royce Merlin aero-engine, the power plant for the Lancaster bomber, in May 1941 cost £7 million to build and equip.[7] By the end of the war it employed 17,316 workers. The purchase price of a Lancaster in 1943 was £42,000, about £2 million in today's money.[8] During the war more than 7,000 were built in Britain alone as well as 6,000 Halifaxes and nearly 2,000 Stirlings.

Building a bomber station cost about £1 million (£59 million today). Bomber Command had started the war with twenty-seven, all with grass runways. In 1944, it had 128, all but two with concrete runways.[9] According to Harris, 'the education of a member of a bomber crew was the most expensive in the world', costing £10,000 (£589,000), 'enough to send ten men to Oxford or Cambridge for three years'.[10] Many of the RAF's eggs had been put in one basket. For better or worse, the air campaign against Germany was a central pillar of British strategy, and the logic was that to weaken it would undermine the whole construct.

This was the thinking that underpinned Churchill's statement of policy delivered to the War Cabinet on the first anniversary of the outbreak of the war, placing the hope of victory on the shoulders of the RAF, and in particular Bomber Command. Despite the abysmal results to date, Churchill was adamant that the way ahead was to 'develop the power to carry an increasing volume of explosives to Germany, so as to pulverize the entire industry and scientific structure on which the war effort and economic life of the enemy depend, while holding him at arm's length from our Island. In no other way at present visible can we hope to overcome the immense military power of Germany ...'[11]

It would be another eighteen months before bombing showed any signs of effectiveness. Despite this delay, the appalling losses in late 1941 that forced Churchill to call a suspension of operations until the following spring, and the huge change for the better in the strategic situation by the entry of first Russia, then America into the war, Britain's leaders stuck to the spirit of the plan. The arrival of the thirty-ton, four-engine bombers, better navigation aids, properly trained crews and a ruthless and energetic leader in the shape of Harris provided the 'power' that Churchill's speech looked forward to. From the summer of 1942 onwards the story can be told in terms of tonnages. In 1940 Bomber Command dropped 13,033 tons of bombs; in 1941, 31,704; in 1942, 45,561; in 1943, 157,457, in 1944, 525,718, and in 1945, up to 1 a.m. on 9 May, 181,740.[12] By the end of the war Bomber Command could deliver in twenty-four hours the same weight of bombs as the Luftwaffe had managed in the whole eight months of the 1940–41 Blitz.[13]

Support for the primacy of bombing was wide and deep. There was plenty of resentment from the other services and inside the RAF itself at Bomber Command's privileged status, but in the civilian world there was near-universal agreement that bombing Germany was the right and obvious thing to do. The consensus spanned the political spectrum and there were as many enthusiastic bombers on the left as on the right. The high-minded Marxist sympathizer Stafford Cripps, Minister of Aircraft Production in 1942, was a fervent supporter of bombing Germany. Another leading Labour intellectual, John Strachey, Eton-educated, a sometime Communist, joined the RAF and served as a public relations officer, broadcasting propaganda about the men of Bomber Command on the BBC.

In early 1942, there was at last something substantial to boast about. It was the raid on Cologne on the night of 30/31 May that demonstrated to the British people, the Germans and the world at large that an important shift had taken place in the direction of the air war. Every serviceable bomber, including aircraft from training units, was dragged in for the first Thousand Bomber Raid. This was the biggest air operation in history and set new records of violence, destroying 13,000 homes, nine hospitals, seventeen churches and numerous other public buildings and killing 469 people, all but fifty-eight of whom were civilians. Forty-three aircraft failed to return – just under 4 per cent of the force. These were the heaviest losses yet suffered by Bomber Command but deemed acceptable, given that the clear conditions favoured not only the bombers but also the German defences.[14]

Cologne was as much a propaganda as a military exercise. Newsreel crews were given access to briefings and filmed aircraft being bombed up. The commentaries that accompanied the reports are remarkably similar in tone and content. There are passing references to Cologne being 'of first importance to German war industry'. The overwhelming message, though, is that this is an act of retribution. The Pathé Gazette report, written and voiced by a veteran American journalist, Quentin Reynolds, started with a comparison based on his own experience of the Blitz. 'A year and a half ago I saw the Nazis concentrating their might on London,' he declaimed. 'From the clouds, hell was let loose … as the flames roared, Londoners set their teeth and took it on the chin. But it wasn't a knock out. It gave birth to a grim determination that the Germans should pay dearly for such destruction. Then at last came the Spring morning when the people of London and other blitzed cities of Britain heard that the Royal Air Force had sent more than a thousand planes over Cologne and the Ruhr, the crews having instructions to "let 'em have it! Right on the chin!" And so it was ... RAF bombers dropped big beautiful bombs, right on the centre of the Nazis' war effort. An uppercut, right on the chin, creating havoc and fear in the hearts of the foolish people who put Hitler in power ...'[15]

The punch line was Harris's. All the newsreels carried footage of him dictating a message to his crews in which he exhorted them to 'press on your attack. If you succeed you will have delivered the most devastating blow against the very vitals of the enemy. Let him have it, right on the chin!' This was followed by a warning to Germany and a statement to the world of Bomber Command's intentions, which would soon be reinforced by the arrival of the air power of the United States Army. 'Cologne, Lübeck, Rostock. Those are only just the beginning. Let the Nazis take good note of the Western horizon. There they will see a cloud, as yet no bigger than a man's hand. But behind that hand lies the whole massive power of the United States of America. When the storm bursts over Germany, they will look back to the days of Lübeck and Rostock and Cologne as a man caught in the blasts of a hurricane will look back to the gentle zephyrs of last summer ...'

It was in this appearance that he delivered his most famous prophecy, all the more effective for being delivered in tones of cold certainty, devoid of histrionics: 'The Nazis entered this war under the rather childish delusion that they were going to bomb everybody else and nobody was going to bomb them ... they sowed the wind, and now they are going to reap the whirlwind.' The biblical theme of great sins inviting greater punishment was a favourite of Harris's. The Allied air attack on Hamburg launched in the last week of July 1943 that killed 30,000 was code-named Operation Gomorrah.

These sentiments were warmly endorsed by figures accepted on the left as moral arbiters, notably George Orwell who, in a BBC broadcast after Cologne, told listeners: 'In 1940, when the Germans were bombing Britain they did not expect retaliation on a very heavy scale ... the people of this country are not revengeful, but they remember what happened to themselves two years ago, and they remember how the Germans talked when they thought themselves safe from retaliation.'[16]

It was quite clear from the coverage what 'retaliation' meant to the Germans on the ground. The British Movietone News report explained that the smoke still covering the city days after the raid had made it impossible to include reconnaissance footage of the damage. Over images of roofless buildings, the voice track continued: 'but from these pictures of previous raid results, it's easy to imagine what Cologne looks like today'.[17] A cheerful airman then reports: 'We certainly gave Cologne a good pasting today. I looked down on the target and it was nothing but a sea of fire.'

The obvious message that mass air raids produced civilian casualties produced no outcry. There were a few brave dissenters who spoke out against area bombing, such as George Bell, the Anglican Bishop of Chichester, and the Labour MP Richard Stokes. But the vast majority agreed with Orwell that the Germans had had it coming, a view that persisted even when the scale of the destruction was revealed. In 1946, the pioneering documentary maker Humphrey Jennings made A Defeated People, which showed the consequences of the Allied victory. It opened with footage of a moonscape of pulverized streets and voiceovers in a variety of accents reflecting what Britons were saying about Germany. The first says: 'They asked for it. They got it!'[18]

The name of Arthur Harris would stick to the bombing war the way that Bernard Montgomery's stuck to El Alamein. It was his good luck to arrive at Bomber Command just as it reached effectiveness. It was his misfortune to be associated forever in everyone's mind as the prime mover behind area bombing, rather than the man who carried it out. If any one senior airman bears responsibility for the policy it is Portal, who was advocating 'a definite attempt with our offensive to affect the morale of the German people' by attacks 'with the prime aim of causing heavy material destruction' as early as October 1940.[19]

Harris complained about the misattribution but accepted there was little hope of correction. Given the gusto with which he entered into his role as the scourge of Germany, it was hardly surprising that he should get the blame rather than the cool, fastidious Portal, who was as surefooted as a chamois on the slippery slopes of power and whose distaste for publicity equalled Harris's enjoyment of it.

Seventy-five years on, Harris seems an unsympathetic figure, brutal of speech and manner and apparently indifferent to the human cost of the bombing campaign, whether of German women and children or his own men. The experience of the bomber crews may have some marked similarities with the lot of infantrymen in the trenches, but Harris was no Douglas Haig. The judgement that matters most to a commander is that of his own troops. 'Butch' won the respect, even the admiration, of many. In the company of men whose emotions were strictly rationed, he could also kindle a strange sort of liking.

Bomber Boys were by and large a bolshie lot. Many of them came from social backgrounds and areas of Britain which gave them no reason to respect the established order or take for granted the good faith or competence of the ruling class. Eric Banks, a Bradford boy who completed a tour as a rear gunner with 166 Squadron, had what was in some ways a typical attitude towards his duties. Brave, resourceful and punctilious when in the air, he resented attempts to impose petty rules and restrictions on the ground and did his best to thwart them. Yet his judgement on Harris was fulsome. 'He was a figure of the highest esteem, almost affection, from his "boys",' he wrote.[20] 'I never saw the legendary leader, neither did I come across anyone else who had caught a glimpse of him. He did not tour around the bomber bases holding impromptu talks with his air and ground crews, sloganizing and entertaining his troops with light-hearted patter. Perhaps he surmised that his minions, young as most were, deserved better. From my small experience, I gained the impression that, to a man, they regarded their commander as one of their own – the highest praise of all.'

This verdict does not sit easily with some of Harris's attitudes and actions. He was opposed, for example, to setting a limit on operational tours, a practice he inherited on taking over. 'I am most unwilling to do anything to foster the idea that our crews are under some description of Trade Union contract to carry out a certain number of carefully-defined operational missions, after which they are free, at any rate for a fixed period, to take no more part in the war,' he wrote to the Air Ministry in February 1942.[21] As was sometimes the case, his habitual sarcasm disguised more nuanced thinking and a willingness to let things lie. In this case, he did nothing to alter the existing arrangement and his real point was that he thought it better to leave the length of a crew's tour for the squadron commander to decide, on the basis that he would know whether or not they had 'done their best'.

So it was with his attitude towards VD. In his letter replying to Sutton's querying of his policy of punishing sufferers with a second tour, he amplified the point made in the original signal to group commanders, and his justifications made a certain harsh sense. 'The personnel concerned must be regarded not as unfortunate individuals [he wrote] but as people who through their own action and their own carelessness ... have broken up a highly skilled and highly trained flying crew. It is not the individual but the crew that matters. These crews are first disrupted and then thrown out of gear perhaps for the rest of their tour. As a consequence, not only is the operational effort of the whole Command seriously reduced, but "patched up" crews are undoubtedly liable to suffer heavier casualties than crews who have been trained and learnt by long experience to work together as a team.'[22]

Cruel though the measure seemed, the Bomber Boys would not have denied the truth of Harris's words. The chemistry of a crew was a mysterious thing. In a brilliant display of imagination, the system allowed each team to select itself, pilot, navigator, bomb aimer and air gunners, milling round in a hangar until they coagulated into a unit in a process often described as resembling a mass blind date. Time and trial were needed to weave the web of trust needed to fly a huge aeroplane efficiently in conditions of extreme danger. The loss of one of the team for whatever reason was bad news, and, as Harris said, possibly fatal.

Norman Lee, a rear gunner with 428 Squadron, had finished three trips with his regular all-NCO crew when they were tasked with a raid on Milan. They were apprehensive about the operation, not just because it meant a ten-hour flight and crossing the Alps twice, but because their regular navigator had gone sick and they were getting a young pilot officer as a replacement. 'This didn't please us much,' he wrote, 'not because he was an officer or because we doubted his technical competence … but because it was unsettling to have a stranger flying with us.'[23]

The outward journey was uneventful and the target was lightly defended. Soon after they turned for home the trouble started. The pilot lost his way and they found themselves over Paris, where 'they gave us a dreadful pasting. The searchlights had us coned for about ten minutes while the flak gunners threw everything they had at us.' The pilot, Johnny Harkins, ended the ordeal by finding sanctuary in a cloud, and eventually they reached the Channel coast. When they eventually landed, 'two of our engines actually died of thirst as we finished our landing run'.

Lee admitted that 'it was probably a bit brutal of us, but I don't think anyone spoke a single word to the poor old navigator after we left the aircraft. There was none of that sense of comradeship that is supposed to be generated by sharing and surmounting common dangers. Or rather that was just the trouble. The comradeship existed, but it was between the regular crew and it didn't include stand-in navigators who lost the way home.'

Almost every account of the experience makes it clear that in the later stages of training and for the duration of the tour, your crew were the most important people in the universe, crowding out thoughts of friends and family; even girlfriend or wife. Often the individual members had little in common and, in other circumstances, had their paths crossed no lasting relationship would have ensued. But as Lee said, shared danger and the responsibility each man shouldered for keeping the others alive created a deep attachment, the quality of which can perhaps only truly be understood by those who experienced it.

Eric Banks considered that joining the crew of Squadron Leader Stowell was 'without doubt the most important decision I ever made'. It was a typical Bomber Command jumble of backgrounds and nationalities. All but the pilot were sergeants. Banks, the wireless operator, had been a clerk before joining up. 'Tubby', the Canadian navigator, interrupted his science studies at university to volunteer. He was 'large, with a rather vacant fixed grin'. The mid-upper gunner was 'Whitey', from Shropshire, who had lied about his age to join the RAF. Jimmy, another Canadian, was a Methodist minister's son whose 'chief interest appeared to be "chicks" with whom he went dancing on just about every free evening'. 'Red', the bomb aimer, was the third Canadian in the crew and Banks's best friend. The last to join was Ernie, the flight engineer, from the East End of London who was 'the most accomplished booze artist I ever met'. He spent every evening 'propping up the bar of some Lincolnshire pub, quietly talking to anyone around drinking one pint every twelve minutes or so, and when the evening came to an end, collecting those of his companions who had fallen by the wayside and ensuring that they reached camp safely'.

Years later he still cherished memories of 'great hilarity, much revelry and above all, the unthinking loyalty and friendship of a small group of youngsters towards each other'. The odd man out was the pilot, who Banks gives the pseudonym 'Squadron Leader Stowell'. He was thirty-six years old, ancient by aircrew standards, a pre-war regular who had volunteered for flying duties with Bomber Command. He was the son of a senior official at the Colonial Office, and 'it soon became evident that he had no idea as to how the vast majority of British citizens lived'. The other crew members regarded Stowell as snobbish and offhand, though Banks charitably excused his manners on the grounds that he could not be blamed for his upbringing. On one of their first outings, however, his attitude provoked a mutiny. While still at the OTU at Peplow, Shropshire, they were returning from a cross-country daytime trip. As they approached the base, 'Tubby' the navigator warned the skipper to gain height as they were in danger of flying into the 1,335-ft-high Wrekin, which lay to the south of the station. Stowell 'replied that this was nonsense and [it] would be another twenty minutes or so before reaching the area of the airfield. He refused to gain altitude but the matter was resolved when the Wrekin appeared.'

After landing, 'Tubby' announced that this was 'the last time I fly with that bastard'. The rest agreed. They decided to report their decision to the Wing Commander in charge of flying training. He listened sympathetically and agreed that Stowell had acted improperly. 'He was naturally loath to break up a crew,' wrote Banks, 'and asked if we would consider continuing with Stowell for the moment until he had a tactful talk with him … we rather doubtfully agreed to this [but he] must have been as good as his word as we never had further nonsense of this sort again.'

Later, while they were doing their conversion course to Lancasters at Lindholme HCU, Stowell made an attempt to be sociable, asking Banks if he might join them on their nightly excursion to the village pub. Banks agreed, though the others received the news without enthusiasm. That evening in the bar 'the customers were as usual thick on the ground. He pushed his way through to us and insisted on buying a round, although we had just been served with our second whiskies.' Banks judged that 'by and large the evening was a success. He chatted amicably with us but we learned nothing about him that we did not already know.' The experiment was not repeated, and he would never be one of the boys.

Nonetheless, when they began their tour of operations flying out of Kirmington in north Lincolnshire with 166 Squadron, the rest of the crew came to respect his courage and skill. In late July the squadron took part in a raid on Le Havre. It was an evening operation but it was still broad daylight when they arrived. 'All went well until we were nearing our target and had commenced the bombing run,' Banks remembered. He was standing in the astrodome to get a view of the heavy flak barrage when he 'happened to glance upwards. To my horror, a Lancaster with bomb doors open was positioned exactly above us and … appeared almost within reach.' The rear gunner, Whitey, had seen it too and screamed a warning over the intercom. Stowell 'could not have known just what had occurred, but he certainly knew panic when he heard it. Our aircraft was thrown wildly to starboard as the bombs hurtled past our port wing. It was a magnificent reaction and Whitey and I breathed again.'

Their relief was premature. Banks assumed the skipper would abort the operation. All the other aircraft had completed their bombing runs and were heading for home. He was astonished to hear Stowell's voice in his earphones. '"We'll have to go around again," he said conversationally. It was as if he was suggesting another round of … golf.'

270 · PATRICK BISHOP

His first thought was that 'there was no way that a sole aircraft could, in daylight, fly through that flak barrage and come out the other side without phenomenal luck. I honestly doubt that I had any great feeling of terror … Possibly I had passed the terror stage.'

With 'Red' the bomb aimer, calling directions, Stowell 'carefully handled the aircraft towards the target. He was quite oblivious to the lethal barrage and seemed no more concerned than any pilot on routine bombing range practice. "Bombs gone!" shouted Red. The aircraft banked steeply to port and in no time we were out of range of the German gunners.' Despite this extraordinary sang-froid, Banks believed there 'was nothing foolhardy about Stowell. He was just doing his job as instructed.'

Halfway through their tour the crew were told out of the blue that Stowell was being promoted and posted away to command 12 Squadron at Wickenby in Lincolnshire and they were to get a new skipper. At first this seemed like good news. Then they reconsidered. He was after all 'a competent pilot and had shown he did not panic in desperate situations … we had completed fifteen ops with Stowell and shared the dangers and worries with him and survived'. Another thought struck them. What if his replacement was 'a gung-ho type who would really be "one of the boys"'? It was a relief when a few days after his departure they received a message that 'Wing Commander Stowell wanted "his boys" at Wickenby', where they would finish their tour, with the CO occasionally flying with them.

Harris believed there were similarities between what his men were doing and the experience of serving as an infantryman on the Western Front. They showed 'the courage of men with long-drawn apprehensions of "going over the top"', he wrote in a memoir, two years after the end of the war.[24] But he pointed out an important distinction. It was 'furthermore, the courage of the small hours, of men virtually alone, for at his battle station, the airman is virtually alone'.

Bomber crews operated in a capsule. On boarding their aircraft, men merged with machines. Flying towards enemy territory in the gathering dusk it was reassuring to see what Les Bartlett of 50 Squadron observed on his maiden op, a trip to Berlin on 22

November 1943. 'At 9,000 feet, still climbing, we break cloud,' he wrote in his diary.[25] 'It is almost dusk yet all around we can see shapes, vague yet resolute, all moving in the same direction. It is rather comforting to know you are not alone in your efforts ...' On their return, as they crossed the English coast, he realized that 'we are in the centre of a great armada, hundreds of little red, green and white navigation lights – actually they've been there all the time, without lights, but of course we couldn't see them.' Once night fell, the darkness swallowed your companions who might reveal themselves only as they loomed out of nowhere on a collision course over the target area or went up in a fireball, struck by flak or a night fighter's cannon shells.

Inside the skin of your Stirling or Halifax or Lancaster speech was strictly rationed. Once an operation began, the banter and easy familiarity ended and all was grave and serious. Outsiders they met in the towns and villages near the stations where they served 'would no doubt regard us as a bunch of happy clowns without a care in the world,' wrote Eric Banks. 'They would not have recognised us if they could have seen us at work. We regarded ourselves and each other as experts, each in his own particular field. And the fooling stopped when we donned our flying kit ...'

It annoyed Norman Lee how 'in films about the war, the crews seem to chatter away over the intercom all the time about popsies, wizard prangs and all the rest of it, always using Christian names and generally giving a rather happy-go-lucky impression'. His crew 'never did this ... we always followed the procedure when we spoke to one another: "rear gunner to pilot"; "pilot to navigator" and so on. No-one was ever addressed by his first name while we were in flight, which is as it should be.'

Personality was replaced by function. It was a lonely business, especially for a rear gunner like Lee, an arse-end Charlie marooned at the extremity of the Halifax connected to his mates only by intercom. The pilot, engineer and navigator were kept constantly busy but for the others there were long periods with nothing to do. Lee boasted that he was entirely without imagination, which he regarded as an attribute rather than a deficiency in his chosen line of work for it meant he hardly ever felt fear. It also meant he suffered more than most from boredom. The business of flying did nothing for him, and it was true that the glamour of aviation soon wore after a few hours in a bomber. 'The alleged poetry and beauty of it all left me cold,' he confessed. 'Going on an op in an aeroplane was just riding to work as far as I was concerned.'

His duties were 'to report flak positions or searchlights but otherwise it was dead quiet apart from the aircraft noise. I used to sing to myself the whole way there and back.' Lee recalled that during his tour in the summer of 1943, the gunners were instructed not to open fire at night fighters unless in dire necessity. 'Shooting enemy fighters down was not what the rear gunner existed for, but bringing the aircraft back,' he wrote. 'The vital part of the job was to spot the night fighters in time for the pilot to take evasive action. Firing your guns at the enemy was only a last resort if you failed to evade him, the point being that when you opened up with your guns you were giving a firework display, so if there was another fighter in the vicinity, he would spot it and join in the party.' After seventeen ops he had 'never fired my guns in anger'.

In his determinedly unheroic memoir, Lee several times makes the point that operations could often go off without the participants feeling any real sense of danger. His first trip with 428 was to Hamburg on 2 August 1943. The weather was atrocious, their Halifax was repeatedly struck by lightning, and of the thirty-two aircraft that set off from their station, Middleton St George in Yorkshire, only a handful reached the target. Lee's crew was not one of them and instead they dropped their bombs on Heligoland. The weather kept the night fighters on the ground and the flak gunners 'couldn't do much that night except poop off a few rounds, more as a gesture than in real hope'. He concluded that 'all in all, I can't say that this first taste of war impressed me very much'. The second and third trips were not much more eventful.

Even when things livened up, Lee felt insulated from events outside the aircraft and a sense of disconnection between the bomber and the bombed. Later, when, after being shot down he fell in with the French resistance, he was able to compare fighting in the air with fighting on the ground. 'Seeing the people you are shooting at makes you dry in the mouth, especially when you hit them,' he wrote. 'Hearing the bullets whistling around your unprotected body is quite another thing from seeing flak from the inside of an aeroplane.'

Little noise penetrated the aircraft because the roar of the engines drowned out everything. 'To us the whole affair was just a silent firework display, like Cinerama with the sound turned off. The searchlights poked about the sky. The flak explosions made puffballs all round. The town below quietly burned and exploded. We were no more than spectators of it all. The only sense of reality came from the smell of cordite produced by the flak bursts, [which] came through despite the oxygen masks.'

This sense of isolation is echoed in the testimony of many Bomber Boys. They were delivering an abstract violence, turning the ground below into a boiling palette of reds and yellows, and it needed an effort of imagination to translate what they saw into dead bodies and shattered buildings. It took personal disaster to puncture the bubble. For Lee and his crew, it came on the night of 4 October 1943. They took off from Middleton St George at 17.25 to bomb Frankfurt. It was a clear evening, which favoured the night fighters who were further helped by marker flares dropped by Path Finder Force aircraft to direct the bomber stream to the target.

They were thirty minutes' flying time from Frankfurt when Lee saw a Junkers 88 about three hundred yards astern. 'I immediately told Johnny using the standard reporting procedure: "Rear gunner to pilot – prepare to corkscrew to starboard. Corkscrew starboard down – go!"' Johnny Harkins threw the aircraft into the approved manoeuvre, which involved falling away in the direction of the attacking fighter, then rolling and climbing. It seemed to be successful. As far as Lee could see, the attacker never opened fire. But 'there must have been another fighter working with him' for the bomber was raked from underneath, and both engines on the starboard fire burst into flames. Lee saw 'the starboard aileron sail past the tail and disappear. As it went, the flames from the engines were shooting past my rear turret on the starboard side. I remember Scotty the flight engineer yelling over the intercom, "the whole bloody aircraft's on fire." Indeed it was. The flames had reached back down the petrol feedlines and were setting the inside fuselage ablaze.'

Nobody panicked. Things were happening too fast for that. Harkins gave the order to bale out and it was every man for himself. Hunched in his position at the back of the aircraft Lee 'centralised the turret, opened the turret doors, grabbed my parachute which was hanging inside the fuselage' and clipped it on. He swung the turret away from the flames roaring down the starboard side and climbed onto the seat. The correct drill was to tumble out backwards but he 'didn't fancy this'. He went out feet first and a few seconds later 'there was a thump and an upward jerk on my chest and shoulders, and there I was dangling by my armpits on a cold night eighteen thousand feet somewhere over Europe ...' All the crew survived. Four were taken prisoner, but Lee and two others avoided capture. He landed near the Germany–Luxembourg border, and was sheltered by the head of the local resistance, who passed him on to the French underground. He would end up fighting with the Maquis in the South of France.

Lee was leaving the bombing war just as it was entering its most intense and costly phase. In November 1943 Harris was given a free hand to launch a series of massive raids on the German capital and other cities that became known as the Battle of Berlin. It lasted until March and aimed to prove once and for all the contention that it was possible to bring about the collapse of the enemy from the air. It was the aerial equivalent of the 'Big Push', beloved of First World War generals, and developed in much the same way. Initial success, raising hopes of a breakthrough, soon subsided. Gains dwindled as deaths rose. For those who took part in it there were none of the longueurs that Lee describes and every night there were dramas and catastrophes.

Les Bartlett arrived at Skellingthorpe in Lincolnshire to join 50 Squadron just as the battle got started. He was the bomb aimer with a crew skippered by Michael Beetham, who would gain a reputation as one of the most able and tenacious pilots in Bomber Command and end up Marshal of the RAF and Chief of the Air Staff. The life he described in his diary is one of almost constant hazard. Almost every operation, even those regarded as a 'piece of cake', resulted in significant losses. Perched in the nose of their Lancaster he had a stark view of the mayhem on the way to the target as night fighters slunk into the bomber stream, dealing death to their unsuspecting victims from below. During fourteen large raids on 'the Big City' between the middle of November 1943 and the end of January 1944, 384 aircraft were lost.[26] The campaign was a failure. As time passed, the raids became less effective and more costly. Most of the victims fell to the reorganized Luftwaffe night-fighter force which by the end could muster nearly 400 aircraft and Berlin, though battered, was still nowhere near surrendering when a halt was called.

The night of 30/31 March 1944 saw the biggest slaughter. The objective was Nuremburg, far away in Bavaria, which so far had been left off the target list. Bartlett recorded that when the crews learned their destination at the briefing, someone remarked: 'Oh this should be nice quiet stooge.' They took off at 10 p.m. and climbed to their operational height over the Channel. The first stage was uneventful. Then, wrote Bartlett, 'as we drew level with the south of the Ruhr Valley, things began to happen.

> Enemy night fighter flares were all around us and in no time at all, combats were taking place and aircraft were going down in flames on all sides. This aggravated the situation because each time a kite hit the deck a great glow lit up the area and night was turned into day making it easier still for the enemy fighters … I can remember looking out at the poor blighters going down and thinking to myself it must be our turn next, just a question of time … a Lancaster appeared on our port beam converging on a collision course, so we dropped a hundred feet or so to let him cross. He was only about two hundred yards on our starboard beam when 'crash' – a string of cannon shells hit him and down he went. The night fighter which got him must have been on our tail at the same time but with so much happening we didn't spot him.

As they altered course to approach Nuremburg, he 'looked down on the starboard beam at the area we had just passed … there were kites burning on the deck all over the place, bombs going off where they had been jettisoned by bombers damaged in combat and fires from their incendiaries across the whole area'. By the end of the night ninety-six aircraft had been lost, the largest number in a single operation in the history of Bomber Command. The catastrophe marked the close of the Battle of Berlin, but failed to shake Harris's conviction that crushing cities was a war-winning strategy.

Sharing such experiences forged a camaraderie which rendered the larger institutional identity of the Air Force remote and insignif-icant. The squadron, an important focus of loyalty for fighter pilots, does not seem to have featured greatly as an emotional point of reference for most bomber crews. A bomber station was a big, impersonal place, swarming with the two or three thousand ground staff needed to keep the fliers in the air. Each squadron had around a hundred and forty aircrew, whereas a fighter unit was a seventh of the size and there were usually two squadrons at each base. In 1943 and early 1944, when the losses were most intense, there was not enough time during the course of a tour to connect with your fellow airmen, who might be chatting in the canteen one day and vanished the next. In the six months from November 1943, during the Battle of Berlin, 50 Squadron lost nineteen crews, and only five completed a tour of operations.

Both earlier and later in Bomber Command's war, when the pace of operations was less hectic, some sort of squadron spirit had a chance to evolve and aircrew might get to know something of the character and quality of their superiors. During the darkest passage of the story, the relationship between directors and actors seems to have become more tenuous, and the crews' sense of identity tighter and more exclusive. You saw the base commander and the squadron commander at operational briefings, and perhaps when there was some administrative or disciplinary business to be dealt with, but the human scale of the enterprise was too big to allow much inti-macy. Norman Lee and his crew 'scarcely saw an officer except at briefings or debriefings'. The commanders who flew disappeared with the same rapidity as everyone else. Five squadrons lost their COs in the first week of the Battle of Berlin.

Norman Lee claimed that talk of 'squadron spirit, morale and so on' was already redundant during his tour of duty with 428 Squadron, which ended halfway through when he was shot down just before the assault on the Big City got properly underway. 'To be frank, there just wasn't any,' he wrote. 'I never cared tuppence about the squadron as such, nor did the rest of our crew. But we did care for each other and this extended to our ground crew as well.' Officially the squadron belonged to the RCAF, but all but two of those flying with Lee were British. The ground crew, however, were Canadians. 'They looked after our aircraft [only] and our confidence in them was total. Nothing, absolutely nothing, was too much trouble, and they nursed our aircraft as if their lives depended on it as much as our own.'

Aircrew and ground crew took turns inviting each other out 'on the beer', a treat the better paid Canadians could afford more easily than the Brits. Lee 'particularly wanted to point this out, not because it rankled with us but because it didn't. We were a happy group together, and if there was indeed on the squadron as a whole anything that could be described as high morale, it was within the individual crews that it was generated.'

The death rate made any wider emotional association almost impossible. In the nine weeks that Lee was in action, 428 Squadron lost twenty-one crews on operations – that is almost the entire strength of an average bomber squadron. The turnover created an atmosphere of anonymity that numbed the emotions. Lee wrote that although 'the empty chairs appeared night after night ... the truth is that in our squadron at least, it didn't much bother anyone – certainly not the crews ... my crew was scarcely on the squadron long enough to get to know anyone properly, and as a matter of fact I don't think many other people were either. Nobody lasted long enough. The disappearance of people whose names you could barely fit to their faces produced little impact. Our feelings were that the other crews were either already there when we arrived so they didn't count, or else they joined us afterwards so they didn't count either.'

Conversely, the death of a member of the group, a rear gunner killed by flak, say, was felt intensely. The only time Lee 'saw a man go to pieces' was on returning from a mid-tour leave. 'There was an air-gunner on the squadron who joined our train at York. He ought to have returned the day before but had some compassionate reason for not having done so. When we got back to Middleton St George he learned that his crew had returned on time, gone on ops that night and gone missing. He had a complete nervous collapse and had to be taken off flying immediately.'

Operational flying created a confidence in your abilities and a faith in the competence of those around you that fostered a disinclination to show unquestioning respect for superiors and deference to orders that seemed pointless or stupid. Eric Banks noted early on in his training that it was those without combat experience who most revered the rules and that the closer you came to operations 'the less the bull'. The training staff seemed to understand that 'the types volunteering for flying duties were not those who would respond with any enthusiasm to the ... theory that only those who would jump to attention when shouted at were fit to fight the Hun'.

The instructors were 'gen men' who knew the reality of what they were preparing their charges for, yet spoke little about their exploits even in the pub. 'Gen men' were the only superiors Bomber Boys were likely to look up to, officers like Flight Lieutenant Les Gray, the signals leader at Wickenby, responsible for the wireless operators and who Banks was told by his colleagues on arrival was 'the best bloke you'll ever come across'. Having completed two tours and won the DFC he need never have flown again. However, against regulations, he had taken 'every opportunity of standing in for any wireless operator, or even gunner, who happened to be unfit for flying', often managing to get the trip credited to the absentee's total. His standing was further cemented by his institution of 'periodic piss-ups' at a hotel on the Lincoln Road, where all wireless operators were welcome provided they could hold their beer.

In this self-confident ambience, where respect was hard-won, Joubert's proposal that an attempt should be made to impose something like pre-war discipline on the crews seems absurd. A less rigid mind might have concluded that such efforts were not only futile but counter-productive. Instead, as his report made clear, during his tour of the bomber stations, where others might have recognized constructive informality, he saw slackness.

On his visit to Wyton, Cambridgeshire, he was unimpressed by the conduct of Wing Commander Tommy Rivett-Carnac who had just finished leading 156 Squadron of the Path Finder Force. 'It would appear that [he] needs training in his duties as commanding officer,' he wrote. 'I was particularly struck by the number of charges preferred by the APM [Assistant Provost Marshal] against the aircrew of his squadron which were dismissed by this officer.'[27] 'I also observed that some aircrew who had bad conduct sheets were nevertheless put up for promotion as a matter of course. In other words, bad behaviour was having no effect whatsoever on their careers.'

Rivett-Carnac was twenty-eight years old, South African-born, had a DFC and bar and was about to be awarded the DSO. As a Cranwell graduate and pre-war professional he might be expected to share Joubert's opinion about the need for firm discipline. Instead he seems to have taken the view that men facing death were entitled to a bit of fun.

The resistance that the aircrews showed to old-fashioned military discipline did not reflect any lack of commitment to their task. Norman Lee, a proud member of the awkward squad, recorded how 'when we were told at briefing … "you're going to the Big City tonight," a great cheer went around the room'. Les Bartlett and his crew could not wait to start their tour of operations. 'Our luck is out,' he wrote in his diary on 10 November 1943, on learning that his crew was not on the list for 50 Squadron's trip to Modane on the French–Italian border. 'What a bind … Good shooting you lucky people!'

It was another week before they were selected. 'Tonight's the night' runs the entry for 17 November. 'You can imagine how excited we felt as we put on our flying kit and drove out to the kite to do our Night Flying Test.' Then at 2 p.m. they were told that ops had been scrubbed due to poor visibility. 'What a disappointment,' he wrote.

Then at last, on 22 November, they made their debut. 'Briefing started at 1.30 pm and what do you think? It's the Big City … Needless to say we were all very excited, because to an experienced crew Berlin is quite an assignment, so you can imagine what we felt like to be doing it as a first trip.'

Sitting in his bombing compartment after take-off his enthusiasm began to falter. 'I plug in my electric suit, make myself comfortable (if that is possible) and let my thoughts wander … I realise what we are out to do and how frightened I really am … In spite of the unsuitable surroundings I say a prayer to ask forgiveness for the murder of so many human beings by the dropping of my bombs, and also a prayer to ask for courage which I seem to lack at the moment, and for a safe flight to enable me to return to the land which I realise I love so much – to relatives and friends and to my wife who means more to me than anything in the world.'

This entry makes it clear that Bartlett was fully aware of what attacking the Big City meant for the population. Lee says that before his first trip to Berlin (on 23 August 1943), 'a ring was drawn around a sector of the city on the briefing map. The briefing officer pointed to it and said: "This is where you bomb and the next time you hit Berlin you'll bomb the area adjacent to it, and so on until the city is completely flattened."'

Lee knew 'perfectly well' that in the attacks on Berlin 'we were being sent to bomb civilians. I can't answer for all the other aircrews but as far as ours was concerned it didn't bother us. We felt the Germans had only themselves to blame. They had started it and now we were finishing it.' Once again the impersonal nature of the bombing war made that understanding easier to live with: 'It wasn't like a couple of infantrymen slugging it out with bayonets. It was just a technical job … We didn't think about the people we were killing because we didn't see them.'

After his moment of reflection on his first trip, Les Bartlett's diary records no further qualms about civilian casualties. His accounts of raids become technical and dispassionate. Describing a trip to Stettin on 5 January 1944 he wrote: 'We settled down to bomb and I did a "bang on" run up on the centre of the city. The raid was highly concentrated and kites were bombing above and below and on all sides of us. Visibility was excellent and I could clearly see whole areas of houses and shops blasted and blazing like an inferno. The place "burned like a bastard" …'[28]

He soon noticed that not everyone shared his eagerness for action. 'Ops tonight but just as we were going out to the kite it was scrubbed,' he wrote on 30 November, a week after. 'Loud cheers. The blokes just ran around in circles, dumped their kit and dashed off to town.' A few days later, after surviving a hair-raising fourth trip to Berlin (he would do ten in all), he and the crew felt the same way. 'Ops were on again but just as we were going out to the kites it was scrubbed and were we glad. We are going on leave in two days' time and feel much safer on the deck until we have had it.'

Operations brought little or no sense of progress. Eric Banks's first trip to Germany was to bomb Stuttgart, and when he left the city was swamped with smoke and fire. When he entered the briefing room the following day 'and saw that Stuttgart was again the target, I naively thought that this was rather overdoing things. From my view on the previous night I expected that the chaos below would be total and that not much would have escaped the attentions of the several hundred bombers.' This was in August of 1944. Stuttgart had first been attacked four years before, and in the first seven months of 1944 had already been subjected to six heavy raids.

In the end, the importance of each operation was that it brought you one step closer to the end of your tour and re-entry to a world where the prospect of a future could reasonably be entertained. That, perhaps, provided the main impetus to keep going. There was, of course, another force at work. The crews had no real choice in the matter. In the First World War dereliction of duty could mean a death sentence.

By 1940 the authorities had devised other deterrents for those who refused to fly on operations. There was an official reluctance to stigmatize men as exhibiting a 'Lack of Moral Fibre' (see page 139), which meant, before more humane procedures were introduced, they were stripped of their rank and placed on menial ground duties at another base. Guidelines emphasized that it was 'highly important ... to eliminate any possibility of medical disability before a member of an aircrew is placed in [the LMF] category'.[29] Between February 1942 and the end of the war, the vast majority of those who dropped out were stated to be suffering from 'neurosis' (8,402) rather than LMF (1,029).

Sometimes, circumstances forced the issue, leading to a court martial. The offence came under the heading of 'failure to carry out a warlike operation'. It seems to have been an unwelcome last resort, and only a handful of cases appear in the records. One trial, on

31 August 1943, gives a grim taste of the pressures brave men were under, and a glimpse of the harsh face authority was prepared to show when it felt an example needed to be set.[30] The case related to four sergeants of 214 Squadron based at Chedburgh in Suffolk, members of the same all-NCO crew. In the last week of July, they had undergone a succession of sticky trips. During a mass raid on Hamburg on 24/25th, an exhaust burst into flames, attracting a night fighter which they managed to drive off. On the return leg, an engine caught fire and they staggered back to base, making an emergency landing which collapsed the undercarriage. Two nights later they were sent to Hamburg again but were forced to turn back when the rear turret jammed. The following night the squadron joined the third great operation in the Battle of Hamburg. After bombing, the crew found themselves apparently alone over the city and were 'coned' in searchlights for eight minutes while flak burst all around, hitting their Stirling in the port wing and tail.

They were coned again over Heligoland, and, almost out of fuel, were redirected to land at Stradishall, the main base. It was 7.15 a.m. before they got to bed. Few were able to sleep. At 2 p.m. they learned they were on ops again that night. Four of the team told their Australian captain they were too 'shaken up' to fly that night. He referred them to their flight commander who was unsympathetic and reported them to the Wing Commander who was Squadron CO.

They explained to him they felt unfit to operate and feared they would endanger each other if ordered to fly. According to one defendant, the CO 'appeared … to have already made up his mind that we were to fly, and that was that, no matter what happened'. By his own admission, the Wing Commander hinted that they faced a firing squad if they refused, warning them: 'Do you realise the maximum penalty for this offence?' It made no difference. Although ordered to operate, they turned up at dispersal without their equipment and were arrested, charged and imprisoned in the guard house for the next thirty days.

The court martial revealed the system at its worst. There were ways to deal with such incidents which, if infrequent, were not uncommon. Flight commanders had the discretion to leave a crew off the battle order if they judged they were reaching the limit of their physical and mental endurance. One easy get-out was to treat the matter as a medical problem and refer the men to the MO. Instead, the CO was recorded in the transcript of the proceedings as having told the bomb aimer when he announced he felt unfit to fly: 'Ridiculous, man! You look all right to me.' The bullying tone of the prosecuting officer, who held the rank of squadron leader but flew a desk in the department of the Advocate General, sounds contemptible to modern ears. He put it to the crew's flight engineer, just nineteen years old: 'When you join the service, you are taught to do what you are told, whatever it may be. It is not for you to set up your own opinion against what you are told to do. Do you agree with that?'

'Yes, sir,' came the humble reply.

None of the accused was refusing to carry on with their tour, just seeking the shortest of respites before taking their place again in the line. 'All I actually needed was a night's sleep,' said the bomb aimer, a London policeman in peacetime. 'I thought I would be all right for the next night.' Instead, he and his comrades were sentenced to 112 days' detention, reduction to the ranks, and utterly undeserved ignominy. The upside was that they lived.

12

'Britain's Best Advertisement'

The shape of the war was always shifting. The flux touched everything: alliances, strategies, technologies, the ebb and flow of battle. The fixed points were the four warlords, Hitler and Stalin, Roosevelt and Churchill, seemingly immoveable above the great floods swirling around their feet.

War accelerates change. Since the start of hostilities, the RAF had raced in weeks and months through evolutionary processes that in peacetime would have taken years, expanding hugely in size and complexity so that in early 1944 it bore little outward resemblance to the Air Force of 1939. Its DNA might remain the same, but the external transformation had been as extraordinary as that of a mayfly, with the drab nymph shucking off its larval case to flutter free, fully formed and something marvellous to behold. The process had been painful and laborious but the suffering was worth it. In the spring of 1944, a year which brought real hope that this might be the last of the war, the RAF was a success that Britain could boast about.

By now it had won the good opinion of those who mattered most: the Americans. In March 1944, it was decided that the RAF would have its own public relations outlet in Washington and the Air Information Office opened two months later. The Wing Commander in charge set out its aims in a long memo. He started by saying how easy he found his current task. 'The raw material provided by the magnificent achievements of the Service and their high and constant news value has hardly needed any processing at all …'[1]

He went on: 'We cannot hope to *enhance* the prestige of the RAF. Throughout the world, it is a household word and in the United

States its reputation is so high that in some quarters it is almost regarded as something apart from, and superior to, Britain. Many people who dislike the British would not say a word against the RAF.' It was 'the service with the highest reputation in the outside world and ... therefore Britain's best advertisement'.

The Wing Commander's problem was that, with a second front about to open, the RAF's great standing might soon be eclipsed as American forces moved to centre stage. He urged his superiors 'to do everything possible to keep the RAF's share in the war from being forgotten by a fickle public'. There was much more at stake here than simply the good name of the Air Force. Underlining his words to reinforce his conviction, he urged that its fame should be broadcast as loudly as possible in order to *enhance British prestige generally and to strengthen Britain's post war authority and influence*.

By now the early days of material shortage and tactical confusion, of blunders, humiliations and debacles were all but forgotten. The bad memories had been wiped away by a record of rising efficiency and steady success, wherever the Air Force operated across the globe. The failure of the Battle of Berlin to bomb Germany into submission did not darken the picture. Harris's grandiose hopes for the campaign had never been officially endorsed and it was relatively easy to present the episode as another phase in the ongoing programme of retribution and attrition, paving the way to victory. Bomber Command was as dear to British civilian hearts as Fighter Command had been in 1940, and the size, brute force and determination of the squadrons impressed American soldiers, politicians and civilians.

The British and American air forces had been working together since the Torch landings in North Africa in December 1942. Relations from the bottom to the top were on the whole reasonably smooth. With the invasion of Sicily, then Italy, the Americans had taken charge of events, but the shift in the balance of power and status had produced remarkably little resentment or obstructionism. The Allies worked together to devise tactics to deal with a fiendishly dogged and inventive enemy. The strategy they developed would be put to good use at the next great test they faced together – the invasion of north-western Europe.

286 · PATRICK BISHOP

The RAF understood that the best way to present its achievements was with a human face attached. The Air Ministry public relations team were often pre-war professionals, with an artistic and technical understanding of what was required. It included a creative writers' unit where the likes of Hilary St George Saunders, a novelist, and John Pudney, a journalist and poet, set talent to work, illuminating and celebrating the work of the Air Force. They were imaginative and willing to take risks, investing time and trust on the basis of instinctive judgements. H. E. Bates, then relatively unknown, was given a rank, a uniform and the run of RAF bases. The result was a series of short stories, published under the pseudonym 'Flying Officer X', which presented heroism in a nuanced and thoughtful way that drew the home front and the battlefield of the air close together.

At a more mundane level, airmen toured war factories, in an effort to link the workers' labours to the progress of the war. It was summed up in a 1944 cartoon by David Langdon, showing a manager briefing a visiting pilot on how to present his spiel: 'Start off with say, a saturation raid on Kiel and then lead up to the float chamber sprocket of our Bigley Carburettor.'

The Air Force was lucky to have in its ranks personalities who were as big and powerful as the aircraft it sent over Germany. At the pinnacle was Guy Gibson, famous for leading the May 1943 Dams Raid. The PR machine moved swiftly to spin propaganda gold from an exploit which displayed Bomber Command as a precise instrument that could strike with devastating effect at the German war machine. He was sent on an initial tour of Britain before heading off in the late summer for a progress through North America.

Gibson was scarcely representative of Bomber Command pilots. He was often touchy, rude and vain, in an environment where teamwork was essential. He was as far from being a typical Bomber Boy as Douglas Bader was from being a typical Fighter Boy. Gibson's reputation has become dented with the passing years and his record as a warrior qualified by his deficiencies as a human being. Richard Morris's 1994 biography made clear the misgivings of his peers. He was a 'bumptious bastard', always straining to prove himself and poor company in a world where conviviality was a religion.[2] Those further down the ladder could take a more forgiving view. Ted Mace, an aircraft electrician, served with Gibson on 106 Squadron. In the summer of 1944 he was climbing into a Lancaster at Coningsby when 'a staff car pulled up alongside and who should be the driver but my old CO Guy Gibson. He recognized me and remarked, "Hallo! One of my old boys." We had quite a conversation ...'[3] The grieving parents of boys taken from them before they were scarcely out of school would never forget the simple, heartfelt handwritten messages he added to the pro-forma letters expressing official regret at their loss.[4]

It was this face that Gibson showed to his American audiences. He sailed for Canada with the Prime Minister and Charles Portal on board the *Queen Mary* in August and began a series of press engagements, VIP encounters and talks. Gibson could be funny and self-deprecating in public, which made the passages of earnestness all the more effective. During one interview, he was asked why he wore two watches. One was in fact a wristband, a relic of his days as a Boy Scout, but Gibson replied disarmingly that 'this one looks good and the other one tells the time accurately'.[5] The little flash of innocence is a reminder that at the time he had just turned twenty-five.

In October, he began a coast-to-coast tour of the United States. In Hollywood, he stayed with Howard Hawks, the film director and powerful industry figure who was keen on making a movie of the Dams Raid. He commissioned a script from Roald Dahl, who, after a hectic career as a fighter pilot in North Africa, Greece and Palestine, had been declared medically unfit for flying duties. He was now a press attaché at the Washington embassy and had already attracted the attention of Walt Disney with his book *The Gremlins*, malign, troll-like creatures that in RAF mythology were blamed for mechanical mishaps.[6] The Dam Busters project died when the script was rejected by Barnes Wallis who thought it absurd, to be successfully resurrected a decade later.[7]

In December, Gibson returned to Britain. He immediately tried to get back on operations but was told instead to take leave and continue his propaganda work, this time writing a book which would be published as *Enemy Coast Ahead*, a frank, powerful

288 · PATRICK BISHOP

account of his war, that is clearly mostly his own work. The attention he had received across the Atlantic had not improved him.
Displays of arrogance and petulance were noted. Arthur Harris
believed that the Americans 'had spoiled young Gibson', and the
decision was taken not to repeat the performance with another
Bomber Command hero and former 617 Squadron commander,
Leonard Cheshire.[8] There was a brief flirtation with politics when,
in February 1944, Gibson accepted an invitation to stand as
Conservative candidate in a by-election at Macclesfield – and then
backed out. His real desire was to return to the fight. His craving
only deepened when the Normandy landings came and went without him playing a part.

His superiors were unwilling to indulge him, for his own good
and for the image of the Air Force. A live hero was worth much more
than a dead one. By string-pulling and persistence, however, he
managed to manoeuvre his way back to the front line. On 19
September 1944, 5 Group were tasked with bombing three objectives in Rheydt and Mönchengladbach. Gibson was named as
master bomber, monitoring the target marking and co-ordinating
the main force bombing. The news was met with 'incredulity' by the
crews taking part. He would be flying a Mosquito, a type he was
relatively unfamiliar with, and orchestrating a complex raid with no
previous experience of such operations.

The squadrons took off from Lincolnshire at dusk. One mishap
followed another. The target marking went awry. Gibson's own
attempt to drop indicators failed when they hung up on release.
Main force aircraft were forced to loiter over the objective, increasing the risk from flak and night fighters. By the time the muddle was
sorted it was too late. The attack was scattered and one of the aiming
points went unbombed. The raiders left at 21.58. Gibson may have
orbited for a minute or two assessing results. What happened next
will probably never be known. Like Richthofen, Mannock, Ball and
other legendary airmen before him, the precise details of Gibson's
end are unclear. He and his navigator, Squadron Leader Jim
Warwick, hit the ground at Steenbergen in Holland at about 22.30.
The Germans cordoned off the area and sifted through the remains.
Gibson was identified by a laundry tag on a sock.[9]

Gibson's death was the final tragedy in what, for all the attention and glory it attracted, seems now like a sad life. Growing up, he hardly ever saw his father, whose relationship with his children was chilly even by the standards of the day, and he shrank from his embarrassing mother who sought solace from her failed marriage in drink. At his public school, St Edward's in Oxford, he failed to read the codes correctly, tried too hard to be liked and was cold-shouldered by the elite he yearned to join. He had few friends and his relationship with his actress wife, Eve, was bumpy and argumentative. The judgement of the historian Malcolm Smith, that Gibson was 'a hollow man, starved of affection … constantly trying to prove himself, truly unexceptional except for a dogged determination and a photogenic smile' seems harsh but probably not inaccurate.[10]

But, then, he never had the chance to develop a core. Gibson was just twenty-one when the war broke out, only twenty-six when he died. He had passed almost all his life in institutions, mixing almost exclusively with men. He could measure his worth only in terms of success in his trade, marked by ever more medals – a VC, DSO and bar, DFC and bar when he died – and the mounting entries in his log book. It was no wonder he was so desperate to get back on operations. The world of death was the only life he knew.

Fame was, by and large, a misfortune. It loaded another burden on men who already had enough to weigh them down. The stories of RAF celebrities rarely had happy endings. Leading Fighter Command poster boys ended up dead, like 'Paddy' Finucane and James Nicholson, the sole Battle of Britain VC, or prisoners of war like Douglas Bader and Bob Stanford Tuck.

Before Gibson, the most famous member of Bomber Command was Percy Charles Pickard. The film maker Harry Watt came across 'Pick' at a London party and asked the RAF to borrow him to play 'Squadron Leader Dickson', captain of F for Freddie in the 1941 hit drama-documentary *Target for Tonight*. Pickard stood out. Hugh Verity, who served with him, saw 'a big man, rather heavily built, with a pointed nose and very fair hair. He smoked a pipe. Whenever possible, on or off duty, he was accompanied by an Old English Sheepdog, Ming.'[11] He was the son of a Sheffield businessman who had moved the family to London. Pick was sent off to Framlingham College in Suffolk, where he was usually bottom of the class – possibly a result of dyslexia rather than inability.[12] He left school to work on the ranch of a school friend in Kenya where he revelled in riding, polo and the outdoor life. He returned to Britain in 1935 and he applied to join the Army. When they rejected him, he tried the RAF and was awarded a short service commission. By the time of the film he was already a veteran, having survived a tour of thirty-one operations flying Wellingtons with 99 Squadron, alongside his navigator, friend and comrade to the end, Alan Broadley.

Pickard was amiable and gregarious. His elder sister Helena was an actress, married to Cedric Hardwicke, a big name of British stage and screen. He and his wife, Dorothy, were happy and well matched. The attention that followed *Target for Tonight* had no apparent effect on him. In all these respects, he was very different from Gibson but they shared one thing in common: a seeming desperation to continue operational flying long after anyone expected them to.

While commanding a Czech squadron, 311, supposedly a 'rest' post, he insisted on going with them on their first raids over Germany. There followed three and a half months with 9 Squadron, in the thick of a grim period of the bomber offensive with heavy losses and few results. By the end of August, he and Broadley had chalked up sixty-four ops together, more than fulfilling their duty and entitling them to move to safer duties.

Neither grabbed the lifeline. In November, he joined 51 Squadron, tasked with high-level photographic reconnaissance. After a few trips, he was detached for a special mission. British scientists were anxious to learn the secrets of the German Würzburg radar system which they blamed for Bomber Command's heavy losses. An airborne raid was planned on the installation at Bruneval, on the heights overlooking the Channel, north of Le Havre. On the night of 27 February 1942, Pickard led the force that dropped a team of commandos on the site. The raid was a complete success. The team returned with vital pieces of the set, as well as a captured German technician, having sustained relatively few casualties.

His next posting was perhaps his most hazardous yet, commanding 161 Squadron which operated out of a clandestine aerodrome at Tempsford in Bedfordshire, ferrying Special Operations Executive agents in and out of occupied France. When Hugh Verity, who had volunteered to fly Lysanders, first met his new CO he noticed that 'though still in his twenties ... he seemed ten years older. One got the impression that he was driving himself hard and burning himself up.'[13]

When that job was finished, he was offered a safe post commanding a non-operational airfield. It was the autumn of 1943 and the RAF was restructuring to prepare for the invasion of northern Europe. The formation of 2nd Tactical Air Force combined squadrons from Fighter Command and light bombers from Bomber Command's 2 Group to create an instrument of integrated air power to support the Allied armies.

Pickard was determined to be part of it. He enlisted the help of an admirer, the 2 Group commander Basil Embry, who put him in charge of 140 Wing made up of three Mosquito squadrons based in Sculthorpe, Norfolk. Embry recognized that there was a problem with the appointment. Pickard's previous experience involved flying heavy bombers at high altitudes, or landing light Lysanders and Hudsons in French fields. The group was engaged in very different operations, screaming in at very low altitudes to hit small, usually well-defended targets. He and Broadley were a team again and Embry sent them off on familiarization trips to start with. On two occasions, they returned with significant damage to their Mosquito.

It seemed to Charles Patterson, by then a pilot with the RAF Film Unit that recorded the group's exploits, that Embry's well-meaning intervention was seriously misjudged. 'It was a wrong decision,' he said years after the war.[14] 'Embry ought to have recognised that after a hundred trips on night bombers there was no basis on which to start off a completely new career on low level daylight bombing ... not only was he operationally tired out – it's asking a lot of a man to adapt to something so completely new.' The signs of exhaustion were obvious. 'He was a nervous wreck. And he was obsessed with getting on operations but his brain was too tired to really sit down and tackle the detail ... his temper was very uncertain ... it was quite obvious that he should have been rested no matter how much he wanted to go on ...'

In February 1944, the group was tasked with a spectacular but extremely delicate mission. In the approach to D-Day, the French resistance grew in importance. They could provide vital intelligence and mount sabotage operations. German efforts to smash local networks intensified as expectation of the landings mounted. The organization in the Pas-de-Calais was hit hard with the arrest of senior figures who faced torture and death. Many were held by the Gestapo in a block in Amiens prison. Early in 1944 a local resist-ance chief begged the SOE in London to mount a rescue mission. The task was passed to 140 Wing.

The plan for Operation Jericho was bold and spectacular. The attack was timed for midday when the guards would be eating and the prisoners back in their cells. Six Mosquitoes from each of the three squadrons would attack in sequence. The first wave would blow holes in the prison outer walls. The second would take out the two guardrooms at either end of the main block. The explosions were expected to shake the cell doors off their hinges. The third wave was to be ordered in only as a last, dreadful resort. If the first attacks failed to breach the walls, the last one would bomb the prison out of existence, killing Germans, but also the French pris-oners who would no longer be able to divulge under torture any details they might know about the landings.[15]

Basil Embry elected to lead the raid himself. He was overruled by his superiors, concerned at the potential loss of one of the key plan-ners for the forthcoming invasion. He handed the job to Pickard. He would be flying with the Australians of 464 Squadron in the second wave, with the New Zealanders of 487 Squadron at the spearhead and 21 Squadron of the RAF in the rear.

The date was set for 17 February but the weather forced a post-ponement. It was no better the following day, but further delay was impossible. Pickard briefed his men at 8 a.m. at their new base at Hunsdon, Herts. They took off at 11 a.m. in a blizzard and were joined by a large force of Typhoon fighter escorts. Snow lay thick around the prison as the first wave of Mosquitoes arrived in two sections of three at a few minutes after midday, seeming to skim the ground as they raced in, dropped their bombs, then pulled up sharply to avoid smashing into the tall prison block beyond. They left behind two large breaches in the northern and eastern walls. The second wave was equally efficient, flattening the guardhouses. Pickard circled above, waiting for the smoke to clear to assess whether the job had been done. It had. There was no need for the third wave and he broadcast the signal, 'Red Daddy, Red Daddy', ordering them to head for home.

As the force turned away, the Mosquito piloted by Ian Ritchie of 464 Squadron was hit by ground fire and crashed at high speed. Ritchie survived but his navigator, Richard Sampson, was killed. Pickard was apparently checking out the wreckage when he was attacked by two Focke-Wulf 190s which had been scrambled from Grévillers airfield, thirty miles to the north-east. He managed to avoid their first attacks. Then a stream of fire blew off the Mosquito's tail and it rolled over and plunged down, crashing in flames near the village of Saint-Gratien.

It had been unwise to linger, but Pickard had not done anything wrong. His death cannot be attributed to the relative unfamiliarity of the aircraft or his inexperience of such operations. He had simply gone on too long and the odds had caught up with him. Charles Patterson later expressed regret that 'a man who'd made a stagger-ingly splendid contribution to the war was denied his future'.[16] Perhaps his fame, an unwillingness to let his public down, might have played a part in driving him back into danger. As he left no record of his thought processes it is impossible to know. One senses, though, that Pick was willingly doing what he felt he had to.

With so many of his friends and colleagues gone before, his own death must have seemed an inevitability. His mother, who was better placed than most to judge, surely got it right in the memorial notice she placed in *The Times* on the first anniversary of his death. As well as commemorating 'our darling "Boy"' and Alan Broadley, it also took the trouble to remember 'his many friends whom he was not afraid to join'.[17]

News of Pickard's death was delayed for a while and did not overshadow the success of the mission. About 400 prisoners escaped and 288 remained at large, including a key resistance leader, and the underground was able to regroup to play a part in the invasion. Inevitably, many were killed in the raid, some shot dead as they ran.

But in the ledger of war it counted as a success and a cheering one. An RAF Film and Photographic Unit Mosquito had been present and the footage was eventually played in cinemas across Britain and the free world. The commentary's praise of the 'perfect discrimination in this, one of the most difficult operations of the war' was no more than the truth.[18] It was a sword thrust in the dark heart of the enemy. The images of the smashed-up prison, swathed in smoke, and the reported sighting of men running through the breached walls were a marvellous symbol of retribution and salvation. Pickard's death was presented as a fitting end. He had 'died leading probably the most successful operation of his gallant and brilliant career' and had 'made sure the RAF paid another debt'. Further superbly executed raids against Gestapo headquarters in Denmark would follow.

The glory reflected from such feats added to the self-esteem of airmen and airwomen at every level, whether they served on the ground or in the air. The men at the top of the RAF were justified in feeling some satisfaction. Most were old enough to remember the struggles of the early years and the hostility they had faced from the soldiers and sailors. The spirit of resentment had not entirely disappeared. In the middle years of the war, in the constant battle for resources, it was usually the RAF which came out on top. The aerial war 'was given priority in materials, facilities for aircraft production and men for aircrew and technical needs'.[19] To the politicians, the Air Force represented value, delivering military results and boosting domestic morale, but also maintaining Britain's standing with the all-important Americans.

It had gone into the war armed with inadequate aircraft and no real understanding of how air power worked. The shock of combat had tested its organization, training methods and fighting techniques, sometimes close to the point of destruction, but it had emerged from each crisis tougher and wiser. Now it had the best machines in the air, a magnificent cadre of well-trained men to operate them, and drills to deal with most eventualities of battle. Luck, inevitably, played a part in the success story. But so, too, did judgement and the quality of the high command. Hectic expansion was possible because of the organizational framework put in place by Trenchard. The great improvement in aircraft was due to shrewd decisions by unsung planners whose names would never be known to the public and in technology to backroom players willing to try anything that offered a chance of success. Human resources were equally well managed, particularly the supply of aircrew, thanks to the foresight shown in schemes like the British Commonwealth Air Training Plan which trained nearly half the pilots, navigators, flight engineers, wireless operators, bomb aimers and air gunners who flew under the RAF standard in the war, in overseas flying schools, most of them in southern Africa and Canada.

After some initial hesitation on the part of Canada, the Dominions had made an extraordinarily generous response to Britain's predicament, and the Air Force had reason to be particularly thankful for their solidarity. The term 'RAF' is used routinely in this book but it is shorthand for what was in many ways an umbrella organization, providing an operational and administrative system covering elements of the Royal Australian, Royal Canadian, Royal New Zealand and South African Air Forces. Of the 487 squadrons in the RAF order of battle in June 1944, 100 were provided by the Dominions (forty-two by Canada, twenty-seven by South Africa, sixteen by Australia, nine by India and six by New Zealand).[20] In addition, there were many Dominion citizens serving in strictly RAF units. Of the 340,000 who served as aircrew in the Second World War, 134,000 men came from British overseas territories. Then there were the airmen from the conquered territories of Europe, the Poles, Czechs, French, Norwegians, Belgians, Dutch, Greeks and Yugoslavs. Their contribution was more than a token. The Poles had fourteen squadrons and 15,000 men in the RAF, which included their own ground staff.

Such a diverse force needed a strong identity to glue it together. The essential element was a sense of belonging to a worthwhile enterprise. In the participants' diaries, letters and memoirs there is a marked pride in their service. RAF life brought a degree of satisfaction that was perhaps harder to find elsewhere. In Bomber Command, despite the paucity of measurable progress, it was a feeling, expressed over and over again, that you were 'taking the fight to the enemy'. That meant striking back, exacting revenge, and perhaps bringing the end of the war a tiny bit closer. Bomber Command and Fighter Command had an intimate relationship with the enemy (Coastal less so). The violence they inflicted was direct and produced instant, if not necessarily lasting, results. In the spring of 1944, the RAF felt it was on the path to victory. As the snot froze in his nostrils, an able seaman looking out at the ice floes of the Arctic from the deck of HMS *Belfast* had been told often enough that if his convoy got through to Arkhangelsk or Murmansk he was making a real contribution to the war effort, but it probably did not seem much like it. A private in the Durham Light Infantry staring up at the peaks of the Gustav Line understood his courage was a factor in the drive to Rome, but what effort would be required for such minuscule observable gain!

Looking down from his Perspex perch in the nose of a Lancaster at the carpet of reds and yellows bubbling below, the bomb aimer knew that he was hurting Germany. Strangely, for all the repetition there was in the work described in Bomber Boys' accounts, a sense of futility is only rarely encountered. In the air war, effort and effect were almost instantaneous, as the cine-camera footage from operations makes dramatically clear. One can feel, at close second hand, the joy of a Coastal Command Wellington crew as their depth charges split the sea around a surfaced U-boat, or the savage thrill of pressing the firing button on the control column of a Typhoon and sending rockets snaking into a line of German trucks.

Many participants often claimed there was nothing personal about the violence. A typical voice was that of Andrew Hendrie, who flew with Coastal Command from 1942 to 1945 and later wrote its history.

'Coastal Command aircrew were concerned not with killing men but with sinking U-boats,' he wrote.[21] Others showed less detachment. Revenge was in the mix of motives. Writing to the parents of Flight Lieutenant Gray Healey, who was shot down by a night fighter during a raid on Essen in January 1943 and killed with the rest of the crew, Guy Gibson told them they could 'rest assured that the boys and I will hit those Huns even harder for doing this to you'.[22] Norman Lee volunteered for Bomber Command largely because his twin brother had done so. While he was still training, he heard that his Lancaster had failed to return from a raid on Wilhelmshaven. 'Although I felt deeply about my brother's death,' he wrote, 'it never occurred to me not to go on flying – rather the reverse. I wanted to get my own back.'[23]

After the Blitz, finer feelings evaporated. One day in the summer of 1941, Charles Patterson caught sight of the human face of the enemy. He had been sent with 114 Squadron on a daylight raid on the Knapsack power station near Cologne. It was a particularly risky operation and he set off with little hope of returning. He was in good spirits as they scudded home unscathed over the flat land near the German–Dutch border. He remembered flying 'on and on over these fields, past little villages and hamlets, the occasional individual diving into a ditch beneath us. Then just before we got to the German border, we flew over a typical German industrialist's Victorian semi-baronial mansion with turrets and things, and a garden … I just got a glimpse beside a cedar tree of a table, large white tablecloth, all laid out for lunch … and a group of people standing round it.

'As we whizzed over the top of this my gunner let fly and broke up the party. He felt that any rich Germans who were living like that … deserved to be shot … that sounds appalling, but at the time it seemed right and proper.'[24]

There were uplifting encounters, too, with people on the ground that reminded Patterson what the war was about. Flying back and forth over Holland as a Film Unit Mosquito pilot accompanying raids, 'a very interesting thing used to happen … when they heard these low-flying aircraft coming towards them they knew they were probably British … the Dutch country people used to run to the doors of their little houses and cottages and open and shut the door so they signalled a flashing light towards us of welcome. It was a very wonderful thing to see them doing this when one realised the terrible risks they were running in doing something that was purely a human gesture. It wasn't of any military value. They weren't damaging the enemy in any way. They were just risking their lives to do no more than wave us a greeting.'

It was the fliers who derived the most fulfilment from their work and who reaped the benefits that flowed from an admiring and thankful nation. A slate-blue uniform with an aircrew brevet meant free drinks in pubs and a privileged claim on female attention in bar, cinema queue and dance hall. Even the Yanks could not compete. Early in 1943, Norman Poole, a Beaufighter navigator, and his pilot friend Archie Mackinnon were on their way to Bristol to pick up a brand-new aircraft when they stopped at Swindon to change trains. A long wait was expected so they headed off in search of a pub. 'At one of the tables were four girls and about half a dozen US servicemen entertaining them,' he remembered.[25] The Americans had already 'established a commanding lead over British service-men in terms of pay, smoothness of uniform and delicious, ration-free goods'. They were also a source of nylon stockings, 'the key to a girl's heart and often a few other closely guarded treasures as well'.

Although Poole and Mackinnon 'didn't have nylons, we had an advantage that others didn't possess. We had "Wings"! We were still the glamour boys of the services and you couldn't blame us for trading on it.' They managed to get a message to the girls that they would 'love to see them outside if they could make their escape. I don't know how they managed it, perhaps a combined expedition to the toilet, but they got away and we joined up not only for another pub but one of them lived nearby ... we got the Bristol train early next morning.'

For the four-fifths of the Air Force who never took to the skies, there was a share of the glory that reflected from the deeds of the aircrews. A squadron fitter or rigger had a relationship with an aeroplane, a pilot or a crew, that connected him with the struggle and gave him a stake in it. The pride that this generated – and the anger if it was felt that their effort was not being valued as it should – were revealed in a report to Mass Observation by the writer Roderic Papineau who, in the summer of 1941, was serving as a leading aircraftman with 256 Squadron, a night-fighter unit based at Squires Gate near Blackpool. He gave a verbatim account of a conversation with Corporal Crump, an 'expert maintenance fitter' who serviced the unit's Defiants. Crump explained that job satisfaction depended on a feeling that his labours had been worth it. When working on the Hurricanes of 111 Squadron at Croydon during the Battle of Britain his experience had been that 'you work on a kite carefully, sweat your guts out and then see it go up, dive on a formation of Jerries and actually watch three or four of them crashing all over the place as a result of your work ... you really feel keen. Next time that kite comes to your hangar for repair or a sixty-hour inspection, you turn her out shit-hot, every nut and bolt an absolute cert.'[26] Nowadays, he found, 'you don't get that incentive. Take "M" for instance. I'd just finished a thirty hour on that machine, taken the whole engine down and worked nearly a hundred hours to get the kite running sweet. Then some half-pissed idiot lands her 30 mph too fast and busts up the whole issue, probably joking about it in some mock-heroic way. I tell you, you don't feel keen on maintenance work unless the pilots are doing something worthwhile.'

Crump could afford to take a stern line as he was about to start aircrew training. The relationship between aircrew and ground crew was complicated. There was an obvious discrepancy in the risks each group faced. Douglas Bader made it clear that he regarded non-fliers as a lesser breed and the relationship between pilot and erk was that of master to servant. Len Hayden described how, while a fitter with 222 Squadron at Duxford in 1940, his flight sergeant told him he would be servicing the aircraft of a new pilot, warning him, 'he has no legs so you will have to assist him into the cockpit.'[27]

The two met on the grass in front of No. 1 Hangar where Bader's new Spitfire was parked. They shook hands. 'Bader then turned to his aircraft, and placing his left foot on the trailing edge and grasping the cockpit ... with his right hand started to heave himself heavenwards, assisted by a hefty shove up the arse by yours truly. This apparently was not what was required because red-faced and in a violent rage he dressed me down with some of the most colourful language I had ever heard. "All I want from you," he raged, "is to stand to attention with your arse to the trailing edge there" – indicating the position with the toe of his shoe.'

Hayden was not the deferential type, a confident craftsman who went on to be a crack motor racing mechanic. Yet he accepted this treatment and 'from then on we became friends'. Bader's arrogance was tempered by his own version of noblesse oblige. In return for

Hayden making sure not only his Spitfire but his MG sports car was in peak condition he would 'always see that the tea and rations brought to us on the airfield were to the best standard', ordering the duty cooks to make fresh tea for his ground crew rather than the 'sewage' they usually served up.

Some testimony reflects unease at the danger deficit. Overall, ground personnel were ten times less likely to die than aircrew. About 93,000 RAF, Dominion and Allied (i.e. Poles, Czechs, French etc.) aircrew were killed in the war on operations or in accidents. About 9,500 officers, NCOs and airmen were killed on the ground.[28] The discrepancy was particularly marked in Bomber Command. Over 55,000 aircrew were killed on operations or in accidents. The total of ground crew deaths in action was 530, a ratio of a hundred to one.[29]

A vague feeling of guilt ripples beneath the surface of the writings of John Sommerfield. In 'Hang Him Up to Dry', a story he wrote in May 1941, the narrator describes one of his ground crew companions laughing about a visit to the funfair in Blackpool and enthusing about a 'wizard bint' he was trailing. 'I lay back on the bunk with a cap over my eyes, half listening, thinking about the pilot and the gunner we had lost the night before, who still lay smouldering in little bits and pieces half a mile down the perimeter road.'[30] Sommerfield presented one pilot he served with as something more than a man of courage but as a paladin who was the embodiment of kindness and decency. In a story based on his ground crew experiences in Burma, he introduces Phil, a Spitfire pilot, 'who made you think of … tennis-playing young men, strolling through peacetime summer evenings down rows of little redbrick houses with gardens in front of them and names like "The Acacias" on the garden gate, of … young men in banks and offices who haven't yet started to take their jobs seriously, who go to musical comedies and come away humming the choruses, whose ambition is a sports car and a girl, or maybe a succession of girls to go with it.'[31] That, he wrote, was 'the sort of young man that so many of the pilots had been', but 'they weren't like that now. The war and their jobs had changed them, really changed what was inside them, as well as the way they talked and behaved.' Phil, however, had retained his innocence and cheerfulness, 'not the protective, wisecracking cheerfulness that most of the others wore like uniform, but simply from an abundance of good humour'.

Phil treats the erks as equals, but the difference between them becomes apparent when he climbs into the cockpit to take his aircraft, whose identity letter is 'L', for a test flight. 'I could see Phil's face bent over the instrument panel, and then he put on his mask and flying helmet. He didn't belong with us any more. Once in the seat, with the airscrew turning and a great torrent of sound pouring away from it, he became someone else, someone remote and inhuman, the brains of the machine.'

Later the same day the squadron is scrambled. The narrator and his companions, who observe the war and the Air Force with smart-aleck wit, are jolted out of their cynical pose.

'We watched them dwindle in the distance until they were out of sight and there was only a faint and distant aerial humming … no-one spoke for a while, our ears strained for sounds from the sky. Tommy said suddenly, "L's got no overload tank you know."

'"He'll be all right," said Slush. "Phil's too sensible to try any hero stuff if he runs into a load of Japs."'

They wait anxiously until at last they see the aircraft returning. Phil's is not among them. At first, they refuse to believe that he has been shot down and cling to the hope he has baled out. But then one of the pilots confirms that he circled the wreckage and saw him 'all burnt up, lying half out of the cockpit'.

The hard-boiled façades melt away. 'Perce shook his large head slowly and disconsolately. "There's no doubt," he said. "That's the way it always is. It's always the best chaps that get knocked off."'

Whether you were flying or not, there seems to have been a degree of connectivity between all parts of the Air Force that reinforced an already vibrant *esprit de corps*. Gladys Partlett joined the WAAF in Brighton in 1942. She wanted to be a driver but the category was full up so she opted to be a cook, 'a decision I never regretted'.[32] The morning shift started at 4.30 a.m. and finished at 2 p.m. She spent her days labouring over cast-iron pots and coal-fired stoves. Food shortages and the demands of mass catering meant the culinary bar was set low and the official RAF cookbook makes grim reading today. Typical is the recipe for faggots which called for '3–5 lbs gristles and rinds. 8 lbs cooked meat. 9 lbs bread. 2 lbs onions. 8 oz faggot seasoning. Method: cook the rinds all day, cool off in cold water and mince finely ...'[33]

Gladys and her colleagues, some of them 'the finest chefs from hotels like the Ritz and the Dorchester', took their duties as seriously as any rigger fitter, pilot or navigator, determined to improve standards and produce the best they could with the means available. The results were impressive. At RAF Stoney Cross in the New Forest they managed to vary breakfast; bacon and (powdered) egg one day, sausage and tinned tomatoes the other, and plentiful bread, margarine and marmalade. For lunch there was fish and chips or steak and kidney with a steamed pudding or semolina to follow.

When she moved to RAF Tarrant Rushton in Dorset in 1944, dinner in the officers' mess 'always began with soup, egg mayonnaise or hors d'oeuvres made from salad, diced beetroot, sardines, grated carrot and cheese. This would be followed by chops ... mixed grills or roasts, served with sauté, creamed or chipped potatoes.' It was a time she would look back on as a great adventure, full of drama, enjoyment and fulfilment. She remembered Stoney Cross as having 'a very happy atmosphere. Often we would sing and everyone in the mess would join in.'

It felt like a community enterprise. The station commander had a Tiger Moth and would fly the cooks over the camp and around the Isle of Wight. At Scampton, crews routinely if unofficially took WAAFs on training flights. Aircraftwoman Morfydd Rose was a waitress in the sergeants' mess. Her boyfriend, Flying Officer Phil Burgess, was a navigator with 617 Squadron and would take part with his crew in the Dams Raid. Morfydd was friendly with Norm Barlow, the Australian captain, and the rest of the team, 'especially Harvey Glinz [the mid-upper gunner] and young Jacky Liddell', the rear gunner. They had two flights together and on one 'I remember Harvey saying, "if you do not have sex with us, we will drop you out of the plane in a parachute". Morfydd replied, '"OK Harvey, you can have first go" ...'[34] Such repartee was par for the course. After flying, the doors of the mess 'would burst open and the aircrews would swarm in, shouting boisterously as we served the meal. We young WAAFs would have to endure a barrage of good-natured banter: "How is your sex life?" "I dreamed about you all night" … "Please serve us in the nude." We took it all in good part, because we knew the great strains they were under …'

Almost all the testimony suggests that fun was as important and vividly remembered a part of the RAF experience as the business of war. It took many shapes and forms, from a beer-fuelled sing-song around a piano in an East Anglia pub to cocktails in the American bar of the Savoy. The diaries of Betty Bullard, a thoughtful WAAF officer who came from a wealthy brewing family in Norwich and served with Transport Command, brim with jolly outings. On 10 April 1942, while serving at Honington, in Suffolk, she and a bunch of friends 'piled into cars' and headed to Norwich where they 'had dinner at The Castle. M got very whistled and I hoped I shouldn't meet anyone I knew. Saw Gledhills [her superior] but fortunately only when the party was behaving quite well and not throwing things about.'[35] On 19 April after a convivial night in the mess a party repaired to a married quarter where they 'drank beer and listened to [the] gramophone and everyone discovered I was ticklish. Oh dear, had a grand evening, a memorable one, but what will I feel like in the morning …' The following day there was 'an excellent lunch' in the mess to welcome a colleague's squadron leader brother with 'asparagus and masses to drink' and amusing anecdotes from Bob Boothby, the roguish Tory politician who was serving on the ground with 9 Squadron at the base. It did appear, as she observed, that 'life seems to be full of parties', and not just for a well-connected young women such as herself but for almost everybody.

The difference was that Betty was well able to handle the relaxation of social restraints that war brought in its wake. For some, the sudden freedom of life away from home was intoxicating but strewn with traps. The impositions and controls of service life were often matched by a lack of restraint off-duty. Every week there were base parties where drink was available. Stern parents and disapproving brothers were out of sight and out of mind and girls found themselves doing things they would never have countenanced before

Betty Bullard

they put on uniform. Sylvia Drake-Brockman, a by no means narrow-minded spinster, who as a senior WAAF officer was in charge of discipline and welfare of hundreds of girls, was shocked by a sight she witnessed after an American base sprang up not far from RAF Moreton-in-Marsh. 'It was positively embarrassing to return to the camp after 10 at night, the road was so full of couples locked in each other's arms,' she wrote.[36]

The result was inevitable at a time when sex education – including that offered to WAAFs – was minimal and contraception was not available to women. Drake-Brockman was much concerned with pregnancies, the rate of which increased as the war went on. Girls often tried to conceal their condition for as long as possible and she instituted a system where NCOs tipped her off if they suspected a case. Once summoned, the WAAF 'generally denied it to begin with but when I asked her to go to the Medical Officer for an examination so that the rumour could be quashed she admitted that the report was correct'.

Under the rules, pregnant women were discharged the service. There was an RAF maternity home for the many who could not bear the shame of going home to have their babies, 'but it was difficult to make use of this as it was so much in demand'. Most of the children seem to have been put up for adoption.

The free-and-easy nature of the wartime RAF was a source of deep concern to some senior officers steeped in the ways of the pre-war service. They watched with alarm as the strict hierarchies of the old RAF blurred, and smartness gave way to 'scruffiness'. Discipline was the responsibility of Edgar Ludlow-Hewitt who in 1940 was appointed the RAF's Inspector General after being removed from Bomber Command. In December 1942, the issue was considered serious enough to merit the appointment of a second IG, Philip Joubert.

Ludlow-Hewitt issued a series of reports bemoaning the decline of standards. He was particularly alarmed at what might be called the increasing civilianization of the Air Force. The tide of newcomers had brought the democratic spirit of an emerging Britain with them, threatening established customs and practices. In the summer of 1942 he complained that 'in many, I might almost say most units of the Air Force today, the NCOs have little disciplinary influence. They are regarded by the men rather as foremen of works in a factory.'[37]

Rank was no longer given automatic deference. 'It is not unusual for a station commander to go into a barrack room, reading room … bar or dining room where the men sitting about do not make a move to acknowledge his presence.' Smartness seemed optional and 'the tendency to scruffiness at home gets worse overseas and men [are] frequently seen on working parades unshaved. Officers, too, often appear unshaved, sometimes with half-grown beards without any reasonable excuse ...'

These worries seem to have been shared by many of those at the top. Commenting on the report, 'Jack' Slessor agreed that NCOs were no longer held in proper esteem. 'When I joined the RFC twenty-seven years ago as a Second Lieutenant, I looked upon a Sergeant or Flight Sergeant as being a hell of a chap and so did the men. Today every RAF station ... is lousy with Sergeants and Flight Sergeants – or rather men with three stripes on their sleeves ... a great many of them are completely undisciplined and they let the side down both in the sergeants' mess and out of it.'

Various remedies were proposed. Men should be 'paraded, inspected and marched to work'. At a high-level meeting in January 1944, it was even suggested that the cartoon character Pilot Officer Percy Prune, the shambolic novice who provided cautionary light relief in the training publication *Tee Emm*, was 'perhaps doing more harm than good'. The time had come 'to introduce a counterpart who should be a smart type with operational experience'.

If any of these measures were tried they seem to have done little good. Two years later, Ludlow-Hewitt was still warning that 'the greatest danger to ... morale is the importation into the service of the factory spirit with its suspicions, selfishness and distrust of authority'.

The truth was, as the Inspector General acknowledged honestly in a letter of June 1944 to a complaining colleague, that there was no link between appearance and efficiency. 'That you see untidy and scruffy airmen in the London streets, and officers as well often enough, does not really indicate low morale but simply ignorance,' he wrote. He went on: 'Indeed the Press seems to take particular pleasure in glorifying the unshaven, so much so that one [has] found again and again, that officers just as much as airmen think that being unshaven and scruffy is the hall mark of the genuine warrior.'

The casual approach to rules and dress, the partying and the urgent, impulsive sexual encounters were as structural an element in the war as bombs and rationing. It was a way of protecting yourself and carrying on against a background of constant tragedies. Those most intimately involved in the fighting added a further layer of insulation. The laconic response to loss has become a cliché of depictions of the RAF's war. It is exemplified by what Brian Kingcome portrayed as 'a typical conversation in a bar or … RAF mess'.[38]

> 'Heard about old Bill?'
> 'No. What's he up to, then?'
> 'Bought it yesterday.'
> 'Really? What happened?'
> 'Bounced by some 109s over Calais. Came down in flames.'
> 'Parachute?'
> 'No. Leastways, no one saw one.'
> 'Tough luck. Nice chap. Time for another?'

The accuracy of this reaction is confirmed by contemporaneous testimony. Sometime early in 1942, Australian navigator Walter 'Roo' Langworthy wrote from his bomber base to his WAAF girlfriend Sylvia Pickering bemoaning his 'miserable misfortune' at having been ordered to attend another funeral parade for a dead colleague.[39] He went on: 'Bad show really – still, that's how it goes. Now for pleasanter topics. Ain't the weather wonderful …'

Stiff upper lips could not be on permanent display. Morfydd Rose remembered standing by in the sergeants' mess to serve the crews their meal after returning from the Dams Raid, when they were told that eight of the aircraft would not be coming back. 'We all burst into tears,' she wrote. 'We looked around the … mess, the tables we had so hopefully laid out for the safe return of our young boys looked empty and pathetic.'[40]

The Second World War was a war of liberation, and liberation came in many forms and on many fronts. The triumph over Nazism brought other victories for freedom in its wake. For lower-class members of the RAF it created a sense of possibility. For those of the ruling class, an acceptance that merit spoke with many accents. Notions of masculine superiority were challenged and demolished by the overwhelming evidence to the contrary provided by a multitude of intelligent, efficient, dutiful and brave women.

The primacy of the white man was among the fallen bastions of pre-war thought. A few Indian pilots had served in the First World

War. The foundation of the Indian Air Force, an auxiliary formation, in 1932 opened the door to more Indian pilots and nine squadrons would fight in the Second World War.

In the RAF itself, pre-war policy had made membership of the white European races a requirement for joining. In October 1939, the need for manpower resulted in the dropping of the colour bar and in November 1940 recruiting began in the West Indies and Africa.[41]

In the Caribbean, the colonial education system stressed a familial link with Britain and many saw it as the mother country. The response was enthusiastic. Many thousands volunteered, of whom more than 400 were accepted as aircrew. Eighty women joined the WAAF. Their motives were the same mixture of idealism and adventurousness that impelled their British counterparts. Ulric Cross was working for the government in the railways department in Port of Spain, Trinidad, when the call came. 'The world was drowning in fascism,' he remembered. 'So I decided to do something about it and volunteer to fight in the RAF.'[42] Cross trained as a navigator, was commissioned and flew with 139 Squadron, Path Finder Force. He had an extraordinary war, flying three tours and eighty trips, including an astonishing twenty-two to Berlin. He finished the war as a squadron leader with a DFC and DSO and went on to a distinguished post-war legal career.

Africa produced only eighty volunteers, a result, it was said, of obstruction by reactionary colonial administrators. About 5,000 volunteers were put to work on the ground, in the West African Air Corps which supported the RAF in bases in Nigeria, the Gold Coast, Sierra Leone and Gambia. One who did make it past the prejudices of the local authorities was Flying Officer Akin Shenbanjo, a wireless operator with 76 Squadron, where his crew named their Halifax after him: 'Achtung! The Black Prince.'[43]

The aircrew came largely from the islands' best schools and the official assessment of their quality was glowing. 'The West Indian personnel selected for training have proved themselves capable of reaching the high technological standard required from operational aircrew and … their discipline, spirit and general conduct is such as to enable them to carry out the ground duties of an officer or NCO with complete satisfaction,' concluded a report in 1944.[44]

This did not mean to say they could be treated entirely as equals. It went on to say that 'colour has not proved a drawback, either to them or their relations with their fellow officers or airmen – except in one respect – they have not proved suitable as captains of aircraft'. The perceived problem was not with them but with the rest of the crew. In a multi-crew aircraft, the pilot was the captain to whom the rest answered. The report considered that 'however good the individual may be, the mere fact that he is coloured may induce a feeling of lack of confidence in the members of the crew. It is a matter entirely beyond the Captain's control and while the feeling may be only subconscious, it will tend to lower the efficiency of the crew as a whole.'

This verdict does not seem to have been translated into strict policy, given the example of Flight Lieutenant Billy Strachan who started off as a wireless operator with 99 and 101 Squadrons and ended as a pilot flying Lancasters with 156 Squadron PFF.

The RAF's reputation as a meritocratic service where ability trumped background was validated by its openness to non-white airmen. Dropping the colour bar was not just a temporary expedient. It marked the advent of a new attitude in which discrimination was officially forbidden. An Air Ministry Confidential Order of June 1944 stated: 'All ranks should clearly understand that there is no colour bar in the Royal Air Force ...' Any instance of 'discrimination on the grounds of colour by white officers or airmen or any attitude of hostility towards personnel of non-European descent should be immediately and severely checked'.[45]

The aircrew volunteers seem to have been accepted easily enough as exotic additions to the rich human mix that peopled the squadrons. Billy Strachan reflected that 'by any reasonable calculation one might have expected me to have suffered, if not discrimination, at least a constant barrage of racist jokes. I can confirm that this did not happen.'[46]

The aircrews' unique shared experience created a mutual understanding that dissolved the barriers of class, education and nationality that might have kept individuals apart in peacetime. It might be hoped that the same would be true of colour. On the ground, the picture is not quite so rosy. There is evidence of white staff bullying and verbally and physically abusing black airmen and unfairly blocking promotions. The victims did not take such treatments meekly and punch-ups ensued.

But the RAF lived up to the credo implicit in the decision to open its ranks. Caribbean aircrew mostly flew bombers, but they served in all the commands except Transport, where they could expect to visit countries where prejudice was entrenched. The islands produced fighter pilots like Flying Officer Jellicoe Scoon who flew Spitfires with 41 Squadron, then Typhoons with 198 Squadron, and Flight Lieutenant David Errol Chance who flew Beaufighters with Coastal Command's 603 Squadron against enemy shipping in the Aegean.

Many of those who survived went on to fame and success after the war. Michael Manley, who served in the RCAF, became Prime Minister of Jamaica. Cy Grant from Guyana was commissioned and served as a navigator with 103 Squadron before being shot down on his third trip during the Battle of the Ruhr. He spent the rest of the war in Stalag Luft III. He decided to stay on in Britain and become a barrister but found the Inns of Court less enlightened than the RAF and gave up the law. Instead, he took to stage and screen and in the 1950s was the first black face to be seen regularly on British TV.

The relative welcome that black volunteers found in the RAF was a pleasant contrast to the violent hostility that African-Americans encountered from their comrades in the armed forces of the United States where segregation was strictly enforced. Air Force policy was far in advance of the attitudes and hiring practices of most British firms of the time. Though it was not mentioned in the report of the Air Information Office in Washington, here was another area in which the RAF could claim to be 'Britain's best advertisement'.

13

Out of Sight

'Today the real adventure starts' reads the entry in Lucian Ercolani's diary for Saturday 12 December 1942. 'Arrived at 99 Squadron – right out in the jungle!'[1] The base was 'just bamboo huts and tents'. The mess bar was a 'tent open one end … a hurricane lamp hanging down … with a semi-circle of chairs'. He found the ramshackle set-up rather stimulating. 'In the evening after dinner, seeing [every-one] standing around under the light with glass in hand, the howls of the jackals outside, discussing the 'morrow's operation was a most impressive scene' as if they were all involved in an '"outpost of Empire" sort of racket'.

Ercolani was twenty-four, and a veteran bomber pilot who had already completed a tour of operations over Germany. Returning from a trip to Berlin in November 1941, his Wellington was hit by flak and most of the mid-section of the fuselage burned away. Despite the damage, he decided to try and make it back to base but was forced to ditch in the Channel. When the aircraft hit the water he was injured and went down with the wreck. Then the cockpit section broke free and bobbed to the surface. Ercolani scrambled out to join the rest of the crew in a dinghy, which floated for three days in the wintry seas undetected by searchers until it washed ashore on the southernmost tip of the Isle of Wight. The exploit earned him an immediate DSO for 'outstanding courage, initiative and devotion to duty'.[2]

Ercolani was the son of a prosperous Italian-born furniture designer and manufacturer who settled in High Wycombe, after moving from Italy in 1910. After Oundle public school, Lucian joined the family business and was all set for a conventional, prosperous life when the war took him off on an entirely different path. Ercolani had no literary pretension but his diaries are a gem. Heartfelt, artless, utterly genuine, they give a rare feel of the actuality of an overlooked campaign, as well as a glimpse into the mind of a decent man, dedicated to a duty that wrenched him from a much-loved wife and cherished family.

He arrived in India at the start of the great Allied push back against the Japanese eruption which had brought the enemy to northern Burma and the gates of the Raj. The fall of Singapore in

Lucian Ercolani with Cynthia at the Palace

February 1942 had been a strategic catastrophe for Britain and a huge psychological blow. The loss of this citadel of the Eastern empire had a chastening effect. There was an initial, abortive offensive to gain a foothold in the Arakan Peninsula in 1943. After that, the campaign of reconquest proceeded patiently. Lessons were learned, preparations were thorough and enough human and material resources dedicated to the enterprise to maximize the chances of success.

In contrast to the handful of squadrons allocated to the defence of Singapore, there would be abundant aircraft and aircrews available to support the armies on the ground and air power in all its forms would play a decisive part in the victory. Like the ground war, the air war in the Burma theatre had its own special character. In the accounts of those who fought it, there are few dogfights; indeed, the Japanese air force plays a minor role and the Allied air force would come to outnumber its opponents by three to one.[3] The most consistent enemies were the weather, the landscape and the logistical problems of mounting complicated missions over great distances, or operating from advanced bases like the one Ercolani arrived in, hacked out of the jungle by coolie labour. The courage of the airmen was measured less in feats of arms than of endurance and fortitude.

Jungle fighting called for a greatly expanded understanding of how air power could be most effectively used. Much of Burma was covered in forests and mountains and was short of roads and railways. There were no formal front lines and the fighting was done in pockets. The fighting would come to coalesce on three fronts in the west, centre and north of upper Burma. Increasingly, as well as providing firepower, the British and American air forces would be involved in moving troops and maintaining air bridges to forces cut off from conventional means of replenishing food, ammunition and medical supplies, as well as flying out casualties. The man who heaved the pallet out of the back of the Dakota to the 12th Army outpost beleaguered in the sea of tropical vegetation below became as essential a player in the enterprise as the fighter pilot or navigator, and the capacity to lift men and things at least as important as the ability to drop bombs.

Ercolani was arriving at 99 Squadron just as the offensive was starting. It was equipped with Wellingtons and tasked with hitting Japanese supply lines and destroying infrastructure. He had recently been promoted squadron leader and would be commanding a flight. He spent a few days getting re-accustomed to the 'good old Wimpey' and flew his first operation on 16 December. The trip was 'a special one … a sort of army co-op affair'. Low cloud meant they failed to locate the target but Ercolani was pleased with his 'damned good' crew. 'The ice is broken, am not as [nervous] as was to begin with – roll on the war,' he wrote on his return.

In his diary entries, faithfully jotted down each night in the early days, Ercolani was honest about his doubts concerning his abilities and acknowledged his fears. The next op was four days later and the familiar butterflies stirred as the hour approached. 'In the morning [I] am dead keen and happy about the trip but by night always [seem] to get a bit apprehensive,' he confessed.

He had been assured on arrival that there was little to fear from the Japanese air force but the previous day a crew had reported having to dive away before finishing their bombing run after five fighters came up to them. On 20 December he was off again to an unspecified target, first flying to an advanced landing ground to refuel. The attacking force failed to form up on the way to their destination and arrived in dribs and drabs. Three of the first were set upon by fighters and he was 'scared as we did our run that fighters would then come after us', but 'nothing happened, took an extra photo and pushed off home, just crawling over the mountains'. Over the target they 'only saw some rather pathetic tracer miles away and three smoke puffs from AA'.

The rocky ridges, rising to nearly 20,000 feet in the north, seemed a much greater hazard than flak or Japanese Zeros. A fortnight later, after returning from an op near Mandalay, he recorded how he 'hated passing over those mountains – a nasty black night and the A/C [aircraft] seeming as though it's never going to make it as the hills get nearer and nearer. Even if you are above them, they still seem to tower above one.' He took to climbing to 14,500 feet to clear features that were reckoned to be 10,000 feet. In the airspace of the uplands he always felt 'a bit of a nag at the back of one's head wondering what we would do if an engine packed up ...'

On the way back from an operation on 12 February he 'heard an A/C send an SOS, then "so long" – we wondered who it was – it made seem crossing the hills all the worse'. It turned out to be P-Peter, captained by a pilot named Watson who had celebrated his twenty-first birthday two days before. Watson managed to land without injury to himself or the crew. They were soon spotted by searching fighters and seem to have made it back to the nearby British lines.

This was remarkable good luck. Anyone surviving a crash was immediately confronted with a new array of deadly dangers: death from starvation, thirst, disease, or the bite of a host of venomous creatures. They could expect no mercy from the Japanese. The torture and execution of Allied airmen was officially sanctioned. One notorious incident exemplified the enemy attitude. On 31 January 1945, a Liberator with a nine-man crew carrying out an intelligence mission monitoring Japanese radar near Rangoon developed engine trouble and the captain ordered the crew to bale out. Six landed in the same area and were reunited. The others were believed to have died in the crash. The survivors headed west in the hope of reaching the coast. They sought help from a village head-man who tipped off the Japanese. The airmen were taken by boat down the Irrawaddy River to the Bassein district. The two officers in the group were taken off to Rangoon for further questioning. The NCOs were kept behind and relentlessly beaten. The worst treat-ment was reserved for the wireless operator, Flight Sergeant Stanley Woodbridge. He knew the codes and wavelengths used for links with ground operators who provided the co-ordinates of Japanese targets. Woodbridge revealed nothing. Eventually all four were beheaded.[4]

Ercolani arrived too early to benefit from a specialist training school set up in Poona to teach jungle survival skills. Before being sent to his squadron, Spitfire pilot Fred Dane completed the gruel-ling course. The school was 'in a large solid building situated in ... hills overlooking dense jungle in all directions. How it got there and who built it in such isolation I never found out.'[5]

The classroom teaching was done by 'primitive natives from the Chin Hills in Northern Burma. They couldn't speak a word of English and all instruction had to be through an interpreter.' They learned how to make cooking utensils out of bamboo, trap and kill small animals including rats and snakes, and build fires to cook them on that gave off no tell-tale smoke. Then it was time to put their skills into practice. Groups of three were 'dropped off in the jungle with water bottles, a compass and a small amount of basic rations. Our base was a four-day trek in an easterly direction and we had to find our way back without maps.' Dane and his companions returned in time, all of them considerably thinner and 'suffering from ticks, bites, bleeding caused by leeches, dozens of insect bites and ... numerous abrasions and sores as the result of forcing a passage through the denser parts of the jungle.' The consensus was that, even with an elaborate survival kit, a pilot 'would have to be very lucky indeed to make it back from any distance in the jungle unless he was fortunate enough to stumble across friendly natives'.

The attitude of the local tribes was uncertain, as Alan Sammons, a Hurricane pilot with 20 Squadron operating out of a tiny forward airstrip on the Bay of Bengal, discovered. On 24 February he and his Canadian partner Eddy Fockler were taking a last stooge round at the end of an offensive recce over the southern tip of Arakan when 'bang – I copped it'.[6] A lucky shot from rifle or machine gun hit the engine coolant pipe line, 'steam flooded the cockpit and I became very warm indeed'. He was too far from friendly territory to reach it before the engine seized up so he headed for the coast and crash-landed in a mangrove swamp on the Mayu River. Amazingly, he was unhurt 'but the poor old kite was quite a wreck. The engine was broken away and was steaming in the swampy water, the wings were torn off and the fuselage was smashed in except for the cockpit.' He 'splashed through the water so that I could wave to Eddy who was circling overhead'. But Eddy failed to spot him. As the Hurricane eventually turned away and dwindled into the distance, Sammons was separated from the British forward position by more than fifty miles of hostile territory with only a rubber dinghy and a handful of Horlicks tablets and glucose sweets to sustain him.

He decided to seek help from the local inhabitants. He set off across the river in the dinghy but tides and currents defeated him and it was the afternoon of the following day before he got ashore and found a village. He waited for dusk, then 'seeing no sign of Japs I … approached the nearest hut around which a crowd soon gathered and with many salaams began to get down to the job of obtaining food and drink which I had been without for twenty-eight hours'. He was eventually given some watery rice, then, by means of sign language, tried to request that they take him by canoe, down the river and up the coast to the British front-line position at Maungdaw, where they would be given 'plenty of money as a reward'. Sammons understood they had agreed to set off with him in the morning. He was still cautious and determined to stay awake but exhaustion overtook him and he dozed off. He was woken up 'by the unpleasantness of a noose being tightened round my neck and several village stalwarts hanging on to me'. They robbed him of his revolver, sheath knife and escape kit, comprising compass, fishing line, matches, water purification tablets, silk scarf with printed map and £6 in silver rupees. He was then tied up 'securely and most uncomfortably' and they set off on a night march to a Japanese outpost where the tribesmen handed him over, receiving four blankets for their efforts.

After a desultory interrogation he was taken on a two-day trek north to what seemed to be a divisional headquarters where other Allied captives were being held. After several months they were moved down to the POW camp at the Central Prison in Rangoon where Sammons spent the next year. The prisoners subsisted on a near-starvation diet and were forbidden to communicate with each other. There were occasional beatings, but most of the suffering was caused by neglect, and the numbers were constantly thinned by deaths from beri-beri and dysentery. Their bony bodies were clothed in rags and maggots seethed in their open sores. In their misery, they showed astounding cheerfulness and ingenuity, using whatever tiny resource came their way to lighten the load of their appalling existences. 'To pass things from one cell to another we would throw a piece of string along … and attach our mess tins to the other end,' wrote Sammons. Smoking was forbidden but the prisoners 'used to make cigarettes from dog ends picked up while cleaning and any little scraps of newspaper'. Not all the guards were brutes. Sometimes, one would give a prisoner a light which he would then pass down the line of cells by means of the string and mess tin.

The dreadful prospect of a crash-landing meant the reliability of aero-engines took on an even greater importance. The ground crews had to be where the aircraft were based, or in the large number of advanced landing grounds that were planted in the middle of nowhere to extend operational reach. This often meant slaving twelve hours a day in sauna-bath humidity under constant attack from voracious insects, eating tinned and dehydrated food and sleeping in airless tents, with no diversions and few opportunities for escape. Ercolani's diary has many words of praise for their efforts and sympathy for their lot. One evening he went to check on a Wellington that needed attention and found 'the three senior NCOs at work on it together. They are an absolutely grand lot, never seen anything like it.'

The constant toing and froing of aircraft meant that even the most remote spots were kept supplied with booze flown in from Calcutta, and the familiar rituals of Air Force revelry were heard amid the steamy heat of the jungle. On 17 February 1943, Ercolani went for a few drinks in the mess, intending to take the 1 a.m. train to Calcutta for a few days' leave but a party developed which was 'such an utter shambles' that he missed it. There were 'chairs, tables, strewn all over the floor – Dicky Richardson with nothing on bar his identity discs. I put up a black – emptied a flower pot over W/C [Wing Commander] of 159. He was a bit cheesed. I don't mind but I do hope it has no repercussions on poor old Barry [his brother who flew with 159 Squadron].'

Leaves, as Ercolani admitted, were not particularly restful and down time could take as much out of you as operations. The routine followed the same lines that the RAF had established in Cairo, Algiers, Naples and any other city or town where there was the remotest possibility of a well-lubricated good time. 'Must say enjoyed the leave – am not really much better for it though,' he recorded early in March 1944. 'We stayed at the Grand Hotel, swam in the Calcutta Swimming Club in the mornings, had lunch time "sessions" which generally ended about four in the afternoon, then rested, or rather recovered – on then, to beat up the town in the evening. Spent a hell of a lot of cash ...'

These excursions to Calcutta seemed only to emphasize the distance from home. The advanced landing grounds were carved out of an exotic landscape that pale-skinned young Britons had only encountered in comic books and films, full of wild beasts and primitive tribesmen. Calcutta, the nearest leave centre, seemed scarcely more civilized. Fred Dane felt 'the whole city seemed to pant in the heat'.[7] Misery was everywhere, worse than anything seen in the African ports of call on the voyage from Britain. He was appalled by the treatment by European and Indian alike of the rickshaw men, 'disease ridden skeletons' suffering from 'tuberculosis, hookworm and many other diseases ... it was not unusual to see the passenger sitting back in the chair ... kick out at the rickshaw wallah because he wasn't moving fast enough'.

One day in September 1943, while driving near Midnapur, Lucian Ercolani 'passed a station where a grain train was in. There were hundreds of Indians; men, women and children roaming around, all armed with staves and knives, some very long and thin, to poke through the doors and pierce the grain sacks so that it runs out. They catch some, then as the train pulls out, they scramble between the lines for the grains ... it is a terrible sight to see some of them, just skin and bones.'

British rule did not seem to have done much for India. Resentment was palpable, and, to most who gave the matter thought, justifiable. The Allied servicemen were occupiers not liberators. Indian soldiers taken prisoner after the loss of Singapore and Malaya, together with thousands of volunteers, were now fighting alongside the Japanese in the Indian National Army, for liberation from British rule. Everyday transactions could be fractious and fraternization was rare. 'The troops treat the Indians, no matter what standing, as dirt,' Ercolani wrote following a riot in a canteen over the price of bananas.

The sour atmosphere intensified the yearning for home. On Easter Sunday 1944, while recovering from a bout of jaundice in the Himalayan hill station of Nainital, where the British went to escape the heat of Delhi, Ercolani was woken by the very English sound of bells tolling in the tower of St John in the Wilderness church. 'It reminded me of home when I used to get up early and go to ... the Communion service with Mummy,' he wrote. 'What peaceful days those now seem. That Sunday morning always used to belong to Mummy and I.'

But more than home Ercolani yearned for his wife. He married Cynthia Douglas in June 1941 and she moved with him from aerodrome to aerodrome during his service in Britain. His diary throbs with the pain of separation. He recorded in bittersweet detail their parting in October 1942, at the door of the cottage they shared in Barton Bendish, Norfolk, when 'just before going we sat in the car ... our last moment together. God, it was terrible. We kissed each other goodbye. She got out of the car with tears just beginning to well out of her eyes and looked in the window of the car and waved. I drove on and waved back through the sunshine roof and had a last glimpse of her standing in the road outside the cottage with her camel coat over her pyjamas.'

It was not quite the final farewell. Flying up to Blackpool, prior to setting sail for the East, he took the aircraft down low over the cottage, just as he used to 'beat up' their lodgings near the base at Stradishall before setting off on an op. She came out, 'jumping up and down and waving goodbye'.

He was oppressed by the same thought that clouded every farewell. 'Will I ever see her again?' It would be nearly three years before they were reunited. Time and distance only seem to have intensified his feelings. Her picture went with him everywhere, the focus of a nightly ritual. 'Said goodnight to Cyn and the photo I took on our anniversary smiled back goodnight.' There are almost daily references to how much he missed her and every good time he recounts is qualified by the thought that it would have been even better if she was there to share it. Cynthia wanted to join the WAAF. He had misgivings, fearing she was too sensitive for service life. She went ahead anyway, trying to wangle a posting to India to be near him. It didn't work out but the story had a happy ending. Despite his fears that they would reunite as strangers, their marriage seems to have successfully picked up where it left off.

Duty offered a shape and purpose to a dislocated existence. In the Far East theatre the ideological element to the conflict was less obvious than it was in Europe and the Mediterranean. The Japanese were ciphers, their culture and beliefs opaque and unknowable, and their cruelty and fanaticism made it hard to regard them as entirely human, 'no better than a horrible animal', concluded Ercolani. He wanted to 'hit them good and hard'. Over Germany he had experienced a 'slightly different feeling ... felt it was a job to be done more than anything else'.

Well-executed operations brought a sense of progress, each one a step nearer home. Ercolani was present from the beginning of the major air effort in Burma until well after the end. When long-range Liberators arrived to beef up the bomber force in September 1943 he moved to the newly formed 355 Squadron, flying missions involving round trips of 2,000 miles against enemy supply routes including the Burma–Siam railway, partly built by the slave labour of Allied prisoners. A year later he returned to 99 Squadron as CO. Although not required to, he led many of the most difficult raids himself, attacking supply dumps, railway targets and enemy headquarters. When, in the spring of 1945, the battle for Burma was won he moved on to command 159 Squadron, part of a target-marking force, engaged in operations that could take more than twenty hours.

His achievements are barely mentioned in the diaries. He took satisfaction in a job well done, though no pleasure in destruction. Early on he was one of three aircraft taking part in a diversionary raid on 'some obscure town' in enemy hands. He wrote later that they 'certainly laced that place up. Felt a bit guilty about it. It was undefended and just sheer butchery. Bombed in two sticks from 3,500 and [machine-gunned]. I didn't like that but the gunners would never have forgiven me if I hadn't [let them].'

Occasionally, though, a glow of professional satisfaction shows through. A raid with 159 Squadron on 13 May 1945 was 'a really successful op. Our job was to destroy a bridge over 1200 miles away – a bomb aimer's dream. It was laid flat and was a wonderful sight. The first few bombs didn't get it, then down it went. We felt like singing ...'

The Burma campaign was just part of the wider, American-led struggle against the Japanese in the Far East. From August 1943, all Allied land, sea and air forces in the operational area covering India, Burma, Malaya, Ceylon, Siam and parts of Sumatra were fused into South East Asia Command, under a British chief, Louis Mountbatten. The air forces were placed under an RAF officer, Richard Peirse, who had made a good recovery after being sacked as C-in-C Bomber Command by Portal in January 1942.[8] His number two was an American, Major General George Stratemeyer, who issued a memorable order of the day establishing the spirit of the joint enterprise. 'We must merge into one unified force,' he declared, 'in thought and in deed, neither English nor American, with the faults of neither and the virtues of both. We must establish in Asia a record of Allied Air Victory of which we can all be proud in the years to come. Let us write it now in the skies over Burma.'[9]

The official history judged that the campaign 'showed how well and gallantly this exhortation was fulfilled'.[10] Nonetheless, command arrangements were notoriously complicated and however well the elements co-operated operationally there were differences of style on the ground that could grate. During a leave in Calcutta Lucian Ercolani bumped into a senior American airman at the 300 Club. 'We were all a bit whissholed and he started to tell us about how damned marvellous the United States Army Air Forces are,' he wrote.[11] 'They seem to get a medal for practically damn-all. There's no doubt they are a good lot of fellows but their standards are so different to ours. He talks of the number of ships he has sunk. When we get down to actual facts he is not so certain. Also they have very little interest … in the RAF, whereas a lot of the RAF boys try to find out all they can from the Yanks. We can't be all that bad … we've been doing the job a lot longer and have far greater experience.'

The landscape of Burma made conventional campaigning impossible. Aircraft became an essential means of moving troops around the battle fronts and keeping them supplied in place. The transportation and logistical capacity provided by aircraft were fundamental to the Allied victory. The first long-range penetration operation mounted by the Chindits in February 1943 was unsustainable without regular air drops by the RAF. The second, which began in

February 1944, relied on American aeroplanes and gliders of the 1st Air Commando Group to insert troops behind enemy lines.

All activity on the ground, offensive or defensive, had to be sustained from the air. In late 1943 the British 14th Army under General Bill Slim launched its great effort to seize back Burma. It started with another attempt to take the Arakan Peninsula led by XV Corps. The Japanese responded with the tactics of infiltrating British lines and threatening encirclement, forcing a withdrawal which had worked well the previous year. They appeared to be about to succeed again, and the headquarters of the 7th Indian Division was overrun. Instead of falling back, though, the threatened units were told to stand and fight. The calculation was that the Allies' great advantage in air power would mean the defenders could be kept supplied with enough rations, ammunition and medical supplies to hold out indefinitely. The Japanese would have to rely on overland transport, which could be disrupted by air attacks, and eventually forced to retire.

So it turned out. The 7th Indian Division withdrew into a jungle compound, 1,200 yards in diameter, which became known as the 'Admin Box', where they staved off the besiegers from 5 to 23 February. In that time, Dakotas flew 714 sorties dropping 2,300 tons of supplies to them and other troops. They faced some initial opposition from Japanese fighters, who were soon driven from the skies by three squadrons of Spitfires operating from airfields around Chittagong. The Japanese losses of about 5,000 men were fewer than those of the Allies. But their methods had been successfully countered and the pattern was set for the remainder of the Burma campaign.

Shortly afterwards, the Japanese launched their own major offensive. Central to the plan was the destruction of the British forces around Imphal, the capital of the state of Manipur, which commanded the approach to Assam and the Raj. Imphal was surrounded in early March, and the strategic town of Kohima to the north on 4 April. The siege of Imphal lasted four months, that of Kohima, eleven weeks. Both were decisive defeats for the Japanese, the largest they had suffered to date, and marked a turning point in the Burma campaign.

Once again, it was resupply by air that determined the outcome. The seventy-six transport aircraft of SEAC, reinforced by twenty C-46 twin-engine Curtiss Commandos diverted from their duties flying over the 'Hump' of the Eastern Himalayas to convoy supplies to the Nationalist Chinese forces of Chiang Kai-shek, kept up a continuous shuttle to the enclaves. They lifted 19,000 tons of materiel, flew in 12,000 fresh men and took out 13,000 casualties and 43,000 non-combatants. The supplies included a million gallons of fuel, a thousand bags of mail and forty million cigarettes.[12]

In these battles and at every stage of the campaign, the 14th Army could rely on the support from the RAF's 3rd Tactical Air Force as well as units of the USAAF Tenth Air Force to provide close air support and act as aerial artillery. Fred Dane arrived in theatre to join 155 Squadron at Meiktila in central Burma just after it fell to the Allies in March 1945. The fourteen pilots were a typical mix of nationalities: two Australians, a New Zealander, a South African and a Canadian, the rest British. They were kept busy, flying up to seventeen sorties a day as the army pushed south down the Sittang River towards Rangoon.

The Spitfires operated in groups of two or four, sometimes eight, depending on the size of the objective, bombing and strafing with cannon fire as the enemy floundered back through the paddy fields. All attacks were at low level. 'Sometimes the target would be a few mud huts, that the Japs had taken and the army wanted destroyed,' Dane wrote.[13] 'Often the only target indicator would be two thin strips of white cloth, some distance apart, pointing towards the enemy strong point. The attacking aircraft would have to judge the interception point and [hit] an unseen target obscured by jungle, perhaps within a few hundred yards of our own troops.'

They had to contend with anti-aircraft fire, often very accurate. The main danger, though, was from the weather, which during the monsoon was more vicious and destructive than anything the Japanese air force could now contrive. The pilots lived in dread of cumulonimbus clouds, huge thunderheads which reared upwards from below rocky ridge lines for 35,000 feet. They 'had the reputation of disintegrating an aircraft unlucky enough to accidentally fly into them', torn apart by drastically varying wind currents. The tropical clouds harboured their own malevolent micro climate, blotting out light, whipping up hailstorms and coating wings with ice. Great banks of 'cumulonims' could stretch for a hundred miles or more, and the only way through was underneath, if the cloud base allowed it. Even then, 'the turbulence, wind shear and buffeting were extreme'. Flying beneath the clouds Dane was once struck by lightning and 'temporarily lost control … the plane was engulfed in a blue haze, mini flashes of lightning [flickered] between the prop blades and the radio was wrecked'.

The push south to the Japanese main base in the port of Rangoon was given added urgency by the fact that American transport aircraft were due to be withdrawn at the end of May for use elsewhere and the prospect of the approaching monsoon. If the city had not fallen by the time the rains came, victory in Burma would be delayed by months. As 14th Army closed from the north, it was decided to mount an amphibious assault from the south. On 1 May, a battalion of Gurkhas parachuted onto flat land near Elephant Point, south-west of Rangoon. At the same time the Royal Navy was tasked with leading a flotilla of seaborne troops up the Rangoon River.

The end was a merciful anti-climax. On the evening of 29 April, after lights out was called in Rangoon jail, one of the prisoners of war, Dick Corbett, had been unable to sleep. He heard the revving of lorries and the smell of burning paper. The guards had gone. Alan Sammons remembered him 'immediately arousing us all and in no time several men were scrambling over the compound and rousing the members of the other blocks'.[14] The senior officer among the prisoners, Wing Commander Lionel Hudson of the Royal Australian Air Force, took charge and a Union Jack used for numerous burial services was hoisted over the prison. A little later a large painted sign appeared on the roof for the benefit of Allied aircraft: JAPS GONE. BRITISH HERE. EXTRACT DIGIT.

14

Black and White

Merston aerodrome used to lie just south of the main Bognor Regis to Chichester road, between the English Channel and the West Sussex Downs. There is no trace of it today. A ghostly airman returning would see only cereal fields flanked by row after row of polytunnels filled with ripening soft fruit; nothing at all that hints at the stupendous enterprise these few acres were once part of. In the early summer of 1944 Merston was a temporary airfield, with two steel mesh runways laid over the dirt, and tents instead of huts for the air and ground staff. It was home to 145 Wing of the RAF, made up of two fighter squadrons manned by the Free French, another, mainly British, Spitfire squadron plus a transport unit flying Douglas DC-3 Dakotas.

On the evening of 5 June, officers were called to a briefing from the CO. Group Captain Adolph 'Sailor' Malan was a celebrated Battle of Britain pilot, a South African of Afrikaner stock. He looked pugnacious with his close-cut blond hair and square jaw and was famous for his aggression in the air. On the ground, he was surprisingly mild and introspective. The audience had a good idea of what he was about to say. 'He came into the tent and informed us, quite quietly, that the show was on,' wrote one of those present, an RAF Regiment officer called John Rolfe to a female friend a year later.[1] 'I can capture the atmosphere easily now. The smell of the tent in the hot sun, and one of the tent flaps banging in the wind. As he spoke we heard the first wave of gliders going over, and suddenly it dawned on me that it was our supreme effort …'

The sound and sight of aeroplanes overhead, of all shapes and sizes and in vast, amazing numbers, would be indelibly imprinted on the memories of everyone in southern England that summer. Thirty-eight years afterwards John Keegan recalled how as a boy he watched the Somerset countryside fill up with the troops and war machines and then, one night, suddenly empty.

> One evening the sky over our house began to fill with the sound of aircraft, which swelled until it overflowed the darkness from edge to edge. Its first tremors had taken my parents into the garden, and as the roar grew I followed and stood between them to gaze awestruck at the constellation of red, green and yellow lights which rode across the heavens and streamed southwards towards the sea. It seemed as if every aircraft in the world was in flight, as wave followed wave without intermission ...[2]

In this first, great southward-heading flock were 1,000 heavy bombers with night-fighter escorts, tasked with pounding the reinforced concrete strong points and gun emplacements of the Atlantic Wall, transports laden with paratroopers and tugs towing gliders crammed with infantrymen. Further north, a decoy operation was underway as 617 squadron, the Dam Busters, scattered bundles of tinfoil Window, which lit up German radar screens, creating the impression of an invasion fleet approaching the Pas de Calais at seven knots and for a few crucial hours sowing confusion about where the real blow was falling.

Just before dawn, it was the turn of the fighters and fighter bombers. At Merston, the pilots were told they would be providing dawn-to-dusk cover of the invasion. They were to operate over Omaha Beach, on the Calvados coast where the Americans met the fiercest resistance of the day. For the airmen looking down, the carpet of ships butting across the Channel was an awesome sight that matched the spectacle the air fleet presented in the skies. Flight Lieutenant Stanley de Vere, a twenty-five-year-old New Zealander fighter pilot who was temporarily on ground control duties, wangled himself onto a patrol in the middle of the afternoon. 'It was amazing,' he wrote in his diary. 'From Portsmouth Harbour and Southampton to the beachhead was [a] lane of every type of craft, from battleships to small infantry landing craft. Warships, from battleships to small corvettes were hurrying around each convoy and fussing like a hen over her chicks. Then just off the beachhead still greater numbers of ships … were lying, the battleships shelling enemy positions on the shore. Saw one destroyer which had been sunk, its funnels and some of the superstructure were showing above the water …'[3]

Ken 'Paddy' French, a Spitfire pilot with 66 Squadron, was thrilled by the panoramic view of the warships belching shells and the landing craft running up the beaches but felt 'strangely detached from it all'.[4] The tongues of flame shooting from gun barrels, the flash of exploding shells, were oddly soundless and it was hard to grasp that the scene was accompanied by 'terrible noise and the fact that thousands of men were dying on the beaches below'.

While marvelling at the armada, French's main thought had been relief that, should he be shot down, there were plenty of boats to pick him up. As it turned out, it was two days before he saw enemy aircraft. Flying back to base with another squadron member after both developed engine trouble, they spotted a pair of Me 109s. They were 'pretty sure they had seen us as they emitted a little puff of smoke indicating that they were accelerating'. But they were speeding away, not towards them. The Luftwaffe, for the moment at least, were in no mood or condition for a fight.

The Allies would enjoy the priceless asset of the freedom of the skies for most of the campaign. Air superiority was a *sine qua non* of the Overlord plan. Lavish air power was essential to cover the landing beaches as the armies struggled ashore, to shield them from the inevitable counter-attacks as they carved out a bridgehead, to prepare the ground for the push forward, and to create the conditions for the breakout that led to victory. Clearly, this called for the closest possible co-operation between land and air, as Bernard Montgomery, commanding the Allied ground forces in Normandy, spelled out in a letter to Miles Dempsey, commander of the British Second Army, a month before the landing. 'I feel very strongly … that we can achieve no real success unless each Army and its accompanying Air Force can weld itself into one entity,' he declared.[5] He looked forward to the continuation of the happy situation that had

Sardonic, humane and a star of the Mediterranean air war. Neville Duke snapped by Cecil Beaton.

Land-air co-operation in action: a Martin Baltimore of 55 Squadron silhouetted above a salvo of exploding bombs, dropped in a joint attack with the USAAF on Rommel's armour during the Battle of Alamein.

Unsung heroes. Short Sunderland and crew. Coastal Command's role in the existential struggle of the Battle of the Atlantic was often overlooked.

Depth charges from a sub-hunting Sunderland of 422 Squadron RCAF rock a U-boat in March 1944.

British industry was harnessed to the needs of the RAF. Here the de Havilland factory is churning out one of its most brilliant and versatile products – the Mosquito.

Ground crew working on a Bristol Beaufighter of 89 Squadron at a remote airstrip. The Burma campaign relied utterly on air power to succeed.

Percy Pickard like Guy Gibson was a favourite of RAF propaganda. Like Gibson, he insisted on returning to ops, and died in action.

Pilots of 132 Squadron with their CO Geoffrey Page (holding map) prepare to attack targets in France in the run-up to D-Day.

The RAF was a multinational, multi-ethnic force. Above, Polish pilots of 303 Squadron. And below, some of the 400 West Indian aircrew volunteers.

Though relations with the Army improved steadily throughout the war, the Air Force would get a large share of the blame for the debacle at Arnhem.

Arming a Typhoon during the Normandy campaign.

Slaughter in a country lane. The devastating result of a 'Tiffy' rocket attack on a German column in the Falaise Pocket.

Job done. Hitler's Berchtesgaden retreat after a last-minute visit by Bomber Command.

Airmen in Austria
studying literature
for the 1945 General
Election. The
democratic spirit of the
wartime RAF would be
echoed in the outcome.

It's a lovely day
tomorrow …

developed in the Middle East and Italy where 'the spirit of unity went right down to the individual soldier and airman'.

The Normandy enterprise would reassemble some of the key players in those campaigns. Arthur Tedder, who had worked side by side with Monty since 1942, was Deputy Supreme Allied Commander and co-ordinator of air activities. The great desert air warrior Arthur Coningham was chief of the RAF's 2nd Tactical Air Force, a huge assembly of light bombers and the new generation of fighter-bombers that would roam the battlefield that summer. Familiarity did not breed affection or respect. As head of the Desert Air Force, Coningham had fallen out badly with Montgomery over his failure to fall on Rommel's retreating army after Alamein. Tedder derided his claims to great generalship and deplored his boastfulness and publicity seeking. In early 1943 he shared his opinion with US General George Patton. Monty, he wrote, was 'a little fellow of average ability who has had such a build-up that he thinks of himself as Napoleon – he is not'.[6] Nothing that happened in Normandy would cause him, or Coningham, to revise their opinions.

The air operations that preceded Overlord were intelligently conceived and executed on a massive scale. Never before had air power been used with such care and in such quantity. The sharp efficiency demonstrated by the Allied air forces before and during the campaign stood out against the duller performance of the forces on the ground. The landings themselves were a brilliant success but thereafter progress disappointed. For all his bold talk, Montgomery showed his habitual caution. His commanders bungled opportunities and misunderstandings and balls-ups abounded. Monty's tricky personality guaranteed trouble with his chief, Eisenhower, and the leading American generals Bradley and Patton. His insistence that everything was going according to his master plan sounded increasingly hollow as weeks passed and the crucial Caen sector, which he had led everyone to believe could be taken on D-Day, remained firmly in German hands.

The Allied armies were up against the most formidable soldiers in the world, courageous and fanatically determined, who made maximum use of the difficult terrain and their still considerable resources, directed by field commanders of the calibre of Erwin Rommel. On the other hand, the invaders had the priceless asset of a huge air force which did everything that was asked of it swiftly and effectively. For months before the first soldiers hit the beaches, the Allied squadrons had been working to a plan that would undermine the Luftwaffe's powers and shape the battlefield to the Allies' liking. Before the air campaign started, the USAAF and Bomber Command launched a week-long assault on German aircraft factories, designed to structurally undermine the Luftwaffe by attacking its industrial base, as well as luring it into an attritional battle to whittle away aircraft and aircrew. The continual losses the German air force suffered on the three fronts it was fighting on in the spring of 1944 meant that, when the time came, it was unable to contribute much to the defence of Normandy, let alone seriously challenge the Allies in the air.

The preparations and the post-invasion air campaign were the responsibility of the Allied Expeditionary Air Force (AEAF) under Trafford Leigh-Mallory, who was moved from Fighter Command to become Commander-in-Chief in November 1943. It grouped together the new formations created for the invasion; the RAF's 2nd Tactical Air Force (2nd TAF) and the United States Ninth Air Force (9th USAF) as well as units of Fighter Command. Leigh-Mallory did not, however, control either Bomber Command or the United States Strategic Air Forces in Europe, which for the time being remained at the disposal of the Combined Chiefs of Staff. He was far from being the ideal man for the job. Many of his British and American peers regarded Leigh-Mallory as uncongenial and incompetent, and friction over control was guaranteed.

AEAF was nonetheless a hive of original thinking. In January 1944, a bombing committee was set up whose members included Professor Solly Zuckerman, a South African-born zoologist who had worked with Tedder in Italy studying the effects of bombardment. He and other experts evolved the 'transportation plan' aimed at paralysing German rail communications by first attacking marshalling yards and maintenance and repair facilities in the wider network, before moving on to tactical targets like bridges, locomotives and rolling stock inside the invasion zone. The certainty of

Fifth wheel. Leigh-Mallory

civilian casualties alarmed politicians, senior airmen and Eisenhower himself. Predictably, the plan was opposed by Arthur Harris and his US counterpart Carl Spaatz on the grounds that it would divert their bombers from their proper function of destroying Germany's industry and undermining civilian morale.

The success of experimental operations in March against rail centres in France and Belgium, significant civilian deaths notwithstanding, persuaded military and political leaders to back it. By

D-Day, eighty railway targets had been attacked and, in the words of the official history, 'the movement of German troops and material by rail had thus become a matter of very great difficulty and hazard … such trains as still ran moved very slowly, were forced to make long detours and travelled only at night. The enemy had no freedom of movement in a large part of France and Belgium and would therefore find it difficult, if not impossible, to marshal troops quickly for a decisive counter attack …'[7]

In the weeks before the landing, airfields, coastal batteries and radar sites were blasted up and down the coast of northern France, and, in the last days, bridges over the Seine. At least as many raids were mounted outside the landing zone as in it. Thus was maintained the deception that the real invasion was aimed at the Pas-de-Calais, a bluff that succeeded beyond the wildest hopes of the Allies, planting a misconception in the Germans' minds that would endure for many weeks after D-Day.

In the spring and early summer of 1944, temporary airfields like Merston sprang up like mushrooms in bucolic corners of southern England. The familiar fighters of the RAF had undergone an evolution. The Spitfires of 66 Squadron could now carry 500lb bombs, to add another dimension to their capabilities. Dive-bombing had come late to the Air Force and it took some time to work out the best method of delivery. 'Paddy' French recalled how initially they would 'fly over the target at 10,000 feet and when we saw it appear behind our wing we would turn over on our backs, going into a steep dive aiming at the target'.[8] At 2,000 feet, the pilot was supposed to 'pull out of the dive and count three seconds' before releasing his bomb, yanking the stick back as the ground approached at 300mph, then swooping upwards again to avoid anti-aircraft fire. At this point, French 'always blacked out because of the G-force but the plane would keep climbing and you would come round again'. He found the technique 'rather haphazard and accuracy could not be guaranteed'. The pilots soon came up with a better method, which was both safer and much more effective: 'We would come right down low and fly the plane directly at the target, and at the last second release the bomb so that it would go straight into the target and at the same time you would lift the plane over the top. You couldn't really miss.'

More formal training was on offer to the men leading the fighter-bomber units. Six months before D-Day, Geoffrey Page, commanding 132 Squadron, was sent on a course at the Fighter Training School at Milfield in Northumberland, which had just opened to teach leaders the special skills needed for close support operations flown from front-line airfields. There was snow on the ground when he arrived which contrasted with 'the cosy warmth of the officers mess'.[9] There he met 'a milling throng of cheerful young men [who] despite their … youth sported the ranks of squadron leaders and wing commanders combined with decorations for gallantry. Together they represented the spearhead of leadership in the air for the coming invasion …'

After breakfast on the first day, they listened to a welcoming speech from a young air commodore who quickly got down to essentials, telling them 'for the next three weeks you will fire your guns and practise dive bombing until it is second nature. On the beaches near here are convoys of … lorries of different shapes and sizes. There are also tanks. These you will attack with cannons and rockets followed by an inspection on foot of the damage caused … you will learn through trial and error the best angle of attack for thin and thick-skinned vehicles. On the bombing ranges you will obtain a proficiency previously thought impossible. You will set a standard for the pilots in your squadron, a standard that you must demand that they in turn attain. You will keep up the highest traditions of the Royal Air Force.'

With the spring, the new techniques were put into practice. On D-Day minus sixty, 66 Squadron bombed a site in a wood near Abbeville. The pilots learned later that it was a launch ramp for the V-1 flying bombs which would later begin cascading on London and the South East. They went off on low-level sweeps, ranging beyond Paris, with orders to engage targets of opportunity, and escorted bombers attacking railway junctions. At the end of May, they struck at radar stations in the Pas-de-Calais, part of an ongoing effort that would end with the destruction of all six long-range scanners south of Boulogne and the reduction of four-fifths of the enemy early warning and gun laying capacity.[10]

The squadron was part of the 2nd TAF which, together with the

9th USAF Force, could muster 2,434 fighters and fighter-bombers and about 700 light and medium bombers. They were reinforced by the might of Bomber Command. For the crews, the diversion away from pulverizing German cities onto tactical targets in France was welcome, bringing relief from their grim nightly routines and generating the feeling that they were making a palpable contribution towards victory. After some initial blustering, Harris accepted the new situation with reasonable grace and would turn out to be a reliable partner to the Overlord armies.

The invasion preparations marked a new and more positive phase of Bomber Command's war. On the night of 5/6 April 144 Lancasters of 5 Group attacked and badly damaged an aircraft factory in Toulouse. The precision of the raid was in part due to the low-level marking carried out by a Mosquito flown by Leonard Cheshire, the innovative and apparently nerveless CO of 617 Squadron. For the next two months, British and American bombers hit railway targets, military bases, arms and ordnance factories, ammunition dumps, and as the date grew closer, coastal batteries and strongpoints. Despite improved accuracy, German reinforced concrete proved highly resistant to destruction and on D-Day damage to the seaward defences was less than the Army commanders had hoped. Despite the steady plastering, enough infrastructure survived to make the American landing at Omaha Beach a bloody affair.

On 5 June, the airmen learned that the prelude was over. The ground crews broke off their normal duties to paint broad black and white stripes around their Spitfires' wings. The livery would let troops on the ground – and trigger-happy gunners on ship or shore who even at this stage in the war would reflexively fire at anything that appeared overhead – know that the machine above was friend, not foe.

The stripes were an unintentional symbol of dramatically changed circumstances, the difference between night and day. The last time the British Army had been in action in France was in June 1940, falling back on the beaches of Dunkirk before an unstoppable enemy under a sky that, to their eyes, the RAF appeared to have vacated. Now they were returning, and no soldier would be able to claim that the Air Force had let them down. The victory that followed was a feat of co-ordination and co-operation involving all arms, but it was only possible because of the Allies' command of the air, a fact that was now apparent to all. At last air power had been accepted, not as an adjunct to the efforts of troops on the ground or ships at sea. It was the ingredient that determined success or failure.

Next to Dwight Eisenhower in the Allied command structure stood the RAF officer who had done more than anyone else to embed this reality in British military thinking. Arthur Tedder first met Ike in North Africa late in 1942 and soon took a professional liking to him. The feeling was mutual, and in time the shared regard developed a human dimension. Tedder's outward amiability masked a temperament that was chilly, sharp and reserved. His feelings for his chief were unusually warm and he chose him as his best man when, after his first wife Rosalinde was killed in a plane crash, he married the vivacious and independent-minded Marie 'Toppy' Black. She shared his affection for the American, writing to her mother: 'I like Ike so much. He is a dear, honest-to-God straight, good man and a very great friend of ours.'[11]

They were excellent partners for a fraught task. The Allies' outward similarities masked acute differences in outlook, approach and the ultimate objectives that lay beyond immediate war aims. They were managing a team that included some monstrous egotists – led by Montgomery for the British and Patton for the Americans. Handling national and personal sensitivities required Olympian tact and iron self-control. Both men possessed them and although the ride was often rocky, their mastery of Alliance diplomacy made a crucial contribution to victory.

In January 1944 Tedder and Coningham were recalled to Britain to join Eisenhower for the countdown to D-Day. They brought with them enormous experience, the glow of victory and a shared outlook. The nature of the air war fought through North Africa, Sicily and Italy had to some extent been formed by Coningham's ideas and leadership. In February 1943, he was given command of the British and American tactical forces in Tunisia. The team carried the Allies through the expulsion of the Axis forces from Tunisia, the Sicily landings and the invasion of Italy. At every stage lessons were learned and technologies and tactics were refined that would be applied triumphantly in the next stage of the air war.

On D-Day, 171 squadrons roamed over the troops toiling ashore. The almost total lack of opposition meant they were barely needed and hopes faded for a decisive first-day battle that would wipe the Luftwaffe from the skies. When dusk fell, the bag was a paltry twelve Junkers 88s.[12] On 10 June, tactical support and air-cover units began to move across the Channel. Waiting for them at Sainte Croix-sur-Mer was an airfield, thrown together from portable components by the RAF Servicing Commandos and Airfield Construction Branch wings. By the time the Normandy campaign was finished there would be thirty-one in the British zone and fifty in the American area of operations, most of them constructed under fire.

For Britain-based ground crews who manned the invasion force bases, Normandy would bring a dramatic change to their routines. Harry Clift, an armourer with 175 Squadron, arrived by Dakota on the morning of 17 June. They touched down at airstrip B5 at Le Fresne-Camilly, north-west of Caen. Before landing they were told to unload as quickly as possible and then carry aboard a party of wounded who would be lying on stretchers by the runway. The aircraft threw up clouds of dust, alerting the German 88mm gunners who opened fire on the runway. He and his comrades scrambled out and flung themselves to the ground 'much to the amusement of the wounded'.[13] The shells landed a hundred yards away and they were assured by the veterans that they would soon get used to it. 'After that we only dropped to the ground for the close ones and ignored the others.'

In sunny weather – by no means constant in a summer of freakish cloud and rain – the thick dust, a compound of limestone and powdered dirt, was a menace. Each take-off and landing would send it swirling around the airfield forcing the armourers to swathe their heads in scarves and shield their eyes with anti-gas goggles to protect them from the blast from the propellers. It worked its way into the 20mm cannon, causing many stoppages and clogging the air intake system of the Merlin engines, so that desert filters from North Africa had to be fitted. The problem would eventually be reduced by laying bitumen-coated strips on the runways and spraying them with water at night.

Life was tough for the crews, working all the hours of daylight, subject to frequent shelling and strafing, sleeping in tents, or at least trying to against a constant background roar of aircraft and artillery. There were many compensating satisfactions. They were right on the front line and the 175 Squadron armourers 'could watch our Typhoons take off ... form up over the sea, fly inland to the target, dive on to their target, release their rockets, pull out of the dive and circle the strip ready to land. It gave us the feeling that we were personally involved in the attack.'

The pilots provided a running commentary on the progress of the battle. Sometimes the ground crews made their own direct contribution. At Le Fresne-Camilly, exasperated at the attentions of the Luftwaffe who would shoot them up on their way back to their bases after attacking the beachhead, they made a gun-pit out of sand bags and installed twin Browning .303s. One day they brought down a marauding Focke-Wulf 190.

For once there was a feeling that, further up the chain, the effort was appreciated. One day they received the ultimate accolade. 'We were told to smarten up and gather at the side of the runway,' Clift recalled. 'When we arrived there we found a large crowd of all ranks who like us were wondering what it was all about.' After a while a light aircraft landed and rolled to a stop nearby. 'In the rear cockpit was Winston Churchill who stood up ... and gave us a pep talk, telling us how he and everyone back home were thinking of us and how proud they all were at the way we were fighting the enemy.'

Harry Clift would go all the way to Germany but it was the first weeks that stuck most vividly in his mind. 'It was hard work, we were in danger most of the time, but we had an important job to do and we were allowed to get on with it without interference or red tape. In those early days we found a feeling of camaraderie between all ranks which was to stay with us throughout the campaign.'

Among the British pilots were many who had been fighting since the beginning of the war. They could remember the daunting odds, the scant resources, the desperation and the exhaustion of the Battle of Britain. Now there was a lavish supply of aeroplanes and pilots and the only shortage was the paucity of enemies to come up and fight. For some, Normandy was an opportunity to pay off old scores.

Geoffrey Page had baled out over the Channel in August 1940. He was badly burned when they picked him up and spent the next two years at Queen Victoria Hospital, East Grinstead, where he was one of the pioneering plastic surgeon Archibald McIndoe's 'guinea pigs', undergoing multiple operations. Sometimes the orderlies would push the patients out onto the hospital lawn, where they watched Spitfires on their way to sweeps over northern France. 'How my heart yearned to be one of them, and not just a burnt cripple,' he wrote.[14] 'I made a bitter vow to myself that, for each operation I underwent, I would destroy one enemy aircraft when I returned to flying.' He overcame many bureaucratic obstacles to get a chance to fulfil this promise and in June arrived in France at the head of 132 Squadron. Initially, he was disappointed by the Luftwaffe's absence and had to content himself shooting up targets of opportunity on the ground. Although he 'exulted in the sight of my cannon shells ripping into the lurching vehicles as they careened about the narrow Normandy lanes like stricken animals, my lust lay in the desire to destroy enemy aircraft'.

Then, one day, while on a test flight with another pilot thirty miles behind the enemy lines, he got his chance, running into a formation of thirty Me 109s near Lisieux. Despite the odds, he plunged to attack. In the dogfight that followed Page was hit by a cannon shell and wounded in the leg. The red mist cleared. He dived to tree-top level, and pulling out, looked round to see only a lone Messerschmitt was now dogging him. 'Hatred brought with it a new strength,' he wrote. His opponent pulled up the nose of his aircraft to get enough deflection on his target. The move was fatal. Already on the point of stalling when the pilot opened fire 'the recoil slowed the [aircraft] sufficiently to flick over and strike the trees twenty feet below. Circling the funeral pyre I watched the column of black smoke rising with morbid fascination.'

For Pierre Clostermann, Normandy represented a further opportunity to restore the honour of France. He was a diplomat's son with family roots in Alsace and Lorraine who was studying aeronautical engineering at California Institute of Technology at the start of the war. Before he could return home, France had fallen. He made a circuitous journey to England, and after training joined first 341

(Alsace) Squadron, before transferring to 602 Squadron, where he flew Spitfires over France. Five days after D-Day, he set foot again in his homeland. The squadron was told to overnight at the landing ground at Bazenville, just south of the British landing beaches. He and his friend Jacques Remlinger were given the honour of putting down first and dressed for the occasion in their best dark blue uniforms. The great moment was a let-down. They landed in a cloud of dust which 'penetrated everywhere, darkened the sky, suffocated us ... for 500 yards round the landing strip all green had disappeared – every growing thing was covered by a thick layer, stirred by the slightest breeze'.[15] Their first night was interrupted by the drone of a twin-engine aircraft and the swish of a falling bomb. 'I dived under a lorry ... the earth quivered, a burning gust of air slapped our faces and glowing splinters bespattered the tent, the trees and the lorry and bounced back sizzling on the dew-covered grass.'

Like the German army, the Luftwaffe used what resources they had to great effect. The narrow bridgehead behind the landing beaches was so choked with troops, ammunition dumps, concentrations of armour and aircraft that, as Clostermann said, 'they could scarcely fail to score a bull practically every time'. The greatest hazards faced by Allied pilots in Normandy were the expertly operated 20mm light flak guns that protected airfields and the 88mm anti-tank guns of the infantry. After the initial avoidance of air-to-air combat, the Germans did come up to fight, sometimes with devastating effect.[16]

The Luftwaffe, though, had no hope of turning the battle. Their enemy overwhelmed them in every department. The first units ashore arrived with radar systems and mobile air–ground control posts, allowing commanders to request air strikes which, most of the time, materialized.

Coningham pressed on with the methods he had developed in North Africa and Italy. The essential challenge of close air support was how to concentrate firepower on tactical targets in the shortest possible time. Coningham's solution was the 'cab rank' system. It involved placing an air controller with the advancing troops, who could call on permanent air patrols loitering on the edge of the battle zone. The aircraft would carry a list of pre-arranged objectives but could be switched immediately if required to targets of opportunity or to relieve an immediate threat.

In Normandy, the system reached its apotheosis, finally fulfilling the devastating potential of air–armour fusion glimpsed on the battlefields of the Western Front a generation earlier. On the road to Berlin, the 'brown jobs' and the Brylcreem Boys marched side by side. On the British side the new methods were incarnated in the muscular form of the Hawker Typhoon (for the Americans it would be the P-47 Thunderbolt), loved by every Allied footslogger, dreaded and hated by his German foe. The 'Tiffy' was a speedier, deadlier descendant of the Fighter Command stalwart of the Battle of Britain. Its development had been marred by technical setbacks and, initially, it earned a reputation among pilots as a killer when put into a dive. By the summer of 1944 it was the perfect machine for the campaign, capable of 400mph and packing firepower that made the eight Browning .303-calibre machine guns of the 1940 Hurricane seem like peashooters.

According to Harry Clift, a typical armament load consisted of 'four boxes of 20 mm ammunition. Each box contained a belt of 140 rounds, made up alternatively of two High Explosive and two Armour Piercing/Incendiary shells throughout the belt.' Next came 'eight rocket motors weighing 20lbs each and already fitted with fins and saddles by the armourers' assistants working at the bomb dump'. Screwed into each was a 60lb High Explosive Warhead. The rockets were mounted on rails under the wings and fired electrically. A newsreel commentary claimed one Tiffy could deliver the equivalent of a destroyer's broadside and just one missile could transform a tank into a hunk of glowing metal.[17]

The Germans received their first taste of what fighter bombers could deliver at dawn on D-Day plus one. The Panzer Lehr division was caught as it moved forward in five columns from Alençon, eighty-five miles south of the beachhead. The attacks went on all morning. Before they had even sighted the invasion forces they had lost ninety supply lorries, forty fuel trucks, eighty-four half-track fighting vehicles and several 88mm guns.

Only five days after the landings, Rommel reported to Field Marshal Keitel that 'the enemy has complete control of the air over the battle area up to a distance of about 100 kilometres behind the front [which] immobilizes almost all traffic by day on roads or in open country … in the country behind, all roads are exposed to continual air attack and it is therefore very difficult to bring up the necessary supplies of fuel and munitions …'[18] Generals were as vulnerable as everyone else. On 17 July, Rommel's staff car was caught in the open by a Spitfire of 412 Squadron, a Canadian unit. Rommel was badly wounded and invalided back to Germany, never to return to the battlefield.

The defenders were under attack on sea as well as land. The attempt by U-boats to stem the flow of men and logistics across the Channel exposed them to the attentions of Coastal Command which, in four days following D-Day, attacked twenty-five submarines, sinking six of them.

The picture on the ground was rather different. The continuing inability of the British to take Caen prompted Leigh-Mallory, eight days after the invasion, to suggest a raid by light and heavy bombers to 'unfreeze' the situation.[19] The tactical use of heavies had been tried before in February during the battle of Monte Cassino in southern Italy when American bombers dropped 1,400 tons of bombs on a hilltop monastery overlooking the Allies' route to Rome. The attack achieved little. There were no troops on hand to follow up and German paratroopers moved into the rubble to establish strong defensive positions. The proposal was rejected by Tedder, apparently on the grounds that Leigh-Mallory was trespassing on Coningham's area of responsibility. Bomber Command and the US Strategic Air Force were anyway opposed to the operation, fearing the front lines were too close and accuracy too questionable to prevent friendly casualties.

Three weeks later, with the capture of Caen no nearer, Montgomery grabbed at Leigh-Mallory's plan. On 7 July, AEAF HQ at Stanmore in Middlesex discussed a request for Bomber Command to blast a path for a renewed assault by carpet-bombing the northern approaches to Caen. Tedder, who had been leading the criticism of Monty, disliked the development, believing it could encourage continual Army requests for heavy bomber support, diverting them from more pressing duties, but did not object.

In one hour on the late evening of 7 July, 457 Bomber Command aircraft dropped 2,363 tons of bombs on northern Caen. The effect was spectacular but the results relatively insignificant. Two days of bitter fighting followed, resulting in the capture of half the city but the bombardment seems to have brought few advantages. apart from boosting morale. There was no proper co-ordination between air and ground and though the defenders were shaken up, few were killed. Showing the same fanatical determination that would mark every stage of the German retreat, they fell back to positions on the south of the city to block any further advance and the strategic position remained the same.

Despite the disappointing results, Montgomery gave a wildly optimistic account of the episode and British and American heavy bombers launched six further massive air raids before German resistance in Normandy cracked. The risk to civilians was obvious. About 3,000 French men, women and children were killed in Caen alone between 6 June and 19 July. The French historian Henri Amouroux put the civilian death toll for the campaign at more than 50,000.[20] The bombs had the same effect on French towns as they did on German ones. About 75 per cent of the fabric of Caen, ancient churches, university and all were demolished by the attacks. Nor were the liberating troops spared from the inevitable inaccuracies. The preparatory bombardment for Operation Cobra, the American attack on Saint-Lô at the end of July, killed about a hundred GIs and wounded another 500.

The effort was an attempt to break out of the cramped hedge and lane 'bocage' of the Cherbourg Pensinsula and into the easier country to the south where the US divisions could sweep west to secure the ports of Brittany and east towards Paris. The massive air assault of 25 July involving 1,500 heavy bombers dropping 3,400 tons of bombs, opened the first big cracks in the German defences.

In early August the US Third Army under Patton had secured Brittany and was ready to swing back to join the First Army, which was now moving eastwards. The end was hastened by a typical intervention from Hitler. Viewing events from his retreat at Berchtesgaden he perceived the desperate situation as 'a unique, never recurring opportunity for a complete reversal of the situation'.[21] He ordered

Panzer units in Normandy into a counter-attack to recapture the neck of the Cherbourg Peninsula and cut off American forces in Brittany. The German Seventh Army moved forward to be enveloped by the advancing Americans as British and Canadian forces moved in behind them. The trap they were caught in would become known as the Falaise Pocket.

On 13 August, Hitler finally accepted reality and gave permission for a fallback to the Seine. The Germans attempted an orderly retreat, delaying their departure. When, on the 17th, they took to the roads leading east and north-east from Falaise, they made a terrible rendezvous with the predators of the 2nd TAF. The retreat was spotted by Wing Commander Charles Green, who reported back to Harry Broadhurst, commanding 83 Group, that he was 'so low I could see not only the black crosses on the vehicles but the square heads of the drivers'. The weather prevented operations that morning but the fleeing Germans came under continuous attack. The official history recorded that 'as evening fell, pilots ... were greeted with a display of white handkerchiefs and cloths waved by despairing drivers. No notice was taken of this attempt to surrender. None of our land forces was anywhere in the neighbourhood to round up the would-be prisoners, and to cease fire would merely have allowed the enemy to move unmolested to the Seine.'

The debris became a war tourist attraction in the days ahead. Airmen had the unusual experience of witnessing the effects of their efforts. Stanley de Vere set off from Falaise hoping to find an abandoned vehicle for the squadron's use. He was out of luck. The road east to Trun, he recorded in his diary, was 'littered with wrecks, nearly all burnt out and some not recognisable as vehicles at all'.[22] Beyond Trun, he saw mounds of dead horses, pressed into service as artillery transport when petrol ran out, and 'the bodies of Germans began to make an appearance ... the sight and smell of these dead Germans didn't worry me much more than if they were horses really'. In a village he came across a 'jerry tank' with 'a body lying over the top of the track, its head and arms hanging down and altogether looking a horrible sight with eyes and mouth gaping and skin quite black ...'

Many vehicles had taken to side roads and farm tracks in a futile attempt to avoid their fate. A witness who was forced to detour because the main road was impassable found 'cars of every description, many of them Citroens, Renaults and other French makes, strewed the fields, mingled with horses dead in the shafts of stolen carts and even old-fashioned traps of two generations ago'.[23] He noticed 'one up to date limousine, painted with the stippled green and brown camouflage affected by the Germans. It contained on the back seat a colonel and his smartly-dressed mistress. Each had been shot through the chest with cannon shells ...' Further on in a leafy lane was a mile-long traffic jam from which all life was extinct. At its head and tail were a smashed-up armoured car. Every vehicle had been hit by rockets. 'Grey-clad, dust-powdered bodies were sprawled everywhere, propped against trees, flopped over driving seats or running boards ...' Pilots flying over the scene the following day reported that even at 15,000 feet the stench of death reached their nostrils.

The carnage in the lane bore the hallmarks of a classic Typhoon attack in which the lead and rear vehicles were rocketed first to immobilize the column which could then be annihilated systematically. There was no escape. Harry Clift recorded that at this phase of the fighting the Typhoon's payload was arranged so that half the rockets were an antipersonnel type 'to explode at ground level and deal with the crew'.[24] If any survivors 'tried to escape by running through the cornfields, they left a trail which could easily be seen from the air. Then they were strafed with cannon fire.'

The fugitives were harried every yard of the way. Sweeping over the small bands of escapees, Geoffrey Page found his anger turning to pity. At first he revelled in the pursuit. When he came across a group of 'arrogant German soldiers, sitting outside on [a] farmhouse steps playing cards' he 'stopped their game with a few hundred rounds of bullets and their arrogance disappeared rapidly'.[25] Then he 'met a man who will haunt me to my dying day'. He calculated that by now he had 'probably killed several hundred people but from the air it was completely impersonal, and made no mental impact'.

When out on a hunt for German aircraft, he saw a small cloud of dust rising, revealing a motorbike and rider. He went down to investigate and saw the bike was camouflaged and the rider wore uniform;

a legitimate military target. 'As I placed the orange reflected dot of my gunsight on the centre of his body, he looked straight up at me, and I knew that the moment of truth had arrived,' he wrote.[26] 'As I stabbed the gun button he threw up his left arm as if to shield his face from the impact. I cursed him … for making such a simple, pathetic human gesture, and loathed myself as I saw man and bike disappear in a torrent of bullets. I returned to base, and found it difficult to talk to anyone for several days. I can still see his face and the raised arm.'

The 2nd TAF averaged 1,200 sorties a day for ten days, turning defeat into headlong retreat. On 25 August, the German garrison in Paris surrendered. The pent-up force of the Allied advance broke free, falling on the backs of the retreating Germans. The pursuers could barely keep up with them. On 3 September, the fifth anniversary of the outbreak of war, Stanley de Vere had gone down with food poisoning. The rest of the squadron were sent off that morning and he wandered down to the flight office to find how they were faring, to hear that they were 'coming back again without having operated'. The reason for their return, he wrote in his diary, 'was that the bomb line had suddenly been moved forward and our boys would have possibly been strafing our forward troops, thinking them to be Huns!'[27]

15

The Hyacinths of Spring

For the Tactical Air Force squadrons keeping step with the advance across Europe, there was plenty of work, bombing and strafing, but ample time off to enjoy the pleasures and privileges accorded to the liberators. Everywhere, they were swamped with gratitude. Paddy French was in a small party sent on a recce to Lille to see if the airfield was fit for occupation by 66 Squadron. It was. Having sent a message to HQ, they 'decided we would smarten up and go into the town'.[1] As they got ready they 'heard sounds outside and found it was the local people starting to gather. There was much hand shaking and shouts of "Vive la France" and "Vive l'Angleterre." We eventually got away and drove into town where we were mobbed. We were eventually rescued by the police …'

John Rolfe of the RAF Regiment wrote to his friend Joan Durnford in Cheshire, describing the reception given to his armoured car unit when it arrived in Ghent early in November with 'people standing at their doors and cheering, waving and blowing kisses – all very embarrassing'. Later he found the 'poor devils … are pathetically anxious to make friends and practically fight each other to give you things they are so grateful …'[2]

The gratitude could become oppressive. Stanley de Vere's Kiwi amiability was tested by a young Frenchman from Lille who took to dropping in on the squadron. 'He has been coming to our quarters to speak to us [bringing] cakes, fruit and tomatoes etc.,' he confided to his diary on 4 October. 'Really very kind of him … but the trouble is he seems to come almost every day and stays a long time talking incessantly … we haven't had the heart to tell him to scram.'[3]

These gifts involved sacrifice. Rolfe reported that the Belgians were 'very short of food – pitifully so … coal is terribly short'. It was 'literally true that a tablet of soap, a bar of chocolate or even twenty cigarettes will get you *anything*'. Yet for all the privations, 'the people will never ask you for anything for services rendered, they just want to be friends'.

De Vere and his comrades were probably too modest to see what heroic figures they cut in the eyes of their Belgian admirer. They were young men like himself, who instead of having to endure the suffering and humiliation of defeat and occupation, were saviours, whose skill, courage and sacrifice had lifted the terrible yoke. The ravages of life under the Germans were all too apparent. Paddy French noticed what looked like a graveyard next to the Lille airfield and a few days later saw people digging there. A man spotted him and came over and told him that the plots contained the bodies of

Brussels breathes again

about eighty men, women and children, hostages murdered by the Germans a few months before. He took him over to one pit and 'apart from the smell it was a horrible sight. The bodies of four men with their hands tied behind their backs.'

The German appetite for destruction seemed insatiable. In Ghent, Rolfe reported, 'the sanitary arrangements leave much to be desired … from what I have learned Jerry connected up the town's main water supply with the sewerage system and then blew the lot sky high. A typical piece of German beastliness.'

The pilots took the opportunity to explore their new surroundings during their frequent downtime before wining and dining at night. A sense that things were settling down was reinforced by the arrival of an inexorable visitor. When 66 Squadron moved to Grimbergen, near Brussels, base personnel were told to stand by to welcome Lord Trenchard. It can only be wondered what, if anything, his presence meant to the young men, many of them Norwegian aircrew. He seemed an 'old man' in the eyes of Paddy French, who Trenchard buttonholed for a few minutes, apparently relieved at finding a native English speaker among the throng of foreigners in Air Force Blue.

The semi-domesticity of life could foster a false sense of security. The Germans were still capable of biting back. On 3 November, with the squadron now based near Brussels, de Vere was tasked with a bombing and strafing attack on Klundert in southern Holland where a German rearguard was holding up the advance. 'We saw lots of planes over the town having their whack and then we started on ours,' he wrote in his diary that night in an entry that reveals the extraordinary proximity that 'close air support' could involve.[4]

'The flak was pretty intense and rather accurate – more than we had expected. I saw streams of it following close behind me several times. Noticed a large vehicle parked in the centre of town, so went down on it using guns and let my bomb go close by, hoping to damage some buildings where the Hun might be. Decided to give the vehicle another dose so came round again and squirted more stuff into it and the street and buildings round about. By the time I was at the bottom of the "pull-out" I was a bit lower than a church steeple and passed close to it. Was thinking what a good thing it was

I didn't fly into it when there was a hell of a thumping bang and my eyes were full of glass splinters. A 20 or 30 mm shell had struck the windscreen and shattered it leaving a hole about 6 inches in diameter … after a few seconds of furious blinking I found I could see OK out of my right eye and fairly well out of the left, but both felt crammed full of this fine glass …' He had a painful journey back to base reflecting 'on how lucky I had just been. A 100th of a second later and the shell would simply have wiped my head off.'

The scale of the task still lying ahead became clear at the end of September at Arnhem. The Allied advance slowed drastically as supply lines lengthened and logistical difficulties multiplied. Resupply was made more difficult by the German strategy of leaving garrisons behind in the French Channel ports with orders to fight to the death. On 4 September, the British Second Army (with assistance from the local resistance) took Antwerp intact, but the Scheldt Estuary on which it lay remained in German hands so that the port facilities could not be exploited.

Eisenhower was determined to maintain the Allied advance on a broad front and urged Montgomery to break through to Antwerp. Monty had his own ideas. He proposed instead 'one really powerful and full-blooded thrust towards Berlin …' commanded, naturally, by himself.[5] It aimed to propel a large force across the waterways guarding the northern frontiers of Germany, thereby circumventing the man-made defences of the Siegfried Line and catching the German army in a pincer movement. The crucial element was surprise, which was to be achieved by the landing of a huge airborne force to seize bridges over the rivers Maas, two branches of the Rhine and several canals and tributaries. This was Operation Market. In Operation Garden, armoured forces would then drive north from Belgium to link up and pour across the captured bridges into Germany to take the Ruhr region whose industries kept the German war effort alive. Largely in the interests of maintaining Allied harmony, Eisenhower agreed.

Operation Market was the greatest air assault attempted to date. Taking part would be 34,600 men of the American 101st and 82nd Airborne Divisions, the British 1st Airborne Division and the Polish Brigade.[6] About 20,000 would jump into their landing zones. The rest would be towed there in gliders. A force of 1,438 Dakotas and 321 converted bombers, plus more than 3,000 gliders, was available. The swift adoption of Montgomery's plan meant preparations were rushed. It was originally sanctioned on 10 September for execution on the 14th but on the 12th it was postponed until the 17th.[7] Thus, the detailed planning took a week compared to the months dedicated to preparing the airborne operations in Sicily and Normandy. The element of shock was diminished by the fact that there were still not enough resources to get all the troops on the ground on the first day, forcing a phased delivery.

The opening moves of Market went well. The great majority of the troops reached their drop zones without meeting significant flak or fighters, and arrived where they were supposed to. The 1st Airborne Division's objective was the road bridge over the Nederrijn (Nether Rhine) in the Dutch city of Arnhem, but the landing zone chosen required a significant march to secure it. The progress of the troops alerted the defenders and by the time they reached the bridge they did not have the numbers to capture it. The heroic debacle that ensued dispelled hope that the war might be over by Christmas.

The operation was described in enthralling detail by Sergeant Arthur Rigby, a member of the Glider Pilot Regiment. Its members were trained by the RAF but controlled by the Army and fought alongside the men they transported. Rigby was disappointed to miss out on the D-Day glider operation and had spent a frustrating summer in England. His account, written while fresh in his mind a few weeks after his capture, records that a number of airborne ops were scheduled and then abruptly cancelled during the period, for 'each time … there was no time to mount it before the ground troops had overrun the ground, so rapid was the advance'.[8] His testimony reveals a high degree of training and competence on the part of the aircrews that absolves them from any blame for the catastrophe.

Rigby remembered a stir at the end of August at his base at Brize Norton, 'suggesting something was afoot'. It was confirmed around 10 September when the group was ordered to move to Manston on the North Foreland in Kent, in order to put their upcoming objective within range of their Albemarle tug aircraft. There they stayed for a week before the target was revealed. They would be transporting the men of the 1st Airborne Division to a Landing Zone (LZ) near Arnhem then joining the operation to capture and hold the bridge until relieved. On the morning of Sunday 17 September, as the sun burned off the mist and with 'everyone in high spirits', they got ready for take-off. Rigby and his co-pilot, Sergeant Ted Healey, were at the controls of their usual glider, an Airspeed Horsa, sixty-seven feet long with an eighty-eight-foot wingspan, which they nicknamed 'Droopy'. They were carrying a six-pounder anti-tank gun and three-man crew plus a jeep to tow it, as well as their own Bren gun, rifle and ammunition.

Marshals orchestrated the complex take-off schedule and at 10.40 a.m. it was their turn. The tug took up the slack on the tow rope and 'the glider started to roll gently forward and to rapidly gain momentum. 20 ... 40 ... 60 ... 80 ... 85 ... 90! Ease back on the column and the old Droop came off the deck as smoothly as she always did and we rose to about fifty feet and settled down at that height until the tug got airborne, and as she did just that, so we started gently to climb ahead of her rise, all very smoothly and gracefully.' From the cockpit, the sky seemed 'literally full of aircraft ... Dakotas, Stirlings, Albemarles, Horsa and Hamilcar gliders, and here and there Typhoon and Thunderbolt fighters sliding around like black and white minnows in a pool of pike'. He was a little nervous crossing the coast but it was only when they passed Nijmegen on their right that they saw the first puffs of flak, far away and ineffectual.

Rigby handed the controls to Ted Healey to take charge of the landing while he cast off the tow rope. Then 'we were in free flight and heading towards the Landing Zone. Everything was quiet ... other than the rushing sound of the wind as we swept on, no gunfire, nothing.'

They landed at 1.20 p.m. in what looked like a potato field in a cloud of dust that left them coughing and spluttering. The back of the Horsa unbolted. The jeep rolled off, they hitched up the gun and took their place in the column in the road next to the LZ. A Hamilcar came in too fast and flipped over, killing everyone on board. It was a routine tragedy and did little to spoil the feeling that everything was going well. A little way away, 'parachute troops were floating down … the sky was full of them'. Apart from the aircraft engines 'there was not a sound, no gunfire … it was as if we had landed in Holland completely unnoticed'.

It was three hours before the force was assembled and ready to move off. Half of the troops were to stay behind together with the Divisional HQ to secure the landing zones and drop zones [DZs] for the second lift due the following day. That meant there were only about 700 men to tackle the objective. The LZs and DZs were seven and in some cases eight miles from Arnhem, well beyond the range of the HQ radios, which, it turned out, were tuned to the wrong frequencies.

Eventually, the column set off, taking a road close to the Rhine which led through the district of Oosterbeek. The weather seemed propitious. It was a 'perfect Sunday afternoon, sunny and warm and very suburbanly quiet. We passed some houses on the way and there were men digging their gardens and mowing their lawns just as though it was quite usual to have an entire airborne division drop in …'

Then people emerged from their houses and 'it was like a royal progress; men, women and children were standing along the pavements and in their front gardens, throwing posies of marigolds to us, giving us apples and bottles of wine, shouting "Welcome! Welcome! Four years we have waited," shaking our hands. Little boys ran along with us, their faces shining.'

Oosterbeek was a few kilometres west of Arnhem. It stood on high ground at the edge of fields that sloped away to the Rhine a mile or two away. A steel cantilevered railway bridge ran across it. They paused while a party of Royal Engineers set off to deal with any demolition charges. They had only gone a very short time when the crackle of rifle and machine guns drifted across the fields. Then there was 'a tremendous roar of explosives and the railway bridge began to collapse in a pall of dust and smoke'.

There followed what seemed to Arthur 'quite a dangerous delay. Quite obviously, the officers in the column were taken by surprise by the sudden appearance of enemy resistance after the quiet start of the operation and it was some time before there was any forward movement.'

After a skirmish on route they arrived at dusk to find Arnhem 'a ghost town'. As they approached the north end of the bridge, the shooting started, with 'terrific crashes and bangs and enormous explosions'. Arthur and Ted helped the gun party manhandle the six-pounder into position. Arthur acted as loader and they opened fire. Their target was 'a concrete pillbox about half-way up the approach ramp to the bridge, from which quite a lot of opposition was emanating and we had to either knock it out or quieten the occupants down while a flame thrower party could get in close enough to deal with it. We pumped three shells into it and the firing died down … we were told to hold our fire and quite suddenly there was an enormous burst of flame and black smoke around the strong point, followed by the most terrifying screaming …'

The clean streets, tidy houses and neatly trimmed gardens of Arnhem became an intimate battleground. Arthur and his fellow glider pilots dodged from house to house, beating back infantry attacks, while each one was gradually demolished around them by tank and artillery fire. It is only on Tuesday 19 September – the third day of the operation – that that there is any mention of aircraft in his account, and the aeroplanes that appeared were German. He recorded that before noon 'the Luftwaffe had a go at us. A gaggle of Messerschmitts came over low over the houses with the cannon and machine guns blazing away, going like the clappers.' One clipped the cathedral spire and crashed, and 'they didn't try anymore strafing after that'. It was not necessary. On Wednesday, as ammunition and all forms of supplies dwindled, casualties mounted, and hopes of the long-promised relief faded, group by group, the gallant band surrendered. The old Army cry, heard at Dunkirk of 'where are the RAF?' does not appear in Arthur Rigby's story. No one could blame him for uttering it.

The Allied air forces' performance would attract much of the blame for the failure of Market Garden. The first, veiled, criticism was voiced three months after the debacle and it came from a very authoritative, if not disinterested, source. In his after-action report of 10 January 1945, the commanding officer of the 1st Airborne Division, Major General Roy Urquhart, chose his words cautiously but their meaning was clear. 'An Airborne Division is designed to fight as a whole,' he wrote.[9] 'If the Division is split and committed to a 2nd lift some 24 hrs later then, owing to the necessity of allotting part of the first lift to protect the DZs and LZs of the following troops, the effective strength for immediate offensive action of the Div is reduced to that of a B[rigade].'

So, the operation had been weakened from the beginning by the failure to deliver all the airborne attackers in one go. It was further undermined by the choice of landing sites, chosen, it appeared, because of appreciations of the strength of anti-aircraft artillery around the target which were 'very pessimistic' as it turned out. 'When the balance sheet of casualties at Arnhem is made,' he ventured, 'it would appear a reasonable risk to have landed the Div much closer to the objective chosen, even in the face of some enemy flak. It has always been the rule when planning that the maximum distance from the LZ or DZ to the objective should not exceed 5 miles. In the ARNHEM operation the distance was 7 miles and in some cases 8 miles. An extra two minutes flying time in the face of flak, if not too severe, would have put the Div – always supposing that the ground was suitable – much nearer its objective. Initial surprise ... was obtained, but the effect ... was lost owing to the time lag of 4hrs before the troops could arrive at the objective.'

Finally, there was the absence of the fighter-bombers which in the campaign so far had been the Army's constant companions. 'Close air support during the first afternoon ... would have been invaluable,' Urquhart wrote. 'If there had been a "cab rank" available, the effect on the enemy would have been considerable. Close air support during the period when the troops were in movement might easily have turned the scale and allowed the whole of 1 Para B[rigade] to have concentrated near the main ARNHEM bridge.'

Successive historians, including loyal friends of the RAF, have largely agreed with the soldier's view. Recently, a strong defence of the Air Force planning and performance by Sebastian Ritchie of the RAF Air Historical Branch makes the case convincingly that culpability for the failure cannot be as neatly assigned as the Airborne version claims and that 'the Allied air forces were not primarily responsible for Market Garden's failure'.[10]

The multitude of what-ifs inherent in Market Garden seem likely to ensure that it will be endlessly and inconclusively debated. The fact was that the Allies did not cross the Rhine until March. In the interim the Germans gathered enough strength to mount a last fightback, on the ground and in the air. On 16 December 1944, the commander-in-chief in the West, Gerd von Rundstedt, launched the fiercest counter-attack since the landings. The thrust through the Ardennes was soon beaten back, with the Allied tactical air forces as well as British and American heavy bombers helping to stop the advance in its tracks by Boxing Day. The Luftwaffe, or what remained of it, played a minor part in the operation. On 1 January, they put in a dramatic appearance.

'Started 1945 in fine fashion,' wrote Stanley de Vere in his diary.[11] He woke up in Brussels having celebrated the New Year with appropriate enthusiasm and after breakfast 'heard the sound of aeroplanes … and a burst of cannon fire … rushed downstairs and out into the street. There, scarcely able to believe my eyes, I saw a number of FW 190s and Me 109s circling low over the city. From the direction of Evere aerodrome came dense clouds of black smoke … after waiting for a few minutes I expected to see swarms of Spitfires etc. nipping in to put a finish to the Huns but I think I saw only one … very little AA could be heard and the cheeky buggers continued milling [around] over the centre of Brussels for about twenty minutes.'

The feeble anti-aircraft fire was evidence of the Allies' low estimate of the threat the Luftwaffe now posed. Before the end of September, 2nd TAF's commander Arthur Coningham had ordered heavy guns to be withdrawn from the airfields and camouflage netting to be sent back to the base depots.[12] His force was now concentrated in a relatively small number of congested bases in Belgium and Holland, presenting an attractive and vulnerable target if the resources could be found to mount an effective assault.

The Luftwaffe took their chance. Planning for Operation Bodenplatte, as it was code-named, began at the start of December. An ill-assorted force of a wide array of types – about 800 aircraft in all – was scraped together, piloted by every man available, from experienced instructor to raw novice. The attacks and air combats that day destroyed about 300 Allied aircraft, as well as killing men on the ground, forty in the British area alone. The operation proved to be a minor setback for the Allies. For the Luftwaffe, it was all but fatal. More than 140 airmen were killed and seventy were captured. The Allied losses were soon made up. The German aircraft and personnel were by now irreplaceable. The Luftwaffe could no longer mount an effective defence of German airspace or interfere significantly when the Rhine was crossed at last. The roof of the Reich had fallen in.

The bombardment of German cities had resumed long before. In mid-September, Arthur Harris was formally released from the clutches of Supreme Headquarters Allied Expeditionary Force in Europe and the heavy bomber squadrons returned to Air Ministry control. Things would not be quite as before. All future operations were required to fit into Eisenhower's overall plans, and heavy bombers provided to support the troops when required. This still left enormous spare capacity. The number of front-line aircraft increased by half in 1944. A single group could now drop as much tonnage as the whole of Bomber Command managed two years earlier.

What to do with all these bombs? Harris was determined to persist with area attacks. But there were now powerful voices with a claim on his squadrons and his formula for success was under challenge. The intention at the top was that Bomber Command should continue focusing on specific targets, in particular synthetic oil production and the Reich's transportation system. Portal and the Air Ministry favoured an emphasis on the former, Tedder and the senior Allied commanders on the ground in Europe, the latter. At the end of September, a directive issued to Bomber Command and the American Eighth Air Force gave priority to oil, with rail and waterway networks and tank and vehicle factories joint second. Harris fell reluctantly into line and railway junctions, canals and synthetic oil plants like the Leuna and Braunkohle refineries joined the target lists alongside the old favourites. Nonetheless, his generous interpretation of the scope of the new orders meant that area attacks would continue until the end.

Almost half the tonnage of bombs dropped by Bomber Command in between 1939 and 1945 was delivered in the last nine months of the war. The opposition was lighter now with the German night-fighter force in decline, and increased accuracy and refined marking meant destruction was maximized.

The defenders could still draw blood. In January 1945, the command lost 179 aircraft in operations against Germany. But the swish of the reaper's scythe was heard less frequently now and the business no longer felt so much like dicing with death.

The vulnerability of German cities was horrifyingly demonstrated on the night of 13/14 February 1945. Dresden has become a symbol of the moral dubiety of the Strategic Air Campaign. In fact, the attack was not intended as an exercise in area bombing. It was an Army support operation, aimed at easing the Soviet advance, and Harris was simply following instructions. Much of the testimony of those who took part conveys a sense that this was just another op, memorable because of the spectacular results and the subsequent furore.

However, there were some who felt unease as Bomber Command turned its attention to places that had until now not been touched. Kelso Robinson, an Australian wireless operator with 550 Squadron, was part of a force tasked to attack railway yards in Hildesheim, in Lower Saxony, on 22 March. No trouble from fighters was expected and they set off in daylight. Robinson felt 'stronger than usual twinges of doubt about the morality of our actions as I saw the town spread out in clear view beneath, a small, clean looking city, apparently undamaged by any previous bombing. Surrounded by fields, it could have been England ...'[13]

But then came a reminder that the war was not yet over. Somehow, their Lancaster got detached from the bomber stream and ended up near the flak defences of Cologne which 'soon had us in their sights ... ominous black puffs of exploding shells began to appear around us as the Germans improved their aim and soon the sound of shrapnel ... like a heavy hailstorm could be heard spattering against the fuselage. Ahead of us, getting slowly closer, was the Rhine, the other side of which lay safety. Our engines were at full power and we were weaving violently to present as difficult a target as possible, but of course there is little sense of speed when travelling at high altitude ... and we seemed to be hanging still in the air, a sitting target.'

He recalled 'having a peculiar detached feeling, not really fear, more a sense of regret that my life was to finish now, with so much unexperienced and unaccomplished. I expected to die, but mercifully did not think of what that might mean, the pain and the terror, perhaps burning alive … I even had a thought for the German gunners, no doubt young men not unlike ourselves, willingly or unwillingly doing their military duty. What a thrill they would get if they were able to send us crashing to the ground in flames.'

The ordeal went on for ten minutes before they crossed the Rhine. They counted more than a hundred holes in the fuselage and tailplane. Their luck had held. Otherwise they might have joined the other eight Lancasters from the squadron lost on operations that month.

Robinson's qualms about Hildesheim were justified. What was meant to be a precise operation turned out to be 'virtually an area attack'.[14] The bombing survey carried out by the RAF after the war reported 70 per cent of the town destroyed, and local records show 1,645 were killed. It was in keeping with the apocalyptic destruction that airmen were now beginning to see close up as the front line moved across Germany.

'During my travels I passed through a number of towns which have featured largely in the news,' wrote John Rolfe of the RAF Regiment to Joan Durnford at the end of April.[15] 'The devastation is terrible. I have seen *nothing* in England to compare with them, not even in the most badly blitzed towns. It really is a terrible sight, Joan, to see a town the size of Sheffield *completely* wiped out, not one house left standing or habitable. Nothing to be seen but piles of rubble and still smoking ruins. The dust and the smells were awful of course …'

Armourer Harry Clift was sent with his squadron to Schleswig in May. On the journey, they breasted a hill 'and there in the valley below lay the city of Hamburg. We were used to seeing the destruction of towns caused by bombing raids but had never seen anything like this. As we drove through the city all the buildings for mile after mile had been reduced to rubble about one storey high. The smell of dead bodies still buried in the rubble was quite sickening.'[16]

When Rolfe saw civilians moving through the ruins, queuing up for food and water, he was 'inclined to feel pity … but I realised that if Jerry had had his way the same scene would have been taking place in England'. Clift had recently encountered a Nazi breeding centre where Aryan women from occupied countries were put to mate with German servicemen, and witnessed the skeletal, pyjama-clad survivors of Belsen. Rolfe had seen photographs of German atrocities committed in France which provoked him to exclaim in one of his letters: 'You could not credit that such deeds could be perpetrated by anyone with the vestige of a soul.'

He was educated, thoughtful, a liberal in politics, yet, viewing the destruction, he had to 'confess to a feeling of savage pleasure at seeing the way the war has recoiled on the German heads'. The belief that this was just retribution is mixed with mystification at the psychological forces that led the Germans to this pass. 'I should like to get behind the German mind and find out what they really think of their Führer and their responsibility for the war,' he wrote to Joan on 24 April 1945. 'If ever we wanted to show the German people as a whole what warfare on their own territory is like then what is happening now will fulfil that want and amply repay them for years of aggression upon other countries. They are getting it back with bags of interest and I rejoice in it. I am glad that the war did not end before we entered Germany.'

There was little chance to ask the defeated directly. Crossing into the occupied zones servicemen were met with large signs warning them against fraternizing with the enemy, though inevitably this was ignored by the adventurous.

Rolfe's first impression was of a people habituated to fear from whichever source it emanated. 'In some places they were disposed to be friendly,' he wrote. More often they were 'scared stiff and hopped out of the way whenever possible ... in one place where we stopped for two days I was told by the Bürgermeister that the people ... were convinced that our purpose was to burn the place down and line [them] up and shoot them.' His initial feeling was that Germany could never recover. The dead towns 'can be completely written off. I can't see that they will ever rise again.' The quiet acceptance in defeat, and the way they were prepared to carry out the orders of their new masters with the same meek efficiency as they had the old seemed contemptible at first. But at the end of July, he wrote admiringly that 'the German capacity for work is phenomenal. They have repaired more damage in Bonn in one month than the French have tackled in a year. What a marvellous thing it would be if this could be turned to work for good instead of aggression ...'

The amount of time devoted to thinking about the future had naturally increased as the end approached. In the course of the war, reflection waxed and waned according to circumstances. In the early days, there are few mentions in the diaries and letters of airmen and women of what it is they are fighting for, apart from survival, the defence of the values of decency and the defeat of an enemy with whom there could be no accommodation. It was this message that Chamberlain had first delivered in his 3 September speech, when he defined the 'evil things' they would be fighting against, and which Churchill had brilliantly developed.

The bigger question, of what they were fighting *for*, did not take long to appear on the public agenda. It was put there by *Picture Post* in its 'Plan for Britain' issue, published in January 1941 which called for a minimum wage, national health service, children's allowances and other reforms which would be formulated officially in the Beveridge Report of November 1942.

Mass Observation tried from time to time to gauge the political mood of the services, by gathering personal reports and commissioning surveys. The results are inevitably patchy and unscientific but nonetheless revealing. In August 1941 John Sommerfeld wrote from his RAF camp to Tom Harrisson of MO, regretting that only 'about one in fifty see a daily paper ... talk about the political aspect of the war is rare and ill-informed'.[17] In July 1944 a campaign began to get servicemen to register as voters, and a brown buff form, No. 2040, was sent to all RAF stations near and far. MO attempted a survey on the registration process across the forces and the results showed a wildly varied picture. In one Army unit with a 'high standard of efficiency', the MO correspondent reported that of the sixty-eight men in his unit only six bothered to fill in the form.[18]

The RAF take-up rates recorded were much higher. In one unit 85 per cent registered, in another 92–95 per cent. This seems to have less to do with the political enthusiasm of the airmen than a policy of encouragement decided on at a reasonably high level. One MO reporter described an officer delivering 'a brief but convincing talk of the desirability of registering ... everything was done to encourage personnel to realise the importance both to themselves and the nation in general'.

A leading aircraftman was quoted as claiming he had 'never previously encountered a body of men so "Left-Wing" as the RAF. I reckon they must be ninety-per cent Left, from officers downwards.' However, the attitude he goes on to describe sounds more cynical than ideological: 'One view I heard recently, "only hypocrites and humbugs stood for parliament so it doesn't matter who we vote for."' It was echoed emphatically by an anonymous WAAF who declared: 'They're all a bleeding lot of swindlers, out for themselves – one's no better than the rest, Conservative or Labour, it's me first every time.'

Behind this general disillusionment lay a vague but powerful feeling that after the war things would have to be different. It is evident in the evening chat of the Far Eastern ground crews counting the days until they can go home, recorded in John Sommerfield's short stories. In 'Worm's Eye View' the narrator and his friend Tommy are chatting on their bunks about post-Demob life. He warns that they may be going back to 'the same sort of job again that we'd had before the war, only for less pay maybe and provided that we're lucky enough to get jobs at all'.[19]

> 'There'll have to be a big change in the way things are done,' Tommy interrupted. 'Everybody feels there's *got* to be a big change.'
>
> How often had I heard that said lately, more and more frequently as time went on ...
>
> 'Yes,' I replied. 'A change is needed and there'll be one all right. But whether it's for the better or worse depends on us, – on us alone.'

The narrator goes outside and stands 'watching the squadron taking off in the brilliant moonlight and drone away into the distance ... though I was very tired I was unwilling to go back to the tent's narrow stuffiness'. Instead he lit a pipe and lay down on the warm sand. 'The past was dead, the future would be as we made it. I rolled over on my stomach and began to write:

> Winter is the time of war
> But a spring comes with hyacinths
> Whose blossoms are the banners of peace
> Foretelling rich harvests of freedom
> For the towns and seasons of our future …

In Europe, the future finally dawned at 2.41 on the morning of 7 May when at Supreme Headquarters Allied Expeditionary Force headquarters in Reims, General Alfred Jodl signed the unconditional surrender documents for all the German armed forces. The joy that erupted took many forms. On VE Day WAAF cook Gladys Partlett left Tarrant Rushton to visit a friend in nearby Wimborne Minster. They pushed a piano into the street and a party began 'in which the whole town seemed to be joining in'.[20] She was on duty to prepare breakfast the following morning. It was impossible to get back to the base that night but she hitched a lift in the morning 'only to find that everyone was drunk. The mess was a mess … aircrew were riding motorcycles through the dining room and the duckpond was full of furniture and drunken officers.'

At Hustedt-Schwerin airfield near Celle, Harry Clift and his comrades started the day with a game of football with the officers, and spent the afternoon drinking hock out of pint mugs. As darkness fell they 'had a huge bonfire and used signal cartridges as fireworks. Someone towed an Me 109 on the bonfire but in their merry state forgot to remove the ammunition.' As the tracer zipped harmlessly into the darkness he looked back to see 'a wonderful sight after so many years of blackout … the lights from the buildings and the tents shining out over the aerodrome'.[21]

Epilogue

Brothers and Sisters

On the damp Saturday afternoon of 8 June 1946, the crowds packing the Mall in London for the first anniversary of Victory in Europe celebrations looked up as the air filled with the rumble of aero-engines sounding from the east. Out of the dishcloth-grey clouds a small shape appeared over Admiralty Arch and flashed past to disappear into the murk above Buckingham Palace. The blunt outlines of a Hurricane were instantly recognizable, an enduring symbol of the guts and skill that had won the Battle of Britain.

It was followed by a stream of 306 aeroplanes large and small, each type reflecting an aspect of the air war. There were Sunderlands from Coastal Command, twelve Lancasters from 35 Squadron of Bomber Command and Spitfires, then Mosquitoes and Beaufighters, the jacks-of-all-trades of the Air Force, Fireflies and Seafires of the Fleet Air Arm. After twenty minutes, the propeller throb was drowned out by the roar of jet engines. The crowds barely had time to register the sleek forms of the new Meteors and Vampires of Fighter Command before they had vanished.

Less than a year after the end of the war, the aircraft that had won it already belonged to a rapidly receding past. The commanding place of air power and the Royal Air Force in the story, though, was already assured. The squadrons had been in action every day of the conflict, often in conjunction with the Army and Navy but much of the time on their own. Victory was the work of many – soldier, sailor, airman and civilian – but, though they did not make the claim themselves, the Air Force can fairly be said to have made the most significant contribution. It was Fighter Command which, in the summer of 1940, kept Britain in the war, creating the essential

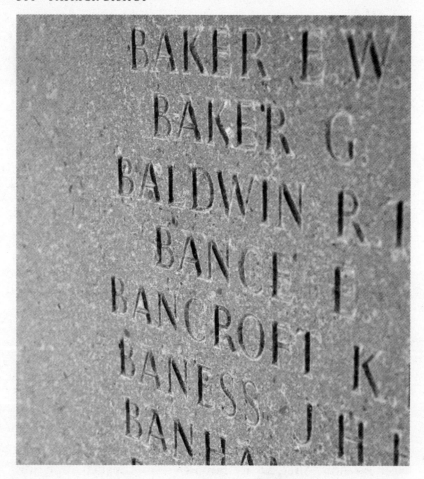

The Many – some of the more than 20,000 dead airmen with no known grave
commemorated at Runnymede

conditions for a landing in north-west Europe and the ultimate defeat of Germany. It was Bomber Command that had led the fight back, taking the war to Germany by the only means available and slowly dismantling its ability to make war. If not for Coastal Command, the struggle to keep the sea lanes open would have been lost and Britain starved into submission. Without the efforts of all arms of the Air Force and the alliance with the USAAF, the invasion of Normandy might have been much bloodier and the march to Berlin a great deal longer. During the conflict, air power had become inextricably fused with action on land and sea and superiority over the enemy in the air accepted as the essential prerequisite for success.

In the course of the war the RAF had grown gigantically. In May 1945, it numbered 1,079,835 men and women, compared with the 173,958 it had started out with, and 9,200 aircraft compared with a front-line strength of 1,911 at the beginning.[1] A tight, white, socially restricted elite had burgeoned into a heterodox host of nationalities, races drawn from every milieu.

The force had expanded to fill the ravenous demands of the war and when it ended much of the organization became redundant. At the same time the factors that had shaped its evolution altered dramatically. The last act of the conflict seemed to spell the end of the era of total warfare and the opening of a new age that required a new air force. On 6 August, the first atomic bomb burst over Hiroshima followed three days later by one on Nagasaki, ending the war with Japan. With the coming of the Cold War, Britain and America would henceforth base their national security on a policy of deterrence with fleets of long-range nuclear bombers at its heart.

The process of dismantling a vast force took time. For most airmen, demobilization could not come fast enough. As Bomber Boy Eric Banks observed, 'whatever [their] RAF experiences, they remained civilians at heart'.[2] Respect for the force, pride in its achievements and gratitude for the friendships forged along the way notwithstanding, they still 'had no interest whatsoever in the peacetime pursuits of the service'.

The slow rate of demobilization was resented, particularly overseas where many had served for years without seeing home or loved ones. In January 1946, a wave of strikes rippled across bases in India, and the Far East. Hundreds of ground staff downed tools in protest at the slow rate of repatriation. The 'factory spirit' feared by Ludlow-Hewitt in his reports on discipline as Inspector General lay dormant in the wartime service. With the overwhelming Labour victory in the 1945 General Election – a result which the Forces vote had done much to bring about – the trade union ethos was everywhere in the ascendant.

The RAF's internal report into the disaffection tried to blame the trouble on a 'well organised minority' of troublemakers and claimed that the episodes had caused a 'serious loss of prestige to the Junior Service at a time when it was universally recognised that Air Power had been one of the deciding factors in World War II'.[3] From the accounts of those involved in the protests, it seems more like the justifiable frustration of patriotic men who had kept their side of the bargain and simply wanted to go home. On the morning of 22 January 1946 Flight Mechanic R. J. Adams and his crewmates reported for duty at the Mauripur base outside Karachi to find 'everything was dead quiet'.[4] On learning that a strike was underway they set off back to their tents but were overtaken by the engineering officer in a jeep who asked them where they were going.

'"Back to the camp sir," said we. "We are on strike." I'm sure had he insisted we would have gone back but he said "OK then" ... he did not make things unpleasant as he could have done. Indeed, there was no unpleasantness at any time during the strike. It was a strange situation for us all. We had been subject to military discipline for years and we knew what we were doing was really mutiny.'

The protest was led by NCOs, none of them pre-war regulars, but seems to have had the sympathy of the officers on the spot. According to Adams 'the organisation and management ... was nothing less than brilliant. Everything had been thought through and acted upon superbly.' The leaders knew very well that Mauripur was an essential link in the airline route operating eastwards from Cairo and on to Singapore and even a short closure could bring chaos. After three days and fervent assurances from visiting senior officers and leading figures in Air Command South East Asia that grievances would be addressed, the strike was called off, mostly with no consequences for the ringleaders. The other protests were similarly dealt with.[5]

The episode was perhaps to be expected. The men on strike were skilled, self-confident and proud. They had accepted service customs and discipline for the duration of hostilities but they had never lost their aversion to bullshit. The slow pace of the demobilization and repatriation programme seemed exactly that.

The RAF had no interest in preserving the more flexible character of the citizen Air Force and was anxious to return as soon as possible to its pre-war, professional identity. The attitude was apparent in ways that were small, but revealing. While the war was on, many bases held dances at which all ranks were welcome. Previously the practice had been for officers to attend NCOs' or airmen's parties by invitation only and then to stay for only a short time.[6] The trend towards more democratic socializing had been noted anxiously by the ever-vigilant Ludlow-Hewitt who warned that, though 'we have to remember … that today we have a citizen Air Force', the matter still 'required careful consideration'. After discussion, it was decided to let the dances continue. After the war the Director General of Personnel, Dermot Boyle, summed up the new mood by stating that though they had served a 'very necessary and useful purpose in wartime' it was now 'common ground that "all ranks" dances are to be deprecated … since they may lead to the inescapable barriers, however intangible they may be, between different ranks being broken down too far, with the result that discipline might suffer'.[7]

Ludlow-Hewitt's strictures seem tinged with nostalgia for the pre-war era. But it was in this, broadened phase of the RAF's life, when Tom, Dick and Harry, Joan, Kath and Betty flooded into its ranks that it lived its hour of greatest glory. Its deeds and triumphs, great and small, were largely the achievements of the birds of passage, and it was the image they created that fired the imagination of Britain and the world.

By 1945 everyone knew about the RAF. Fighter Command's victory in the summer of 1940 was famous not merely as a military success but as a triumph of the spirit and the brave, apparently carefree young pilots were the embodiment of the values they were willing to die for.

With Bomber Command, the picture was more complicated. Their achievements soon came to be questioned on the grounds of both utility and morality. The RAF's own post-war survey showed that, until the last period of the campaign, the spectacular destruction meted out had not had quite the devastating effect on industrial production that had been expected. The conclusion drawn by some critics, that the strategic bombing campaign was a massive waste of life and effort, was however inaccurate and unjust.

The bomber cult that shaped pre-war development, misguided though it seems in hindsight, made sense to many at the time, and once the commitment to strategic bombing was made there was no real choice but to stick to the plan. Trial, error and the acceleration of technology that always comes with war meant that by the end the prophecy was fulfilled. In the judgement of the official historians, whose four-volume account of the history treated Harris and the bomber zealots with admirably stern detachment, 'both cumulatively in largely indirect ways and eventually in a more immediate and direct manner, strategic bombing ... made a contribution to victory which was decisive'.[8]

The charge that the huge civilian casualties resulting from area bombing amounted to an Allied war crime came later, in time to trouble the old age of brave men who had not welcomed war and had no say in how it was conducted. Kelso Robinson was unusual in admitting to 'nagging doubts about the morality of what I was doing' during his tour of operations in 1944–5, which included the raid on Dresden.[9] However he 'fairly easily assuaged my conscience by reflecting that what we were doing was carrying out the policy of the highest in the land ... and supported almost completely by the public at large'. Looking back half a century later, he wrote: 'I do not think my viewpoint has changed. In spite of the horror, the indiscriminate killing and maiming ... I think the bombing policy was probably right. War is horrible ... once a nation has become involved in a war it is the responsibility of the political leaders and commanders to win ... as quickly as possible and with minimum casualties to their own side. It is not possible to fight and win a war under some kind of Marquis of Queensbury rules.'

If the man who directed the policy, and pressed on with it even when Churchill's enthusiasm cooled, had any qualms, he kept them to himself. What went on behind Peter Portal's hooded eyes would remain his secret. It was not necessary to penetrate his thought processes to appreciate his brilliance. The youngest of the wartime service chiefs, he was the coolest and shrewdest, the unflappable opposite of hot-tempered Alan Brooke, apparently inexhaustible when Dudley Pound was visibly flagging. These qualities would be much needed in his dealings with his peers. As late as the summer of 1942, he was still fending off Army and Navy efforts to bend the Air Force to their wills. The Royal Marine General Sir Leslie Hollis, who observed him in conference with the Chiefs of Staff, 'never saw him ruffled, even under vicious and uninformed attacks on the Air Force. He would sit surveying the critic coldly from beneath his heavy-lidded eyes, never raising his voice or losing his temper, but replying to rhetoric with facts.'[10]

Portal was the best chief the service could have hoped for, and among the men he presided over were several superbly suited to their place and time. Tedder, Dowding and Harris were very different men. They seem granite figures now, terrifying in their certainty. What they shared was a certain clairvoyance, and the enormous energy and self-belief needed to push their vision through the thickets of the decision-making process and make it a reality. Their service was well rewarded. They ended up heaped with honours bestowed by Britain and her grateful allies. Portal had already been made a Marshal of the Royal Air Force in January 1944. In August 1945 he became a baron and in January 1946 a viscount, as well as being awarded the Order of Merit, to join the row upon row of silverware that jangled on his chest.[11]

For the mass of those who served, their reward was their memories. The war diverted them from a course whose direction was largely set by their background and education, taking them down unexpected paths and into unusual company. 'I quite enjoy the idea of not knowing what will happen to me,' wrote Betty Bullard in her diary eleven days after the outbreak of war.[12] Her career in the WAAF would bring responsibilities, adventures and friendships that a woman of her background would never have experienced in peacetime. 'Sergeants party tonight which I rather enjoyed' ran a typical entry a few years later.

For women who had hitherto served only under men, serving with them could prove a liberation and a validation of their worth. Sylvia Drake-Brockman discovered a new self as a highly efficient WAAF officer, as competent at giving orders as acting on them. In the RAF she found men who treated her as something approaching an equal. Among her papers is a letter she clearly cherished, from Group Captain Peter Jones, the station commander at West Kirby, a despatch centre for personnel going overseas, received after she had been posted away in his absence. 'Dear D-B,' it read. 'It was a shock to come back and find no wise woman to greet me. I shall miss you and you must know that I have appreciated our talks together about all sorts of subjects …'[13]

For hundreds of thousands of ordinary people who in peacetime could expect only a small ration of excitement and fulfilment, war was the great opportunity. It swept away the restricted vistas of normal life, revealing possibilities that were unimaginable hitherto. Fred Dane, who fantasized about being an RAF pilot growing up in west London in the 1930s, remembered a moment when he was just completing his training at an OTU in Egypt. He wrote: 'I was stooging around at 30,000 feet in clear, blue empty sky, wallowing a little in the rarefied atmosphere and admiring the magnificent view across to Ismaelia, the Suez Canal, on to the Sinai Desert and then to the minute curve of the earth on the far horizon. In that grand isolation, it occurred to me that had it not been for the war, instead of flying a Spitfire high over the desert of Egypt I should probably be working at a bench in some dreary factory on the Perivale Trading Estate.'[14]

The Second World War is lodged in our collective memory as the Good War. For all its contradictions, confusions and bitter ironies, it was the closest thing to a clear-cut moral conflict that we are likely to see. The sense that the effort was being made in the name of decency permeates the testimony of the ordinary players in the struggle. Everyone who wrote anything about their war refers to a feeling of solidarity that incubated among people who in other circumstances would probably have never mixed, a sense that, even in such socially stratified times, what combined people was greater than what separated them. For those in the front line, the camaraderie had a special quality that only they could feel, and which endured long afterwards. 'I am a shy man,' wrote Kelso Robinson, 'but I can go to a meeting of former aircrew whom I do not know and immediately feel at home. It's not that we talk about the war, but the sense of a shared extraordinary experience gives us a feeling of common brotherhood.'[15]

It was made more intense by the ghostly presence of the absentees. In all 102,592 British, Dominion and Allied personnel were killed serving in the wartime RAF.[16] Another 31,011 were wounded.

The balance of casualties in favour of death reveals the thick layer of added hazard involved in fighting in aeroplanes. By choosing to serve in the air they had identified themselves as adventurous and high-spirited, ready for challenges and thirsty for life; just the people needed to build a new world from the rubble of the old.

Acknowledgements

In this book I have tried whenever possible to draw on contemporaneous sources – letters, diaries, as well as official documents, etc. – supplemented by post-facto recollections and memoirs. So my first thanks – sadly posthumous in most cases now – are to all those men and women at every level of the wartime RAF who felt moved to write down their experiences. Why one person chooses to record events and another not is a mystery. I am just grateful that the impulse exists. Tattered journals, pale blue notepaper with the RAF crest, flimsy airmail letter-cards and faded ink are for me the mother lode as I go about my historical prospecting. Every nugget has value. Much of the writing has a freshness and honesty that is sometimes lacking in professional accounts. All of it reinforces my continuing wonderment at the qualities and achievements of an extraordinary generation of men and women. I am consequently very grateful to those families who, understanding the importance of their loved ones' testimony, added its riches to the public trove of stories.

My thanks are therefore also due to the staffs of the libraries who curate and manage the material and who have been so helpful to me during my researches. I'm particularly indebted to Peter Devitt of the Royal Air Force Museum at Hendon, for his enthusiasm for the project and his many insights and observations, which illuminated what is a very large landscape. The Liddle Collection in the Brotherton Library at Leeds University was a rich source of new material and the team there made my life a lot easier with their professionalism and courtesy. The early period research owes a lot to Tim Pierce and the staff at the College Hall Library, Cranwell. Alina Nachescu and Cristina Neagu at the Portal Archive at Christ

Church College, Oxford, were unfailingly helpful. Thanks too once again, to the staffs of the Imperial War Museum, the National Archives, the British Library and the London Library.

A big thank you too to old friends for encouragement, help and advice, notably Maurice Byrne in Dublin and Richard Foreman, Sebastian Cox, Head of the Air Historical Branch of the RAF, and John Nichol in the UK. Dr Robert Owen, the official historian of 617 Squadron, did me the huge service of reading the manuscript, criticizing and correcting to greatly beneficial effect. For those errors that remain, the fault is mine.

As always the HarperCollins team was a joy to work with. To Arabella Pike, Richard Collins, Iain Hunt, Julian Humphries and Helen Ellis, my sincere gratitude for your talent, good-natured professionalism and generosity in smoothing the way.

Notes

PROLOGUE: FIRSTWAY

1. The National Archive [TNA] AIR 41/9.
2. Vincent Orange, *Tedder: Quietly in Command*, Frank Cass, 2004, p. 242.
3. Ibid., p. 152.
4. TNA AIR 41/9.
5. Susan Ottaway, *Dambuster: A Life of Guy Gibson VC*, Pen and Sword, 2003, p. 136.
6. Sir Charles Webster and Noble Frankland, *The Strategic Air Offensive Against Germany, 1939–1945*, HMSO, 1961, vol. IV, p. 456.
7. www.tophilo.com
8. Roger A. Freeman, *The Mighty Eighth: A History of the Units, Men and Machines of the US 8th Air Force*, Cassell, 2000, p. 2.
9. *Picture Post*, Saturday 8 October 1938.
10. *Men of the RAF*, Oxford University Press, 1942, p. 78.
11. John Keegan, *Six Armies in Normandy*, Book Club Associates, 1982, p. 9.
12. *Picture Post*, 7 October 1939.
13. Ibid., 28 October 1939.
14. Diary of John Thornley, Mass Observation Archive, University of Sussex, Diarist No. 5212.
15. Bernard Fergusson, preface to Sir John Kennedy, *The Business of War*, Hutchinson, 1957, p. xix.
16. *Picture Post*, 28 October 1939.

1: THE BIG ONE

1. Fred Whitfield, *We Sat Alone, Diary of Rear Gunner*, unpublished manuscript, Liddle Collection, Brotherton Library, University of Leeds.
2. TNA AIR 14/3135.
3. Whitfield, op. cit.
4. Ibid.
5. Imperial War Museum [IWM] Sound Archive 2207.
6. Patrick Otter, *Lincolnshire Airfields in the Second World War*, Countryside Books, 2002, p. 29.
7. IWM Sound Archive 2207.
8. Wikipedia: 'Consolidated B-24 Liberator'.
9. IWM Sound Archive 2207.
10. Alan Cooper, *Beyond the Dams to the Tirpitz*, Goodall Publications, 1991, p. 158.
11. Martin Filler, *Hanging Out With Hitler*, New York Review of Books, 17 December 2015–13 January 2016.
12. Despina Stratigakos, *Hitler At Home*, Yale University Press, 2015, p. 81.
13. Willi Frischauer, *Goering*, Odhams Press, 1951, p. 261.
14. IWM Sound Archive 2207.
15. 9 Squadron Operations Record Book [ORB], 9 Squadron Archive, RAF Marham.
16. IWM Sound Archive 2207.
17. 9 Squadron ORB.
18. Whitfield, op. cit.
19. Emmy Goering, *My Life with Goering*, David Bruce and Watson, 1972, p. 124.

20. Irmgard Hunt, *On Hitler's Mountain: Overcoming the Legacy of a Nazi Childhood*, William Morrow, 2005, pp. 220–3.
21. Whitfield, op. cit.

2: A COTTAGE OR A CASTLE?

1. Recollections of Group Captain Arnold Wall, RAF Museum, Hendon.
2. Sir John Slessor, *The Central Blue: Recollections and Reflections*, Cassell, 1956, p. 31.
3. Maurice Dean, *The Royal Air Force and Two World Wars*, Cassell, 1979, p. 20.
4. Malcolm Smith, *British Air Strategy Between the Wars*, Oxford, 1984, p. 18.
5. TNA AIR 1/29/15/1/141/3 (3625).
6. TNA T 161/282 (3657).
7. Slessor, op. cit., p. 45.
8. Viscount Portal Archive, Christ Church College, Oxford.
9. Henry Probert, *High Commanders of the Royal Air Force*, HMSO, 1991, p. 4.
10. Ibid., p. xxi.
11. Smith, op. cit., pp. 23, 43.
12. Ibid., p. 42.
13. Wall, op. cit.
14. By Leo Amery, Under Secretary for the Colonial Office [Wikipedia: Somaliland Campaign 1920].
15. H. Montgomery Hyde, *British Air Policy Between the Wars*, Heinemann, 1976, p. 230.
16. Sir Philip Joubert de la Ferté, *The Third Service, The Story behind the Royal Air Force*, Thames & Hudson, 1955, p. 70.
17. *Journal of the Royal Air Force College*, vol. XV, Spring 1935, no 1.
18. All the following statistics are based on an analysis of data contained in the *List of Graduates, The Royal Air Force College Cranwell, February 5 1920–December 18 1962*, published by the Old Cranwellian Association.
19. Brian Kingcome, *A Willingness to Die*, Tempus, 1999, p. 19.
20. Tony Mansell, *Flying Start: educational and social factors in the recruitment of pilots of the Royal Air Force in the interwar years*, History of Education, 1997, vol. 26, no. 1, pp. 71–90.
21. Analysis of List of Graduates.
22. Peter Townsend, *Time and Chance*, Book Club Associates, 1978, p. 57.
23. Kingcome, op. cit., pp. 34–5.
24. Tim Vigors, *Life's Too Short to Cry*, Grub Street, 2006, p. 61.
25. Kingcome, op. cit., p. 24.
26. *Journal of the RAF College*, vol. XV, Spring 1935, no 1.
27. Townsend, op. cit., p. 110.
28. Kingcome, op. cit., p. 36.
29. Townsend, op. cit., p. 74.
30. Analysis of List of Graduates.
31. John James, *The Paladins, a social history of the RAF up to the outbreak of World War II*, Macdonald, 1990, p. 106.
32. 'The RAF of the Future' by Major C. C. Turner, *Journal of the Royal Air Force College*, vol. XIV, Spring 1934.
33. John Terraine, *The Right of the Line, The Royal Air Force in the European War, 1939–1945*, Hodder & Stoughton, 1985, p. 4.
34. James, op. cit., p. 113.
35. Hubert Rawlinson, *Chronicles of a Trenchard's Brat by 565663*, unpublished manuscript, RAF Museum, Hendon, B683.
36. James, op. cit., p. 108.
37. Analysis of List of Graduates.
38. Ibid.
39. James, op. cit., p. 113.
40. TNA AIR 32/15. Air Historical Branch Monograph: History of Flying Training, Part II: Organisation.
41. Probert, op. cit., p. 24.
42. Townsend, op. cit., p. 120.

3: SMOKE AND MIRRORS

1. Sir John Slessor, *The Central Blue*, Cassell, 1956, p. 163.
2. Malcolm Smith, *British Air Strategy Between the Wars*, Oxford, 1984, p. 336.

3. For a full analysis see Smith, op. cit., pp. 44–75.
4. Ibid., p. 6.
5. The full transcript can be read on www.emersonkent.com
6. Slessor, op. cit., p. 167.
7. Ibid., p. 204.
8. Though information from the air raids on Barcelona in March 1938 was used by the Home Office to try and determine casualty rates in an all-out German air assault. David Edgerton, *Britain's War Machine*, Penguin, 2012, p. 36.
9. *Chief of Staff, the Diaries of Lieutenant-General Sir Henry Pownall*, edited by Brian Bond, Leo Cooper, vol. I, *1933–1940*, p. 38.
10. Ibid., p. 49.
11. Ibid., p. 135.
12. *The War Narrative of Major General Sir John Kennedy*, William Morrow, New York, 1958, p. 7.
13. Ibid.
14. Pownall, op. cit., p. 203.
15. Kennedy, op. cit., p. 36.
16. Ibid., p. 37.
17. Ironside claimed that Hore-Belisha's limited grasp had led to a crucial misunderstanding when discussing with General Gamelin the time it took to build a 'pillbox' strongpoint. The minister thought he said three days when the Frenchman had said three weeks. The resulting controversy ended in Hore-Belisha's departure from the War Office.
18. See 'Double Lives – a history of sex and secrecy at Westminster', Michael Bloch, *Guardian*, 16 May 2015.
19. TNA AIR 6/39.
20. H. Montgomery Hyde, *British Air Policy Between the Wars*, Heinemann, 1976, Appendices VII and VIII.
21. Philip Joubert de la Ferté, *The Third Service*, Thames & Hudson, 1955, p. 126.
22. Montgomery Hyde, op. cit., p. 462.
23. Slessor, op. cit., p. 159.
24. *The Times*, 19 October 1937.
25. David Irving, *The Rise and Fall of the Luftwaffe: The Life of Erhard Milch*, Weidenfeld & Nicolson, 1973, p. 58.
26. *The Times*, 20 October 1937.
27. Richard G. Smith, *Hornchurch Scramble*, Grub Street, 2000, p. 32.
28. *Flight*, 23 October 1937.
29. Montgomery Hyde, op. cit., p. 395.
30. Slessor, op. cit., p. 158.
31. Montgomery Hyde, op. cit., p. 407.
32. Ibid., p. 418.
33. John Terraine, *The Right of the Line*, Hodder & Stoughton, 1985, p. 76.
34. Denis Richards and Hilary St George Saunders, *The Royal Air Force 1939–1945*, vol. I, p. 63.
35. Montgomery Hyde, op. cit., p. 361.
36. TNA AIR 8/226.
37. Ibid.
38. Andrew Boyle, *Trenchard*, Collins, 1962, p. 710.

4: BRYLCREEM BOYS

1. Eric Partridge, *A Concise Dictionary of Slang and Unconventional English*, Routledge, 1989.
2. After the war he had a distinguished career as a psychologist.
3. Richard Passmore, *Blenheim Boy*, Thomas Harmsworth, 1981, p. 14.
4. TNA AIR 20/8992. The precise figure is 1,201,106.
5. TNA AIR 32/15.
6. Ibid.
7. I am indebted to Dr Tony Mansell for the insights in his paper 'Flying Start: educational and social factors in the recruitment of the Royal Air Force in the interwar years', in *History of Education*, 1997, vol. 26, no. 1, pp. 71–90.
8. TNA AIR 32/15.
9. Sir John Slessor, *The Central Blue*, Cassell, 1956, p. 160.
10. Vincent Orange, *Tedder: Quietly in Command*, Frank Cass, 2004, p. 36.
11. Ibid.
12. John Terraine, *The Right of the Line*, Hodder & Stoughton, 1985, p. 43.
13. Peter Townsend, *Time and Chance*, Book Club Associates, 1978, p. 95.

14. TNA AIR 32/15.
15. Mansell, op. cit., p. 87.
16. TNA AIR 32/15.
17. John Llewellyn Rhys, *England Is My Village*, Faber & Faber, 1942, pp. 76–7.
18. Ibid., pp. 23–4.
19. Analysis of data from Ken Wynn, *Men of the Battle of Britain*, Gliddon Books, 1989.
20. TNA AIR 41/9.
21. Colin Cruddas, *Those Fabulous Flying Years, Joy Riding and Flying Circuses Between the Wars*, Air Britain, 203, p. 52.
22. Ibid., p. 58.
23. Charles Fenwick, *Dear Mother*, unpublished memoir, p. 4.
24. IWM Images, PST 14624.
25. Len Hayden, unpublished memoirs, RAF Museum, Hendon.
26. IWM Documents 4207.
27. TNA AIR 6/56.
28. TNA AIR 6/41.
29. IWM Sound Archive 008901/16.
30. TNA AIR 6/27.
31. IWM Sound Archive 12217.
32. IWM Sound Archive 10961.
33. Christopher Foxley-Norris, *A Lighter Shade of Blue*, Ian Allen, 1978, p. 8.
34. Interview with the author.
35. AVM Smyth, *Abrupt Sierras*, Wilton, 2001, p. 49.
36. Interview with the author.
37. IWM Sound Archive 8901/16.
38. A. W. T. Tedder, *With Prejudice: The War Memoirs of Marshal of the Royal Air Force Lord Tedder*, Cassell, 1966, p. 5.
39. Bob Doe, *Fighter Pilot*, Spellmount, 1991, p. 7.
40. Edward Hearn, *The Chronicle of a Passer By*, unpublished memoir.
41. TNA AIR 6/27.
42. Ibid.

5: 'THERE'S SOMETHING IN THE AIR'

1. Roger Broad, *Conscription in Britain: The Militarisation of a Generation*, Routledge, 2006, p. 144. The RAF would remain the most popular choice until late 1942 when it was overtaken by the Navy (see Table VI in H. M. D. Parker, below, for figures).
2. H. M. D. Parker, *Manpower: A study of War Time Policy and Administration*, HMSO, 1957, Table VI.
3. TNA AIR 20/8992.
4. Ibid.
5. Ibid.
6. Broad, op. cit., p. 146.
7. House of Commons Library, Social and General Statistics SN/SG/4252.
8. F. S. Reed, '*One Scruffy Erk*', unpublished memoir, RAF Museum, Hendon, X001–2307.
9. 'Lawson Memorandum', RAF Air Historical Branch, Northolt, Middlesex.
10. Denis Richards, *The Royal Air Force 1939–45*, vol. I, *The Fight at Odds*, HMSO, 1953, p. 229.
11. John Sommerfield, letter to Tom Harrisson, 27 November 1940, Mass Observation Archive [MOA], University of Sussex.
12. TNA AIR 20/8992.
13. IWM Sound Archive 32219.
14. TNA AIR 20/8992.
15. Diary of John Thornley, MOA, Diarist No. 5212.
16. Norman Lee [with Geoffrey French], *Lower Crust War*, unpublished memoir, Liddle Collection, Brotherton Library, University of Leeds.
17. Sam Pritchard, unpublished memoir, RAF Museum, Hendon.
18. Ibid.
19. Ibid.
20. Edward Mace, unpublished memoirs of RAF service, Liddle Collection, Brotherton Library, University of Leeds.
21. Lee, op. cit.
22. Letter from John Sommerfield to Tom Harrisson, MOA.
23. John Sommerfield, *The Survivors*, John Lehmann, 1947, p. 141.
24. MOA, Sussex.
25. Eric Partridge, *A Dictionary of RAF Slang*, Michael Joseph, 1945, p. 8.
26. 9 Squadron Line Book, RAF Marham.
27. *Picture Post*, 28 October 1939.

28. James Hampton, *Selected for Aircrew*, Air Research Publications, 1993, p. 116. He added that, had he done so, he would probably 'not be here today'.
29. Letters of Edwin Thomas, IWM 67/281/1.
30. *Sunday Express*, 31 December 1939.
31. S. P. Mackenzie, *British War Films, 1939–45, The Cinema and the Services*, Hambledon, 2001, pp. 33–4.
32. IWM 67/281/1.
33. TNA AIR 20/8992.
34. John Frayn Turner, *The WAAF at War*, Pen and Sword, 2011, p. 129.
35. Sylvia Drake-Brockman, *Memories of the Women's Auxiliary Air Force 1940–1946*, unpublished memoir, RAF Museum, Hendon.
36. Marjorie Hazell, *All The Same Buttons*, unpublished memoir, RAF Museum, Hendon.
37. Initial WAAF policy was that women would be posted to a base near their homes.

6: 'TRAGIC, CRIMINALLY TRAGIC'

1. Sir John Slessor, *The Central Blue*, Cassell, 1956, p. 234.
2. Guy Gibson, *Enemy Coast Ahead*, Crecy, 2003, p. 30.
3. Peter Johnson, *The Withered Garland, Reflections and Doubts of a Bomber*, New European Publications, 1995, pp. 132–3.
4. Peter Townsend, *Time and Chance*, Book Club Associates, 1978, p. 102.
5. Tim Vigors, *Life's Too Short to Cry*, Grub Street, 2006, p. 78.
6. John Terraine, *The Right of the Line*, Hodder & Stoughton, 1985, p. xi.
7. Slessor, op. cit., p. 234.
8. Stephen Bungay, *The Most Dangerous Enemy*, Aurum Press, 2001, p. 93.
9. TNA AIR 41/4 [RAF Air Historical Branch, Flying Training 1934–42].
10. Mark Barber, *RAF Fighter Command Pilot, The Western Front 1939–42*, Osprey, 2012, p. 14.
11. TNA AIR 41/4.
12. Ibid.
13. Ibid.
14. Ibid.
15. Sir Charles Webster and Noble Frankland, *The Strategic Air Offensive Against Germany*, HMSO, 1961, vol. I, p. 112.
16. Ibid., I, p. 205.
17. Ibid., I, pp. 179–80.
18. Jonathan Falconer, *Bomber Command Handbook*, Sutton Publishing, 1998, p. 41.
19. Hubert R. Allen, *British Bombing Policy During the Second World War*, Fonthill, 2016, p. 75.
20. TNA AIR 6/39.
21. Webster and Frankland, op. cit., I, p. 116.
22. Terraine, op. cit., p. 88.
23. TNA AIR 6/39.
24. Webster and Frankland, op. cit., IV, pp. 99–102.
25. Slessor, op. cit., pp. 205–6.
26. Denis Richards, *Royal Air Force, 1939–45*, HMSO, 1953, vol. I, p. 38.
27. Webster and Frankland, op. cit., I, pp. 116–17.
28. Richards, op. cit., p. 38.
29. Eric Banks, *The Laughing Boys*, unpublished memoir, Liddle Collection, Brotherton Library, University of Leeds.
30. Norman Lee, *Lower Crust War*, unpublished memoir, Liddle Collection, Brotherton Library, University of Leeds.
31. Falconer, op. cit., p. 77.
32. Allen, op. cit., p. 77.
33. Martin Middlebrook and Chris Everitt, *The Bomber Command War Diaries, An Operational Reference Book, 1939–1945*, Penguin, 1990, p. 12.
34. *Daily Telegraph*, 9 September 1939.
35. Webster and Frankland, op. cit., I, p. 203.
36. Lord Portal Archive, Christ Church College, Oxford.
37. Lord Portal Archive, Christ Church College, Oxford. AVM William Yool interview with Denis Richards 6/10/72. The anecdote recalls the opening scene in Powell and Pressburger's *The Life and Death of Colonel Blimp*.

38. Lord Portal Archive, Christ Church College, Oxford. AVM Hugh Walmsley interview with Denis Richards.
39. Lord Portal Archive, Christ Church College, Oxford.
40. *RAF College Cadet Magazine*, vol. 1, April 1921, No. 2.
41. AVM Smyth, *Abrupt Sierras*, Wilton, 1965, p. 84.
42. IWM Sound Archive 11772.
43. Richards, op. cit., p. 109.
44. Webster and Frankland, op. cit., I, pp. 118–19.
45. Richards, op. cit., p. 110.
46. Ibid., p. 116.
47. Papers of Len Clarke, RAF Museum, Hendon.
48. Richards, op. cit., p. 142.
49. Christopher Foxley-Norris, *A Lighter Shade of Blue*, Ian Allen, 1978, p. 16.
50. Recollections of Group Captain Arnold Wall, RAF Museum, Hendon.
51. TNA AIR 20/4325.
52. Slessor, op. cit., p. 367.
53. Foxley-Norris, op. cit., p. 16.

7: THE BATTLE

1. Diary of James Barclay, RAF Museum, Hendon.
2. The full despatch is available on www.spitfiresite.com
3. TNA AIR 6/41.
4. TNA AIR 6/70.
5. Barclay, op. cit.
6. Private Papers of Pilot Officer D. H. Wissler, IWM Documents 786.
7. Barclay, op. cit.
8. Ibid.
9. Letters of Denys Mileham, Mileham family archive.
10. War Diary of No. 73 Squadron RAF July 1940–January 1941. IWM Documents 9422.
11. IWM Sound Archive 12217.
12. Letter included in 73 Squadron War Diary, op. cit.
13. George Barclay [edited by Humphrey Wynn], *Angels 22: A Self-Portrait of a Fighter Pilot*, Arrow, 1977, p. 89.
14. Group Captain R. Deacon Elliot, Unofficial History of 72 Squadron, RAF Museum, Hendon.
15. AIR 16/1032.
16. Cecil Beaton, *Winged Squadron*, Hutchinson, 1942, p. 6.
17. Paul Richey, *Fighter Pilot*, Guild, 1990, p. 143.
18. Deacon Elliot, op. cit.
19. Kenneth G. Wynn, *Men of the Battle of Britain*, Gliddon, 1989.
20. Deacon Elliot, op. cit.
21. Barclay, *Angels 22*, p. 101.
22. Leng, op. cit.
23. Barclay, *Angels 22*, p. 103.
24. Beaton, op. cit., p. 6.
25. Mackenzie, op. cit., p. 45.
26. Ibid., p. 38.

8: FIGHTING THE NIGHT

1. Private Papers of Squadron Leader H. E. Bodien DFC, IWM Documents 17660.
2. Denis Richards, *Royal Air Force 1939–45*, HMSO, 1953, vol. I, p. 201.
3. Ibid., p. 206.
4. AVM Desmond Hughes, *Unfinished Memoirs: A personal history*, unpublished MS in possession of author.
5. Hughes, op. cit.
6. Richards, op. cit., p. 204.
7. Hughes, op. cit.
8. Bodien, op. cit.
9. John Golley, *John 'Cat's Eyes' Cunningham, The Aviation Legend*, Airlife, 1999, pp. 34–5.
10. IWM Sound Archive recording 12155.
11. Golley, op. cit., p. 38.
12. Richards, op. cit., p. 215.
13. Golley, op. cit., p. 53.
14. Home Intelligence weekly report 4 October, 1940. Mass Observation Archive, University of Sussex.
15. Home Intelligence Report, 11–18 December, 1940. MOA.
16. Civilian Attitudes to the Navy compared with the Army and RAF. MOA.
17. Home Intelligence Report, 11–18 December, 1940. MOA.

18. Brian Kingcome, *A Willingness to Die*, Tempus, 1999, pp. 14–15.
19. S. P. Mackenzie, *British War Films, 1939–45*, Hambledon, 2001, p. 39.
20. *Winged Words: Our Airmen Speak for Themselves*, PRO, 1941, pp. 99–100.
21. *Picture Post*, 14 September 1940.
22. Home Intelligence Report, 12–19 March, 1941. MOA.
23. Home Intelligence Report, 26 March–2 April, 1941. MOA.
24. Sir Charles Webster and Noble Frankland, *The Strategic Air Offensive Against Germany, 1939–1945*, HMSO, 1961, vol. I, p. 153.
25. Ibid., p. 154.
26. Ibid., p. 157.
27. *Dictionary of National Biography*, 'Newall, Cyril Lewis Norton' by Vincent Orange.
28. Private Papers of E. F. Fry DFM, IWM Documents 15155.
29. Michael Paris, 'The RAF on Screen', *History Today*, vol. 40, issue 8, August 1990.
30. Richards, op. cit., p. 383.
31. Sholto Douglas, *Years of Command*, Collins, 1966, p. 114.
32. Richards, op. cit., p. 384.
33. Ibid., pp. 384–5.
34. Ibid., p. 385.
35. Donald Caldwell, *The JG 26 War Diary*, vol. I, *1929–1942*, Grub Street, 1996, p. 199.
36. Cuthbert Orde, *Pilots of Fighter Command*, Harrap, 1942, p. 32.
37. Figures from Maurice Byrne in his review of Anthony Cooper, *Paddy Finucane and the Legend of the Kenley Wing*, Foothill, 2016, p. 175.
38. Anthony Cooper, *Paddy Finucane and the Legend of the Kenley Wing*, op. cit., pp. 175–7.

9: TEN MILLION MILES OF SEA

1. readings rafbf.org
2. John Terraine, *The Right of the Line, The Royal Air Force in the European War 1939–1945*, Hodder & Stoughton, 1985, p. 226.
3. Andrew Hendrie, *The Cinderella Service, RAF Coastal Command 1939–1945*, Pen and Sword, 2010, p. 27.
4. Sir Philip Joubert de la Ferté, *The Third Service*, Thames & Hudson, 1955, p. 132.
5. Tony Spooner, *In Full Flight*, Wingham Press, 1991, p. 116.
6. Group Captain Guy Bolland, unpublished memoir, RAF Museum, Hendon.
7. See Roy Conyers Nesbit, *An Expendable Squadron, The Story of 217 Squadron, Coastal Command, 1939–1945*, Pen and Sword, 2014, for a full account.
8. Bolland, op. cit.
9. *The Gazette*, 13 March 1942.
10. Air Ministry, *Coastal Command*, HMSO, 1942, pp. 28–9.
11. TNA AIR 2/5995.
12. Spooner, op. cit., p. 156.
13. *Coastal Command*, HMSO, pp. 28–9.
14. Spooner, op. cit., p. 158.
15. Hendrie, op. cit., p. 208.
16. Denis Richards, *Royal Air Force, 1939–45*, HMSO, 1953, I, p. 227.
17. Spooner, op. cit., p. 159.
18. *Coastal Command*, HMSO, p. 66.
19. Terraine, op. cit., p. 230.
20. *Coastal Command*, HMSO, p. 101.
21. Ibid., p. 101.
22. Joubert, op. cit., p. 155.
23. Webster and Frankland, op. cit., I, p. 327.
24. Ibid., p. 325.
25. Terraine, op. cit., p. 452.
26. Webster and Frankland, op. cit., 1, p. 340.
27. Ibid., pp. 341–3.
28. Stafford Cripps set out the arguments in a general form in a debate in the House of Commons.
29. Terraine, op. cit., p. 402.
30. Ibid., p. 403.
31. Tony Spooner, op. cit., p. 238.
32. Wikipedia, 'Leigh Light'.
33. Spooner, op. cit., p. 245.
34. Hendry, op. cit., p. 230.
35. Sir John Slessor, *The Central Blue*, Cassell, 1956, p. 468.

CHAPTER TEN: THE BLUE

1. Sam Pritchard, *By the Centre*, unpublished memoir, RAF Museum, Hendon.
2. 'Bobby Gibbes Writes on Fear' [From 'You Live But Once' by Wing Commander Robert H. Gibbes, www.3squadron.org.au].
3. Denis Richards, *Royal Air Force, 1939–45*, HMSO, 1953, p. 242.
4. John Terraine, *The Right of the Line*, Hodder & Stoughton, 1985, p. 304.
5. Vincent Orange, 'Sir Arthur Coningham,' *Dictionary of National Biography*.
6. Philip Guedalla, *Middle East 1940–1942, A Study in Air Power*, Hodder & Stoughton, 1944, p. 83.
7. Terraine, op. cit., p. 313.
8. Guedalla, op. cit., p. 157.
9. Terraine, op. cit., p. 309.
10. Denis Richards and Hilary St George Saunders, *Royal Air Force 1939–1945*, HMSO, 1954, vol. II, p. 163.
11. Ibid., II, p. 166.
12. A. W. T. Tedder, *With Prejudice, The War Memoirs of Marshal of the Royal Air Force Lord Tedder*, Cassell, 1966, p. 82.
13. Ibid., p. 95.
14. Ibid., p. 107.
15. Ibid., p. 70.
16. Ibid., p. 93.
17. Ibid., p. 101.
18. Ibid., p. 95.
19. Ibid., p. 105.
20. Ibid., p. 107.
21. Papers of J. Pickering, 1939–45 RAF, Liddle Collection, Brotherton Library, University of Leeds.
22. Ibid.
23. Pritchard, op. cit.
24. Pritchard, op. cit.
25. Pritchard, op. cit.
26. Brian Kingcome, *A Willingness to Die*, Tempus, 1999, p. 145.
27. Papers of Kathleen Bishop.
28. Pritchard, op. cit.
29. Tedder, op. cit., p. 165.
30. Family anecdote.
31. Pritchard, op. cit.
32. See Tedder, op. cit., pp. 176–90 for his account of this episode.
33. Ibid., p. 198.
34. *The War Diaries of Neville Duke, 1941–1944*, edited by Norman Franks, Grub Street, 1995, p. 32.
35. Pritchard, op. cit.
36. Wing Commander Norman Poole, unpublished memoirs, RAF Museum, Hendon.
37. Diary of W. J. Corbin, 1939–45 RAF, Liddle Collection, Brotherton Library, University of Leeds.
38. Pritchard, op. cit.
39. John Frayn Turner, *The WAAF at War*, Pen and Sword, 2011, pp. 169–70.
40. Corbin, op. cit.
41. Duke, op. cit., p. 45.
42. Tedder, op. cit., p. 200.
43. Pritchard, op. cit.

11: 'EAT, DRINK AND BE MERRY ...'

1. TNA AIR 2/5995. Maudling would go on to become a Conservative politician, serving as Chancellor of the Exchequer, 1962–4. He volunteered for the RAF at the start of the war but was rejected for flying duties because of poor eyesight and served in intelligence before going to work for Sinclair.
2. TNA AIR 2/5995. Sir Harold Whittingham, Director General of Medical Services RAF to Sir Bertine Sutton, 27 December 1943 (3759).
3. All references to correspondence on the controversy are from AIR 2/5995 'Control of Venereal Diseases in the RAF – Proposed Defence Regulations' unless end note number indicates otherwise.
4. Mark K. Wells, *Courage in Air Warfare*, Cass, 1995, p. 127.
5. Ibid.
6. TNA AIR 20/2860.
7. David Edgerton, *Britain's War Machine*, Penguin, 2012, pp. 202–3.
8. Ibid., p. 364.
9. Ibid., p. 199.
10. Sir Arthur Harris, *Bomber Offensive*, Pen and Sword, 2005, p. 98.

11. Denis Richards, *Royal Air Force 1939–1945*, HMSO, 1953, p. 229.
12. Sir Charles Webster and Noble Frankland, *The Strategic Air Offensive Against Germany*, HMSO, 1961, vol. IV, Appendix 44.
13. Edgerton, op. cit., p. 285.
14. Martin Middlebrook and Chris Everitt, *The Bomber Command War Diaries, An Operational Reference Book, 1939–1945*, Penguin, 1985, p. 272.
15. YouTube, 'On The Chin', 1942.
16. Patrick Bishop, *Bomber Boys: Fighting Back 1940–45*, Harper Press, 2007, p. 100.
17. YouTube, British Movietone News, 'Gigantic 1,000 Bomber Raid', 1942.
18. Philip M. Taylor, *Munitions of the Mind, A History of Propaganda from the Ancient World to the Present Day*, Manchester University Press, 1990, p. 233.
19. Bishop, op. cit., p. 72.
20. Eric Banks, *The Laughing Boys*, unpublished memoir, Liddle Collection, Brotherton Library, University of Leeds.
21. Wells, op. cit., p. 126.
22. TNA AIR 2/5995.
23. Norman Lee and Geoffrey French, *The Lower Crust War*, unpublished memoir, Liddle Collection, Brotherton Library, University of Leeds.
24. Harris, op. cit., p. 267.
25. Diary of Flight Lieutenant Les Bartlett, Liddle Collection, Brotherton Library, University of Leeds.
26. Middlebrook and Everitt, op. cit., p. 448.
27. TNA AIR 8/730 5777.
28. Bartlett, op. cit.
29. See my *Bomber Boys*, pp. 247–55 for a full discussion of the subject.
30. TNA AIR 18/15 et al.

12: 'BRITAIN'S BEST ADVERTISEMENT'

1. TNA AIR 41/9 RAF Air Historical Branch, 'Propaganda and Publicity'.
2. See Malcolm Smith's verdict in *History*, vol. 82, no. 267 (July 1997), pp. 540–41.
3. Edward Mace, unpublished memoirs, Liddle Collection, Brotherton Library, University of Leeds.
4. Susan Ottaway, *Dambuster: A Life of Guy Gibson VC*, Pen and Sword, 2003, p. 95.
5. Ibid., p. 130.
6. Dahl's story *The Gremlins* based on the RAF name for mythical creatures blamed for mechanical glitches on aircraft was bought and developed by Disney though no film appeared.
7. Richard Morris, with Colin Dobinson, *Guy Gibson*, Viking, 1994, pp. 207–8.
8. Ibid., p. 210.
9. Ibid., pp. 284–5.
10. Smith, op. cit.
11. Hugh Verity, *We Landed by Moonlight*, Air Data Publications, 1995, p. 13.
12. Adrian Orchard, Group Captain Percy Charles 'Pick' Pickard www.oldframlinghamian.com
13. Verity, op. cit., p. 13.
14. IWM Sound Archive 8901.
15. Orchard, op. cit.
16. Patterson, op. cit.
17. *The Times*, 19 February 1945.
18. Pathé News, 'The Jailbreakers', www.youtube.com
19. Roger Broad, *Conscription in Britain 1939–1963: The Militarisation of a Generation*, Routledge, 2006, p. 50.
20. Hilary St George Saunders, *Royal Air Force, 1939–45*, HMSO, 1954, vol. III, p. 370.
21. Andrew Hendrie, *The Cinderella Service*, Pen and Sword, 2010, p. 129.
22. Ottaway, op. cit., p. 95.
23. Norman Lee and Geoffrey French, *The Lower Crust War*, unpublished memoir, Liddle Collection, Brotherton Library, University of Leeds.
24. Patterson, op. cit.
25. Wing Commander Norman Poole, unpublished memoir, RAF Museum, Hendon.

26. Roderic Papineau report to Tom Harrisson, 18 June 1941, Mass Observation Archive, University of Sussex.
27. Hayden, op. cit.
28. TNA AIR 20/6211.
29. Sir Charles Webster and Noble Frankland, *The Strategic Air Offensive Against Germany, 1939–1945*, HMSO, 1961, vol. IV, Appendix 41.
30. Roderic Papineau, MOA, University of Sussex.
31. John Sommerfield, *The Survivors*, John Lehmann, 1947, p. 76.
32. G. M. Partlett, *Memories of the WAAF 1942–1946*, unpublished memoir, Liddle Collection, Brotherton Library, University of Leeds.
33. RAF Manual of Cooking and Dietary, April 1942, in Partlett file, Liddle Collection, Brotherton Library, University of Leeds.
34. Morfydd Brooks, Letter to Dr Peter Liddle, 30.05.1997, Liddle Collection, Brotherton Library, University of Leeds.
35. Diaries of Betty Bullard, Liddle Collection, Brotherton Library, University of Leeds.
36. Sylvia Drake-Brockman, *Memories of the Women's Auxiliary Air Force, 1940–1946*, unpublished memoir, RAF Museum, Hendon.
37. TNA AIR 20/4583.
38. Brian Kingcome, *A Willingness to Die*, Tempus, 1999, p. 149.
39. Mrs Sylvia Watts, letters and memorabilia, Liddle Collection, Brotherton Library, University of Leeds.
40. Morfydd Rose, op. cit.
41. RAF Museum online exhibition, 'Pilots of the Caribbean', www.rafmuseum.org.uk
42. www.caribbeanaircrew-ww2.com
43. RAF Museum online exhibition.
44. Kurt Burling, 'Flyers of the Caribbean,' 13 November 2014, BBC London Online.
45. RAF Museum online exhibition.
46. Ibid.

13: OUT OF SIGHT

1. Diaries of Wing Commander L. B. Ercolani, IWM Documents 15352.
2. Obituary, 'Wing Commander Lucian Ercolani', *Daily Telegraph*, 7 April 2010.
3. Brian Bond and Kyoichi Tachikawa, *British and Japanese Leadership in the Far Eastern War*, Frank Cass, 2004, pp. 124–6.
4. www.aircrewremembered.com. Woodbridge was later honoured with the award of the George Cross. Two of his executioners were tried for war crimes and hanged in Rangoon in 1947.
5. F. Dane, unpublished memoir, IWM Documents 18824.
6. A. B. Sammons, 'Experiences as a Jap Prisoner of War', IWM Documents 2525.
7. Dane, op. cit.
8. His comeback would be hampered somewhat by his affair with Lady [Jessie] Auchinleck, wife of Field Marshal Sir Claude Auchinleck, the Army commander in India.
9. Hilary St George Saunders, *Royal Air Force, 1939–45*, HMSO, 1954, vol. III, p. 310.
10. Ibid.
11. Ercolani, op. cit.
12. Battle of Imphal, Wikipedia.
13. Dane, op. cit.
14. Sammons, op. cit.

14: BLACK AND WHITE

1. Letters of Flight Lieutenant John Rolfe, RAF Museum, Hendon.
2. John Keegan, *Six Armies in Normandy*, Book Club Associates, 1982, pp. 14–15.
3. Diary of Flight Lieutenant Stanley Bruce de Vere, IWM Documents 17213.
4. Ken 'Paddy' French, *My Early Life*, unpublished memoir, RAF Museum, Hendon.
5. Carlo D'Este, *Decision in Normandy*, Collins, 1983, Appendix A.

6. Vincent Orange, *Tedder: Quietly in Command*, Frank Cass, 2004, p. 218.
7. Hilary St George Saunders, *Royal Air Force, 1939–45*, HMSO, 1954, vol. III, p. 89.
8. French, op. cit.
9. Geoffrey Page, *Shot Down in Flames*, Grub Street, 1999, p. 134.
10. St George Saunders, op. cit., p. 95.
11. Vincent Orange, op. cit., p. 233.
12. St George Saunders, op. cit., p. 115.
13. Private Papers of H. E. Clift, IWM Documents 12270.
14. Page, op. cit., p. 116.
15. Pierre Clostermann, *The Big Show*, Weidenfeld & Nicolson, 2004, p. 171.
16. D'Este, op. cit., Appendix B.
17. YouTube, British Movietone News 'The RAF's Airborne Artillery'.
18. St George Saunders, op. cit., p. 123.
19. D'Este, op. cit., pp. 225–8.
20. The Bombing of Normandy, Wikipedia.
21. St George Saunders, op. cit., p. 136.
22. De Vere, op. cit.
23. St George Saunders, op. cit., p. 136.
24. Clift, op. cit.
25. Page, op. cit., p. 149.
26. Ibid., p. 150.
27. De Vere, op. cit.

15: THE HYACINTHS OF SPRING

1. Ken 'Paddy' French, *My Early Life*, unpublished memoir, RAF Museum, Hendon.
2. Letters of Flight Lieutenant John Rolfe, RAF Museum, Hendon.
3. Diary of Flight Lieutenant Stanley Bruce de Vere, Diaries, IWM Documents 17213.
4. Ibid.
5. Sebastian Ritchie, *Arnhem, Myth and Reality: Airborne Warfare, Air Power and the Failure of Operation Market Garden*, Robert Hale, 2011, p. 90.
6. Operation Market Garden, Wikipedia.
7. Ritchie, op. cit., p. 12.

8. Sergeant Arthur Rigby, War Time Log, Liddle Collection, Brotherton Library, University of Leeds.
9. Ritchie, op. cit., p. 16.
10. Ibid., p. 257.
11. De Vere, op. cit.
12. Hilary St George Saunders, *Royal Air Force 1939–45*, HMSO, 1954, vol. III, p. 208.
13. Kelso Robinson, unpublished memoir, Liddle Collection, Brotherton Library, University of Leeds.
14. Middlebrook and Everitt, op. cit., p. 685.
15. Rolfe, op. cit.
16. Private Papers of H. E. Clift, IWM Documents 12270.
17. Mass Observation Archive, University of Sussex.
18. The Forces Vote: A Mass Observation Report, 19 July, 1944. MOA, University of Sussex.
19. John Sommerfield, *The Survivors*, John Lehmann, 1947, pp. 27–30.
20. G. M. Partlett, *Memories of the WAAF 1942–1946*, unpublished memoir, Liddle Collection, Brotherton Library, University of Leeds.
21. Clift, op. cit.

EPILOGUE: BROTHERS AND SISTERS

1. Hilary St George Saunders, *Royal Air Force 1939–45*, HMSO, 1954, vol. III, p. 371.
2. Eric Banks, *The Laughing Boys*, unpublished memoir, Liddle Collection, Brotherton Library, University of Leeds.
3. TNA AIR 23/1986.
4. Eyewitness recollections of the airmen's strike at Mauripur, Karachi, in 1946 by ex LAC T. J. Adams, RAF Museum, Hendon.
5. An AC2, N. H. Cymbalist was imprisoned for ten years for promoting a strike at Base Headquarters, Singapore, but, after a few months, the sentence was quashed.
6. TNA AIR 57/2.
7. Ibid.

8. Sir Charles Webster and Noble Frankland, *The Strategic Air Offensive Against Germany, 1939–1945*, HMSO, 1961, vol. III, p. 310.

9. Kelso Robinson, unpublished memoir, Liddle Collection, Brotherton Library, University of Leeds.

10. Denis Richards, *Portal of Hungerford*, Heinemann, 1977, p. 204.

11. Harris was said to have been passed over for a peerage at the end of the war but maintained he had never wanted one. Churchill offered to ennoble him in 1951 but he declined, accepting instead a baronetcy.

12. Diaries of Betty Bullard, Liddle Collection, Brotherton Library, University of Leeds.

13. Sylvia Drake-Brockman, *Memories of the Women's Auxiliary Air Force, 1940–1946*, unpublished memoir, RAF Museum, Hendon.

14. F. Dane, unpublished memoir, IWM Documents, 18824.

15. Robinson, op. cit.

16. TNA AIR 20/6211. The figures are as of 31 May 1947. Another 117 from all categories are listed as missing.

Illustration Credits

Hugh Trenchard inspects men of the RAF Regiment (© *Imperial War Museums, CH 8705*)

RAF recruits signing up (*Photo by M. McNeill/Fox Photos/Getty Images*)

WAAF camera gun technicians (*Photo by © Hulton-Deutsch Collection/CORBIS/Corbis via Getty Images*)

Hugh Dowding with Fighter Boys (© *Imperial War Museums, CH 16283*)

Spitfires in formation (*Photo by Fg Off. B. J. Daventry/IWM via Getty Images*)

George Barclay with 249 Squadron comrades (*ww2images.com*)

Paddy Finucane at RAF Kenley, 20 September 1941 (*Pictorial Press Ltd/Alamy Stock Photo*)

Eric Lock drawn by Cuthbert Orde (© *Imperial War Museums, ART LD 2363*)

'Peter' Portal (*Photo by: Universal History Archive/UIG via Getty Images*)

Arthur Harris (© *Imperial War Museums, TR 1092*)

AVRO Lancaster (*Photo by Hulton Archive/Getty Images*)

Aircrew prepare to board a Short Stirling, 1942 (*Photo by Charles E. Brown/IWM via Getty Images*)

Vickers Wellingtons in formation (*Photo by Charles E. Brown/Royal Air Force Museum/Getty Images*)

Arthur Tedder (© *Imperial War Museums, TR 1487*)

Arthur 'Mary' Coningham (© *Imperial War Museums, TR 1497*)

Neville Duke (© *Imperial War Museums, HU 112294*)

Martin Baltimore of 55 Squadron (© *Imperial War Museums, CM 3844*)

Short Sunderland and crew (*Photo by Fox Photos/Hulton Archive/Getty Images*)

Sub-hunting Sunderland attacking U-boat, March 1944 (© *Imperial War Museums, C 4287*)

RAF Mosquitos at the de Havilland factory (© *Imperial War Museums, TR 1426*)

Bristol Beaufighter of 89 Squadron (© *Imperial War Museums, CF 511*)

Percy Pickard (© *Imperial War Museums, HU 98865*)

Pilots of 132 Squadron with CO Geoffrey Page (© *Imperial War Museums, CH 12889*)

Polish pilots of 303 Squadron (*Photo by Fox Photos/Hulton Archive/ Getty Images*)

Paratroopers, planes and gliders litter the skies during Operation Market Garden in September 1944 (*Photo by* © *CORBIS/Corbis via Getty Images*)

Arming a Typhoon during the Normandy campaign (*Photo by Fox Photos/Getty Images*)

Slaughter in a country lane, Falaise Pocket (© *Imperial War Museums, CL 910*)

Hitler's Berchtesgarden retreat after visit by Bomber Command (*Photo by* © *Hulton-Deutsch Collection/CORBIS/Corbis via Getty Images*)

Airmen in Austria studying literature for the 1945 General Election (© *Imperial War Museums, CL 2980*)

It's a lovely day tomorrow, celebrations in Whitehall (*Photo by Fox Photos/Getty Images*)

Index

Royal Air Force (*cont ...*)
149 Squadron 16–17, 58, 119; 150 Squadron 127; 151 Squadron 165; 155 Squadron 324; 156 Squadron 278, 309; 159 Squadron 321; 161 Squadron 290–1; 175 Squadron 336, 337; 198 Squadron 310; 214 Squadron 124, 182–4, 186, 282, 297; 216 Squadron 221; 217 Squadron (Coastal Command) 88, 202, 202–4; 221 Squadron (Coastal Command) 211; 222 Squadron 299; 249 Squadron 134–5, 153; 256 Squadron 93, 298; 257 Squadron 156–7; 263 Squadron 125; 264 Squadron 167, 168, 169, 170; 311 Squadron (Czech Squadron) 290; 341 (Alsace) Squadron 338–9; 355 Squadron 321; 412 Squadron 341; 428 Squadron 92, 272, 276–7; 464 Squadron 292, 293; 487 Squadron 292; 502 Squadron (Coastal Command) 211; 601 Squadron, Auxiliaries (County of London) 56, 70; 602 Squadron 339; 603 Squadron (Coastal Command) 310; 604 Squadron 172–3, 175; 611 Squadron 191–2, 193; 617 Squadron (Dam Busters) 15–16, 17, 82, 288, 327; 619 Squadron 23

Royal Air Force: American view of 1–4; assessment of 363–5, 367–9; attitude to violence and shared fulfilment in the work 295–9; Battle of Britain effect 164, 178; Brylcreem Boys 65, 340; cab rank system 339–40; cheerful fatalism of 28; colour, nationality and diversity in 295, 307–11; considered unstuffy, modern and competent 3–4, 6; and cult of the bomber 51–3, 62–4, 112, 367–8; death, survival and friendships 100, 145–6, 147–9, 370–1; demobilization and disaffection 365–7; dilution of old pre-war elite 140–1; dominant role of 4; drinking and socialising 141–5, 298; expansion, independence and professionalism of 16–17, 29–31, 49, 69–70, 114; fact-finding tours of 5–6; favoured status of 49–50, 298; and feelings of revenge and retaliation 184–5, 295–7; female responses to 6–7, 9, 94–5, 298; film-makers interest in 78–80; geographical reach and spread 92–3; glamorous image and appeal of 7, 28–9, 65, 72–5, 76, 80, 94, 95–7, 298; identity and loyalty focused on the squadron 153; incidence of VD in 252–9; interest in politics 360–1; leadership of 31–5, 153–5; losses, failures and inadequacies 127–33, 191–6; mobilization of 106–9; need for determination and flying ability 149–51; need for numerical and technological parity with the Luftwaffe 56–64; nicknamed 'The Firm' 94; official publications on 76; origins of the blue uniform and the ensign 25–8; *Per Ardua ad Astra* as motto of 30; pervading mood of cheerfulness in 145–7; portrayals in novels and biographies 70–2, 75–6; in the press and media 4–5, 6–7, 94–5; progress to a squadron 97–100; proportion of ground staff to aviators 87–9; provide essential air support in the Far East 321–5; publicity machine 78–80, 176–7, 178–84; relationship between ground crew and aircrew 299–301; relationship with the other services 31, 53–4, 126, 198, 294; relationship with politicians 54–5; scruffiness, deference and discipline in 305–7; sense of belonging and identity 295–6; slang 93–4; success of 35–6, 294–5; transformation of 48; as umbrella organization 295; unassailable reputation 7–8; vibrant *esprit de corps* in 301–7; virtues, qualities and deferential attitudes 146–7; weaknesses in 111–20; wishes to return to pre-war professional identity 366–7; women in 301–5, 307, 369–70

Royal Army Clothing Department 31
Royal Australian Air Force (RAAF) 224, 295, 325

PATRICK BISHOP

TARGET TIRPITZ

X-CRAFT, AGENTS AND DAMBUSTERS – THE EPIC QUEST TO DESTROY HITLER'S MIGHTIEST WARSHIP

WILLIAM
COLLINS

To Tony and Mary

Contents

Illustrations

Kapitän zur See Karl Topp on the navigation bridge of Tirpitz. (*The Trustees of the Imperial War Museum, London, HU 50747*)

Injured observer Dunworth being carried from his Albacore, March 1942 (*The Trustees of the Imperial War Museum, London, A 7902*)

Ice-caked deck of British warship in Northern Waters, 1942. (*Topham/AP/TopFoto. co.uk*)

Admiral Sir Dudley Pound walking to No. 10 with Winston Churchill. (© *Associated Newspapers/Daily Mail/Rex Features*)

Admiral Sir John Tovey. (*Süddeutsche Zeitung Photo/Scherl*)

Escorts and merchant ships of convoy PQ.17 at Hvalfjord, May 1942. (*The Trustees of the Imperial War Museum, London, A 8953*)

Tirpitz steaming through Altafjord, 16 March 1944. (*John Asmussen, www.bismarck-class.dk*)

RAF reconnaissance picture of Tirpitz in Trondheim. (*ww2images.com*)

Bjorn Rorholt. (*Private Collection*)

Tirpitz at anchor off Kaafjord, 4 July 1942. (*The Trustees of the Imperial War Museum, London, HU 50983*)

Mark Two Human Torpedo, 1942. (*ww2images.com*)

X-10 with Sub-Lieutenant Page on the casing. (*The Royal Navy Submarine Museum*)

Interior of X-craft with Sub Lt. 'Robbie' Robinson. (*The Royal Navy Submarine Museum*)

X-craft commanding officers before departure on Operation Source. (*The Royal Navy Submarine Museum*)

Tirpitz moored in Kaafjord. (*Popperfoto/Getty Images*)

View from Tirpitz of the X-Craft attack. (*ww2images.com*)

X-craft survivor John Lorimer on board Tirpitz after capture. (*ww2images.com*)

Donald Cameron with Godfrey Place after their release from a German PoW camp. (*Popperfoto/Getty Images*)

Wildcat on deck. (*ww2images.com*)

Barracudas landing on HMS *Formidable*, August 1944. (*The Trustees of the Imperial War Museum, London, A 25443*)

Christmas in the seamen's mess on Tirpitz, 1942. (*The Trustees of the Imperial War Museum, London, HU 50938*)

Seamen drinking beer on Tirpitz. (*The Trustees of the Imperial War Museum, London, HU 50766*)

Vice Admiral Oskar Kummetz on deck with Raeder and Admiral Otto Schniewind during an inspection trip to Norway. (*akg-images/ullstein bild*)

Aerial still of RAF attacks on Tirpitz, 15 September 1944. (*ww2images.com*)

Group photo of Flight Officer C. H. Giersch, Flight Lieutenant Bruce A. Buckham, Flight Officer D. A. Nolan, Squadron Leader A. G. Williams, Flight Officer D. A. Daniell and Wing Commander James B. Tait. (*AP/Press Association Images*)

James Tait with pipe. (*Courtesy Peter Tait*)

Woodsman's picture of the final attack through trees, November 1944. (*Private collection*)

Aerial photo of final attack taken from Flight Lieutenant Knights' Lancaster. (*ww2images.com*)

Tait pictured with Cochrane at the Tirpitz celebrations. (*Courtesy Peter Tait*)

Capsized Tirpitz with bomb crater in foreground. (*Popperfoto/Getty Images*)

Maps

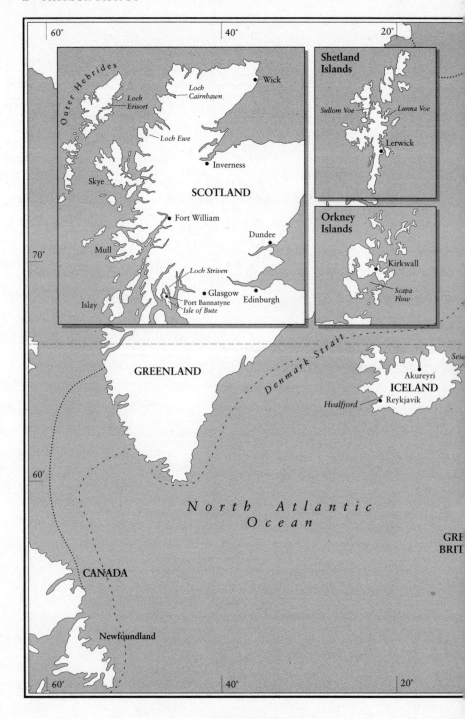

60°   40°   20°

Outer Hebrides

Wick

Loch
Cairnbawn

Loch
Erisort

Loch Ewe

Inverness

Skye

SCOTLAND

70°

Fort William

Dundee

Mull

Loch Striven

Glasgow

Islay

Port Bannatyne   Edinburgh
Isle of Bute

Shetland
Islands

Sullom Voe   Lunna Voe

Lerwick

Orkney
Islands

Kirkwall

Scapa
Flow

GREENLAND

Denmark Strait

Akureyri   Seið

ICELAND

Hvalfjord   Reykjavik

60°

North Atlantic
Ocean

GRE
BRIT

CANADA

Newfoundland

60°   40°   20°

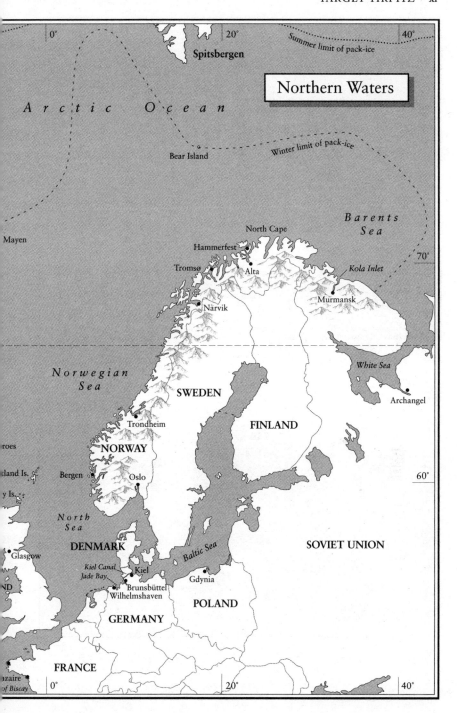

0° 20° 40°

Spitsbergen

Summer limit of pack-ice

Northern Waters

A r c t i c   O c e a n

Winter limit of pack-ice

Bear Island

B a r e n t s
S e a

Mayen

North Cape

Hammerfest

70°

Tromsø   Alta

Kola Inlet

Narvik

Murmansk

White Sea

N o r w e g i a n
S e a

SWEDEN

Archangel

Trondheim

FINLAND

roes

NORWAY

land Is.

60°

Bergen   Oslo

y Is.

N o r t h
S e a

DENMARK

Baltic Sea

SOVIET UNION

Glasgow

Kiel Canal   Kiel
Jade Bay

Gdynia

ND

Brunsbüttel
Wilhelmshaven

POLAND

40°

GERMANY

FRANCE

azaire

0°   20°   40°
of Biscay

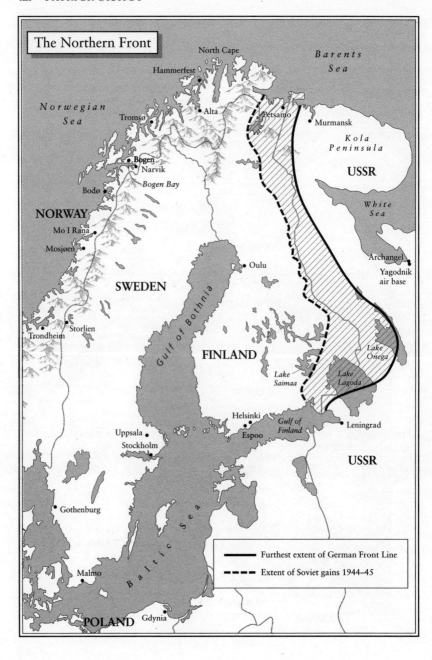

The Northern Front

North Cape

Barents
Sea

Hammerfest

Norwegian
Sea

Tromsø

Alta

Petsamo

Murmansk

Kola
Peninsula

Bogen
Narvik

Bogen Bay

USSR

Bodø

White
Sea

NORWAY

Mo I Rana

Mosjøen

Oulu

Archangel

Yagodnik
air base

SWEDEN

Gulf of Bothnia

Trondheim

Storlien

FINLAND

Lake
Saimaa

Lake
Onega

Lake
Ladoga

Uppsala

Stockholm

Helsinki

Espoo

Gulf of
Finland

Leningrad

USSR

Gothenburg

Baltic Sea

Malmo

Furthest extent of German Front Line

Extent of Soviet gains 1944–45

POLAND   Gdynia

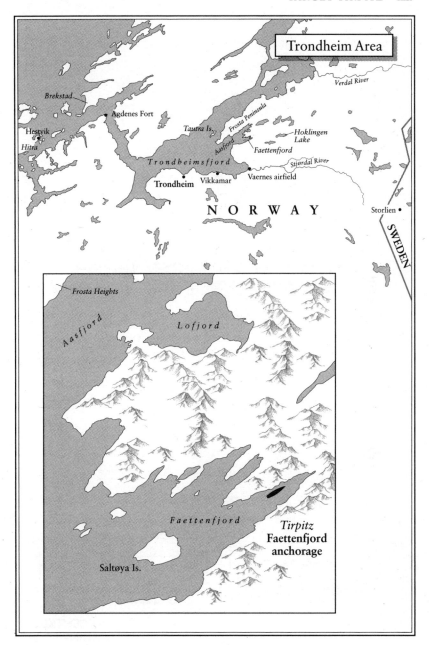

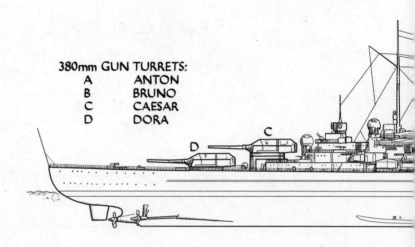

380mm GUN TURRETS:
A   ANTON
B   BRUNO
C   CAESAR
D   DORA

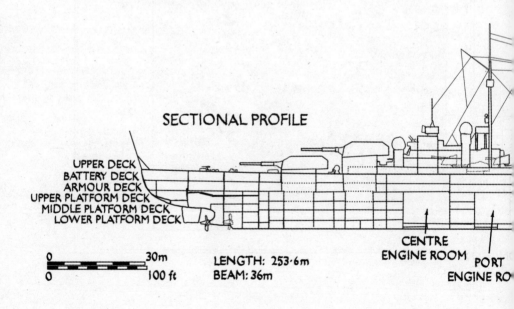

SECTIONAL PROFILE

UPPER DECK
BATTERY DECK
ARMOUR DECK
UPPER PLATFORM DECK
MIDDLE PLATFORM DECK
LOWER PLATFORM DECK

CENTRE
ENGINE ROOM   PORT
ENGINE RO

0   30m
0   100 ft

LENGTH: 253·6m
BEAM: 36m

BATTLESHIP *TIRPITZ*

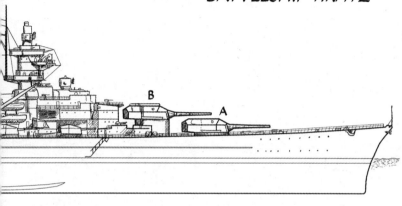

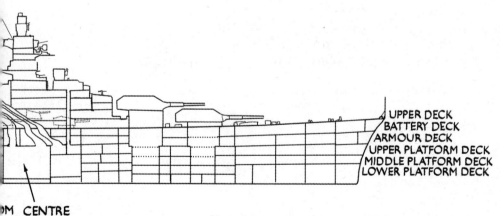

UPPER DECK
BATTERY DECK
ARMOUR DECK
UPPER PLATFORM DECK
MIDDLE PLATFORM DECK
LOWER PLATFORM DECK

M CENTRE
BOILER ROOM
(no.2)

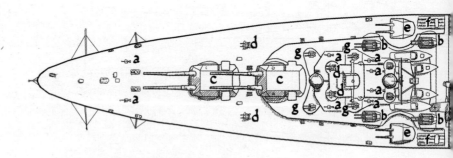

a 20 mm/L65 MG C/30 Single
b 105 mm/L65 SK-C/37
c 380 mm/L48.5 SK-C/34
d 20 mm/L65 MG C/38 Quadruple

TIRPITZ ARMAMENT
MARCH 1943

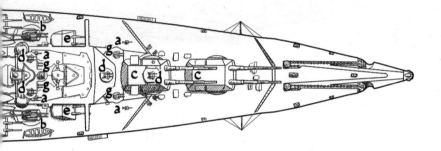

e   150 mm/L55 SK-C/28 End Turret
f   G7a T1 (Torpedo Launcher)
g   37 mm/L83 SK-C/30
h   150 mm/L55 SK-C/28 Middle Turret

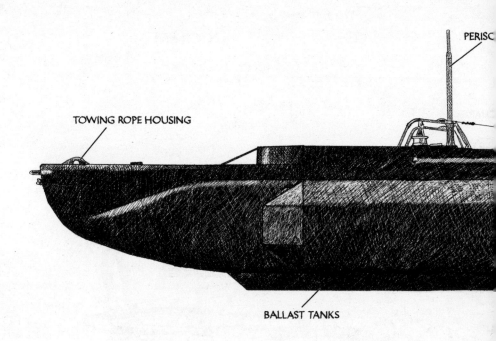

TOWING ROPE HOUSING

PERISC

BALLAST TANKS

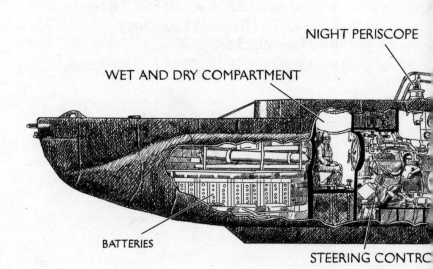

NIGHT PERISCOPE

WET AND DRY COMPARTMENT

BATTERIES

STEERING CONTRO

X-CRAFT

CHARGE

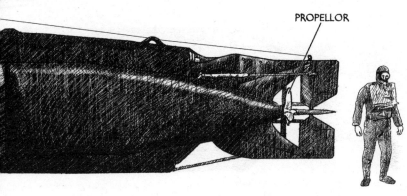

PROPELLOR

RISCOPE

HYDROPLANE AND MAIN MOTOR CONTROLS

AFTER HATCH

DIESEL ENGINE

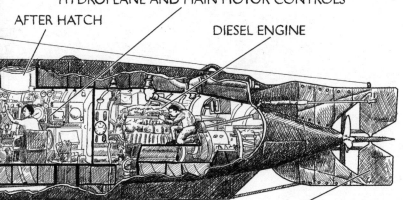

RUDDER AND HYDROPLANES

Ranks of the Kriegsmarine

SEAMEN

Matrose	Ordinary Seaman
Matrosen-Gefreiter	Able Seaman
Matrosen-Obergefreiter	Leading Seaman
Matrosen-Hauptgefreiter	Senior Leading Seaman

WARRANT OFFICERS

Bootsmann	Boatswain
Oberbootsmann	Chief Boatswain
Stabsoberbootsmann	Senior Chief Boatswain

OFFICERS

Fähnrich zur See	Midshipman
Oberfähnrich zur See	Sub-Lieutenant
Leutnant zur See	Lieutenant (Junior)
Oberleutnant zur See	Lieutenant (Senior)
Kapitänleutnant	Lieutenant Commander
Korvettenkapitän	Commander
Fregattenkapitän	Captain (Junior)
Kapitän zur See	Captain (Senior)
Konteradmiral	Rear Admiral
Vizeadmiral	Vice Admiral
Generaladmiral	No equivalent
Grossadmiral	Admiral of the Fleet

Prologue

The shortest memorandum in Winston Churchill's vast wartime output of queries, instructions and exhortations is three words long. On Monday, 14 December 1942 he wrote to the First Sea Lord, Sir Dudley Pound, demanding: 'Where is TIRPITZ?' The reply was reassuring. She was stuck safely in a Norwegian fjord near Trondheim undergoing repairs. Far from getting ready for a potentially devastating sortie, the crew was busy decorating the messes in preparation for Christmas.

The terse tone of the memo reveals a tremor of alarm. Churchill's manner, both real and contrived, radiated unflappability, even in the face of towering danger. Yet throughout her life this one battleship, the last of Hitler's fleet, could disturb his calm, nagging at his thoughts when it might be imagined he had bigger concerns to worry about. His wish to see it sunk, or at least disabled, bordered on the obsessive. The archives contain a stream of calls for action addressed to admirals and air marshals. A note from Churchill's office dated 22 January 1942 reports that 'the Prime Minister rang up the First Sea Lord and instructed him to see tonight the Chief of the Air Staff and concert means for making an attack on the TIRPITZ'. It goes on to record his opinion 'that the crippling of this ship would alter the entire face of the naval war and that the loss of 100 machines or 500 airmen would be well compensated for'.

In the cruel ledger of war, this, at the time, would have counted as a bargain. The destruction of no other enemy asset would absorb so many resources and so much time and energy. As long as *Tirpitz* was afloat she cast a shadow over British naval planning, mesmerizing the Home Fleet and forcing its most powerful ships to keep a constant watch against a breakout into the Atlantic where, in the anxious eyes of those watching her, she might cut Britain's transatlantic lifeline.

Fear of her destructive power inspired a heroic feat of arms, the blowing up of the St Nazaire dock in March 1942, thus depriving the battleship of a haven should it ever make it into the Atlantic. It also triggered the shaming decision a few months later to abandon Convoy PQ.17 to its fate when it was thought that *Tirpitz* was at sea.

The effort to deal with her was unrelenting. Between October 1940 and November 1944 she was the target of twenty-four major air and sea operations. They ranged from conventional attacks by heavy bombers to innovative operations by human torpedoes and midget submarines that even in wartime seemed suicidally risky. Churchill's proddings produced other even more hazardous and fanciful schemes that, mercifully, were never implemented.

Whether the prize was worth the cost is open to question. Churchill's determination, though, ensured that it would be paid in full. The actions that followed produced one of the great dramas of the war, touching the limits of human courage and folly. This is it.

1

The Belly of the Beast

At 8.30 on the morning of 12 November 1944, the gun crews and lookouts on the decks of the battleship *Tirpitz* stood at their action stations staring intently into the eastern sky. It was a crisp, clear day. The sunlight sparkled on the waters of the Norwegian fjord in which they lay anchored, close to a small, humped island, smudged with the first snow of winter. A few minutes before there had been a clamour of bells and blaring loudspeakers as an air raid warning was announced.

Below deck in the gunnery fire control section a young midshipman called Alfred Zuba was reading a book on German history when the alarm was sounded. He put it aside and waited for information about the approaching aircraft to start crackling in the earphones clamped to his head. The first report placed the raiders less than twenty miles away to the south-east, flying at an estimated 9,000 feet. The details changed fast. The aircraft were closing rapidly. Like everyone on board, he knew what they were – Lancaster bombers, carrying big new bombs that exploded with the destructive power of an earthquake. Nonetheless, he felt confident. *Tirpitz* had seen off a similar attack a fortnight before and there was a squadron of fighter aircraft nearby to protect her. As yet, though, there was no sign that they were flying to the rescue. When the raiders were nearly thirteen miles away the ship opened fire on the attackers. The first salvo erupted from 'Anton' and 'Bruno', the forward turrets each housing two 15-inch guns hurling shells weighing almost a ton each with a force that made *Tirpitz* vibrate like a tuning fork.

Above decks, men were shouting and pointing excitedly at a cluster of small dots, black and ominous against the innocent blue of the sky. The heavy anti-aircraft guns and the light flak opened up and the stink of burnt powder filled the air.

Then, over the industrial thud of artillery and the clatter of cascading shell cases, a different noise was heard. A deep, elemental thunderclap rolled over the decks and echoed through the passageways and stairwells. It was followed by another. It seemed to Zuba that the great craft was 'staggering'. She was being 'shaken by giant fists'.

In an instant the atmosphere of quiet efficiency inside the steel walls of his battle station was swept away and everywhere was 'disorder, confusion, mess, chaos – the bedlam of near and distant noises'. The deck below him began to tilt and he had to cling to a bulkhead to stop himself falling. He called the central flak control station but got only silence. Nearby, Oberleutnant zur See* Ludwig Mettegang, a twenty-three-year-old communications officer, was scrambling up the sloping floor to reach the emergency telephone that connected with the bridge. This line was still working. Mettegang demanded information and instructions, shouting to be heard over the din of explosions and the shriek of tortured metal. The thirty men around him, crouching in the gathering darkness as the lights flickered and died, watched and listened. They were on the lowest deck of the ship. To reach the outside world meant climbing through four levels up a succession of ladders. Mettegang turned to them with some dismaying news. The orders from the bridge were that they were to stay at their posts. Then came 'new terrific hits, new gigantic shakings'. Mettegang was shouting 'get out! Now!'

Zuba 'tore the phones from my head. I took my gas mask and rushed to the emergency exit. Fifteen, twenty men were standing there. Everybody wants to go up, wants to get out – out to life, to escape from death! But there is only room for one at a time … so we are standing there and waiting for our turn.'

As he shuffled forward he could feel the 'bottom burning under our feet'. Then it was his turn and he was 'clambering through, along the pitch-dark narrow hold' that led to the gun deck. As he reached

* See Ranks of the Kriegsmarine, p. xxiii, for equivalent British rank.

the next hatchway the ship made another sickening lurch. He slid down the linoleum-covered floor, slippery with oil and water, away from the exit. Water was tumbling into the compartment, 'black and oily', reaching up to his chest. He felt 'death take hold of me with iron hands'. He yelled for a lifebelt but no one could help. He scrabbled on the slick lino as 'more and more water comes streaming in, holds me tight and does not let me go'. He could feel the shock of more explosions shaking the ship. At last he 'found a handhold and pulled myself up. A comrade stretched out his hand to me so I could reach a ventilator [pipe].' The respite was short. The ship slumped again. The pipe that had been upright was now horizontal and he was hanging above the water swirling below. The weight of his sodden clothes was dragging him down and he could 'literally feel the strength draining out of my fingers'. Zuba had decided that 'a few minutes then it will be over' when the ship shifted again. His dangling feet found another pipe and he was standing upright once more. Someone was shouting that everyone should go back through the emergency exit. He could see the opening but to reach it he would have to leap six feet over the inky, freezing water. He braced to jump, knowing that, if he fell short, 'death was waiting underneath … my knees were trembling'. In this fatal moment an absurd concern floated into his mind. Somewhere along the way he had lost his cap. He pushed the thought aside and jumped. Then he was hauling himself through the hatchway. There was a thud as another man landed behind him, missed his footing and slipped, leaving him hanging there with the water lapping at his feet. Zuba went back to help him. He recognized him, a seaman called Hegendorf. The ordeal was only beginning but Hegendorf had already had enough. 'He was crying "Let me go, I must die." "Don't talk nonsense," I answered. I pulled him out through the hatchway. He was very heavy. Then we closed the exit to stop the water.'

They climbed through the bowels of the ship, collecting other survivors on the way, until they reached a messroom. A young sub-lieutenant, Willi Völsing, the senior officer in the gunnery fire control section, took charge. He told Zuba and the others to stay put while he took a party off to search for a way out. They sat down to wait. At least they were out of the water and had air to breathe. Someone found a battery lamp which gave a little light. There was silence. They 'tried to be calm. Nobody wanted to show what they were thinking about.' The one exception was Hegendorf who was a 'bundle of nerves'. Zuba tried to calm him down. He took no notice, only stopping when Völsing returned and warned him that he would shoot him if he did not shut up.

Völsing took Zuba aside 'and said to me in a low voice, "It's no use. We can't get out. We've been searching everywhere."' For the benefit of the others though, the sub-lieutenant put on a brave face, announcing loudly: '"We'll find some way out. I won't abandon this fight."' Now Zuba took over the search. He and his team found their way into the A Deck radio room where there were more survivors whom he led back to join the others. During their search they had found another lamp, and some dry clothes. Zuba stripped off his uniform and put on white underpants, green trousers and a blue mechanic's jacket, which made him look 'like a comic actor'. They had also found bread, coffee, cognac, sweets and a large box of cigarettes.

For a while their fear lifted and their spirits rose. 'Suddenly someone said, "Good Lord, today is my birthday." We all congratulated him.' It seemed to Zuba, though, that many were thinking 'let us hope your birthday is not your death day as well'. The 'birthday boy was allowed to take the first big swig. Then it was the turn of the others.'

They sat, warmed by the cognac, chewing coffee beans. One of the wireless operators, 'a regular brick, calmness itself', gave an optimistic assessment of their situation. He was sure that everything was being done to save them – they would have to be patient until the cutting gear arrived. The ship was 118 feet wide and the water she lay in was shallow. Now that she had turned turtle, 'there is always going to be a bit sticking out of the water'.

Soon afterwards the wireless operator's prediction seemed about to come true. Zuba heard 'a knocking somewhere – bang, bang, bang'. Someone seized a fire extinguisher and began knocking back, but the noises got weaker and faded away. Their spirits slumped again. They sat in the cold metal box, each alone with his thoughts. Zuba worried how his mother would take the news of his death. His brother had been killed a year and three days before on the Eastern Front. What would the effect be on his fiancée Ruth who, when he had told her that he was being posted to *Tirpitz*, 'was glad because she thought that being on a battleship was safer'?

Someone blurted out, '"If I get out of here I will get married at once." Now they all start saying what they intend to do if they get out'. While the others gabbled, though, hope was ebbing from Zuba. He could hear the rush of water. Then one of the radio operators noticed it, too. He began asking 'again and again, "is the water rising?"' The others told him to shut up. They sat sunk in silence. Then, over the sinister gurgling, they heard men calling out.

They shouted back together, 'where are you?'. A chorus of voices came back but the reply was indistinct. The yelling continued. Finally they understood what they were saying. Their unseen comrades were trapped in Switch Room 3. Zuba and his companions shouted back that they were in the forward mess, but there was no answering call. They sank back into silence.

Then, someone thought they heard other voices, and a sharp hissing noise. It sounded, he said, like gas from an oxyacetylene torch. To Zuba, though, it seemed more likely to be the rustle of invading water. Others, though, seized on this rope end of hope. A leading seaman took the fire extinguisher and smashed through the compartment wall nearest to where the noise was coming from, only to be faced with a slab of thick steel. Zuba could hear the hissing more clearly now. It was stopping and starting. He began to think that 'it could come from cutting apparatus … again there is hissing, crackling and banging'.

They started yelling again, 'shouting "hurry up, the water is rising"'. Their room was still dry but they could see the compartment below them filling up. Zuba felt they were 'in a running race with death'. The torch noises were getting closer, though. Someone 'puts his hand on the steel wall. It is quite warm. "Hurry!" we shout'.

Then, a molten red spot appeared on the wall, followed by a shower of sparks. They shouted with joy 'like little boys', as the

The last berth

glowing line crept along the wall. They were 'staring at it, drinking in every centimetre of its growth', when 'suddenly the hissing stopped. We heard voices moving away. There was a deathly silence around us.'

The captives shouted in dismay. They screamed and banged on the cold steel walls of their prison, but 'there is no answer, only the echo of our desperate shouting'. In the darkness below they could make out a 'mirror of black gleaming water' rising towards them.

Just as despair settled over him, Zuba heard more banging and sparks sprayed from the wall. A molten spot reappeared and slowly traced a glowing rectangle. There was a clang of falling metal and faces appeared in the hole. Their saviours looked 'as if they had come from another world'. The hole was only sixteen inches wide. Each man had to be pushed and pulled through it. They emerged into another space with a ladder leading upwards. When Zuba reached the top he saw a square in the metal above him and, through it, the sky. It was evening. The stars 'were twinkling, a sight I will never forget'. He climbed up, and out into freezing night, 'standing free and saved and sucking ... air into my lungs'.

He was standing on a vast expanse of red-leaded metal. It took him a moment to realize it was the hull of the ship. As he was led away a soldier told him why the rescue had been broken off. Working in the cramped space between the hull and the lower deck, the welders had started to pass out from lack of oxygen. The twenty survivors were put on a launch and taken off to another ship, where they were fed and bathed and clothed. Zuba was anxious to know the fate of the men he was with when the ship began to topple. Leutnant Mettegang was still missing, believed trapped with twenty-four men. Next day, when Zuba asked again for news, he was told they were dead. According to the story that went around, the rescue team had been able to hear the trapped men but not to reach them. They had been singing 'Deutschland, Deutschland, Über Alles' before they suffocated.[1]

2

Wilhelmshaven, Saturday, 1 April 1939

Adolf Hitler descended from a Mercedes limousine and strode along the dockside beneath the slipway supporting the gigantic hull. His face wore an expression of childish delight as he looked up at the soaring flank of his new battleship, then turned to salute the crowds packed in thousands in orderly squares alongside. They had been brought in from all over Germany's ever-expanding territories to provide the numbers needed for a theatrical display of might and played their part enthusiastically, cheering, waving swastika pennants, pressing forward for a glimpse of the leader as he strode past.

He skipped up the steps to a high platform raised before the bow. It was a bright, sunny day but a cold wind whipping in from Jade Bay snapped at the flags and bunting and rattled the still-bare branches of the trees. Surrounding him on the platform was a cluster of admirals and generals. Among them, wearing a cloche hat and a fur stole, stood a lone woman. Frau Ilse von Hassell was there to name the ship in honour of her father, Admiral Alfred von Tirpitz, the architect of the Imperial German navy. She was a reluctant participant. Her husband Ulrich, a diplomat, had watched the ascent of the Nazis with dismay. The head of the modern German fleet, Admiral Erich Raeder, had first asked Tirpitz's seventy-eight-year-old widow Marie to perform the ceremony but she claimed to be too old and infirm to attend. He turned next to Ilse and her younger sister Margot but they too declined. Ilse recalled that he then 'sent a second appeal, urgently demanding my presence. It was practically an order. I need not explain … what such an order meant in those times in Germany.'[1]

The Führer and the admiral's daughter stood in the blustery wind for a minute or so in uncomfortable silence. Eventually he looked down at the sea of joyful, upturned faces and, 'in a sort of monotone', murmured: 'I have sent trains to all parts of Germany, of Austria, of Czechoslovakia. It is the best propaganda.' An official called her forward to the microphone. In a clear voice she declared: 'By order of the Führer and Supreme Commander of the Wehrmacht, I christen you with the name "Tirpitz".' The bottle swung and smashed. A large, hand-lettered sign reading TIRPITZ in Gothic script was lowered over the side. Then the hull began to move slowly, gathering speed as it went, stern-first down Slipway No. 2 hitting the basin in a maelstrom of churning water. Only the steel vanes welded onto the sides, sticking out like elephant's ears, prevented a collision with the far jetty. The cheers of the crowd mingled with 'Deutschland Über Alles' blaring from loudspeakers as the notables descended the steps and were driven to the town hall square for the next event.

The day was charged with nervous expectation. The world was watching Wilhelmshaven. Europe was sliding towards war and Hitler's words might give a sign of how fast or slow the catastrophe would be in coming. The omens were not good. The previous day Britain had abandoned its policy of appeasement. The decision had been forced by Hitler's demand that Poland hand over the free city of Danzig, prised from Germany by the Treaty of Versailles. The Prime Minister, Neville Chamberlain, who stood by timidly as the Reich swallowed Austria and Czechoslovakia, had at last made a stand, telling the House of Commons that Britain and France would lend Poland 'all the support in their power' if Germany attacked.

The volte-face triggered a Wagnerian rage. Hitler had hoped he would not have to go to war against the British. Admiral Canaris, the head of German Military Intelligence who was with him when the news came through, watched as he pounded his fists on a marble table, his face contorted with anger, shouting that he would 'cook them a stew they'll choke on'.[2] At around noon, Hitler began the speech everyone was waiting for. Wilhelmshaven's main square had been decked out Nuremberg-style with flags and banners. Reporters in the press area noticed something they had not seen before at such events. Hitler was standing behind a curved glass screen, apparently designed to protect him from an assassin's bullet.

His speech was long and disjointed, now soft, now hard, swinging between cajolery and bluster. Its main theme, though, was Britain, or 'England' as Germans chose to call it. The change of heart in London amounted to a declaration of enmity. Instead of staying on the sidelines as Hitler had hoped, Britain, its army and above all its navy would now have to be counted in the forces arrayed against his plans for European domination.

He started by reopening an old wound. He reminded the crowd that during the last war the British had 'systematically' encircled Germany, imposing a 'hunger blockade' that had resulted in hundreds of thousands of deaths. Now, by blocking her efforts to reclaim her historic territories, she was seeking to do so again. Germany, he warned, was 'not going to put up in the long run with a policy of intimidation or … of encirclement'.

The warning was reinforced by a threat aimed at the British navy – which had enforced the wartime blockade. Only four years before, Britain and Germany had agreed a naval pact that limited the size of the German fleet. It had been based, he said, 'on the fervent desire we all possess never to go to war with England'. He went on: 'If this wish no longer exists in England, then the practical condition for this agreement is removed.' The German people would be 'quite content to put up with this. We are so sure of ourselves because we are so strong and we are strong because we are united.'[3]

The speech ended in a volley of 'sieg heils'. Hitler was driven away to board a launch which sped out into the sparkling waters of Jade Bay, carrying him to the battle cruiser *Scharnhorst*, which had gone into service less than three months before and seemed to embody all the power and vigour of the new order. There he was met by Erich Raeder, carrying the baton which marked his promotion that day to the rank of Grossadmiral – the highest pinnacle of the naval hierarchy.

At 2.30 p.m. they sat down to eat flanked by admirals and generals, past and present. The exaltation that flooded through Hitler during great public performances had subsided and he appeared

Erich Raeder with grossadmiral's baton

subdued. 'He arrived, saluted, sat down, spoke to his neighbours and disappeared as he had arrived,' wrote Ulrich von Hassell* in his diary. 'He said not a word to any of the old officers, nor did he even look them in the eye.'[4]

After lunch Hitler was ferried to another ship, the *Robert Ley*, a large liner that took party loyalists on holiday cruises. He stayed on board throughout Sunday, while the ship tacked back and forth in the waters off Wilhelmshaven, escorted by *Scharnhorst* and a pair of

---

* Von Hassell was a conservative patriot who had been wounded in the First World War and still carried a French bullet in his heart. He was executed for his part in the 20 July 1944 plot to assassinate Hitler.

destroyers. To amuse the Führer, Raeder at one point ordered the battle cruiser to steer directly at the liner, only swerving away at the last minute.[5]

These carefree activities seemed calculated to demonstrate Hitler's lack of concern at the new international developments. Whether he understood their full import for the navy he was reviewing was open to question. Naval matters played a subordinate role in Hitler's military calculations, an attitude he did not bother to disguise. He was a soldier not a sailor. Throughout the time at Wilhelmshaven he had worn a brown greatcoat and tunic, the colour of the Flanders mud he had fought in bravely which stood out against the navy blue and gold braid of the attendant admirals. He came from land-locked Austria and was often seasick on his occasional voyages aboard the state yacht *Grille*.

Grossadmiral Raeder, though, was disturbed by the turn that events had taken. He had been born sixty-three years before in Hamburg, the son of a devoutly Christian teacher, and entered the Naval College at Kiel at eighteen. The Dreadnought era was approaching when great battleships, bristling with guns and laden with armour plating, were the peak of naval power and prestige. He fought the British at Dogger Bank and Jutland and stayed on in the navy, serving the Weimar Republic loyally. In 1928 he was appointed Commander-in-Chief of the Kriegsmarine.

Raeder kept his distance from Hitler until he came to power. His first impression of him was favourable. Hitler seemed to him 'an outstanding personality with a real claim to leadership'.[6] He had gained the Führer's confidence and, once the strategic decisions had been taken, been given a free hand and a generous budget to build up the navy. Hitler had been presented with two choices for his navy. The first proposed a cheap, light, flexible force, centred on submarines and the small but powerfully armed long-range cruisers that the British had nicknamed 'pocket battleships'. This plan had no pretensions to challenging Britain as a naval power but carried great potential to harm her. The second was to build a big fleet of modern surface ships that would establish Germany as a world maritime force. He had chosen the grandiose option, with Raeder's approval. The result was 'Plan-Z', which had been finally agreed by Hitler only two months before. It envisaged a fleet with ten battleships at its core and four aircraft carriers to provide the air power that was becoming a vital adjunct of naval operations. Supporting them would be fifteen pocket battleships, over a hundred cruisers and destroyers and an underwater strength of more than 250 U-boats.

A force of this size would take up to ten years to build. The plan had been designed on the assumption, reinforced by frequent assurances from Hitler, that a war with Britain was still well over the horizon. Only four years before, the two countries had signed the Anglo-German Naval Agreement, mentioned by Hitler in his speech. Germany agreed to limit its surface shipbuilding programme to 35 per cent of the British fleet. In submarines, it was permitted 45 per cent of the Royal Navy's tonnage, with a clause allowing it to rise to parity in special circumstances. The deal was negotiated in a friendly atmosphere. Historically, both sides had felt respect for one another. When the commander of the British Fleet at Jutland, Lord Jellicoe, died in November 1935, Raeder ordered all German warships to fly their flags at half-mast.

A confrontation with the Royal Navy had seemed a distant prospect when Plan Z was being worked out. Now, with Chamberlain's guarantee to the Poles, it loomed suddenly and alarmingly into view. Raeder's exalted title scarcely reflected the might of his fleet. As he waved his landlubber leader off at the end of his Wilhelmshaven jaunt, he knew very well that he had limited assets with which to face the coming crisis.

The German fleet that spring had only two big ships in service – the battle cruisers *Scharnhorst* and *Gneisenau*, both displacing 32,000 tons.* There was a heavy cruiser, the 14,000-ton *Admiral Hipper*, which would be joined in the coming year by two ships of the same class, the *Blücher* and the *Prinz Eugen*. Three pocket battleships were in commission, the *Deutschland*, *Admiral Graf Spee* and *Admiral*

---

* All displacements are given as standard, minus the weight of fuel, water and stores that would be carried on voyage.

Scheer. Despite displacing only 12,000 tons, they packed heavy fire-power in their six 11-inch guns. Of the four planned aircraft carriers only one, the *Graf Zeppelin*, had been laid down, but years of work remained. As for submarines, about fifty would be ready for operations by the end of the summer.

In numerical terms, this was a tiny force when compared with the Royal Navy. It could muster twelve battleships with five more on the way, four battle cruisers, six aircraft carriers with another six building, and twenty-four heavy cruisers. It was only below the waves that numbers were equal.

But strength was not measured in numbers alone. The qualitative difference between the two fleets went a long way towards correcting the quantitative imbalance. The core of the German fleet was modern, whereas many of the British ships dated back to the previous war and only some of them had been updated. The new ships in the pipeline were inferior to their German counterparts. Britain, it would often be lamented in the years to come, had played the game when it came to honouring the various limitations agreements it had entered into in the inter-war years. The Germans had, systematically and ruthlessly, cheated.

All their large ships were bigger than they were supposed to be. The *Scharnhorst* and *Gneisenau* were actually 6,000 tons heavier than officially claimed. The extra weight came from the thick armour plating which reduced the danger from the heavier guns of the British battle cruisers. They were also faster than claimed and could muster thirty-one knots, which gave them the edge over their counterparts if forced to run.

It was in the top class – the battleships – that German superiority was most marked. Since *Tirpitz* and her sister ship *Bismarck* were laid down in 1936, the Germany Embassy in London, on Raeder's instructions, had lied to the Foreign Office about their specifications. Instead of being 35,000 tons, the upper limit agreed in the Anglo-German Naval Agreement, they would both weigh in at 42,500 tons. The British stuck to the rules. As a result the battleships under construction of the King George V (KGV) class were nearly 12 per cent lighter.

It was not merely a question of size. When finished, *Tirpitz* and *Bismarck* would best the Royal Navy's new ships in every department. They each mounted eight 15-inch guns against the 14-inch main armament of the *King George V*. They were faster and could travel far greater distances without refuelling. They were also immensely well protected, with thick layers of steel armour encasing decks and hull, turrets, engine rooms and magazines. It was often said by their enemies that the Germans had declared their battleships 'unsinkable'. The claim does not seem to have been made officially. Their constructors revealed after the war that the Kriegsmarine often intervened during the building of *Tirpitz* and *Bismarck* to 'raise their levels of unsinkability'.[7] The result was that, in the case of *Tirpitz*, 40 per cent of her overall weight was made up of armour plating. The belief grew that *Tirpitz* and *Bismarck* could survive any torpedo, shell or bomb that British ships or aircraft could hurl at them, and it was not unfounded. The British navy had been starved of funds in the post-war years, and little effort had been put into developing new weaponry. Torpedoes and shells carried feeble charges and lacked penetrative power. The greatest failure to keep pace with technological developments lay in the area of naval aviation. The Admiralty was only now regaining control of the Fleet Air Arm from the RAF, whose equipment programmes had given priority to fighters and bombers. The navy was entering the war equipped with biplanes that looked like survivors from the previous conflict.

Even with his long-term plan in tatters and *Tirpitz* and *Bismarck* still far from completion, Raeder could still cause Britain great harm. The Royal Navy suffered from a crucial strategic disadvantage. Britain depended for survival on its seaborne trade. The navy had the duty of protecting a web of routes that stretched to all corners of the globe. Germany, as a continental power, was far less reliant on overseas supplies. If it came to war, its navy's responsibility was clearer and narrower. Its function was not to protect but to attack, ravaging the sea lanes that linked Britain to the rest of the world.

As the countdown to hostilities accelerated, it was powerful German warships rather than the U-boat fleet that the Admiralty most feared. 'Nothing would paralyse our supply system and seaborne trade so successfully,' wrote the First Sea Lord Sir Dudley Pound, just before the outbreak, 'as attack by surface raiders.' It was to their detection, pursuit and destruction that the Home Fleet turned as the long overture finished and the curtain went up on the war.

3

Swordfish

Caked with the salt of the northern seas, her flanks streaked with rust, HMS *Suffolk* slid gratefully towards the Icelandic haven of Hvalfjord. The heavy cruiser had been patrolling the Denmark Strait between Greenland and Iceland and her crew were looking forward to a quiet evening in harbour. Then a signal arrived warning them that their respite might be a short one. *Bismarck*, the ship they had been watching for, had been sighted at the Norwegian port of Bergen.

On arrival in Hvalfjordur *Suffolk* went straight off to refuel. The company were eating supper when another signal arrived. They were to return immediately to the Denmark Strait. The following morning, Friday, 23 May 1941, they met up with their sister ship *Norfolk* in the harbour at Isafjordur on the north-west coast of Iceland and headed off to take up their patrolling positions. The Strait was the most distant of the possible routes German warships could take from their own ports to the Atlantic. It was 300 miles long and 180 miles wide at its narrowest point, but even at this time of year it was still choked with pack ice which stretched eighty miles eastward from the Greenland coast.

The cruisers spent the day criss-crossing the sleeve of green water, flecked with floes, but saw nothing. Then, early that evening, the voice of Captain Robert Ellis sounded over the tannoy. He broadcast news that was both exciting and alarming. *Bismarck* had left Bergen. Her destination was unknown but there was a strong chance she was heading their way. The ship's officers did not allow the revelation to disturb their sangfroid. They gathered, as usual, in the wardroom for a drink before dinner. The captain had just walked in to join them when a klaxon blared, calling all hands to their action stations. The officers slammed down their sherries and pink gins and dashed to their posts. 'It was the enemy!' Lieutenant Commander Charles Collett recorded afterwards. '[And] they were only six miles away, slinking along the edge of the ice in a snowstorm.'[1]

The moment that Winston Churchill and the Admiralty had been waiting for had arrived. *Bismarck* was at sea. Simultaneously, a great threat and a great opportunity had materialized. Sinking her would count as a magnificent naval victory. It would also provide some longed-for good news after a succession of setbacks, failures and disappointments. The relief of surviving the Battle of Britain had given way to the bleak realization of the nation's isolation and the immensity of the difficulties ahead. The country was now engaged in another struggle for existence, which Churchill had christened the Battle of the Atlantic. Having failed to bring Britain to terms by the threat of invasion, Germany had switched strategy and was trying to starve her into submission, by cutting the lifelines that connected her with the rest of the world. Churchill was to judge later that 'amid the torrent of violent events one anxiety reigned supreme ... dominating all our power to carry on the war, or even keep ourselves alive, lay mastery of the ocean routes and the free approach and entry to our ports'.

It was the navy's principal duty to defend these routes but the task was overwhelming. It no longer had the resources of the French fleet, a large part of which lay at the bottom of Mers-el-Kebir harbour, sunk by British guns. America gave all the help it could, but had yet to enter the war. Early engagements, in the battle for Norway and on the high seas, had failed to neutralize the threat from the German navy. Instead, in the spring of 1941, the Kriegsmarine was setting the pace in the struggle.

The main battleground was the vital sea lanes of the North Atlantic. In March and April 1941, nearly half a million tons of Allied shipping had been sent to the bottom. Most of it was sunk by U-boats, whose effectiveness had been badly underestimated by a complacent Admiralty in the interwar years. Until now the surface raiders that Admiral Pound had feared would 'paralyse' the sea lanes had played a secondary part in the campaign. That seemed about to change. A foray by the battle cruisers *Scharnhorst* and *Gneisenau* in February and March had resulted in the destruction or capture of twenty-two ships totalling 115,600 tons. Now it was *Bismarck*'s turn and the transatlantic convoys, already ravaged by bombardment from land-based bombers and ambush by prowling U-boats, would be at the mercy of the most powerful German warship yet put to sea.

When the news of the sighting came through, Churchill was embarked on a weekend at Chequers with his wife Clementine, his daughter Sarah and her husband, the comedian Vic Oliver, as well as the devoted Major General Hastings 'Pug' Ismay, his Chief of Staff as Minister of Defence. He had also invited Averell Harriman, President Roosevelt's special representative. Before dinner that Friday night the Prime Minister was pondering a stream of unwelcome reports from Crete. British resistance to the German invasion was faltering. After a poor start, the Germans were recovering. Paratroopers seized the vital airfield at Maleme and reinforcements were flying in. Luftwaffe fighters had begun to arrive that day as well as artillery units. *Bismarck*'s detection raised hopes that some better tidings might be on the way. Churchill waited up until 3 a.m., for the latest developments, but eventually gave up and went to bed.

The *Bismarck*'s breakout had been expected for days. An initial report from Captain Henry Denham, the busy British naval attaché in neutral Sweden, that the battleship had left the Baltic was soon reinforced by sightings by RAF reconnaissance flights and German naval signals decrypted by the Bletchley Park code breakers.

The question was, which way would she come? There were two possibilities. She could aim for the Denmark Strait. Or she could take the shorter route and dart at the gap between the Faroes and Iceland. The Commander of the Home Fleet Sir John Tovey had dispatched *Norfolk* and *Suffolk* under the command of Rear Admiral William Wake-Walker to deal with the first eventuality. At the same time he had detached a squadron under Vice Admiral Lancelot Holland consisting of the battle cruiser *Hood*, the battleship *Prince of Wales* and six destroyers to plug the Faroes–Shetlands gap.

This was at first sight a formidable force. *Hood* was the biggest ship in the British fleet. *Prince of Wales* was brand new – so new that she had yet to complete working up and still had workers from Vickers Armstrongs and Cammell Laird on board when she sailed. On the evening of 22 May Tovey himself left Scapa Flow aboard his flagship *King George V*, and together with the aircraft carrier *Victorious* led the Home Fleet westwards.

With the assets at his disposal, Tovey had every chance of intercepting *Bismarck* and bringing her to action. It was a thrilling prospect. Great sea actions were rare, yet they were the unspoken end of all naval training and preparation. From early puberty, naval cadets were steeped in the legends of Trafalgar and the Armada. Below decks, the pride in tradition though more subdued was present nonetheless. An epic battle offered those who fought in it the chance of distinction and to those who directed it the prospect of greatness. Tovey knew that if he sank the *Bismarck* his place in the Royal Navy's history was assured. He accepted, too, that his peers were harsh judges and failure would bring ignominy.

The odds on an interception were in his favour. Even so, there was still a good chance that *Bismarck* would reach the Atlantic unscathed. It had happened before. In February, *Scharnhorst* and *Gneisenau* had evaded the Home Fleet to squeeze through the Faroes–Iceland gap to begin their Atlantic raid. If *Bismarck* repeated the feat, a ripe cluster of targets awaited her. There were eleven convoys plying the Atlantic, some of them perilously close to *Bismarck*'s likely point of arrival in the ocean's northern reaches.

It was important for Hitler's long-term war plans that the battleship made it through. He was about to turn his armies eastwards against the Soviet Union and he needed a cowed and docile Europe at his back. The war at sea presented the best chance of bringing his last enemy in the west to heel. The original operation, codenamed Rheinübung, or Rhine Exercise, had been correspondingly ambitious. Admiral Raeder's plan had been to combine his four biggest ships in a powerful task force that could, temporarily at least, cause a suspension of the convoys, cutting off Britain's maritime life-support system. *Bismarck* and *Tirpitz* would sail from Germany, and meet up with *Gneisenau* and *Scharnhorst*, now lying at Brest on the French Atlantic coast. One by one, though, his force had been whit-tled away. A lucky torpedo dropped by a Beaufort of RAF Coastal Command had done *Gneisenau* enough damage to put her out of action for six months. Then it was discovered that the boilers power-ing *Scharnhorst*'s steam turbines needed replacing. The battleships would have to operate on their own. For both it would be their first operation.

There was one more blow to fall. *Tirpitz*'s progress from launch to commissioning had been slower than her sister's. She had finally gone into service on 25 February that year. Spring sea trials in the Baltic had revealed numerous niggling mechanical difficulties. Raeder decided he dare not risk her on a long and testing operation. The decision dismayed the crew and their new commander, Kapitän zur See Karl Topp. When Hitler paid a visit to the battleships as they lay at Gotenhafen, as the Germans called the Polish Baltic port of Gdynia, a fortnight before Rhine Exercise was to start, Topp begged him to overrule Raeder. Hitler refused. When *Bismarck* left Gotenhafen just before noon on 18 May, she had with her only a single big ship consort – the 14,000-ton heavy cruiser *Prinz Eugen* which, although new, had limited firepower and a short range.

The operation was led by Admiral Günther Lütjens, the commander of the German fleet. His reputation stood high. It was he who had led *Gneisenau* and *Scharnhorst* during their late winter rampage. Lütjens' down-turned mouth and hard eyes seldom broke into a smile. He looked what he was – cold, proud and utterly confi-dent of his abilities, rarely feeling the necessity to explain critical decisions to those above or below him. His abilities were tied to a strict sense of duty. He could be relied on to follow the spirit of his orders even when he doubted their wisdom. Lütjens was quite aware of the dangers ahead. His ship outclassed anything in the British fleet. But the task force he was commanding had shrunk to a fraction of its original strength. It seemed to him probable – even inevitable – that it would eventually be overwhelmed by weight of numbers. Before the start of Rheinübung he had called on a friend at Raeder's Berlin headquarters to say goodbye. 'I'll never come back,' he told him, in a matter-of-fact voice.[2]

The mood aboard *Bismarck*, though, was buoyant. The ship thrummed with excitement and anticipation as she headed out towards the Norwegian Sea. At noon, over the loudspeakers, the ship's commander, Kapitän Ernst Lindemann, at last told the 2,221 officers and men on board where they were going. 'The day we have longed for so eagerly has at last arrived,' he said. 'The moment when we can lead our proud ship against the enemy. Our objective is commerce raiding in the Atlantic imperilling England's existence.' He signed off with 'the hunter's toast, good hunting and a good bag!' There was to be nothing sporting about their methods, however. The orders Lindemann had been given included an instruction that 'the work of destruction is not to be delayed by life-saving activities'.[3]

Two days later, Lütjens' task force was two hundred miles off the Norwegian coast. Just after noon, ignoring the preferences of the headquarters staff who favoured the Faroes–Iceland passage, he decided he would take the long way round to the Atlantic. He ordered course to be set for the Denmark Strait, hoping that the fog, snow and rain that was gathering in the west would cloak his movements.

At 7.11 p.m. on 23 May, as the task force steamed at a brisk twenty-seven knots with the black peaks of Iceland to port and the antiseptic blue of the Greenland pack ice to starboard, lookouts picked up an ominous shape among the shifting banks of fog. It was the *Suffolk*. The flimsy hope of concealment was gone and, whether it came soon or late, everyone realized that a battle was now all but inevitable.

Suffolk's lookouts had also sighted their enemy. The first reaction was alarm. *Bismarck* and *Prinz Eugen* were only six miles away, and the battleship's guns would make short work of her. It seemed to Charles Collett that 'at that short range [she] could have blown us out of the water'. But nothing happened. Lütjens gave the commander of *Prinz Eugen*, Kapitän Helmuth Brinkmann, permission to fire but the target was too indistinct. *Suffolk* was able to turn away rapidly into the mist and wireless the momentous news. When it reached Tovey, he ordered the Home Fleet to alter course to the north-west to bring them to an intercepting point south of the Denmark Strait. Aboard the *Hood*, Holland had also picked up the sighting report. He, too, changed course and steamed at full speed on a line that he hoped would bring his ship and the *Prince of Wales* across the path of the raiders as they emerged from the Strait at about 5.30 on the morning of 24 May.

Throughout the night, *Suffolk* and *Norfolk* kept a high-speed tail on *Bismarck* and *Prinz Eugen*, helped by the *Suffolk*'s new Type 284 long-range search radar. It was a delicate business, requiring them to keep close enough to stay in radar range but beyond the reach of German shells. At one point the 15-inch guns of *Bismarck* flamed out of the murk sending five salvoes in the direction of *Norfolk* but they fell wide and she suffered only minor damage. There was a frantic ninety minutes when the cruisers lost the scent but then, Collett recorded, they were 'rewarded in the early morning by seeing, mere smudges on the horizon, the *Hood* and the *Prince of Wales* to the eastward and the German ships, by now also specks on the horizon (as we had opened our distance as it became lighter) to the southward'. The sight of the British ships was 'a great relief ... it meant that our main job was completed successfully and that there was little likelihood of the German ships turning round and engaging us – always a distinct possibility whilst we were shadowing'. Collett, in his air defence role, had a station on the upper works with all-round vision. It gave him a grandstand view of what happened next.

As dawn came up on 24 May, *Prinz Eugen* and *Bismarck* emerged at high speed from the southern end of the Denmark Strait. *Hood* and *Prince of Wales* were closing with them from the east at an angle. At 5.35 a.m. a lookout in the crow's nest of the *Prince of Wales* saw smoke on the north-west horizon and yelled down the voice pipe to the bridge that the enemy was in sight. Seven minutes earlier the *Prinz Eugen* had already spotted distant ships off her port bow. The two forces plunged towards each other on a converging course and at 5.52 a.m., at a range of over thirteen miles, *Hood*, in the lead, opened fire with four shells from her 15-inch guns. Holland gave the order to engage the left-hand ship. He had picked the wrong one. It was *Prinz Eugen*, a much less dangerous adversary than *Bismarck*. Captain John Leach in *Prince of Wales* did not make the same mistake and engaged *Bismarck*. The *Hood*'s salvoes missed their target. *Prince of Wales*'s 14-inch guns scored three hits on *Bismarck*, the last bursting through the hull below the water line and doing considerable damage.

Lütjens, on *Bismarck*, held his fire. Then, at 5.55 a.m., he ordered both ships to aim at *Hood*. At least one shell hit her, starting a fire. *Hood* and *Prince of Wales* now turned to port to bring their main aft guns to bear. As they did so a salvo from *Bismarck* crashed around *Hood* amidships. One shell appeared to hit just behind the main-mast. Collett, watching from *Suffolk*, saw 'a terrific sheet of scarlet flame suddenly reach up high into the heavens … and then die down to be followed by billowing clouds of thick black smoke'. He knew at once that a magazine had gone up and that 'this must be an end to her'.[4]

So it was. On board *Prince of Wales* a young midshipman, G. P. Allen, was at his station in the Upper Plot, the chart room just below the bridge. His duties including recording events in the ship's log as they were called down on the voice pipe from above by the naviga-tor. He remembered later how 'the *Hood* was only a few cable lengths away on our port bow when at 06.02 I heard "*Hood* hit," at 06.04 I heard "*Hood* on fire" and at 06.05 "*Hood* sunk."'[5] As Allen, whose nineteenth birthday it was that day, struggled to absorb the information a shell impacted a few yards over his head, smashing into the bridge and killing two of his fellow midshipmen. The Upper Plot was connected to the bridge by a funnel through which the captain could peer down to check the ship's progress on the chart stretched out below. The shell had blown the top off the funnel and 'blood began to drip steadily onto the chart table. We caught the drips in a half-empty jug of cocoa'. The *Prince of Wales* was by now in no fit state to fight back. She had been hit seven times by the German ships. Two of her ten 14-inch guns were out of action – not because of the damage wrought by the German ships but because they were still not properly installed when the order came to sail. Captain Leach 'very wisely' in Allen's view decided that he risked losing his ship without any chance of damaging the enemy. He turned her away, made smoke and ran for safety.

The loss of the *Hood* was heard with disbelief among the rest of the fleet. One minute it had been on the surface firing its guns. The next it had disappeared along with all but three of its 1,419-strong crew. The 'mighty *Hood*' as she was known to the Royal Navy was the symbol of Britain's maritime power, whose appearance in the great ports of the world on flag-flying visits sent a message that, despite the challenges from rising powers, the navy still ruled the waves.

The catastrophe sent a shudder through the surrounding ships. Patrick Mullins, an ambitious and well-read young ordinary seaman with the Home Fleet on board *Repulse*, wrote later that it was 'difficult to comprehend the effect that the sudden loss of this great, glamorous and handsome ship had [on us]. Suspension of belief was the first reaction, followed by awe and then by the realization that now it was up to us … suddenly our side did not look nearly so strong.'[6]

Tovey, aboard *King George V*, heard the news in a stark signal sent from the *Norfolk* stating simply, '*Hood* has blown up.' Soon it reached the Admiralty who passed it on to Chequers. 'Pug' Ismay was woken by the sound of voices and got out of bed 'to see the Prime Minister's back disappearing down the corridor'. Averell Harriman's bedroom door was open and Ismay went in. He was told that Churchill had arrived a few minutes before 'in a yellow sweater, covering a short nightshirt, his pink legs exposed', muttering '"Hell of a battle. The *Hood* is sunk, hell of a battle."'[7]

The news should not have come as such a great surprise. *Hood* was bound to come off worst in a contest with a strongly armoured opponent whose guns could comfortably outreach her own. She was a battle cruiser not a battleship, and now, at the age of twenty-one, a relatively elderly one at that. Her 42,100-ton displacement made her the biggest ship in the navy. But at the time she was designed, the existing technology did not allow her to carry eight

15-inch guns as well as heavy armour. Subsequent refits had failed to add adequate protection. Her deck armour was an inch thick in places and only three inches thick over the magazines where the shells and charges were stored. *Bismarck*'s deck was plated all over with between 4.2 and 4.7 inches of Krupp steel. *Hood* was highly vulnerable to *Bismarck*'s shells, especially if they were fired at a high trajectory. It was recognized that 'plunging fire', as it was called, would slice easily through her armour decking. Holland had known this better than anyone. Yet he had chosen to gamble at intercepting his adversary sideways-on, laying himself open to the battleship's broadsides rather than getting ahead of the German force and confronting it head-on – which would have reduced the size of the target he presented.

The battle, though, had not been altogether one-sided. The three shells that *Prince of Wales* managed to land on *Bismarck* knocked out one of her electrical plants, flooding a boiler room and rupturing fuel tanks. She could now only manage a maximum speed of twenty-eight knots, trailing an iridescent banner of spilled oil in her wake. In this state a prolonged raiding expedition was out of the question.

Lütjens was faced with two choices. He could turn round and go home, having scored a memorable victory, and await further chances for glory. Or he could hold course and seek the safety of the French coast to recuperate. It was a desperate dilemma. If he carried on, he knew that his ships were in a race against the avenging forces of the British fleet, and that the chances of interception were high. Turning back was equally perilous. The navy would be alerted and waiting. So, too, would the air force, whose bombers were within easy reach of his homeward routes. He chose to press on, aiming to run for St Nazaire at the mouth of the Loire, where there was a dry dock big enough to carry out repairs.

The Brittany ports were still nearly two thousand miles away and two enemy naval forces were converging on the German ships. Trailing doggedly in their wakes as they pressed on southwards were the *Suffolk*, *Norfolk* and *Prince of Wales*. By now, Tovey and the Home Fleet were hurrying south-west on a course which he hoped would place his ships in a position to cut off Lütjens' retreat at about 9 a.m. the following day.

Bismarck ploughed on through worsening weather. Her bows were 3 degrees down in the water, the result of a hit in the foredeck from a shell fired by the *Prince of Wales*. The *Prinz Eugen*, though, was unscathed. As long as she was tied to *Bismarck* her chances of remaining so diminished. On the afternoon of the 24th, Lütjens decided to set her free. He signalled her commander Kapitän zur See Helmuth Brinkmann his intention to take advantage of the next squall to turn to westwards in the hope of shaking off *Suffolk* and *Norfolk*. The *Prinz Eugen* was to carry on the Atlantic raiding mission alone. *Bismarck* briefly turned on her pursuers to buy time for her consort while she got away.

That evening she was butting westwards through heavy weather when Tovey decided to throw the aircraft aboard the carrier *Victorious* into the hunt. At 10 p.m. a small force of Swordfish torpedo bombers and Fulmar fighter reconnaissance aircraft flew off into a storm-swept night. Despite the conditions they tracked down the *Bismarck*

Fairey Swordfish

120 miles ahead. One Swordfish got off a torpedo that struck the hull. The point of impact was at the thickest part of the armoured belt and the damage was slight. The explosion, however, shook loose the collision mats sealing the earlier damage, causing renewed flooding and pushing the battleship further down at the bows.

As Sunday, 25 May dawned, the *Bismarck*'s luck turned. Frantic work by the crew had restored some speed. Her pursuers, though, had been forced to slow down. On entering the broad waters of the North Atlantic, *Suffolk* and *Norfolk* began to zigzag to shake off any waiting U-boats. By 3 a.m. they had lost radar contact with their quarry. Without the tracking reports of the heavy cruisers to assist him, the great prize might slip from Tovey's grasp. It was an appalling prospect.

He had been asleep in his sea cabin on *King George V*, about a hundred miles to the south and east of where *Bismarck* was last sighted when he was shaken awake with the bad news. He climbed up through two decks to the plotting office for a staff conference. His ships were now widely dispersed and half of them were running low on fuel. The weather was bad and promised to worsen, cutting down the chances of either the aircraft aboard *Victorious* or coastal-based long-range reconnaissance planes spotting *Bismarck*.

In the absence of real information about her condition, there were two eventualities to consider. *Bismarck* might be undamaged, in which case she would be heading west to carry out her raiding mission. Or she might be in trouble and heading east towards a French port. He decided to concentrate his forces on searching to the west. In the meantime, more ships were approaching from the south which could help comb the east.

Force H, an ad hoc fleet which operated out of Gibraltar under the command of Vice Admiral Sir James Somerville, had been ordered north to join the hunt. At its core were Somerville's flagship, the ageing battle cruiser *Renown*, the heavy cruiser *Dorsetshire* and the light cruiser *Sheffield*. Most importantly for what was to come, it included an aircraft carrier, the *Ark Royal*, with twenty Swordfish torpedo bombers aboard, crewed by men who had seen much action in the Mediterranean.

For a while it seemed the pursuers had regained the scent. Lütjens, unaware that he had shaken off the pursuit, radioed a situation signal to the Naval Group Command West headquarters in Paris. It was picked up by HF/DF receivers at British shore stations and, although it would take time for the code to be broken, it at least gave an indication of *Bismarck*'s whereabouts. She was somewhere to Tovey's east but more than that was impossible to say. Tovey and his staff took the view that she was heading for home and hurried back on his own track away from his quarry.

As the morning advanced, the level of desperation rose. The damp, showery weather over Buckinghamshire matched the grey mood inside Chequers. To Churchill, *Bismarck*'s disappearance was an avoidable disaster. She should have been finished off when the chance arose in the Denmark Strait. His anger fell on Admiral Wake-Walker, and Captain Leach of the *Prince of Wales*, who in Churchill's opinion should have carried on engaging *Bismarck* even if to do so invited disaster. At around noon he returned to London and throughout the rest of the day made frequent, scowling appearances in the Admiralty's Operational Control Centre, greatly intensifying the anxieties of the staff as they struggled to make sense of the situation.[8]

For the rest of the day *Bismarck*'s chances improved with each passing hour. An increase in German naval and air force radio traffic along the Brittany coast eventually persuaded the Admiralty that the battleship was heading to Brest or St Nazaire, and orders were issued to change course, but hours of steaming time had been lost and one by one the British ships were breaking off the search as they headed off to refuel.[9] *Bismarck*'s precise course was not known. Reconnaissance flights by RAF Coastal Command had turned up nothing and the weather was worsening, with thick cloud and low visibility forecast.

By mid-morning on Monday, 26 May, *Bismarck* was only a day from safety. The mood on board was lightening. They might not have reaped the glory promised by Kapitän Lindemann at the start of the voyage, but they would be content with survival. Even so, there was no slackening of concentration among the ship's anti-aircraft crews. At 10.30 they caught a glimpse of a large twin-engined aircraft through a hole in the blanket of cloud overhead. The alarm was sounded and the thud of outgoing flak could be heard over the rising wind.

The aeroplane was a PBY Catalina long-range reconnaissance seaplane. It was operated by Coastal Command's 209 Squadron and had taken off on a search mission from the base at Loch Erne in Northern Ireland at 3.45 that morning. It was an Anglo-American effort. Flying Officer Dennis Briggs was accompanied by Ensign Leonard B. Smith of the US Navy who had volunteered to go with an assignment of Catalinas, supplied under the Lend-Lease agreement, to train up British crews. His mission stretched the boundaries of his duties, but was in keeping with President Roosevelt's determination to offer Churchill every assistance short of formally entering the war on Britain's side.

Smith had seen the ship through a patch of clear sky from ten miles away and he and Briggs had brought it in through the murk hoping to track it from a safe distance. Instead they had emerged directly overhead providing the anti-aircraft gunners with a few seconds of point-blank firing time. Bullets and shells punched through wings and fuselage and one shell punctured the floor of the pilots' cabin. But then they were smothered once again in cloud, and radioing back the sensational news. *Bismarck* had been found and from now on she would be tracked by shadowing aircraft.

For those on board there was still hope. They were 790 miles north-west of Brest at the time of the sighting and they did not need to reach port to find relative safety. The U-boats and the Focke-Wulf Condor bombers operating from the Brittany coast were daunting deterrents to the British pursuers. By now most of the heavy ships had departed in search of fuel, leaving only *King George V* and *Rodney*, and they were far away, too far to make an interception if *Bismarck* maintained her speed.

That left Somerville's Force H, which was approaching *Bismarck* from the south. The *Ark Royal* was less than a hundred miles from the battleship at the time of the Catalina sighting. Her Swordfish had been searching in the same area and soon sighted their quarry.

There was no question of engaging. Somerville's flagship, *Renown*, was an old-fashioned battle cruiser and no match for the *Bismarck*, even in her damaged state. Nor were the cruisers *Dorsetshire* and *Sheffield*. At noon, Somerville detached *Sheffield* to pick up *Bismarck*'s trail with instructions to follow her at a safe distance.

He calculated that the best chance lay in an aerial attack that would slow her down and allow Tovey to catch up. 'Slim' Somerville was a popular commander, who sometimes took exercise before breakfast by rowing a skiff round his ships. His Fleet Air Arm crews thought he had a better understanding of the uses of aircraft than most admirals. He had learned to fly himself and sometimes flew as a passenger on training flights 'just for fun'.[10]

Perhaps his Swordfish, flimsy and insubstantial though they seemed against the power of the elements and the might of their opponent, might complete the job themselves. 'With any luck we may be able to finish her before the Home Fleet arrives,' he said in a message to the crews.

At 2.50 p.m., fifteen Swordfish from 818 and 820 Squadrons took off to attempt an attack. The weather all day had been atrocious. Even the *Ark Royal*, which reared sixty feet above the waves in calm seas, had green water coursing over her bow. The crews stepped out onto the bucking deck and groped their way to their aircraft. 'The after end of the flight deck ... was pitching something like fifty feet up and down,' recalled Sub-Lieutenant Charles Friend, an observer. 'The take offs were awesome in the extreme. The aircraft, as their throttles were opened, instead of charging forward on a level deck were at one moment breasting a slippery slope and the next plunging downhill towards the huge seas ahead and below.'

The force was led by Lieutenant Commander James Stewart-Moore, who flew as an observer. He was eager and confident as he prepared to take off. He admired Somerville and was anxious to do him proud as 'he took good care of us and we did our best for him'.[11] The mission seemed 'fairly straightforward'. One of the Swordfish in his flight was equipped with radar which would aid the hunt. At the pre-operational briefing he was assured that there were no British ships in the search area which was 'a great help as it meant we did not have to identify the ships before we started our attack'.

Despite the howling Force 8 gale all the aircraft got off safely. The radar-equipped machine led the way. It was operated by the observer, Sub-Lieutenant N. C. Cooper. There was no wireless communication between aircraft and crews relied on hand signals. 'After a while I saw Cooper waving to me,' Stewart-Moore recalled. Cooper indicated that the set had picked up something twenty miles away to starboard. This was puzzling. The position did not seem to correspond with the last known course of the *Bismarck*. Nonetheless, as Stewart-Moore had been told there were no British ships in the area, 'it had to be German'. As they swooped down through the clouds to torpedo-dropping height, keeping close together, 'everything looked promising'.

But as soon as they were clear of the clouds, his pilot, Lieutenant Hugh de Graff Hunter, 'called to me down the voice pipe, "It's the *Sheffield*"'. Instead of *Bismarck*, they had come across the cruiser Somerville had detached to shadow her. Hunter waggled his wings furiously to alert the other aircraft but it was too late. One by one, they dropped their 'kippers', as they called their torpedoes, while their commander 'watched from above, horrified and praying for a miracle'.

To his enormous relief 'the miracle department was paying attention to incoming prayers and the miracle was provided at once. Without any apparent reason, all the torpedoes except one or two, blew up within half a minute of striking the water.'

Back on board *Ark Royal* they were met with 'profuse apologies' for the intelligence cock-up. Plans were already in place for another strike. Stewart-Moore was anxious to alert his superiors about the premature detonation of the torpedoes. They were the standard 18-inch-diameter model, but equipped with an innovative Duplex magnetic firing pistol. When these were fitted, the torpedoes were set to run just below the target ship. The pistol was activated by the sudden change in the magnetic field surrounding the torpedo, made by the steel hull. The ship then caught the full force of the subsequent blast. The old-fashioned pistols were activated by the torpedo colliding with its target. The disadvantage was that much of the force of the explosion was vented uselessly into the atmosphere.

Stewart-Moore guessed that the Duplex mechanisms had been disoriented by the heavy swell, causing them to go off early. The contact pistols stood a much better chance in the rough seas. He found it very hard to get anyone to listen to him, however. Eventually it was Somerville himself, a torpedo specialist in his early days, who ordered the detonators to be changed for the next attack.

Six sub-flights of Swordfish, fifteen aircraft in all, were lined up for another attempt before night fell. The attack was led by Lieutenant Commander Tim Coode, of 818 Squadron. His wing-man was a twenty-one-year-old Scotsman, Sub-Lieutenant John 'Jock' Moffat. He felt the full weight of the expectations pressing down on him and his comrades. 'It was all on us now,' he remembered. 'It was a question of salvaging our reputations. There was serious concern that we didn't make a mess of this again. By now we were under no illusions about how important this was to the Navy and to Churchill and we felt under enormous pressure to pull it off.'[12]

As the Swordfish were brought up from the hangars below, the weather worsened steadily. On the flight deck 'the wind hit you like a hammer, threatening to knock you down ... the deck crews were really struggling with the aircraft, spray was coming over the side and the waves were breaking over the front of the flight deck'. The 22,000-ton *Ark Royal* was bucking and sliding as he took off. 'I felt that I was being thrown into the air rather than lifting off,' he wrote. 'I was struggling to control the aircraft while the wheels were still on the deck, watching for a sideways gust that might push me into the bridge, praying that we would clear the tops of the mountainous waves.'

They were helped on their way by the Deck Control Officer, Lieutenant Commander Pat Stringer, who, at well over six feet tall, had to be anchored with a harness to a stanchion to avoid being blown overboard. Stringer had an instinctive understanding of the ship's position in relation to the sea. 'He would signal to start the take off when he sensed that the ship was at the bottom of a big wave so that even if I thought that I was taking off downhill, the bows would swing up at the last moment and I would be flying above the big Atlantic swell rather than into it.'

Eventually all the aircraft were airborne and after forming up together headed off. Moffat tucked in behind Coode and within a few minutes they had found – and correctly identified – *Sheffield*. The signal lamp winking from the deck told them that *Bismarck* was only twelve miles ahead. They were flying low, at 500 feet, and Coode ordered them to climb to 6,000 feet. They broke through a thick blanket of cloud into clear, freezing air. Moffat's first concern was the ice forming on the leading edges of his wings and main struts. It was quickly overtaken by alarm at the black smoke from exploding shells mushrooming all around them. 'We knew then that *Bismarck* was nearby and we assumed she had found us on her radar.' Coode signalled them to form a line astern and they dived through the cloud. Almost immediately they lost sight of each other. When Moffat broke out of the cloud at 300 feet he found he was alone.

In the pre-operational briefing the pilots had been given a detailed plan of attack. It followed the standard Fleet Air Arm method for firing torpedoes at ships at sea. The first three flights were to come in on the port beam from differing bearings. The second wave would do the same on the starboard side. The intention was to force the anti-aircraft gunners to divide their attentions between two targets and to bracket the ship with torpedoes, severely restricting its ability to steer out of their path.

Any chance of this happening had now vanished. There were no other aircraft in sight. Moffat glanced around. There, about two miles away to the east, was the *Bismarck*. 'Even at this distance the brute seemed enormous to me,' he recalled. He turned to his right towards her. Almost immediately 'there was a red glow in the clouds ahead of me about a hundred yards away as anti-aircraft shells exploded'. Then the gunners were aiming just ahead of him and their fire threw up 'walls of water' in his path. Two shells erupted next to and below the Swordfish, knocking it 90 degrees off course.

Moffat dropped to fifty feet, just above the height where he might catch a wave and cartwheel in to the sea.

This seemed to be below the angle at which the flak guns could operate but, in their place, cannon and machine guns were pumping out red tracer which flowed towards Moffat and his two-man crew 'in a torrent'. As he raced towards the target he felt that 'every gun on the ship was aiming at me'. He could not believe that he was flying straight into the hail of fire. 'Every instinct was screaming at me to duck, turn away, do anything.' But he suppressed his fear and pressed grimly on as the target grew larger and larger.

His training taught him to assess the speed of the ship under attack and fire ahead, using a simple marked rod mounted horizontally along the top of the cockpit to calculate the correct distance to lay off. With *Bismarck* looming ahead of him, Moffat felt he could not miss. 'I thought, I'm still flying. If I can get rid of this torpedo and get the hell out of here, we might survive.' He was about to press the release button on the throttle when he heard his observer, Sub-Lieutenant John 'Dusty' Miller, shouting 'Not yet, John, not yet!' Moffat looked back to see Miller's 'backside in the air … there he was hanging over the side and his head [was] down underneath the aeroplane and he was shouting "not yet!"' Moffat realized what was going on. 'It dawned on me that if I dropped that torpedo and it struck the top of a wave it could go anywhere but where it's supposed to.' Miller was waiting for a trough. Then 'he shouted "let her go!" and the next [moment he] was saying "John, we've got a runner."'

Relieved of the torpedo's ton weight, the Swordfish leapt upwards and it was all Moffat could do to wrestle it down below the gunfire streaming overhead. It would have taken ninety seconds to follow the track of the torpedo to the target. Hanging around meant certain death. Moffat put the Swordfish into a 'ski turn. I gave the engine full lick and I stood on my left rudder and I shuddered round flat.' It was a manoeuvre that only the slow-moving Swordfish could pull off and it kept them down beneath the lowest elevation of the guns. He headed away at maximum speed, keeping low until he judged it was safe to climb into the cover of the clouds. He had no idea of whether his torpedo had found its target or not.

There was one last hazard to face. When he reached *Ark Royal* the deck was still heaving. As he finally touched down 'there was nothing more welcoming than the thump of the wheels on the deck and the clatter of the hook catching on the arrestor wire'. Clambering down from the cockpit he felt light-headed from adrenalin and fatigue. He told the debriefers the little he could, then headed below for a special meal which he was too tense to eat.

The mood among the crews was subdued. Everyone had been disoriented by the cloud and the attacks had all taken place in ones and twos. Only two, possibly three torpedoes had been seen to hit the target. That was not a cause for celebration. *Bismarck*'s thick armour meant that even a direct hit amidships would not necessarily prove fatal, as the attacks from *Victorious* had shown. Moffat thought he might have been responsible for one recorded strike. A pilot who followed him in saw a torpedo exploding two-thirds of the way down the port side.

Visibility was too bad for another attempt that night but they would be sent off again the following morning. Someone remarked gloomily that 'the Light Brigade had only been asked to do it once'. Then a stream of information started to arrive that lifted their spirits. *Sheffield* signalled that the *Bismarck* had slowed down. Then came the astonishing news that she had turned round and was heading straight towards the battleship *King George V*, which was approaching from the north. A little later, two Swordfish returned to *Ark Royal* from a long reconnaissance to report that *Bismarck* had lost speed and had steamed round in two full circles. HMS *Zulu*, which by now had arrived on the scene, confirmed it: *Bismarck* had been stopped, less than five hundred miles from the French coast.

Moffat learned later that it was probably his torpedo that had stopped her. It had exploded at the battleship's stern, jamming her rudders at 12 degrees and making steering impossible. With that, *Bismarck*'s fate was sealed. Throughout the night she was subjected to repeated torpedo attacks from fast destroyers which had now caught up. In the morning, *King George V* and *Rodney* arrived and closed for the kill. The end was never in doubt but it still took forty-five minutes of pounding from the two British battleships and the

ABOVE: Hitler arrives at Wilhelmshaven dockyard. On the right, Frau Ilse von Hassell, daughter of Admiral Alfred von Tirpitz.

BELOW: 'It is the best propaganda.' Thousands of Nazi supporters brought in by bus and train gather to greet the Führer.

LEFT: Master and Commander: Karl Topp's brilliant seamanship earned him the respect of the crew.

BELOW: Sub-Lieutenant A.G. Dunworth is carried from his Albacore after being wounded in the thighs during the attack on *Tirpitz* on 9 March 1942.

ABOVE: The Cruel Sea: ice cakes the deck of a British warship in the winter of 1942.

ABOVE: Churchill's anchor: the First Sea Lord, Dudley Pound, with the Prime Minister, on their way to Downing Street.

ABOVE: *Bismarck*'s nemesis: Admiral Sir John Tovey.

ABOVE: Eve of destruction: escorts and merchantmen of Convoy PQ.17 in Hvalfjord.

ABOVE: Reconnaissance photograph taken shortly after *Tirpitz* arrived in her Faettenfjord berth.

LEFT: *Tirpitz* being put through her paces in Altafjord in March 1944.

BELOW: Agent Extraordinary: the young Bjørn Rørholt.

ABOVE: Arctic summer: *Tirpitz* in Altafjord, July 1942.

BELOW: Human Torpedo with charioteers in training, 1942.

ABOVE: *X-10* departs Loch Cairnbawn under tow. Sub-Lieutenant Page (the passage CO) is on the casing.

BELOW: Interior of X-craft with Sub-Lieutenant R.G. 'Robbie' Robertson at the controls.

ABOVE: X-craft crew commanders. (*Left to right*) Hudspeth, McFarlane, Martin, Place and Cameron.

BELOW: *Tirpitz* in Kaafjord, shortly before Operation Source.

heavy cruiser *Dorsetshire* before the *Bismarck*'s big guns stopped firing. By then Lütjens was dead, probably killed when a shell from *King George V* hit the bridge. *Dorsetshire* administered the coup de grâce. An able seaman on board, A. E. Franklin, watched two 21-inch torpedoes leave the cruiser's tubes then saw 'a tremendous explosion … the fish having truly planted themselves in the bowels of the *Bismarck* far below the water line amidships'. *Dorsetshire* closed to 1,000 yards to deliver another torpedo which struck squarely on the port side.

John Moffat was flying overhead when she went down. He saw a sight 'that … remained etched in my mind ever since. This enormous vessel, over 800 feet long, her gun turrets smashed, her bridge and upper works like a jagged ruin, slowly, frighteningly toppled over, smashing down into the sea and her great hull was revealed, the plates and bilge keels glistening dark red as the oily sea covered her. Still leaping from her were men, sailors and there were hundreds more in the sea, some desperately struggling for their lives, some already inert tossed by the waves as they floated face down.' Moffat was pierced by the knowledge that 'there was nothing that I could do to save even a single one'. *Bismarck* finally sank, stern first, at 10.39 a.m., four hundred miles west of Brest, an hour and fifty minutes after the battle was joined.

Only 118 of the 2,224 men on board were saved. Most were taken aboard the *Dorsetshire*. Franklin recorded that with 'the battle finished, the humanitarian instinct rises above the feeling of revenge and destruction … ropes come from nowhere. Willing hands rush to haul on board the survivors.'[13] But then came a warning that an enemy submarine was in the area. The rescue work broke off and *Dorsetshire* and the destroyer *Maori*, which was also standing by, made for safety, leaving hundreds of men bobbing in the oil-stained sea to await death.

The relief in London was immense. Churchill's desperation for a victory had caused him to issue some unfortunate instructions. The night before the end Tovey had signalled that he might have to break off the chase. *King George V*'s fuel bunkers were draining fast and if they ran dry his flagship would be dead in the water, at the mercy of any prowling U-boat. Churchill's response, passed on by Pound, was that '*Bismarck* must be sunk at all costs and if to do this it is necessary for the *King George V* to be remain on scene then she must do so, even if it subsequently means towing *King George V*'. Tovey was to describe this later as 'the stupidest and most ill-considered signal ever made',[14] and the exchange deepened the mistrust developing between the two men.

Churchill broke the news to the nation in dramatic style. He was on his feet in Church House, where House of Commons business was conducted while bomb damage to the Palace of Westminster was repaired, describing the battle raging in the Atlantic when there was a commotion and a messenger handed him a piece of paper. He sat down, scanned it and got up again. 'I have just received news that the *Bismarck* is sunk,' he announced and the assembly erupted in a roar of applause.

There was much to celebrate. *Hood* had been avenged and a serious threat to Britain's war effort neutralized. While the nation savoured the victory, satisfaction in the Cabinet and the Admiralty was tempered by the understanding that it had been a close-run thing, revealing many weaknesses in the navy's armoury.

It had taken six battleships and battle cruisers, two aircraft carriers, thirteen cruisers and twenty-one destroyers to bring the *Bismarck* down. Most of the torpedoes of the Fleet Air Arm's obsolescent aircraft had bounced off her and it was a lucky strike that doomed her. Of the 2,876 shells fired by the fleet, only 200–300 hit the target. Even when utterly at the mercy of her pursuers, *Bismarck* had proved extremely hard to kill. What, then, would it take to seal the fate of her surviving sister, *Tirpitz*?

4

Trondheim

Flight Lieutenant A. F. P. Fane was turning his Spitfire for home after a frustrating reconnaissance flight over the eastern end of Trondheimsfjord in central Norway when he glimpsed a large shape in the confused pattern of grey seas, dishcloth clouds and white-capped hills below. 'I saw something like a ship hidden in the shadow of the far end,' he recorded in a neat, pencilled hand in his diary. It was so large that he thought he was mistaken and it 'must be an island'. He went down for a closer look. 'By God it's a ship – it's *the* ship,' he wrote. He 'rolled onto my side to have a good look and remember saying out loud, "my God I believe I've found it!" I couldn't believe my eyes or my luck.'[1]

Fane's delight at his coup wore off as he struggled to reach home. The cloud pressed down to 600 feet and he was flying into 'a hell of a wind from the south'. Twenty minutes after he should have landed he was 'getting really worried'. There was still no sign of land and he was down to his last twenty gallons of fuel – less than half an hour's flying time. Then a gap appeared in the cloud and he recognized Scapa Flow. He turned south and scraped down at Skitten, a satellite field near Wick. A little later he was back at base telling his flight commander Tony Hill that 'I'd thought I'd found the old Rowboat but could not believe it'. He 'hopped about on one foot then the other waiting for photos to be developed. When film was ready tore in to look at negatives.' He was still worried that 'maybe I'd missed the b--- thing. NO! there it was – no doubt now, it was the TURPITZ [*sic*] all right.'

Fane, a dashing thirty-year-old who was a Grand Prix racing driver before the war, had been sent with C Flight of No. 1 Photographic Reconnaissance Unit (PRU) to Wick on the north

Flight Lieutenant A. F. P. Fane

Scottish coast on 21 January 1942 with the specific job of searching for *Tirpitz*. Now, only two days later, he had found her, tucked into Faettenfjord, a finger of deep water forty miles from the open sea.

Churchill received the news with great excitement. He immediately ordered the Chiefs of Staff to draw up plans for *Tirpitz* to be bombed. 'The destruction or even the crippling of this ship is the greatest event at sea at the present time,' he told them. 'No other target is comparable to it.' A successful attack would mean that 'the entire naval situation throughout the world would be altered', freeing the Royal Navy to assert itself in the Pacific against Japan, which had now entered the war. He concluded: 'The whole strategy of the war turns at this period on this ship, which is holding four times the number of British capital ships paralysed, to say nothing of the two new American battleships retained in the Atlantic. I regard the matter as of the highest urgency and importance.'[2]

The dramatic tone of the memo made it apparent that the removal of *Bismarck* had done nothing to diminish Churchill's concern about Hitler's remaining battleship. During the second half of 1941, the PRU had kept a continuous watch on *Tirpitz*, flying regular reconnaissance missions over Kiel, her home port for the period. Failure to spot her, during one of her frequent excursions on sea trials, generated a flurry of alarm. Even when safely in view, she still exercised a peculiar menace. At the beginning of August, Churchill set off on board HMS *Prince of Wales* for his first wartime conference with President Roosevelt at Placentia Bay, Newfoundland. A surveillance flight had located *Tirpitz* at Kiel on 6 August, much too far away to pose any threat, yet speculation persisted that she might attempt an ambush. Colonel Ian Jacob, an astute staff officer on board *Prince of Wales*, noted in his diary that 'the Prime Minister did not seem to worry in the least, and he is secretly hoping the *Tirpitz* will come out and have a dart at him'.[3]

As the summer turned to autumn, worry about the battleship's whereabouts and intentions continued to distract the navy, tying up, as the Prime Minister noted in his memo to the Chiefs, a disproportionate number of capital ships, as well as part of the American naval task force which, from September 1941, was based in Iceland to assist the Home Fleet. The Admiralty believed that three battleships were needed on standby to overwhelm *Tirpitz* were she to break out. Churchill thought the caution overdone, complaining to Pound that this was an 'excessive provision' and 'incomparably more lavish than anything we have been able to indulge in so far in this war'.[4]

He was nonetheless impressed with the influence *Tirpitz* was able to assert. This attitude led to what can be counted as *Tirpitz*'s first indirect success of the war – a result that was achieved without her having to leave port. During the 1930s Churchill had paid little attention to the maritime threat posed by Japan, despite the fact that it was in the process of building a powerful fleet. He continued to underestimate the danger until early 1941when he first admitted, in a letter to Roosevelt that 'the weight of the Japanese Navy, if thrown against us, would confront us with situations beyond the scope of our naval reserves'. As the year advanced and this dire prospect grew more likely, he considered moving a battleship of the most modern King George V [KVG] class to the East to deter Japan. The hope was that it would exercise the same mesmeric effect on the Japanese navy as *Tirpitz* did on the Home Fleet. '*Tirpitz* is doing to us exactly what a "KGV" in the Indian Ocean would do to the Japanese Navy,' he wrote to Pound on 29 August 1941. 'It exercises a vague, general fear and menaces all points at once. It appears and disappears, causing immediate reactions and perturbations on the other side.'[5]

By October he had settled on sending the *Prince of Wales* and in the War Cabinet discussion of 17 October he again cited the 'example of the battleship *Tirpitz* which … compelled us to keep on guard a force three times her weight in addition [to the] United States forces patrolling the Atlantic'.[6]

Prince of Wales was duly dispatched to Singapore on 23 October, over the strong objections of the Admiralty, which feared that *Tirpitz* might attempt a breakout at any minute. She sailed first to Ceylon where she met up with the ageing battle cruiser *Repulse*. On 2 December they arrived in Singapore. Their deterrence mission was long obsolete. Five days afterwards the Japanese attacked Pearl Harbor and launched an invasion fleet towards Malaya. *Prince of Wales* and *Repulse* set out to intercept it. On 10 December, both ships were sunk within an hour of each other by Japanese torpedo bombers, a disaster that plunged the nation into gloom, temporarily extinguishing the hope aroused by the arrival of the United States into the war.

Though Churchill and the admirals were not to know it, *Tirpitz* represented no threat at all during the second half of 1941. Having lost *Bismarck*, Raeder was taking all care of his single greatest resource and the tests and trials to establish her sea- and battleworthiness that filled the rest of the year were rigorous even by peacetime standards. While the Home Fleet steeled itself for the battleship's appearance she was engaged in a leisurely working-up programme cruising back and forth between Baltic ports.

The fate of her sister ship *Bismarck* seems to have had surprisingly little effect on the morale of the ship's company. Onboard routine and the spirit of the ship were described in great detail by the administration officer, Korvettenkapitän Kurt Voigt in his letters home to his wife Erika, or 'Klösel' as he affectionately called her. He was a member of the Prussian professional middle class who had joined the navy in 1917 and carried on as a career officer in the interwar years. Voigt comes across in his correspondence as a decent man, a loving husband and father and a considerate boss. He was now in early middle age, considerably older than the rest of the crew. He nonetheless showed a boyish pride in his association with

Karl Topp (*left*) and Kurt Voigt

a famous vessel. Like everyone, the first thing that struck him about *Tirpitz* was its immensity, after which the First World War era battle-ship *Schlesien* seemed 'a ludicrous trawler'.[7]

He arrived on board at the end of September, as the ship stood off the Aaland Islands, the Baltic archipelago at the mouth of the Gulf of Bothnia. *Tirpitz* was the core of a force that included the pocket battleship *Admiral Scheer* and four light cruisers. Since June, Germany had been at war with the Soviet Union and the fleet was assembled to deter Russian warships from venturing out from Kronstadt. The Soviet ships stayed put and there is no sense at all of impending action in Voigt's accounts of onboard life. Instead his letters are taken up with marvelling at the comfort and modernity of his surroundings. 'My room is considerably bigger than what I'm used to,' he wrote on 7 October after *Tirpitz* had returned to Gdynia. '[There's] a chair with leather-type upholstery for visitors, a comfort-able writing chair, a square table, lace curtains on the portholes and the sides, all in cream.' He also had a telephone 'that communicates with all officers and other stations. There's an entire phone book for this little city.'

The latter was an exaggeration but *Tirpitz* certainly had the facil-ities of a fair-sized village or small town. There was a hairdressing salon with five barbers, a bakery, a cinema well stocked with newish films, and a printing press which churned out regular editions of the onboard newspaper *Der Scheinwerfer* (The Searchlight). Officers took their meals in a mess that was like 'a large and imposing restaurant with ceiling lighting'. The food was plentiful and pretty good. His first meal on board was 'excellent' – lentil soup followed by roast meat. During the Baltic autumn there were luxuries to supplement the staples of meat, tinned fish and potatoes and 'now and again we get beautiful apples, tomatoes and grapes'.

There was also plenty to drink. At his first meeting with Kapitän Karl Topp, he was offered sparkling wine then whisky. He had encountered him before and found him 'not much changed except a bit greyer'. Topp was extremely welcoming. 'He was friendly and spent a lot of time talking to me,' he reported to Erika on 1 October. The following day he comments again on his friendliness and observes proudly that 'he treats me with respect … something the others remarked on'.

Voigt's evident admiration for his captain appears to have been shared by most of the men on board. Karl Topp was forty-five years old when he took formal command of *Tirpitz* on 25 January 1941. He was born in Vörde in Prussian Westphalia, the son of a clergyman, and joined the Imperial navy when he was nineteen, serving in submarines during the First World War. At its close he was first officer of a U-boat in the Mediterranean which succeeded, through sinkings and minelaying, in forcing the temporary closure of the port of Marseilles. His captain was Martin Niemöller, then a fierce nationalist who went on to become a Lutheran pastor and anti-Nazi theologian.

Topp was one of the lucky ones who managed to stay on in the service during the harsh and chaotic Weimar years. He combined virtuoso seamanship with technical knowledge and specialized in military shipbuilding. He was stocky with a broad, meaty face and bright blue eyes. His manner was calm and methodical. He radiated authority, leavened with humour and consideration for his men. The weather was bitter on 25 February 1941, the day *Tirpitz* was officially commissioned. One of the engine room officers, Georg Schlegel, remembered that 'we all went to the top deck and it was snowing and very cold. The Commander kept it short so that we didn't have to stand in the snow so long. The flag was hoisted and that was that.'[8] Touches like that generated affection as well as respect among the ship's company, who had given him the nickname 'Charlie'.

Topp commanded a crew of 2,608, made up of 108 officers and 2,500 men. Most of them were young and inexperienced. Among them, though, was a core of sailors who had experienced the full trauma of war at sea. They were survivors of the heavy cruiser *Blücher*, the newest ship in the Kriegsmarine which had been sunk by shore-based gun and torpedo batteries as she sailed into Oslofjord during the invasion of Norway in April 1940 – an event as shocking and unexpected as the loss of *Hood* was to be for the British. *Tirpitz* seemed immune from such a catastrophe. Everyone on board took comfort from the ship's armadillo hide of steel armour and the huge guns, encased in turrets named Anton, Bruno, Caesar and Dora. 'The many, very heavy guns give a sense of absolute safety,' wrote Voigt to Erika in Berlin. The sheer size seemed to promise security, as reflected in the metaphors of impregnability that crop up again and again in his correspondence. The ship was a 'fortress', a 'slab of granite'.

Tirpitz, though, was an offensive not a defensive weapon. In the aftermath of the *Bismarck* disaster there was uncertainty as to how she should now be used. The loss had jolted Hitler into action. Admiral Raeder noted that the Führer abandoned laissez-faire and now became 'much more critical and more inclined to insist on his own views than before'.[9]

The battleground for which *Tirpitz* had originally been intended no longer seemed attractive. America's full entry into the war in December 1941 made the Atlantic a much more dangerous place for surface ships. The *Scharnhorst* and the *Gneisenau* were still in the area, lying up at Brest, where they were harassed by Bomber Command and afflicted by mechanical problems that delayed their return to operational health. *Tirpitz* was still not at battle readiness and, even if she were, would face a dangerous voyage to a French Atlantic port and be exposed to RAF attack once she got there. If a raiding force did venture out its operations would be circumscribed by a dire shortage of oil. All in all, Atlantic operations by large ships seemed to offer more danger than they did reward.[10]

Hitler's thoughts turned instead to Norway, which Germany had held since the spring of 1940. He regarded its possession as a strategic necessity. Norway commanded the Reich's northern approaches. It was also vital for the transportation of essential iron ore supplies from Sweden. During 1941 he grew increasingly worried that Germany might be about to lose it. Hitler harboured a persistent suspicion – which sometimes seemed to shade into obsession – that Britain planned to invade Norway. A series of increasingly daring raids by British and Norwegian commandos on the Lofoten Islands, Spitsbergen and Bear Island, and Vaagsøy on the mainland, raised the possibility that a landing in Norway might be imminent. The prospect of losing Narvik was particularly alarming. It was the only ice-free port in the area, through which Swedish ore could be shipped to German war factories all year round.

On 13 November Hitler met Raeder at the Wolfschanze, a head-quarters in East Prussia from where he oversaw the war on the Eastern Front. It was decided to transfer *Tirpitz* from the Baltic to Trondheim. Hitler was now of the opinion that 'every ship which is not stationed in Norway is in the wrong place'.[11] *Scharnhorst* and *Gneisenau* would be moved north when the circumstances allowed.

Raeder doubted there was any real danger of a British attack on Norway. It was another example of Hitler's exasperating belief in instinct over logical assessment. However, the move had his approval. He, too, had come to believe that the Atlantic was too dangerous for extended raiding operations. Northern waters offered a more advantageous battleground for his big ships. From Norwegian ports they could sally forth against the Arctic convoys which, in response to Stalin's appeals to Churchill and Roosevelt, were ferrying substantial war supplies round the North Cape to the Russian ports of Murmansk and Archangel. The first had sailed from Iceland on 21 August, six more followed by the end of the year and many more were expected in 1942.

The goal of strangling Britain had diminished in importance. The great struggle now was with the Soviet Union and *Tirpitz* could make an important contribution to the war on the Eastern Front. The holds of the cargo ships plying the Atlantic and Arctic oceans were crammed with tanks, aircraft, lorries, engines, guns and ammunition, shoring up Soviet resistance to the German onslaught. It was far more efficient to destroy them on the high seas than on the battlefield, and each ship sent to the bottom by the navy saved many Wehrmacht and Luftwaffe lives.

The mere presence of *Tirpitz* and the other big units in northern waters would also add greatly to the Royal Navy's already crushing burden of duty. The convoys needed heavy protection and a substantial force of capital ships, destroyers, minesweepers, anti-aircraft vessels and submarines would have to shield them as they came and went. Even if the German ships never left port they would act as a 'fleet in being', forcing the enemy to maintain a countervailing force in the area, tying up valuable units that could be put to much-needed use elsewhere.

Raeder summarized his intentions in his sailing orders. Her new home was to be Trondheim, halfway down Norway's western coast. From there she was to 'protect our position in the Norwegian and Arctic areas by threatening the flank of enemy operations against the northern Norwegian areas and by attacking White Sea convoys … to tie down enemy forces in the Atlantic so they cannot operate in the Mediterranean, the Indian Ocean or the Pacific'.[12] *Tirpitz* would be supported by the pocket battleship *Admiral Scheer* and the heavy cruiser *Prinz Eugen* which would soon be on their way from Germany.

Tirpitz left Gdynia on the Polish Baltic coast on the afternoon of 12 January 1942. At seven o'clock the following morning she arrived at Holtenau at the eastern end of the Kiel Canal which linked the Baltic to the North Sea. There she unloaded stores and equipment in order to lighten the load and ease the passage through the water-way. On board, excitement was mounting. After nearly a year of working-up exercises the preparations seemed to be over and operations about to begin. 'Nobody knew anything,' remembered Adalbert Brünner, a young midshipman who had joined the ship the previous autumn. 'Everybody hoped we were off on a *Gneisenau* or *Bismarck* type of operation.' The crew wondered whether 'we were on our way to the Atlantic … the ship was humming with rumours.'[13] It seemed barely possible that her broad beam would be able to squeeze through the canal. Water from the wash overflowed the banks and it appeared to Brünner as they passed under the high bridge at Rendsburg, halfway along the route, 'one could almost shake hands with the pedestrians'.

That evening *Tirpitz* arrived at Brunsbüttel at the mouth of the Elbe at the western end of the canal where she took on fuel and reloaded the cargo previously taken off. The following day she steamed out into the North Sea. It was there that the crew finally heard of their destination. They were going to Norway not the

Atlantic. The news did nothing to deflate spirits. Either way they would soon be in action. To some, the move seemed predestined. By a curious chance, the ship's symbol was the curved prow of a Viking longship.

It was deep midwinter, and the weather was on their side. Before setting off, Navy Group North reassured Topp that the forecast was bad for central England and Scotland, 'with poor take-off conditions'.[14] His ship stood a good chance of getting to Trondheim without being spotted by reconnaissance aircraft. On 15 January *Tirpitz* was on her way. The seas were so rough that the escorting destroyers were unable to keep pace and had to follow in the battleship's wake as it sliced through the waves close to its top speed of just over thirty knots.[15] Then, on the morning of 16 January, those on deck caught their first sight of the Norwegian coast. 'It was hung with cloud, sombre, covered with snow,' remembered Brünner. 'It was a strange sight for all of us, scattered houses which didn't look as if they were connected up by roads – it seemed like the quintessence of loneliness.'[16]

In the afternoon they turned to starboard and passed between the low headlands at the entrance to Trondheimsfjord which plunged for eighty miles east and north into the Norwegian mainland. Their final destination was a narrow finger of water at the south-eastern end – Faettenfjord. It was only about three-quarters of a mile across at its widest, with a small island, Saltøya, planted at the entrance, and it took great skill to bring *Tirpitz* in. Topp managed the feat easily. 'The commander simply made fast there without any pilot ships or tugs,' said Georg Schlegel. 'He was the best. He could really drive that ship.'[17]

In Faettenfjord a berth had already been prepared with two massive concrete capstans sunk into the rocks on the northern side of the fjord as mooring points. The crew were immediately set to work stretching grey camouflage nets over the length and breadth of the ship, which they covered with fir branches cut from the forest that covered the hill above. Soon *Tirpitz* was cloaked in a dusting of snow and its outlines melted into the monochrome landscape of hill and water.

The anchorage had been well chosen. *Tirpitz* was tucked into the tail of the inlet. The hills standing 400 to 600 feet above plunged straight into the water, making a natural mooring deep enough to take the ship's nearly thirty-four-feet draught. There was another ridge on the southern shore, about 700 feet high. Any attacking aircraft would have to approach from the western, seaward side, making the task of the defenders much easier. The ship was protected by clusters of anti-aircraft batteries mounting sixteen 105mm, forty-four 20mm and eight 37mm guns sited to give an all-round field of fire. Within a few days more flak batteries had been placed on the slopes above it as well as chemical smoke generators that could pump out a thick, protective pall within minutes. Soon afterwards it was fully protected by attack from the water by steel anti-submarine and anti-torpedo nets, hung at right angles, a hundred yards from the stern, which faced backwards towards the mouth of Faettenfjord.

Topp and his superiors were certain that the British would soon learn about the new whereabouts of the *Tirpitz* and immediately attack her. Thanks to Fane's reconnaissance flight of 23 January, the battleship had indeed been found. The Admiralty and Air Ministry now set to finding a plan that would satisfy the Prime Minister's impatient demand that it should be sunk without further ado. In his instructions, Churchill had raised the possibility of an attack by carrier-borne torpedo planes. That would mean sailing a carrier close enough to put their aircraft within range of the target. To do so would expose the carrier and its escorts to great risk from the Lufwaffe's Ju88 and Ju87 bombers and dive-bombers and Heinkel 111 torpedo planes that had begun to arrive in the region in response to Hitler's new focus on Norway. Even if the Fleet Air Arm's Swordfish and Albacore biplanes made it to Faettenfjord, the narrowness of the anchorage made it extremely unlikely they would be able to hit the target.

It was left to Bomber Command to come up with something. *Tirpitz* lay at the extreme limit of the range of even the four-engine bombers that had now come into service. To reach the target and return safely home they would have to take off from bases in

Scotland. The operation that ensued was given the name 'Oiled'. It was undertaken in a spirit of hope rather than expectation. The RAF had long been aware that it lacked the means to pose a deadly threat to large German warships. Since the second day of the war it had been trying to sink them, with very little success. *Tirpitz* herself had been the object of five operations while lying at Wilhelmshaven and Kiel. The results were negligible, even when large numbers of aircraft were involved. On the night of 20/21 June 1941, a force of 115 Wellingtons, Hampdens, Whitleys, Stirlings and Halifaxes set off for Kiel to 'identify and bomb the *Tirpitz*'. Not one aircraft succeeded in doing so.[18]

At this stage navigational aids were still primitive and it was a considerable achievement to find the target. Even then, the chances of hitting it were small. Bomb sights were simple and hopelessly inaccurate. To limit the risk from flak, aircraft had to drop their bombs from heights of 10,000 feet or more. To hit a target as tiny as the deck of a warship from this range was a considerable feat. When bombs did strike they were unlikely to cause fatal damage. Once again, post-war economies had held back research and development and RAF aircraft went into the new conflict with much the same ordnance as they had carried in 1918. The biggest bomb the twin-engined Whitleys, Hampdens and Blenheims in service at the start of the war could carry weighed 500lb of which only a third was explosive charge. Bomber crews sometimes endured the heartbreak and frustration of struggling through flak and fighters to strike their target, only to be let down by their weapons. Such was the experience of the fifteen Halifaxes of 35 and 76 Squadrons which broke through fierce fighter opposition to hit *Scharnhorst* where she lay at La Pallice on the French Atlantic coast on 24 July 1941. Three armour-piercing bombs passed through the ship without exploding. Another two bombs did detonate but the damage was repairable and *Scharnhorst* was ready for action again in four months. If the quality of the crews' weapons had matched their skill and courage, she should have been sent to the bottom.

The nine Halifaxes and seven Stirlings from 15 and 149 Squadrons which took off in the early hours of 30 January from

Lossiemouth, on the north-east coast of Scotland, to attack *Tirpitz* were almost certainly destined to fail. So it turned out. The weather was terrible. Only two aircraft managed to find Trondheim where they dropped their bombs without effect over some unidentified shipping. One Stirling was shot down. Churchill's incessant prodding meant it unlikely that the failure would deter further attempts. On 22 February Bomber Command got a forceful and ruthless new commander, Sir Arthur Harris, who was anxious to impress. There would be two more attempts by the RAF to sink *Tirpitz* in Faettenfjord before the start of the summer.

The ship was now under regular surveillance. A picture taken by a PRU overflight on 15 February shows it lying at its usual berth, the long, finely tapered bow flaring out into a broad 118-foot beam. It looks safe and secure inside its protective netting, with a cluster of small maintenance and supply craft huddled around it feeding its needs, and a sheet of snow on its upper surfaces. The photographic intelligence was soon supplemented by reports from Norwegian agents in the area.

They were operating in an extremely risky environment. By now the German occupation had set hard over Trondheim and the surrounding area. The army had garrisoned the town. Navy control boats plied the length of Trondheimsfjord checking fishing boats and cargo vessels while bigger ships stood sentry at the entrance. In their wake came the Gestapo, led by Obersturmbannführer Gerhard Flesch, who arrived in October 1941. He took over the local prison as his headquarters and set up a concentration camp at Falstad, near Levanger, north-east of Trondheim.

Trondheim was historically and economically important. Norwegian kings were still crowned there in the Gothic cathedral of Nidaros whose triple spires poke elegantly above the merchant houses and leafy squares of the old town. The banks of the Nidelva river, which snakes around the centre, were lined with slipways, small canning factories and warehouses, painted yellow and red and topped with steep-pitched, corrugated-iron roofs. The smells of the sea – drying nets, fish, salt, tar and diesel oil – hung pleasantly over the town.

A small minority of Norwegians had welcomed the arrival of the Germans. The Norwegian Nazi Party, led by Vikdun Quisling, had a presence in the area. Over time they planted their supporters in influential jobs in schools, hospitals and local administration. They forced the Protestant bishop from the cathedral and a collaborator was installed in his place.

With his arrival, congregations dwindled. It was the young who seemed to feel the German presence most, especially the students at the Institute of Technology, an imposing granite pile, which had been training architects and engineers since 1910. The Gestapo were quick to suppress displays of patriotism. Gestures of defiance, though, hardly posed a threat. Their main concern was enemy agents who could pass on intelligence about German dispositions and movements, particularly the activities of *Tirpitz* which now lay only fifteen miles to the east of the town.

British intelligence agencies set about establishing a network of agents under the Germans' noses, in Trondheim and other key points along the Norwegian coastline. Their activities were to provide a continuous stream of human intelligence, gathered by direct observation. It was extremely valuable. Despite the aerial reconnaissance and the watch kept by British submarines at the sea entrance to Trondheimsfjord, bad weather meant that there were frequent holes in the surveillance. Agents could fill the gaps. *Tirpitz* had only one route to the sea – westwards along the fjord. This took it right past the 50,000 inhabitants of Trondheim, which lay on the southern shore. There were further settlements strung along either side of the fjord. Reliable agents equipped with radios would be able to alert the Admiralty to any significant comings or goings.

Shortly after the battleship's arrival, Bjørn Rørholt, a twenty-two-year-old Royal Norwegian Navy lieutenant, exiled in London after escaping the Gestapo, was called to Admiralty Headquarters in London. Rørholt came from a patriotic military background. His father Arnold was an early member of the resistance and had been taken hostage after Bjørn had fled Norway. Bjørn had studied radio communications at the Institute of Technology in Trondheim and joined the Norwegian Military Academy at the outbreak of the war. He was taken prisoner during the invasion fighting but was released in the autumn of 1940 and returned to his studies at the Institute.

By then a clandestine radio service was already in operation. The British Secret Intelligence Service (SIS) had helped set up two stations for broadcasting information back to London. One, code-named Skylark-A, was in Oslo. The other, Skylark-B, was in Trondheim, under the direction of Erik Welle-Strand who was also based at the Institute. The students formed a pool of potential spies and saboteurs. Their natural patriotism was sharpened by resentment at the German presence which, despite the theoretical kinship the invaders felt for their fellow Aryans, was clumsy and arrogant. When black-bordered notices appeared around the town announcing the first executions of resistants, indignation curdled into hatred.

Skylark-B sent back important information on troop and naval movements. It took a year for the Gestapo to track the transmitter down. Rørholt had just finished a transmission when the secret police arrived. He said later he escaped 'after an unintentional shooting match with the Germans ... most of the others were captured. Since I had escaped the Germans blamed me for most of what had been done.'[19] He made his way to neutral Sweden and then on to Britain where he joined the Norwegian navy. There he teamed up with Polish officers and technicians in a workshop near London working on miniature radio transmitters. Now the Admiralty was asking him to go back to Norway. His task was to set up another, more comprehensive radio network, to spy on *Tirpitz*. Even though he was well known to the Gestapo and his father was a hostage in their hands, he agreed.

He had one night to spend in London before flying to Shetland where the exiled Norwegian resistance had a base. He drew some money from a bank in the City and had a lavish dinner at the Savoy. Two days later, on 20 January, with a Lieutenant John Turner, on attachment to Naval Intelligence, he flew to Lerwick. They put up at the Queens Hotel and spent days discussing the details of the operation. Rørholt was to travel by sea to Trondheim, carrying a number of transmitters powerful enough to send a signal to Naval Intelligence headquarters. He was to identify potential agents in useful locations who would then make regular reports of enemy activity in their areas, particularly anything related to *Tirpitz*.

Rørholt was taken to Norway by a seaman called Leif Larsen. Larsen was thirty-six years old, quiet and modest, a brilliant sailor and a natural and inspirational leader. He had learned his craft as master of a small passenger ship that plied the southern Norwegian coast and had an intimate knowledge of its confused contours of islands and inlets. He escaped from Norway in February 1941 aboard a fishing boat, the *Motig 1*, and joined an outfit set up by the Special Operations Executive, the Norwegian Naval Independent Unit. It operated a ferry service using disguised fishing vessels carrying agents and saboteurs to and from the Norwegian coast and became famous as the 'Shetland Bus'.

There was a six-day wait before the weather allowed them to sail. Rørholt used the time to dye his blond hair black. It was not much of a disguise, as the suspiciously raven locks clashed with his blue Scandinavian eyes. They set off on Saturday, 26 January 1942 on the cutter *Feie* with the aim of landing Rørholt south of Trondheim. The improvement in the weather had been minimal. It was freezing cold and the boat was battered by heavy seas. By the halfway mark, water had leaked into the fuel tanks, causing the engine to cut out repeatedly. At one point Larsen had to hoist canvas to make any progress while he carried out repairs. With the engine back in service they butted on. The motor cut out again. When he went to raise the sails they refused to budge. The rigging was solid with frozen spray. After more work on the engine it eventually spluttered into action and they finally reached the shore, numb, exhausted and seasick after thirty-six hours on the water.

They anchored in the lee of an island to wait for daylight. There they were discovered by some friendly fishermen who warned them that the Germans had set up a new control point on the route they had been planning to take. They changed their plans and diverted to an island farther south which was home to one of the *Feie*'s crewmen. His father had a boat there, which was well known in local waters. They could put Rørholt aboard and with luck he would be able to slip through the German control.

The new route would take them past another island where Larsen had previously landed an agent, who had been equipped with a transmitter. He was anxious to hear how he was getting on. They soon found the agent but he had bad news. He had failed to make any contact with Britain. He had come to the conclusion that the radio was faulty and had been trying to arrange a voyage back to Shetland.

Rørholt cast his expert eye over the set it but could not find the fault. He decided to try one of his own radios. Again, he failed to get a response on any of the agreed frequencies. The three of them came to the same dismaying conclusion. The radios were useless. They would have to go back.

There was no improvement in conditions on the voyage home. They struggled through heavy seas, nauseous from the motion of the ship and frozen stiff by the wind and flying spray. The engine played up constantly. They were blown off course and instead of making for Lerwick, Larsen decided it was easier to head for the haven of Lunna Voe. On 30 January the *Feie* made harbour in a snowstorm.

The failure had at least taught some lessons. The transmitters were too unwieldy and unreliable to justify the risks entailed in operating them. Rørholt remembered the miniaturized set he had seen his Polish colleagues experimenting with in London. 'It had slightly less power than the others but it had an ingenious antenna arrangement which made up for it and it fitted in a briefcase of normal dimensions,' he said. 'However I had not been able to take that set as it was a prototype. Now I decided that I was definitely going to get that set and some others if possible. That was why my only concern when we reached Lunna was to get to London as quickly as possible.'

There were some bureaucratic difficulties in his way. Arriving in London, he was once again refused the use of the Polish transmitters. According to the subsequent legend, Rørholt decided simply to steal some of them. He returned to Shetland and on 11 February set off for Norway. Larsen was at the helm once more. This time he had a more reliable craft, the *Arthur*, which he had liberated to escape back to Shetland after a previous escapade. Rørholt was now 'Rolf Christiansen'. There were two other agents making the trip, including Odd Sørli who would play a major role in the *Tirpitz* story. The crossing was rough but uneventful. On 13 February he arrived in the Trondheim area to begin his vital mission.

The dangers he faced were considerable. Ranged against him and the men he hoped to recruit was a strong force of professionals unconstrained by moral scruples, led by Gerhard Flesch. Flesch did not look or sound like the conventional image of a secret policeman. He had warm eyes and a mouth that in photographs seems always to be smiling. He was born in the city of Posen, the Polish Poznán, in 1909, when it was still part of the German empire. He joined the Nazi Party in 1933 while a law student. By 1936 he had joined the Gestapo and had the job of monitoring Germany's religious sects. He was part of the organization that operated in the Sudetenland and later Bohemia and Moravia following their occupation. After the invasion of Poland in September 1939 he returned to his hometown where he was leader of an *Einsatzkommando* which started the work of exterminating the 3,000 or so Jews who still lived in the city.

Flesch had help from local collaborators. The most enthusiastic was Henry Rinnan. Rinnan belonged to the category of misfits and sociopaths to be found throughout the occupied territories for whom the arrival of the Nazis was a liberation. He was born into a poor family in Levanger, north of Trondheim, on 14 May 1915, the oldest of seven children. He was short, five feet three inches, and dark-haired, in a land of large, healthy blonds, which marked him out for ridicule and teasing. His early life was a story of disappointment and disgrace. He got a job working at his uncle's petrol station but was sacked for stealing. He was twenty-one at the time, and married. To make restitution he was forced to sell all the household goods he had acquired on hire purchase. When the war began he tried to join the Finnish forces resisting the Soviet invasion but was turned down on the grounds of his puny physique. He served as a lorry driver in the

Norwegian army, in April 1940 ferrying weapons around Trondheim. Two months later he was working as a car salesman.

The Germans had arrived in town and his employer gave a party to which some of them were invited. The invaders seemed friendly enough and Rinnan responded warmly. Three days later he was summoned to the Hotel Phoenix in Trondheim where he met a Gestapo official called Gerhard Stubs. By the time he left he had become an agent and received his first reward – a hundred krone note. As the Gestapo's first local employee he was agent 001 and had the alias 'Lola'. The attention revived his withered self-esteem. With the money he bought a new suit. There was little work for him, though, until the arrival of Flesch who gave him the task of infiltrating communities in the districts surrounding the town. He had another Norwegian to assist him, a former Trondheim policeman called Ivan Grande, and together they built up a network of informers and *agents provocateurs*.

The open atmosphere of a town where everybody knew and largely trusted everyone else had been corrupted and the Trondheim that Rørholt and his companions were heading for was tainted with fear and suspicion. They arrived by passenger steamer after being dropped off on an outlying island. He later recounted how, when disembarking, a German soldier offered to carry his suitcase. The weight of it surprised him. Inside were three miniaturized transmitters which he now set about distributing. There was one man whom Rørholt was sure he could trust. Birger Grønn was the manager of the dockyard. He had learned where *Tirpitz* was anchored from one of his engineers who lived near Faettenfjord. While cycling to work along the road that ran along the southern shore he had been amazed to see the battleship looming out of the morning gloom.

Grønn set out to investigate. Posing as an innocent passerby he took note of the piers being built on either side of the water and the flak batteries installed on the hill beneath which the ship was anchored. To increase the hazards, the Germans had also strung steel hawsers from the ridge to the high ground on the southern side. He sketched the detail in a notebook and returned to Trondheim.

Rørholt already knew Grønn from his student days at the Institute. As soon as he arrived in Trondheim he went to see him, taking a taxi to his house in a suburb in the hills above the town. They discussed the best vantage points for the three transmitters. Ideally, one should be on hand near Faettenfjord, one in Trondheim and one at the mouth of Trondheimsfjord, through which *Tirpitz* would have to pass on its way to the open sea. Grønn told him of a man who might be willing to cover the latter location.

Magne Hassel lived at Agdenes, near the old fortress that commanded the seaward approaches to the city. Grønn knew his brother Arne who was one of his welders at the port. Before Rørholt's arrival he had telephoned Hassel to gauge his willingness to cooperate, and he had agreed to the assignment. The problem for Rørholt was how to get a transmitter to him. The headland at Agdenes was in a closed military area.

Rørholt soon established a useful cover. He arranged a job as an insurance salesman with the firm of Tobias Lund. He equipped himself with brochures which he packed in a cardboard suitcase, hiding the transmitter underneath, and set off for Agdenes. After talking his way through the checkpoint he was taken to see the commander, a naval officer. He was friendly and swallowed Rørholt's story that he was in the area to visit clients but had only just arrived from Oslo and had not had time to get clearance from the German authorities at Trondheim. He even expressed interest in a policy himself. Rørholt was unsure whether or not he was joking. He replied with a straight face that his firm did not insure the lives of German officers as 'the risk is too great'. The commander laughed and sent him on his way with a sailor escort.

He found Hassel's green-painted mill house looking out over the mouth of the fjord and left the sailor at the gate. Hassel had been warned of the visit by his brother and was waiting. He was ready to help but explained that he did not know Morse code. Rørholt gave him a card with a simple code. One signal meant that *Tirpitz* had put to sea. Another, that it had returned. A third gave warning that other major ships had left the fjord. They hid the transmitter under the floorboards. Over the next thirteen months Hassel would diligently record *Tirpitz*'s comings and goings, providing invaluable real-time intelligence that the Admiralty could match against information gleaned from signals intercepts and Enigma decrypts.

Rørholt, meanwhile, was given a lift back to Trondheim on a naval motorboat thanks to the courteous fort commander. He stayed on in Trondheim recruiting several more volunteers. They would be required to transmit more detailed data than the simple reports that Hassel would provide. To do that they needed training. Rørholt made arrangements for them to meet up with the Shetland Bus network and they were taken by fishing boat to England to undergo short courses in wireless telegraphy.

British intelligence was going to need all the help it could get in Norway. On the night of 11 February, the move to shift the main elements of the German surface fleet northwards took a dramatic step forward, when *Scharnhorst* and *Gneisenau*, together with the heavy cruiser *Prinz Eugen*, nosed out of Brest and headed for home ports. The force was commanded by Vizeadmiral Otto Ciliax who had replaced Lütjens as Commander of Battleships after his death. With the fate of *Bismarck* in mind, Hitler had forbidden it to return to Germany via the Atlantic. Instead it was to take the direct route through the Channel. It was an intelligently calculated risk. The nearest British battleships were at Scapa Flow and the Luftwaffe had air bases the length of the northern European coastline which could provide cover. British intelligence had anticipated the move but had not expected the ships to dare negotiate the narrows of the Strait of Dover in daylight. It was twelve hours before the German fleet was spotted, crossing the Bay of Seine. The combined efforts of navy torpedo boats, Fleet Air Arm and RAF torpedo planes, fighters and bombers and the army's shore batteries failed to stop the escapers. Night had fallen and they were off the Dutch coast before they suffered a setback. *Scharnhorst* and *Gneisenau* were both damaged by mines but were still able to make their way to Wilhelmshaven from where they arrived at the mouth of the Elbe at 7 a.m. on 13 February.

The Channel Dash was regarded at home and abroad as a humiliation for the British navy. From the Kriegsmarine's perspective, though, it represented, as the German Naval Staff admitted in their summary of the outcome, 'a tactical victory but a strategic retreat'.[20] There were no German capital ships left in French Atlantic ports to menace the convoys. That was now left to the U-boats, which continued through the spring and summer to savage the Atlantic convoys.

Henceforth, the big units of the German fleet would be concentrating on a different target. A week after reaching Germany, Ciliax took *Prinz Eugen*, accompanied by the pocket battleship *Admiral Scheer* and the destroyers *Hermann Schoemann*, *Friedrich Ihn* and *Z-25*, and headed for Trondheim. Enigma intercepts told the Admiralty of their departure, and four submarines were waiting for them outside Trondheimsfjord. HMS *Trident* managed to hit *Prinz Eugen*'s rudder with a torpedo but she was still able to make it to Aasfjord, just west of Faettenfjord, by midnight on 23 February. Rørholt watched them arrive. 'We have got the two babies. They are safe and sound with their other playmates,' he signalled.

Their presence in Norway made the Atlantic a safer place, but it greatly increased the dangers to the Arctic convoys. A powerful squadron, led by *Tirpitz*, was now concentrated at the eastern end of Trondheimsfjord. It could not be long before it ventured out.

5

'A wonderful chance'

In the first two months of 1942, nine Allied convoys crossed the Arctic Ocean, going to and from Russia. The voyage tested the seamanship and character of the crews to the limit. In the freezing heart of winter, the sea lapping the polar ice cap was the grimmest place on earth. They travelled in darkness, relieved only by a few hours of wan twilight in the middle of the day, through fog-smothered and snow-swept waters seething with submerged growlers and jagged floes that could rip through the hull of a merchantman like a tin opener. Sudden storms whipped placid seas into cliffs of angry water, seventy feet high, tearing the formation apart and scattering ships far and wide. Strange effects compounded the literal truth that they were sailing to the end of the world. Cold air settling on warmer water created wraiths of mist that made it seem that the sea was boiling. On a clear night the Northern Lights flickered mystically in the black, star-dusted canopy above, filling those who looked up at it with awe and apprehension.[1]

The narrowness of the waters east of Bear Island meant that ships could not turn into the waves and meet heavy seas bow-on as they did in the Atlantic. Instead, they were rocked from side to side, rolling as much as 30 degrees to port and starboard. Temperatures could plunge to sixty below, sheathing the upper deck with ice which the crew attacked with axes and steam hoses to prevent the added weight tipping the ship over. Able Seaman Bill Smith, who made the voyage aboard the anti-submarine sloop HMS *Magpie*, recalled how eyebrows, eyelashes and nasal hair froze solid, 'like needles'. Men came off watch with their faces covered in blood from rubbing their noses without thinking.[2]

These were not waters into which sailors ventured happily and the First Sea Lord, Sir Dudley Pound, and the Home Fleet commander, Sir John Tovey, had opposed the Arctic convoys. They argued instead that supplies to the Soviet Union should be sent via the Persian Gulf which, though longer and slower, would cost fewer ships and lives.

Churchill overruled them. His motives were political as well as practical. As the summer of 1941 faded, German armies prepared to close on Moscow, and Stalin needed swift and solid proof that Britain and America were genuine allies. The first convoy sailed on 21 August 1941, opening a pipeline which, with some significant interruptions, gushed tanks, aircraft and stores to the – largely ungrateful – Soviets until the last days of the war

There were frequent differences between Churchill and some of the admirals. On the whole his relations with Pound were good – a result, said critics, of the First Sea Lord's emollient and accommodating attitude – and his opposition to the convoys was soon forgotten. The clash with Tovey, though, merely deepened Churchill's irritation with the Commander-in-Chief of the Home Fleet. Even as an adolescent at Dartmouth, 'Jack' Tovey had been marked for the top and he had a stubborn faith in himself and his judgement. He was also deeply religious and if he had to choose between the will of his Maker and the dictates of the Prime Minister, God was always going to trump Churchill.

Tovey's robust integrity had caused problems with Pound in the aftermath of the *Bismarck* episode. With the Prime Minister's encouragement, the First Sea Lord had proposed disciplining senior officers for their alleged timidity during the battle of the Denmark Strait. He started moves to bring court-martial proceedings against the commander of the *Prince of Wales*, Captain John Leach, and Rear Admiral William Wake-Walker, who took command of the force after Admiral Holland went down in the *Hood*. It was Wake-Walker who ordered *Prince of Wales* to break off the action against *Bismarck* on the grounds that she was bound to come off worse. Tovey agreed with the decision. He let it be known that if proceedings were brought he would resign and appoint himself 'prisoner's friend' at the service of the accused and Pound was forced to drop proceedings.

Churchill interpreted this behaviour as evidence of cautiousness rather than moral fortitude. Even though he had – after some initial dithering – put Tovey in charge of the Home Fleet, he came to regard him as lacking in offensive spirit, the military quality that he prized above all others. By the beginning of 1942 he was complaining to Pound about Tovey's 'negative, unenterprising and narrow-minded' attitude.[3] Tovey, for his part, had a professional's contempt for Churchill's continuous interventions, which often seemed wildly at odds with reality. After an early meeting he wrote to his friend Vice Admiral Sir Andrew Cunningham expressing surprise at the Prime Minister's 'astonishing statements about naval warfare both at home and abroad'.[4] Cunningham shared his view, confiding in a letter to an aunt that Churchill was 'a bad strategist but doesn't know it and nobody has the courage to stand up to him'.[5]

Churchill had served two stints as First Lord of the Admiralty, first in 1914–15 and then from September 1939 until arriving at Downing Street in May 1940. Like Hitler, he had an extraordinary capacity for absorbing facts and few matters, great or small, escaped his attention. There was no phony war at sea and the first weeks of the naval conflict were fraught with drama and incident. Churchill nonetheless found time on 21 November 1939, a day when the new cruiser HMS *Belfast* had had her back broken by a German mine in the home waters of the Firth of Forth, to dictate a memo on the question of whether having a cockney accent should be an impediment to rising up the service (it should not). His experience, and his image of himself as a born warrior, persuaded him that his judgement was at least equal to that of the admirals. There were enough occasions when he was demonstrably right and they were wrong to confirm him in this view.

Churchill's intention to keep the Arctic convoys sailing at regular intervals throughout the year presented Tovey with a continuing logistical migraine. He did not have the ships to provide a strong escorting force as well as mounting an effective guard on the northern passages to the Atlantic. The lengthening hours of daylight made the voyage increasingly hazardous. In the first few months of 1942, the convoys had got off lightly. Only one destroyer and one merchantman had been sunk and several convoys had passed undetected. The concealing robe of darkness, though, was slipping away. The same was not true of the polar ice cap, which would take several more months to retreat, forcing the convoys to pass through narrow waters patrolled by U-boats and within easy reach of the newly arrived Luftwaffe reinforcements on land. Tovey voiced his fears but Churchill was adamant that the risks were acceptable and the convoys would sail.

Tovey could take some comfort in the thought that a great opportunity had arisen from the new situation. *Tirpitz* was now in Norway, with the pocket battleship *Admiral Scheer* to support her. Another convoy was due to set to sail at the beginning of March. Surely they would venture out to attack it, providing him with the chance to bring off an extraordinary coup? He had already sent *Bismarck* to the bottom. Now he was well placed to sink her sister. It was a thrilling prospect, and he was eager to seize it. So, too, was Churchill. The Prime Minister's fascination with *Tirpitz* was unabated. On 27 January he had taken the trouble to complain to Alexander about the waste of time involved in signalmen, cipher staff and typists referring to the ship as 'Admiral von Tirpitz' in every signal when 'surely TIRPITZ is good enough for the beast'.[6] Now there was a chance that the beast might come out to fight. On 3 March he once again emphasized *Tirpitz*'s great significance in the strategic picture, telling the War Cabinet Defence Committee that she was 'the most important vessel in the naval situation today', and that 'her elimination would profoundly affect the course of the war'.[7]

By then, a new convoy, PQ.12, was already at sea. It had set sail on 1 March, with seventeen vessels from Iceland, bound for Murmansk. At the same time, Convoy QP.8, made up of fifteen ships which had made the journey earlier, set off from Murmansk for home. The lurking presence of the Trondheim squadron meant that, for the first time, the movement in both directions would be covered by the main body of the Home Fleet. PQ.12 would have a close escort comprising a cruiser, *Kenya*, two destroyers, *Oribi* and

Offa, and several Norwegian whaling vessels converted to hunt submarines. A larger force consisting of the battleship *Duke of York*, the battle cruiser *Renown* and six destroyers, commanded by Vice Admiral Alban Curteis, had put to sea from Iceland on 3 March to cover from a distance. Tovey, on board *King George V*, followed two days later from Scapa Flow, together with the cruiser *Berwick* and six destroyers. To provide air cover and to attack any German shipping, the 29,500-ton carrier HMS *Victorious* sailed with them. She was fast, modern and could accommodate thirty-six aircraft. It was a lavish use of the Home Fleet's stretched resources. Altogether, the thirty-two merchantmen in the outward and inward convoys would be protected by forty-two escorts.

Around noon on 5 March 1942 one of the Luftwaffe long-range Focke-Wulf Condors that scoured the northern sea routes for enemy convoys saw ships sailing eastwards near Jan Mayen Island, a barren lump of rock in the middle of the Norwegian Sea about 350 nautical miles north-east of Iceland. The news was passed on to the headquarters of Naval Group North, at Kiel. Its commander, Generaladmiral Rolf Carls, eagerly signalled the naval staff in Berlin for permission to attack.

Raeder, with Hitler's blessing, gave permission. Here, at last, was a chance for *Tirpitz* to do something to justify its existence. The Kriegsmarine's big ships soaked up enormous amounts of materiel and manpower that were much needed elsewhere yet had made little difference so far to the war at sea. It was becoming clear from the battle in the Atlantic that submarines and aeroplanes were far more effective than surface vessels at the business of ravaging allied seaborne commerce. By now U-boats had destroyed more than five and a half million tons of Allied merchant shipping. Enemy aircraft had accounted for nearly two million tons. Warship raiders, however, had managed only to sink seventy-three ships totalling a paltry 363,146 tons. Submarines and aircraft had also proved a deadlier enemy to the Royal Navy's big ships than their opposite numbers in the Kriegsmarine's surface fleet. Of the eight battleships, battle cruisers and aircraft carriers lost to enemy action in the war to date, only two had been sunk by gunfire.

Raeder, though, was cautious. The prize of destroying the convoy was not worth the risk of the loss of his battleship. Vizeadmiral Ciliax, in command of the operation, was told that he was to avoid confronting enemy forces unless it was absolutely necessary to complete the destruction of PQ.12. Even then, he was to engage only if he was confident that he was facing an equal or inferior force.

There was plenty of time for an interception and nothing to be gained by an early appearance that would give the enemy time to react. It was not until the following morning that *Tirpitz* slipped her moorings at Faettenfjord and set off westwards into Trondheimsfjord. Darting ahead were the slim shapes of the destroyers *Hermann Schoemann*, *Friedrich Ihn* and *Z-25*. Snapping in the wind, high on the mast, flew the flag of Otto Ciliax, flushed with success from the Channel Dash and as anxious as Tovey for another triumph.

That afternoon *Tirpitz* passed the Agdenes fortress and steered round the Brekstad headland and out into the open sea. Norwegian agents onshore seem either to have missed her passing or their reports did not reach London in time, for the first sighting was made by one of the British submarines, now on regular picket duty off the entrance to Trondheimsfjord. Lieutenant Dick Raikes was patrolling in *Seawolf*, trying to stay hidden on a 'horribly flat sea' from the German aircraft that appeared frequently overhead, when, just before 6 p.m., the submarine's hydrophones picked up the ominous churning of big propellers. He stayed on the surface long enough to glimpse the foretop and funnel of a large warship which he immediately took to be *Tirpitz*. He dived and set off towards her but 'never got within ten miles of her'. It was, as he reflected later, as well that he did not for the destroyers and the escorting aircraft circling the squadron would have made short work of *Seawolf*.[8]

He broke off the chase to report the news to London. Nerves everywhere, in the Admiralty, in Downing Street and on all the ships at sea, were already strained in expectation. The Condor's signal had been picked up and decoded. Just after midnight, Raikes' confirmation that *Tirpitz* had been unable to resist the temptation presented by PQ.12 was in Tovey's hands aboard *King George V* and he paused to consider his options.

Tirpitz was at sea but what about her companions? *Prinz Eugen* was still out of the picture, thanks to the damage done by a torpedo from HMS *Trident* on the journey to Trondheimsfjord, but where was the *Admiral Scheer*? The answer was that she was still at anchor, immobilised by the caution of Raeder who was worried that she was too slow to take part in the operation. Tovey continued to worry about a big ship breakout into the Atlantic. There was a danger that one enemy ship might engage the convoy, diverting the attention away from the other while it raced for the North Atlantic. He considered dividing his force to cover both possibilities but an intervention from the Admiralty stopped this line of thought. They were sharply aware of the threat posed by the Luftwaffe squadrons now based in the area. The navy's losses from air attack in Norway, Dunkirk and Crete had taught them a painful lesson. Tovey was told to keep his fleet concentrated under the protective air umbrella provided by the Fulmar fighters aboard *Victorious*.

Fleet Air Squadrons 817 and 832 made up the striking force that would be thrown at German shipping. They were equipped with Fairey Albacore torpedo planes, the replacement for the Swordfish. The RAF's interwar control of naval aviation had meant that the navy had inherited a service that was dismally lacking in aircraft and weapons capable of taking on ships. For the first years of the war the men of the Fleet Air Arm were stuck with inadequate and ill-equipped aeroplanes which they flew with extraordinary élan and determination despite being profoundly aware of their shortcomings.

Sub-Lieutenant Charles Friend had just arrived on 832 Squadron, his latest posting in an incident-packed war that included having taken part in the air attacks on *Bismarck*. He was a reservist, a 'hostilities only' volunteer. Like many young men of the time he was fascinated by flying and in 1939 had given up his job as a lab assistant at the Paint Research Station in Teddington, Middlesex, to join the Fleet Air Arm. Friend was a grammar school boy, intelligent and lively. He brought a healthy dose of civilian scepticism with him into the enclosed world of the professional navy. On the whole, though, he found his new life congenial. 'I had been made aware of the military virtues of obedience and loyalty in my family and school life as most of us had at the time,' he wrote later. 'The loss of complete independence in service life at all levels was compensated for by an abiding sense of belonging to an organization with a purpose.'[9] In the early spring of 1942 he was just twenty-one but had already seen enough action to furnish several military careers. As well as the *Bismarck* operation, he had watched the sinking of the French fleet at Mers-el-Kebir, hunted submarines in the Atlantic and been aboard the carrier *Ark Royal* when she was sunk by a U-boat in the Mediterranean in November 1941.

Friend was an observer and most of his flying had been done in Swordfishes. He found the Albacore 'like a first class version of the Swordfish. It was an improvement on the dear old Stringbag because it had a more powerful engine and it was more aerodynamically efficient.' Unlike the 'Stringbag' it had an enclosed and heated cockpit which represented an enormous improvement to the lives of the crew, particularly in the savage conditions of the Arctic. It also had an automatic life raft ejection system which triggered in the event of the aircraft ditching. One innovation was particularly welcome. The installation of a 'P Tube' meant they could relieve themselves in comfort. In the Swordfish, the crew had to make do by filling the empty containers of aluminium dust markers or flame floats, used to determine wind direction and tide speed, before flinging them overboard. It was important to choose the right side, 'because over the wrong one, the slipstream opened them and showered the contents back into the cockpit'.

The Albacore already bore an air of obsolescence. It was a biplane and its fixed undercarriage hung below, dragging through the air and slowing it down. Even with the extra horsepower offered by its new 1,065-horsepower Bristol Taurus II fourteen-cylinder radial engine it could still only manage a top speed of 150 knots (172mph) in straight and level flight. Its usual speed was a mere 90 knots (103mph), which made the observer's job of navigating easier but severely limited its searching capabilities especially when the wind was against it. Some pilots felt the controls were heavier than those of the Swordfish and it was harder to take evasive action after dropping a torpedo.[10]

There were other antiquated touches. The pilot's seat was just ahead of the upper mainplane and a long fuel tank separated him from the observer. Communication was via a Gosport speaking tube – a simple length of flexible pipe. Pilots often forgot to connect them. According to Friend, to gain the attention of the man at the controls of a Swordfish 'one simply reached over and banged his head'. In Albacores, though, 'we all carried a long garden cane to reach forward past the tank to tap him on the shoulder'. Detailed messages were written down and passed forward in an empty Very signal cartridge stuck on the end of the stick.

Contact between aircraft and back to the ship was by radio and conducted in Morse code and was only used to report a sighting of the enemy or in extreme emergency. The Aldis lamp was still a useful tool to signal from air to deck or to other aircraft. When flying in formation they 'resorted to making Morse with a swung forearm – "zogging" it was called'. As protection the Albacore had one fixed forward firing .303 machine gun in the starboard wing operated by the pilot. The rear cockpit was fitted with twin Vickers K guns operated by a third member of the crew, which delivered more firepower than the Swordfish's single Lewis gun.

Compared with the Luftwaffe's sleek Condors and Heinkels, compared with the Japanese Mitsubishi torpedo and bomber aircraft, the 'Applecore' was slow and feebly armed. Thus equipped, the Fleet Air Arm could hope to achieve little. Given the quality of its aircraft, it had performed remarkably well. So far, the FAA actions had sunk three Italian battleships and six destroyers, as well as a German light cruiser, largely thanks to the skill and boldness of the crews. These qualities were about to be tested again as the British fleet and the *Tirpitz* squadron headed towards what all involved believed would be an epic encounter.

By the evening of 6 March, *Tirpitz* was steaming north-eastwards up the Norwegian coast at a steady twenty-three knots through heavy seas before turning due north at midnight. At ten the next morning an attempt was made to send two of the battleship's four Arado seaplanes off to try and locate the convoy. The Arado 196 was a robust, fast and well-armed monoplane designed for reconnaissance. It carried a pilot and an observer who also operated the guns. It was equipped with two floats and got airborne by being fired off the deck by a thirty-four-yard-long catapult that could be extended telescopically over the side. Its main shortcoming was that on returning it had to land on the water as near as it could to the ship's side, to be lifted back aboard by a crane. In anything other than calm conditions, this was a difficult and dangerous manoeuvre.

Arados had folding wings and were usually housed below decks. The *Tirpitz* aircraft, though, were parked on deck. It was appallingly cold and snow gusted over the heaving, iron-grey seas. When the crews inspected their aeroplanes they found the wings were coated in ice. Flying was impossible. There would be no aerial reconnaissance that day. Ciliax did the next best thing and detached the three destroyers to head off north-north-west, while he took *Tirpitz* on a north-westerly heading, judging that one or other force would sail across the route the convoy would take.

Tovey had been moving steadily in the opposite direction, with the intention of putting a defensive shield of warships between the expected German line of approach and the convoy. Like Ciliax, he was operating blind. The weather brought no advantages to either side. The Albacores aboard *Victorious* had iced up, just like the *Tirpitz's* Arados. There was no way of tracking the enemy from the air, and no other technological aids to decision-making to fill the information gap. Radar only stretched to the horizon. The great boon of Ultra had its limitations. The Kriegsmarine used an Enigma encrypting machine which had a different key system to that used by the army and air force. The code breakers at Bletchley Park found naval intercepts more difficult to decipher. It was sometimes twelve hours between a message being picked up and the decrypted content arriving at the Admiralty's Operational Intelligence Centre (OIC), and so far there was nothing to reveal Ciliax's intentions.

As the forenoon of 7 March wore on, both admirals were sifting their options in a manner that would have been familiar to a fighting captain of Nelson's era. Into their calculations went the state of the sea and the weather, the speed and capabilities of the enemy force and, not least, their own assessment of the character and propensities of their opponent. Tovey's intention was not only to protect PQ.12 but to lure *Tirpitz* and her companions into a battle which he hoped would end in her destruction. Ciliax was content with doing the maximum damage to the convoy.

It was likened later to a gigantic game of blind man's buff, as both commanders groped through the great wastes of empty water, swept by frequent squalls and blizzards. Through the middle hours of the day both forces held their headings, waiting for a development that would propel them on a more promising course. While they did so, the returning Convoy QP.8, travelling westwards, and the outgoing ships of PQ.12, crossed through each other's lines in a snowstorm.

Though they did not know it, the hunters and the hunted were close to brushing each other. *Z-25*, the destroyer Ciliax had sent off earlier in the day to find PQ.12, had passed only ten miles from the home-bound QP.8 but in the snow and gloom had failed to see its smoke. As the afternoon wore on visibility improved and the weather quietened. Another destroyer, the *Friedrich Ihn*, saw a smudge of smoke on the horizon and hurried off to investigate. The smoke was trailing from the funnel of the slow-moving Russian cargo ship *Izhora*, a straggler from QP.8. She was pathetically easy meat. At about 4.30 p.m. a torpedo from the destroyer hit her square on the port side. A photograph taken from the decks of the attacker shows a fierce fire burning amidships and black and grey smoke swirling above and behind. In the next one the bow has already disappeared beneath the surface of the sea which is now flat calm. *Tirpitz* hurried to join the destroyers as the *Izhora* went down, but the job was done and there was no need for her to fire her guns. Before the stricken merchantman disappeared, her radio operator managed to get off a distress signal which was picked up by the Home Fleet.

Tovey now had a rough idea of the enemy's position. It was supplemented by wireless bearings of an unidentified ship, which

The end of the *Izhora*

might have been the *Tirpitz*, which led him to take the main body of the fleet off eastwards towards Bear Island in pursuit. In case this proved to be a false scent, and the battleship had turned for home, he detached six destroyers to hunt along a line stretching from the last position of the *Izhora* to Trondheim. Tovey kept up his search to the east until midnight, then turned south so that he could stay in touch with his destroyers and place *Victorious* in a position where her aircraft could set off on an aerial reconnaissance in the morning.

Ciliax was still intent on attacking PQ.12. By the evening of 7 March, his destroyers were running low on oil. There was no accompanying tanker to allow them to refuel at sea. Ciliax ordered *Friedrich Ihn* back to Narvik to replenish and rejoin him as soon as possible. The other two destroyers tried twice to refuel from *Tirpitz*'s bunkers but it was impossible to hook up the hoses in the heavy swell. They were sent back to Tromsø to fill up.

The following morning, 8 March, he carried on the hunt with *Tirpitz* alone. He ordered Topp to turn due north towards Bear

Island, calculating this would put him ahead of the advancing convoy. Once there, they turned again, heading south-west on a zigzag course which Ciliax believed would bring him onto a collision course with his prey. He was sure his instinct was right and the crew were called to action stations. But as the tension mounted and Topp and his men steeled themselves for their first battle, the convoy was steaming safely eighty miles to the north.

PQ.12 had been warned of the ambush. An Enigma intercept had reached the OIC which gave notice of Ciliax's move towards Bear Island and the news was passed on in enough time for the convoy to steer away from danger, moving north along the edge of the Arctic pack ice.[11] It was yet another example of the blessings of Ultra. Had the intercept not been made, the merchantmen might well have sailed into *Tirpitz*'s guns while Tovey's fleet was still two hundred miles away. By now Tovey had concluded that *Tirpitz* had eluded him and was on her way back to port. He intended to take the fleet back westwards to Iceland to replenish his destroyers. The new intelligence reached him in the late afternoon and at 5.30 p.m. he turned his ships round and headed north-east again in the direction of Bear Island.

Ciliax had spent a frustrating time steaming along his chosen line of interception. At 8 p.m. he finally decided to give up the hunt and return south to Norway. He signalled his intentions back to Kiel. The message was duly intercepted and passed to the Bletchley Park decrypters who worked frantically to crack it in time for it to be put to maximum use. By the early hours of 9 March, the information that the German fleet was on its way reached Tovey. At 2.40 a.m. he ordered the fleet around and steered south-east as fast as his ships were able in an attempt to cut off Ciliax and his force before they reached safety.

It was too late to catch them and bring them to battle. The aircraft aboard *Victorious* provided a strike force that could land a significant blow, however. By skill or luck, some of the Albacores' torpedoes might find their target, slowing *Tirpitz* enough for the Home Fleet to catch her, presenting Tovey with the chance to crown his earlier triumph against *Bismarck*.

As the minutes passed the prospects of success seemed to grow. An Ultra signal reached Tovey from London giving further, invaluable details. An intercepted message from Naval Group North in Kiel gave the position, off the Lofoten Islands, where *Tirpitz* was to rendezvous with its replenished destroyers at 7 a.m. At 3.16 a.m. the information was passed to Captain Henry Bovell, the commander of *Victorious*, with the order 'report proposals'.[12] Charles Friend was in the Operations Room when the new information arrived. '[It] said in effect that *Tirpitz* would be in a stated position just off Vestfjord which leads up to Narvik,' he wrote. He remembered that it also gave the battleship's speed and course. The precision prompted him to think 'that to have such prior knowledge Admiral Tovey must have had a spy on board *Tirpitz*'.[13] It was only some time after the war was over that those who had fought in it finally learned of the existence of Ultra.

It was still too dark to fly but Bovell assured Tovey that operations would begin at first light. He signalled back: 'Propose fly off searching force of six aircraft at 0630 ... fly off striking force of 12 as soon as ranged about 0730.' The Albacore crews were woken at 5.30 a.m. Seventy minutes later, three aircraft each from 817 and 832 Squadrons left the carrier to comb the waters to the south-east. By now *Tirpitz* had been reunited with one of its destroyers, the *Friedrich Ihn*, returned from refuelling at Narvik, and was west of the Lofotens, steaming hard for home. Over the horizon, only 115 miles to the west-north-west, sailed the Home Fleet.

The Albacores climbed through patchy cloud and gusting snow into a lightening sky. At 8.03 a.m. Sub-Lieutenant Tommy Miller piloting the lead Albacore spotted *Tirpitz* ploughing through the leaden seas. The trim hull of the *Friedrich Ihn*, tiny in comparison, skimmed along beside it, a mile or so to the west.

He radioed back the news. The twelve Albacores of the strike force were waiting for the signal to go. Before they flew off Tovey left them in no doubt of the hopes that they carried with them. 'A wonderful chance which may achieve most valuable results,' he signalled. 'God be with you.'

For a few minutes after Miller's aircraft had made contact, the battleship sailed blindly on. The mood on board *Tirpitz* was subdued. After years of preparations and months of anticipation the ship's first foray had been desperately disappointing. For all the expenditure of energy and adrenalin, for all the massive consumption of scarce fuel oil, the expedition had resulted only in the sinking of a single merchant ship. At the moment the Albacores arrived, Ciliax was having breakfast in his quarters and Topp was resting in the lookout room. The ship was in the temporary charge of the navigating officer, Korvettenkapitän Gerhard Bidlingmaier, who was writing up his log when he heard a shout of 'aircraft astern!' and ran to the bridge.

He ordered the ship to full speed and the Arados into the air. All over *Tirpitz*, alarm bells clanged and men ran to their action stations. Ciliax abandoned his breakfast and Topp his rest and they rushed to the bridge. It was clear that a torpedo attack was imminent. Ciliax took the decision to stay on the same heading until the Arados were airborne then change course and run for the shelter of Vestfjord which lay behind the Lofotens and led into the haven of Narvik.

Only one Arado managed to take off. It turned towards the pursuers, dodging in and out of the drifting cloud cover, apparently directed towards the shadowers by *Tirpitz*'s radar. One of the Albacore's gunners opened fire but without serious effect. The Arado was more successful. One Albacore was hit and the observer, Sub-Lieutenant A. G. Dunworth, wounded in the thighs. Despite the attentions of the Arado, the shadowers stuck with the battleship, and at 8.30 a.m. radioed back her change of course towards the narrow entrance of the Moskenes Strait which opened into Vestfjord.

The strike force, formed up into four sub-flights of three aircraft, was now heading straight for *Tirpitz*. It was led by Lieutenant Commander Bill Lucas of 832 Squadron. Lucas was the most senior pilot in the force. He was not, though, the most experienced. He had arrived on the squadron only a few weeks before to replace Lieutenant Commander Peter Plugge who had disappeared with his crew in atrocious weather off the Norwegian coast on a futile search for the *Prinz Eugen* as it sailed for Trondheim. According to Charles Friend, Lucas was an 'unknown quantity'. In contrast, his subordinate in the operation, Lieutenant Commander Peter Sugden of 817 Squadron, had been flying operationally for two years and had won the DFC.

At 8.40 a.m. Lucas sighted the target in the distance, creaming strongly through the corrugated seas, and the Albacores fell in behind. It seemed to Friend that it was taking an eternity to reach it. They were 'flying upwind against a thirty-five knot wind and ninety knots air speed, to a target which was steaming directly downwind at twenty-five knots. Our closing speed was therefore thirty knots – about the speed at which one carelessly drives in a built up area.'

On spotting the target Lucas had taken them up to 3,500 feet, hoping the scattered cloud would mask their approach. Friend found that, as they climbed, ice began to form on the wings. 'The huge ship seemed to be there for hours as we crawled towards her,' he recalled, 'although it was only ten minutes from sighting to attack.'

The subflight led by Lucas was approaching *Tirpitz* on the port side. The other three were to starboard. The recommended drill for a squadron-strength, twelve-aircraft torpedo attack on a ship was for the force to overhaul the target then turn back onto it. Two subflights were to attack on the port quarter and two on the starboard, dropping their torpedoes in a fan-shaped pattern from a height of fifty to a hundred feet across her bows. This would cover a ninety-degree arc, making it difficult for a big ship to take evasive action and greatly increasing the chances of a hit. The method had its dangers. The quarter attack exposed the aircraft to the ship's guns which were presented with an ideal opportunity as the pilots approached, flying straight and level, low and slow, to drop their torpedoes at an optimum range of between 800 and 1,000 yards.

Lucas, however, decided against the textbook approach. They were only catching up at a rate of a mile every two minutes and the danger of icing up was increasing. He gave the order for each subflight to attack in its own time, choosing its own trajectory. The concentration of force mustered by a coordinated attack was now lost. If a torpedo did hit *Tirpitz* it would be more by luck than design.

Lucas led his sub-flight in first. As he got closer there was a break in the cloud which he thought would expose their position. He decided on an immediate attack from the side rather than a head-on approach. At 9.18 a.m. the three Albacores dropped almost to sea level and released their torpedoes. According to Friend the others watched the attack with 'astonishment … the subflight was led down immediately on *Tirpitz*'s port beam leaving the other three [subflights] badly placed should she turn to port which she forthwith did'.[14] Lucas claimed, no doubt sincerely, that he had released his torpedoes from 1,000 yards, the outer limit if there was to be any chance of success. Friend's account says it was closer to a mile.

From the bridge, Topp could see the torpedoes hit the water and head towards his ship at forty knots. Without hesitation he shouted to the helmsman to wrench the ship hard to port. His instruction was countermanded immediately by Ciliax, standing alongside him, who ordered the helmsman to steer to starboard. There was a moment of silence. The Topp spoke quietly but firmly. 'I am in command of this ship, sir, not you,' he told his chief, and repeated his order. The helmsman obeyed. A photograph, crisscrossed by the rigging of the wings of the Albacore from which it was taken, shows the ship turning with a tightness that seems extraordinary given its size, making a near semi-circle in the water.[15] The torpedoes from Lucas's flight cruised harmlessly astern, with the nearest one passing 150 yards away. The second 817 subflight now crossed over to the port side and launched another broadside attack.

All the *Tirpitz*'s many guns were blazing in unison, supported by those of the *Friedrich Ihn*, but the pilots stuck to their course, releasing their torpedoes at 1,000 yards. Once again, they missed. The two remaining 817 Squadron flights under Sugden had anticipated the first evasive action and cut the corner of the turn to port to place themselves ahead. But *Tirpitz* now changed course again and swung sharply to starboard, taking her back on an easterly tack. Instead of a frontal attack they were forced to come at her from behind.

The 817 Squadron crews were heading into a blizzard of shells and bullets. Film taken from deck level shows two low-flying Albacores desperately clawing for height as gunfire whips up ramparts of spray in the sea right behind them. A close-quarters attack was suicidal. 'With shots from her coming all around us I dropped my torpedo at almost extreme range,' admitted an 817 pilot, Lieutenant Commander John Stenning, later.[16] One Albacore of 832 Squadron and another of 817 Squadron were hit just as they released their torpedoes and tumbled into the sea. There was no chance of rescue by the fleeing battleship and all six on board were killed or drowned.

Despite the furious defence they encountered, the attackers came remarkably close to scoring a hit. According to the *Tirpitz* log, three of the torpedoes went wide, but a fourth passed ten yards from the stern. A near miss, though, counted for nothing. The determination and sacrifice was in vain. No damage had been done to the target. The only German casualties of the attack were three men wounded by machine-gun fire from the Albacores.

As the torpedo planes dwindled into the distance, relief swept the ship. The decks jingled with shell cases. In the brief action, *Tirpitz's* sixteen large-calibre 105mm flak guns, the size of field artillery, had fired off 345 rounds. The 37mm light flak guns had got through 897 rounds and the 20mm guns 3,372. The ship's eight gigantic guns had also been fired in anger for the first time, loosing off two broadsides against their flimsy attackers. Ciliax made amends to Topp for his intervention. 'Well done, captain,' he said in front of the rest of the officers on the bridge. 'You fought your ship magnificently.' Exercising his prerogative as fleet commander he made an immediate award to Topp of the Iron Cross, taking off his own and pinning it on the captain.[17]

The surviving aircraft arrived back on the carrier at 11.00 a.m. to a cold reception. 'The processes of debriefing and dissection of the fiasco ended in the surviving crews being mustered on the quarterdeck of *Victorious* to be addressed by senior officers in a very recriminatory way,' Charles Friend remembered. 'We received for our efforts and the loss of six men what can only be described in the naval slang of the time as a "severe bottle". Friend considered his superiors' disappointment as 'natural'. But he judged that 'their humanity seemed to have left them at that time'.[18]

Lucas was criticized by Bovell for launching his attack prematurely. He went on to conclude that 'all aircraft were deceived by Tirpitz's large size and dropped their torpedoes at too great a range'.[19] A fairer criticism would have been of the system which placed Lucas in charge, even though he had received no training for such an operation and had never flown in action with his men before that day. In the judgement of the official historian of the war at sea, 'to be called on to carry out so critical an operation in such circumstances was a very severe, even unfair test'.[20]

It was, as Tovey had said, a wonderful chance. But God was not on his side that day and the opportunity had been lost. For a few hours Tirpitz had been uniquely vulnerable, in open sea, with only her own guns and those of a single destroyer to defend her. There was some consolation in the safe arrival of PQ.12 at Murmansk on 12 March. But weighed in the scales of war, Tovey regarded the sinking of Tirpitz as 'of incomparably greater importance ... than the safety of any convoy'. To him the battleship remained a mortal menace, whose removal was worth gamble and risk.[21] The moment had passed and there was no knowing when it would come again. As Tirpitz slipped into the safety of the sheltered anchorage at Bogen, near Narvik, the Home Fleet, with Victorious, headed disconsolately back to Scapa Flow.

The game was not quite over. The Bogen Bay anchorage provided only a temporary haven. If she lingered, Tirpitz could find herself bottled up by a blockading force stationed at the exit where the narrow Vestfjord met the sea, and vulnerable to air attack. Group Headquarters in Kiel ordered her back to Trondheim. She left at eleven o'clock on the night of 12 March, accompanied by five destroyers. They had been due to sail early on the 13th, but Topp, chastened perhaps by the near miss of the torpedo, superstitiously brought the departure forward.

They picked their way through the inner leads and raced south, through foggy seas, keeping a watch for mines. Though those on board did not know it, there were other dangers lurking. Once again Ultra had given warning of the movement. A flotilla of eight destroyers from Scapa Flow arrived off the coast between Bodø and Trondheim at 1.30 a.m. and steered north into the path of the oncoming *Tirpitz*. By 3.30 a.m., they had to turn away, so as to be clear of the coast when dawn came up, exposing them to Luftwaffe attack.[22]

Tirpitz steamed southwards, hugging the coast through fog and snow, passing close to four waiting submarines deployed tactically at points along the way where she had to leave the shelter of the leads for the open sea. By nine o'clock on the evening of 13 March, she was back in her anchorage in Faettenfjord. The thick weather persisted. It was not until six days later that a reconnaissance flight confirmed that *Tirpitz* had returned home.

The failure to nail *Tirpitz* was badly received in Downing Street. On 13 March, Churchill sent Pound a message asking him to 'kindly let me have a report on the air attack on TIRPITZ, explaining how it was that 12 of our machines managed to get no hits as compared with the extraordinary efficiency of the Japanese attack on PRINCE OF WALES and REPULSE'.[23] The underlying explanation, as he knew well, was that the Japanese had the aeroplanes and weapons to wage successful war at sea. The FAA was paying the price of its neglect. Its aircraft were outmoded and outclassed and, in the rapid expansion now going on, training had been rushed and units diluted with untested new arrivals. The debacle hastened efforts to repair these weaknesses, so that the next time the FAA met the *Tirpitz* the results would be different. In the meantime, Churchill could take satisfaction from an operation that was very much to his taste.

6

'A somewhat desperate venture'

Tirpitz and all the Kriegsmarine's other large units were now grouped in northern waters, but at the Admiralty the fear persisted that at some point they would return to the Atlantic. If they did, the expectation was that they would then make their base in France. The journey home after a raiding expedition, for refit and repair, would be extremely hazardous. It would make more sense to operate from ports on the Bay of Biscay, and in particular St Nazaire.

St Nazaire lies five miles along the northern bank of the mouth of the Loire where it meets the Atlantic Ocean. It housed a complex of reinforced concrete pens from which German U-boats sallied out against Allied shipping. It was also home to the world's biggest dry dock, built between 1928 and 1932 for the construction of the great French luxury liner SS *Normandie*. The dock was the only one on the Atlantic coast large enough to handle a big battleship. It was where Admiral Lütjens had been heading when the *Bismarck* was damaged and was the obvious place from which *Tirpitz* could lunge at the transatlantic convoys.

Hitler by now had no intention of risking *Tirpitz* on a long-range mission. Raeder agreed with him. Her performance against PQ.12 was disappointing. Nonetheless, she was providing a great service tying up a large portion of the Home Fleet which otherwise might be operating to greater effect in the Mediterranean or Far East. U-boats were, anyway, sinking large amounts of transatlantic Allied shipping every day without any help from the surface fleet – 1.2 million tons were lost in the first three months of 1942.

In these circumstances, the U-boat pens at St Nazaire would appear a more vital target than the dry dock. The port had already been subjected to air attack. In the spring of 1941, as the crisis of the

Battle of Britain faded and the Battle of the Atlantic intensified, Churchill had demanded a maximum effort from the RAF against the two enemy weapons that were wreaking most of the destruction. His words were repeated in the directive handed to Bomber Command: 'We must take the offensive against the U-boat and the Focke-Wulf (Condor) wherever we can and whenever we can.'[1] St Nazaire was listed as a target. It was not until the next year that regular raids were launched. The bombing was inaccurate and ineffective and operations were restricted by Churchill's instruction that aircraft were to attack only when visibility was good enough to minimize the risk to French civilians. A chance had been missed. By March 1942, nine out of fourteen planned submarine pens were finished. Shielded from bombs by massive layers of ferro-concrete, there was no hope of destroying them from the air. A land attack would take enormous resources and involve considerable losses.

The pens, then, were too tough a target, whichever way they were approached. The *Normandie* dock, however – even in the changed circumstances of early 1942 – still appeared a worthwhile proposition. The shift of all Hitler's big ships northwards that was completed with the *Scharnhorst* and *Gneisenau*'s dash through the Channel had not been interpreted in the Admiralty as meaning that the Kriegsmarine's surface ships would no longer venture south.

Fear of the *Tirpitz*'s destructive capabilities remained as intense as ever. As long as the facilities at St Nazaire were intact, the possibility existed that a raiding force with *Tirpitz* at its heart would launch into the North Atlantic, laying waste to the convoys and diverting most of the Home Fleet into the effort to hunt it down. The destruction of the *Normandie* dock would shut down that possibility for ever.

In January 1942, following a conversation with Churchill, Sir Dudley Pound asked the Admiralty's Plans Division to examine the possibilities. They in turn asked the newly appointed Chief of the Combined Operations Headquarters, Lord Louis Mountbatten, to devise a solution. Combined Ops was an inter-service organization tasked with devising disruptive raids that would harry and unnerve Axis forces. It could call on the troops of the Special Service Brigade's Commandos, set up after the fall of France by Churchill to 'develop a reign of terror down the enemy coast'. But it had no real resources of its own and was dependent on the cooperation of the other services, which was by no means automatically forthcoming.

Over the next weeks Mountbatten and his team drew up a plan of outrageous boldness. It depended on speed, surprise and devastating force and was just the sort of operation that delighted Churchill, appealing to his romantic weakness for the dash of pre-industrial-era soldiering. If successful, it would have very welcome psychological as well as material results. With the Soviet Union and the United States as allies, Britain was no longer alone. On land and sea, though, the war was not going well. As Commander Robert Ryder, who would lead the naval force in the attack, observed, 'some feat of arms that would hearten the country in such a dark hour' was an added good reason for the great risks involved.[2]

The *Normandie* dock was 1,148 feet long and 164 feet wide with lock gates, known as caissons, at each end. It ran at a slant with one end opening into an inner port basin, the Bassin de Penhoët. The other connected to the river. The caissons were made of hollow steel sections and were thirty-five feet thick.

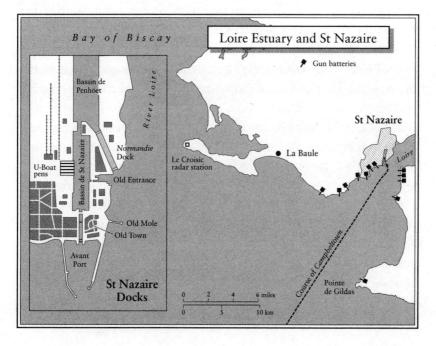

The basic plan was to sail an old destroyer, the *Campbeltown*, accompanied by eighteen shallow-draught launches, up the Loire estuary to St Nazaire and drive her at full speed through the lock gates. Next, 277 commandos, split into eighteen teams, would set about destroying the dock machinery. Then, time-delayed fuses would detonate the four and a half tons of Amatol high explosive packed into the *Campbeltown*, destroying the dock.

The commandos at the heart of the operation were all volunteers, dedicated, skilful and aggressive. In the six weeks they had to prepare, the teams trained with an intensity that reflected the hardening professionalism and determination of the British war effort, carrying out dummy runs in the port facilities at Cardiff and Southampton. In Southampton they had the advantage of familiarizing themselves with the King George V Dry Dock which was an almost exact replica of the one they were going to attack.

The force was led by Lieutenant Colonel Charles 'Charlie' Newman of 2 Commando, which provided most of the troops. Newman was an amiable and good-natured thirty-seven-year-old, who was married with four children and a fifth on the way. He had been a successful civil engineer before the war, though, as well as a Territorial Army officer. Much of the rest of his spare time was spent playing rugby, golf and the piano. He smoked a pipe and reminded one of his young volunteers of a 'benign elephant ... due to the downward curve of his prominent broken nose', the result of his time as an amateur boxer.[3]

A week before the operation was due to begin, Newman returned from a meeting with the Chief of Combined Operations and addressed his commandos frankly. One of his men recalled him telling them that Mountbatten was confident that they would 'get in and do the job'. He made it clear, though, that 'we cannot hold much hope of you getting out again'. Newman also passed on Mountbatten's offer that 'any man could volunteer out of the forthcoming operation should he wish to do so. Charlie though was wasting his time ... Everyone stayed put, satisfied in their work and of course labouring under that strange illusion – their own immortality.'[4]

The flotilla set off from Falmouth on the afternoon of 26 March, escorted by two destroyers. The *Campbeltown* was in her second incarnation. In her previous life she had been USS *Buchanan* of the United States Navy and had been transferred to Britain as part of the Destroyers for Bases Agreement, earlier in the war. She was captained by Lieutenant Commander Stephen 'Sam' Beattie, a thirty-three-year-old Welshman who was to win the Victoria Cross for his part in the raid. The rest of the flotilla was made up of sixteen wooden-hulled motor launches, one small MGB (motor gunboat) and one MTB (motor torpedo boat) to provide covering fire and to evacuate the survivors of the raiding party.

The raid was to open spectacularly with the *Campbeltown* driving at full speed into the southern caisson, lodging herself firmly in the middle of the structure to cause maximum devastation when the twenty-four Mk VII depth charges she was carrying, each weighing 400lb, exploded. They were packed into a steel tank and concreted over and fitted with long-delay fuses timed to detonate after eight hours.

Then it was the turn of the commandos. The teams were divided into three groups, one on the *Campbeltown* and the other two on the launches. They were to storm ashore and set about their demolition tasks. Each team was divided into two, with one half laying their charges while the others held off the defenders with guns and grenades.

The force on board *Campbeltown* had the mission of wrecking the machines that operated the *Normandie* dock – the pumphouse and winding sheds that filled and emptied the basin. They were also tasked with destroying the northern caisson. The other two groups were to be landed to the west at the Old Mole and the Old Entrance to smash up bridges and locks. In the unlikely event of the operation going perfectly to plan, they would then seal off the area to allow an orderly evacuation on the motorboats. Finally, the flotilla's MTB was to fire torpedoes at the lock leading to the main dock, the Bassin de St Nazaire, on which the submarine pens lay.

The mission bordered on the suicidal as all who took part in it knew. Major Bill Copland, Newman's second in command and a forty-four-year-old veteran of the First World War, who was leading the group embarked on the *Campbeltown*, spelled out the likely consequences in a farewell letter to his wife Ethel. 'My dearest,' he wrote. 'I have to write this letter although God knows I hope you never receive it – which you only will if I don't come back. We sail in a day or two on a somewhat desperate venture, but one of high purpose. If we succeed, and only the worst of ill-luck will stop us, then we shall have struck a great blow for the cause of freedom. Remember too that if I do get blotted out I shall probably die in good company, for never did a finer crowd set out on a doughtier task.'[5]

The force sailed south-west, across the English Channel, then south round the Brittany Peninsula and into the Bay of Biscay, taking a meandering route and keeping well out to sea to disguise their ultimate destination. The *Campbeltown* had been given a quick cosmetic refit to try and alter her lines to something resembling a German warship, reducing her four funnels to two. All in the flotilla flew Kriegsmarine ensigns, weathered and tattered for authenticity.

The assumption was that sooner or later they would be spotted by an enemy vessel or aeroplane and on the morning of the 27th they were. They were 160 miles south-west of St Nazaire and just turning back towards the coast when they sighted a U-boat that was making its way back to port. One of the destroyers gave chase and dropped depth charges but the submarine got away. Its radio message reporting the encounter led the German naval command onshore to conclude that the British force was on passage to Gibraltar or on a minelaying mission.

The expedition's luck had held but the hazards were only just beginning. Even with surprise on its side the risk of catastrophe was high. The area around St Nazaire was heavily protected by gun emplacements operated by German naval troops. To reach St Nazaire they had first to sail past the heavy seaward defences set up at the mouth of the Loire. There were forty-three guns ranging from 75mm artillery pieces to hefty 240mm howitzers mounted on railway trucks. Closer to the port they would face flak batteries equipped with 40mm, 37mm and 20mm cannon. The port itself was defended by a thousand men and studded with pillboxes and strongpoints, while harbour defence boats patrolled the waters outside. The whole area could be lit up at night by searchlights sweeping the docks and waterways. If the men charged with the defence of St Nazaire failed in their duty there were another 5,000 German troops based in the town to fall back on.

The purpose of all these precautions was not, however, solely to protect the *Normandie* dock. In the minds of the Germans, the most important potential target were the submarine pens which lay on the west side of the Bassin de St Nazaire, surrounded by flak batteries and searchlights.

Moored inside the pens were the craft of the 7th Submarine Flotilla. More U-boats were on the way and the facilities were being extended to accommodate the 6th Flotilla which was in the process of transferring from the Baltic. The day before the raid, the officer commanding the U-Boat fleet, Vizeadmiral Karl Dönitz, had inspected the defences together with the commander of the 7th Flotilla, Kapitänleutnant Herbert Sohler. He asked him what he would do if the 'English' attacked. Sohler replied that it was 'out of the question' as they would never be able to reach the harbour'.[6]

On the evening of 27 March, the attacking force turned to make its last approach and headed towards the mouth of the Loire. The destroyer escorts slid away and the raiders were on their own. They were led by the MGB with Colonel Newman and Commander Ryder on board. Immediately behind came *Campbeltown* with the other motor launches arrayed in two columns on either side with a tail of three bringing up the rear. Most were wooden-built Fairmile 'Bs'. They were 112 feet long and nearly twenty feet wide and their two 600-horsepower engines could push them through the water at twenty knots. Extra guns had been fitted for the operation. They had two 20mm Oerlikon cannons mounted fore and aft with two .303 machine guns on the bridge.

As the little fleet progressed, those on board could hear the rumble of explosions. A bombing raid was included in the plan, timed for just before midnight. It was a diversionary effort with thirty-five Whitleys and twenty-seven Wellingtons taking part. According to Ryder, 'it was hoped that under the general confusion caused by this air raid, directed right on the waterfront, our landing would be comparatively unopposed'. However, in keeping with Churchill's concerns about French civilian casualties, the crews were under instruction to bomb only if they could see their targets. The blanket of cloud made identification impossible. Only four aircraft dropped their bombs and the main result of the raid was to sharpen the Germans reflexes and arouse their suspicions.

'In effect, the raid raised the alarm,' wrote Ryder later. 'Every gun was manned; patrols, fire parties and others had fallen in, and the gun control and look out system [was] thoroughly on the alert ... thus the surface attackers reaped every disadvantage in having their attack heavily opposed by an enemy fully prepared.'[7]

The very feebleness of the attack had made the defenders suspicious. Kapitän zur See Karl-Conrad Mecke, who commanded the naval flak brigade responsible for the close defence of the port, noticed that the bombs were seemingly dropping at random and warned everyone to be on their guard against a possible assault by parachute troops or an attack from the sea.

By now the raiders were past the radar station at Le Croisic and inside the estuary. Just after 12.30 a.m. they passed a grim monument to disaster. The hull of the SS *Lancastria* loomed out of the water, lying where she had been sunk in June 1940, with a loss of four thousand lives evacuating the last British troops from France. Sam Beattie handled the *Campbeltown* deftly, taking advantage of the spring tide to steer her through the shallow waters on the western side of the approach, avoiding the central channel.

The modified destroyer drew only eleven feet of water. Twice its hull scraped against the muddy estuary bottom but she slithered on. At 12.45 a.m. they swept past the 75mm guns on the Pointe de Gildas without challenge. Looking back from his gunboat at the head of the column, Ryder found it 'difficult to imagine there could be any successful deception. Each craft, with her silvery bow wave, stood out clear and bright.' It was too good to last. 'This is a queer do,' remarked Lieutenant Tom Boyd, a twenty-seven-year-old commanding one of the launches, to his coxswain. 'It'll be a bloody sight queerer soon,' came the reply.[8]

Once a searchlight flashed across the water, passed them, and went out. Then, just before 1.20 a.m., a lookout noticed the shapes gliding through the darkness and radioed the harbour commander's headquarters with the news that a flotilla of unidentified vessels was heading upriver. The report was dismissed at first. When the sighting reached the cautious Mecke, however, he put all units on alert. All along the banks of the river searchlight batteries flicked on. The Kriegsmarine ensigns streaming from the masts of the destroyers and motor launches caused some hesitation. There were a few warning bursts. Sliding along in his launch tucked in on the starboard side of *Campbeltown*, Lieutenant Commander Billie Stephens was beguiled by the sight of tracer. 'It was a beautiful bright red colour and as it sailed towards us I couldn't imagine that if it hit us it was going to harm us ... very shortly afterwards I was disillusioned.'[9]

Twice they were challenged from the shore. Standing next to Ryder in the MGB leading the flotilla was Leading Signalman F. C. Pike, who was trained in German morse. He signalled back 'wait' then gave the call sign of a German motor torpedo boat obtained from naval intelligence, followed by the message: 'Two craft damaged by enemy action. Request permission to proceed to harbour without delay.' The lights went off, the firing stopped and the flotilla carried on. Then, at 1.28 a.m., when the force was less than a mile from the harbour, the Germans realized their mistake.

'All at once the searchlights came on us again and the guns commenced to open fire in real earnest,' recalled Stephens. 'Things were getting pretty hot. *Campbeltown* was hit again and again and anything which missed her stern was passing mighty close to us.' The British gunners were giving as good as they got. They were 'magnificent and continued to fire quickly and with accuracy and when one was killed or wounded, another stepped up, took his place and continued'.

Campbeltown was closing rapidly on the lock. Beattie ordered the White Ensign to be run up and went full steam ahead for the gates. The incoming fire was devastating. The helmsman was killed at the wheel. His place was taken by the quartermaster and he too soon fell dead. Another stepped forward, the expedition's explosives expert Lieutenant Nigel Tibbets who had just set the timers for the detonation of the three tonnes of TNT that lay concreted into the hold. The MGB leading the charge veered aside as planned, leaving *Campbeltown* a clear run. The view ahead, though, was obscured by an explosion, sparked by an incoming round which hit the main gun, killing the crew and a number of commandos sheltering on the foredeck.

Then the smoke cleared and Beattie could see the caisson ahead of him only a few hundred yards away. The *Campbeltown* was crashing along at a boiler-bursting twenty knots. Her bows ripped through the heavy steel net rigged up to protect the gates from torpedoes. Then, in a cacophony of screeching metal, she buried herself in the southern lock gates. The commandos leapt down while Beattie gave the order to evacuate and prepared to scuttle the ship so that it settled on the harbour bed, blocking the lock gates. Even if the explosives failed to ignite, it would still render the dock unusable for a long time to come. With the destroyer wedged tight into the caisson, the MTB was free to fire its time-delayed torpedoes at the lock gates that led into the Bassin de St Nazaire. They hit their target and sank to the bottom.

The commandos on board the destroyer now set about their tasks. One group under Lieutenant Johnny Roderick jumped down from the starboard side. They silenced a gun emplacement and a bunker and moved on to their objective, a complex of underground fuel tanks to the south of the dock. Charges were laid but the fuel failed to ignite. They pulled back to provide flank protection for the other teams in the area.

Captain Donald Roy, a proud Highlander who had dressed in a kilt for battle, led his group off the port side of *Campbeltown*. Their job was to attack the guns on top of the pumphouse, which lay alongside the *Normandie* dock. The pumphouse, which emptied the dock of water after a ship sailed in, was the second most vital objective after the caissons. When Roy's group reached the guns, though, the defenders had fled, and they retreated a few hundred yards south to the Old Entrance bridge. Their task was to hold the bridge until the demolition teams working in the dock finished their work

HMS *Campbeltown*, wedged in the *Normandie* dock gates

and had retreated over it to the Old Mole, sticking out into the river on the south-west side of the port. From there, according to the plan, they would be picked up by the motor launches to run the gauntlet back to the sea. Then the bridge would be blown.

Now it was the turn of Lieutenant Stuart Chant's demolition team to move into the pumphouse. He had been wounded in the legs in the fight on the way in, and so had his number two, Lance-Sergeant Bill Chamberlain. They hobbled to the entrance and blew the door. Leaving Chamberlain on guard, Chant led his other three sergeants down the steps and, thanks to their endless practices, they were able quickly to plant their charges around the machinery before retreating to a safe distance. A few minutes later the pumphouse erupted with a colossal bang. They picked their way through the swirling smoke and dust to check the damage. The pumphouse was a wreck. The floor had collapsed and two of the electric motors powering the impeller pumps lay toppled in the basement. To complete the destruction they set fire to the oil pooling in the debris and retreated towards the Old Entrance bridge.

By now, another team led by Lieutenant Chris Smalley had left the ship and made its way to the winding shed operating the dock gates, which lay along a small canal that ran from the caisson. It was undefended and they had no difficulty blowing it up. Other groups were making their way to the northern end of the dock to deal with the other caisson and its winding gear. They ran into fierce fire from a gun emplacement which they eventually cleared with hand grenades. When the team placing the charges on the caisson reached the lock gates they came under more heavy fire. Despite the bullets sparking off the machinery and ricocheting from the concrete of the dock, they succeeded in placing their charges in the water in front of the caisson where it plunged into the Bassin de Penhoët. It was impossible, though, to lift the access cover that would allow them to lower explosives into the hollow interior of the caisson, thereby guaranteeing its demolition. As the fire grew hotter they were forced to blow up the existing charges and retreat. Another team success-fully destroyed the winding shed and the force withdrew south to try and reach the Old Mole to be taken off.

Colonel Newman had got ashore safely and was trying to direct the operation from the German Dockyard HQ. The attack on the dock had achieved almost all its objectives. But elsewhere there was chaos and failure and everywhere there was death.

The attack on the *Normandie* dock was to have been supple-mented by a commando landing on and around the Old Mole. The motor launches were supposed to put ashore demolition and protection teams which would lay waste to the facilities at the southern end of the port. Of the six boats that attempted to do so, only one succeeded. As Billie Stephens led the force towards the objective it seemed that, although his launch had 'been hit a number of times, [we] were still quite seaworthy and whilst we had some wounded, they were none of them serious'. But then 'our luck turned and they got us twice at point-blank range with something very large … the results were sudden and disastrous'. Both engines and the steering had gone and the boat was swung hard to port by the impact of the shells, which brought it up sharply alongside the Old Mole. A few of the commandos managed to scramble ashore. So did Stephens' signalman, but he was killed before a line could reach him to make the launch fast. Instead it bounced back from the wall of the Mole and into a curtain of point-blank fire from a 20mm gun ashore. 'The damage was simply frightful,' said Stephens. 'There was virtually no engine room left and some incendiaries must have hit our tanks because we were blazing fiercely.'

He gave the order to abandon ship and they lowered the Carley Float life rafts. The murderous gunfire had died away, 'it being only too obvious to the enemy that we had already "had it"'. There was not enough room for everyone and Stephens decided to swim. He had sensibly packed a hipflask. 'After a very long pull at my flask I slid over the bows on a line and into the water and my God it was cold.' He set off, 'quite slowly and casually' at first because the shore was only sixty or seventy yards distant. Then he felt the current carrying him away and had to kick off the flying boots he was wearing to struggle against it. 'I had to fight to stop myself panicking,' he wrote. 'Slowly I began to make headway. Time seemed interminable, but I suppose I had only been in the water seven or eight minutes when I reached a small slipway and having arrived at it I just lay there half in and out of the water and quite exhausted.' With the others, he tried to join up with the party ashore but it was hopeless. They were stranded and weaponless and at 2.30 a.m. they were all taken prisoner.

At the back of the flotilla the story was the same. Philip Dark was first lieutenant aboard ML 306, in the rear of the port column. It was carrying three officers, ten ratings and fifteen commandos. By the time they reached their objective Dark had been wounded and as they drew near the Old Mole 'it was apparent that there was no way that we could get alongside as there was a [Motor Launch] burning on either side'.[10] They decided, reluctantly, to withdraw as there was no chance of landing the troops.

The dockyard was now illuminated by a ghastly chiaroscuro of dancing flames, gusting smoke and glittering tracer. Flaming boats glowed on the water and the screams of burning and drowning men mixed with the thud of heavy machine guns. To stay meant certain death or injury. They 'proceeded down the Loire at 18 knots'. Occasionally the boat would be bathed in the stark white of a searchlight or a round from one of the shore batteries would plunge in the water nearby. Just before dawn, they sighted three enemy destroyers. They tried to creep away but were 'immediately illuminated' by a searchlight on the last ship. Almost as it caught them it went out, extinguished by a burst of Bren gun fire from Sergeant Tom Durrant, one of the commandos aboard. In the firefight that ensued, the destroyer tried to ram the launch. The captain, Lieutenant Ian Henderson, brought the wheel over to lessen the impact but it was still enough to throw several men in the water. One managed to climb back on board but his foot had been half-severed by a propeller. The destroyer now opened up with its 4-inch guns 'which rapidly reduced us to a shambles. The coxswain was killed by a shell bursting in the wheel house. Another landed in the bridge, killing Ian and knocking me into a corner.' By the end only Tom Durrant was left, firing doggedly back despite his wounds, until he too stopped.

The destroyer took the survivors off. Dark was impressed with the crew's courtesy and compassion. There was no doctor aboard but Dark had studied medicine before the war so the Germans helped him to do what he could to patch up his shipmates before starting on the German wounded. Durrant was 'conscious but bespattered with shrapnel. He suffered but bore up incredibly.' He died of his wounds ashore. Dark later remembered the time as 'a sordid, rather ghastly dream of blood everywhere and torn flesh soaking blankets and bunks and human beings no longer real people.'

Later, though, there was a moment of satisfaction. Dark was in the middle of a conversation with a German doctor who had come on board who was 'expressing the sentiment of how mad our raid had been [when] there was an almighty explosion [and] the ship shuddered from stem to stern'. It was 10.15 and the *Campbeltown* had gone up. He was told by a brother officer who was on deck at the time that 'nothing was left of the ship or dock gates. Huge concrete slabs were thrown into the air like so much chaff.' The prisoners, huddled under guard ashore, heard and felt it, too. It was some compensation. Gratitude at having survived when so many others were dead was starting to be replaced by the depressing realization that they would be spending the rest of the war in captivity.

The explosion set the seal on the success of the mission. The *Normandie* basin was destroyed and would not be repaired until after the war. The operation had cost many lives. Of the 611 men who took part, 105 sailors and 64 commandos were killed. Townspeople and forced labourers had also been gunned down by panicking Germans. The courage and determination of the raiders was reflected in the number of medals awarded to the living and the dead. Five of the participants won the Victoria Cross, including Tom Durrant.

The dead were among the most spirited, intelligent and skilful warriors of their generation. In the minds of the planners, though, the losses had been proportionate given the perceived importance of the objectives and the success in achieving them. As a comparison, three months later, on the night of 25/26 June, Bomber Command lost 48 aircraft and 208 highly trained airmen in a single raid on Bremen, which destroyed many houses but had little lasting effect on the shipyards and aircraft factories.

The St Nazaire raid demonstrated imagination and cunning, great intelligence in the way that difficulties were foreseen and overcome, patience and thoroughness in the preparations and ruthless determination to see the plan through. The question was whether the target was worth it. As far as the Germans were concerned, the *Normandie* dock was of secondary value. Their chief concern was the submarine pens, and on the morning of 28 March they stood unscathed.

In Britain, the raid was celebrated as a triumph. It provided a feast of propaganda at a time when good news was still rare. The target that had inspired the operation, though, remained untouched, and seemed untouchable. Tucked snugly inside Faettenfjord, *Tirpitz* was immune to attack by conventional submarines or torpedo planes. It was time for a new approach.

7

Smoke and Fog

With the move to Trondheim, the hope that the RAF might be able to inflict significant damage on *Tirpitz* seemed to have receded further. It did not, though, stop it trying. In February 1942, the Air Ministry came up with a proposal to overcome the fact that Trondheim was beyond the range of their available bombers. The plan was to take Beaufort aircraft from Coastal Command's 217 Squadron and modify them, stripping out all but the most essential equipment. They would then take off from RAF Wick in north-east Scotland, fly to Trondheim and attack Faettenfjord. After that they would either continue to neutral Sweden, where the crews would take to their parachutes leaving the aircraft to crash, or turn round and head out to sea. When their fuel ran out they would bale out. Naval vessels, so the theory ran, would be standing by to rescue them. Work was well advanced on modifying the aircraft before this mad idea was abandoned.

The new four-engined Halifaxes and Lancasters which began to arrive at Bomber Command squadrons in 1942 did have the legs to get to Trondheim and back. There were serious doubts, though, about their ability to hit such a small target as the deck of a battleship. Another problem was the limitations of the bombs then available. Despite their names, the 500lb semi-armour-piercing (SAP) and 2,000lb armour-piercing (AP) bombs had had little success in penetrating the well-armoured craft of the modern German fleet. Any that landed on *Tirpitz* were likely to bounce off. According to naval intelligence, she had two armoured decks. The upper was 2 inches thick. The lower was 3.2 inches thick and 4.3 over the magazines and engine rooms. The side armour was calculated at 12.6 inches. These figures are not far from the truth. The side plating was in fact 13 inches, the upper deck 2 inches and the main deck 3.7–4.9 inches. Even at the lower assessment, the bombs were almost certain to fail.

In the spring of 1942, Bomber Command took delivery of a new bomb which it was hoped might bring results. The Mark XIX spherical contact mine was a modified anti-shipping weapon. Its horns were removed, its casing toughened to withstand the impact of being dropped from a great height and the explosive charge boosted from 100lb of Amatol to 770lb. It was given the unconvincing name 'roly-poly'. The aim was not to hit the ship but to drop the mine so that it rolled underneath the hull. It was detonated by a Mark XIV hydrostatic pistol, activated by water pressure. It was estimated that, if delivered accurately and set to go off at the right depth, it would rip a giant hole in what was supposed to be Tirpitz's most vulnerable point – her bottom.

Delivering the weapon on target, though, posed a number of problems. The mine was aerodynamically awkward. It was round and weighed 1000lb. Initial tests revealed that it was hopelessly inaccurate when dropped at normal bombing heights. After further experimentation it was decided that to have any chance of being effective the crews would have to bomb at no higher than 600 feet.

That was asking a great deal. The Faettenfjord anchorage was narrow and sheltered on three sides by hills. Flak emplacements on the slopes reinforced the ship's own strong anti-aircraft defences. To drop their mines, pilots would have to hold their Halifaxes straight and level for the final approach. It was a prospect to test the strongest nerves. 'Such an operation would be quite possible with a helicopter,' judged Don Bennett, one of the pilots tasked with carrying it out. 'But to do it in four-engined bombers was, to say the least, a little difficult.'[1]

Air Marshal Sir Arthur Harris, the new chief of Bomber Command, believed a daylight operation would have no chance of success and result in heavy losses. They would have to attack at night. On 13 March, the Chief of the Air Staff, Air Chief Marshal Portal, told Churchill that Bomber Command would make an attempt at the next full moon, using the new mines to 'do serious underwater damage'.

'Bomber' Harris

The task was given to 10, 35 and 76 Squadrons based at Leeming and Linton-on-Ouse in North Yorkshire, and Middleton St George in County Durham. The operational order instructing them described their target as 'one of the most powerful war vessels afloat … its presence in these waters apart from the constant menace to our convoys [has] a widespread influence on the strategical situation at sea'. Its destruction or crippling 'would have a profound effect on the whole course of the war, the importance of which cannot be overstated'.

A total of thirty-two aircraft were to take part. They would launch from Lossiemouth, Kinloss and Tain on the north-east coast of Scotland. The ten Halifaxes from 10 Squadron and ten of the twelve from 35 Squadron would each carry four mines and ninety 4lb incendiary bombs. The other two 35 Squadron bombers would be loaded with 50lb incendiaries. The ten aeroplanes from 76 Squadron would each take one 4,000lb High Capacity blast bomb, and four 500lb or 250lb general purpose bombs to inflict damage on the superstructure. The 10 Squadron crews were to try to drop their mines in sticks at intervals of 100 feet, and those of 35 Squadron at 200 feet. The large incendiaries would be dropped 50 feet apart. The distance from northern Scotland was 1,300 miles. Every aircraft would carry 1,872 gallons of fuel and the trip was expected to take eight to eight and a half hours in total.

The attack required great skill, precision and nerve. The danger from the anti-aircraft guns was augmented by the threat from the nearby aerodrome at Vaernes, only eight miles south of Faettenfjord. There were thought to be about sixty fighters there, Me 110s and, more worryingly, Me 109s for whom the heavily laden bombers would be easy prey. The attackers were unlikely to have surprise on their side. The German radar chains would pick up any aircraft approaching from seaward flying higher than 1,500 feet. To divert the defenders' attention, a parallel raid was ordered. Two of the new Lancasters from 5 Group were scheduled to bomb Vaernes aerodrome before the main attack went in.

Despite the trickiness of the operation, preparations were minimal. Sergeant Ian Hewitt, a navigator on 35 Squadron who would fly in S-Sugar on the raid, remembered carrying out only 'two or three practice bombing exercises' on the ranges near their Linton base, 'diving down from 2,000 to 250 feet and dropping a practice bomb'.[2]

In the days before the scheduled operation, Spitfires from Number 1 PRU flew repeated sorties over the area. The battleship's arrival back in Faettenfjord on 13 March had been reported by local agents but bad weather prevented a reconnaissance flight until five days later.

The pilots were from the unit's C Flight, based at Wick, and A. F. P. Fane, who had been the first to spot *Tirpitz* when it arrived in Trondheim in January, was among them. Fane was a veteran now, who had notched up fifteen trips to Norway by the time the big raid was scheduled. The duties of the PRU were tough. The weather conditions were frequently dreadful. Pilots had to contend with dense cloud that concealed the hills and peaks of the Norwegian coast and fjords. The conditions at their home base were hardly better. The round trip took about four and a half hours. Exhausted pilots often spent the last part of their mission desperately searching for a gap in the cloud through which they could spot a landmark that could guide them home. Often it was the Orkneys that provided the fix. If they missed them, which was all too easy to do, there was nothing ahead except thousands of miles of ocean.

Sometimes pilots and aircraft just disappeared. On 18 March Fane wrote that one of his comrades, Flight Sergeant Tommy Tomlinson, 'took off for Bergen and did not return. Weather here bloody ... land and sea search made around these parts but nothing seen.'[3] It was not just the weather that posed a threat. On 5 March, Fane noted in his diary: 'Sandy Gunn missing. Took off for Trondheim. No news. No plot of him coming back.' Next day he recorded that 'German wireless reported that "an English fighter was shot down by AA over the Norwegian coast and the pilot was a prisoner of war"'.

Fane had his own encounter with the German defences fifteen days later. He was flying through brilliant, clear skies over Aasfjord where *Tirpitz* and two destroyers were resting in the inlets after their outing against PQ.12. He had run in low over the ships and taken several 'obliques', framed to show as much of the side view of the vessels as possible. He had 'just started a second run [and] was flying bang into the sun when I suddenly saw a [Messerschmitt] 109E practically formating on me to starboard. [I] nearly jumped out of the aeroplane with shock.' Fane reckoned that his attacker must have approached him from underneath as he 'kept a reasonably good look out'. He 'closed throttle and turned on his tail – that shook him. He took violent avoiding action. Felt better but was soon really upset by seeing a second Me 109 which was following the first one 1000 yards behind and 500 feet above. He immediately dived to make a beam attack. That was fairly easy to cope with as I turned into him and shot underneath long before he could get his guns on.'

Fane then 'took a quick look around to see if there were any more about. Thank God that was all.' Nonetheless he was 'worried about where the first one had got to so instead of heading straight for home went into a screaming, climbing turn back into the sun. Sure enough they were both still turning back towards me but the important thing was that they were well below me.' Showing remarkable coolness, Fane then 'went straight toward them and inside their turn and went screaming into the sun and never saw them again.'

Fane's sangfroid was all the more remarkable given than he had nothing to defend himself with. PRU aircraft were not armed. The guns had been stripped out to reduce weight and allow for the fitting of long-range tanks. The camera itself was mounted vertically on a frame inside the fuselage and behind the pilot's seat. It was bulky, with a thirty-six-inch lens, set at a slight angle. It took film strips nine inches wide that could record an area three miles across. By overlapping the photographs and using a stereoscope, a three-dimensional image was produced. The modified Spitfires did have speed on their side. The aluminium skin of the fuselage and wings was buffed to a sheen and coated with a special pale blue-green eggshell paint called 'camotint'. The refinements reduced drag and allowed them to reach 400mph.

By 28 March the Halifaxes and their crews detailed for the big raid had been moved to their bases in northern Scotland and the full moon was looming. The PRU was under even more pressure than usual to bring back good photographs. 'Hell of a flap on because we have not been able to cover Trondheim for seven days now owing to lousy weather,' wrote Fane in his diary. His CO Tony Hill was on leave and he found himself in charge and having to deal with impatient 'Group Captains, Air Commodores, Air Marshals, Admirals and the like who seem to take it as a personal insult that the poor little Spittie can't get through fog, hail, snow, rain, cloud and mountains'.

That morning Fane took it upon himself to deliver the goods. He took off at 7.30 and climbed up through the all-enveloping cloud and headed north-east. The skies cleared over Trondheim. He took some photographs of the seaplane base at Hommelvik, just to the south of Faettenfjord, then got lost in a snowstorm. When he emerged an anti-aircraft battery opened fire.

He 'dived onto [the] ground and tore round the countryside at 0 feet, 2850 revs and +9 boost doing about 300[mph]'. He picked up a landmark on the shore of Aasfjord and swung into Faettenfjord. There was *Tirpitz*. He flew in parallel to it, then 'screamed round to the left and shot [over] the top of it, in a vertical bank, taking one oblique photo'. Then he 'dropped to the water and flew towards Trondheim'. By now the anti-aircraft batteries along the shores of Faettenfjord were waiting for him and as he skimmed along he saw 'flak from both banks … splashing in the water both sides'. He bobbed up and down 'from 100 feet to 0 feet'. A speedboat lay dead ahead coming towards him. It 'nearly upset getting out my way. I expect he thought I was going to fire at him.' He thought the sight was 'damn funny. I hope it had the Admiral in it.'

Despite these adventures he was still on the lookout for targets. He ran into another snowstorm and emerged to see a large warship in the waters below. He turned round to photograph it. Fane was skilled at ship recognition. He knew as he pressed the shutter button that he was filming the heavy cruiser *Admiral Hipper*, which had arrived a week before from Brunsbüttel. *Admiral Scheer* and *Prinz Eugen* were already in place, lying in Lofjord, just north of *Tirpitz*. Together they made a formidable force. The urgency of the Bomber Command effort sharpened.

The attack was scheduled to start on the evening of 30 March. The operation began to fall apart even before it had begun. The Lancaster raid on Vaernes airport was abandoned after one of the two aircraft taking part crashed at Woodhall Spa when taking off to join the main force in Scotland. The thirty-four Halifaxes nonetheless set off into skies thickly blanketed with cloud just after 6 p.m. When they reached the target area there was nothing to aim at. No one claimed to have seen *Tirpitz*. They could only guess her whereabouts from the muzzle flashes from the flak batteries and the glow of search-lights in the murk below. Only three of the aircraft dropped bombs. Four Halifaxes were shot down in the area of Trondheim. Another two crashed into the sea on the way home.

The episode only emphasized the extreme difficulty of hitting *Tirpitz* in her Faettenfjord berth. The determination to keep trying was unabated, however. The PRU continued to fly sorties and take casualties. On 4 April, Flight Sergeant Mervyn Jones, who had been given leave from his navigation course to ride the 1940 Grand National winner Bogstar, was shot down and killed. Two days later C Flight were replaced by B Flight and returned to Benson. Fane had flown thirteen reconnaissance missions. On ten of them he had managed to photograph the targets. Given the frequently atrocious weather and the strength of the local defences, this was an outstanding record and he had been congratulated by the Commander in Chief of Coastal Command, Sir Philip Joubert de la Ferté, who assured him he was 'fully aware of the skill and daring necessary' to bring the pictures home. But Fane knew that the odds against his survival shortened inexorably the more he flew. He categorized three of the trips as 'dicing' – the pilot's term for a sortie when the conditions were so bad that whether or not you returned was a matter of fate. Just over three months later his luck ran out. He was killed when his Spitfire crashed in bad weather near Great Shelford in Cambridgeshire, returning from a trip photographing Flensburg.

Between 8 April and the end of the month the PRU mounted eighteen sorties, only failing to operate when the weather was impossible. Such was the preoccupation with *Tirpitz*'s activities that on some days they flew three separate missions. On 16 April, pictures showing her 'emitting smoke' as if in preparation for a voyage caused anxiety but she stayed put for the next few days. There was more concern on 24 April when it was reported that she was 'almost free from camouflage netting', suggesting again that she was getting ready to put to sea.[4] Again it was a false alarm. The next 'reccos' showed the camouflage was not only back in place but had been supplemented by more nets and rafts. Local agents reported that the defences were being steadily strengthened with additional anti-submarine and torpedo nets draped on floats in a curtain a hundred yards from the vessel. She now had an all-round anti-aircraft defence from flak and searchlight batteries set in concrete emplacements on either side of the fjord to supplement her own onboard guns, as well as smoke generators to brew up an artificial fog as thick as the natural one that had thwarted the Halifax attack of 30/31 March.

Despite these hazards and obstacles, another attempt was scheduled for the end of April. It would follow the same lines as the original plan, using the same squadrons and taking off from the same north Scotland airfields. There were some refinements, though, which asked even more of the crews than the original orders. The initial attack would be launched by 76 Squadron and twelve Lancasters from 44 and 97 Squadrons. They were to drop 4,000lb blast bombs on *Tirpitz* from 6,000 feet then hang around overhead seeking flak and searchlight emplacements on which to unload their four 500 pounders. There would be no shortage of targets. Intelligence estimates reckoned there were twenty-four heavy anti-aircraft artillery pieces in the immediate area and possibly twice as many light guns. This was a tall order at any time and in any place, let alone the narrow declivity of Faettenfjord at night.

Then it was the turn of 10 and 35 Squadrons. They were to approach from the west at a new, even lower height of 150–200 feet. Each of the twenty Halifaxes would carry four of the Mark XIX 'roly-poly' spherical mines which they were expected to deposit 'close to the stern and between the ship and the shore' at 100 and 200 feet intervals.[5] The crews were told at the briefing that 'one mine directly under the stern will damage propellers and rudders, thus making it necessary to tow the battleship back to a major naval depot for repairs – a battleship in tow would be a set up for our air and naval forces'.[6] According to Wing Commander Don Bennett, who led 10 Squadron on the raid, the crews were assured that 'the mines, rolled down the surface of the mountain which was very steep, sloping under the base of the ship, could have burst the hull from below. That was the theory of it ... All we had to do was drop these mines between ship and shore and they would go down and do their stuff and when they got to a certain depth they would go off.' The briefing notes for the operation say only that the mines were to be dropped behind the stern of the ship – which faced the approaching aircraft. Either way, it was an unlikely proposition.

The tail of Faettenfjord where *Tirpitz* lay was only 350 yards across. The gap between the hull and the northern shore, where it plunged almost vertically into the water, was ten yards wide. The berth, as Dudley Pound pointed out later, was the maritime equivalent of a slit trench.[7] To slot the mines neatly into the gap would require a degree of accuracy that was unheard of at this stage of the war. With bombs gone, the aircraft were to execute a tight turn to the north, over the 700-foot ridge above Faettenfjord and into neighbouring Lofjord, where *Scharnhorst*, *Prinz Eugen* and *Hipper* were anchored in a small, natural harbour. These were designated as secondary targets if the attack on the *Tirpitz* proved impossible. Like *Tirpitz* they bristled with anti-aircraft guns which would be trained on the skies once the raid began.

The crews were left in no doubt about the importance of the mission. Senior naval officers made a morale-boosting visit to Kinloss and Churchill sent a message assuring the participants '[you] will be proud to tell your grandchildren'.[8] The operation was planned for 25 April but fog along the north Scottish coast forced cancellation. It was the same story the following night. The crews relieved their anxieties with beer and horseplay. On the morning of Monday, 27 April a PRU flight reported all the warships in their usual anchorages. There was some good news from Vaernes airport. There was no sign of the thirty Me 109s that were thought to be there. Then the meteorological forecast arrived, predicting reasonable weather. The raid was on.

The bombers started taking off from the three bases just after 8 p.m. Around the time of their expected arrival, Coastal Command aircraft would distract the radar stations in the target area by carrying out small diversionary attacks on aerodromes. For once the weather was perfect. 'The night was calm, the sea was dead flat,' remembered Don Bennett. The full moon glittered on the water and lit up the mountains ahead like a stage set. It was perfect bombing weather. But they were also ideal conditions for the defenders who were now coming to readiness all along the approach path.

The Germans had plenty of notice of the bombers' arrival. At 11.08 p.m. local time, the radar station at Kristiansund had warned of approaching four-engined aircraft and by 11.30 p.m. *Tirpitz* was at action stations. Just before midnight the first aircraft loomed into view and the guns began to thump.

The first to arrive were the Lancasters of 44 and 97 Squadrons and the Halifaxes of 78 Squadron which approached from the south side of Trondheimsfjord and began their run-in. The route brought them close to Vaernes aerodrome at 12,000 feet, where flak began to burst around them. They then dived to 7,500 feet and began the run-in down Faettenfjord into the dazzle of the searchlights and the fire blossoming at the end. The lead Lancaster managed to drop its 4,000lb bomb over the ship then turn sharply to port releasing its four remaining bombs on the guns on the hillside as it went.

Down below the men operating the smoke generators frantically fed canisters of chlorosulphonic acid into the machines and a white pall began to smother the outlines of the ship. The rest of the lead force followed, dropping their bombs over the rapidly disappearing form of the *Tirpitz*, or aiming at the flashes from the barrels of the anti-aircraft guns pumping out shells below.

The flak was already taking its toll of the second wave. Don Bennett's Halifax was still forty miles from the target when he started to take hits from a shore battery. Bennett was an Australian with a reputation for technical brilliance and outstanding flying ability which was matched by his self-confidence and willingness to clash with his superiors if he thought he was in the right. He had broken several flying records and already distinguished himself in wartime by organizing a mass ferry service of aircraft across the Atlantic. He had reached the conclusion that the bombing campaign at the time was 'a complete failure'. To improve Bomber Command's dismal performance he had come up with the idea of a vanguard that would identify and mark targets for a following stream of bombers to attack. The idea was eventually adopted as Pathfinder Force and Bennett would be its first commander and remain in charge of it for most of the war.

Given his experiences that night, he believed that he was extremely lucky to have survived to take up his post. As he approached the target, the fire started by the flak began to take hold. 'I was a flamer so I was picked on all the way,' he remembered.[9] He pressed on, identifying another island which had been chosen as the starting point for a 'stopwatch run' which relied on exact speed, height and timing to take the aircraft to the precise point when the four mines on board should be dropped.

When he reached Faettenfjord, though, he found 'fog filling the whole of the fjord' and all he could make out of the *Tirpitz* was the masts sticking through the blanket of smoke. Braving the flak erupting through the murk, he went round for a second run, which was also 'pretty hopeless'.

By now the aircraft was burning fiercely and he gave the order to bale out. The others scrambled for the hatches snapping on their parachute packs as they went. Bennett's, though, was out of reach. He was 'sitting in my seat in a flaming aircraft and a very hot one, ready to do what? Bail out without a parachute?' Mercifully the flight engineer, Flight Sergeant J. Colgan, turned back to hand Bennett his parachute even as the Halifax went into its final, screaming descent. As he struggled up from his seat, scrabbling to clip on the pack, 'the starboard wing folded up and I got out in a hurry and pulled the plug immediately. I didn't count to three seconds or anything like that and hit the deck just as it opened. If I'd counted the three seconds I wouldn't have made it.' He landed in thick snow and was buried up to his neck.

The crew of another Halifax, S-Sugar from 35 Squadron, got a better look at the target as they skimmed in below the hills of the fjord. 'We went down to forty feet,' said Rear Gunner Ron Wilson. 'The flak was coming both down at us and up at us. I was firing at cliffs and boats as we went by. Then the skipper said, here's the *Tirpitz* now, and I went beserk on the guns and sprayed [her] from stem to stern.'[10] Immediately after, the bomber was hit by flak.

'There was a great bang and the starboard engine caught fire,' remembered Ian Hewitt, S-Sugar's navigator. 'There was no hope of flying on to Sweden let alone returning to Scotland.' They were too low to bail out. The captain, Flight Lieutenant Don MacIntyre, began to search for a stretch of water. Soon what looked like a lake gleamed out of the darkness below. As they touched down, they realized they had landed on ice. 'The aircraft skidded along for about a couple of miles before coming to rest and slowly began to sink.' Hewitt scrambled out of the upper hatch and onto the wing.

He discovered then that one of the oddities of war was 'the virtual impossibility of keeping farce out of the most dramatic situations'. As he jumped off the wing he fell straight through the ice. As they fished him out, 'the rest of the crew who saw the funny side of the situation before I did, began to laugh'. Soaked and freezing, he set off with the others in what they hoped was the direction of the Swedish border. *

Despite the flak and the fog, the forty-one crews that reached the Norwegian coast had pressed home their attack with remarkable persistence. Thirty-two claimed to have dropped their bombs on *Tirpitz*, though very few of the crews admitted actually to have seen her. Three others said they had attacked other targets. One late arriving 76 Squadron Halifax reported bombing *Prinz Eugen* and *Scheer* in Lofjord.

All the effort produced no result. *Tirpitz* was unharmed. The Mark XIX mines had failed completely. Six aircraft were brought down and fifteen airmen killed. By a stroke of luck that contradicted all the odds, eighteen of the thirty-three men shot down survived to be taken prisoner, or, like Bennett, managed to escape. He struggled from his snowdrift to see the wreck of his Halifax glowing in the distance. He could hear dogs barking and knew that German soldiers would soon be upon him. 'The dogs were my main worry,' he recalled. 'To get away from the dogs I would have to cross a stream.' There was one nearby but it was not an inviting prospect. 'The water in the stream was flowing … but the banks were eight or ten feet wide [and made of] of ice. You had to slide across the ice into the water and then get out the other side.' By now he had met up with his wireless operator, Sergeant C. Forbes. They found a stretch with trees on both banks. 'We slid down the ice hanging onto the tree branches and waded through the water and then on the other side, the branches in one place were where we could grab them so we dragged ourselves across the ice. That shook off the dogs.'

* After the landing the burning bomber melted through the ice and settled on bottom of the lake. It was recovered in 1973 and is now on display at the RAF Museum at Hendon.

They now headed east towards the Swedish border which lay tantalizingly close, less then fifty miles away. Sweden was neutral. If they made it they would be interned, but it was better than ending up in a PoW camp. The journey would take them over more freezing rivers and up and down snow-choked valleys. After two days they had still not reached the frontier. They were tired and hungry and desperate when they emerged from the woods to see a farmhouse on the side of a hill with lights in the window and smoke drifting from the chimney. 'We were in a pretty far gone state,' Bennett remembered. He was still concerned, though, that the inhabitants might turn them in to the Germans so he told Forbes to be ready to run if they got an unfriendly reception. The man who came to the door took a look at the shivering, half-starved visitors and invited them in. 'He was able to speak English,' said Bennett. 'He'd lived in Australia and was generally wonderful. They gave us some of the very little food they had, laid us on the floor in front of a wood stove and gave us two hours sleep, the only sleep we got in three days.'

After their brief rest the farmer handed them on to another local man who was to take them to the frontier, guiding them through the German patrols. They walked through the darkness and as dawn came up they could see the rock cairns planted with the Norwegian and Swedish flags that marked the frontier. They spent an anxious half-hour trekking across an open snowfield. Then they were inside the border and a little later were picked up at the ski resort of Storlien.

Ian Hewitt had also managed to make it across the border. Soon after leaving their burning aircraft the six-man crew had split up. Hewitt and the wireless operator Dave Perry set off with their pilot Don MacIntyre, a Canadian from New Brunswick, who was 'used to snow'. They, too, received help from Norwegians along the way who gave them food and showed them the route.

On crossing the frontier they knocked on a farmhouse door. The inhabitants 'made us quite welcome, gave us a meal and rang the local police'. They were then taken off to the local jail by the police who treated them courteously and hospitably.[11]

Bennett and Forbes were put in an internment camp in central Sweden. Bennett was suffering from frostbite and had lost a lot of weight. The other internees donated part of their rations, which included silver fox meat, to help him recover. Bennett's relief at his deliverance did not last long. He was determined to get back to the war. The British legation in Oslo sent an official to see him. He was not impressed. 'They'd sent up a relatively junior man,' he said. A few days later, though, he had more visitors. Two women and a Swede arrived with a message that Count Bernadotte, the eminent Swedish diplomat later assasinated by Zionists, wished to see him in Stockholm, to clarify his situation. The hopes that were raised by the intervention evaporated when he arrived. According to Bennett's bad-tempered account, Bernadotte seemed strangely unhelpful. Bennett had constructed a complicated argument claiming that the laws of internment did not apply to his case. When Bernadotte disagreed he threatened him with legal action.

Faced with Bennett's brusque determination and clear willingness to cause the maximum trouble to get his way, Bernadotte gave in. Bennett was released into the custody of the British ambassador and promptly sent a signal to London asking for an aircraft to take him home. One was soon on its way. 'The ambassador was furious,' said Bennett. 'He'd been trying to get one for months and months, [then] some little whippersnapper of a wing commander comes along and gets one straight away.' The reason for the swift response was that Bennett was urgently wanted at home to start forming the Pathfinder Force. The ambassador, though, 'was not to be allowed into that secret.'[12] Within thirty days of baling out he was back in Britain. Hewitt, Perry and MacIntyre followed soon after.

Despite the dismal results of the raid, twenty-three Halifaxes from 10, 35 and 76 Squadrons and eleven Lancasters from 44 and 97 Squadrons had taken off from Scotland again the following night. Once again the same method of attack was used. Once again the onboard defences of *Tirpitz*, the shore batteries and above all the smoke machines combined to thwart it. Forty-eight 'roly-poly' mines were dropped. None of them did any damage. The closest one landed seventy yards from the starboard beam of the ship. The

Germans recovered eight of them caught in the trees in the steep hill against which the battleship was anchored. Two Halifaxes from 35 Squadron were shot down by flak, which appeared capable of offering enough protection to the ships for there to be no real necessity for fighter cover. Three men were killed, but, again, and unusually, nine more survived to become PoWs.

Bennett arrived home in a black mood. He returned to 10 Squadron to find it under the temporary command of a twenty-five-year old wing commander called James Tait, who had already established a reputation for skill, courage and coolness. 'Father said drily that he'd managed to do some useful work with the squadron while Bennett was away,' said his son, Peter Tait. 'Bennett was rather a prickly character. So he didn't actually take it as a joke.'[13] Two and a half years later, Tait would pull off what Bennett had failed to achieve.

The operation left some lasting bitterness in Bennett's combative mind. He accused Naval Intelligence of failing the bomber crews on two crucial points. First, they had wrongly assumed that, despite the thick armour plate on its hull and deck, Tirpitz had a 'soft belly' that would be vulnerable to the 'roly-polys'. 'We now know that nothing would have touched the "soft belly" of the Tirpitz,' he said many years after the event. He also claimed that the crews had not been warned about the Tirpitz's smoke generators – even though their existence was well known to the navy. They were 'wrong in letting us go into an area where there was going to be this fog without telling us,' he said. 'And they knew, which I discovered afterwards. So we had plenty to complain about with Royal Navy planning.'[14]

8

Provoking Nemesis

The navy looked ahead to the summer of 1942 with apprehension. The failure to sink *Tirpitz* in March meant the Russian convoys would need constant protection. As the days lengthened and the nights shrank, the risks from surface ships, submarines and aircraft multiplied. Yet there seemed no likelihood that the sailings would be suspended. The Red Army sorely needed the tanks, trucks and aircraft in the merchantmen's holds. The cargoes also carried great political significance.

By keeping the pipeline open, Britain and America demonstrated their commitment to the Soviet Union at a time when it was paying the terrible price of fighting the Germans, practically alone. In the absence of a second front in Europe, the convoys were proof of British and American willingness to accept a share of the costs of going to war with Hitler.

President Roosevelt had insisted that the sailings continued, and contributed a US Navy task force of a battleship and two cruisers to help with escort duties. The reinforcements did little to calm the Admiralty's fears. On 18 May the First Sea Lord, Sir Dudley Pound, sent a worried message to the Commander-in-Chief of the United States Fleet, Admiral Ernest King. 'The whole thing is a most unsound operation with the dice loaded against us in every direction,' he wrote.[1] King was a difficult character, whose Anglophobe tendencies had been nurtured during a period seconded to a British warship during the First World War. However, he agreed with Pound. So did every sailor who sailed in the convoys. Even as he argued, Pound knew that his protest was in vain.

Churchill had accepted that the necessity to appease Stalin outweighed the dangers of maintaining the shuttle. On 17 May he wrote to the Chiefs of Staff underlining that 'not only Premier Stalin but President Roosevelt will object very much to our desisting from running the convoys now. The Russians are in heavy action, and will expect us to run the risk and pay the price entailed by our contribution.' The USSR's attitude had nonetheless been ungracious and uncooperative. It was a constant complaint of the Allies that the Soviets seemed unwilling or unable to deploy their own navy and air force to provide cover for the convoys at their end of the route, where about a fifth of the losses occurred. Eight days before, in a letter to Stalin, Churchill had felt compelled to be 'quite frank and [emphasize] the need for increasing the assistance given by the USSR naval and air forces in helping to get these convoys through safely.'[2] The Soviets thawed sufficiently to allow two RAF squadrons equipped with American Catalina flying boats to operate from bases in north Russia and patrol the Norway coast.

Pound was writing at the end of a string of disasters that had struck in the Arctic since the *Tirpitz*'s sortie against PQ.12. The next pair of convoys to sail were the outgoing PQ.13, and QP.12, which would cross with it as it returned home. Of the nineteen ships in PQ.13, five were sunk: two by aircraft, two by U-boats and one by a destroyer. In addition, two escorting warships, the cruiser *Trinidad* and the destroyer *Eclipse*, had been damaged – the *Trinidad* bizarrely by its own torpedo which turned round after its steering mechanism was disorientated by the freezing water. An enemy destroyer and a U-boat had been sunk. But if the value of the operation was judged in material terms alone, the convoy would have to be marked as a failure. Pound repeated his misgivings to the Defence Committee in early April but to no avail. He had been accused by some in the navy of being too pliant in the face of political demands. He was not so now. It was as if he sensed the disaster in the offing.

At Roosevelt's insistence, the next convoy, PQ.14, was larger than its predecessor. Of the twenty-four ships that sailed, sixteen turned back when they ran into heavy ice. Of those that battled on, one was sunk by a U-boat. The returning convoy, QP.10, lost four of its sixteen ships.

PQ.15 and QP.11 were made up of twenty-five and thirteen ships respectively. They sailed at the end of April. A large force was in place to protect them, including the cruiser *Edinburgh*, the flagship of Rear Admiral Stuart Bonham-Carter. While zigzagging in front of the homecoming convoy she was hit by a torpedo fired by a U-boat and had to limp the 250 miles to Murmansk with her stern blown away, unable to steer except on her engines. German destroyers caught up with her and in the fight that followed the *Edinburgh* was caught amidships by another torpedo and almost cut in half. Two of her destroyer escorts, *Forester* and *Foresight*, were also badly hit. Despite being barely afloat, the *Edinburgh*'s gunners succeeded in fatally damaging the destroyer *Hermann Schoemann*. It hardly compensated for the loss of the *Edinburgh*, which was eventually abandoned and sent to the bottom with a friendly torpedo. She was followed, on 15 May, by another cruiser, the *Trinidad*, which was attacked by a lone Junkers 88 dive-bomber as she headed home from Murmansk. Again the ship was abandoned and then sunk to deny her to the enemy.

The next pair of convoys fared slightly better. PQ.16 had thirty-five ships, the largest number yet sailed. The returning QP.12 had fifteen. The homecoming journey was mercifully uneventful. The Germans reserved their energy for PQ.16. After the two convoys passed each other on 25 May, the Murmansk-bound ships were subjected to almost continuous air assaults with Heinkel 111 torpedo planes taking turns with Junkers 88 dive-bombers. On one day, 27 May, 108 attacks took place. Four of the merchantmen were sunk. Two others, and a Polish-manned destroyer, the *Garland*, were badly damaged.

Among the submarines protecting the convoy was HMS *Seawolf*, commanded by Lieutenant Commander Dick Raikes, who had raised the alarm when *Tirpitz* left Trondheim in March. During the first two days out, the seas were clogged with fog which increased the risk of collisions but at least hid the ships from the eyes of German reconnaissance aircraft. As soon as it cleared, they were joined by a Focke-Wulf long-range spotter which circled out of range of the guns. Raikes recalled later that 'from then until arrival in Russia, one of these planes was always with us, "homing" the enemy aircraft from the many airfields in Norway.'[3]

The submarines were under instructions to attempt to sink any surface raiders with their torpedoes but to dive if the convoy was attacked from the air. It was soon clear that the orders were impracticable. After submerging following the first actions and finding himself miles astern of the convoy, Raikes resurfaced and signalled to the close escort commander, Captain Dickie Onslow, on board the fleet destroyer *Ashanti*, 'in the event of future air attack, intend to remain on the surface.' Back came the wry reply: 'So do I.'*

For the next five days everyone involved in PQ.16 lived in a state of adrenalin-soaked anxiety as each attack arrived, or nervous trepidation as they waited for the next one to develop. They were naked on the water, illuminated by a merciless sun that never fully set. 'The convoy was attacked practically without a pause by high level bombers, dive bombers and torpedo-carrying bombers,' Raikes remembered. The U-boats stayed away at first. Then, on the third day, just as Raikes was heading to his bunk for a rest he was 'summoned back to the bridge to see a U-boat torpedo narrowly missing my stern. It was running shallow and nearly all guns in the convoy were firing at the spume to try and explode it.' Raikes had on board a new sub-lieutenant who remained 'commendably unmoved by the whole experience and announced that the spume was caused not by a torpedo but by an Arctic whale. He had just said the word "whale" when the torpedo hit a large Russian ship carrying ammunition.'

The normally insouciant Raikes reported that 'we were all shaken by this as the Russian ship was only about three hundred yards from us and after an instantaneous change to white heat, exploded and totally disappeared in a few seconds. It was blown into tiny smithereens and didn't even leave any traces of wreckage of the surface.'

It was not long before Raikes had recovered his normal, jokey composure. 'After three or four days watching the Focke-Wulf aircraft

---

* A witty signal is highly prized in the navy and these *bons mots* have been attributed to other captains.

circling the convoy and knowing we were powerless to do anything about it, I told the signalman to call it up on the signal lamp. I made "you are making me dizzy. Please go round the other way." To my great surprise he replied "Certainly." And did so.' The last leg was as harrowing as the rest of the trip. The exhausted survivors endured their last air attack 'within a dozen miles of a Russian fighter airfield. Not a single fighter came to our assistance.' It confirmed his view of his Soviet brothers-in-arms. 'Bastards,' he wrote.

The convoy had lost seven ships and four escorts, with many more damaged. They had managed to shoot down twenty German aircraft. Nonetheless, Raikes and every other sailor took satisfaction in the fact that the convoy had got through, 'albeit to a thoroughly ungrateful ally'.[4]

The sunken ships were carrying valuable war materiel and 77 aircraft, 147 tanks and 770 military vehicles were now on the bottom of the Arctic Ocean. It amounted to a quarter of the cargo. In a single day, a few Luftwaffe aircraft had disposed of materiel that it might take an armoured brigade a month to destroy, and they had done so at relatively little cost.

The danger from the air was already plain. After the experiences of PQ.15 the Commander-in-Chief of the Home Fleet, Sir John Tovey, had agreed with Admiral Bonham-Carter that unless the airfields from which the Luftwaffe operated in northern Norway could be knocked out or the convoys allowed the cover of darkness, the whole punishing exercise should stop. 'If they must continue for political reasons, very serious and heavy losses must be expected,' he wrote.[5] Like his chief, Admiral Pound, he believed that the strategic situation was 'wholly favourable to the enemy'.

In the Admiralty, preparations for the next convoy took place in an atmosphere of impending disaster. The official historian of the war at sea, Captain Stephen Roskill, wrote that 'it was plain to all involved in the work of planning the convoys and the associated fleet movements and in the long drawn out anxieties of their execution, that we were gambling with fate to an extent that was bound, sooner or later, to provoke nemesis. All realised that a disaster was likely; but when, and on which convoy would it fall?'[6]

There was a brief lull before the tempest blew up. In early June 1942, the demands of Malta took priority over the Arctic convoys. Ships were detached from the Home Fleet to protect the 'Pedestal' convoy, carrying vital supplies to the besieged island. By the end of the month they were back in Scapa Flow waiting for the Russian convoys to resume.

The next eastbound convoy was coded PQ.17 and was made up of thirty-five vessels. The homecoming QP.13, which it would cross, had thirty-six. Both were set to depart on 27 June. They would be sailing in virtually continuous daylight. To compensate, they would have a formidable force to protect them, bolstered by the US Navy's Task Force 99 under the command of Rear Admiral Robert C. Giffen. It was made up of Giffen's flagship, the battleship USS *Washington*, two cruisers, the *Wichita* and the *Tuscaloosa*, and some destroyers. For the first time in the war, substantial American forces had been placed under British command.

The crew of the *Wichita* included a film star. Lieutenant Douglas Fairbanks Jnr was thirty-five years old, and an established Hollywood actor with a marriage to Joan Crawford behind him. He spent some of his youth in Britain and moved easily in upper-class and royal circles. He was a friend of the Duke of Kent and had met his brother, King George VI. He was equally well connected at home. Roosevelt sent him in 1941 as a special envoy to South America.

Fairbanks was unusually politically committed for an actor of the period, particularly for a star of the American film industry where commercial concerns steered studios away from subjects that might alienate any section of the mass audience. From the outset, he had been disturbed at the rise of fascism in Europe. He was friendly with two rising talents of the Conservative Party, Anthony Eden and Duff Cooper, both of whom resigned over the government's appeasement policy. Fairbanks attributed his political awareness to 'an accumulation of anger at the whole Nazi system and what it threatened, not to Britain or to my country in particular, but in terms of what it threatened to the world and to what that world had built up over two thousand years'.[7]

His transatlantic sympathies convinced him that strong joint action by Britain and America was the only way to confront the menace. He propagated his pro-British views in speeches and letters to newspapers and even in his choice of roles. In 1938, at the height of the Munich crisis, *Gunga Din*, which grafted Kipling's famous poem onto his story 'Soldiers Three', was screened in cinemas across Britain and America. A critic, Paul Holt, wrote in the *Daily Express*: 'I don't have a doubt that in these days of power politics and propaganda, this tale of tough and stupid British soldiery, grinning heroes with cropped hair and thick necks, is as valuable to this country as a thousand front-line bombers. Particularly when our friends the Americans have got it into their skulls that this country is soft and

decadent.'[8] In fact, Fairbanks' support brought him a certain amount of resentment in an America where anti-British feeling and the spirit of isolationism were strong.

He was already a reservist in the US Navy at the start of the war. When America entered it, he was sent to join the staff of Mountbatten's Combined Operations Headquarters. By the spring of 1942 he was putting his belief in Anglo-American cooperation into practical effect, as a member of the screening force that would protect PQ.17. and QP.13.

The operation represented far more than a political gesture. It was one of the most valuable convoys ever to go to sea, with an estimated worth of £200 million. On board were nearly 300 aircraft, 600 tanks, 400 lorries and 150,000 tons of general cargo. Together it amounted to enough materiel to equip an army of 50,000 men.[9]

It was a lot to risk given the perils facing the operation. The experience of PQ.16 had shown what German aeroplanes could do. Hitler had kept a promise to Raeder to provide extra aircraft for Norway and by now there were 250 on hand in four bases in northern Norway to locate and bomb Allied shipping. The menace from U-boats and torpedo boats was also obvious. And now there was a fourth element of German military power on hand. At the end of March the heavy cruiser *Hipper*, a veteran of the Norway campaign and several Atlantic sorties, arrived to join *Tirpitz* in Trondheim. The pocket battleships *Scheer* and *Lützow* were already in the area as well as three destroyer flotillas. Together they would form a fleet under the command of Generaladmiral Otto Schniewind, who until then had been chief of the Kriegsmarine's naval operations. So far a surface force of this size had not been used in combination with aircraft and submarines in an attack on a convoy. As preparations for PQ.17 continued, there was disturbing news that the situation could be about to change.

A 'most immediate' signal dated 18 June arrived at the Admiralty from Captain Henry Denham, the British naval attaché, who under the terms of Swedish neutrality was allowed to operate, albeit under serious restrictions, in Stockholm. Despite these difficulties he had befriended a sympathetic officer high up in Swedish intelligence who had called him to his office to provide him with some startling information. Denham rushed back to the British Legation to draft his report which was encoded and radioed to London at 7 p.m. 'Following is German plan of attack on next Arctic convoy,' he announced in his coded telegram. 'It is hoped to obtain early reconnaissance report when eastbound convoy reaches vicinity of Jan Mayen. Bombing attacks from aircraft based in North Norway will then commence.'

He went on to predict the naval movements that would follow.

1. Pocket battleships with six destroyers will proceed move to Altenfjord … [Altafjord]
2. *Tirpitz* with *Hipper*, two destroyers and three torpedo boats will proceed to Narvik area, probably Bogenfjord. Naval forces may be expected to operate from their anchorages once convoy has reached 5 degrees east. The intention for the two groups of surface forces is to make a rendezvous on the Bear Island meridian and to make a simultaneous attack on convoy supported by U-boats and aircraft.[10]

He graded the information 'A.3', indicating that the source was utterly reliable but the information was uncheckable. The chances were it was solid. The German teleprinter lines to north Norway passed through Sweden, and the Swedes had cracked the codes. Denham's stock was high. It was his report the previous year that had alerted the Admiralty to the move north by *Bismarck* and *Prinz Eugen*.

There was no question of cancelling the convoy. To do so would be to confirm that, merely as the core of a 'fleet in being', *Tirpitz* was able to shut down one of the Soviet Union's main supply lines and throw more grit in its already abrasive relationship with its Western allies. With mounting unease preparations went ahead.

Despite the misgivings of Pound and his team there was nothing inevitable about the disaster that was about to occur. In certain circumstances, the sailing of Convoy PQ.17 might have been the occasion for a great victory. The escorting force should have been more than a match for the Germans.

Altogether there were forty-five surface ships in the force, more than one for each of the thirty-three merchantmen. In addition, thirteen submarines, including two supplied by the Soviets, would be mounting patrols. The fleet was split into three. The convoy would have a close escort of nineteen vessels, under Commander Jack Broome in the destroyer *Keppel*. It was made up of six destroyers, four corvettes and two submarines, plus two anti-aircraft ships, two anti-submarine trawlers and three minesweepers. They in turn would be covered by a cruiser squadron comprising the *London*, *Norfolk*, *Wichita* and *Tuscaloosa*, commanded by Rear Admiral Sir Louis Hamilton, scion of an old naval family, who in line with the navy's fondness for nicknames was widely known as 'Turtle'. Three destroyers were in attendance.

Beyond these two groups, roaming at a distance in the waters around Jan Mayen Island, poised to launch into action as the situation dictated, was the British battle fleet under Tovey, who was flying his flag in the battleship *Duke of York*. Alongside him was Rear Admiral Giffen in the *Washington*, plus two British cruisers, the *Nigeria* and the *Cumberland*, and the aircraft carrier *Victorious*, together with fourteen destroyers.

The surface fleet would protect the convoy from heavy attack during the western leg of its journey from Iceland to Bear Island, a barren block of rock and ice about 280 nautical miles (310 statute miles) north of Norway, lying on the western edge of the Barents Sea. Captain Broome's destroyers would huddle around the merchantmen while Admiral Hamilton's cruiser squadron hovered protectively in the distance. Tovey and the Home Fleet would be following at one further remove, ready to intervene if needed. Once the convoy passed Bear Island, PQ.17 would have to rely on the close escort and accompanying submarines to defend it from surface attack.

The orders contained some elasticity. The cruisers could go beyond Bear Island – as far as latitude 25 degrees east – if a German surface force emerged to threaten the convoy. There was, however, a proviso. No confrontation was sanctioned unless the cruisers had a chance of winning the ensuing fight. In other words, they were forbidden to sail into battle if *Tirpitz* was present.

Tovey had no quarrel with this restriction. He had always been opposed to the idea of sending cruisers to escort convoys into the Barents Sea. They were highly vulnerable to attack by land-based bombers and torpedo planes and U-boats and if they were damaged it was a long, slow and dangerous journey to Murmansk where the repair facilities were, anyway, inadequate. This view had only been strengthened by the recent examples of the *Trinidad* and the *Edinburgh*. He had other objections, though, which he aired in telephone conversations from his base in Scapa Flow to Pound at the Admiralty. He argued that the convoy was too big for the size of the escort that had been provided. He proposed that it should be split up and sent in two sailings – a solution that would have doubled both risk and effort. Pound overruled him, as Tovey must have known he would.

His main concern, though, was an alarming detail of the plan which emerged in his phone exchanges.[11] Pound told him that if *Tirpitz* did appear, and if he thought the convoy was facing likely annihilation, he would consider ordering it to scatter. The logic was that the German attackers would find it easier to destroy a concentrated formation of ships than have to go to the inconvenience of hunting down individual vessels. The dispersed merchantmen would therefore have a better chance of survival on their own.

Tovey seems to have been genuinely shocked and surprised by this statement. It ran against the lessons of all recent experience. The examples of convoy traffic in all the oceans where the war at sea had so far been fought had been that as long as ships maintained discipline and close order, the escorts could provide some sort of effective protection for the merchantmen. Once the formation dissolved, each scattered ship was easy meat for whichever U-boat, aeroplane or surface vessel came across it. Tovey did not mince his words when he gave his reaction to his chief. He let it be known later that he told Pound that if the order was ever given, it would result in 'sheer, bloody murder'.[12]

Hindsight has made Tovey's judgement seem darkly prophetic. His own feeling, though, was that *Tirpitz* was unlikely to venture out. His reading of the German admirals' minds was that they would not risk sending their last remaining battleship into the perilous waters of the Barents Sea where she would be beyond the protection of land-based aircraft. The Germans had no aircraft carrier in their fleet. One was supposed to be under construction – the *Graf Zeppelin*. Despite Raeder's urging and Hitler's acquiescence, it was still far from completion. The German admirals considered *Tirpitz* had been lucky to escape the Swordfish attacks at the end of her March excursion. A sortie against another convoy would expose her to the same risk.

Nonetheless, if she did venture out, Tovey would be happy to see her. It would provide an opportunity for another epic battle like the one he had fought against *Bismarck*. He regarded escort duties as a departure from the real business of naval warfare, which was to close with the enemy fleet and destroy it. Tovey nurtured the hope that *Tirpitz* could be enticed into an encounter that he was sure he would win. A victory would bring enormous benefits. The risk to the convoys would now be manageable. And the large number of naval resources, now passively engaged in containing the *Tirpitz*, could be used much more effectively elsewhere.

What was needed was a deception that would persuade the Germans that they had no choice but to send their last battleship to sea. Several weeks before the convoy sailed, Tovey began to work on a subterfuge by which *Tirpitz* might be brought to battle. Sixty-one years after the event, declassified documents in the Public Record Office revealed an extraordinary intervention by the Home Fleet commander to mount a spoof operation to lure the German fleet towards the coast of Iceland where his ships would be waiting to pounce. The papers make it clear that it was Tovey himself who approached MI5 with the ruse, which was codenamed 'Plan Tarantula'. A meeting was held at MI5 headquarters in Broadway, central London, on 29 May 1942, a month before the convoy sailed. The minutes, stamped 'Most Secret' and typed on flimsy paper, state that 'the object of the plan which has been conceived by C-in-C

Home Fleet is primarily to assist the passage of a convoy (PQ-17)*
from Iceland to Russia … it is hoped that if this plan is successful,
the Home Fleet will be able to bring the German fleet to battle.'[13]

Tovey's idea was to 'inform the Germans that a convoy is assembling in Iceland and that another convoy is assembling in Scapa
Flow and that it is believed that these two convoys may in all probability be taking troops to effect a landing on the Norwegian coast'.
The minutes note that 'it is known that the Germans are at the
present moment in an extreme state of agitation for fear lest an
attack should be made by us on the Norwegian coast'. The false story
was to be fed to the Germans by two agents, 'Land Spider' and
'Mutt', who had been recruited by German intelligence to report on
convoy movements from Iceland but had been turned by the British.

At that stage the two convoys were expected to sail on 11 June. As
the date approached, the two double agents were to start sending
coded wireless reports to their controllers leaking details of the
supposed invasion convoy. The plan was based on the premise that
the Germans would find it impossible to ignore the threat and sail
out to intercept the convoys, which the reports would say were to be
protected only by light escorts. Once the Germans were at sea, the
convoy would turn back towards Iceland, luring their pursuers to
where the Home Fleet and its American allies would be waiting to
annihilate them.

Tovey's gambit started to play out. The plan was subsequently
revised and it was not Land Spider or Mutt but another agent who
laid the bait. 'Cobweb' was Ib Arnason Riis, a seaman born in
Denmark to Icelandic parents who had been recruited by the
Abwehr German military intelligence organization while demoral-
ized and unemployed in Copenhagen in 1940. In April 1942 he was
landed by submarine in Iceland with a cover story that he was a
returning refugee from occupied Denmark. He was provided with a
radio, a code book based on the Penguin edition of Maxim Gorky's
Leaves from My Diary and $1,800 largely in $50 notes. His instructions were to find out everything he could about aerodromes,

* Brackets in original document.

industrial and military sites and shipping movements, particularly anything concerning the convoys. Soon after his arrival, however, he 'took the first opportunity of reporting his presence to the British authorities and readily accepted the proposal that he should work as a double agent'. Under the supervision of two MI5 officers he began to make wireless transmissions to his Abwehr controllers.

The Germans declined the bait. A dummy convoy of minesweepers and colliers escorted by two light cruisers and five destroyers did sail from Scapa Flow but it provoked no reaction. The Germans had either failed to locate it, or, if they had, chosen to ignore it. It was always unlikely that Admiral Raeder would abandon the policy of caution, bordering on timidity, that had governed all *Tirpitz*'s movements, and sail into waters where the strategic balance tilted back strongly in the Allies' favour. Even if he had, it was almost certain that Hitler, who admitted that, however bold he might be in his approach to land warfare he was a 'coward at sea', would overrule him.

Despite the wariness of the high command, the appetite for action among crews and commanders was strong. The concentration of *Tirpitz* and *Hipper*, *Scheer* and *Lützow* so close to the convoy routes created an atmosphere of expectation. The men and those who led them chafed at inaction and were anxious to justify their existence. The reinforcements of aircraft and an increase in the submarine strength in the Arctic boosted their advantages. The arguments for a sortie were further strengthened by the allocation of 15,000 tons of scarce fuel oil for fleet operations in June.[14]

The objectives, nonetheless, remained modest. Operations would only be sanctioned if they carried a good chance of cheap and relatively risk-free success. Hitler had told Raeder that when the next convoy sailed, no move was to be made against it until the Luftwaffe had located and attacked any British aircraft carriers in the escorting force. The order virtually ruled out any chance of the *Tirpitz* or any other heavy ship attacking the convoy. By the time the Luftwaffe's task was completed, it might be too late for the big surface ships to close with their targets. Raeder hoped to increase his room for manoeuvre by moving his big ships to anchorages in the far north of Norway as soon as a convoy was sighted, to be in a better position to strike when it passed by. That was not to say that he was anxious for a fight. He, too, believed that a major naval setback at this stage of the war would be disastrous and his views conditioned the attitude of Naval Group North at Kiel.

Excitement grew aboard *Tirpitz* when Generaladmiral Schniewind arrived to take up command of his fleet. On 30 May, Raeder visited Trondheim to discuss future operations. On 14 June, the plan – the one that Denham in Stockholm had passed on to London – was settled. At that time, Schniewind's force was split in two. One group, clustered around the *Lützow* and the *Scheer*, under the command of Vizeadmiral Oskar Kummetz, was in Narvik with a flotilla of destroyers. *Tirpitz* and *Hipper* lay near Trondheim with two flotillas. It was decided that as soon as the convoy was known to be on its way, the Narvik force would move to Altafjord in the far north. The Trondheim group would sail for Vestfjord, which led into Narvik. The two squadrons would set sail from their new locations once the convoy passed the meridian of 5 degrees east, meeting a hundred miles north of Norway's most northerly point, the North Cape. They would attack when the convoy was in the Barents Sea, east of Bear Island, between the 20 degree and 30 degree meridians. The British fleet had never sailed that far east, and the planners assumed, correctly, that they would not do so now. The German ships, submarines and aircraft would then be in a position to destroy the merchantmen in their own time. Admiral Carls would have overall control of the operation from Naval Group North in Kiel. He in turn would be in touch with Vizeadmiral Krancke – Raeder's representative at Hitler's headquarters in Berlin. The operation carried the codename Rösselsprung – the Knight's Move. The Führer was shown the plan and approved it in principle, though the fleet would have to await his order before putting to sea. *Tirpitz* was set for its long overdue triumph.

PQ.17 left on the afternoon of 27 June 1942. The thirty-five merchant ships sailed from the anchorage of Hvalfjord, an inlet to the north of Reykjavik, in line ahead and when they reached the open sea arranged themselves in nine columns. They were sailing to

Archangel, further than Murmansk, which had been put out of action by heavy air raids. There was something very touching about the sight. It was impossible not to feel a stirring of pity at their pathetic vulnerability. Douglas Fairbanks recorded in his diary how he watched them 'waddle out to sea like so many dirty ducks. Everyone who was watching them paid a silent tribute and offered some half-thought prayer.'[15]

For the next four days they steamed to the north-east at a steady nine knots. The sky was overcast and a mist often covered the flat sea. The disadvantage the convoy faced in operating in continuous daylight was counterbalanced a little by the fact that the Arctic ice cap had retreated in the summer sun and it was now possible to sail north of Bear Island. The route was longer but it meant that the ships were further away from the Luftwaffe's Norwegian bases. On 30 June, the long-range close escort under the command of Jack Broome joined them. It was made up of six destroyers, led by his ship *Keppel*, four corvettes and two submarines as well as two anti-aircraft ships, the *Palomares* and the *Pozarica*. There were also three rescue ships to take on survivors from ships that had been sunk.

Pozarica was a 1,900-ton converted cargo ship commanded by Captain E. D. W. Lawford with a crew of about three hundred, many of them young and green. Among them was Godfrey Winn, travelling as a war correspondent for Beaverbrook Newspapers. Winn was thirty-four years old and a star Fleet Street columnist and feature writer whose sensitive persona and confiding style made him a favourite with women readers. He had been an actor and retained a rather camp manner. He was brave and determined and had just volunteered for service in the navy as an ordinary seaman when he was diverted onto PQ.17.

On the afternoon of 1 July, the day after the close escort joined the convoy, he was called onto deck to see an ominous sight. A 'half-glimpsed presence [was] zooming about in the fog, which turned out to be a German recco plane and which sent a shiver down our spines.' It was a Blohm and Voss 138 seaplane, nicknamed the Flying Clog by the Luftwaffe for its clunky profile. The *Pozarica*'s crew christened it, and the others that followed, 'Snoopy Joe'. They understood, as they watched it curve 'round the horizon, now reappearing, now disappearing again in the veils of mist, and always just out of range of our guns, that she was not wasting time, but was busy counting the number of ships and their escorts and wirelessing back to her base in Norway the exact composition of the convoy'.[16]

So it was. The aircraft's report was relayed to U-456, one of a string of submarines keeping a standing patrol in expectation of the next convoy. Aircraft and submarines now started the long hunt that preceded the kill, with all the patience and efficiency of predators of the African plains.

The initial sighting produced a flurry of aerial attacks but they were efficiently beaten off by the escort's anti-aircraft guns. On the afternoon of 2 July, PQ.17 and QP.13 crossed each other north-east of Jan Mayen Island. That evening there was another unsuccessful torpedo plane attack and an enemy plane was shot down. By now the cruiser fleet under 'Turtle' Hamilton was overhauling the convoy, steaming forty miles to the north of its route, hoping to keep out of sight of German reconnaissance aircraft. That evening, the elements sided with the convoy and a fog rolled in that persisted until well into the following morning.

Far to the south, though, the German fleet was on the move. *Tirpitz* and *Hipper* had left Trondheim as planned on the evening of 2 July and by the following day had reached the Lofoten Islands off Narvik. The *Scheer* had also moved from Narvik to Altafjord, leaving behind its partner, the *Lützow*, which, along with three destroyers from the *Tirpitz* group, ran aground near Narvik and played no further part in the proceedings. At 7 a.m. on 3 July, PQ.17 turned due east towards the Barents Sea. An Admiralty update reported that the ice cap had retreated further than earlier thought and Hamilton proposed that the convoy swing to the north to put yet more distance between it and the mainland. Broome, though, was anxious to press on and altered course only slightly. At 10.15 p.m. the convoy was thirty miles north of Bear Island and crossing into the perilous waters of the Barents Sea.

Hamilton's orders had allowed him to accompany the convoy east of Bear Island to a limit of 25 degrees if he saw fit. He decided to do so. The sailors aboard the convoy had reason to feel reasonably optimistic as they steamed through the twilight and the welcome embrace of a fog. The Luftwaffe's attentions, though, were unrelenting. Early on the morning of 4 July, a single torpedo plane managed to find a hole in the low cloud and swooped through to cripple an American merchantman, the *Christopher Newport*, which had to be abandoned. This setback did nothing to dent the conviction of the escorting force that when the serious attacks began, as everyone knew they soon would, they would be able to deal with them. Hamilton had noted the date and sent Captain Hill on *Wichita* congratulations. Hill had replied 'Independence Day always requires large fireworks. I trust you will not disappoint us.'

At noon that day Hamilton was told by the Admiralty that he could keep company with the convoy past the 25 degrees east meridian if he saw fit. Tovey, however, issued a qualification to the message. He told Hamilton that 'once the convoy is east of 25° East or earlier at your discretion you are to leave the Barents Sea unless assured by Admiralty that *Tirpitz* cannot be met'.

The whereabouts of *Tirpitz* was now of paramount importance to the dispositions of the convoy and the ships that were there to protect it. The ships at sea had no direct information of their own apart from the evidence of their own eyes and radar. Their intelligence came primarily from the Admiralty and they were reliant on what they were fed and the interpretation that had been put on it in London.

At 6 p.m. on 4 July, Hamilton reported back that he intended to leave the convoy at 10 p.m. The signal came back from the Admiralty that 'further information may be available shortly. Remain with convoy pending further instructions.' The implication was that there were new developments concerning the German surface fleet which would determine the cruiser squadron's next move.

A little after the exchange, the attacks anticipated earlier in the day arrived and the Independence Day fireworks began. The convoy's radio operators had been picking up signals from U-boat and aircraft homing beacons since mid-afternoon. At 4.45 p.m. Broome ordered his ships to close in on the convoy to provide anti-aircraft support and soon afterwards the first wave of Heinkel He 115 torpedo bombers, equipped with floats, arrived. On board *Pozarica*, Godfrey Winn, pressed back against the narrow passage-way, watched 'the surging throng, rushing upwards to Action Stations, putting on their tin hats as they went, cursing and blasting but no sign of panic'. The ammunition crews supplying the ship's fourteen guns were 'stripped and ready for loading an endless relay of shells onto the pulleys that would take them to the guns'. They were 'naked to the waist, sweating like cattle, blind'. For two hours the Heinkels buzzed around, trying to penetrate the curtain of fire thrown up by the escorts. They dropped torpedoes but most were ranged too far to have any effect. Winn watched one cruise by, 'its wash like that of a porpoise'.

The *Pozarica* claimed no hits but Winn saw an aeroplane in the water about four miles away. 'A few minutes later, a sister plane landed beside it, and picked up the pilot from his rubber dinghy. We all saw the rescue quite clearly through our glasses.' He thought it 'pretty cool – and you couldn't help admiring the manoeuvre, even though regretting it meant another pilot was safe to bomb us again.' The effect of the attack was 'like champagne on the ship's company. They had come through their first challenge without loss of face, and many of those lads had never been to sea, let alone battle.'[17]

The elation was short-lived. At 8.15 p.m., German aircraft were back. The first attack by Junkers 88 bombers was driven off but then the Heinkels returned again. This time they split into two groups which massed to attack the convoy on the starboard bow and quar-ter. The convoy was lucky to have the American destroyer *Wainwright* alongside which had left Hamilton's cruiser squadron to refuel from one of the convoy's oilers.

She steamed at full speed to where the aircraft attacking on the bow were grouping, with all guns firing. One Heinkel was shot down and none of the torpedoes that were dropped found a mark.

The second group, however, managed to break through the wall of anti-aircraft fire, and drop at least twenty torpedoes. Once a torpedo was in the water it was still possible to deflect it with machine-gun fire and several were knocked off course. Three got through, hitting a Russian tanker, the *Azerbaijan*, and two cargo ships, the *Navarino* and the *William Hooper*. The *Azerbaijan*, which had at least one woman among the crew, was, in the words of Broome, 'holed but happy' and able to make nine knots, so she stayed with the convoy. Two of the Heinkels were shot down, one of them hitting the sea close to the freighter *El Capitan*. There was to be no rescue for them. The men on the freighter's deck shouted abuse at the doomed airmen as their burning airframe slid under the waves.

The rescue ships moved in to pick up survivors from the *Navarino* and *William Hooper* and convoy and escorts resumed the plod eastwards. By now the men who sailed in the convoys and those who protected them were hardened to sinkings. These were to be expected and by the arithmetic of such operations the loss of three ships was unremarkable. The convoy was now less than a thousand miles from its destination. Confidence was high. In Broome's estimation the feeling was that, 'provided the ammunition lasted, PQ.17 could get anywhere'.[18]

9

'A heart-shaking decision'

The mood in London was far less confident. At about the time the attacks were going in, Pound was in the middle of a conference in the Admiralty to assess a situation that seemed to him to be increasingly loaded with danger.

His main concern was not the air attacks and the U-boat menace but the possibility that *Tirpitz* and her companions were about to enter the picture. The Admiralty's knowledge of her whereabouts had been patchy from the beginning. Between 1 July and the morning of 4 July, the RAF Catalinas now operating out of north Russia had been providing thorough reconnaissance cover of the fjords and coastline of Norway. But there had been a gap in surveillance between the hours of 11 a.m. and 5 p.m., due to one of the aircraft breaking down. By the time the flights resumed, Pound was in an agony of uncertainty. The last sighting of *Scheer* and *Lützow* had been at Vestfjord when they were photographed leaving from Narvik. There was nothing to show where they had gone. The expectation was that they had moved to Altafjord, near the tip of northern Norway. As for *Tirpitz* and *Hipper*, they had last been heard of on the afternoon of 3 July when all that was known was that they had left Trondheim. In the absence of any hard facts Pound had only suppositions and his own instincts to help him decide what to do next. It was entirely possible that during the surveillance blackout, all four heavy warships were at sea and steaming at full speed towards PQ.17.

By the time the conference started the picture had cleared a little. In his signal to Hamilton, sent just before 7 p.m., Pound had stated that 'further information may be available shortly' and ordered him to stay with the convoy for the time being. This referred to the

137

message Pound had just received from Bletchley Park that the German naval codes for the twenty-four-hour period ending at noon that day had been broken and the details would be at the Admiralty soon. The decrypt included a signal from the Kriegsmarine's Naval Group North headquarters in Kiel revealing that *Tirpitz* and *Hipper* were expected to arrive in Altafjord that morning, that is the forenoon of 4 July, and their destroyers had been ordered to top up with fuel. It was now 8 p.m. Anything could have happened in the meantime.

Once he received the report, Pound made some rapid calculations with dividers and chart. The squadron would probably need a few hours to turn around in Altafjord. If it then set off at an easy cruising speed of twenty-eight knots it would be in position to intercept the convoy at about two o'clock on the morning of 5 July. There was no doubt that if that happened, the German fleet would win the ensuing battle. Its guns were bigger and its ships were faster. Broome's close escort could be dealt with at long range without the destroyers' guns being able to land a single shell on their attackers. The convoy would be destroyed in minutes and if Hamilton's cruisers sailed to the rescue they, too, would be outgunned, outranged and outmanoeuvred. If that was the case, then Pound believed he had no choice but to order the escort to turn away to avoid annihilation and for the convoy to then scatter, leaving every ship to make its own, plodding run for the nearest Russian port.

There was nothing in the decrypt, though, to suggest that a foray by the German ships into the Arctic Ocean was imminent. Pound needed expert advice. He left his office to pay a visit to the intelligence officer with responsibility for the Kriegsmarine's large units, Paymaster Commander Norman Denning. Denning was the son of a Hampshire draper who had been forced on account of his poor eyesight to make his way up the navy ranks in non-operational jobs.* He had promoted the use of systematic intelligence analysis

---

* Norman Denning was one of a trio of remarkable brothers. 'Tom' Denning became Master of the Rolls, Britain's senior law officer, Reginald joined the army and ended up a lieutenant-general and Norman finished his career a vice admiral.

in the shaping of operational decisions, and had championed the cause of the Photographic Reconnaissance Unit. He now presided over the Operational Intelligence Centre, inside the squat, bomb-proof bunker of the Admiralty Citadel that since 1940 has disfig-ured the northern side of Horse Guards Parade.

Denning was a master of his craft and his opinion was worth a great deal. He recalled later how 'the First Sea Lord came down to my room … at about seven o clock in the evening, and he wanted to know what *Tirpitz* was doing. From one source and another I was able to assure [him] that as far as I was concerned *Tirpitz* was still safely in Altenfjord [*sic*]. He seemed to accept that at the time and when he left my room I was fairly convinced that he had taken it in.'[1]

Denning did not spell out the reasons for his judgement and Pound did not ask for them. His opinion was based on several factors. For one thing, the decrypted signals from Naval Group North had not warned U-boats operating in the area of the presence of friendly ships – standard practice in order to prevent them from attacking their own side. Nor had the Royal Navy submarines patrol-ling off the narrow inlets that led from Altafjord to the open sea reported any movement. A Norwegian agent was in place at the entrance to Altafjord. There had been no radio message from him saying that the battleships had put to sea. Lastly, there was none of the high volume of the radio signals buzzing back and forth between Naval Group North and the ships that were to be expected before a large sortie.

This was perhaps the most difficult decision Pound had had to make in his career. He was a quiet man in a service in which senior officers tended to be loud and colourful. His silence made him enig-matic. The night would deepen the mystery about Pound's character and thought processes.

The crucial conference took place at 8 p.m. Pound sat down with about a dozen of his officers and asked each of them in turn their opinion as to what should be done next. No formal record has survived of the meeting but some versions relate that several present took the view that the time had not come to disperse the ships. The

Vice Chief of the Naval Staff, Vice Admiral Sir Henry Moore, was said to have argued that, if the order was to be given, it should be given soon. The further east the convoy steamed the more it would be constrained by the ice cap and the less sea room it would have in which to scatter.[2]

Pound was faced with an appalling choice. The sequence of events as it had developed so far seemed to lead inexorably to a sortie by the German fleet which, without some fateful intervention, would surely result in catastrophe. Everything the Germans had done so far had conformed to the plan outlined in the intercepted orders obtained by Captain Denham the previous month. They had spoken of 'simultaneous attacks by two surface groups supported by U-boats and aircraft when on the meridian of Bear Island'. All the elements were in place. All logic suggested that an attack was imminent. But what if it was not? Pound knew very well that if he ordered the convoy to scatter he was sending at least some of the ships to extinction.

One account of the conference described Pound closing his eyes, and keeping them closed for so long that an officer present worried that his chief, who was known to be a sick and exhausted man, had fallen asleep. But then he opened them again. 'The convoy is to disperse,' he said.

Once the decision was made a volley of brief, ominous signals was fired at the fleet. The first, timed at 9.11 p.m., was marked SECRET. MOST IMMEDIATE. It directed: 'Cruiser Force to withdraw Westward at high speed.' The second, timed twelve minutes later, offered a sort of explanation and was rated SECRET. IMMEDIATE. 'Owing to threat from surface ships convoy is to disperse and proceed to Russian ports.' The third, sent at 9.36 p.m., reverted to the level of MOST IMMEDIATE. 'Convoy is to scatter,' it ordered.

When the orders arrived at the fleet they were met with disbelief. Jack Broome recalled that it came 'out of the blue' and 'shook us all to the core. We'd got no reason to believe there was anything to scatter about.' His reaction was that 'this could only mean one thing. That *Tirpitz* was here, she was on the horizon. Up went all our glasses focussing on various quarters of the horizon. I remember expecting someone to say, "there she is! There's a gun flash" – something like that. But there was nothing. The waters around were empty.'

Grimly and reluctantly Broome called for the flags signalling the order to scatter to be hoisted. Soon after, he noticed that on the *River Afton*, the merchantman in which the convoy's commander, Commodore John Dowding RNR, was sailing, there were no flags flying in response. Broome 'thought, well there's no time to lose. She might be on us and I shot into the convoy in *Keppel*, went alongside the Commodore and switched on my loudhailer.' He saw the commodore standing on the bridge wing and asked him if he had received the order to scatter. Dowding had seen it, but 'he simply couldn't believe it. You see we'd just been through the air attack and we'd done jolly well. Everybody was on their toes and full of beans.' Broome persuaded Dowding that the order was correct and he 'finally hoisted the signal. I said, I'm sorry about this, it looks like being a bloody business and he said something like "good-bye and good hunting".'

The Admiralty's signal had said nothing about what the destroyers should do. It seemed to Broome, though, that if a battle with the German force was imminent, they should be alongside Hamilton's cruiser force to face it. He signalled to the other destroyers to join *Keppel* and they set off on a direct heading westwards. Every man on board the warships felt the weight of what they were doing. 'There was no doubt about it,' said Broome later. 'They were all feeling the same as I was. Going on the opposite course to this scattering convoy, ships we were supposed to be looking after, going the other way, watching them get smaller on the horizon. That was terrible.'[3] The convoy was not completely naked. Broome ordered the two anti-aircraft ships, including *Pozarica*, and the twelve anti-submarine corvettes, minesweepers and armed trawlers, to carry on.

On board the US cruiser *Wichita* there was 'stunned shock', Douglas Fairbanks recalled. 'We felt there must have been some error in transmitting the signal.' When it became clear that there had been no mistake, the Americans blamed their allies. His shipmates 'were particularly bitter, cursing the British for what they believed was running away in the face of a good battle which we had a chance of surviving. We resented leaving the defenceless merchant ships to straggle at nine and ten knots through icy water, which we knew from experience would not permit survival for more than a very limited time.' The latter was a reference to the loss of two of *Wichita*'s observation pilots who had died of exposure before they could be rescued after crashing. The Americans' anger was 'made more intense by the philosophic and good natured spirit in which the merchant ships received the order and saw us turn tail'.[4]

Deep inside the Admiralty Citadel, Norman Denning heard the news of the order to scatter from his superior, Rear Admiral Clayton. He was now sure that *Tirpitz* had not left Altafjord. There was still a telling absence of the radio chatter from Naval Group North which would have been picked up if a big raid had been in progress. His belief was confirmed when a decrypt arrived from Bletchley of a signal from Admiral Schmundt, the officer commanding Northern Waters at Narvik. It was addressed to the *Eisteufel* (Ice Devil) submarine group waiting for the convoy in the Barents Sea and stated: 'No own naval forces in the operational area.' With the arrival of the new information Denning decided to take the initiative. He asked Clayton to take the evidence to Pound and try and get him to reverse the order. Clayton did so. Pound, though, was unmoved. Clayton returned to Denning and told him: 'Father's made his decision and he's not going to change it now.'[5]

It is hard not to sympathize with Pound's predicament and easy to imagine the immense burden of anxiety weighing down on him as he struggled to make up his mind. He was a sick man, in constant pain from an arthritic hip, which stopped him sleeping, and suffering from a brain tumour. The tumour had been diagnosed in 1939 but Pound had tried to suppress the discovery. Everyone in the Admiralty knew, nonetheless, that he was desperately ill. Pat Trehearne, a young female clerk in the cipher office, remembers 'a grey figure, descending the main staircase, having to lean on the railing for support'.[6]

Pound faced a dilemma that would mean lost lives whichever way it was resolved. Churchill described it later as a 'heart-shaking' decision.[7] Yet it was clear, almost from the outset, that he had made a strange choice. Stephen Roskill, the naval officer who was given the first unrestricted access to the signals traffic and related documents covering the disaster, wrote that 'whilst making every allowance for the strain and anxiety felt in London, it is hard to justify such an intervention, made in such a way. If it was felt that dispersing the convoy would turn out to be the less perilous action, such a proposal, and the grounds on which it was made, could justifiably have been sent to the responsible officers for them to carry out or not as they saw fit.' Roskill, who spoke to all the commanders at sea, concluded that if Tovey, Hamilton and Broome had been in possession of the very sparse information on which Pound and his staff had been making their calculations 'it is beyond doubt ... the convoy and the escort would have been kept together'. As it was, the three signals taken together seemed to convey that the 'further information' mentioned earlier had now arrived and that the fleet was in imminent danger of attack from *Tirpitz* which made it imperative for the cruisers to cut and run.[8]

None of those things were true. As the merchantmen chugged stoically on, watching their escorts dwindle to nothing on the western horizon, *Tirpitz* and the fleet were still stuck in Altafjord. On board, crews were straining to get into action. But a flurry of mistaken information had meant that Raeder, in Berlin, still hesitated to go to Hitler for the approval to let them off the leash. On the night of 3 July, while *Tirpitz* and *Hipper* were on their way to Altafjord, a reconnaissance aircraft had sighted Hamilton's cruiser squadron and reported back that it contained a battleship. Hitler had insisted that no operations were to take place if there was a battleship in the British force. The error was corrected by another pilot the following day, only to be repeated again in a report from a shadowing U-boat. To add to the confusion, at 6.30 p.m. on 4 July another reconnaissance flight reported seeing 'torpedo planes' near the cruiser squadron. They were, in fact, spotter planes from the *Wichita* but Raeder could not discount the possibility that they had flown off an aircraft carrier – the presence of which would, again on Hitler's orders, mean an attack was ruled out.

It was not until 6.55 the following morning, when a Luftwaffe flight came across the Home Fleet 200 miles north-west of Bear Island, that he felt confident enough to commit his big ships to action. The pilot reported that the British force was steering south-west, towards home, and that the aircraft carrier *Victorious* was with it. There were now eight hundred miles of sea between Tovey and the point where the German fleet would intercept the convoy. That meant the Home Fleet was still at least thirty hours away. The dangers were minimal. Even so, when Raeder issued his orders, after first passing them to Hitler for his blessing, they were cluttered with warnings and provisos. Schniewind was advised that 'a brief operation with partial success is more important than a total victory involving major expenditure of time. Report at once if over-flown by enemy aircraft. Do not hesitate to break off operation if situation doubtful. On no account grant enemy success against fleet nucleus.'9

By the time the orders arrived Schniewind had given in to his frustration and *Tirpitz* was already under way, leaving Altafjord just before noon on 5 July. By 3 p.m. she was cruising at twenty-five knots heading east-north-east into the Barents Sea. It was not long before she was sighted. A Soviet submarine, *K-21*, spotted her off the North Cape. The captain fired his torpedoes and signalled excitedly that two had hit but it was wishful thinking. The *Tirpitz* swept on unharmed. An hour afterwards, an RAF spotter plane operating from Murmansk picked up the German battle fleet parting the waves below. Two hours later again, the British submarine *Unshaken* saw her at a distance, too far away to engage.

The main concern of Schniewind and his men was that there would be no ships left to sink by the time they arrived. The excitement of anticipated action, though, did not last long. The signals from the British spotter plane and submarine had been intercepted and reported to Kiel and Berlin. It was now the Germans' turn to overestimate the aggressive intentions of their enemy. Now that the British knew *Tirpitz* was at sea, they might decide to turn round and go after her. The risk was slight but it was not one Raeder was prepared to take. At 9 p.m. he radioed Schniewind and told him that he was breaking off the operation. The red pennant signalling a 180 degree turn was hoisted. In the early hours of 6 July the dejected crews arrived back into Altafjord.

For everyone from Schniewind down, the exercise had been another anti-climax. The Knight's Move had turned out to be a feint. It was, though, a spectacularly successful one. Without firing her guns, the German fleet had scored a remarkable physical and moral victory. All across the Barents Sea merchantmen were being hunted down while British and American warships fled in the opposite direction from the shadow of the *Tirpitz*.

The scattered merchantmen were now virtually defenceless. A welcome fog had descended just after the order to scatter had been given but by 2 a.m. on 5 July it had lifted. 'Snoopy Joe' appeared over *Pozarica*. Godfrey Winn asked one of his shipmates what he thought their chances were now. He replied, 'about fifty-fifty if we are rather lucky'.[10]

At breakfast time the sinkings began. The 6,645-ton *Empire Byron* was the first to go. Her master was the convoy's rear commodore, Captain John Wharton. She was carrying a cargo of the new Churchill tanks and a REME officer, Captain John Rimington, was aboard to give technical advice to the Soviets. Wharton had collapsed in an exhausted sleep in an armchair in his day room on the bridge after thirty-six hours at action stations when Kapitänleutnant Bielfeld in U-703 launched his first two torpedoes at extreme range. They passed harmlessly ahead, unnoticed by the crew. Two more also missed. The fifth, though, struck the engine room. Wharton slept through the explosion and had to be shaken awake by his gunnery officer. Outside the crew were frantically lowering the lifeboats. There was no escape for the sailors trapped below by the explosion and their screams mingled with the shouts of those on deck as they struggled to get the boats into the water.

Wharton stayed on the bridge long enough to destroy all documents then dived into the icy water. He was picked up by a raft and then put aboard one of the lifeboats. He ordered everyone to concentrate in two of the boats, one of which had an engine. Bodies were clustered face down in the sea around. As they moved away from the *Empire Byron*, the boiler exploded, ripping open the hull and the trapped men were dragged into the depths. Eighteen gunners and sailors were dead, but forty-two were now huddled in the lifeboats watching the black, glistening hull of the U-boat that had sunk them emerge from the sea and head towards them. A tall blond man, an officer they assumed, had descended from the conning tower to the submarine's deck accompanied by a rating with a machine gun. When the U-boat drew up he demanded to know which of them was the captain. Wharton had told his men not to reveal his identity. After failing to correctly identify him the blond officer ordered Rimington, who stood out in a new white duffel coat, to climb aboard. Then they were given tins of biscuits, apple juice and a piece of sausage and informed that the nearest landfall was 250 miles to the south. They handed back the engineer who had been taken below after his rescue. He told his crewmates that the U-boat commander had said he was sorry to sink the ship but it had been his duty.[11]

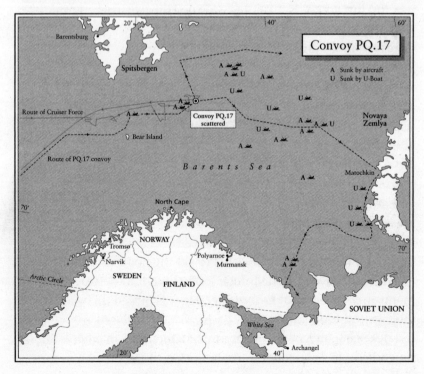

There were several instances of the German air force and navy showing humanity towards their victims. The forty-one survivors of the American merchantman *Carlton* assumed the worst when a Heinkel torpedo plane returning from a sortie swooped down and began to circle them. But then it put down nearby and taxied over to the lifeboats. The pilot signalled to them that he could take three passengers. Two of the seamen managed to make it aboard. The third was too heavy to haul himself onto the float. Two hours later a Dornier 24 hospital plane landed and took off ten more. Later, two more rescue aircraft took off another twelve. The last pilot warned those left that there would be no more flights. The remaining seventeen rigged a sail and steered towards Russia.

For those who survived the sinkings, another ordeal was beginning. William Kenyon, a merchant seaman, managed to get aboard a lifeboat but the drinking water soon ran out. 'We were reduced to drinking our own urine,' he remembered. One man went mad with thirst. They soon noticed a strange phenomenon. 'When you haven't had anything to drink for a few days, you find that your tongue swells up and protrudes from your mouth and this ... is how we all looked. There were thirty-seven men in this boat, sitting with their tongues sticking out of their mouths.'[12]

Of the thirty-two ships which sailed on alone into the Barents Sea, thirteen were sunk by aircraft and ten by U-boats. Altogether, only thirteen ships survived. The material losses were enormous. Out of the 594 tanks aboard, 430 were lost. Of the 297 aircraft, all but 87 went to the bottom. So, too, did 3,350 of the 4,246 vehicles and 99,316 tons of the 156,492 tons of food, steel plate, ammunition and other much-needed cargo. One hundred and fifty-three seamen lost their lives. They died quickly in the initial explosions or the first contact with the icy sea, and slowly, succumbing to exposure, wounds and burns as they drifted in the perpetual, pearly light.

The German navy and air force had won a significant victory and at a tiny cost. None of their ships were lost and only 5 of the 202 aircraft that took part in the attacks were shot down. The disaster did not bring the convoys to an immediate halt. One more, PQ.18, sailed early in September. After ten of its ships were sunk, further

A steamship from PQ.17 falls victim to the U-boats

sailings to Russia were suspended until winter darkness increased the odds of survival.

The disaster and the cutting of the supply route inevitably caused bitterness between the Soviets and their allies. 'Has the British Navy no sense of glory,' taunted Stalin in a message to Churchill on 16 August while the pain of the catastrophe was still raw.[13] That was to be expected. But the episode also created suspicion and hostility between the Americans and their new comrades. This was the first time in the war that the British and American navies had worked together on a big operation and it had ended in disaster. Douglas Fairbanks recorded how back 'in the officers mess at Scapa, after rather too many beakers, there was much mutual recrimination and many hard words were passed. These were finally resolved in cursing the Admiralty and their inability to judge a tactical situation from a lot of pins on a board more than a thousand miles away. It was a pusillanimous defeat and a shocking error of judgement.' The same verdict was delivered by virtually everyone who had not been directly involved in the decision. 'The order to scatter the convoy had been premature,' wrote Tovey in his dispatch covering the episode. 'Its results were disastrous.'

The decision had finally been taken by one man. Pound had chosen to make it alone, declining to press for all relevant details from Denning and neglecting to share what information he did have with his admirals at sea who would surely have gone against the decision to scatter if they had been aware of the full intelligence picture. As Hamilton remarked, plaintively and with restraint in a letter to Tovey, 'it would have been of great assistance to me had I known that the Admiralty possessed no further information on the movements of the enemy's heavy units other than I had already received'. Like everyone involved in the responsibility he was haunted by the thought that he should have acted differently. 'I suppose I ought to have been a Nelson,' he remarked to his flag captain. 'I ought to have disregarded the Admiralty's signals.'[14]

It was Pound who had the most to regret. Yet initially, at least, little blame landed on him. The First Sea Lord made no move to accept culpability and Churchill seemed reluctant to chastise his old friend. In his account of the episode given after the war, he offered an explanation for Pound's actions, saying he would 'probably not have sent such vehement orders if only our own British warships had been concerned'. There were American ships to think of, too, and 'the idea that our first large joint Anglo-American operation under British command should involve the destruction of the two United States cruisers as well as our own may well have disturbed [his] poise'.[15] Pound himself gave a version of events that offered a crucial but unsubstantiated explanation. On 1 August he told the Cabinet that on the night of 3/4 July, the day before the order to disperse was given, 'the Admiralty had had information ... that the TIRPITZ, having eluded our waiting submarines, would, if she continued on her course, be in a position to attack the convoy early the following morning'.[16] As Stephen Roskill noted after his unrestricted trawl through the papers, 'the existence of such precise intelligence has not been confirmed by post war research'.[17] Pound also offered the War Cabinet a tacit excuse for the urgent wording of the 'scatter' order. It was phrased like that because the convoy was travelling so slowly and would need as much warning as possible. It was not intended to suggest that 'it was about to be attacked at any moment'.

Pound died fifteen months after the debacle. His achievements would always be overshadowed by the disaster of PQ.17. Each year for many years to come the date of 4 July would revive bitter memories among the merchant seamen seething at what they regarded as a great betrayal. There were many within the Royal Navy who accepted the charge. Vice Admiral Bill O'Brien, who served as a young officer on HMS *Offa*, one of the close escort destroyers, remarked years later: 'I have never been able to rejoice with my American Friends on Independence Day, because July 4 is to me a day to hang my head in grief for all the men who lost their lives on Convoy PQ.17, and in shame at one of the bleakest episodes in Royal Navy history, when the warships deserted the merchant ships and left them to their fate for in simple terms, that is what we were obliged to do.'[18]

10

A Ha'porth of Tar

One morning in April 1942, a lorry arrived at a deserted corner of Portsmouth naval base. Canvas screens were moved aside and the truck drove in and pulled up next to Horsea Lake, a seawater basin used for diving exercises. The screens were dragged back again to hide what followed from the sight of passers-by. A strange-looking torpedo-shaped craft was manhandled off the back and winched off the deck. Two men, encased in canvas and rubber suits, lowered themselves into the water, pulled themselves on board and sat astride it, one behind the other. A small launch carrying two men in naval uniform towed it out into the middle. For the next half an hour they watched closely and made notes as the men in the water struggled to get the craft to do what it was supposed to.

The vessel was a prototype of a new secret weapon. The navy called it a 'chariot'. It was officially known as a Mark I Human Torpedo, a name that fairly described its look and function. The tests now under way were the result of another of Churchill's interventions. A few months earlier, on 18 January 1942, he sent a memo to the Chiefs of Staff Committee asking them to 'please report what is being done to emulate the exploits of the Italians in Alexandria Harbour and similar methods of this kind'. It ended on an irritable note: 'Is there any reason why we should be incapable of the same kind of scientific aggressive action that the Italians have shown? One would have thought we should have been in the lead.'[1]

Churchill and the Admiralty had been unpleasantly surprised by a display of ingenuity by the Italian navy a month before. On 19 December 1941, three 'human torpedoes' were launched from an Italian submarine at the entrance to Alexandria harbour where the British Mediterranean Fleet was at anchor. They crept in while the boom was open to allow some ships to enter and clamped delayed action mines on the undersides of the battleships *Queen Elizabeth* and *Valiant*. Both were seriously damaged and knocked out of action for many months. If the enemy could do this to our battleships, Churchill wanted to know, why should we not do it to theirs?

The idea of a human torpedo had been around since the beginning of the century. In 1909 a retired British naval officer, Commander Godfrey Herbert, had designed a one-man craft which he called the 'Devastator'. Its prospectus advertised it as a 'means for propelling against an enemy ship or other target a large quantity of high explosive, and of effecting this with great economy of material and personnel'. He had presented his idea to the Admiralty before and during the First World War only for it to be turned down by, among others, Winston Churchill, then First Lord of the Admiralty and the navy's political master.[2]

In the interwar years the idea had gained credibility and champions. They included Sir Max Horton, who had commanded one of the first ocean-going British submarines, HMS *E9* at the start of the First World War. He had provided an early demonstration of the effects small submersible vessels could have on big surface ships. On 11 September 1914, *E9* met SMS *Hela*, a German light cruiser, off Heligoland and fired two torpedoes, sending her to the bottom. After a day evading vengeful Germans, he returned safely to Harwich and sailed into harbour with the Jolly Roger flying from the conning tower – a grim tradition maintained by submariners right up to the sinking of the Argentinian cruiser *Belgrano* by HMS *Conqueror* in 1982.

By the end of 1940 Horton was head of the Royal Navy's submarine service. He had already commissioned experiments to develop the original ideas and among those involved was the father of the concept, Godfrey Herbert. As well as human torpedoes, Horton was also keen to produce a 'midget submarine' that could attack ships while they were in harbour. The arrival of effective defences like booms and heavy steel mesh anti-submarine and anti-torpedo nets meant that conventional submarines were incapable of carrying out close attacks. Midget submarines – X-Craft as they came to be called – were intended to have a much longer range than the chariot and would take more time to develop. By the beginning of February 1942, though, Horton was working on operational plans involving both craft.

The new vessels would need specialized crews. To find men with the right temperament Horton issued an appeal for 'volunteers for hazardous service'. The terminology was deliberately vague to disguise the nature of the duties. Those who answered were driven by boredom, ambition or a thirst for adventure and by April more than thirty had been selected. Among them were Lieutenant Chuck Bonnell, a Canadian, and Petty Officer Jim Warren, a former submariner, the pair given the job of testing the prototype chariot in Horsea Lake.

The men watching them were also submariners, appointed by Horton to supervise the training of volunteers. Commander Geoffrey 'Slasher' Sladen had already had an outstanding war. A few months earlier he had been in command of the submarine *Trident* when it badly damaged *Prinz Eugen* with a torpedo on passage to join *Tirpitz* at Trondheim. He was six feet tall, a talented sportsman with four England rugby caps who also kept goal for his submarine's football team. He was boisterous, noisy and impatient with anyone who showed what he regarded as a lack of zeal or efficiency.

Commander William 'Tiny' Fell was a New Zealander. He was short, quiet and courteous. His outlook, though, was just as aggressive as 'Slasher' Sladen's. He had already won a Distinguished Service Cross for leading fireship raids against German shipping gathering in French ports in the summer of 1940 for an invasion that never came.

The prototype whose trials he and Sladen was overseeing was codenamed 'Cassidy' and built of wood. It was supposed to replicate some of the functions of the final version. The design was based on the pre-war experiments and some features copied from an Italian human torpedo salvaged by navy divers after a failed attack in Gibraltar. When completed it would be just over twenty-two feet long and weigh, with its warhead, 3,500lb. It was driven by a propeller, powered by a large electric battery, which could push it along at three knots for a maximum distance of eighteen miles. The man in front sat behind a cowling which shielded an illuminated instrument console with compass. He steered to port and starboard and moved the chariot up and down by pushing and pulling at a joystick which operated the rudder and hydroplane fins mounted at the rear. The man behind was charged with navigation and cutting through nets. He also had the task of fixing the chariot's detachable warhead, clamped on the nose, to the hull of the target ship. Pumps and a compressed air system filled and emptied the ballast tank that sank the chariot below the waves or raised it to the surface. There were also two smaller tanks in which the water level could be adjusted to trim the craft to achieve the best balance and the smoothest forward progress.

Warren and Bonnell's instructions were to open the vent in the main ballast tank which stuck up like a hump between the forward and after seats, set the hydroplanes to dive and slide thirty feet to the bottom of the harbour. They were equipped with breathing apparatus and two bottles of oxygen. Their nostrils were clamped shut with nose clips and they inhaled through a mouthpiece gripped in their mouths. They were to communicate with the surface by tugging on a lifeline, using simple signals. 'Cassidy', though, showed no signs of wanting to submerge. It was only after many pounds of lead had been loaded onto the hull that it eventually slipped under the surface and settled on the rock, mud and seaweed of the bottom. Fell and Sladen soon realized what was causing the problem. They had already conducted an initial test suspended by a gantry in a large tank. The tank was full of freshwater and far less buoyant than the brine of Horsea Lake.

So the development of the new weapon went on, a continuous, frequently hazardous, process of trial and error. A crucial problem which had to be solved if the charioteers were to go to war was finding a breathing apparatus that met their particular needs. To reach their target undetected and dive to place their charge they might have to travel at depths of thirty feet and more and stay underwater for up to six hours. Oxygen was the obvious breathing medium as it produced no telltale bubbles. However, thirty feet was considered to be the maximum depth at which it could be used. Beyond that the diver was liable to suffer convulsions and blackouts, ending in death.

The Admiralty's Experimental Diving Unit began work with a specialist firm of diving equipment manufacturers, Siebe, Gorman, to see if the boundaries could be stretched. The unit moved its headquarters to the company's works in Tolworth, Surrey. There, the company's scientists worked with the hazardous service volunteers to explore the limits of physical endurance. According to the firm's chairman, Sir Robert Davis, what followed 'was probably the most exhaustive programme of human experiments ever attempted on one aspect of diving'. In all it involved more than a thousand dives to depths considered 'toxic'. Many of the divers suffered convulsions or passed out, yet carried on, showing 'great courage in submitting themselves cheerfully to these experiments, in spite of the risk and unpleasantness of the job'. They invented a mythical monster to represent the ever-present threat of toxicity, 'Oxygen Pete', who lurked at the bottom of the high-pressure water chamber, waiting to snare them.[3]

One difficulty was overcome with the unwitting assistance of the German air force. The breathing apparatus's steel oxygen cylinders were found to interfere with the chariot's compass. Alloy cylinders would get round the problem but none were then being manufactured in Britain. Then someone remembered that German bombers carried their oxygen supply in aluminium alloy bottles of almost exactly the right shape and size. 'Fortunately the Royal Air Force maintained its toll of the Luftwaffe at a sufficiently high rate to meet the needs of the Human Torpedo scheme ... until production of similar cylinders could be started in England,' noted Sir Robert.

The charioteers were clad in rubberized cotton 'diving dress' but extra clothing was also needed to withstand the extreme cold of a northern Norwegian winter without adding too much bulk. In the end they settled for silk underwear with padded kapok vests and trousers for another light layer of insulation. The quest for satisfactory gloves ended in failure, despite the efforts of guinea pigs who sat with their hands immersed in crushed iced to reproduce the right level of numbness. Most of the charioteers simply coated their fingers with a thick layer of 'Peddo' grease.

Diving was a miserable business. Somehow water always managed to seep through the seals of the .one-piece dry suits and they had earned the nickname 'clammy death'. They were also bulky and cumbersome. Getting into one was painful and needed the assistance of a 'dresser'. It involved squeezing your head into a thick, tightly fitting rubber hood and forcing your hands through watertight cuffs that cut off circulation.

The volunteers were officially part of the Experimental Submarine Flotilla based at Fort Blockhouse, the Royal Navy's Portsmouth submarine base at Gosport, opposite Portsmouth. By the start of the summer, the pool of recruits had grown to twenty-four RNVR officers, mostly young sub-lieutenants and lieutenants, and thirty-one ratings, some of whom had exchanged safer berths as cooks and signalmen to answer Horton's call. Two army officers had also found their way to Portsmouth.

In June most of them transferred to the opposite end of the country. Trainees and instructors moved by train and ship to set up an operational training base at Loch Erisort, on the Outer Hebridean island of Lewis. The remoteness of the spot was suited to the tight secrecy that had been imposed on the project. It also meant there were few distractions from the continuous drills. Stornoway, the island's capital, was picturesque but sedate. It was a stronghold of the puritanical Free Church of Scotland and had more kirks than pubs.

The volunteers still had to practise on 'Cassidy', the faithful wooden prototype. Shortly after the group moved north, though, another experiment was carried out in Portsmouth with a new, metal-hulled model which became known as 'The Real One'. The final trial, with Sladen in the forward seat, took place in front of a VIP audience which included Sir Max Horton and Admiral Ernest King, the prickly Commander-in-Chief of the US Fleet. The 'Real

One' behaved immaculately, diving, manoeuvring and surfacing to order. King was sceptical. For Sladen and his chief, though, the display seemed to prove that the experiment had produced a weapon of real value. It was soon on its way to Lewis for an intense period of further training in preparation for serious operations.

Throughout the summer the teams underwent a punishing regime designed to give them an instinctive ability to handle the craft under any conditions and difficulties. It was a wretched process, chilly and uncomfortable and fraught with continuous dangers. The occasional pleasure of drifting serenely beneath the choppy surface of the loch was outweighed by the misery of enduring, for several hours at a time, tight-fitting nose clamps while biting hard on a large steel and rubber oxygen mouthpiece which left the gums bruised and bloody.

The physical strains were matched by psychological pressures. It took a particular form of mental toughness to withstand the rigours of training. The divers operated in an atmosphere in which the potential for catastrophe was always present. Their survival depended on new and complicated equipment which could go wrong at any time. When accidents happened, there was often no explanation. The first fatal casualty had occurred before they left Portsmouth. Lieutenant P. C. A. Browning had been doing a routine dive in perfect conditions when one of the attendants who kept a constant watch found there was no answering tug when he pulled on the lifeline. That was not a cause for immediate concern as it was relatively easy for a diver in difficulties simply to jettison his lead-weighted boots and kick himself to the surface. After a few minutes with no sign of Browning, sound signals were broadcast underwater, ordering him to abandon the dive. There was no response. When the body was recovered by divers there was no clue as to how he had met his end.

The volunteers soon discovered that Loch Erisort brought its own peculiar dangers. A chariot could be cruising along at three knots, well trimmed, and at a comfortable depth suspended between surface and bottom, then suddenly plunge sharply away. The result was a drastic and alarming surge in pressure. The divers felt their eardrums bulge, their joints throb with pain and their lungs flatten against their ribs.

The explanation was simple. Close to the rocky banks, the salt-water of the loch was thinned out by streams which fed in fresh-water, causing a dramatic change in buoyancy. Divers were briefed to expect it. It still required steely composure to follow the correct drill. The first step was to hang on as the chariot began a vertiginous drop of up to a hundred feet towards the loch floor. They were then to wrench open the bypass valve of their oxygen tubes and gasp in the extra gas needed to breathe at extreme depth, allowing some to escape so that it formed a cushion between their faces and the glass visor of the helmet, now crushed by four atmospheres of pressure against their lips and noses. At the same time they were to swallow and breathe hard through their nostrils, squeezed shut by a clip, to combat the agonizing pressure on their eardrums. Once these steps were taken they were to carry on until they were out of the freshwa-ter patch and back in the seawater which would waft them upwards.

At depths of more than forty feet there was a tendency to black out. At least three-quarters of those under training did so at one time or another. The convention was to treat it as an occupational hazard, even a joke. For all the discomforts and dangers, for all the trepidation that was inevitably felt as they tried to imagine what it was that they would be expected to do when they finally went on operations, the number of dropouts was tiny.

Once they had mastered the chariot, volunteers moved on to dealing with the obstacles they would have to overcome to reach their targets. Once again they had to find their own solutions. All surface warships were now draped around with defensive nets if they were lying at anchor for any time. There were two types. One was a criss-cross curtain of steel wire, heavy enough to deter a marauding submarine and deep enough almost to touch the bottom. The second was made out of steel rings and was designed to stop torpedoes. Nets were strung on jack stays and hung on buoys in the loch for the teams to practise on.

It was the number two's job to wield the heavy metal cutters stowed in the bo'sun's locker behind him while his number one kept the chariot steady. The anti-submarine nets were relatively easy to cut through. The anti-torpedo defences were like outsize chain mail and defeated the cutters. The only way past was to dive under them.

Another difficulty was how to attach the chariot's warhead to the target's hull. Again, the crews and their tutors were operating in unknown territory. Dummy attacks were tried on HMS *Titania*, the flotilla depot ship, anchored at Loch Erisort. Eventually, a method evolved. The chariot approached the ship well below the waterline and, when it met the hull, slid underneath. The next step was to detach the clamps holding the warhead to the nose of the chariot. It was packed with 600lbs of explosive and fitted with a time-delay fuse. The number two charioteer then heaved it into position, fixed it to the hull with magnets and set the timer. When the job was done the next thing to do was get away as fast and far as possible before the charge went up. The chariots did not have the legs to get back to the mother ships that had delivered them to the target area. The only option left was to head for land and make for neutral territory. In order to prepare his men for life on the run, Sladen devised an exhausting series of exercises in the scree, peat and heather around Loch Erisort.

Despite the secrecy surrounding the project it seemed obvious to the volunteers that they were being trained to attack the big German ships now lying in the Norwegian fjords and above all *Tirpitz*. Sladen wanted to see his men in action as soon as possible. He was concerned that after three months of intensive training they were beginning to lose their 'snap'. Almost as soon as the crews arrived in Scotland, moves were under way to put them to use. The failure of the April air attacks followed by the catastrophe of PQ.17 had increased determination to deal with *Tirpitz*. At the Admiralty, the belief grew that the chariots should be given a chance to show what they could do. If they did not succeed, then the midget submarines still in development could be tried at a later date.

A plan was already in the making. In the middle of June, the operational commander of the submarine service, Rear Admiral Sir Claud Barry, had instructed one of his officers, Captain Lord

Ashbourne, to work with the Special Operations Executive (SOE) on plans to attack the *Tirpitz* in Faettenfjord. SOE was set up by Churchill in the grim days of July 1940 to establish espionage networks and promote sabotage behind enemy lines. The organization was closely involved with the activities of the Shetland Bus operation and had a Norwegian Section headed by Lieutenant Colonel John Wilson, who had been a luminary of the Boy Scout movement before arriving in the cloak-and-dagger world of SOE. Ashbourne and Wilson began to work on a proposal. It was clear from the beginning that for the plan to succeed it would require the help of the Norwegian resistance – at home and abroad.

The first problem to overcome was how to get the chariots – whose range was severely limited – close enough to carry out the attack. One proposal was to drop the men and craft at night by parachute from a Halifax bomber. Another was to land them by Sunderland flying boat and five were converted for the purpose. The first idea was abandoned when someone pointed out that it was unlikely that the crews would be able be able to find their craft in water in darkness. The second was jettisoned when it was realized there was little chance of making a landing undetected.[4] Attention turned to getting the chariots in place by boat. With intelligence provided by the Norwegian underground, a plan emerged to sail teams and machines to the coastal island of Frøya, west of Trondheimsfjord. There they would transfer to a boat supplied by a local resistance sympathizer, which would then bluff its way past the German controls at the mouth of Trondheimsfjord and sail in, with the chariots in tow underwater. The chariots and crews would take to the water to be dropped at the island of Tautra, just to the north of Faettenfjord, where they were just close enough to the anchorage to carry out the attack on their own.

Once Ashbourne and Wilson's plan had been approved by Sir Dudley Pound it was transmitted in code to E. S. Nielsen, a Norwegian consular official in Stockholm. He had escaped from Norway earlier in the war and was now charged with looking after refugees. He also acted as a link between local resistance groups and the outside world. Nielsen arranged for an agent, Arne Christiansen, to travel to Trondheim to seek the help of the Rørholt network. The network included Birger Grønn, manager of the dockyard, and Herbert Helgesen, the boss of a sausage factory, who posed as a friend of the Germans. They would be in a position to find out the precise details of restrictions and regulations and the documentation required to get round them. Christiansen would then try and find a fisherman in Frøya who was willing to take the huge risks involved in smuggling the chariot team under the noses of the Germans to Faettenfjord.

The attack was initially set for the start of October and given the codename Title. However the sortie against Convoy PQ.17 and *Tirpitz*'s subsequent return to Narvik made that date uncertain. The high tempo of training was unaffected. The crews were given a fortnight's leave in mid-August. They returned to a different headquarters, at Loch Cairnbawn, south of Cape Wrath in the far north of Scotland. It was deep enough to accommodate one of the Royal Navy's biggest and most modern ships, HMS *Howe*, a 'KGV'-class battleship. *Howe* was on loan for a few days so that the chariots could mount a practice attack on her. She had a draught of 10.5 metres (34 feet), deeper than the 9.9 metres drawn by *Tirpitz*. This was significant. If the chariots were to approach in the agreed fashion, they would have to descend to below thirty feet, the danger level for oxygen toxicity.

For the exercise the *Howe* was moored tight to the shore, protected on the seaward side by two layers of nets. Hydrophones were extended into the water to detect any disturbance below the surface and a patrol boat plied the water around the ship. Seven chariots would take part in the dummy attack. Their orders were simply to 'get your charge under the *Howe* and get away undetected'. The crews left the depot ship *Titania* at quarter-of-an-hour intervals under cover of darkness and dived half a mile from the target. The first chariot was manned by Sub-Lieutenant George Goss and Leading Seaman Trevethian. They noticed that one net did not stretch all the way to the shore so came in behind it, dived under the second barrier and placed their charge under the stern of the *Howe*.

The second team negotiated the nets without trouble and clamped their warhead in place with magnets amidships. The third pair also got in and out successfully. The fourth team hit immediate difficulties when a wire on the nets punctured breathing equipment. They managed to withdraw without being seen. The fifth team had problems with its securing magnets and could not attach the warhead but managed to escape unseen. The next pair got into an unexpected patch of freshwater and plunged seventy feet to the bottom, damaging their eardrums. They decided not to risk compromising the presence of the other craft and returned to the *Titania*. The last was piloted by Lieutenant Jock Kerr, who had volunteered for hazardous duties from the Highland Light Infantry five months before. He took his craft so far down that it bumped the bottom. A blast of compressed air sent it floating upwards to stop against the vast hull of the *Howe*. The charges were placed and Kerr made his escape, only to be spotted by the patrol launch on the surface. To everyone watching and taking part, the exercise had proved the feasibility of an attack by human torpedoes on large enemy vessels. Another exercise was held the following night with four teams. All four got through but two were spotted as they got away. The exercise only reinforced the positive mood.

A death on the third and final night dampened spirits. Sub-Lieutenant Jack Grogan, a South African reservist, and Able Seaman 'Geordie' Worthy dived steeply to get beneath the *Howe*'s hull. There, Grogan blacked out. Worthy moved forward and, while he held Grogan upright, managed to manoeuvre the chariot out from under the battleship and up to the surface. It was too late to save Grogan. The loss did not alter the judgement that the chariots were now ready for action.

Since returning from its foray against PQ.17, *Tirpitz* had spent the rest of July and the whole of August and September in Bogen Bay, the deep, sheltered anchorage on the north shore of the approach to Narvik. There had been a surge of excitement when it was thought that she might put to sea against convoy PQ.18, which sailed from Iceland early in September. It soon subsided. The experiences of July suggested strongly that aircraft and U-boats could wreak sufficient havoc without it being necessary to risk the Kriegsmarine's greatest asset. So it proved to be and bombers and submarines accounted for ten of the convoy's forty-five ships.

Tirpitz had been operational for more than a year. Despite having taken part in only two operations she was already due for a refit. Raeder wanted to bring her back to a modern dockyard in a German port with full facilities but Hitler objected, fearing an attack on the homeward voyage. The work would have to be done in Norwegian waters. Bogen Bay was unsuitable. The decision was made to move back to Faettenfjord. First, though, her old berth would have to be improved for the refit to be carried out.

Preparations for Operation Title had continued during *Tirpitz*'s absence. The fact that shore-based anti-aircraft batteries were still in place around Faettenfjord persuaded the Admiralty and SOE planners that the battleship would at some point return there. However, some alterations were needed to the plan. Arne Christiansen, the agent sent from Stockholm to alert the local underground, had failed to find anyone on the island of Frøya willing to allow his boat to be used to carry the chariots and their crews to the target area. A man who he had been told might cooperate had refused, on the understandable grounds that he feared for his family's safety if things went wrong.[5]

Colonel Wilson now favoured using one of the Shetland Bus fleet for the whole operation. Earlier that year, Sub-Lieutenant David Howarth, a young naval officer working with the Norwegians, had come up with a scheme for using one of the cutters based at Lunna Voe for a torpedo attack on *Tirpitz*. He tried the idea on Leif Larsen, who had landed Bjorn Rørholt near Trondheim earlier in the year. Larsen agreed it was feasible and volunteered his services. Howarth passed the idea on to the Admiralty where, as he later wrote, it 'disappeared into the administrative maze and was never heard of again'.[6]

Larsen was already something of a legend. His extraordinary skill and courage made him stand out, even from the company of the Norwegian exiles, themselves a brave and determined bunch. He was the ideal man for the job. Major L. H. Mitchell, who ran the

Shetland Bus operation, sounded him out and he signed up immediately for what would be his most alarming mission to date.

It was left to him to choose a crew. The three men who came to
mind were his friend Palmer Bjørnøy, to serve as the ship's engineer,
Johannes Kalve, whose worth he knew from several shared Shetland
Bus operations as deckhand, and Roald Strand, a trained radio
telegraphist. When he approached them he could not divulge the
details of the operation, but he warned them that the chances of
returning alive were limited. They all accepted the mission. After
some deliberation it was decided to use his own boat, the *Arthur*.
Work began on adapting her for the job. Two chariots would be
used in the attack. They would make the first part of the journey on
deck and new hoisting gear was engineered to lift them on and off.
For the last part of the journey, a hundred-mile voyage through the
islands and inner leads, into Trondheimsfjord, they would be towed
underneath the boat with steel hawsers. Two massive eye bolts were
machined with threaded ends that meant they could be screwed

Leif Larsen

together through a hole bored through the solid oak of the *Arthur*'s keel. Steel cables were then shackled to each of the eye bolts. These would be connected to eye bolts in the nose of the warheads. It was essential that the work was sound and Larsen himself fixed the keel housing.

Below deck, a secret compartment was built to hide the four chariot crewmen and two dressers who would help them into their diving gear, in the quite likely event of the *Arthur* being stopped and searched by the guard vessels that plied the approaches. Larsen's cover story would be that he was on his way to Trondheim to deliver a cargo of peat, a commodity regularly traded between the coastal islands and the mainland. The hold would be stacked with sacks of the stuff, and with the chariots' warheads buried underneath.

Documents were needed to fool the German bureaucracy. The *Arthur* would have to pass the guards keeping watch from a boat lying off Agdenes at the entrance to Trondheimsfjord, who checked the papers of all who came and went. The Trondheim underground leaders Grønn and Helgesen had been asked to discover what was required. The list was long: registration papers for the boat, identification cards for Larsen and the crew, bills of lading signed by the German harbourmasters of all the ports they had visited in the last three months and authority to enter the fjord, which was a closed military area. As well as this essential information, the agents were also able to supply some of the blank documents. An agent, Odd Sørli, who had accompanied Rørholt on his first trip and was now in Stockholm, travelled to Trondheim at the end of September to collect them.

Safely back in Sweden, he flew to London, disguised as a Lutheran pastor, carrying the papers and details of the underground group's arrangements for helping the attack party to escape after the operation. After dropping the chariots and their crews, the Norwegians and the two remaining Britons were to scuttle the *Arthur* and row in the boat's dinghy to the southern shore of Trondheimsfjord and hide in a hay lorry. After the charioteers had landed, both groups would be collected by the resistance and driven to the Swedish frontier.

The preparations and trials continued until the last minute with scrupulous attention to detail. The *Arthur* was given the identity of a boat similar in size and appearance picked from the Norwegian fishing boat register. Messages were passed to the Trondheim agents to check it was still in service. The registration documents were rubbed to authentic griminess, then stamped with forged stamps and signed with forged harbourmasters' signatures. 'When they were finished,' said Howarth, 'they were masterpieces.'[7]

In the first week of October, the *Arthur* sailed with the crew selected by Larsen to Loch Cairnbawn for a final dummy run. Here the Norwegians met the men they would be carrying. The final selection had now been made. One chariot would be crewed by Sub-Lieutenant William Brewster and Able Seaman A. Brown, both of whom answered to the name of 'Jock'. Sergeant Don Craig, an early volunteer from the Royal Engineers, and Able Seaman Bob Evans made up the other team. Able Seamen Billy Tebb, a cockney wit, and Malcolm Causer, who had been brought up in Brazil but returned home to volunteer at the outbreak of war, would be travelling with them as spare crew and dressers. The target for the exercise was the battleship *Nelson* and Sir Max Horton was on board to see how it went. At midnight the day after Larsen's arrival, the exercise began. To replicate conditions as closely as possible, the *Arthur* stopped several miles away from the *Nelson*, and the chariot crews prepared to descend into the loch and under the boat. 'A little splash was heard as the four men of the deep let themselves glide down into the coal black sea to disappear from sight,' Larsen wrote later. 'It was quiet on board while the fellows worked under the bottom of the vessel and unshackled the Chariot ... the only thing that could be seen was the phosphorescence and ripples which rose up. Then one machine bobbed up a little way from the side of the vessel. Evans and Craig were holding on to the sides of it and had to [struggle] to mount. Then the other machine appeared.'[8]

That night both teams managed to cut through two curtains of nets draped around the ship, dived underneath a third, laid their mock charges and withdrew, without being spotted. A few days later, *Arthur* and the charioteers returned to Lunna Voe to await the order to sail.

Tirpitz arrived back in Faettenfjord from Narvik late on 23 October. The following day it was spotted by a PRU reconnaissance flight. On 25 October a signal arrived in Lunna Voe from Admiral Horton: 'Carry out Operation TITLE – target *Tirpitz* in Faettenfjord. D-Day October 31st.' That gave them six days to get there.

The *Arthur* left Lunna Voe at mid-morning on Monday, 26 October. Crown Prince Olaf of Norway waved them off in the autumn sunshine. The fine weather soon faded. Rain fell and a strong wind blew in from the north-east. The boat plunged and shuddered as it drove through the head-on seas. Even the Norwegians were feeling seasick. They still managed to toast Brewster's twenty-fifth birthday with a tot of gin. It was not until midday on Wednesday, 28 October, that Kalve spotted white-capped mountains through gaps in the curtain of fog ahead. As they got closer Larsen identified them as the range that overlooked the town of Bud, south of Kristiansund. Soon afterwards the engine faltered and stopped. 'We lay for three hours in sight of land, completely helpless,' wrote Brewster later. 'This was of course rather worrying in broad daylight but no-one came near us.'[9] They hoisted a sail to make way while Bjørnøy worked on the engine. After a few hours it was working again and they were steering north-east towards the island of Edøy where, according to their cover story, they had taken on their cargo of peat. At eight next morning, as dawn was painting the snow on the hills pink, they anchored in a small bay on an islet west of Edøy, at the entrance to the complex of shoals, skerries and minefields that led into Trondheimsfjord.

This was the end of the first leg of the journey. It was now time to lower the chariots over the side and lash them to the hull for the next stage of the voyage. The crew and teams got to work, untying the ropes and removing the tarpaulins and burrowing into the peat in the hold to retrieve the warheads.

As they did so, a German aircraft appeared in the distance and flew straight towards them. They only just had time to haul the covers back over the chariots when it noticed them and swooped down to take a better look. The British scrambled below deck. The Norwegians put on a display of nonchalance for the benefit of the pilot circling sixty feet above, fussing with the net they had dropped over the back. Kalve added authenticity by urinating casually into the sea from the bow. The spotter plane left.

As they resumed work, another aircraft appeared, took another look at them and droned off. There were several more visits that morning. Finally, there was a long enough lull for them to risk another attempt. The warheads were brought up from below and fixed to the noses. When the first chariot was hoisted up on the derrick it was clear to Brewster that the heavy swell in the bay would make it extremely difficult to get it into the water. 'It should have been about an hour's job,' wrote Brewster later, 'but it took a devil of a lot longer.'[10] In the choppy sea the *Arthur* started to drag her anchor. There was nothing for it but to set off again, trailing the chariots behind, to seek a better haven.

Night was falling when they found one and 'after much cursing and mucking about' made the boat fast to the beach. The chariot-eers went below to get some sleep. At five o'clock in the pre-dawn darkness of Friday, 30 October, they tried again. Tebb and Causer helped Brewster and Evans into their diving gear and they slipped into the water. They checked the electric motor and instruments then pushed and pulled the craft seven feet below the surface and fixed them under the keel. They lashed ropes underneath which were fixed to cleats on deck to hold the chariots horizontal. They had just got back on board when the *Arthur* became the subject of more unwanted attention. A rowing boat was approaching, with an old man at the oars. He drew up alongside, held onto the starboard rail and began a desultory conversation with Larsen.

It was clear that he was in no hurry to leave. He kept up a steady flow of awkward questions, which Larsen, with increasing annoy-ance and alarm, managed to parry. As they talked, the old man noticed the chariots gleaming in the clear, shallow water. He bent down to get a better look. When the visitor asked what they were Larsen replied that they were mine-exploding devices. Comprehension dawned on the old man's face. 'You fellows go about with the Germans, perhaps?' he asked. Larsen admitted this was the case.[11]

The old man now felt on good enough terms to ask if they could spare any butter. Larsen obliged. As the man prepared to row away, Larsen asked him where he lived and whether he had a family. He supplied the information happily, adding that his daughter lived nearby. In a flash Larsen's friendly manner evaporated. If he breathed a word of what he had seen that morning, he snarled, he and his daughter would pay for his indiscretion with their lives. The old man seized the oars and rowed away, pausing now and again to shout back assurances that he would keep his mouth shut.

Before setting off again, they went over the ship searching for anything incriminating – such as Larsen's British-made pipe – and threw it over the side in a weighted sack. The transmitter, which was one of the most up to date yet produced, was also ditched. The machine gun they had been given in case of emergencies, rucksacks and emergency provisions for their getaway they stowed in the secret compartment.

There were now less than forty-eight hours to go to the attack. Before they approached Trondheimsfjord there was an important call to make. Larsen headed for the fishing village of Hestvik, on the island of Hitra, fifteen miles west of the mainland. Sørli had made contact with a local storekeeper called Nils Strøm who had promised to help out with details of German activities.

On the way the engine began to knock ominously again. Bjørnøy, the engineer, examined it and diagnosed a damaged piston. Unless it was repaired the *Arthur* would never make it to Trondheimsfjord. They reached Hestvik at eleven that night. Larsen told Bjørnøy to strip the cylinder while he and Strand went to find Nils Strøm. There had been a festival that day and people were still on the streets. When Larsen stopped someone to ask for directions to the store he found he was talking to Strøm's son who took him to the shop. A pre-arranged question and answer had been supplied to both Larsen and Strøm which would establish each party's bona fides. But when Larsen uttered the crucial words 'Do you need any peat?', Strøm failed to respond to his cue. After some farcical toing and froing, the penny dropped and Strøm got on with filling Larsen and Strand in on the latest details of the German checks.

They returned to the boat to bad news. Bjørnøy had discovered that the piston was cracked and would not last much longer. They needed a replacement, or at least the chance to make a repair. Strøm had a solution. The village blacksmith was a reliable man. He would be willing to give Bjørnøy the use of his forge to try and mend it. They woke him up and he let them into his workshop where, for two hours, the engineer hammered away. They returned to the boat and reassembled the engine. When they fired it up the following morning Bjørnøy's verdict was that it would get them to their destination.

At 9 a.m. on Saturday, 31 October, they left Hestvik on the last and most dangerous stage of the voyage. From now on they must expect to be stopped and questioned by the Germans at any moment. The British group hid in the secret compartment, machine gun at the ready. The Norwegians had pistols hidden under their jerseys. Just before ten o'clock, as they chugged through smooth waters off Trondheimsfjord, a German patrol vessel spotted the *Arthur* and swung towards her. It passed with barely a glance. The cutter was indistinguishable from hundreds of others that worked between the islands and the mainland, fishing and trading.

The inevitable encounter came as they approached the mouth of Trondheimsfjord. The entrance was watched by the Germans from the fortress at Agdenes on the southern side and several observation posts and gun batteries. As they moved slowly towards it, a converted trawler with a gun mounted in the bows sailed towards them. Larsen called a warning to the six Britons below, handed the wheel to Bjørnøy and composed himself.

His main concern was the dead calm of the water. With no breeze to ruffle the surface, the chariots might well be visible hanging down from the keel. His anxiety mounted as he noticed a sailor in the bow of the guard ship staring down at the waterline as the *Arthur* approached. It seemed he was about to say something when the *Arthur*'s hawser landed on his shoulders, thrown aboard by Kalve, who was standing in the bows. The sailor lost interest. The *Arthur* came alongside and the chariots were once again hidden from the Germans' sight.

The lieutenant in charge was brisk and thorough. He jumped aboard and began to examine Larsen's documents, carefully comparing the signatures on the papers with his own records. Crammed in their hiding place between the bulwarks, the chariot teams and the dressers could hear the exchanges between the two in a mixture of German and Norwegian. At last the officer seemed satisfied. He thawed and began to chat. He inquired conversationally whether Larsen knew his old school friend Leutnant Ormann, the harbourmaster at Kristiansund, which, according to the documents, had been their last port of call? Larsen mumbled that he did. Was it a trick question? He braced himself for the shout of triumph as the German unmasked him. It never came. The officer was rattling on about the strange coincidences that occurred in wartime and his sorrow that the threat of a British invasion had forced Germany to take over Larsen's country. At last he handed back the documents and after a quick examination of the peat in the hold, he climbed back onto the guard ship and waved them on. The *Arthur*'s propellers turned, the water boiled, hiding the submerged chariots and the boat moved slowly into Trondheimsfjord.

Five hours later, with dusk falling, Larsen thought it safe to allow the men below a spell on deck. The Britons emerged from the hold. They were passing Trondheim where the spires of the cathedral stood out dark against the fading sky. 'The weather was quite fine,' wrote Brewster. 'There were many friendly-looking lights flickering ashore. There certainly didn't seem to be very much concern about black-out. And so we continued peacefully.'[12] There were now less than twenty miles to the island of Tautra where they would unharness the chariots. It was time to get ready. Craig and Evans went back down with Tebb and Causer and began the laborious business of dressing.

Next, it was Brewster and Brown's turn. Brewster found it hard to stay on his feet. A north-easterly wind had got up and the *Arthur* was thumped and shaken by the waves driving into her bow. Then, Brewster heard 'a succession of sharp bumps. The chariots were being swung up against the keel.' They were in the grip of a full-blown storm. Larsen slowed the *Arthur* to reduce drag. There was no question of seeking shelter until the weather calmed. They would be bound to be discovered. Brewster decided that 'the only advice we could give ourselves was to "press on regardless"'. Larsen explained that these sudden storms often blew themselves out as quickly as they had brewed up. They were only an hour or two away from *Tirpitz*. If they maintained the speed they would still get there in time to launch their attack before daybreak. Brewster and Brown carried on dressing.

They were almost finished when it happened. 'We heard a loud, grinding tearing noise,' remembered Brewster. 'The vessel jerked and shuddered. Something pretty substantial had fouled the propeller. We all guessed what it had been – one of the chariots.' It was a blow – but not a fatal one. The remaining chariot could still carry out a successful attack. They steered towards the shore, in search of shelter to check underneath. Bob Evans was fully dressed and ready to dive. When they reached calmer water Larsen hove to and Evans slipped over the side. When he reappeared he reported the heart-sinking news that there was 'nothing there at all'.

'We were dismayed,' wrote Brewster. 'The chariots were gone and the attempt was off. I don't think anyone has ever been so disappointed as we were that night. We were ten miles from the pride of the German Navy; all our obstacles were behind us; and we might as well have been at the North Pole. Looking back I don't remember one single curse. We were all too unhappy for that.'[13]

Larsen worried that the disaster was somehow his fault. Evans reassured him that it was the bolts on the warheads of the chariots that had sheared off, not the fastenings on the *Arthur*'s hull, which were still intact and trailing the steel hawsers. It was irrelevant now. All the training, all the preparations, the painstaking intelligence gathering and the bold subterfuge had been for nothing. *Tirpitz* had been spared by a lucky change in the weather and faulty workmanship.

There was no time to brood. They were immediately absorbed with the problem of how to get away. The original escape plan was now unworkable. It was nearly twelve hours until their rendezvous with the local underground and they could not scuttle the *Arthur* so near the shore without a high risk of alerting the Germans. Nor could they go back the way they had come as there was no pass from the German authorities in Trondheim to allow them past the controls at Agdenes and no receipt for the peat they were supposed to be delivering. Bjørnøy reported that the engine was, anyway, on its last legs. There seemed to be no alternative to Larsen's proposal to continue eastwards to where the fjord swung north, which would bring them closer to the Swedish border. Then they would find a quiet place to sink the faithful *Arthur*, put ashore in the dinghy and start trekking to the frontier.

They abandoned ship in the channel between Tautra and the Frosta peninsula, just north of Faettenfjord, a few miles from where the crew of the *Tirpitz* were standing watch, relaxing off duty or sleeping. They collected their iron rations, maps and a revolver apiece and rowed ashore in two parties, as the *Arthur* slipped beneath the now calm waters of the fjord.

It was one o clock on the morning of 1 November 1942. They had no choice but to start moving and keep going as long as they could. They were exhausted, weighed down by fatigue and a feeling of failure. Larsen assumed leadership of the band of ten. It was his country and the four Norwegians had the most to lose. They were wearing their sea clothes: jackets, jerseys and sea boots. If captured in the company of the British, they would be shot as irregulars. The British, clad in submariners' jackets and naval battledress, comforted themselves with the thought that they at least had the protection of their uniforms.

The tip of the peninsula sloped down gently to the sea. To the east, though, the land rose steeply to a 700-foot ridge, covered with pine trees and bushes interspersed with patches of snow and ice-covered rock. They walked for a while through the darkness, passing an aerodrome. Ten men together made a conspicuous sight. They were reasonably safe in the dark but when day broke they would have to split up. As the sky lightened Larsen called a halt. They slept huddled together against the piercing cold, taking turns to stand watch. At midday they set off again. This time they were in two groups. Larsen led one, with Don Craig as his second in command, together with Bob Evans, Bill Tebb and Roald Strand. Jock Brewster took charge of the other, with Jock Brown, Malcolm Causer, Johannes Kalve and Palmer Bjørnøy. Each man had biscuits, chocolate, a tube of condensed milk, two tins of corned beef and three of sardines. The leaders had a map and compass.

It was fifty miles as the crow flies to the Swedish frontier, sixty-five with detours to avoid villages. The going would be hard all the way but the toughest part would come at the end, when they had to cross the plateau between the Verdal and Stjørdal valleys, 3,300 feet high, covered in snow and scoured by wind. They decided to take separate routes. Larsen's group turned inland. Brewster and his men followed the coast. For a while they kept in sight of each other. Then Larsen's team rounded a hillside and disappeared. The path that Brewster was following began to rise. It was cold but sunny. They were making good progress. They reached the top of the Frosta heights and looked down at the granite-blue waters below. There, tucked securely into the sheltering bowl of Lofjord, were the outlines of a warship. The pocket battleship *Admiral Scheer* lay at anchor, covered with skilfully painted grey and white nets and tarpaulins to blend in with the surrounding land and sea. Apart from some German sailors, enjoying a walk along a path on the slope below them, they saw no one. That night they broke into a hut and collapsed into sleep without bothering to post sentries. 'We were all pretty weary and I suppose we took very few precautions,' wrote Brewster. 'The nature of the whole business was such that it would have been impossible not to leave something to chance. We preferred to put speed before everything else, even at the cost of running some rather unwise risks during the daylight hours.'[14]

The luck they had trusted to held. The following night they risked knocking on the door of a farmhouse and the farmer took them in, fed them soup, eggs and potatoes and gave them beds in his hayloft, in the full knowledge that this hospitality, if discovered, was likely to cost him dearly. The next night they came across a hunting cabin, where they found butter and flour. They mixed them up with the condensed milk from their ration packs and wolfed down a meal of flapjacks.

They reached Sweden on the morning of Thursday, 5 November after struggling overnight over the final range of mountains, wading through wind-whipped snow. Later that day they reached a small village and reported their arrival at the local police station. 'We were glad to give ourselves up,' wrote Brewster. 'We were dishevelled, hungry and wearing ten days' growth of beard.' Apart from Causer they were all in reasonable condition. He was 'in a bad way. He had been in pretty bad pain for the last couple of days but had said nothing about it. It was frostbite of course.' The police were friendly. They sent for a doctor and Causer was taken away for hospital treatment. The policemen told them that another British party had crossed the border that morning.

The Larsen group also owed their escape to the kindness of Norwegian strangers. Their journey had been harsh but they had not hit trouble until the final stretch. Just before they reached the frontier, floundering along in soft snow as they turned a bend in the road they came face to face with a German military policeman accompanied by a member of Hirden, Quisling's paramilitary organization. There was no chance to escape. They were questioned briefly and arrested. As they were marched away, Billy Tebb pulled out his concealed gun and opened fire. In the ensuing fight the German was killed and the collaborator ran off. Bob Evans, though, had been hit. Accounts of the seriousness of his injuries are confused. There were many German troops in the area and to hang around meant certain capture. The decision was taken to leave Evans behind. They reasoned that as a uniformed combatant he would receive proper treatment and the status of a prisoner of war.

Instead, after being nursed back to health Evans was handed over to the Trondheim Gestapo chief, Gerhard Flesch. He was then loaned to senior Kriegsmarine officers, questioned about the details of the operation, and handed back to Flesch. His naval interrogators can have been in no doubt what would happen next. The submariner's jacket had proved no protection. On 19 January 1943, Bob Evans was shot in Oslo as a saboteur. He was twenty years old. The execution was approved by the chief of the German High Command, Field Marshal Keitel.*[15]

His companions crossed the border within a mile of the Brewster party. The two groups were reunited at the police station then locked up in a village house for two days, before being moved to an internment camp outside Stockholm. Ten days later they were freed into the custody of the British Mission. Everyone was repatriated over the following days. After a pleasant time in a nice hotel, eating, drinking and sightseeing, Brewster was flown back to Scotland, arriving in Leuchars on 17 November. Larsen went back to Shetland. The operation was marked as a gallant failure. Rear Admiral Sir Claud Barry, who had taken over as Flag Officer Submarines, declared that 'the achievement of penetrating to within ten miles of the berth occupied by the *Tirpitz* represents, on the part of the personnel and particularly that of the Norwegians, a fine example of cold-blooded courage'.[16] Brewster was awarded the DSC. Larsen received the Conspicuous Gallantry Medal.

All the praise, and all the laurels, could not mask the fact that the operation had been an appalling waste of effort. Great ingenuity and technical skill had gone into the plan. Many men in Norway and Britain had risked their lives to realize it. By the end it stood a real chance of success. Despite the meticulousness of the preparations and the determination to leave nothing to chance, one vital detail had been neglected. The fate of the mission hung on two shackles. When they snapped, a great opportunity was squandered.

The episode passed unnoticed by the men on board *Tirpitz* who went about their duties in ignorance of the dramas taking place around them. It was only a few days after the date of the intended attack that the discovery of the partially sunk hulk of the *Arthur* off Tautra island revealed the danger they had been in. The news caused a welcome stir. It was a rare moment of excitement in the routine of shipboard life.

---

* The episode was used as evidence in the post-war trials of Flesch and Keitel which ended with their executions.

11

The Iron Castle

A miasma of boredom hung over the decks and messrooms of *Tirpitz*. The crew's frustration at their inactivity was tempered by awareness that they were living a pampered existence. The knowledge produced mixed emotions. 'We are living like lords,' wrote the ship's administration officer, Kurt Voigt, guiltily to his wife early in 1942. His conscience had been pricked by an article in a weekly magazine describing how 'millions on the Eastern Front have to hunker down in snowstorms next to the horses'.[1]

Moored in Faettenfjord, and later further north at Bogen and Kaafjord, the Russian Front was not far. As they ate their three meals a day with only the faint prospect of an air raid to concern them, the crew had every reason to count themselves lucky. The ship had become their universe. On first setting eyes on the *Tirpitz*, most had been struck by its immensity. Once on board they continued to be awed by the scale of everything about her. Klaus Rohwedder, a young conscript, was 'stunned. Everywhere there was noise; rumbling, humming. I was quite disoriented by the size and the noise'.[2]

The ship swallowed them up. They lived a life that was strangely disconnected from their surroundings. Above deck they looked out on a timeless landscape of rock, wood and water, where nature ruled and the red-roofed timber houses of the local people seemed no more substantial than lichen on a tree trunk. Below, everything was mechanized and modern. They passed their leisure hours at hobbies, sport and games, watching films and newsreels in the ship's cinema, reading a book from the library or leafing through the ship's newspaper, *Der Scheinwerfer*. It was tepid stuff, four pages of improving articles on subjects like the history of chess, caricatures of onboard personalities, little poems sent in by the crew and feeble jokes. Among the cartoons and word puzzles, though, there were uncomfortable reminders of the outside world. While they were stagnating in a Norwegian fjord, their fellow sailors were carrying the war to the enemy. 'In the last few days and weeks, a fanfare of special reports has called the German people to the radio,' ran the main article of the issue of 17 April 1942. 'The familiar words: "German U-boats have sunk … off the American coast …" have revealed the amount of tonnage dispatched into the deep by the German U-boat weapon, far from their home bases.'

Apart from the tedium, there was nothing to complain about. The accommodation was spacious by maritime standards. Kapitän Topp's quarters were palatial, a large day cabin and a sleeping cabin with bathroom attached. There was a similar suite reserved for visiting admirals. The two were separated by a large saloon which doubled as a dining and conference room. His senior officers all had their own cabins complete with washbasin and table. Junior officers shared and the men slept below decks in hammocks. Each night everyone drifted off to sleep to the husky voice of Lale Andersen crooning 'Lili Marleen' over the loudspeakers.

The hardships of war barely touched them. Voigt had responsibility for the company's victuals and comforts and seems to have had considerable success finding supplies. His letters home are full of descriptions of food and drink. 'I ate a pound of crabs for dinner

Killing time. A seaman displays a model of his ship

tonight, quite fresh from the fish market in the town,' he wrote on 20 February. 'On the other hand I did not get any lunch.' Skipping a meal does not seem to have been a regular occurrence. Early on he complains that he is 'getting fatter, though it has not yet become ridiculous'. His duties took him ashore regularly. When *Tirpitz* was

'Unter der Laterne …' Lale Andersen

in Faettenfjord he held meetings with army colleagues at their head-quarters in Trondheim. They had set themselves up at the city's best hotel, the elegant stucco-fronted Britannia, and took their meals in the glass-domed palm court. On 6 February 1942 he drove slowly with Topp and a party of the ship's senior officers along the icebound road that ran along the south side of Trondheimsfjord to have dinner with the army brass. 'We were received in the hall by many army people in a very friendly way,' he wrote. 'Charming waitresses in white and black outfits handed us a welcome drink. The prettiest were engaged to German soldiers. Then we started the food which was extremely tasty: first Irish stew, then bread and sausage or roll-mop herrings.' Afterwards they 'spread out on the charming furnish-ings' to drink coffee, beer and champagne. 'There is a rather classy standard of living here,' he noted. 'Three women were with us, offic-ers' daughters who were working with the army.' They were 'very disappointed' when the party had to break up at 11 p.m. in order for the visitors to return to their ship. The trip back took two hours 'through the white moonscape, over hill and dale, as well as a short further journey to get on board'.

If Voigt lived well he did his best to see that the men did, too. Just before setting off for Norway, in the depths of a north German winter, he had managed to lay his hands on supplies of apples, oranges and walnuts. Once in Trondheim such exotic treats were unobtainable. He did what he could with local markets, buying in cod, halibut and herrings and, when the weather improved, fresh vegetables. He bought some pigs which were reared ashore and planted a kitchen garden to provide salad. Potatoes were a staple of the company's diet and they had brought an enormous quantity with them from Germany in two holds on the deck next to the funnel. Voigt records that in one hold alone there were '450 zent-ner', that is, more than twenty-two tons. Keeping them from going rotten was a constant preoccupation. Electric heaters from the cabins were requisitioned to prevent the cargo from freezing.

Voigt's purchasing trips brought him into contact with the local people and he found them courteous and often hospitable. On 21 April he went for a stroll ashore, climbing up the hillside above the anchorage by way of a fifty-metre path that a work party had cut into the rock. They came across a farmstead where they had heard 'there was milk to be had. On the barren meadow in front of the house a couple of sprightly lads were jumping about with a pointer dog. To the great joy of one of them we played football with him. We then went into the very basic house and asked for some milk. A friendly woman was just cleaning the tidy living room but stopped immediately and brought us a couple of stools. Then a friendly girl aged about sixteen with very thin legs brought over a small table with a cloth on it and put a large jug with two glasses on a tray on top of it. Everything was simple, the furniture simply painted, meagre like the land, but the people are friendly … I left quite soon but the milk tasted fantastic.'

Living close to the ship, the farmers had little choice but to be amiable and the German sailors were, anyway, on their best behaviour, paying for everything or offering cigarettes, schnapps or other luxuries in exchange for some milk, eggs or butter. Other Norwegians, though, were genuinely welcoming. While *Tirpitz* was anchored at Bogen in the mid- to late summer of 1942, Voigt made the acquaintance of 'an intelligent, once beautiful' woman, the wife of a prosperous farmer. On his first visit she 'prepared coffee in the main room' which, unlike the spare surroundings of the Faettenfjord homestead, was full of 'highly polished furniture beneath wood-panelled walls'. He noticed a bookcase filled with 'well-read volumes, the history of the area, a large dictionary and a copy of *Mein Kampf* in Norwegian'. The lady sent him away with two cauliflowers, some cream and two eggs. Later, at her invitation, he went back 'to dine on chicken and mushrooms'. A few days later he visited the farm again and met the farmer ('a Quisling') with whom he made a deal to supply cauliflower to the ship. The farmer's wife gave him 'some lovely milk and green plums from the south of the country' as a parting gift. Later she sent a present of flowers to the ship and another invitation to dine.

Voigt's impressions of Norway and the Norwegians were positive. He found Trondheim dreary in its wartime austerity and complained about the 'lazy buggers' who were too idle to shovel the snow from the precincts of the cathedral. On the whole he subscribed to the official view that the local inhabitants were pretty much like himself and his kin – good Aryans with the potential to become honorary citizens. One day in mid-September he went ashore at Bogen with two of the ship's doctors to forage for wild mushrooms, strawberries and raspberries. They went past a farmyard where four children were playing. Among them was a girl of seven or eight who 'ran up and astonished us with her beauty and queenly bearing and expression as only a northern German can demonstrate'. They gave her a sweet and 'it was a delight for us to see the way in which this girl took [it] and ate it'. The contrast with an encounter at a nearby dockside three days later could not have been greater. There, as he supervised the loading of supplies, he watched 'Russian prisoners stamping up and down the quayside, most of them with Mongol features, taking in the strange world around them with wounded, animal eyes'.

Voigt's job meant he had more contact with Norwegians than most. While *Tirpitz* was at Trondheim, ordinary crew members were allowed into town once a fortnight. There was little opportunity, though, to engage in the traditional pastimes of sailors on a run ashore. Military policemen kept a close eye on them and instead of whiling away their time in bars and brothels the only entertainment on offer was at the 'German House' which had formerly been a Masonic lodge. It had a reading room, two cafeterias and a concert hall, where faded variety performers turned up from time to time. The strongest drinks were cocoa and coffee. The hundred or so German women, imported to carry out secretarial duties at the military headquarters, 'lived like nuns' according to Voigt and had to seek official permission to go out on dates. He himself formed a friendship with a Fraülein Francke, a thirty-year-old spinster who, despite a limp, was 'not ugly and quite nice'. Together they enjoyed meals, strolls in the country and skiing trips.

Without distraction it was easy to succumb to what the crew called 'Polarkoller' – polar fever. The sense of confinement was reflected in the ways they referred to their ship. The young midshipman Adalbert Brünner called it the 'iron box', Voigt the 'iron castle'.

Kapitän Topp saw their frustration and worried. Boredom was not merely irksome. It could be dangerous. A stale ship's company could easily turn uncooperative, even hostile. The memory of the Kiel mutiny in 1918, when the lower ranks of the Kriegsmarine who had been sitting idle in harbour for two years refused orders to put to sea on a last foray against the Royal Navy, was still fresh. Admiral Raeder ordered a leaflet to be printed and distributed to all officers with instructions on how to identify and suppress trouble. The ship's executive officer, Fregattenkapitän Paul Düwel, had responsibility for onboard discipline and instructed officers and NCOs to report any whispers of subversion to him.

At the same time Topp did everything he could to keep his 2,400 men occupied. He encouraged them to go ashore to climb the hills around Faettenfjord, or hunt for gulls' eggs in nests that were identified using the ship's powerful Zeiss optics. Rat hunting was another diversion. Despite all precautions, the ship was plagued with them. 'They had already come on board via the steel cables in Germany,' remembered Herbert Ludwig, a young anti-aircraft gunner. 'Many more came on board in Norway since there was always something to eat. They gnawed our bread sacks open at night and helped themselves. The creatures travelled through the ship via the air ducts. My hammock, a metre under the deck, was right under an air duct opening. One morning I found a rat in my hammock. Whether I crushed it or whether my shipmates had put it there I do not know. But I eagerly claimed the five marks we were given when we handed in a dead rat.'[3]

Topp did not stand on his dignity and, when the occasion warranted it, could take a joke. He hated beards, once ordering a subordinate who dared to grow one 'to take that sauerkraut off your face'. Shortly after arriving in Trondheim, the men manoeuvred him into growing one himself by promising to pay a sizeable sum into an army charity if he did so. If he refused, he would have to make an even bigger donation. 'Those of us who knew our Charley Topp knew what an ordeal this was for him,' remembered Brünner. 'I can't remember him giving us blacker looks.' He gamely wore the whiskers for four weeks before shaving them off on Army Day, the climax

of the money-raising activities. The Tag der Wehrmacht was celebrated on 22 March. Before the war it had been a recruiting event
but on board *Tirpitz* it had, according to Brünner, developed into an
occasion for institutionalized high-jinks. 'On that day we had a
fool's licence towards our superiors' he wrote. 'We celebrated with a
great deal of tomfoolery and mischief making.'

Topp set the tone by playing a harmonica over the ship's tannoy.
The ship's chaplain broadcast extracts from a saucy book. Rank was
turned on its head. Senior officers served as waiters in the canteens
and NCOs scrubbed tables and the medical officers were ordered by
their charges to report sick.[4]

Topp had early on spotted the recreational potential of the small
island of Saltøya, a mile or so astern of the ship at the entrance of
the fjord. He requisitioned it and work parties were moved in to
spruce it up. A cluster of dilapidated buildings which had once
housed a sanatorium were refurbished to provide sleeping huts and
a mess. The teams built log cabins, painted them bright colours and
named them after their officers. They decorated two of them, the
Hindenburglager and the Krillstube, in the style of rustic inns to
remind them of home.[5]

The centre was officially opened on 30 May 1942 with beer and
snacks, including stuffed gulls' eggs, cocktail sausages, potato salad
and beer, while the ship's orchestra played on the island's band-
stand.[6] The crew nicknamed the place 'Tipito', a Germano-
Norwegian approximation of 'Tirpitz Island'. It was, said Brünner, 'a
small holiday encampment'. The sailors went there to 'take it easy
– pursue a hobby or go swimming. In short, to forget everyday life.'

There were, however, rules. Notices posted around the place
detailed a long list of *verboten* activities including smoking in the
huts, picking flowers, collecting gulls' eggs without authorization,
pulling branches off trees, trading with Norwegians and receiving
guests who were not Germans. This last restriction was to bring
about the end of the idyll. Soon crew members were arranging to
ferry in girls from Trondheim and the surrounding area. The forbidden revels came to light when a fisherman who had carried some of
the guests to and from the island was arrested for stealing supplies

from the stores. At the hearing he revealed the goings-on. The head-quarters at Trondheim ordered Tipito to be closed down.[7]

During the sojourn at Bogen in the summer of 1942 there were concert parties and rowing races and football tournaments with teams drawn from each of the ship's company's twelve 'divisions'. One of the officers constructed a puppet theatre. On 21 August, after a dinner of 'herrings and new potatoes soaked in butter', Voigt watched a 'charming puppet show … the figures were half the size of a human and fantastically realistic'. It was 'a brilliant performance that released waves of laughter'. Heinz Assman, who took over from Düwel as executive officer after the return to Trondheim, was a piano virtuoso and had a concert grand brought on board on which he gave regular recitals.

All this relentless displacement activity was no substitute for the excitement of operations. Topp tried to keep his crew honed with the sort of drills that precede a major sortie. Brünner described how they would haul in the anchors to the frantic waltz tempo of the 'Lampenputzer Galopp' blaring from the loudspeakers. 'But then nothing happened,' he wrote wistfully. 'Every "anchors aweigh" was just an exercise.'

Everyone wanted action. The desire was natural. By the end of 1942, the captain and many of the crew had been on board for nearly two years. They had taken part in innumerable exercises and dummy runs. Yet in all that time they had put to sea only twice with the intention of engaging the enemy. It was an inglorious situation. At times it felt ignominious. Every day news trickled in of the epic struggle taking place a few hundred miles away to the east. Many of the crews had families back in Germany's big cities who were in greater danger than they were. By now Bomber Command was getting into its stride. The first thousand-bomber raid had struck Cologne on the night of 30/31 May, killing at least 469. On the night of 14/15 September, Wilhelmshaven, where *Tirpitz* had started life, suffered its worst raid to date. Seventy-seven people were killed. Voigt's mother lived there but had been out of town at the time. He saw the headlines on the report of the attack in an old newspaper. He told his wife how he read it 'with great trepidation, but no-one we know was listed … the old city hall was destroyed along with a load of damage in the Villen quarter [in the centre of town]. How sorry I feel for the people.'

The growing frequency and power of the raids only sharpened the desire to fight. Beyond the placid fjords of Norway the war had intensified into a struggle for Germany's existence in which it seemed that everyone but the *Tirpitz* and her crew were involved. Any doubts about Hitler appear to have been overtaken by the need to win the struggle – or at least to survive. There seems, anyway, to have been little antipathy towards the Führer. The detached, maritime nature of the Kriegsmarine and the fact that its traditions predated the arrival of the Nazis had given it a degree of independence that its commander, Raeder, fought to protect. That did not mean that its sailors were not good and obedient patriots. Hitler's portrait hung in Topp's day cabin, next to that of Admiral von Tirpitz, wearing full dress uniform and the Grand Cross of the Imperial Eagle, looking stern and patriarchal with his bald skull and long, forked beard. The Führer's picture also hung in the messes, one of which was decorated with exhortations – 'Our leader's struggle is our struggle' and 'Our leader's faith is our faith'. On Hitler's birthday, Topp gave a speech to the entire crew and the officers toasted their leader's health in sparkling wine.

But despite routine displays of patriotism, it was impossible for some to suppress doubts as to where the Führer was leading Germany. Karl Voigt was a thoughtful man who appreciated good books, films and music and took a keen interest in his surroundings. He was also a loyal German. But in his letters to his wife, buried among the endearments and minutiae of his existence it is possible to detect a murmur of doubt as to whether the war was worth it.

One day in August the reality of the war in the east was brought home to him again when one of the ship's doctors showed him photographs in a medical journal of soldiers whose eyes had been damaged in action. 'My God, how appalling' he wrote to his wife. 'How much men suffer today at the effects of this horrible war where the heroic sudden death seems more merciful than the alternative.' He predicts that 'every day in the East will one day be engraved in golden letters in a history of Germany'. But he goes on to wonder, 'what are they compared to what these battles have done to the mothers, the women and the brides of the dead and badly wounded heroes?'[8] He was ready to fight if the circumstances arose. It was not to be. At the end of October he left the ship to be reunited with his beloved 'Klösel' and his family in Berlin.

The mood of frustration led directly to one episode which provided a stark reminder to all on board that they were in the business of life and death. One morning in August 1942, while *Tirpitz* lay at Bogen bay, the early muster revealed that one of the crew was missing. His name was Bernhard Turowsky. He was eighteen years old and served as a gunner on a flak battery. Inquiries revealed that he had last been seen the previous afternoon. The ship was searched but there was no sign of him.

The authorities on shore were alerted and after four days Turowsky, wearing civvies and guarded by two military policemen, was dragged back on board showing signs of having been beaten. He had been captured thirty miles away, close to the Swedish border. He was carrying a compass and pistol, stolen, it turned out, from one of the ship's Arado pilots.

A few days after his capture, Turowsky appeared before a court martial convened in the main lecture hall. He was condemned to death with the sentence to be carried out the following day. That night, Turowsky was allowed to eat a last supper with his comrades. Among them was Herbert Ludwig, who knew and liked the condemned man. 'They had cut all the buttons off his uniform and removed the swastika,' he recalled. 'He had ordered himself a good meal as his final wish and, to our astonishment, had eaten quietly with no complaining or recriminations. We said our good-byes full of emotion. We, not he, had tears in our eyes.'[9]

The motives that led Turowsky to swim ashore and head for the border, fully aware of the penalty for desertion, remain unclear. He was reported to have told the court martial that he was driven by simple boredom. A story went round the ship that he was intending to head for the United States – either to join up with the Allies or deliver a plea for peace, according to who was telling it. Ludwig maintained that 'he was badly bullied by his battery officer'. However, Hein Hellendoorn, a flak artillery officer, friendly with the officer who defended Turowsky, 'never heard that he had a difficult time on board'.[10]

On 4 September the sentence was carried out in front of the entire ship's company. The ship's log recorded a cloudy day and a choppy sea. The execution was timed at 3.50 in the afternoon. Shortly before, Turowsky was brought up from below, blindfolded and led to a point behind the after gun turret. The firing squad was made up of eight men from Turowksy's battery. One of the rifles was loaded with blank ammunition. Turowsky was tied to a rail. Pastor Müller, the ship's chaplain, spoke a few words of comfort and asked him if he had anything to say. Turowsky simply thanked the pastor for his kindness. 'At the command "Fire" his body straightened and fell to one side,' remembered Ludwig. His corpse was taken to a military cemetery ashore but the authorities there refused to bury it. It was returned to the ship and later sewn into a weighted sack and dropped into the fjord.[11]

Tirpitz's time at Bogen was by then coming to a close. Despite her inactivity and a careful regime of maintenance, she was due for a major overhaul. A report drawn up by the ship's technical officers on 15 September 1942 listed a large number of necessary repairs and improvements, ranging from the engines and guns to the fresh-water drinking tanks and fire extinguishers. The hull's magnetic field also had to be neutralized to prevent it triggering mines – 'degaussed' in technical parlance. Proper port facilities were required to do the job properly and they were not available in the Narvik area. After Hitler again judged the risk of sailing her to Germany was too great, she set off back to Trondheim, weighing anchor on 23 October, and arriving in Faettenfjord the following day.

Two days later the *Arthur* put to sea from Lunna Voe with the chariots and their crew on their mission to destroy the battleship. In the flap that followed the failed attack, *Tirpitz* started to shift her mooring frequently, moving around a succession of berths, all at the eastern end of Trondheimsfjord, and divers made regular inspections of the hull. At the end of November a PRU reconnaissance flight reported seeing her at Lofjord, the neighbouring narrow inlet to the north. Her hull was painted in dazzle camouflage with broad black diagonal strips on the port side at the bow and the stern, designed to make her look considerably shorter than her true length. Another ship, identified as the *Stavangerfjord*, a depot ship for the workers brought in from the Kiel dockyard to carry out the refit, was alongside. A few days later a local agent reported the presence of a 100-ton floating crane and that major repairs were under way.[12] The work threw the orderly world of the ship into chaos. 'The noise really was appalling, fraying our nerves,' Adalbert Brünner remembered. 'It was astonishing how poorly sound-proofed [the] iron box was. Everywhere you turned there was something in the way: cabling, air and gas pipes, transformers, tools of every kind and, lastly, the workers themselves.' By 17 December, the refit was completed and the workers had all gone home.

Tirpitz was at full readiness once more and the mood on board was optimistic as Christmas approached. The crew threw their energies into celebrating it in style. A tall fir tree was erected on the after deck and decorations festooned every cabin, mess and gangway. 'Snow lay deep all around and stillness settled on the landscape,' wrote Brünner. 'It was like going back to childhood days.' On Christmas Day, Topp stood on the after deck in the thin grey northern daylight, beneath the tree flickering with candles, and gave a speech which 'emphasized the Christian nature of the holiday'. Then, apart from those on watch, the company settled down to enjoy themselves. They ate and drank and listened to a concert given by a mixed choir.

There were more celebrations on New Year's Eve. There was a special dinner and every man got a bottle of wine, extra tobacco, a packet of sweets and a book. In the wardroom they held a mock trial and one of the officers did an impression of the Führer. At midnight Topp addressed the company over the tannoy. He repeated the message in his New Year greetings card, distributed to all the crew, in which he spoke frankly about the frustrations of the last twelve months and his hopes for the time to come. He recalled the adventures 'we all dreamed about during the dash from Wilhelmshaven to Trondheim ... sorties to the northern seas, the Arctic seas, the North Atlantic and the coast of France' where they would find 'success and the laurels of victory'. Instead, they had been denied 'a free ranging war against merchant vessels on the vast extending oceans'. There was, however, nothing to be done. 'We grit our teeth and bow to the decision of our superiors, even if it is often difficult. We are soldiers and we obey.' His message finished on a rousing note: 'Let us enter the New Year as Adolf Hitler's truest and best soldiers, with unyielding faith in our victory and Germany's future, and with the sure expectation that the great hour when we can prove ourselves will arrive.'

As the festivities continued, five hundred miles to the north other German ships were locked in battle. In the Barents Sea, a force led by the heavy cruiser *Admiral Hipper* had clashed with British escorts protecting the second part of convoy JW.51B, on its way to Murmansk. The German force was led by Vizeadmiral Oskar Kummetz, the Kriegsmarine's commander of cruisers. The convoy had been sighted by a U-boat on 30 December. Kummetz was on board *Hipper* at Altafjord and immediately put to sea. He had with him the pocket battleship *Lützow* and six destroyers. Ranged against them were two British cruisers, the *Sheffield* and the *Jamaica*, and six destroyers. The German ships were bigger and better armed than their British opponents and when battle was first joined they seemed sure to overwhelm the convoy and its escorts. In the middle of the morning of 31 December, in the brief and thin mid-winter twilight, the destroyer escort was attacked by *Hipper* from the north. HMS *Onslow* was hit and the escort commander, Captain Sherbrooke, badly wounded. A little later, *Lützow* appeared on the convoy's southern flank but instead of attacking immediately her captain decided to hold back until the weather improved. *Hipper*'s guns, meanwhile, sank the minesweeper *Bramble* and crippled the destroyer *Achates*, which had been laying down smoke to conceal the convoy.

Just as a massacre seemed imminent, the British cruisers arrived and opened fire on the *Hipper*. They were mounting 6-inch guns, against the enemy's 8-inch main armament. They nonetheless managed to do enough damage to force Kummetz to retire.[13] The cruisers then sighted two of the German destroyers and attacked, sinking the *Friedrich Eckholt*. Shortly afterwards, Kummetz ordered his squadron back to port. The *Sheffield* and the *Jamaica* gave chase but, by 2 p.m., *Hipper* had been swallowed up by the Arctic darkness. The British could feel considerable satisfaction at the outcome. They had held off a significantly more powerful force for the loss of one minesweeper sunk and one destroyer damaged. All fourteen ships of the convoy had escaped serious damage and continued to Murmansk unmolested to join the fifteen others that had arrived safely on Christmas Day.

For the German navy, the Battle of the Barents Sea, as it became known, was a humiliation. Hitler's anger at the outcome created a crisis that was to affect profoundly the future of the Kriegsmarine. In the weeks that followed, *Tirpitz* was in greater danger than it had ever faced its short life. The threat, though, came not from the enemy but from its own commander-in-chief.

12

Enter the Lion

It took a while for the storm to break in Berlin. The initial reports of the battle had been sketchy but promising. A U-boat reported back from the Barents Sea that the enemy convoy was under attack and Hitler settled back 'in delighted impatience', according to Raeder, to hear the details of its complete destruction. The news, though, was slow in coming. Kummetz maintained radio silence on the way back to Altafjord. Once he got there, his report was delayed by a breakdown on the teleprinter line from north Norway.

Instead, Hitler learned the truth via the BBC, which announced that the raiders had broken off their attack and the convoy had got through without loss. Hitler assumed that he had been kept in the dark about the failure and 'flew into a towering rage'. Raeder's liaison officer at headquarters told him that 'in the first outburst of anger, Hitler had expressed his views on the uselessness of our heavy ships and caused them to be recorded in the war log as his considered opinions'.[1] The judgement had been gestating for some time. Six weeks before, on 14 November 1942, he had met Raeder at Berchtesgaden and questioned him as to why the Kriegsmarine's big ships had done nothing since July. Raeder had a reasonable excuse. The navy was being starved of fuel. Operations involving the large surface units used up vast quantities of precious oil. The sortie by the *Tirpitz* squadron in March against the convoy PQ.12 had swallowed 8,000 tons, equivalent to one month's production from the Romanian oil fields. The Battle of the Barents Sea seemed to suggest that even when capital ships were allowed off the leash, the results hardly justified the material costs.

Raeder was told to report at once at the Führer's headquarters. He managed to delay for a few days, excusing himself on the grounds that he needed to acquaint himself with all the facts of the episode. On 6 January he met Hitler at the Wolfschanze (Wolf's Lair), the Führer's heavily protected headquarters buried among woods and lakes near Rastenburg in East Prussia where he oversaw the campaign on the Russian Front.[2] It was soon clear that Hitler's views had not softened. He subjected Raeder to a lecture that lasted more than an hour, much of which consisted of a 'spiteful and quite unobjective attack on the Navy', Hitler coming close to accusing his commanders of cowardice. The navy's performance in the Barents Sea, he said, was 'typical of German ships, just the opposite of the British who, true to their tradition, fought to the bitter end'.[3]

'Apart from the submarine arm, he could not find a good word to say about the German Navy throughout its whole history,' wrote Raeder. 'Our heavy ships – which had always particularly interested Hitler and of which he had once been particularly proud – were now condemned as useless.' Not only did they not do anything, they required constant protection by the Luftwaffe and by smaller vessels. In the event of an Allied attack on Norway, a scenario that continued to loom large in Hitler's imagination, the air force would be much better employed attacking an invading fleet than shielding the battleships. He had therefore come to the conclusion that the Kriegsmarine's heavy ships had no further role to play in the war. They were to be taken out of commission and broken up. Their guns would be salvaged and mounted in shore batteries where they might actually do some good. His resolve was 'firm and unalterable'.[4]

This was an extraordinary proposal, even for Adolf Hitler. The big ships were the Kriegsmarine's sceptre, orb and crown. *Tirpitz*, in the words of Topp's New Year message, was 'still the strongest and sharpest sword in the German armoury'. Now it seemed it was to be melted down. German workmen would voluntarily carry out a task that the Royal Navy and Air Force had spent hundreds of lives and untold effort failing to achieve.

As Raeder listened silently to the diatribe he thought he detected the malign influence of Hermann Göring, who frequently denounced the failings of the navy and army to Hitler in order to enhance the achievements of his Luftwaffe. He disagreed profoundly with everything that was said. The modern Kriegsmarine was largely Raeder's creation and Hitler was intent on dismantling his life's work. The rant had convinced him that he could not continue as head of the German navy. Listening to it had been a disturbing experience. Hitler had 'been very excited, and from time to time had allowed himself to go further than he had ever gone before in his dealings with me'. Raeder, the chilly Prussian, judged that 'the fact that he had allowed himself to lose his self-control in my presence showed me clearly that he regarded the differences between us as more than purely objective'.

He asked for a private audience and Field Marshal Keitel, who was also present, and the two stenographers recording the proceedings left the room. Raeder then told Hitler he wanted to stand down as Supreme Commander of the Navy as he clearly no longer enjoyed his confidence. 'As always when he found himself resolutely opposed,' Raeder recalled, 'Hitler now climbed down and tried to qualify his previous observations.' It was too late. Raeder's stiff mind was made up. A few days later he wrote a memorandum setting out his views on the role of capital ships in which he argued strongly for their retention. He also made two recommendations as to who should succeed him. His first choice was Admiral Rolf Carls, who commanded Naval Group North. The other was the head of the U-boat service, Karl Dönitz. Hitler chose Dönitz.

It was decided that Raeder would soldier on until the end of the month, allowing him to complete ten years at the top under the Hitler regime. This could be presented as a suitable milestone for retirement and minimize the impression that the relationship had ended in bad blood.

His replacement was another Prussian who in later life was candid about the effects his background and upbringing had in determining his outlook and actions. Dönitz came from a long line of modest landowners, yeomen rather than Junkers, whose estate lay close to the River Elbe on the frontier with Poland. Later generations had produced clergymen, men of letters and military officers. Dönitz's father, Emil, had been an engineer. He wrote later that 'as a family we were devoid of any sense of personal individuality'. Instead they were 'deeply conscious of the corporate spirit of the Prussian community to which we belonged'. When he entered the navy, in 1910, 'both the exercise and the acceptance of discipline came quite naturally to me. As a child I had been imbued with the conviction that fulfilment of my duty came before everything else.'[5]

This attitude made it possible for him to accept the elemental changes to Germany brought about by the arrival of Hitler without deviating from the career course he had set himself. Nor did his subsequent disagreements with the direction in which the Führer was taking Germany deflect him from pursuing his tasks with extraordinary drive and efficiency.

He joined the Imperial submarine service in October 1916. Two years later, with the end of the war only a month away, he was commanding *UB-68* in the Mediterranean when it was sunk by British ships after being forced to surface in the middle of a convoy. He and the other survivors were picked up by a destroyer and taken to a prisoner-of-war camp on Malta. When he returned to Germany in July 1919 he found the country in chaos. He was twenty-seven years old. All the notions of duty, national unity and patriotism that had underpinned his short life seemed to have been swept away and replaced with shrill factionalism. Like Raeder he was able to hang onto his commission, which kept him afloat during the years of unemployment and inflation. He moved up the service ladder, holding a series of staff jobs including one dealing with political developments which affected the navy, as well as discipline and the application of military law.

He struggled to remain aloof from party politics. Members of the armed forces were not allowed to vote, a circumstance that later proved useful to those wishing to distance themselves from the Nazi regime. Dönitz admitted frankly, though, that he had welcomed the arrival of Hitler. In the street-fighting years of the late twenties and thirties when left- and right-wing thugs battled in German cities, he found himself taking part in conferences on how the armed forces would react to a complete disintegration of internal order, a prospect that often looked quite likely. As the German nation moved to the extremes of the political spectrum and the moderate centre shrivelled, a civil war could not be ruled out. The military was simply not strong enough to hold the ring. They would have to choose their side. 'That they could not come down on the side of the Communists was obvious,' wrote Dönitz after the war. 'It was as a result of this process of reasoning that they welcomed the appointment of Hitler as German Chancellor.'

Dönitz himself 'believed that Germany had chosen the right path'. Nonetheless there would be occasional points of friction between the navy and the Nazi Party, and in particular the SA. When Hitler moved against them in the 1934 Night of the Long Knives Dönitz regarded the bloody purge as an unfortunate necessity. The Kristallnacht outrage caused him a mild crisis of conscience. Like Günther Lütjens, he wrote a letter of protest to Raeder who endorsed the sentiments and passed them upwards to the Führer.

He had not welcomed the coming of war, fearing that Hitler had failed to understand the dangers of taking on Britain and its navy. It was 'with a feeling of extreme scepticism' that he learned of the 'allegedly unavoidable attack on Poland', and the declaration of war by Britain and France that followed, although anticipated, was 'a bitter blow'. Even so, he believed that it was 'the moral obligation of every fighting man unreservedly to support the government of his country when it goes to war'. He maintained this attitude to the end.

Despite his reluctance to engage in a war with Britain, Dönitz had strong ideas on how it should be fought. He advocated a concentrated campaign against her transatlantic shipping using U-boats. In October 1939 he was appointed Rear Admiral Commanding Submarines and in a position to prove his point. He brought a hunter's instinct to the business of tracking down and destroying merchant ships as they plodded gamely across the great grey plains of the Atlantic, organizing his submarines into 'wolf packs' which, once they had found their victims, would hang around for days, appearing and disappearing, picking them off with cold, lupine efficiency. His men called him after another predator.

His nickname was *der Löwe*, the lion. His tactics were highly success-ful. During the course of 1942, U-boats sank nearly eight million tons of Allied shipping, at one point reducing Britain's stocks of commercial oil to two months' supply.

With this background, Dönitz might be expected to share Hitler's pungent views on the utility of submarines and the uselessness of the big ships. At their first meeting at the Wolfschanze on 30 January 1943, Hitler repeated again his determination to scrap the surface fleet. When he asked for Dönitz's views, the new Chief of the Navy did not immediately concur with the plan but said that he did not feel qualified to give a response and needed time to study the details.

Dönitz was nonetheless inclined to go along with Hitler's wishes. On 8 February, he returned to Rastenburg to present detailed proposals.[6] Most of the big ships were to be paid off. He asked for complete priority to be given to U-boat construction, maintenance and repair and for his ships to be provided with adequate air cover by the Luftwaffe – a request that Raeder had forlornly repeated on numerous occasions with limited results.[7] He also asserted his sole right to order such surface units of the Kriegsmarine that remained after the reorganization to sally out on operations and laid down the principle that, when in action, commanders should be left alone to fight without interference from above.

Back in Berlin, as he worked his way through the details of the plan, unwelcome doubts stirred in Dönitz's mind. He had before him Raeder's memorandum on the subject, drawn up as his last act as Commander-in-Chief. Raeder maintained that despite their record of inactivity the heavy ships in Norway were making an important contribution to the war effort. As long as the main body of the surface fleet was in the northern fjords, the Allies were obliged to maintain at least an equal number of capital ships in northern Scotland and Iceland. While holding themselves ready for a break-out, they could not be put to more effective use in either the Mediterranean, where their presence would help greatly to secure the Allies' communications, or the Pacific, where they would add to the difficulties of Hitler's Japanese partners.

ABOVE: *X-7* under fire. The target float where Place stepped off is on the left.

ABOVE: A wary-looking John Lorimer on the deck of *Tirpitz*, shortly after capture.

ABOVE: Captains Courageous: Place and Cameron after their release.

ABOVE: Touchdown: Wildcat, just after landing.

BELOW: Barracudas landing on HMS *Formidable* during Operation Goodwood.

Der Glaube des Führers ist unser Glaube,

Der Kampf des Führers – ist unser Kampf.

ABOVE: Christmas Day in the seamen's mess 1942. 'The Führer's Faith is Our Faith' and 'The Führer's Struggle is Our Struggle' say the slogans on the wall.

BELOW: Battleship *Bierstube*. Life was good for the crew of *Tirpitz* – while on the Eastern Front their comrades froze.

LEFT: Grossadmiral Erich Räder (*foreground*) next to Admiral Otto Schniewind and Vizeadmiral Oskar Kummetz (*right*), on board *Tirpitz* to discuss plans for 'Rösselsprung.' Topp is smiling in the background.

BELOW: Lancaster silhouetted over Kaafjord during the attack on 15 September 1944.

ABOVE: The men who sank the *Tirpitz* – and the men who filmed it. (*Left to right*) Flight Lieutenant Eric Giersch, Flight Lieutenant Bruce Buckham, Flying Officer Dennis Nolan, Squadron Leader Bill Williams, Flying Officer 'Danny' Daniel and Wing Commander James Tait.

RIGHT: 'Essentially a shy person': the young 'Willie' Tait.

BELOW: Unique photograph of the moment of *Tirpitz*'s death, taken by a woodcutter looking south from Tromsø.

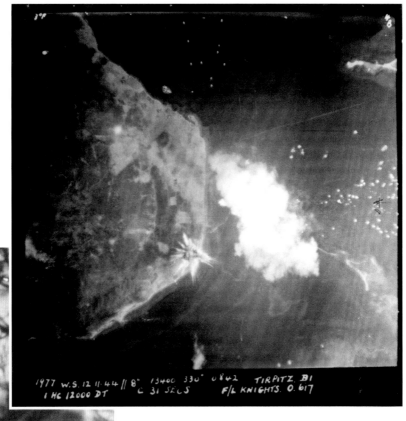

1977 W.S. 12·11·44 // 8" 13400 330° 0842   TIRPITZ. BI
1 HC 12000 DT   C 31 SECS   F/L KNIGHTS. O.617

ABOVE: The opening of the final attack, seen from the Lancaster of Bobby Knights.

BELOW: A muted celebration. Tait on the terrace at Petwood with 5 Group Commander Sir Ralph Cochrane.

Last resting place. Looking out from Haakøy at the hull, with Tallboy crater in the foreground.

This was not an argument for continued passivity. In the same document Raeder advocated more vigorous action by the big ships. It was Hitler himself who had handicapped offensive operations by insisting that the battle fleet could only venture out when there were no aircraft carriers among the enemy forces.

Further restrictions were imposed by the dearth of aircraft in the area to provide reconnaissance and to cover the ships when they were at sea. The aircraft that had been switched to Norway to support the shift of the surface fleet northwards had since been moved away to answer the pressing needs of the army in North Africa and on the Eastern Front. In December 1942, there were only fourteen serviceable Me 109 fighters available in the Trondheim area.[8] Progress on the building of the navy's sole aircraft carrier, *Graf Zeppelin*, had always been jerky as priority was given to more pressing work like building U-boats. In February 1943 it stopped altogether. For all these handicaps, Raeder managed to finish his memorandum on a positive note. 'The possibility of scoring a success most certainly exists,' he wrote, 'provided that the fleet remains constantly on the alert for every possible contingency and waits for the favourable opportunity. Even without adequate air cover and reconnaissance, opportunities will always occur when, by making full use of favourable conditions, we can achieve surprise and strike a worthwhile blow.'[9]

Dönitz was persuaded. 'As a result of this further scrutiny,' he wrote, 'I came to the conclusion that withdrawing these ships from service would not result in any appreciable increase in either manpower or material, and that the implementation of the project could not but react politically and militarily to our disadvantage.' Actually dismantling them as Hitler had proposed 'was an even less attractive solution for it made considerable claims on labour and technical rescources'.[10]

The change of heart was unfortunate. Hitler's reaction to such a swift volte-face was not hard to imagine. Before committing himself, Dönitz took soundings from his senior commanders, to see if they agreed with Raeder's analysis, particularly on the question of the fleet being put to more active use. Both the Admiral Commanding the

Fleet, Otto Schniewind, and Admiral Kummetz agreed that 'the ships, given a favourable opportunity, could undoubtedly still be committed to battle'.[11]

Dönitz revised his plans accordingly. On 26 February he travelled to another Eastern Front headquarters, Vinnitsa, on the western borders of Ukraine, to announce the result of his deliberations and to put his case to the Führer. He started incontroversially by saying that the heavy cruiser *Hipper* and the light cruisers *Leipzig* and *Köln* had outlived their usefulness and would be decommissioned. The same went for the antiquated battleships *Schlesien* and *Schleswig-Holstein*.

But while he was willing to pay off some of the surface fleet he was not going to agree to scrapping all of it. The Russian convoys, he declared, made excellent targets and he considered it his duty to relieve the pressure on Germany's soldiers on the Eastern Front by attacking them. He therefore proposed sending the *Scharnhorst*, currently lying in the Baltic, to join *Tirpitz* and *Lützow* in Norway. Together with six destroyers they would make a formidable force to menace the Arctic routes.

Dönitz was effectively asking his leader to revoke his 'firm and unalterable' decision and cancel his orders to scrap the surface fleet. The response was predictable. The Führer was 'highly astonished and indignant'. He was 'disagreeably surprised since he had not expected that I, as the former Flag Officer, Submarines, and the man who had always pressed for the expansion of the U-boat war would adopt this attitude'. Dönitz was now subjected to a Force 9 tantrum in which Hitler denounced the crews of his capital ships whom he presented as enjoying an extended winter holiday while their comrades froze and died in the east.[12] Eventually, though, his anger subsided. He could not risk another resignation by the head of the navy so soon after Raeder's departure. Hitler, wrote Dönitz 'very grudgingly agreed, and I was ungraciously dismissed'.

It had taken some courage to contradict the wishes of a leader as capricious as Hitler and Dönitz wondered for a while whether his 'days as Commander-in-Chief were not already numbered'. The crisis, though, had passed. Soon afterwards, Dönitz issued a directive in which he defined the role of the Norway-based fleet and the conditions under which it could go into action.

Its purpose was to defend Norway against invasion and attack Arctic convoys when the chance arose. Dönitz admitted that the restricted and clearly finite resources the German navy could muster meant opportunities would be limited, given the strong escorts the enemy were sending. If a lightly or undefended convoy did appear, however, the chance 'must be seized with determination'. The directive also kept alive the possibility that it might become necessary to attack heavily escorted convoys with all available forces 'if the convoy in question is deemed to be of such value that its destruction is of primary importance to the situation as a whole'.[13]

These instructions created an atmosphere of imminent action. Spring was creeping across the north and change was in the air. The *Tirpitz* was undergoing a transformation. Her atmosphere and moods, the outlook and way of life of her crew had, to a significant degree, been determined by the character of her master. On 21 February, Kapitän Topp left the ship for the last time. In keeping with tradition he was rowed ashore by midshipmen while the crew waved blue gingham sheets from the top decks until he was out of sight. He had been promoted to rear admiral and was heading off to a staff job in Berlin. His replacement was Kapitän zur See Hans Meyer, who lacked Topp's flamboyance. One sleeve of his uniform was pinned to his tunic. He had lost an arm fighting with the right-wing Freikorps against the Spartacist revolutionaries during the uprising of 1919.[14] After Topp, Adalbert Brünner, who served as Meyer's adjutant, found him 'a more quiet person. He was a man of genuine modesty and integrity.'[15]

The feeling that events were gathering pace intensified when, in March 1943, *Tirpitz* was ordered northwards to a base closer to the convoy routes. She stopped first in the familiar waters of Bogen Bay. Spring was early and Brünner remembered it as a 'sublimely beautiful day'. Basking in the welcome sunlight he felt he was on a 'Strength through Joy cruise in the high northern spring' rather than on a battleship. The stay was short. *Tirpitz* was soon on her way again and this time to a new and remote location. On 24 March

Hans Meyer

1943 she dropped anchor in Kaafjord, a narrow spur of Altafjord, a large inlet that pierced the coast of Finnmark, close to Norway's most Arctic extremity, the North Cape. It seemed to Brünner that it was hard to find a place much further away from what the sailors regarded as civilization. The nearest town was Alta, a much smaller and less sophisticated place than Trondheim. It was too far 'even for seasoned seamen to reach by foot', and even if they had, 'they would certainly not have found any kind of Reeperbahn there'.

On the other hand, there were signs that other excitements might be in the offing. By the end of March the surrounding waters were thick with warships. Alongside *Tirpitz* were the *Lützow* and the *Scharnhorst* which, after two attempts to break through from the Baltic to the North Sea had finally made it to northern Norway. The fleet was supplemented by destroyers and torpedo craft as well as eighty U-boats which had been made available for operations in the area. The force in Altafjord became known as the Northern Task Force and was put under the command of Admiral Oskar Kummetz.

In Britain, the drama of Raeder's departure and Dönitz's promotion had been followed closely. The concentration of forces in northern Norway led the Admiralty to an obvious conclusion. It seemed to Admiral Tovey that Dönitz was more inclined than his predecessor to take risks and there was now a greater prospect that *Tirpitz* and the other big ships might dare a convoy attack. There was even a chance that the enemy might 'venture all on a desperate breakout' into the Atlantic, a development that would not be unwelcome. Tovey felt that with the new circumstances came 'a chance for us to accept fleet action under conditions of exceptional favour'. In other words, there was now perhaps an opportunity for a full-blooded high seas battle.[16]

For *Tirpitz* to be tempted out, though, there had to be a target. After the successful arrival in Murmansk of the second half of convoy JW.51 following the Battle of the Barents Sea, the pressure from the Soviet Union to keep the supplies coming was unrelenting. Stalin's demanding voice was amplified by his ambassador in London, Ivan Maisky, whose tone and persistence grated on Churchill's nerves. On 9 January 1943, he told the Foreign Secretary Anthony Eden that 'Maisky should be told that I am getting to the end of my tether with these repeated Russian naggings and that it is not the slightest use trying to knock me about any more'.[17]

Even so, another small convoy, the fourteen-ship JW.52, sailed that month. The Arctic darkness kept air attacks to a minimum and the seas were unseasonably kind. The passage was swift and the escort kept the U-boats at bay, aided by the new direction-finding wireless reception equipment which intercepted submarine signals and pinpointed their whereabouts. All but one ship, which turned back early, reached the Kola Inlet safely on 27 January. After a two-day rest the three cruisers, which had shepherded them all the way through, escorted the returning convoy RA.52 home, losing one of the eleven ships to a U-boat on the way.

The next east-bound convoy, JW.53, was made up of twenty-eight ships and sailed from Iceland in mid-February. By now the darkness was receding and a stronger 'summer-scale' escort was thought necessary. The convoy was covered by three cruisers with a large force of bigger ships waiting at a distance to intervene if needed. This time heavy gales scattered the merchantmen. Twenty-two were rounded up and continued on their way. Despite a following pack of U-boats and occasional bombing raids, all reached port safely. The returning convoy was not so lucky. It was shaken apart in a heavy gale. U-boats closed in on the isolated merchantmen, sinking three, and another foundered in the wild seas.

The risks to the convoys mounted as the days grew longer. As well as the submarines and aircraft, the escorts now had to contend with the threat from *Tirpitz* and her companions, lurking in Altafjord. From now on, dispatching a convoy carried the risk of a clash between the escorts and the *Tirpitz* squadron. It was a prospect that Tovey was happy to consider if the battle took place at a meridian of the Allies' choosing, preferably west of Bear Island where the full power of the covering force could be applied without too much danger from aerial attack. That seemed unlikely, however. The expectation had to be that Dönitz would wait until the convoy was deep in the Barents Sea, and inside the Luftwaffe's striking range, before launching an attack.

Tovey's misgivings were reinforced by the behaviour of his Soviet allies. The Russians seemed to regard civility, let alone camaraderie, as a sign of weakness. In the first few months of 1943 they ground down the sympathy of their Allied partners with a campaign of obstruction. Two British wireless stations in northern Russia were closed down without explanation and RAF ground crews needed to service the aircraft that flew from bases in the area were refused entry.

The question of how far into the year to keep the convoys running was eventually decided by Dönitz. In March 1943, the Battle of the Atlantic approached its climax. Dönitz threw all his submarines into an effort to cut the transatlantic lifeline. The immensity of the odds dwarfed all other considerations. Every ship available was needed to stem the losses that the wolf packs were inflicting. The next planned outgoing and returning convoys were cancelled. Churchill explained the decision in a letter to Roosevelt, who had maintained firm pressure on Britain to keep the convoys sailing whenever possible. In the middle of March one of the biggest convoy battles of the war was fought in the North Atlantic. Dönitz concentrated a force of forty U-boats against convoys HX.229 and SC.122 sailing from New York. In two days, they sank seventeen ships. The disaster, wrote Churchill, was 'a final proof that our escorts are everywhere too thin. The strain on the British Navy is becoming intolerable.' Roosevelt was sympathetic. At the end of March, convoys to the Arctic were postponed and the ships that would have protected them were transferred from the Home Fleet to Western Approaches Command, which had responsibility for the Atlantic routes. It would be the autumn before another Arctic convoy set sail.[18]

On board *Tirpitz* and the other warships in Altafjord, the days of perpetual daylight dragged by. The commanders struggled to find new ways to lift the blanket of boredom. There were berry- and mushroom-gathering expeditions ashore. An athletics tournament, the Polar Championships, was mounted on a gravel playing field on the shore of Kaafjord. The truly desperate could enrol in a raffia-weaving course. None of these diversions was likely to prove satisfying for long. News of the destruction raining down on their homes was reaching the sailors, many of whom came from the industrial towns of the Ruhr. The commander of the *Scharnhorst*, Kapitän zur See Friedrich Huffmeier, noted the 'uncomfortable feeling we have that up here in the north we are much safer than are our loved ones, exposed as they are to constant bombing attacks'. Frustration stoked the urge to strike back. 'The desire to avenge these attacks on families and friends with the aid of the ships or in some other way is very widespread.'[19]

Back in Berlin, Dönitz was equally anxious to give the crews something to do. At last a target came to mind. Spitsbergen is a large, mountainous island of 15,000 square miles, part of the Svalbard archipelago, lying 450 miles north of the North Cape. The Norwegian and Russian communities that made a living working in the islands' coal mines had been evacuated at the start of the war. Since then it had been reoccupied by the Allies who set up a meteorological station at Barentsburg, monitoring weather, sea temperature, ice formations and the like and radioing reports back to Britain. It was a dismal place, a sprawl of huts and machinery, dotted with coal heaps, one of which had been set on fire in late 1941 and was still sullenly burning. In September 1943 it was manned by a force of 134 Norwegian soldiers, mostly former seamen who had received basic training in Scotland, together with nine officers and men from the Norwegian navy. Five British ratings and an RNVR liaison officer were also stationed there.

Spitsbergen was of minimal strategic importance. Its destruction hardly justified the large amounts of precious fuel that would be used to get the fleet there and back. Dönitz, however, considered an attack worthwhile as it 'gave the [*Tirpitz*] group and the destroyers attached to it a chance to work together'.[20]

The action was more like an exercise than a real operation of war. The risks were minimal. The fleet could be back in port by the time the British ships put to sea to catch them. The men on *Tirpitz* were nonetheless delighted when on 6 September, with Admiral Kummetz aboard, they put to sea together with *Scharnhorst* and an escort of ten destroyers. They had not been told their destination. The news that they were on their way to Spitsbergen did not dampen their spirits. 'Our excitement ran high,' remembered Adalbert Brünner. As they approached Barentsburg on 8 September, Kummetz ordered all the ships to run up the white ensign as a *ruse de guerre*. The deception was hardly necessary. The tiny force was in no position to resist the might of the two biggest ships in the German navy.

The garrison had been told that they would receive ample warning of any German attempt to take the base as it would be impossible for a major seaborne operation to go undetected. In the event of a landing, they were to destroy sensitive equipment and retreat to the interior. A raid by U-boats was thought more probable. The inhabitants had three 4-inch naval guns and and eight Bofors and Oerlikon anti-aircraft cannon with which to defend themselves.

On the night of 7 September, Esmond Dabner, a Navy code specialist, ate a supper of boiled beef and dumplings with the rest of the British team before retiring to bed in his hut at 11.30. Dabner was a quiet, scholarly man who had been quite content with his pre-war existence as a clerk with the Midland Bank. Like hundreds of thousands like him, the coming of war swept him from his comfortable obscurity into a world of peril and adventure. After his capture he wrote down his experiences in one of the wartime logs for British prisoners, sent out to PoW camps by the YMCA via the Red Cross in Geneva. On the first page he inscribed Lord Macaulay's famous words about the global effects of the ambitions of Frederick the Great: 'The evils produced by his wickedness were felt in lands where the name of Prussia was unknown, and in order that he might rob a neighbour whom he had promised to defend, black men fought on the coast of Coromandel, and red men scalped each other by the Great Lakes of North America.'

Reflecting on the fortunes of war and the strange circumstances in which he found himself, Dabner wondered if the British team, composed of 'a librarian, an insurance official, two commercial men and two bank clerks, who drew graphs by the light of the Midnight Sun' were the counterpart of those 'black men' and Spitsbergen was their Coromandel.

At 2.30 on the morning of Wednesday, 8 September he was woken by Duggie Arthur, another member of the British team, with the news that ships had been seen in the approaches to Barentsburg. The assumption was that they were British but the order had been given to sound the alarm. Dabner dressed and made his way to the mustering point at the wireless station. On his way he saw the ships in the distance and was 'somewhat shaken to hear gunfire'.[21] The party had their steel helmets but not their rifles and mountain packs which were stored in the research station. It looked as if they had left it too late to retrieve them. Dabner could see the ships looming in the bay now. It seemed to him that the wisest course of action would be to beat a rapid retreat. Instead, the light guns on the shore were pumping shells at two German destroyers, the Z29 and the Z33, which were rapidly approaching the dock.

'The inevitable reply to this was a hail of missiles which left us with no alternative but to lie down in a small gulley,' he wrote. On board *Tirpitz* the crew watched delightedly as the turrets of Anton and Bruno, Caesar and Dora swivelled, the muzzles of the 15-inch guns belched smoke and flame and the air wobbled as the shells reduced the shore installations 'to matchwood', according to Adalbert Brünner who was among the spectators.

Very soon the shore batteries were silenced, but not before they had managed to score some hits on the two destroyers, forcing Z33, the second in line, to falter and then turn away. Peering up from his gulley, Dabner saw 'the greater part of Barentsburg in flames'. Z29 had now docked and advance parties were swarming ashore, moving through the coal and slag heaps while the covering volleys from the destroyers whistled overhead. They 'proceeded to spread fire to such few places that had so far escaped it and to ferret out the occupants'. Two Arado seaplanes from *Tirpitz* flew back and forth spraying machine-gun bullets. Soon the defenders' fire slackened then stopped altogether. Engineer teams started to lay charges to demolish the settlement's installations.

Dabner and his companions saw that flames were creeping closer to an ammunition store near to their hiding place and decided it was time to move. They split up, heading for the higher ground. Dabner, together with his commander, Lieutenant Watson, Duggie Arthur and two Norwegians took cover in a disused mine entrance. Watson told Dabner to stay put and ran down the hill with Arthur to the research station which was still intact. Dabner emerged from the mine and watched them enter the building. He heard later that they had managed to destroy some records and put the transmitter out of commission. They sloshed petrol around the rooms, set fire to it then ran out of the building straight into the arms of the

Barentsburg

Germans. Dabner considered following them at a distance but 'there seemed little sense in all keeping close together, encouraging as that would have been'.

Looking down at the base he was 'very much aware of the hopelessness of our situation. Everything was burning. *Tirpitz* fired an occasional salvo from her big guns, not now towards Barentsburg, fortunately.' Instead they were concentrating their fire on the coal tips and oil depots. Some of the landing party had reached the slopes behind the settlement. Dabner decided that 'there was no alternative but to go to ground'. He returned to the mine and lay face down inside the entrance. The two Norwegians stood behind him. 'Two hand grenades settled our business,' he wrote. 'All three of us were hit. Looking up I saw four German soldiers some 6–8 yards away. It appeared to be time to go. We went.'

They were taken down the hill to the jetty at gunpoint, hobbling from their wounds. The journey 'seemed like a dream'. They had not gone far when Dabner had 'the unhappy experience of seeing the body of my good friend David Rae', one of the British party, lying on the ground. At the jetty they were put on a destroyer. Another Briton, Stan Johnson, was already aboard. He had been with Rae when he was shot but was 'not allowed to do anything for him'. Lieutenant Watson and Duggie Arthur arrived shortly after. Dabner's wounds were hurting him. He had more than a dozen grenade splinters in his legs. He was given treatment by 'a very pleasant German' who told him that they would be moving to the more spacious surroundings of the *Tirpitz*. Sure enough, a little later he was lashed to a stretcher and lowered into a launch flying a Red Cross flag where other casualties, including a badly wounded German, were waiting.

They drew alongside the huge flank of the battleship and were hauled aboard. Dabner took a final look back at the 'island of pointed mountains' where he had spent the last three months. Then he was hurried along the deck to the sound of clicking cameras as the crew snapped away, and down into a comfortable bed in the *Tirpitz*'s well-appointed hospital.

The ships did not linger. They were eager to reach the safety of Altafjord before a British force could mount a retaliatory operation. The Home Fleet did put to sea when news reached the Admiralty of the raid but it sooned turned back when it was accepted that there was no chance of an interception. The weather turned bad on the return but Brünner and his shipmates noted proudly that the ship barely seemed to notice. 'Our Toni Paula [as the crew affectionately nicknamed the ship] made its way sedately, even though she was under full steam, towards the Norwegian coast.' Some booty had found its way aboard, mostly Russian cigarettes. A mysterious chest seemed at first as if it might hold something more interesting. 'It looked amazing, with illegible Russian writing all over its tin cladding,' remembered Brünner. Once it was opened up, it was found to contain nothing but salt. It might have been a metaphor for the Spitsbergen operation. Despite the unimportance of the action, however, Brünner and the rest of the crew were in high spirits. 'Now there was something new to talk about on board,' he wrote. 'Nothing earth-shattering had occurred but *something* had happened.' As they neared their haven they were left wondering whether their adventure was not the prelude to 'a great endgame'.[22]

13

Madmen

The Spitsbergen raid was essentially a morale-raising exercise. It was also a provocation. It had the effect of drawing attention once again to the threat still posed by *Tirpitz*. Churchill needed no reminding. Throughout 1943 the ship had broken into his thoughts, often when it might be imagined there were greater matters at stake. On 16 February, he sent a sharp note to Pound at the Admiralty, Harris at Bomber Command and Mountbatten at Combined Operations, asking if they had 'given up all plans for doing anything to *Tirpitz* while she is at Trondheim? … it is a terrible thing that this prize should be waiting and no-one able to think of a way of winning it.'[1] It fell to Pound to reply on 15 April with a six-page situation report. There were in fact several plans, he reported. The navy was pressing forward with its midget submarines and human torpedoes and the RAF was experimenting with a new bomb – 'Highball' – designed by Barnes Wallis, which it was hoped could be put to use against the battleship. It was based on the same concept as his 'bouncing bomb' which would be used a month later in the raid on the Ruhr dams. None of these weapons, though, was ready for use and the problems of getting at *Tirpitz* were as great as ever. Slotted into her Faettenfjord anchorage, protected by flak, fighters and smokescreen, 'the ship could hardly be in a less vulnerable situation'.[2]

Churchill was not placated. On 1 May he told his scientific adviser Lord Cherwell that he was thinking of asking Pound for a monthly report on the anti-*Tirpitz* activities. 'This will keep things lively,' he promised.[3] A few days later another nagging missive was on its way. 'I trust all concerned are alive to the importance of sinking this ship,' he minuted the First Sea Lord, 'and that it is realised that reasonable losses must be risked in order to do so.'[4]

At this point it was the navy that felt the pressure for results most. Bomber Command was entering into the most terrible phase of its campaign to smash Germany from the air and Harris could reasonably argue that he had other priorities. The navy was also locked in its own mortal battle in the Atlantic. However, there was pride at stake. The failures to bring *Tirpitz* to action on the high seas or to blow her up in her anchorage rankled at the Admiralty, deepening the determination to finish the job.

By late summer it seemed that unorthodox tactics with unconventional weapons still carried the best hope of success. The gallant failure of Larsen and the charioteers in October 1942 had not dampened enthusiasm for human torpedoes and they would go on to be used in further operations in the Mediterranean and the Far East.

In the case of *Tirpitz*, though, it was time for midget submarines to have their chance. There were now two types in existence. The Welman was a one-man submarine developed by the SOE's Technical Section following a request from the Admiralty for new ideas on dealing with *Tirpitz*. It never seemed a very convincing weapon. An early version envisaged human propulsion with the operator pedalling the craft like a bicycle. Later models lacked a periscope and vision was restricted to glass panels in the small conning tower, which made navigation almost impossible.

X-Craft seemed a much better proposition. A prototype had been launched in conditions of great secrecy at Portsmouth in March 1942 and intensive trials and modifications had been going on ever since. They could travel almost a hundred miles submerged and carry two concrete detatchable charges, clamped port and starboard to the hull, each containing two tons of Amatol explosive – surely enough to penetrate even the *Tirpitz*'s far from soft underbelly. They were fifty-one feet long – small enough to reduce the chances of detection and sufficiently manoeuvrable to find a way through or around the mines and nets festooned about the battleship.

During the spring and summer of 1943 work continued on an attack plan. It would be carried out by teams drawn from the body of men who, like the charioteers, had answered the Admiralty's call for 'volunteers for hazardous operations'. The response had been good and a steady flow of officers and ratings had been put through special training at Portsmouth. They were a diverse bunch, ranging from seasoned merchant seamen to adventure-seeking playboys and included South Africans, Irishmen, Frenchmen and Australians, among them a young reserve officer called Maxwell Shean.

Shean was twenty-four and had been brought up in Perth, where his father taught him how to sail and build small boats. He was mechanically minded and was halfway through an engineering course at the University of Western Australia when war broke out. Shean had never been to Britain; nor had his immediate family, yet he 'felt a great affinity for England'. His uncle had fought in the Great War and been grotesquely disfigured by a wound to the face. Shean did not feel inclined to follow him into the colours. Then came the disaster of Dunkirk. 'You couldn't ignore that,' he said later. 'Until that time I had confidence [we could] keep the Germans at bay.'

He went with a friend to the Australian navy depot in Fremantle and tried to join up. They were told it would be better for them and the navy if they first finished their degrees. But their initiative had

Max Shean

214 · PATRICK BISHOP

made them restless. When an advertisment appeared calling for volunteers with sailing experience to be trained for anti-submarine operations they both applied. This time they were accepted and after initial training in Sydney were on their way to Britain aboard a refrigerator ship loaded with frozen lamb. Shean's first posting was as a sub-lieutenant to HMS *Bluebell*, an anti-submarine corvette, based in a Blitz-scarred Liverpool. At school and at home, the old country had been 'presented as a fairyland. Everything in England was beautiful. But Liverpool didn't look pretty at all. It looked desperate and I hated it.'[5]

Bluebell was on convoy duty, covering the sailings to and from Gibraltar. For fifteen months Shean endured the harrowing routine. 'I was homesick and I was seasick and those two don't go well together,' he remembered. 'I used to go up on the bridge with oilskins, sou'wester and a bucket. It was very hard to hold up your dignity as an officer when you go up there with a bucket in your hand.' The first trip was a 'dream run', and the U-boats left them alone. The return journey was different. Shean was on the middle watch, from midnight to four in the morning. 'The graveyard watch they called it. You turned in as soon as you had your supper and tried to get a bit of sleep.' It was during the pre-watch rest period that the U-boats would attack. 'You'd hear the explosion, hear the odd crump, and then ten seconds later the alarm bells would ring – action stations. You always slept in your clothes. You'd turn out of your bunk, put on your oilskins because it was always wet up top, dash up there and see a ship burning in the distance.'

Sometimes, as the nearest ship to the stricken vessel, they would race to pick up survivors. 'All merchant seamen had little red lights on their shoulders. You would see a forest of red lights. We would pull them out with boat hooks … grab them and haul them up.' They would 'finish up with a dozen chaps lying on deck vomiting'. Some would die and later be buried at sea. 'You couldn't hang around to get everyone. The captain had to decide to move on, otherwise you would be the target. It was very depressing.' Shean spent fifteen months with *Bluebell*. When he left he 'felt as though I was leaving home. I felt sort of homesick again.'

While ashore in Liverpool in mid-1942 he had seen an Admiralty Fleet Order calling for volunteers from officers and ratings for 'special and hazardous service'. It specified that they should be less than twenty-four years old, unmarried, good swimmers and 'of strong and enduring physique'. The order gave no more details of what the duty would entail and Shean had thought little of it. Back on board *Bluebell* the captain, Lieutenant Geoffrey Walker, told him that he intended to volunteer. 'Obviously he wanted a response to this,' he recalled. 'I thought as quickly as possible.' He was coming to the end of his time on *Bluebell*. He would soon be moved to another post. At least by volunteering he was able 'to choose my shift rather than where anybody else thought best so I said right, put my name down too please.'

Shean and Walker were called to HMS *Dolphin*, the home of the navy's submarine service in Portsmouth, for interview. Walker was rejected on the grounds that he could not be spared from convoy duty. Shean was accepted. By now he had been told that the mysterious new mission was connected with midget submersibles. He was going from hunting submarines to sailing in them.

Shean started his initial training in August 1942 at HMS *Dolphin*. It involved repeated practices with the Davis Submarine Escape Apparatus – the invention of Sir Robert Davis of Siebe, Gorman. This comprised an oxygen bottle strapped to the wearer's front and connected by tubes to a lung-like rubber breathing bag and a tight-fitting face mask. The flow was controlled by a tap. Trainees were placed into a diving tank about forty feet wide and thirty feet deep which was filled with tepid water, and made to carry out tasks while instructors watched through windows set in the side. The drill doubled as a psychological as well as a physical test. It was easy to panic as the tank flooded. Some volunteers soon realized they would never be able to control their fears and dropped out.

As the course progressed, they were allowed to know the basics of the mission they were training for. They were going to be sent to attack enemy ships in harbour. They also learned more about the craft they would be operating in. 'We were told that these small submarines, which were called X-Craft, were fitted with equipment to enhance their chances of entering and leaving an enemy harbour undetected and that provided we weren't detected we had a pretty good chance of successful attack and retreat. It wasn't a suicide mission. The risks were pretty high but the reward was great.'

John Lorimer was another of the assorted company of volunteers. He was tall and lean and blessed with a sense of the absurd, a valuable asset in the world he was joining. He was born in Kelso, the son of a Scottish doctor who had served in the navy in the previous war and later set up practice in Norfolk. Lorimer had tried for Dartmouth at the age of twelve but narrowly missed selection. In 1940, aged eighteen, he joined up as an ordinary seaman and spent six months on a destroyer shepherding convoys through the Channel, 'going very slowly as the Germans lobbed shells over', before being commissioned as a sub-lieutenant. Early in 1942 the Admiralty's appeal caught his eye. Almost seventy years later he could still not identify what it was that made him or his comrades respond. 'Perhaps we were all mad,' he said.[6]

The majority of those in training were officers but there were a substantial number of non-comissioned volunteers. Vernon 'Ginger' Coles had left a boring job as a toolmaker apprentice in a tin box factory in Reading to join the Royal Navy at the age of seventeen in July 1938. He had been in the thick of the Norway campaign on the destroyer *Faulknor*, and had seen more action in the Mediterranean. After a spell in Portsmouth qualifying as an engine room artificer (ERA) – the technicians who kept the navy moving – he felt that 'after all the excitement we had had in the *Faulknor* it was a bit boring to be stuck in a naval barracks not knowing what ship you were going to get on'. Egged on by a Glaswegian messmate and fortified by a session in the pub the pair signed up for the submarine service. After five trips to sea he was still in search of more excitement. In September 1942 he saw an appeal for ERA volunteers for special service. 'I looked at this and thought "Shall I or shan't I? Shall I or shan't I?" And in the end I thought, yeah, I'll have a go.' Like Lorimer – like everyone it seemed – he was unable to understand exactly why, when danger was already freely available, he chose to seek out more. It was out of 'excitement or stupidity, call it what you will,' he said many years later. 'When you're twenty-two years old, you look at life differently.'[7]

In the autumn of 1942 work was continuing on two prototypes, X-3 and X-4, developed at Varley Marine in their Hamble works, round the corner from Portsmouth. Command of X-3 had been given to Donald Cameron, a lieutenant in the Royal Navy Reserve. He was twenty-six, and past the official upper age limit, a detail the selectors chose to overlook. He was born in Carluke, in the Lanarkshire coalfields, and went to school at Shawlands Academy in Glasgow, leaving at seventeen to go to sea with a local shipping company, the Baron Line, where he earned a reputation as a brilliant navigator. He was commissioned in the Royal Naval Reserve in 1939 but brought a merchant marine officer's sometimes sceptical outlook to the service and its ways. He was serving on the submarine HMS *Sturgeon* when he volunteered for hazardous duties. Cameron never spoke about his reasons for doing so. To his son, Iain, he was 'a natural loner. That doesn't mean he wasn't perfectly gregarious on occasion but he preferred to be on his own and to be his own boss.'[8] He also had a romantic streak, reflected in his love of the Scottish Highlands and in the thoughtful and whimsical letters he wrote to his wife.

Cameron had spent much of 1942 in Portsmouth carrying out the secret initial trials on the prototype. He had been obliged to move out of the mess to escape the curiosity of his companions and had found digs in a large house on the Hamble belonging to a widow called Mrs Kilpatrick. Soon Cameron was ensconced and courting her eighteen-year-old daughter, Eve, a driver with the WRNS. They found they both liked the same things. 'We got on,' she remembered many years after their first meeting. 'He painted watercolours beautifully.'[9] Romance worked fast in wartime and they soon got engaged. The selection criteria had specified that candidates be single but the Admiralty was sensible enough not to interfere. They were married in June 1942.

By the end of 1942, the other prototype, X-4, was in the hands of Godfrey Place. Place was a regular RN officer among a host of RNVR reservists. He was the son of a barrister who had served in the

trenches and emerged with an MC and a DSO. At fourteen he was
sent to Dartmouth and come out top of his class. He had a reputation for mild eccentricity, 'the scruffiest naval officer I have ever
seen', according to Lorimer, with a habit of making off with other
people's kit. He was on the cruiser *Newcastle* when the war broke
out but joined the submarine service in 1941 and served in the
Mediterranean aboard *Urge* and *Una*. After a spell as liaison officer
in the Polish submarine *Sokol* he joined *Unbeaten* as first lieutenant
and won a Distinguished Service Cross after sinking the Italian
U-boat *Guglielmotti*.

As the summer of 1942 faded, the X-Craft operation moved
north. Real training was about to begin in the waters of Loch Striven,
a narrow seawater inlet plunging between the hills of the Cowal
peninsula in Argyllshire, that replicated the conditions of a
Norwegian fjord. On his way to the station for the train to Glasgow,
Max Shean walked past HMS *Victory* sitting in her place of honour
in a dry dock. He was wondering what he had let himself in for. 'I
thought, I'm not in the right group here. This is not me. I'm not that
sort of person.' As he approached the ship he saw that it had been
damaged by one of the many bombs the Germans dropped on
Portsmouth. He climbed down under the concrete plinth on which
the hull rested. Looking up, he noticed a 'fragment of the oak hanging off the keel'. He 'reached up and broke it off and stuck it in my
pocket … that was my treasure. [It] made me feel a little bit better.'

The 12th Submarine Flotilla, as the force was now called, was
billeted in the Kyles Hydropathic Hotel on the island of Bute. It was
a grey-stone Edwardian structure, overlooking the small fishing
village of Port Bannatyne, where in peacetime rheumatics had gone
for the curative effects of the waters. There were fifty in the group,
and, despite Shean's fears, no easily definable 'sort of person'. What
did bind them together was a certain restlessness, a taste for adventure and a willingness to take mighty risks.

The early exercises had followed the usual process of trial and
error with the usual quota of hair-raising accidents. On 4 November
1942, John Lorimer took *X-3* for a training dive with two other
volunteers, Sub-Lieutenants 'Taffy' Laites and Len Gay. Training

took place in a deserted stretch of Loch Striven, which was hidden from Port Bannatyne across the water by a convenient headland. They boarded the craft, wriggled through the hatch and stood by to submerge. Lorimer opened the valves to flood the buoyancy tanks and, in a disconcerting symphony of gurgling and gulping noises, the hull began to sink. As they slid below the surface, water started to cascade through the hull. The valve shutting off the induction pipe that vented diesel fumes when running the engine at periscope depth had stuck open.

Things happened quickly after that. Lorimer recalled that as they struggled to staunch the flow, X-3 tipped up and 'went down arse first into 120 feet of water'. He ordered the ballast tanks to be blown, which would have taken them safely back to the surface. But as the others scrabbled for the spanner to turn the wheel, it dropped between the deck boards and into the bilges. The vertiginous descent continued, with water coursing through the control room and into the engine room in the stern. 'X-3 was terribly badly designed, as it had the batteries aft,' Lorimer recalled. As the seawater mixed with the battery acid, clouds of poisonous chlorine gas began to form, and soon the control room was filling up.

At the same time a shudder ran through the craft and the lights went out. They had hit the bottom of Loch Striven. Lorimer heard himself telling the others, in a remarkably calm voice, to don their Davis Submarine Escape Apparatus (DSEA). They had one set each, plus a spare. These would save them from the poisonous effects of the chlorine gas and give them enough breathing time while the hull filled up and the water pressure inside and out equalized sufficiently for them to get out.

The important thing was not to panic. Panic made you breathe faster and rapid breathing burned precious oxygen. The others sat as still as they could and tried to control their bodies and their imaginations. Lorimer unscrewed the hatch cover, opened the seacocks and sat back as the seawater bubbled in and crept up around them. 'I was quite convinced I was going to die,' he remembered later. 'I was sitting in this bloody thing for an hour as the water was coming up, waiting until we could open the hatch. I was thinking, well, my parents will get a telegram tomorrow, telling them it's the end of their little son.' He realized with some surprise that he 'wasn't frightened.'[10]

It took forty minutes for the compartment to fill up. They sat there in the dark listening to the beat of blood in their ears struggling to keep their breathing shallow, regular and economical. They were 120 feet under the sea, and they felt the water clasp them tight as it crept up their bodies. Before he was completely submerged, Lorimer removed his mouthpiece and gave the pair their final instructions. Gay was to go first, then Laites.

Eventually, when the compartment was three-quarters full, the pressure inside and outside the hull equalized and the water stopped rising. Gay stood up and pushed at the hatch cover overhead. It was hard work and he was down to his last few lungfuls of oxygen before he forced it open. Water rushed in. He pulled himself through the hole and shot upwards in a cloud of bubbles. Now it was Laites's turn. Lorimer could see nothing. He waited for him to push past but there was no movement. He began a groping search of the control room and his hands closed on an inert figure. Laites's oxygen had given out. Lorimer's mind raced furiously in what he later called a 'miserable debate' with himself. His own oxygen was almost exhausted. If he tried to help Laites he would use up what was left in his cylinder manhandling him through the hatch. If he abandoned him, though, he would save himself.

Lorimer made his decision. He remembered the spare apparatus. He tore Laites's useless oxygen set from his face and hurriedly attached the new one. He switched on the supply but it seemed to make no difference. Laites didn't move. He hooked his hands under his thighs and pushed him towards the hatch. As he shoved him through, the oxygen set was torn off. At least he was free now and on his way to the surface. Lorimer followed him, then kicked towards the pale ceiling of sunlight tilting and shimmering overhead. 'I was unconscious I think when I went up,' he recalled, 'but I held up, and the gunner's mate who pulled me out said "You're bloody lucky, sir, because there was only one 'guff' of oxygen left in your cylinder". It was forty-eight hours later, when the adrenalin had worn off, that the full scale of the drama struck him. He had been strangely calm throughout the ordeal but now 'by God ... I was shit-scared'.[11] Gay and Laites put in for a transfer. Lorimer, though, decided to stay on. After a week's leave he was back in training.

The following month, *X-4* suffered a fatal mishap. Godfrey Place and his crew were on exercise in the Sound of Bute when a storm blew up and Sub-Lieutenant Morgan Thomas was washed out of the W&D compartment and drowned. The waves swamped the compartment, tipping the craft almost perpendicular and trapping Place and ERA Willie Whitley for two hours.

It was a relief when, in January 1943, the new, modified X-Craft began arriving from the Vickers-Armstrongs yard in Barrow-in-Furness. The prototypes had not inspired much confidence when the volunteers got their first look at them. Ginger Coles had been taken with some fellow volunteers to see *X-4*, lying in an unassembled state in a heavily guarded workshop in Portsmouth Dockyard. 'Our stomachs turned upside down when we saw the size of her,' he recalled. Lorimer had reacted the same way, 'thinking how incredibly small everything looked and wondering how such a frail craft was expected to cross the North Sea'.[12] The improved versions seemed quite impressive, however, and Lorimer, who had been to Barrow-in-Furness to take delivery of *X-6*, judged that 'Vickers had done a good job'.

They were indeed midgets, far smaller than the navy's conventional submarines. S- and T-class subs, of the type they would work alongside, were twenty-seven and forty times heavier respectively. The only area in which X-Craft matched their big sisters was in their ability to reach safely the same sort of depths. Otherwise they were slower, managing only a maximum speed of 6.5 knots on the surface and 5.5 knots submerged against a T-class submarine's fifteen knots above the water and nine knots below.

From the outside, an X-Craft looked like a cigar tube, tapered at both ends. Unlike a conventional submarine, it lacked a conning tower. A narrow deck ran along the top of the hull, pierced by a forward and aft hatch and cluttered with lockers and shackles. It submerged and surfaced by means of three ballast tanks, fore, aft and amidships. They were filled by opening seacocks and pumped out with compressed air cylinders. It could go down as far as 300 feet. Below that depth the seams would burst and the hull crumple, squeezed flat by the pressure of the water. Submerged, it was propelled by an electric fan motor driven by two large batteries. On the surface it was pushed along by a diesel engine, the same type that powered London double-decker buses, which also recharged the electric batteries. Aquaplanes were used to manoeuvre the craft up and down when cruising below the surface and small trimming tanks could be emptied and filled to keep it straight and level. The periscope was slender to reduce the chances of detection. It allowed the captain a limited view of what was going on around him. There was a second, short periscope, used to observe and direct the diver as he went about cutting the nets. Unlike conventional submarines, X-Craft had no guns or torpedo tubes. Their sole weapons were the two charges or mines, each weighing four tons in total including explosive, which fitted snugly over the curved sides of the hull. They were released by turning a small wheel inside the control room. As they came away, a copper strip peeled off, unsealing a buoyancy chamber which filled up with water, sinking the charge to the bottom. There it would lie until exploded by a clock timing device, set before release.

You could fit five X-Craft alongside the hull of a T-class submarine with plenty of room to spare. All submarines were cramped but these felt like coffins and great self-control was needed to suppress the claustrophobia that most felt at their first submersion. Even with the improvements, it took great deftness to manoeuvre around the tiny control room amidships where the four-man crew had to live and work. The only place where it was just possible to stand upright was under the dome of the periscope. Elsewhere, the widest point was only four and a half feet high or wide and the crew scrambled and crawled to get around.

The captain sat at a tiny chart table next to the periscope, from where he navigated the craft through the shoals and skerries, nets and minefields they would meet on the way to the target. The first officer's post was an arm's length away at the after end of the control room, monitoring the gauges, wheels and levers that controlled the direction, speed and trim of the craft. The ERA shifted around, maintaining the instruments and engines. With the diesel and electric motors, the wiring and the mechanics, there were an extraordinary number of things to go wrong. To reach the diesel engine in the stern he had to crawl through a two-foot-wide hatch, lying flat on the fuel tank to work in spaces where clearance was only a few inches. The diver, meanwhile, helped out with all the jobs when not performing his specialized task.

The suffocating proximity, the intense interdependence on which success and survival depended, engendered an egalitarian atmosphere. According to John Lorimer, it ran 'through the whole submarine service … from the captain down to the ship's cook you're all equally responsible. You make one mistake and you kill the rest. You're a great team of chums and you call each other by Christian names.'[13]

Sleeping, eating and ablutions arrangements were all improvised and spartan. There was room for one man, two at a pinch, to stretch out on the boards that covered the big batteries, now shifted to the bow. In the control room amidships, there was a gap on the port side. As Max Shean discovered, by putting your head under the chart table and arranging your legs around the pipes and pumps it was possible to get some rest. 'For all the inconvenience of this bunk,' he wrote, 'the few odd hours, or even minutes, which I was able to spend in this position were golden.'[14] They ate prepared meals, heated up on a carpenter's double-boiler glue pot. The head was an Elsan, located in the wet and dry (W&D) compartment in the forward section from which the diver left and re-entered. The air they breathed was cleaned by a Protosorb filter which was reasonably efficient. Submariners tried to be as fastidious as conditions allowed. But life below the waves was not for hygiene fetishists.

Crews would be spending a lot of time aboard. To carry out the attack, the X-Craft first had to get to their targets. Various means of transporting them to Norway were examined, including dropping them from aircraft. It was decided in the end to tow them to the target area behind full-sized submarines. The voyage would take at least five days using passage crews for the first stage, leaving the operational crews fresh for the attack.

In the wardroom at the Kyles Hydro on Bute, renamed HMS *Varbel* after Commanders Cromwell Varley and T. I. S. 'Tizzy' Bell, who had designed and supervised the building of *X-3* and *X-4*, the young men smoked, drank weak, wartime beer and wrestled with the problems that the training exercises continually threw up. They had also been given the use of Ardtaraig House, a shooting lodge at the northern end of Loch Striven. Eventually it was leased to the navy and became 'Varbel II', and the flotilla's diving training centre. 'Life there was much more informal and rural,' remembered Peter Philip, one of the team, 'with cows, sheep and poultry on our doorstep, home grown dairy produce and vegetables, and mugs of beer and long yarns round the roaring log fire at night.'[15] Bell was a fitness enthusiast and encouraged long, early-morning runs. Shean joined the runners but recorded that there was 'another school of thought that argued that the best way to train for life in a poorly-ventilated submarine was to take all the rest available and to spend off-duty time becoming accustomed to a self-generated tobacco fug before the log fire in the officers' mess, sipping gin'.[16]

Eve Cameron, by now 'rather pregnant and fat', was given leave from the WRNS to spend a few weeks with her husband. They were given a room in a gamekeeper's cottage on the 'Varbel II' estate. The project was still top secret and those engaged in it were forbidden from discussing it even with their spouses. Eve had picked up enough during her travels around Portsmouth to have a shrewd idea of what was involved. One Sunday morning they were sitting in their little room. Don was reading the paper which contained an article on the Japanese navy's midget submarines. She could not resist telling her husband 'I know what you're up to.'[17]

For the attack to succeed, they had to find a way through the nets that protected *Tirpitz*. It was standard practice on both sides to drape steel mesh around larger surface vessels if they were at anchor for anything but the shortest periods. The X-Craft had to penetrate an outer perimeter of anti-submarine netting, then a curtain of nine-inch steel hoops suspended from buoys like chain mail to stop torpedoes. There was no question of cutting through the anti-torpedo netting: the hydraulic shears available were not strong enough. The available intelligence suggested that the German nets were the same as the Royal Navy's which only stretched about ten feet below the draught of a ship. It was thought to be relatively easy simply to steer underneath them.

The submarine nets could hang much lower, however, too deep for an X-Craft to dive beneath. They were made of thick steel wire woven together in a diamond pattern. These would have to be cut. It was the diver's job to exit the craft, retrieve the cutter stowed in a locker on the front deck and shear through the wire. He then shepherded the X-Craft through the gap before rejoining the boat. He entered and left the craft via the Wet and Dry compartment. This was a watertight tank situated below the forward hatch, just big enough for a man to crouch inside.

The diver first had to struggle into his two-piece rubber and canvas diving suit. Then he strapped his breathing apparatus onto his chest and inserted the mouthpiece which, to Max Shean, always 'felt that it was lubricated with the previous wearer's saliva'. He then climbed into the tank and began to pump in water from the number two main ballast tank directly below into the W&D compartment.

Shean had done his initial diving training in Loch Striven in an old-fashioned, all-over suit complete with metal and glass helmet and brass breast and back plates. He had quite enjoyed the experience, taking the opportunity to collect scallops from the loch floor to augment the 'Varbel' rations. Initial anxieties were calmed by the shimmering light of the sky through the water above which was 'always friendly and always there. If things go wrong you can come to the surface'. The first time he experienced the inside of a mock-up W&D suspended from a pontoon, he hated it. 'You're filled up with water and you're in this steel compartment. It's pitch dark and you're under water. It's the most unnatural set of conditions you can imagine … at that time you wish you'd never been born.'[18]

As the 'water rose to visor level there was a natural tendency to panic'. He resisted it successfully only to feel another 'shock to my feeling of well-being' as the water covered his head. It was a relief when the tank was full and the water pressure equalized. When he pushed the overhead hatch to make his escape, though, 'nothing happened'. After forcing himself to relax he tried again and 'suddenly all was light. It was like Wagner's Sunrise that preceded Siegfried's Rhine Journey.' He 'floated up, shut the hatch … and swam to the surface'. Soon afterwards he had to reverse the process. Getting back in was no easier than getting out. The outside hatch opened smoothly enough but closing it again 'was the most difficult act of all'. The diver was weightless and had to wedge himself inside the walls of the W&D and struggle to force down the lid. Eventually he was able to close the hatch and open the valves to pump the compartment dry.[19]

The attack had initially been scheduled for March when the Arctic night would still be long enough to provide protection. The ninth of March was considered the last practical date when the mission could go ahead. As well as the cover of darkness there would be a glimmer of moonlight to help the X-Craft on their final approach.[20] But as the date drew nearer it was clear that more preparations were needed. Several practical problems remained. Among them were the difficulties the crews were having with the anti-submarine nets. As the summer arrived, the craft were taking too long to wriggle through the holes cut by the divers. Several divers had blacked out during exercises. One had died. On 31 May, Sub-Lieutenant David Locke surfaced after a test dive in X-7, gave a thumbs-up sign then disappeared, the victim, apparently, of 'Oxygen Pete'. 'It upset me no end,' said John Lorimer. 'He and I had joined the Navy together.'

Further exercises were cancelled until a safer method of net-cutting had been found. Shean was summoned by Commander D. C. Ingram, one of the triumvirate who ran the 12th Submarine flotilla, and told to take command of X-5 and work out a solution to a problem that now looked as if it might scupper the entire operation. He was to 'concentrate on net cutting until you've solved it'.[21] He relished the job. It was 'interesting, challenging, exciting and sufficiently uncertain to inspire the boldest with a sense of care and awareness'. He would be working with Sub-Lieutenant Henry Henty-Creer, as his number two. Henty-Creer was another Australian, the son of a naval officer. He was twenty-two years old, sandy-haired and dashing. He had worked in the film business before signing up for the navy in the autumn of 1940. His last assignment had been in Canada shooting *49th Parallel*, a Michael Powell and Emeric Pressburger production starring Laurence Olivier and Leslie Howard, designed to persuade an as yet undecided America to join the war. After selection for officer training, he passed out near the top of his intake and volunteered for hazardous duty.

Apart from their Australian birth and a shared taste for adventure, the two men had little in common. Where Shean was scientific and methodical, Henty-Creer was romantic and rash. While Shean kept to himself in the mess, 'Henty' was the life and soul of the party, amusing senior officers with jokes and tales of his colourful and glamorous life. Opposites often worked well together in wartime. Men who in peacetime would have been unlikely to meet, or if they had, given each other a wide berth, frequently formed effective teams when flung together by the crisis, supplementing and cancelling out each other's strengths and weaknesses. This was not to be the case with Shean and Henty-Creer.

They started their task by interviewing all the divers. Shean discovered that cutting the nets was relatively easy. The difficulty was doing it in such a way that the X-Craft could then slip through without fouling on the wires. He devised a means of making the minimum number of cuts to produce the maximum-sized hole, and a drill by which the diver made hand signals to the captain, watching through the auxiliary periscope, to ensure the craft was trimmed straight and level and less liable to snag when it passed through.

Soon afterwards, with Henty-Creer, an ERA and a stoker, he boarded *X-5* to put it to the test. Henty-Creer volunteered to make the first attempt. 'That was typical,' said Shean many years later. His partner, he said, 'was a very proud fellow' who always needed to be 'centre, stage-front'. Shean let him have his way. They dived to thirty feet and Henty-Creer struggled into his diving suit and climbed into the W&D compartment. Above, on the grey surface of the loch, a naval rescue boat with a diver on board looked out for any signs of trouble.

At first all went well. The operation of the W&D valves could be monitored from outside and Henty seemed to be doing the right things in the right order, beginning with pumping the compartment full of water. Then Shean noticed that he was 'starting to do some strange things with the valves'. He took over and reversed the valves so that the water could be pumped out again. When he opened the door 'there was Henty obviously having a fit so I pulled him into the control room, pulled out his mouthpiece and opened his visor and got him breathing ...'. There was something wrong with the breathing apparatus. Shean took the craft to the surface, put Henty-Creer on board the rescue boat and helped him out of his suit. He made a rapid recovery and insisted he was fit to carry on the exercise. This time he would keep the craft steady while Shean did the cutting.

Shean managed to exit the W&D compartment without difficulty. First he signalled to Henty-Creer to trim the craft level. Then he retrieved the hydraulic cutter from its locker and began work. 'With a steady hiss the blade moved slowly out from its guide toward the wire held in the hook. When they met, the blade continued as if there were no wire. Crunch, snap and the wire fell apart.'[22] He made three more cuts. The hole widened and Shean watched X-5 slip through, 'nice and easily, nice and slow. All around the green water was very clear and it was a magnificent sight to see.'[23] When he emerged from the W&D compartment, Henty-Creer told him that the whole operation had taken twelve minutes.

When the other crews followed the procedure they had equal success. The way was now clear for the final preparations for the attack. In July 1943 the flotilla shifted its base, this time to Loch Cairnbawn, on the west coast of the Scottish Highlands. From there, six X-Craft would set off on their extraordinary mission. The plan for the operation, codenamed 'Source', was now approaching completion. *Tirpitz*, which had settled into its anchorage at Kaafjord and looked liable to remain there for some time, was the main target. But *Scharnhorst* was also in the area. With any luck the X-Craft might dispose of Hitler's last operational battle cruiser as well as his last battleship.

They would be towed into place by six S- and T-class submarines, which, after slipping their charges, would stand by to pick up the crews when they returned from their mission. The submarines also had a secondary mission. If the attacks caused *Tirpitz* to run for the safety of the high seas they would be there to cut her off.

Each X-Craft would be manned by a passage crew during the initial voyage. They would then hand over to the operational crew travelling aboard the mother submarine, which would carry out the attack. Tests were conducted to monitor the endurance of men cooped up in a tiny craft for long periods. 'We did a six-day trial to see if we could stand it,' remembered John Lorimer. 'Just tooling around the Isle of Bute, six days non-stop.' They were fortified with Benzedrine pills, which 'kept you awake if you wanted to be awake but if you wanted to go to sleep you could sleep'.[24]

Towing trials with HMS *Tuna* revealed that the passage crew's task would not be easy. Shean found that 'in the first minutes we had bother keeping the X-Craft under control'. It had a tendency to 'porpoise, that is to go deep until they get to the stage where the tow pulls them up again, then … break surface and go deep again'. As it reared and plunged, the crew and any loose objects were 'apt to slide along the deck'. They eventually found that by constantly trimming the tanks and keeping to a depth of forty or fifty feet it was possible to maintain fairly smooth progress. Preventing 'porpoising', though, was going to need constant vigilance.

Another source of trouble was the tow cable itself. Despite the ingenuity that went into the design of midget submarines, little thought was given to this most basic aspect of the operation. The debacle of the chariot operation the previous year had revealed painfully the fact that the fate of the mission could hinge literally on the fastening linking the weapon to the towing vessel. Yet at this stage the only material made available for the vital task of towing was manila hemp. The success of the mission was to a large extent dependent on a 600-foot length of rope. It was clear from the outset that the manila tows were less than trustworthy. According to Vernon Coles, during the final exercises they were 'breaking wholesale … they didn't last more than four or five days. We persevered with these things. They put bigger ones on and they still broke.'[25] The crews were told 'not to worry because the towing submarine had a spare cable.' It did not take much imagination to envisage the difficulties of reuniting with the towing submarine if the cable snapped, or the problems of connecting a new line in anything but perfect conditions.

Everyone knew that more robust and reliable cables existed. The RAF had developed nylon ropes with the strength and elasticity to tow gliders. Only three reached the flotilla. When they arrived, Don Cameron made sure he got one for X-6. The others went to X-5 and X-10 while the rest had to make do with something that would have been recognizable to the crew of the Victory or the Golden Hind.

In July, the final crew selection was made for passage and operation crews. Don Cameron and John Lorimer would be sailing with Sub-Lieutenant Richard Kendall as diver and ERA Edmund Goddard as engineer in X-6. Dickie Kendall was slim and athletic, just twenty-one, a public schoolboy who had joined the navy as a rating at the outbreak of war and served on a destroyer before being commissioned and moving to submarines. He had impressed Cameron who had managed to wrest him away from X-10, where he was originally supposed to go. Eddie Goddard, who had been educated at St Edward's School, Oxford, was notable for his jet-black hair, good nature and extraordinary ability to keep things working. For six weeks they lived side by side with the other crews in a large house near the loch, repeating drills and exercises until they had the unthinking familiarity of instinct. Godfrey Place, now a married man, having just wed his sweetheart, Anthea Tickler, a Wren who worked in the coding office at 'Varbel', would lead X-7 on the attack. Two Australians, Brian 'Digger' McFarlane, a short, cheerful regular navy officer from Victoria, and Ken Hudspeth, were in operational charge of X-8 and X-10.

Initially it seemed that Max Shean's training had been in vain. To his annoyance, Henty-Creer would be captain of X-5 on the attack. Shean believed that 'Henty' had used his 'winning personality' to 'obtain command'. He had 'a flair for top billing and would not be happy playing second fiddle to anyone for long.'[26] Then a last-minute decision by two French crew members to pull out meant Shean would go after all. Together with Vernon Coles he got what the navy called a 'pierhead jump', landing aboard *X-9* under Terry Martin.

By the end of August a date had been set and all further leave was cancelled. Operation Source would begin on 20 September. At this time of the year, nights were long enough to provide some cover but the Arctic autumn with its storms and gales had not yet set in.[27]

Contingency plans were made in case *Tirpitz* moved to Narvik or Trondheim but three PRU flights on 14, 15 and 21 August reported that she was in her 'usual berth' in Kaafjord, where she had been for the last five months. Not only *Scharnhorst*, but the pocket battleship *Lützow* was there, too. Work intensified on amassing the latest data on the defences the X-Craft would have to contend with. Photographic reconnaissance was reinforced by the evidence of agents on the ground. Early in August, at the instigation of MI6 and the Norwegian intelligence service in London, a twenty-three-year-old student called Torbjørn Johansen was sent to the area from his home in Tromsø. He took the coastal steamer to Alteidet then cycled more than sixty miles to Alta. The road took him past Kaafjord and the *Tirpitz*, *Scharnhorst* and *Lützow*. He hid among the rocks and undergrowth of the hillside and hurriedly sketched locations, net arrangements and the positions of surrounding gun emplacements. His sharp eyes caught a detail that would prove vital. The double anti-submarine net that was supposed to close the entrance to the fjord was left partly open on the south-eastern side to allow ships to come and go.

Johansen was also tasked with trying to obtain water samples from Kaafjord to establish its salinity and buoyancy. With extraordinary coolness he set off in a boat, equipped with a rod and a set of containers. 'He went all round the fjord fishing and secretly scooping up samples,' remembered another young member of the Tromsø resistance, Terje Jacobsen. 'Every time he caught a fish the Germans watching him from the ships' rails applauded.'[28] Johansen returned to Tromsø where his brother Einar operated the clandestine radio post. The basic information was radioed back to Britain.

The maps and samples went by courier to Stockholm, then on to London.

Unknown to him, another agent was also operating in the area. Torstein Raaby had established his resistance credentials while working in the meteorological station on Jan Mayen Island in the winter of 1941–2 and had used the cover to send reports of German reconnaissance flights and submarine movements to Britain. He had moved to Tromsø where he operated a clandestine radio station but fled to Sweden after a tip-off that the Gestapo were onto him. In March 1943 he reached Britain and spent four months training before being sent back by the Admiralty to conduct close surveillance of the German ships in the Alta area. He was landed by Norwegian submarine south of Trondheim, equipped with eight special transmitter-receiver sets and a large bundle of cash, and made his way north.

In Alta he teamed up with an old friend, Karl Rasmussen, who worked in the municipal roads department, and Harry Pettersen, who ran a taxi service in the town. Much of Pettersen's trade was ferrying junior officers back and forth to *Tirpitz* and their chatter helped to build the picture of the routines, dispositions and atmosphere on board. The town had five thousand inhabitants, small enough for the two men to know who they could trust. There was no shortage of informants. Local women boarded *Tirpitz* every day to clean and work in the galleys. They noted new developments and monitored the notices on the bulletin board. The information was collated and fed to Raaby, whom Rasmussen had fixed up with a job in the roads department. At night he sent his reports via a transmitter hidden in his office, which he hooked up to an aerial conveniently erected by a German officer billeted next door.[29]

All was set for the final preparations. On Sunday, 5 September, the X-Craft were winched on board the flotilla's depot ship HMS *Bonaventure* to be provisioned and fuelled and fitted with their side charges. As the charges were being fitted to *X-6*, sparks from a welder's torch started a fire on deck. The workforce fled in all directions and it was left to John Lorimer to find a hose and douse the blaze – unnecessarily, as it turned out, for a detonator was needed for the explosive to go up. That evening the crews received their first detailed briefing on their targets.

It was the first time they had been officially informed of the ultimate purpose of all their exhausting and dangerous preparations. Most of them had already guessed the targets but it was nonetheless a solemn moment. They were about to attempt one of the boldest strokes of the naval war. Success would bring them fame and glory. It would also make a large and measurable contribution to the war effort. Lorimer wrote later about the sense of 'tremendous responsibility' that descended on the crews. 'If they succeeded in destroying or crippling the *Tirpitz*, the British Home Fleet could give its protection to the U-boat-haunted Atlantic convoys and the lives of thousands of merchant seamen might be saved.'[30] The air of arousal and apprehension that precedes a great adventure hung over the base. 'The adrenalin started flowing,' remembered Ginger Coles. 'The boats were ready, the crews were ready ... everyone was keen to go.'[31]

On 7 September, a PRU Spitfire took off from Vaenga airfield near Murmansk, where the Russians had granted the RAF facilities, and headed to Kaafjord to confirm that *Tirpitz* was where it should be. Instead of the familiar outlines, the pilot saw a much smaller shape in the water which he identified as the *Lützow*. The news caused alarm when it reached London the following morning. As the Admiralty's intelligence staff sifted the possible scenarios, *Tirpitz* was bombarding the shore installations of Spitsbergen. It took a few hours before they learned of the operation. The question now was whether the force would return to Altafjord or head for Narvik or Trondheim. Another flight on 9 September gave no clue. *Lützow* still sat inside *Tirpitz*'s old berth. It was only on Friday, 10 September that a PRU Spitfire sighted the battleship and the rest of the squadron safely back in their old anchorages. Operation Source was set in motion.

The Commander of Submarines, Admiral Claude Barry, flew to Loch Cairnbawn, anxious to be there to 'witness the start of this great enterprise'. He invited the captains of the operational and passage crews to dine with him that night on the *Titania*, the depot

234 · PATRICK BISHOP

ship for the big submarines towing the X-Craft. The navy's social codes may have dissolved during the eighteen months of training, but they were back in evidence on the eve of battle. 'The officers had a wonderful party in the wardroom,' remembered Ginger Coles, 'but not we people on the lower deck.' Instead, the six ERAs were given the use of 'a little cowshed on the beach where a barrel of beer was put and a Naafi manager and we had mud up to our ankles. That was our farewell party to go on the attack.'[32]

When the hilarity generated by alcohol and excitement had subsided fears and doubts edged in. Ralph Mortiboys, the fourth member of Henty-Creer's crew on X-5, missed the cowshed party. A premonition had warned him he would not return from Kaafjord and he stayed aboard *Bonaventure* to write to his widowed mother.[33] Don Cameron had been keeping a log of the preparations for Operation Source. It was intended for Eve, now back in Portsmouth with their seven-month-old son, 'for your enjoyment I hope, and for Iain's when he is old enough to take an interest in such matters'. The talk at Admiral Barry's dinner had been 'very optimistic, perhaps a trifle too much so'. He emerged from it into a 'lively, clear night, moon almost full', promising 'good weather ahead, thank God'. After a few more drinks with his comrades he turned in 'for my last night in a comfortable bed'.

The following day, the good weather that Cameron hoped for failed to materialize. There was a strong south-westerly breeze and the sea was choppy. He brought in X-6 to complete victualling and congratulated himself on having secured one of the 'extra strong' nylon towing ropes. He made out his will and visited the paymaster 'in case something goes wrong'. He felt, he confessed, 'rather sheepish but best to be on the safe side'. There was a last flurry of chart and photograph consultations before a quiet lunch. Then came the final inspection of his boat before Lieutenant 'Willie' Wilson and the passage crew went aboard. At 4 p.m. they led the flotilla out of the loch. Cameron looked back at his native land from the conning tower of the towing submarine, HMS *Truculent*. As they rounded the point and headed for the open sea he felt 'slightly depressed' that he had mislaid a lucky red cap. He comforted himself with the reassuring presence of a little wooden dog, 'Bungay', Eve's first present to him, which he always carried in his pocket. 'Why should I, a product of modern civilization, be affected by such things?' he wondered. 'No logic in it, but there it is. I look at the familiar hills and islands and wonder when I shall see them again. Said a little prayer for all of us darling ...'

14

The Great Adventure

One by one, over the next eighteen hours, the submarine pairs made their way out to sea. They would be travelling on the same course, in parallel and ten miles apart. The route would take them north, leaving Cape Wrath and the Scottish mainland to starboard, passing between the Faroes and the Shetland Islands then turning north-east towards Norway's Arctic coast.

Admiral Barry went out in *Bonaventure*'s launch to wave them off and wish them a 'grand trip'. He regarded the expedition as 'undoubtedly one of the most hazardous enterprises undertaken in [the] war'. He recalled later that 'any doubts I might have entertained about its outcome could not possibly have survived the infectious confidence of these young men who were just leaving us. They were like boys on the last day of school, their spirits ran so high.'[1] The crews did nothing to dispel this fantasy. Lieutenant Martin Jupp, the captain of HMS *Syrtis*, towing *X-9*, had brought along an old-fashioned car horn which he honked from the conning tower as they left. When Barry came alongside and called out 'good luck and a safe return' he gave a few more blasts and shouted back 'Thank you sir. If we have any trouble we'll take a taxi.'[2]

There were a few initial dramas as the passage crews adjusted to the business of steering while being dragged fifty or sixty feet below the waves by a 200-yard-long line attached to the parent ship on the surface. Their work was uncomfortable and exhausting. Towing vessel and charge never seemed to move smoothly together. In rough weather the X-Craft slid up and down as the submarine negotiated the peaks and troughs of the oncoming or following seas, sending everything that was not tied down tumbling around the control room and pitching the crew against the many sharp and hard surfaces.

As there was no need for a diver, it had been decided that a crew of only three would suffice. This, it soon became clear, was a mistake. The weight of work meant there was little time for rest or to maintain the interior, which needed constant wiping down to prevent electrical failures. Of the two men on duty, one spent his time watching the dials on the ballast tanks, the depth gauges and the bubble of the inclinometer which showed the angle of the hull, for any deviation from the norm. Failure to react quickly could easily result in catastrophe. The other was kept busy steering and checking and maintaining the circuits and motors.

In between tasks, they ate, quite well in the circumstances. They heated up tomato soup, tinned lambs' tongues, peas and baked beans in the carpenter's glue pot that served as a stove, and finished off with canned blackberries, loganberries and condensed milk. Cooking added to the sheen of condensation which dripped down every surface, reappearing almost as soon as it was dried. The damp was all-pervading, the air hot and fetid. The only escape was the blissful fifteen minutes they spent above water when, every six hours or so, the craft surfaced to 'guff through' the living space with fresh air and to run the diesel engine to recharge the batteries. Real sleep was almost impossible. Rather, they dozed, stretched out on the pallet in the forward battery compartment. When exhaustion approached, there was Benzedrine to help.

They met their privations with good humour and stoicism. On the morning of the fourth day of the voyage, the captain of *X-7*, Peter Philip, who in his previous existence had been 'Uncle Peter', the presenter of South African radio's *Children's Hour*, recorded his tribulations as the weather worsened. 'We are rolling as well as pitching and every few minutes our bows are hauled over to port with a corkscrew motion. We heel over and rise, then go down in a power dive. Perfectly bloody. I expect the tow to part at any moment. Also I have a vague suspicion that one if not both of our side charges have gone or are at least flooded.' He ended with a cheery 'heigh ho'.

Philip was wrong about the side charges but his fears about the manila tow rope would prove correct. At 4.50 the same afternoon he felt something ominous in the way the craft was moving and a few moments later the stern dipped down and began a steady descent. He gave the order to blow the ballast tanks and after a few heart-pounding moments the bows rose again. They emerged into grey, jagged waves that crashed over the hull, coursing down the hatch when Philip pushed open the cover. He fought his way out and forward along the casing to see the reassuring bulk of *Stubborn* ahead. A lookout had spotted the line break and the submarine had already hoved to. A rubber dinghy was launched with *X-7*s operational diver, Bob Aitken, on board. Clutching a line attached to the replacement tow, he let the wind and waves carry him the seventy feet to *X-7* where Philip was clinging to the upper casing. He hurled the line and Philip miraculously caught it and made it fast. Now Aitken had somehow to row back, against the run of the seas, to *Stubborn*. There were no willing hands to pull him back to the mother ship as the line connecting him to the submarine had

HMS *Stubborn*

snapped. He could see only one solution. He reached down and grabbed the waterlogged manila tow rope he had just delivered and, hand over hand, hauled himself back to the ship.

Earlier in the day, at 4 a.m., *X-8* had also come adrift. In this case, though, it took *Sea Nymph*, the towing submarine, two hours to notice. The captain, Lieutenant John Oakley, ordered the ship around in the hope that his charge had surfaced and proceeded on the same heading. By noon there was still no sign of *X-8*, and in the high wind and rough seas the chances of sighting her were small. The signs were ominous. Then, by an extraordinary stroke of luck, *X-8* was spotted. It was *Stubborn* who encountered her, not once but twice. On the first occasion the submarine mistook her for a U-boat and dived. The second sighting occurred as she came into view just as *Stubborn* was passing the replacement tow to *X-7*. This time there was no mistake and *Stubborn*'s captain, Lieutenant Arthur Duff, yelled through a megaphone to Jack Smart, the passage crew commander, to proceed northward with him on a course of 046 degrees until daybreak, by which time he would have alerted *Sea Nymph* and arranged a rendezvous. The wind whipped his words away. Smart misheard and understood he was to steer 146 degrees. The compass is divided into 360 degrees with 0 degrees as north, 90 degrees east, 180 degrees south and 270 degrees west. The mistaken course now steered by Smart took him further and further away from his saviour.

When dawn broke at 3 a.m. on Thursday, 16 September, Duff scanned the surrounding water in vain. Soon after, *Sea Nymph* appeared. Duff had little information to offer and all Oakley could do was head southward in the hope of another miraculous encounter. Fourteen hours later it came. At 5 p.m., *X-8* was sighted. The crew were crushed by fatigue. There was no question of them carrying on. On board *Sea Nymph*, Digger McFarlane decided that the operational crew would have to take over.

X-9 was also being towed by a hemp line. At 1.20 on the morning of Thursday, 16 September, she came up for the obligatory fifteen minutes to ventilate and recharge, and then submerged. There was no communication between her and *Syrtis* when either was dived as the telephone line had snapped the day before – manila stretched while the wire did not. A signal for resurfacing had been arranged: three grenades dropped in the water. Shortly after 9 a.m. the explosions went off for *X-9* to come up again. When, after fifteen minutes, she still had not appeared, the crew began hauling in the tow. Their alarm mounted as they felt no resistance. Another line had parted. The urgent need now was for *Syrtis* to retrace her course in the hope of seeing her charge on the surface but as the rope was hauled in it snagged around the submarine's port propeller. It fell to Max Shean, as *X-9*'s diver, to try and free it. Shean put on his diving suit which was uninsulated and gave no protection from the bone-numbing cold of the sea. Nor was it fitted with sinking weights. They improvised with lumps of steel from the engine room and he was lowered overboard. Lieutenant Jupp urged him 'to be quick [as] if we were surprised by enemy aircraft we would have to dive immediately'. He 'climbed, with a lifeline attached, onto the after hydroplanes, switched to oxygen and launched myself under the North Atlantic Ocean. It was cold. When my face went under it took my breath away. I was floating. The weights were not only too light but loose as well.'

He tried to force himself under. 'The water was absolutely clear. In the few moments that I could remain submerged I noted the shafts of sunlight descending into the depths. It made me feel giddy. I tried to see the propellers but as *Syrtis* pitched in the heavy swell, the hydroplanes smacked the surface with an almighty splash which forced me to the surface again.'

Shean was proud of his skill and sangfroid, which he had demonstrated over and over again in training, but this was not Loch Striven and he was wearing the wrong kit. His suit was acting like a life jacket, buoying him up, pushing him to the surface with every swell. As he tried again and again to fight his way under, he knew that, unless he succeeded, the submarine would be half crippled, relying on the starboard propeller alone to make progress. He swam clear of the hydroplanes and forced himself under again. The light filtering down lit up the stern and this time he was able to see the propeller clearly. The rope was looped loosely round the screw. He broke the surface and directed the crew as they pulled and pushed at the line until it floated free.

The submarine was at last able to go in search of its lost ward. It swung round and set off with all speed the way it had come. Six hours passed, then a lookout spotted a long oil slick staining the surface. There was no point in searching further. Sub-Lieutenant Edward Kearon, Able Seaman Harry Harte and Stoker First Class George Hollett were gone.

Shean and the X-9 operational crew felt a double jolt of sorrow. They had shared the rigours of training together and the pleasures of relaxation. Shean had a common bond with the commander, 'Paddy' Kearon, 'a cheerful Irishman, short, slightly on the heavy side of average, fair with a broad countenance and a smile to go with it'. Kearon's girlfriend was a Wren and based at Dundee where Shean's girlfriend, Mary, was also posted. On his last leave he had done Shean a favour and delivered a letter to her for him. He remembered 'Darkie' Harte as a 'quiet industrious Londoner', and 'Ginger' Hollett as a 'ball of fire, always cheerful, always doing something in the boat of his own initiative; a very good submariner'. But there was another element to their dismay. The loss of X-9 meant the end of their hopes of glory. Their part in the enterprise was over.* Syrtis proceeded north to a point inside the Arctic Circle where it was safe to radio the news of the loss to the Admiralty.

There were more setbacks to come. When Digger McFarlane and the operational crew boarded X-8 later that Thursday afternoon to relieve the exhausted passage team, they soon discovered major problems. Water was leaking into the empty ballast tank on the charge on the starboard side, spoiling the balance and creating an alarming list. No amount of trimming helped. McFarlane decided to jettison it, reckoning that they could still carry out their attack with the remaining one. He set the timing device to 'safe', which should have meant that the charge sank harmlessly to the ocean

---

* There were to be more frustrations for Syrtis. A little later she twice encountered the same unsuspecting U-boat but was forced to hold fire for fear of compromising the Tirpitz operation.

Attack and passage crew for *X-8*: McFarlane is top row, second from left

floor. They felt the craft rock over to port as the weight dropped away, and adjusted the ballast chambers to compensate. Fifteen minutes later they were knocked off their feet by a massive shock. Somehow, the charge had exploded. McFarlane hurriedly checked the controls. No harm seemed to have been done. They started off again. As the hours passed, the craft began to develop a list again, this time to port. They carried on, trimming as best they could, but it was no good. It seemed that the blast had damaged the copper strips sealing the buoyancy chamber on the other charge, which also began to fill up with water. McFarlane decided that it, too, would have to go. This time he was taking no chances. He set the timer to two hours and sent it to the bottom. Up above, *Sea Nymph* had been told by telephone what was going on. She moved away at nine knots in order to get them both to a safe distance before the Amatex went up.

At the set hour the charge went off with spectacular force. Even at such a distance, the shock wave reverberated through X-8's casing, buckling the seams. Inside, the wiring sparked and crackled as circuits shorted, pipes burst and the W&D compartment started to fill up with water. The shock was felt on board *Sea Nymph* but when her commander, Lieutenant Oakley, tried calling his charge on the telephone he heard only the hiss of static. Some hours later the line miraculously came to life again. McFarlane reported that the midget submarine was slowly filling up with water. They struggled on but it was clear the end was approaching. He took her to the surface and opened the hatch. X-8 was in no condition to continue. Oakley brought his submarine alongside her. He shouted to McFarlane that he was launching a dinghy to take them off. There was one last thing left for the crew to do. 'Scuttle her,' he ordered. 'The show's over.'[3]

It was now Saturday, 18 September. They had been at sea for a week. Of the six X-Craft that had set out four were left and they had not yet reached their slipping positions off the Norwegian coast, when the submarines would say goodbye to their charges and they would continue alone. There was still every hope that the remaining craft could carry out a successful attack. The losses, though, meant that the plan would have to be revised. Two overflights by PRU Spitfires on Tuesday, 14 September had revealed that *Tirpitz* remained in her usual place, inside her net cages in an anchorage thirty fathoms deep, on the western shore of Kaafjord. It was a snug berth. The fjord was only a thousand yards wide and the shore curved protectively around the battleship. *Scharnhorst* lay at the entrance, in deeper water, behind the Auskarneset headland. The third target, *Lützow*, was in Langefjord, another inlet of Altafjord, nine miles to the north.

On the basis of this information the Admiralty had chosen Target Plan Four from the range of options before them. Under this, X-5, X-6 and X-7 would go for *Tirpitz*. X-9 and X-10 would attack *Scharnhorst* and X-8 the *Lützow*. With the losses, the plan now changed. *Tirpitz* remained the great prize and Henty-Creer, Cameron and Place would concentrate on her. Hudspeth would have to tackle *Scharnhorst* alone and *Lützow* was struck off the list. It meant little to the overall success of the operation. The pocket battleship was the least of the targets and on its own represented little threat.

In Kaafjord the mood of celebration that had pervaded *Tirpitz* since the Spitsbergen raid lingered. The crew were still disposing of some of the loot captured from the Barentsburg stores. The haul included chocolate, butter and Russian cigarettes. The goods went back and forth, won and lost in the poker schools that assembled all over the ship.

Beer and schnapps flowed at celebrations to mark the many gongs awarded. Four hundred Iron Crosses, Second Class, were distributed to crew members. Only 162 had gone to seamen on the *Scharnhorst*, a disparity that caused some ill feeling among the crew. Neither ship had played much of a part in the attack. What fighting there had been had largely been done by the destroyers *Z29* and *Z31*. Nonetheless, the crew of *Scharnhorst* felt the *Tirpitz*'s share of decorations unmerited. In the course of the war, the battle cruiser had seen far more action than the battleship. She had sunk the aircraft carrier HMS *Glorious*, spent two months of 1941 roaming the Atlantic and pulled off the Channel Dash. *Tirpitz* had sunk nothing and never strayed more than a few days' sail from her safe Nordic havens. Relations between the two units were already cool. *Scharnhorst* sailors did not regard *Tirpitz* as a happy ship. Their views were coloured by reports from stokers loaned to the battleship who returned from time to time to drink with their old messmates and complain about Kapitän Meyer's disciplinarian attitude.

The awards were indeed extravagant. The operation had been virtually risk-free, compared with the dangers facing troops on the Eastern Front. The boost to morale, though, was thought to justify the largesse. The outing had provided a welcome outlet for the sailors' energies. Admiral Kummetz, the Northern task Force commander, who was flying his flag in *Tirpitz*, was convinced that more such sorties were needed, not just to raise spirits but to improve efficiency. 'I cannot emphasize how important it is to mount frequent operations of this kind that last for several days,' he wrote to naval headquarters. 'They are essential to the maintenance of the Battle Group's effectiveness and striking power.' He had been disturbed to read in his commander's reports of the Spitsbergen action that during the voyage north 'a lot of men became seasick when the height of the waves was no more than two to three metres'. He concluded that 'a Battle Group that never leaves its base loses its edge. It will never be capable of meeting major challenges.'[4]

The desire for more operations clashed with practical realities. All big warships required perpetual attention if they were to remain effective. This was not just a matter of continuous, minor running repairs but regular, exhaustive overhauls. At the same time as he was urging more action, Kummetz recommended that, with winter closing in, it was a good time to send *Tirpitz* for another refit. Long nights and the likely bad weather, he believed, would provide enough protection for her to make the passage safely to a German yard.

As the crew of *Tirpitz* basked in the fading afterglow of their modest adventure, the men sent to destroy them were getting ready to say goodbye to the submarines. On Sunday, 19 September, the captain of *Truculent*, Lieutenant Robbie Alexander, held a service in the control room. The submarine was now submerged to avoid detection from German aircraft operating from the Norwegian coast. The crew of *X-6*, Don Cameron, John Lorimer, Eddie Goddard and Dickie Kendall, by now bristling with ten days' growth of beard, stood with hands clasped and heads lowered and listened to the captain reading from the Book of Common Prayer. He had chosen the Naval Prayer, with its appeal to God to 'preserve us from the dangers of the sea and the violence of our enemies', and its heartfelt wish 'that we return in safety to enjoy the blessings of the land'.

Cameron recorded in his private log how he looked round at his crew and marvelled at how confident they seemed. 'Is it a pose or do they really feel that way?' he wondered. 'If so, I envy them. I have that just-before-the-battle-mother feeling. Wonder how they will bear up under fire ...' The difference between the exercises in Port Bannatyne and Loch Cairnbawn, where, 'if things went wrong, up you popped and came alongside *Bonaventure* for a gin', and the real thing was all too apparent. His thoughts went back to his wife and infant son, waiting for him in Portsmouth. 'I can't help thinking what the feelings of my next of kin will be if I make a hash of things,' he wrote.[5]

Later, in the dying light of the evening, *X-6*'s passage crew surfaced for the last time. A rubber dinghy carrying Cameron and Goddard set off from *Truculent* through steep waves and icy spray. The captain, Lieutenant 'Willie' Wilson, emerged from the hatch and clung to the air induction trunk as the little craft rocked and wallowed. It seemed to Cameron that 'in the half light of an Arctic night, Willie [looked] pretty shagged'.[6] Wilson made his report to the new captain. The ballast tank of the starboard charge was beginning to let in water and the gland that sheathed the main periscope was leaking slightly. Otherwise, *X-6* was in good shape. There were stilted farewells and Wilson, together with another crew member, Bill Oxley, scrambled onto the dinghy and were hauled back to the relative luxury of *Truculent*. The voyage had lasted nine days. They were stiff, dirty and all but wiped out.

Lorimer and Kendall were waiting on the casing. Standing there in the desolation of an Arctic autumn twilight, Lorimer was swept suddenly by doubt. 'I lost my nerve,' he recalled. 'Then the [rubber] dinghy came alongside the stern of *Truculent*, and after Wilson and Oxley climbed out, I thought I heard air escaping from it. In fact I insisted it was leaking, but the seaman lending a hand quite rightly assured me that the noise was the water rising and falling over the stern of *Truculent* and running out of the holes in the casing.' Once aboard the dinghy he 'felt much better, the seamen wishing me "good luck" and "see you in two days time sir". Then there wasn't time for any more doubts.'[7]

With John McGregor, the last member of the passage crew, safely away in the dinghy they were on their own. Cameron set about trying to deal with the problems caused by the leak in the starboard charge. The craft had a list of 15 degrees. That would make manoeuvring it very difficult, especially in the fresher water of Kaafjord which was sixty miles from the open sea. He decided to throw overboard all surplus supplies, including the prized tins of Florida orange juice, and shift the rest to the port side in an attempt to correct the list. Then he had a proper look around his boat. He was pleasantly surprised at its condition. 'Wilson and his crew must have had a field day before handing over,' he wrote. 'Everything was spic and span. There was a little dampness on the hull, and except for the leak in the top periscope gland, she appeared first rate. The list decreased to 10 degrees when submerged, and one got used to it in time.'[8]

By the dawn of Monday, 20 September, all four operational crews were on board, ready to move to their respective slipping positions where they would part company with their parent submarines and continue the journey alone. The submarines, meanwhile, would wait offshore to pick up the crews when – and if – they returned. At 11 a.m. *Stubborn*, which was towing her charge, *X-7*, spotted a contact mine which had broken loose from its mooring bobbing ominously in the water ahead. They watched as it slipped by, the detonator horns almost brushing the hull. Once past them, though, the mooring wire caught in the rope towing *X-7*. Soon the mine was hooked over the bows of the midget submarine. By now the commander, Godfrey Place, had emerged to see what was going on. He saw, rising and falling in front of him, the spherical steel casing and sinister spikes that, if they struck hard enough, would put an end not only to him and his craft but to *Stubborn* as well. Peter Philip, who had commanded *X-7* on passage, watched from *Stubborn*'s conning tower as Place inched to the bow and put one sea boot tentatively against the mine 'a little as if he were shooing off a small animal'. He gave it a shove but it was no good. The mooring cable was wrapped firmly round the tow. He bent down and started laboriously to disentangle it, while the men of *Stubborn* looked on in horrified fascination. It took him seven minutes. Then he grasped the prongs and gave a hefty push. It floated harmlessly away, to relieved cheers from the conning tower. 'That's the first time I've ever shoved a mine clear by its horns,' he called back.

Just before 7 p.m., with dusk yet to descend, *Stubborn* hauled in the tow rope and *X-7* slipped free. Philip and the others waved goodbye as 'she disappeared inshore, creaming along on her engine, bound for the Great Adventure'. Elsewhere, as darkness gathered, the other remaining craft said farewell to their big sisters. They were now less than a hundred miles from Kaafjord, where *Tirpitz* lay at anchor, ignorant of the attempt being made on her life.

15

'A bloody great bang'

The little submarines were on their own now, but Don Cameron, aboard *X-6*, felt a curious sense of relief at the parting of the ways. 'Free at last and left to my own resources,' he wrote in his private log. 'Monarch of all I survey, a little tin god in a little tin fish.' They had agreed on 'patrol routine' while surfaced, with two men on watch for two hours at a time while the other two tried to sleep. Cameron stayed on top for the first watch, crouched in the open hatch above the wet and dry compartment, chilled by the evening air and soaked by the freezing spray, occasionally touching 'Bungay', his doggy talisman, for reassurance and watching the water ahead. He felt 'very much alone' but also 'quite excited … at the prospect before us, and only hope that everything will be OK'.

The first obstacle was the minefields laid off Sørøy Island, which guarded the entrance to Stjern Sound, leading to the inner fjords in which the German fleet lay. The dangers were relatively slight. Mines were designed to blow up big ships and were anchored well below the surface. It was estimated that the X-Craft's shallow draught would mean they would skate over the top without disturbing them.

So it turned out. Shortly after 9 p.m. they were clear of the mines. Cameron watched a 'wonderful display of Northern Lights' which pulsed mysteriously in the heavens at this time of the year. The night passed quietly. *X-6* was listing to 10 degrees now as the starboard charge slowly filled with water but she handled reasonably well. They travelled submerged most of the time, and at 1 p.m. passed into Altafjord. They were now only about fifteen miles from Kaafjord and *Tirpitz*. It had been agreed that the four craft would rendezvous in the waters between the small islands of Tømmelholm and Brattholm, five miles north of Auskarneset, the headland that stuck out into the entrance to Kaafjord. At 6.30 p.m., Cameron brought X-6 to the surface. He felt an air of 'great tension in the craft' as he opened the hatch and crawled out onto the casing to have a look. It was a 'beautiful evening, atmosphere clear and everything still'. He could see the lights of Alta and the German logistics base at Bossekop glimmering on the edge of the water to the south. He decided to find a quiet bay on Brattholm where they could ventilate and recharge in peace. They were hove to twenty yards from the shore when light blazed from among the trees and voices drifted over from an unseen house. Cameron decided they were unlikely to have been spotted and stayed put. Then, a small vessel with the sleek lines of a torpedo boat appeared, heading in their direction. Dickie Kendall was looking forward to the eggs, cocoa, cheese and sardines that John Lorimer was busy preparing when the hatch crashed down and Cameron reappeared shouting for them to cut engines and dive. Kendall remembered later how they could hear the sound of the engines getting nearer, 'straight towards us. Twenty feet. Nearly on us – had they seen us? Thud, thud, thud of the twin propellers – 40 feet. We waited for the crushing effect of depth-charges. None came, and gradually the noise died away'. Cameron took her up again. Dinner lay spread over the control room floor.

They stayed on the surface for the rest of the night undisturbed. Cameron sat on the casing and brooded about what lay ahead. To the south, searchlights illuminated the boom that lay across the entrance to Kaafjord. Thanks to the efforts of the Norwegian resistance and the RAF's photographic reconnaissance from Russia they knew that it was not as formidable as it seemed. The constant traffic of boats ferrying supplies from the logistical base at Bossekop to the ships in the anchorage meant it was too much trouble to keep opening and closing it so a gap was always left at the southern end. Cameron noticed the headlights of a car bouncing off the hillside as it made its way along the shore road and amused himself with the thought that it might be carrying Admiral Kummetz himself. The moon was rising above the mountains and 'everything was brushed with silver'. He wondered if his wife Eve would be looking up at it from her home overlooking the Solent and if his infant son Iain was behaving himself. He felt 'very homesick indeed'. The 'elation of sitting in the middle of [the] enemy fleet's anchorage vied with [the] feeling of a small boy very much alone and wanting

Donald Cameron VC

someone to talk to'. He cheered himself up with 'visions of my leave and the thought of having waited two years for this ...'.[1]

At midnight Lorimer took over and Cameron went below. He busied himself setting the timings on the side charges. He had decided on a six-hour delay. This would give him plenty of time to escape through the boom where he could hide in the broad waters of Altafjord when the inevitable hunt began, before heading to the open sea and the waiting submarines. He started with the starboard charge. Despite being flooded, the clock worked perfectly and he switched it to a six-hour setting. When he tried to do the same on the port charge, though, the fuses blew. The timer was now jammed at a mere two hours, leaving scant time to escape the tight confines of Kaafjord before the explosive went up. In addition, a hole had appeared in the number one ballast tank in the bows which meant that, unless fully submerged, they left a trail of bubbles on the surface which might be noticed by an alert seaman on board one of the many boats lying in Kaafjord.

There was yet another cause for concern. There was no sign of the other X-Craft in the surrounding waters. The surviving crews had not been told that X-9 had sunk without trace and that X-8 had been scuttled. Admiral Barry had decided to withhold the information about these mishaps on the grounds that it 'might have had a slightly dampening effect.'[2] Cameron had no means of communicating with the other craft to find out where they had got to. A rendezvous was not essential for the attack to go ahead but it was certainly desirable. It would mean they could coordinate their movements to all arrive in the target area at the same time. If they could get in together undetected, they would retain the great advantage of surprise and the combined effect of their charges would maximize the damage to the target.

There were many imponderables that Cameron had to weigh as the night wore on. He did his thinking on the casing as the night sky lightened. He reckoned that if he did attack on his own 'and was successful, only one of my charges might explode but the gaff would be blown and the enemy on the lookout for [the others]. If I waited for a day, the others could make their attacks and I could limp around and perhaps do a little damage.' On the other hand, there was no indication that they had made it as far as he had and they might be in a worse state than he was. To add to his troubles, the periscope was leaking and misting up constantly. Soon it might be completely unserviceable, and an attack would be out of the question. He decided that there was really only one course of action. *X-6* would have to press on alone.

In fact, Cameron did have company that night. Godfrey Place and *X-7* were lying on the bottom of Altafjord, just on the other side of Brattholm. After slipping from *Stubborn* they had negotiated the minefield without incident. Off the island of Sørøy, Place had caught a glimpse of Henty-Creer, crouched in the hatch of *X-5*. They had yelled across the waves, wishing each other 'good luck and good hunting'. Then each was lost to the other in the darkness. It was the last time anyone would see Henty. The voyage into the fjords went smoothly. The main excitement was the sight of a large ship lying off Arøya Island at the north of Altafjord. It looked like *Scharnhorst*. If that was the case, she would not be where she was supposed to be, lying in her usual anchorage in the lee of Auskarneset, when *X-10* launched her attack.

Henty

At that moment, though, *X-10* was in no position to menace anyone. Ken Hudspeth and his crew had got into difficulties almost immediately after casting off from *Sceptre*. The passage crew reported problems with the periscope when they handed over on the evening of Sunday, 20 September. By early on Monday the electric motor that hoisted the heavy mechanism up and down had failed and it was stuck fast. The electrically powered gyro compass, which kept true north no matter how the craft was configured and by which the crew steered when submerged, was wandering. At this point it would have been reasonable to decide that *X-10* was in no condition to continue. There was nothing in Hudspeth's background or pre-war career to suggest an unusually developed determination to get to grips with the mother country's enemies. He was the son of a technical school principal and when the war broke out was headmaster of a small school in the idyllic far south of Tasmania.

Instead of turning back, he decided to find a quiet anchorage off the island of Stjernøy where they could carry out running repairs. They headed for the inlet of Smalfjord on the north coast. *X-10* arrived at 7 a.m. and sank to the sandy bottom at the head of the fjord. They spent all day dismantling the periscope motor, then drying, greasing and reassembling it. They did the same with the gyro compass. When they tried them out they were still in less than proper working order. Hudspeth nonetheless gave the order to carry on and just before midnight they entered the northern end of Altafjord.

Ninety minutes later they were forced to dive when they found themselves on a course with an oncoming enemy ship. They levelled out at fifty feet and tried to continue steering by the gyro compass. Once more, it started to wander wildly. There was no way of knowing which direction they were travelling in and nothing to do but to go up again. As they neared the surface, Hudspeth tried to raise the periscope. There was a burst of sparks and the smell of burned rubber filled the control area. The hoisting motor had gone again.

Hudspeth was forced to bring the craft up to vent the smoke. He climbed out onto the casing and looked around. Dawn was now breaking. Kaafjord was only about five miles away. Close by he could see the island of Tømmelholm. He steered the craft towards it then dived to the bottom, nearly two hundred feet down, just to the south-east of the island. They began the repair work all over again. The attack was due to start in a couple of hours. Judging by the time the job had taken before, it seemed impossible they would be there at the start. Cut off from any knowledge of the whereabouts or state of the others, unaware that *Scharnhorst* was no longer there for them to attack, Hudspeth still believed his duty lay in carrying on.

Cameron and Place were by now both entering the final stage of their missions. Admiral Barry's orders had forbidden an attack before 1 a.m. to allow all craft time to get into position.[3] Shortly after the deadline passed, Place gave the order to blow the tanks and she rose from her resting place on the bottom off Brattholm and steered south-west towards Kaafjord's narrow mouth. As they approached the boom he brought her up to periscope depth and took a look around. The Auskarneset headland lay dead ahead, and stretching across the water below it the boom. As predicted, and as hoped for, it lay partially open at the southern end. Half submerged, with a complete absence of drama, *X-7* slipped through the gap and into the narrow sleeve of water that held their target.

The relief of the entry was soon dissipated by the sight of a mine-sweeper coming towards them, heading for the gate in the boom. Place gave the order to dive and they sank rapidly to a depth of seventy-five feet. They moved slowly ahead. After a few minutes they stopped. Something was blocking their way. It was too soft to be a rock. Place decided they had hit an anti-torpedo net. His guess was correct. It was not one of the *Tirpitz*'s defences but was surrounding the empty berth where *Lützow* had until recently been moored. There they remained stuck for what Place later called 'a rather exasperating hour', nosing forward and reversing, manoeuvring in every direction the steering allowed. Then, when they were starting to despair, they were suddenly free. The pulling and pushing had shaken the gyro compass off the gimbals that held it level. To continue the attack they needed to see their way. Place took the craft cautiously to the surface. Then, with only the periscope showing, they steered towards the corner of the fjord where *Tirpitz* lay, protected by a layer of anti-torpedo nets.[4]

Cameron and the crew of *X-6* set off from their lying-up position a little after *X-7*, at 1.30 a.m. The list caused by the flooded starboard charge had got worse and when Cameron tested the periscope he found it was virtually useless. There was a 'green film over the eyepiece except for a tiny pin hole in the top left hand corner'.

By 4.45 a.m. they were approaching the boom. A trawler was just ahead of them, travelling in the same direction. Cameron took his chance and brought *X-6* to the surface, fired up the diesel and tucked in behind it, trusting that their low silhouette would be lost in the white water churned up by the ship's propellers. There were men on deck, making a lot of noise. They seemed to be sailors, returning from a night out. If so, they were in no state to notice the dark shape in their wake.

As the trawler chugged away, Cameron looked around at the flat waters of Kaafjord, dotted with nearly twenty vessels including the 23,000-ton supply ship *Nordmark*, and studded with buoys holding up torpedo nets. Nowhere was there any sign of alarm. In the near distance, only a couple of miles away, the bulk of the *Tirpitz* stood out in the clear morning light. They sank to periscope depth and resumed groping their way forward.

Aboard *Tirpitz*, another working day had begun with its usual routines. At 5 a.m. hands were called to their posts. On shore the anti-aircraft batteries came to full readiness. A launch made its way to the anti-torpedo net, at a point nearest the port bow of the battle-ship which jutted towards the entrance to Kaafjord. The men on board unhooked the net from its buoys and peeled it back, effectively opening a door that would allow small craft to pass in and out. At the same time, the hydrophones that had been listening for suspicious sounds in the surrounding waters were switched off. Both these measures, as Admiral Kummetz was keen to point out in his subsequent report, were perfectly defensible. Leaving an entrance in the net barrier by day was 'in keeping with the existing situation of constant boat traffic', he wrote. The hydrophone operators would have 'lost their alertness' if kept at their posts twenty-four hours a day and there were anyway not enough trained men for non-stop surveillance. Kummetz conceded that the British had demonstrated their ability to launch unorthodox seaborne attacks in 1942 with the unsuccessful attack by 'torpedo riders' at Faettenfjord. But the idea that they could launch another one at such long range and succeed in penetrating the successive lines of defences was assumed, he said, to be 'out of the question'.[5] His main concern continued to be attack from the air, and he had faith in the effectiveness of the anti-aircraft defences.

That morning Kummetz rose, dressed in breeches and riding boots and ate breakfast. He was intending to start his day as he did most mornings with a ride along the shore, and there was nothing to suggest he should alter his routine. He would be going home soon. His request for leave had been granted and he would spend the winter with his family in Berlin, exchanging the gloom of an Arctic winter for the dangers of the increasingly battered capital. Although the news had not yet been made public, most of his Battle Group would also be departing. The order had already been given for *Lützow* to sail to the Baltic for an overhaul. It was expected that *Tirpitz* would follow in November, leaving *Scharnhorst* as the sole big ship on active service in the far north.

As he set off for his morning hack, *X-6* and *X-7* were slowly closing his ship. On *X-6* the periscope was playing up again. Cameron dived the craft and started to clean the delinquent part. The others watched with a 'look of dejection'. He shared their dread that the great enterprise was about to collapse. 'We had waited and trained for two years for this show and at the last moment, faulty workmanship or bad joss was doing its best to deprive us of it all.' He felt a 'bloody-minded' determination not to be thwarted. He replaced the eyepiece, brought *X-6* towards the surface and tried to raise the periscope again. There was a shower of sparks, a puff of smoke and a stink of burning rubber. Just as in *X-10*, the hoisting motor had burned out. The constant breakdowns were, as John Lorimer said later, hardly surprising. After all the working-up trials and the long voyage from Scotland, *X-6* was just 'knackered'. Edmund Goddard had another go at mending it. After more stripping and reassembling he and Cameron succeeded in restoring the viewfinder to a condition when it was just possible to make out vague shapes in the surrounding water. They edged towards the northern bank of the fjord.

There was only one obstacle now separating them from their target – the anti-torpedo barrier. The nets were curtains of circular steel grommets, a hand's width in diameter. They were impossible to cut through but the intelligence briefings had said there would be no need. Torpedoes ran at shallow depths. The anchorage in which *Tirpitz* lay was thirty fathoms – 180 feet. It was calculated that the nets would hang down no more than fifty feet, leaving ample room for the midget submarines to pass beneath them.

Shortly before 7 a.m., *X-6* was creeping along at two knots, just below periscope depth. Through the small glass scuttles set in the hull Cameron could make out the bank rising on his starboard side 'and a few fish'. There was a black shape overhead, 'shaped like a pontoon with wires hanging from it'. They nosed forward gingerly and gently rose to the surface. The periscope was hopelessly fogged but Cameron could just discern some 'dark blobs' which he took to be the floats holding up the anti-torpedo net. There seemed to be a gap. He 'pushed towards a space in this chain' and suddenly they were in open water. *X-6* had found the gate in the net through which a small picket boat had just passed. To his port side, less than two hundred yards away, lay the bow of the *Tirpitz*.

Cameron kept on his course, moving parallel to the battleship's flank. His intention was to veer sharply to the left, to bring himself under the stern, then slide along the keel to drop his first charge, as instructed, under the after big gun turrets – Caesar and Dora – and then move on to Anton and Bruno. Placed there, the explosions would break the battleship's back, an injury from which it could never recover. As *X-6* started to turn, there was a sickening collision that sent all four of them reeling. They had struck an uncharted rock. The impact pushed them upwards and the bow broke the glassy surface of the fjord in a swirl of foam and bubbles. Cameron threw *X-6* into reverse and she slid below again into deeper water. It was 7.07 a.m.

There were twenty-four men posted as lookouts on the deck of *Tirpitz* and several saw the commotion in the water. The shape they glimpsed, twenty yards from the shore, was black and sleek. Among the witnesses was a flak gunner who shouted a warning to his battery commander, Leutnant zur See Hein Hellendoorn. Hellendoorn swept his binoculars to the spot his gunner pointed out. There was nothing there now. Hellendoorn was sceptical. It seemed impossible that a submarine could have penetrated this deep into their defences. Elsewhere others who had seen the apparition were being mocked for mistaking a large fish for a U-boat.

But then, five minutes later, the shape appeared again. This time it was only sixty or so yards from the ship and, as the ship's diary noted, it was clearly recognizable as a 'briefly surfaced mini submarine'. The ship now erupted in a flurry of excited energy. The siren sounded five times, the signal for all the watertight bulkheads to be closed. The ship's first officer, Kapitän zur See Wolf Junge, hurried down from the bridge to the commander's cabin where Kapitän Meyer had just finished breakfast, and told him that a small U-boat had been sighted inside the anti-torpedo net. Meyer was sceptical but hurried out on deck.

By now everyone on board was blazing into the water with rifles and some were throwing grenades at the black shape in the water. The ship's guns were useless. The submarine was too close to the hull for them to be brought to bear. Meyer ordered an Arado plane off to search for other submarines and the door in the nets was closed. At the same time he called for steam so that they could escape the anchorage. No tugs were available and *Tirpitz* would have to make her own way out.[6]

Oberleutnant zur See Herbert Leine, who had been on his way to relieve the officer of the watch when the drama erupted, rounded up some men and set off in a launch from the stern of the ship, armed with rifles, and steered for *X-6*, which was now only fifty yards from the side and heading for the bow. The boarding party peppered the hull with rifle fire and lobbed grenades, but to little effect. The craft slid below the surface again to reappear thirty yards from the stern. As the launch sped towards it, they saw a hatch on the casing clang open. One by one, four men emerged, raising their arms in surrender.

Leine ordered his men to hold their fire and warily they bore down on X-6. One of the sailors jumped across and made fast a tow line. The casing was awash with water. Without saying a word to their captors, Cameron, Lorimer, Kendall and Goddard stepped into the launch. Leine then attempted to tow the craft away from the battleship. The ship's diary recorded that they had only gone twenty metres when it became apparent that 'since the valves had been opened the submarine could not be captured'. It then 'sank having been towed some fifty metres'.[7]

Cameron and the crew sat huddled in the launch, recovering from the most frantic ten minutes of their lives. After hitting the rock and shooting to the surface, they had dived again to seventy feet. The gyro compass was swinging wildly and Cameron had to guess which course would take him under the target. They could see nothing out of the scuttles. He tried a different tack, only to get fouled in some wires hanging down from the ship's port side.[8] They pushed forward and pulled back, blowing water from the ballast tanks, but to no avail. Then, suddenly, they were free and X-6 rose uncontrollably to where the crew of Tirpitz were now waiting with guns trained. They broke the water into a blizzard of small-arms fire and hurled grenades. 'They seemed to think they were under attack from a fleet of midget submarines,' said John Lorimer. 'They were shooting at anything that moved, even seagulls.'[9] Cameron remembered the bullets bouncing off harmlessly but making 'a helluva noise, like a lone dockyard riveter'. As they were shielded by the ship's overhanging bulk, most of the grenades 'plopped ... into the water and exploded well out of effective range'.[10]

They dived once more. This was their last chance to drop their charges. X-6 was now pointing away from the ship so Cameron called for reverse and a minute later the craft was scraping and bumping under the hull. They had arrived at the front of the ship, abreast of Bruno, the second of the two forward big gun turrets. It was as good as they could have hoped for. Cameron gave the order to let go both the charges. Kendall took the port side release wheel and Lorimer the starboard and they started to turn. A moment later the charges dropped away and slithered down the hull to settle nearly 100 feet below, close to the port bow. Freed of their weight, the craft rose sharply. There was no chance of escape now. X-6 was blind and leaking. The boom would be closed and every ship in Kaafjord would be looking for them. Depth charges would soon be plunging around them and the end would come in a crump of buckling seams and a rush of freezing water. It was time to surrender. They set about smashing instruments and burning their maps and charts. Then they pumped in air and X-6 surfaced for the last time. Just before they opened the hatch Cameron gave the order to open all the valves.

At about the time that X-6 had first been spotted, X-7 reached the anti-torpedo net, a few hundred yards in front of the ship's bow. Place timed the charges to go up in one hour – a very short setting if they were to get away – and descended to seventy-five feet, expecting to clear the bottom of the barrier. The net, though, was still there. He dived deeper, to ninety feet, but the result was the same. He reversed, moved forward, then, after what he later described as 'a little wriggling', they were free again and in the clear – whether he had found the boat gate or slipped through an unforeseen gap he was never able to decide. 'We came right up to the surface, not more than thirty yards from *Tirpitz* with no more nets ahead of us,' he said. 'We went straight for her. We collided with her just below the surface and slid gently underneath.' They let go the first starboard charge on the port side of the fore end of the ship near where Cameron's mines dropped earlier. Then they slid another 150 to 200 feet along the bottom and dropped the second charge amidships. As they did, they heard the sound of muffled explosions booming through the water – the sound of the grenades being hurled from the deck at X-6. The crew's satisfaction at having dropped their explosives was tempered by the realization of what would happen when they went off. The seconds were hurrying past.

If they were still there when the charges blew, the blasts were likely to kill them all. But as they tried to escape they 'ran into one net, got out of it and were at once in another'.

Their exertions were draining their oxygen supply. Eventually, in desperation, Place came up as near to the surface as he dared and tried a new technique. Putting the motor full ahead, he took a run at the line of floats from which the net was suspended and slid up and over. They had emerged on the battleship's starboard bow. By now the decks of *Tirpitz* were crowded with watching sailors and *X-7* was hit by a squall of gunfire which forced her under again. She dived to 120 feet. Without the compass, they had no clue as to which way to head to get away. Despite the certainty of being shot at, they would have to ascend to periscope depth. Place recalled later that, when they reached sixty feet, 'it was extremely discouraging … to run into yet another net'. They were still wrestling with it when, at 8.12 a.m., the explosion came. Instead of crushing them, the blast shook them free from the net. They surfaced briefly, and Place was dismayed to see that *Tirpitz* was still afloat. They dived again to 120 feet and wondered what to do next. They had suffered some damage from the blast but the hull was intact, and the engine seemed to be unharmed. Place announced they would try to make a run for it on the surface. It was, as everyone knew, a forlorn hope.

They broke the surface to *Tirpitz*'s starboard, a hundred metres from the net and were immediately engaged by machine guns and flak. Unlike the rifle bullets that had ricocheted harmlessly off *X-6*, the heavier rounds drove through *X-7*'s hull. She dived but as they went down, water gushed in through the holes and she was forced to the surface, to meet another wave of fire. Again they dived but Place had accepted the inevitable. Whoever went through the hatch first to signal their surrender was placing himself in mortal danger. It was the captain's job. Place pushed open the cover and scrambled out. In one hand he waved a white submariner's sweater. The gunners ignored it. Rounds clanged and whined off the casing. The boat was still moving forward. It was heading for a large raft, used as a platform for target practice. The bow slid underneath and Place leapt onto it. Behind him, water sluiced into the hatch of *X-7* and she began to sink. The firing died away. Place was safe but, beneath the platform, his boat was going down for the last time.

Cameron and his crew were taken aboard *Tirpitz* and marched to an upper deck where the ship's English-speaking intelligence officer, Rolf Woytschekowski-Emden, began to interrogate them. Cameron found the atmosphere 'rather frigid'. Presumably because of the great distances involved, his questioner 'would not believe we were British and maintained we were either Russian or Norwegian saboteurs'. The ship's diary noted that 'from the demeanour of the prisoners on board it is to be assumed that the submarine has completed its mission'. That was, they guessed, to lay explosive charges under or at least near the ship.

The crew were now working frantically to shift the ship away from where the first X-Craft had been seen – and where the charges had presumably been dropped. In the absence of power or tugs, they used the anchor cables to shift her, slackening the port line and hauling in the starboard hawser to winch her sixty yards further away from the shore.

It was too late. At 8.12 the diary recorded 'two heavy detonations'. The entire 50,000-ton weight of the *Tirpitz*, ship, men and stores, 'bounced vertically and sharply'. The blasts were almost simultaneous. The charges had been designed so that an explosion by one would detonate any others in the vicinity. The shock waves surfed through bulkheads and down passageways, ripping up decking and slamming men into hard metal. On deck, a twenty-two-year-old seaman, Fritz Adler, was flipped into the air, landing on his head on a mound of anchor chain to be killed instantly. Others suffered broken limbs and cracked skulls. The real damage, though, was to the ship. The forward charges split the port side plating but it was *X-7*'s charge amidships that did the greatest harm, tearing a gash more than twenty feet long, swamping the port outer compartments and partially flooding engine rooms. Everywhere electrical synapses crackled and shorted and all the lights went out.

Kendall had been held on the quarterdeck with Goddard when the others were taken below. He later recalled how his 'knees buckled as the explosion hurled the ship out of the water'. All around there was 'complete chaos. Seamen ran in all directions … injured men were being brought up on deck. Machine gunners imagined they saw submarines everywhere … it was impossible to take it all in. All around was confusion … I suddenly felt tired to death, yet with a wonderful feeling of relief.'[11] John Lorimer was in the captain's cabin being interrogated in pidgin English by Kapitän Meyer when he felt a 'bloody great bang. He went flying one side of the desk and I went flying the other.'[12]

Until now his captors had been proper and correct. With the blast, however, the mood darkened. The interview came to an abrupt halt. Lorimer's guards dragged him back up to the others on the quarterdeck where 'all hell was reigning. Sailors were rushing about. There was a lot of fist shaking and all the guns seemed to be firing.'[13] Cameron also rejoined them and they were lined up against a bulkhead, facing a squad of men carrying machine guns. Lorimer was sure this was the end. 'They were very angry,' he said. He was convinced that 'we were lined up to be shot'. The officer in charge, pistol menacingly in hand, kept demanding to know how many other submarines were out in the fjord. Then, the angry voices quietened. Admiral Kummetz had arrived. He heard the explosions from the shore while on his early morning ride and hurried back to his flagship. Still wearing his jodhpurs and boots, he swept past the four men, but paused to talk to the officer in charge. It seemed to Lorimer that he was saying 'you can't shoot these men, they're prisoners'. Tempers calmed and, as the admiral hurried off to confer with Meyer, Lorimer felt they were safe.[14]

The dramas of the morning were not over. At 08.43 a third submarine was spotted, beyond the torpedo net, 600 metres away on the far side of the fjord. Fifty-six hours after she was last sighted, in the minefield at the start of the voyage, X-5 had reappeared. The guns opened up again. The ship's log noted laconically that the intruder was 'hit in several places. Probably sinking.'[15] John Lorimer was standing under guard on the quarterdeck when its periscope showed above the 'millpond' calm of the fjord. He saw it take a 'direct hit with a 4-inch shell'. He was in no doubt that he had witnessed 'the end of Henty-Creer'.[16] It was the end, too, of Sub-Lieutenants Tom Nelson and Alastair Malcolm and Ralph Mortiboys, the ERA who had missed the eve-of-operation party at Loch Cairnbawn to write a last letter to his mother. His premonition had proved correct.[17]

As the first rush of alarm on board subsided, and the crew busied themselves with emergency repairs, the Germans broke off the interrogation. Woytschekowski-Emden had the four taken to a mess deck where they were given coffee and schnapps. They were provided with hammocks and told they were free to sleep. Before they settled down to their first proper rest in seventy-two hours, Place arrived, clad in the long johns and sea boots he had been wearing when he clambered onto the target platform.

A little later they were joined by another of their comrades. Lieutenant Bob Aitken, X-7's number three, had been picked up in the fjord at 11.25. He was alone. He was too exhausted to speak at first but later, when they had woken from their deep sleep, he told the story of what happened after the craft disappeared under the waters of the fjord.

The ballast tanks had been holed by gunfire and she immediately sank 120 feet to the bottom. Lieutenant Bill Whittam, the second in command, took charge. There was no question of making another attempt to surface. The craft was finished. Whittam and the ERA, Willie Whitley, started to put on their Davis escape kit. Aitken, the only trained diver, climbed into his rubber tunic and waist-high boots. He strapped on his breathing apparatus. It contained a large and a small oxygen cylinder connected by a rubber pipe to the face mask. It also carried two 'oxylets' to inflate a buoyancy bag incorporated in the DSEA and turn it into a life jacket in an emergency. They could provide a few extra lungfuls of oxygen. He made sure that the others had their escape kits on correctly. Then they tried to work out how they were going to get out.

The obvious exit was by the W&D compartment, but it was too late for that now. It took at least half an hour for the chamber to fill up with water. It seemed to Aitken that it was better to flood the entire craft and leave via both the W&D and control room hatches.

Whittam agreed and they opened the seacocks. While they waited they rehearsed the drill. It was immediately clear that it wouldn't work. In the tiny space it was impossible for the three men, two kitted out in their DSEA gear and one swaddled in a diving suit, to get past each other. Whittam ruled that as Aitken was nearest the W&D chamber he should exit first, waiting outside to help the next man through.

The water gushing in was agonizingly cold, colder than anything they had experienced in Scotland. As it crept up their legs, Whittam and Whitley climbed onto seats, bending double under the low upper casing. The process was desperately slow. After thirty minutes the water reached an electrical circuit. The fuse wires spluttered in a spurt of flame and gas began to leak from the batteries. It was time to switch on their breathing apparatus. They stood now in total darkness, listening to the groaning of stressed metal and the sound of their own breathing. They fought to suppress the ghastly scenarios bubbling in their imaginations, willing themselves to stay calm.

Minute by minute the water crept up their bodies until it reached chest level. 'Its icy grip was like a vice,' remembered Aitken. *X-7* had filled with enough water for him to think it worth trying to raise the W&D hatch, but 'the pressure wasn't balanced yet. I had to go on waiting.' His main oxygen bottle was nearly empty. He groped his way back into the control room to where he had last seen Whitley, propped against the periscope, to ask for a hand with the lid. He reached out to touch him but there was nobody there. Then his foot touched something solid. Whitley was on the floor. He 'leant over and put my hand on his face, his chest, his oxygen bottle. The breathing bag was empty, flat, completely flat. The two emergency oxylets were empty too. Poor old Whitley couldn't be still alive, and even if he was, I couldn't hope to lift him ...' He moved forward, groping vainly in the freezing water for Bill Whittam. He was down to his last few lungfuls of oxygen. He remembered 'scrambling back into the escape compartment for one more go at the hatch. Then things went black and I must have fainted.' When he came to he was speeding upwards towards the sunlit canopy of the surface where a launch from *Tirpitz* hauled him aboard.[18]

The next day they were transferred to Tromsø hospital before being sent on to Germany for further interrogation. It was four months before Eve Cameron heard the news that her husband was alive and a prisoner of war. She was pushing Iain in his pram along the seafront near her home overlooking the Hamble when she saw 'the telegram man, on a bicycle go past. I thought, I bet that's for me.' She did not draw the obvious conclusion. 'I knew that if anyone would come through it, it would be him,' she said.[19] Donald's lucky charm 'Bungay' had worked. The Germans found it when they searched him. It was listed along with his fountain pen, pencil and lighter as a 'pipe tamper, wooden, mastiff'.[20]

The Admiralty had to wait several days before learning of the outcome of the raid. A planned overflight on the day of the operation failed and the PRU reconnaissance on 23 September showed *Tirpitz* in her usual place but with no obvious sign of damage. The following day, a radio news bulletin from Berlin announced that an attack by British submarines 'of the smallest type' had taken place but failed. This was the first indication that the attack had in fact taken place.

No photographic reconnaissance was possible between 24 and 26 September. On the evening of the 28th, though, pictures taken showed a two-mile-wide oil slick issuing from the ship. Then, on 30 September, there was came cheering news. *X-10* had spent the day of the attack lying on the bottom near Tømmelholm, four and a half miles from the entrance to Kaafjord, while repairs to the periscope persisted. By the time darkness fell, they were still without a working periscope or compass. That only left them the option of a suicidal approach on the surface. Ken Hudspeth reluctantly abandoned the attack. After many hazards and hardships they made their rendezvous with their mother submarine, *Stubborn*, on 30 September. They were able to pass on to the Admiralty the very welcome information that at the time the attack was scheduled for, the thump of big explosions had reached their anchorage.

When Admiral Barry's first dispatch on the operation appeared on 8 November, he was still only able to say of the results achieved by the X-Craft that 'it may well be that the damage done was

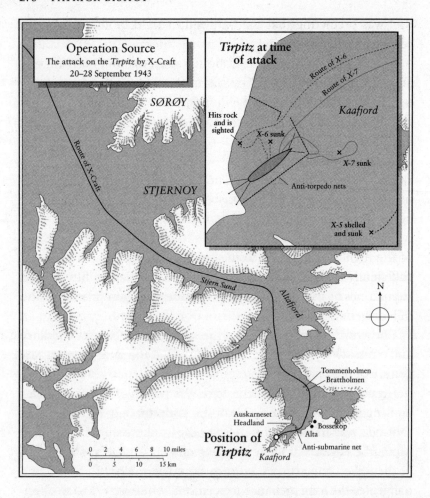

Operation Source
The attack on the *Tirpitz* by X-Craft
20–28 September 1943

SØRØY

Tirpitz at time
of attack

Route of X-6

Route of X-7

Kaafjord

Hits rock
and is
sighted

X-6 sunk

Route of X-Craft

X-7 sunk

STJERNOY

Anti-torpedo nets

X-5 shelled
and sunk

Stjern Sund

Altafjord

N

Tommenholmen
Brattholmen

Auskarneset
Headland

Bossekop

Alta

Position of
Tirpitz

Anti-submarine net

Kaafjord

0   2   4   6   8   10 miles

0   5   10   15 km

considerable'. Barry's guess was correct. Beneath the serene exterior
she presented to the overflying PRU cameras, *Tirpitz* was a mess. The
first reports calculated that 800 cubic metres of water had swamped
the lower decks, contaminating fuel and freshwater tanks. All but
one of the eight motors of the generators providing the ship's electricity were knocked out. Without electricity the boilers could not
be fired and the ship was, for the time being, crippled. One of the
after gun turrets, housing two of the ship's main 15-inch guns, had
been lifted out of its bearings by the blast and was now inoperable.
With no electricity, the fire control systems and electrical range find-
ers were useless. By the end of November the navy headquarters in

Kiel was predicting that the battleship would be 'out of use for several months' to come.

What Barry was in no doubt about was the extraordinary bravery and determination shown by his men. 'It is clear,' his dispatch concluded, 'that courage and enterprise of the very highest order in the close presence of the enemy were shown by these very gallant gentlemen, whose daring attack will go down as one of the most courageous acts of all time.'

The Germans, too, could not hide their admiration. In the words of the official report on the attack, their British enemy had once again shown himself 'a master of cunning and devious weaponry which he is not afraid to deploy in situations where the stakes are of the highest order if he thinks the goal is worth it.'[21] Hitler was sufficiently impressed to approve the construction of fifty midget submarines as well as 'one-man torpedoes' to counter an invasion of Northern Europe.[22]

Churchill had followed eagerly the progress of Operation Source and emissaries from the Admiralty provided verbal updates. As the picture of the operation filled out, he was anxious to broadcast the tidings of a venture that exemplified the virtues of daring, courage and ingenuity that he held dear. On the morning of Tuesday, 12 October, readers of The Times learned of a 'very gallant enterprise' involving 'hazards of the first order'.

Men like Ginger Coles, who had endured all the hardship and dangers of the long preparations, received the news with mixed feelings. For him, the raid had been only a partial success. 'I honestly thought that Tirpitz would have been blown sky high and if everything had gone according to plan she would have been,' he reflected. That the operation had not played out perfectly was hardly unexpected. It was a military cliché that no plan survived contact with reality. The X-Craft crews, though, were cheated of a more complete victory by avoidable mistakes. Equipped with nylon tow ropes, perhaps all six would have made it into Kaafjord. The chances of success would surely have been further improved if they had taken the shorter passage from a base in the Shetland Islands rather then setting out from the mainland of Scotland.

In Churchill's eyes, though, a partial success was better than none. *Tirpitz* had been hurt more grievously by Operation Source than by any previous attempt against her. This was, he wrote, 'an agreeable new fact' in his calculations as to how best to pursue the war in northern waters.

16

North Cape

For Churchill, the crippling of *Tirpitz* had come at a fortunate moment. It offered the chance of – at least temporary – relief from the stream of complaint issuing from Moscow concerning the Arctic convoys. There had been no sailings during the spring and summer of 1943. The middle of the year saw the climax of the Battle of the Atlantic. There was no question of the Royal Navy's warships being diverted to escort duties in northern waters while the outcome hung in the balance. The result was that by the beginning of the autumn only a third of the volume of the previous year's supplies had been delivered to northern Russian ports.[1] This was bad news for Stalin. The tide had turned on the Eastern Front and he needed American and British tanks and aircraft if his armies were to exploit their gains.* He was deaf to the Allies' excuses and Churchill and Roosevelt were subjected to continual badgering from Moscow as to when the convoys would resume. By the end of the summer, Allied air and sea countermeasures had begun to alter the balance in the Atlantic and pressure on the Home Fleet eased. Assets would now be available for convoy duty. The fact that *Tirpitz* was *hors de combat* reduced further the risks of the enterprise. Churchill was eager to resume sailings and had already been pressing the navy to reopen the Murmansk pipeline.

An era was ending at the Admiralty. Dudley Pound was dying, in the same dutiful and uncomplaining way that he had lived. The brain tumour he tried to conceal could no longer be hidden. On 25

---

* There were alternative overland routes to the Soviet Union via Persia and Vladivostok but they took longer and the railways could not shift the same quantities as ships.

...ing the QUADRANT meeting in Quebec where
...velt and their staffs discussed the forthcoming
...ope, he turned down a fishing trip with his fellow
...if, saying 'he did not feel well enough to accompany
... had in fact suffered a stroke, but carried on to Washington
...he conference moved there. On 7 September he visited
...chill in his bed-sitting room in the White House 'and said
abruptly, "Prime Minister, I have come to resign. I have had a stroke
and my right side is largely paralysed. I thought it would pass off,
but it gets worse every day and I am no longer fit for duty."[3] He died
the following month, on 21 October, Trafalgar Day, to be replaced
eventually by Sir Andrew Cunningham, a far more sceptical and
combative personality.

In the interim, the Vice Chief of the Naval Staff, Sir Neville Syfret,
stood in. On 25 September, he received a message from the Prime
Minister asserting the duty 'if humanly possible' of restarting the
Arctic convoys and running one full-sized sailing a month, from
November until March. Churchill found the response 'not satisfactory'. The Admiralty remained doubtful. They were unconvinced
that the benefits merited the risk involved, and it was by no means
clear that the Battle of the Atlantic was yet won. With the 'agreeable
new fact' that *Tirpitz* was no longer a menace, the admirals' resistance could not be sustained for long and on 1 October Churchill
sent a long telegram to Stalin telling him 'with very great pleasure'
that the convoys would resume in November. He made it clear that
while this did not constitute a binding contract it was 'a declaration
of our solemn and earnest resolve'.

He took the opportunity to try and extract something in return
for the Allies' largesse. Relations between British units in north
Russia and their hosts were fractious. The Soviets seemed to regard
their allies as potential fifth columnists rather than friends. They
made endless difficulties about issuing visas. Those who obtained
them, and made the journey to the bleak waters and dreary tundra
of the White Sea and Kola Peninsula, had to endure numerous petty
restrictions on their actions and movements and constant interference from officials.

One incident in particular had raised British hackles. In July and August 1943 the cargo ship *Dover Hill*, which had been stuck in Russia since February when the convoys were suspended, was lying in Ekonomiya on the North Dvina river. There was nothing much to do and the hours hung heavy on the crew. One day, the ship's bo'sun was returning from a run ashore when he met a local who harangued him over Britain's supposed failure to support its Soviet allies. In the ensuing row, the bo'sun laid his critic out. He was then accosted by two militiamen who tried to arrest him. The *Dover Hill*'s cook, passing by, came to his rescue and a brawl ensued. Both Britons were finally subdued. Elsewhere it would have amounted to no more than a quayside mêlée. Here, it quickly developed into a diplomatic incident. Unfortunately for the bo'sun, the man he assaulted was a local Communist Party official. He and the cook were sentenced respectively to seven and four years in prison.

Churchill touched on the case in the long list of requests for better cooperation that he attached to the telegram. It included an easing of visa restrictions and an end to bureaucratic bullying, measures he judged 'modest … considering the efforts we were now to make'.[4] Stalin did not agree. He fired back a telegram, smoking with real or manufactured indignation, describing Churchill's unwillingness to make a contractual obligation to sail the convoys as 'a kind of threat addressed to the USSR'. Familiar though he was with the marshal's violent language, Churchill was surprised and even hurt. For once his professional equanimity was jolted. He told the new Soviet ambassador to London, Fyodor Gousev, that he would not formally accept the telegram and handed it back to him, saying the Foreign Secretary Anthony Eden would deal with the contents on his forthcoming trip to Moscow. His patience with Stalin was reaching exhaustion point. He wrote to Roosevelt, telling him of the exchange with 'Uncle Joe', the ironic nickname they had given their sinister ally. 'The Soviet machine is quite convinced it can get everything by bullying,' he said. 'I am sure it is a matter of some importance to show that this is not necessarily always true.'[5]

In his determination to face Stalin down he was now prepared to countenance cancelling the Arctic convoys. 'It would be a great

Eden, 'to be freed from the burden of these
    ... oring our men home from North Russia.' He
    ... his is what [the Soviets] really mean and want, we
    ... ge them.'[6]

... cooled. Churchill decided against sending an inflamma-
... ry he had drafted in response to Stalin's insulting message.
... just as well. When Eden reached Moscow he found the Soviet
... ood had softened. On 22 October he met Stalin and told him of
Churchill's anger at the telegram with its implication of bad faith.
Eden reported back to London that 'the Marshal said that this had
not been intended'. He acknowledged the bad blood between
British and Soviet personnel in north Russia but lamented that 'if
only our people ... had treated his people as equals none of these
difficulties would have arisen'. If the British were prepared to do
that, then 'we could have as much personnel as we liked'.[7]

The meeting generated a more cooperative spirit and some of the
British grievances were redressed. As an earnest of good faith, the
brawling bo'sun and cook of the *Dover Castle* were freed. By a
combination of courtesy and resolve, Churchill had forced Stalin
into a retreat and to offer the nearest thing to an apology he was
capable of making. There was nothing now to stop the convoys
sailing.

On 15 November, the first half of convoy JW.54A left Loch Ewe
for Iceland. Then, covered by a strong escort and protected by cloud
and mist from the eyes of the Luftwaffe, it set off for the Arctic.
Eleven days later all nineteen ships had docked in Murmansk and
Archangel without loss. The second half of the convoy, JW.54B, set
out a week later and arrived unharmed. Two homecoming convoys,
RA.54A and RA.54B, also made the trip safely.

The news that the convoys were sailing again was received with
alarm in Germany. By the autumn of 1943 Hitler was retreating on
all fronts. The 'one bright spot' – as he had described it – provided
by the successes of the U-boats in the Atlantic had faded as the
Allied navies gained the upper hand in the battle of attrition. The
German army had been driven out of North Africa and Allied forces
were ashore in Italy. In the east, the Red Army was clawing back the

conquered territories, smashing the Wehrmacht at Kursk and Kharkov, while in the air great masses of Yak fighters were clearing the Luftwaffe from the skies. The reconnection of a supply line that would further strengthen the hand of the Soviet forces could not be overlooked. Forceful, even desperate action was needed to shut it off. In the circumstances, the chronic caution that had characterized the attitude of Hitler and his admirals towards their fleet in the north would have to be abandoned.

As it was, there were few assets to bring into play. Not only was *Tirpitz* out of the reckoning. So, too, was *Lützow*, which had quit Narvik on 26 September to return to the Baltic for a refit, dodging a force of Fleet Air Arm torpedo bombers on the way. The only large ship remaining was *Scharnhorst*, still lying at Kaafjord after escaping the attentions of the X-Craft.

It was Dönitz's unenviable duty to report on the X-Craft attack to Hitler in Berlin, three days after the event. He spread out the maps and took him through the operation, emphasizing carefully the extensive precautions that had been in place to protect the ship. The Führer took the news surprisingly well. No explosion of rage was recorded, and Hitler listened as it was explained that extensive repairs were needed if *Tirpitz* was ever to put to sea again.

In Dönitz's opinion there was no question of towing her back to Germany. It had been proposed, before the attack, that she would sail back to home waters for a refit. Admiral Kummetz had considered this feasible as winter and darkness would shield her from Allied attacks. That might be so if she sailed under her own power. Under tow she would be easy meat for British aircraft and submarines. Hitler agreed that the work would somehow have to be done in Kaafjord and experts from the Wilhelmshaven dockyard were soon on their way to decide if this was possible.[8]

The question remained of how to close off the Murmansk pipeline which was flowing abundantly once again. On 12 December, nineteen British and American merchantmen left Loch Ewe in a convoy designated JW.55A. The second half of the convoy, JW.55B, was due to sail eight days later. At Iceland they picked up an escort of eight destroyers while three cruisers, *Belfast*, *Norfolk* and *Sheffield*, under the command of Vice Admiral Robert Burnett, provided distant cover. When it appeared that the convoy had been sighted by a German reconnaissance flight, Admiral Sir Bruce Fraser, who had taken over command of the Home Fleet from Tovey in May, put to sea in his flagship *Duke of York*, accompanied by the cruiser *Jamaica* and the destroyers *Savage, Scorpion, Saumarez* and the Royal Norwegian Navy's *Stord*.

Fraser was hoping that the temptation presented by the convoy would be irresistible and a German force, possibly led by *Scharnhorst*, would put to sea. The sighting seems to have come too late for the Kriegsmarine to react and the convoy passed unchallenged. Fraser stayed with it throughout, taking his squadron all the way to the Kola inlet on which Murmansk lay, arriving on 16 December. It was the first time the Russians had seen a capital ship of the Home Fleet. Fraser had spent six weeks in a Bolshevik prisoner-of-war camp in

Bruce Fraser adds rum to the Christmas pudding on the *Duke of York*

Baku after being captured in the Black Sea during Britain's intervention in the Russian civil war, a fact that made him an object of particular suspicion to the pathologically mistrustful Soviet Commander-in-Chief, Admiral Arseni Golovko. Like many Communist officers and officials in northern Russia he resented bitterly the need to seek capitalist largesse. By the end of the trip, though, Golovko's Arctic hostility had thawed a little. On paying a call on Fraser aboard *Duke of York*, he was surprised when a member of Fraser's staff immediately brought up the business of his chief's incarceration by the Reds. He went on to say that Fraser was grateful for the experience. 'This time I really was astonished,' recalled Golovko. The 'triumphant' officer went on to explain that 'Admiral Fraser was badly fed in the prison where he was confined and this enabled him to recover from an ulcer that was plaguing him'. Fraser 'who was present throughout the conversation confirmed this with a smile'.

With this sally, the admiral and his team seem to have located the Russians' well-concealed sense of humour and for the duration of the visit ideological differences diminished and they were sea dogs together. 'Like a good host Fraser showed me over the whole ship, which indeed made a powerful impression [wrote Golovko] and even invited me into the ship's bakery where we were regaled with some good newly baked buns. After eating one I praised both it and the bakers, little suspecting that this would lead to a surprise. When we had disembarked from the battleship a bulky sack was lowered onto the deck of the launch containing a vast quantity of buns. What you might call the acme of hospitality!'

The following day Fraser and his staff returned the visit. Golovko gave a dinner in their honour and afterwards there was a concert by the fleet choir. 'The visitors were delighted,' he remembered 'especially by the dances and the few songs sung in English. They even entreated me to let them take the choir to Scapa Flow and Rosyth for a fortnight. All in all we received our British visitors as real allies.'[9]

Fraser now returned to Akureyri in Iceland to refuel and await developments. He did not have to wait long. On 19 and 20

Red Admiral: Arseni Golovko

December, Dönitz and other members of the high command met at Hitler's Wolfschanze HQ in East Prussia to discuss the coming year. All theatres of war were reviewed and the preoccupations of everyone present were overwhelmingly defensive. Dönitz's report was pessimistic. He bemoaned the 'wholly inadequate' long-range air reconnaissance that was vital if his U-boats were to return to the offensive in the Atlantic, and the shortcomings of naval radar which by now was significantly inferior to that in use in the Allies' ships. Despite these problems, he ended on a belligerent note. He told Hitler that 'if a successful operation seems assured', he would send the fleet to sea against the next Allied convoy that sailed for Russia.

Even so, there were doubts among Dönitz's own staff as to whether these circumstances would ever arise. The concealing darkness and storms of winter made air reconnaissance very difficult. If a convoy was spotted and tracked, the attackers would almost certainly have to contend with a strong escort as well as carrier-borne aircraft. The Kriegsmarine had only one big ship in play – *Scharnhorst*. Caution argued for leaving her in Kaafjord and mounting a small-scale foray with destroyers alone against the next convoy.[10]

Dönitz, though, was inclined to be bold. The pressure to act was of his own making. It was he who had persuaded Hitler not to scrap the surface fleet after the debacle of the Battle of the Barents Sea the previous Christmas and had promised him that it would be put to aggressive use. Sending *Scharnhorst* to sea might be a gamble, but the stakes were high. A successful attack would not only assist the German armies struggling through another horrific winter. With luck it might also lead to a further suspension of the Arctic convoys, and perhaps a crisis in the relationship between 'Uncle Joe' and his partners.

Another opportunity to strike was beckoning. On 20 December, the nineteen ships of JW.55B, the second half of the convoy, left Loch Ewe and sailed east. On 22 December they were spotted by a Luftwaffe aircraft on a meteorological flight. The next day the convoy was attacked by a force of Ju88s, without result. At the same time, U-boats had fallen in behind it, launching an attack that was beaten off by the escorts' depth charges.

The following day, an Ultra decrypt revealed that *Scharnhorst* had been put on three hours' notice to sail. Fraser and the Home Fleet were in Iceland. The moment he had been waiting for had arrived. Bruce Fraser entered Dartmouth in 1904. He was fifteen years old, the son of General Alexander Fraser of the Royal Engineers, a distinguished empire builder who constructed railways, lighthouses and docks the length and breadth of the Indian subcontinent. Almost from the beginning young Bruce was marked down for a distinguished career. His superiors' confidential reports as he ascended the hierarchy praised his zeal, intelligence and tact. The only fault his senior officer could find with him after he completed two years commanding the light cruiser HMS *Effingham* in 1932 was that 'with his kindly disposition he is apt to allow his heart to rule his head in dealing with his subordinates'.[11]

Those aboard *Duke of York* found him friendly and informal, puffing on a pipe as he did his rounds, dressed for comfort rather than smartness. 'He was the ideal commander,' remembered Julian Richards, an eighteen-year-old midshipman. 'He would spend the first part of the day … just talking to ship's companies and captains, and giving them the lowdown about his intentions. In the afternoon he would spend two or three hours thinking things over in his own mind, preparing for all eventualities. He was the sort of laid-back commander who let people get on with their work and not harry them all the time as others did.'[12]

On the afternoon of 23 December he ordered a top-up of the bunkers and went ashore for a walk to clear his head with the *Duke of York*'s commanding officer, Captain Guy Russell. Back on board he ordered the Royal Marine band up on deck to play Christmas carols. The familiar tunes, with their powerful reminders of hearth and home, 'brought tears to your eyes,' he recalled later.[13] At 23.00 hours that night of 23 December, preceded by four destroyers and with the cruiser *Jamaica* following behind, *Duke of York* put to sea. As well as his own squadron, which he designated Force Two, he also had at his disposal Burnett's cruisers – Force One – which had turned round after delivering the previous convoy and were now headed west to cover JW.55B.

The convoy steamed eastwards throughout Christmas Eve at no more than eight knots, protected by the Royal Navy destroyers *Onslow*, *Onslaught*, *Orwell*, *Impulsive* and *Scourge* and the Canadian navy's 'Tribals', *Haida*, *Huron* and *Iroquois*. The weather was terrible. A gale was blowing from the south, driving huge seas against the flanks of the merchantmen and their escorts. None of them displaced more than 10,000 tons and they were thrown from wave top to trough in sickening succession with no hope in the forecasts of an improvement. As she hurried to catch up from the west, even the *Duke of York* was suffering. The pounding of the sea as it swept over the low bow tore away Oerlikon anti-aircraft guns mounted forward and icy water poured into the bolt holes left in the decks, drenching those below. Julian Richards was in charge of two of the guns. 'Anything that was loose on the upper deck went overboard,' he remembered. Even a big ship like the the *Duke of York* was 'plunging and rocking'. For insulation from the force eight and nine winds those on deck had a duffel coat, layers of pullovers, long stockings and gumboots. A woolly hat, though, 'was not part of the official uniform ... a balaclava, knitted by mummy, was essential'.[14]

The Germans had been shadowing the convoy by air and U-boat since Christmas Eve but, by lunchtime on Christmas Day, a decision to attack had still not been taken. The situation seemed to match Dönitz's criteria for a successful operation. At this point it was not known that Fraser had put to sea. On the available facts, the convoy's escort was no match for the *Scharnhorst*. The target's speed and course were established and the wall of polar ice encroaching from the north limited its room for evasive action. Air reconnaissance had not discovered any heavy enemy unit in the vicinity. That did not mean that there was not a battleship lurking out there somewhere. Dönitz calculated that, even if there were, 'it must have been a long way from the convoy, and the *Scharnhorst* seemed to have every chance of delivering a rapid and successful attack'. Dönitz and the naval staff agreed that 'here was a splendid chance for the *Scharnhorst*'. He sent the order for the battle cruiser and the 4th Destroyer Flotilla to put to sea.[15]

Scharnhorst was at anchor in Langefjord when the news came through. Vizeadmiral Erich Bey, who was in temporary command of the northern task force while Kummetz carried on his home leave, was not on board, however. He was a dozen miles to the south, in a *Tirpitz* stateroom, sitting down to Christmas lunch with Kapitän Meyer. The crew of *Scharnhorst* seem also to have been in festive mood, despite the heightened state of alert. Survivors later told their interrogators that they had 'been looking forward to a cheerful and relaxed Christmas'. Some of them had spent the morning skiing and extra rations of sweets and cigarettes were handed out, overseen by their commander, Kapitän zur See Fritz Hintze, a popular figure who was admired by his men for his attention to their welfare.[16]

At 3 p.m. the order came to prepare to weigh anchor. Shortly afterwards, Bey arrived from *Tirpitz* aboard a tug, and at 7 p.m. *Scharnhorst* steamed north-west up Altafjord with five destroyers leading the way. Once clear of the coast, they headed due north, straining to make twenty-five knots in the dark, wind-humped seas. The launch of the operation produced a quickening of signals flying through the freezing ether between the ship and headquarters in Kiel. In Hut 8 at Bletchley Park, the naval team worked intently, deciphering the traffic and passing it on to London. At 4 a.m. on Boxing Day, as the morning watch relieved the middle watch aboard *Duke of York*, Fraser was handed a slip of paper which read: 'Admiralty appreciate that *Scharnhorst* is now at sea'.

The news sent a ripple of excitement through the ship. The convoy and its escorts were now fifty miles south of Bear Island, butting along at eight knots and heading east-north-east. Ahead, 150 miles to the north-east, the cruisers of Force One – *Belfast*, *Norfolk* and *Sheffield* – were hurrying in their direction. Behind, just over two hundred miles away, approaching from the south-west, further support was on its way from *Duke of York*, the light cruiser *Jamaica* and their four destroyers.

As *Scharnhorst* steamed northwards her destroyers were finding it hard to keep up. Their upper works were encrusted with frozen brine and they were being jostled by a heavy following sea. Bey had reported his problems back to base, only for Dönitz to reply that if the flotilla could not maintain speed, *Scharnhorst* should attack the convoy alone.

At 7.30 a.m., when there was still no sign of the convoy, he detached his destroyers and sent them off on a search to the west. *Scharnhorst*, meanwhile, followed on a zigzag course behind. The first leg of the manoeuvre put the ship on a northward tack. *Scharnhorst* was now on a collision course with the advancing cruisers of Burnett's Force One.

At 8.45 a blip on a cathode screen aboard Burnett's flagship *Belfast* revealed a single ship steaming slightly north of west. The vessel was only fourteen miles away. At 9.21 lookouts on *Sheffield* glimpsed the outlines of a large ship, ghostly in the murk, on the port beam, about seven miles away. There was no doubt what it was. The signal lamps flashed the message to Burnett: 'Enemy in sight'.

At this point, *Scharnhorst* was outnumbered but she was not outgunned. She mounted nine 11-inch and twelve 5.9-inch guns. The heaviest guns the cruisers could muster were the eight 8-inchers on *Norfolk*. *Belfast* and *Sheffield* each had twelve 6-inch guns. The superior reach and power of *Scharnhorst*'s main armament should have been enough for her to do serious damage to one or more of the cruisers without getting within range of their weapons. Her slight edge in speed gave her the advantage in a chase. But Bey and Hintze were hindered by a serious handicap. The limited range of their radar compared with the British equipment meant they were unlikely to sight the enemy before the enemy sighted them. At 9.24 a.m. the gloom was pierced by the first star shell, fired from *Belfast* to light up the target. A few minutes later real shells were plunging into the surrounding waters.

Scharnhorst was just turning south when she was spotted, and the shells from *Belfast* and *Sheffield* all missed. *Norfolk* was luckier. Her radar-controlled 8-inch guns fired six broadsides and scored three hits. One smashed *Scharnhorst*'s main radar aerial and another wrecked the port high-angle gunnery director. In a few minutes her armament advantage had been severely reduced and she was now operating in semi-blindness.

Bey ran for it. He turned *Scharnhorst* south-east, and hurried off at thirty knots, making smoke as he went. Despite the encounter, he was still determined to attack the convoy. He ordered his destroyers to steer north-east on a heading which he believed would take them onto the southern flank of the convoy. He, meanwhile, would race round to the far side, to attack it from the north.

Burnett decided not to give chase. His ships were too slow to overhaul their quarry. He guessed, correctly, that *Scharnhorst* was still full of fight and would make another attempt on the convoy. His place was therefore alongside the merchantmen, and he ordered his squadron north and west, from where JW.55B was approaching.

The news that Force One had lost touch with the enemy and was returning to the convoy was received with dismay by Fraser aboard the *Duke of York*. It seemed to him that *Scharnhorst* was more likely to return to Norway rather than continue the operation. A German flying boat had spotted Fraser's flagship. News of the presence of a battleship in the area would surely cause Bey to beat a rapid retreat. If so, Fraser was still too far away to cut off her off. The prospect of glory was fading. Fraser could not hide his chagrin. At 10.57, nearly an hour after the engagement had ended, he signalled to Burnett: 'Unless touch can be regained by some unit, there is no chance of my finding enemy.'

Bey had indeed received a report of the flying boat sighting but it was shorn of a crucial detail which Dönitz was later to claim could, had it been included, have altered the whole course of the drama. At 11 a.m. he had been told that five warships had been seen far to the north-west of the North Cape. The original report had included the information that one of the vessels was 'apparently a big ship'. This detail had been removed by the senior air officer before relaying it to naval headquarters on the grounds that he did not wish to pass on what he regarded as conjecture.

The result was confusion. Admiral Schniewind at Naval Group North in Kiel made the incorrect guess that the ships were probably the destroyers Bey had sent off when they could not keep up with him, and therefore no threat. Dönitz maintained that, had he been given the full message, he would 'probably have immediately ordered the operation to be abandoned'. What Bey made of the information is unknown. Whatever his appreciation of the situation, he decided to carry on.[17] By noon *Scharnhorst* was to the north and east of the convoy. So, too, were Burnett's cruisers. Once again it was the *Belfast* radar operators who picked up a lone ship on their screens, and the *Sheffield*'s lookouts who first laid eyes on the target. At 12.21 the signal lamp once more flashed the message: 'Enemy in sight'.

Burnett gave the order to engage. At the same time he sent his destroyers darting forward, seeking a line on which they could fire their torpedoes. The sight of the advancing destroyers resulted in *Scharnhorst* making several violent course changes, before heading away on an east-south-east heading. As the first shells crashed around her she returned fire, concentrating on *Norfolk* whose shells were not propelled with flash-suppressing charges. The great tongues of flame leaping from her guns lit her up and gave the German gunners, working without radar, a point for their optics to range on. Their aim was good enough to land one 11-inch shell which struck a gun turret and knocked out the cruiser's main radar sets, killing seven and seriously wounding five more.

Scharnhorst did not linger. She broke away, heading south-east, piling on as many knots as her turbines could muster. Once again her superior speed told and she was soon lost in the gloom and smoke. Although being slowly outdistanced, the cruisers were still able to shadow her for the next few hours by radar, and even as *Scharnhorst* was escaping from one set of pursuers she was running straight into the path of another.

By now Fraser was in a position to cut off her escape. His frustration had given away to cautiously rising hopes as he traced Burnett's reports onto the chart before him. Then, at 4.17 p.m., a bright point of light glowed on the *Duke of York*'s long-distance radar screen. *Scharnhorst* was just over twenty-five miles away. When the distance had closed to eleven miles, he ordered his destroyers to prepare their torpedoes but to await his signal to attack.

It was only when the two ships were seven miles apart that he swung *Duke of York* onto a starboard course to give all his guns and those of *Jamaica* behind him their chance. The bombardment opened with a salvo of star shells which hung in the dark sky, bathing the sea in a flat, harsh light. There, outlined like a great silver ghost, was the *Scharnhorst*. She had been taken by surprise. Her guns were still pointing forward and aft, away from her nemesis. At 4.51 p.m., *Duke of York* shook with the recoil of a full broadside. Shells flew from her ten 14-inch guns on an almost flat trajectory towards their target. One struck *Scharnhorst*'s forward turret, wrecking it. The ship swung away from its attackers, heading northwards – back towards the guns of the shadowing cruisers of Force One. Soon she was under fire from *Belfast* and *Norfolk* and turned to the east, still firing at her pursuers from her rear turret as she fled. *Scharnhorst* still retained one advantage: she was a full four knots faster than *Duke*

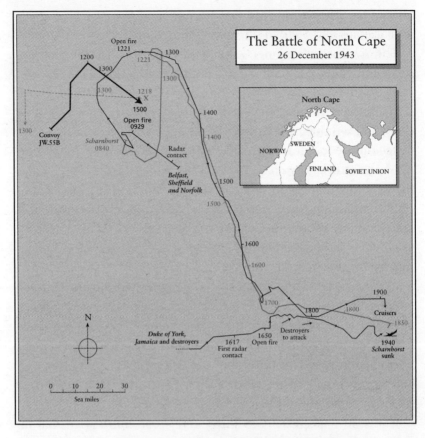

of York. As she pulled away, *Duke of York* fired broadside after broadside. The shocks swept through the ship, smashing the valves in the gunnery radar system, temporarily disabling it.

One of the 14-inch shells struck *Scharnhorst*'s starboard boiler room, slowing her down to ten knots until the steam pipes were jury-rigged to bring her back up to twenty-two knots. It was enough to draw her out of range. At 6.20 p.m., after firing fifty-two broadsides, the *Duke of York*'s guns ceased firing and her exhausted crews slumped back in a despondent daze. It seemed to be all over. Fraser signalled Burnett that he 'saw little hope of catching *Scharnhorst* and am proceeding to support convoy'. His destroyers, though, had not given up hope. Despite the heavy seas they had managed to gain on the battle cruiser. Just as Fraser had decided pursuit was hopeless they arrived astern of *Scharnhorst* and began manoeuvring to launch attacks on either beam, with *Savage* and *Saumarez* on the port side and *Scorpion* and *Stord* to starboard.

The *Scharnhorst*'s gunners soon picked up the port-side attackers but, blinded by star shell, failed to notice the approach from starboard until the destroyers were only two miles away. Hintze swung his ship towards them in an effort to comb the tracks of the torpedoes that would soon be racing her way. He almost succeeded. Sixteen torpedoes leaped from the tubes of *Scorpion* and *Stord*, and only one struck. The change of course, though, brought him into the arcs of the torpedo tubes of *Savage* and *Saumarez*. At almost point-blank range they loosed off twelve torpedoes. Two exploded, knocking out another boiler room and bending a propeller shaft. *Scharnhorst* shuddered and slowed. Soon she was rolling and pitching, barely able to scrape ten knots. *Duke of York* and *Jamaica* swept towards her, opening fire again at six miles. Burnett's cruisers, moving to join up with the Commander-in-Chief's squadron, joined in. Under the pounding she staggered and slowed. The cruisers moved forward and lanced her burning sides with torpedoes. Then it was the turn of the Force One destroyers.

The decks of *Scharnhorst* were strewn with the dead and dying. Among them, the survivors, smoke-blackened and deafened, mustered to abandon ship. She was wallowing, almost on her beam ends. Hintze, who had led them with perhaps more kindness than skill, was fatherly to the end. 'Don't go overboard to starboard,' he told them through a megaphone. 'Go over from the port side and slide from the rail into the water. Don't forget to inflate your lifejackets and now one after the other, over the rail.'[18]

On the deck of *Duke of York*, Julian Richards could no longer see the outlines of the stricken ship, 'just a lot of smoke and a lot of flame'.[19] Witnesses spoke of a dull underwater explosion. Then the black night absorbed the last, flickering flames and there was nothing. Bey's last signal, addressed to Hitler, had announced 'we shall fight to the last shell'. There was no doubt about his bravery or the courage of his men. But in truth he had mishandled an engagement that had offered a significant chance of success. Certainly among the survivors there was bitterness that she had not put up a better show.

After an hour of searching, only thirty-six men, all ratings or petty officers, were picked up. They had been lucky enough to clamber into a life raft. The rest of the 1,765 ship's company were dead, either killed in action or frozen and drowned within a minute of entering the sea.

Scharnhorst had taken a lot of sinking. She had probably received thirteen full hits from *Duke of York*'s 14-inch guns and about as many from the smaller armament of the cruisers, as well as eleven torpedo strikes, and yet she had not blown up. 'Once again,' remarked Stephen Roskill, 'the ability of the Germans to build tremendously stout ships had been demonstrated.'[20]

The loss shook the German fleet. Dönitz struggled to understand why Bey broke off the first fight of the day when, in his judgement, he had it in his power to overwhelm Burnett and his cruisers. 'The correct thing to have done ... would have been to continue the fight and finish off the weaker British forces, particularly as it was plain that they had already been hard hit,' he wrote. 'Had this been done an excellent opportunity would ... have been created for a successful attack on the convoy.' Why, when he fled after the second clash, did he not use his advantage of speed and weight to steer a westerly course into the wind and heavy sea that would have made it very difficult for the lightly built British cruisers and destroyers to keep in contact?[21] The answer would never be known. Bey and Hintze had been swallowed by the Barents Sea.

17

Tungsten

A hundred miles to the south, the crew of *Tirpitz* heard the news and shuddered. The death of *Scharnhorst* 'cast a long shadow over the ship's company', remembered Adalbert Brünner. Among the dead were some of their own comrades who had been lent to the battle cruiser to fill in for men absent on leave.[1] Now *Tirpitz* stood alone, the last of Hitler's capital ships left in commission. A soubriquet began to attach to her – the 'lonely queen of the North'. It was obvious to all on board that their enemies must once again be eyeing her up for annihilation. The tiny shape of reconnaissance Spitfires overhead provided regular reminders that the RAF was following every step of their ship's return to seaworthiness. So, too, were the Norwegians.

The information gleaned from photo reconnaissance and signals interceptions was being supplemented by the eyewitness reports of Norwegian agents. In February 1944 Terje Jacobsen set off from his home in Tromsø on a mission to check on the progress of repairs. He had just turned nineteen and had joined the local resistance network as soon as the occupation began. He was blond, blue-eyed and athletic, the Nordic type that some Germans liked to think of as kin.

Jacobsen had no natural antipathy towards them. He had visited Germany before the war and spoke the language fluently. It was the behaviour of the occupation forces in Tromsø that drove him into the resistance. 'You could practically hear the screams from the Gestapo headquarters in the street,' he remembered.[2] Even in one of the furthest outposts of their territories, the Nazis hunted their victims with appalling zeal. On 18 June 1941, the Gestapo began to arrest Tromsø's Jews. There were only eighteen of them and eventually all were picked up and sent to Auschwitz. The youngest was two and half years old. None survived the war. Among them was Conrad Caplan, a schoolfriend of Jacobsen's, whose father owned a department store. 'He was one of the happiest boys in the class,' he remembered. He perished on 10 January 1945, seventeen days before Soviet troops liberated the camp.

Jacobsen's mission was explained to him by his controller in Tromsø, a policeman called Olaf Aasegg. British and Norwegian intelligence in London wanted detailed information on the condition of *Tirpitz* after the X-Craft attack, and the progress of repairs. He was to go first to Alta, then Kaafjord. If questioned, he was to say he was visiting a friend from Tromsø who, conveniently, lived in the area. To get to Alta he would take one of the steamers that plied the coast to the little port of Alteidet then continue by road to Isnestoften, at the head of Altafjord, to take another boat to Alta where a local contact would take care of him.

The first boat was full of German soldiers. Jacobsen got into conversation with a young SS officer who was impressed by his command of German. Their matey conversation was observed by the boat's captain, a relation of Jacobsen's on his mother's side who 'looked at me as if he would gladly throw me overboard'. On arrival there was no public transport. The German officer offered his Norwegian friend a lift and Jacobsen spent the night as his guest in a barracks. At Isnestoften he took another steamer and met another German, a naïve, well-mannered young man of his own age who was surprised to see him reading a book of German poetry. The poet was Heinrich Heine, a Jew whose books had been burned by the Nazis. 'He had never heard of him,' said Jacobsen.

At Alta he went to the house of Freddie Tscholari, a friend from Tromsø. Tscholari was head of the telegraph office. He found him a bed in official accommodation and lent him his bicycle to make the journey to Kaafjord, five or six miles away. The following day he set off on the icy road. As he was labouring up to the head of the pass that led down to Kaafjord, he turned a bend and there before him were a group of German soldiers, some of them high-ranking, judging by the red tabs on their lapels. Jacobsen had learned that 'the Germans weren't stupid but they had one weak point and that was their superiority complex'. He decided to play on it. 'I looked a bit dumb and I had this fur hat down on my ears. I looked at this German guard rather stupidly and said "Do you have any cigarettes?"'. He was rewarded with 'a kick in the behind' and an order to clear off.

At the top of the pass he had 'a beautiful view of the whole scene. It was very impressive.' The battleship lay in its usual haven in the lee of the hills on the north-west side of the fjord. Nearby loomed a floating crane, the repair ship *Neumark*, and next to it the *Monte Rosa*, a former liner that was now the home of eight hundred workers from the Blohm and Voss Hamburg shipyard. It was the same ship that earlier in the war had carried his friend Conrad Caplan and many other Jews on the first leg of their journey to the death camps. Even at this distance he could sense the bustle and energy below. He lingered as long as he dared, memorizing as much detail as he could. Back in Alta he made notes and sketches that were smuggled by rail to the Norwegian Embassy in neutral Sweden, then on to London. On a second trip he learned from one of the local contractors technical details about the repair programme. It was going very well. On his third visit, in March 1944, Jacobsen witnessed the battleship heading out into Altafjord for initial speed and gunnery trials. His reports reinforced the intelligence gleaned from the Enigma transmissions passing back and forth between Kaafjord and Germany. On 17 March the battleship reported that its 'hull, guns and power installation were from a material point of view fully operationally effective'.[3] It was clear that the 'period of easement' welcomed by Churchill was over.

Three convoys had sailed to north Russia in the first three months of 1944 and three sailed back. Exceptionally bad weather shielded them from the Luftwaffe but not from U-boat wolf packs which harried them all the way. The submarines had only limited success, sinking a total of four merchantmen and two destroyers. The relatively light losses were a tribute to the determination of the escorting destroyers, corvettes and carriers, whose Fleet Air Arm crews were sometimes so frozen at the end of their sorties that they had to be lifted from their cockpits.[4]

With *Tirpitz* out of action, the Admiralty had not judged it necessary to cover the movements with battleships and cruisers. Now that she was back in commission, she reassumed the function of a 'fleet in being' and once again the navy felt compelled to maintain a counter-force to deal with her if she ventured out. The Allies now dominated the seas of the northern hemisphere. They had contained the U-boat threat in the North Atlantic and neutralized the Italian fleet to give them command of the Mediterranean. Apart from *Tirpitz*, the German surface fleet had been reduced to two pocket battleships – the *Lützow* and the *Scheer* – and the heavy cruiser *Prinz Eugen*, all now skulking in the Baltic, and a few training ships. Yet despite this overwhelming superiority, Churchill and the Admiralty remained greatly impressed by the battleship's menace.

The importance they bestowed on it reflected a new perception. As well as threatening the convoys, *Tirpitz* appeared to pose another potential danger. The invasion of Normandy was approaching. As long as she remained afloat, she would absorb naval assets that were essential for the success of the landings. If left unguarded, she could sail south to perhaps sink a troopship crossing the Atlantic, or when the landings began, menace the invasion fleet. As the repair work reached completion, *Tirpitz* loomed again in the Admiralty's imaginations.

It seemed clear that it was the navy that would have to deal with her. There was little enthusiasm in the RAF for an air attack, and none at all from Arthur Harris at Bomber Command. He had decided that the long distances involved and the strength of the battleship's anti-aircraft defences meant there was no more chance of his crews succeeding in 1944 where they had failed in 1942. He, anyway, had no wish to divert them from what he considered their primary task of smashing German cities. He had sidestepped nimbly Churchill's demands for action, suggesting that the US Army Air Force's Flying Fortresses with their superior bombsights were better placed to do the job. If, however, *Tirpitz* was to return to Germany, he graciously offered to mount 'the heaviest possible attacks against the German port where she lies'.[5]

The RAF had already been drawn into one abortive effort to finish off *Tirpitz*. In the spring of 1943 a new weapon appeared which promised to succeed where conventional bombs – and the hopeless spherical 'roly-poly' mine – had signally failed. Its creator was Barnes Wallis whose bouncing bomb was dropped by 617 Squadron – the Dambusters – on their spectacular raid of 16/17 May. The new invention, codenamed 'Highball', was based on the same principle. It was cylinder-shaped, weighed half a ton and contained a 500lb charge. Wallis saw it as a naval weapon and hopes soon rose that it might be used to the same devastating effect on *Tirpitz* as its sister had on the Möhne and Eder dams.

A new Coastal Command squadron, 618, was formed in April 1943 at Skitten, near Wick, in north-eastern Scotland and began secret preparations for an attack, codenamed Operation Servant. Specially converted Mosquito Mark IVs dropped Highballs in dummy runs on the old French battleship *Courbet* in Loch Striven but the results were disappointing. Plans were nonetheless made for twenty Mosquitoes to attack *Tirpitz* in Kaafjord that summer, operating – if the Russians agreed – from the Vaenga airbase. It was shelved when Coastal Command's chief, Air Marshal Sir John Slessor, ruled that it was 'not a reasonably practical operation of war' given the difficulties of delivering a Highball on target in the narrow confines of the fjord and the likelihood of high casualties at the hands of the ship's anti-aircraft defences.[6]

There was another alternative. The north Russian airfields were only three hundred miles from the target. The British Senior Naval Officer in the area, Rear Admiral Ernest Archer, spent the first few months of the year issuing 'almost daily' requests to Admiral Golovko for action. The only result was a half-hearted effort launched on the full moon night of 10/11 February by fifteen aircraft each carrying a 2,000lb bomb. Snow blotted Kaafjord and only four of the raiders dropped their bombs, none of which did any damage.

At the turn of the year, the Fleet Air Arm seemed to offer the navy the best hope of success. British naval aviation had at last struggled into the modern era. It had a new monoplane torpedo bomber, the all-metal Fairey Barracuda II, which replaced the wood and canvas

Albacore biplanes. The specification for an up-to-date torpedo bomber had been issued in 1937 but the priority given to production of RAF aircraft meant that it did not start reaching the FAA's squadrons until January 1943. It performed best as a dive-bomber, helped by large flaps that held it steady as it swooped on its target. The Barracudas were supported by a new generation of very effective carrier-borne fighters, American-manufactured Corsairs, Wildcats and Hellcats.

The FAA had been the target of some sniping from Churchill, who in July 1943 flicked an ill-considered memo at the stolid First Lord of the Admiralty, Albert Alexander, noting the 'rather pregnant fact' that out of the service's 45,000 officers and ratings, 'only thirty should have been killed, missing or prisoners during the three months ending April 30'. It seemed 'clear proof of how very rarely [the FAA] is brought into contact with the enemy'. This was despite the 'immense demands ... made on us by the Fleet Air Arm in respect of men and machines'.[7]

It fell to the Fifth Sea Lord, Vice Admiral D. W. Boyd, to draw up a response. Boyd was 'naturally astonished at the spirit of the Prime Minister's minute'. The draft reply, coldly indignant in tone, claimed that it was 'a matter beyond dispute that, in proportion to its size, the Fleet Air Arm has given bigger results than any branch of any other service'. In the end Alexander decided against rising to the provocation.[8] It was action not words that were needed. The fact was that at the time of Churchill's memo it had been more than a year since the Fleet Air Arm had sunk a ship – a Vichy French armed merchant cruiser, the *Bougainville*, off Madagascar. The resurrection of the *Tirpitz* threat would give the navy the chance to show what its aviators could do.

The initial plan was to hit *Tirpitz* in her Kaafjord anchorage early in March 1944, just before repair work was expected to end. The attack would be spearheaded by two striking forces, embarked on the big fleet carriers *Furious* and *Victorious*. Each one would be made up of twenty-one Barracudas. They would be protected by an escort of forty fighters, some on the fleet carriers and the rest on three smaller escort carriers, *Emperor*, *Pursuer* and *Searcher*. The fleet itself

HMS *Victorious*

would be protected from air and submarine attack by more fighters on board *Furious* and another carrier, *Fencer*. The operation carried the codename Tungsten.

Despite the large scale of the enterprise, the Home Fleet commander Bruce Fraser seems to have had little faith in its chances, and, according to the First Sea Lord, Andrew Cunningham, had to be 'practically bludgeoned' into agreeing to it.[9] As it was, he handed over responsibility for Tungsten to his number two, Vice Admiral Sir Henry Moore.

Intense preparations for Tungsten began in February. Crews flew from Hatston in the Orkneys for exercises around Loch Eriboll, in north-west Scotland. The steep surrounding hills could pass for Kaafjord and the Barracuda crews got busy accustoming themselves to the manoeuvres needed to reach the anchorage, line up on the target, complete the dive and slip back over the hill tops and out of reach of the anti-aircraft batteries bristling on ship and shore.

Barracudas carried a crew of three: a pilot, a navigator and a telegraphist air gunner (TAG), who sat, one behind the other, in the long cockpit. For Alan Thomson, a twenty-two-year-old Glaswegian, flying as a TAG with 830 Squadron, the exercises were the overture to his first big operation. In the loch 'was an island. There was an area laid out, about 900 feet by ninety and we practised bombing that first with practice bombs, then with a 500-pounder.' As yet the target was a secret but the crews did not need to be told. 'There were not many things that were 900 feet by 90 feet so we knew where we were going'.[10]

As was often the case, training activities were almost as perilous as the real thing. One misty morning they were flying over the loch when they glimpsed a tug in the waters below. They had not been told to expect any shipping in the area. A few seconds later, shells were whistling around them as a nearby warship which had just come into view opened up with a broadside aimed at the target that the tug was trailing.

The Barracudas were flown by 827 and 830 Squadrons of the FAA's 8 Torpedo Bomber Wing, and 829 and 831 Squadrons from 52 Wing. Normally, 8 Wing was based on *Furious* and 52 Wing on *Victorious*. Moore wanted the wings to operate as complete units, but embarking them together on their mother ships meant the time needed to take off and form up from a single flight deck would delay and complicate proceedings. He decided that 827 would sail on *Victorious* alongside 829. And 830 Squadron on *Furious* with 831 Squadron. At the given time, the squadrons of each wing would take off from their respective carrier, join up in the air and set off. The attack would be made in two waves, starting with 8 Wing. The strike forces would be protected from fighter attack by a top cover of Corsairs from *Victorious* and a close escort of sixty Hellcats and Wildcats from the other carriers, which would shoot up anti-aircraft batteries on ship and shore and strafe *Tirpitz* from stem to stern

This was a huge and novel operation, 'of a character which hitherto had not been attempted by Allied aircraft in the European theatre', in the words of Captain Michael Denny, commander of *Victorious*. It was the first time in the war that such a large force of dive-bombers had been launched at a single ship. The weight of numbers was supplemented by a correspondingly powerful load of ordnance. The shortcomings of British bomb design had finally been addressed and the Barracudas would be carrying bomb loads which, it was promised, had the capacity to cut through *Tirpitz's* thick carapace. To reach the battleship's vital parts a bomb had to plunge through two layers of deck then penetrate the armoured deck which ran along the waterline, protecting the engine and boiler rooms and the magazines. According to the intelligence estimate, the steel plating was three and a quarter inches thick over machinery and four and a quarter inches over her magazines.

A new bomb – the 1,600lb AP (armour-piercing) was now available which, it was claimed, could penetrate at least the lighter layer of armour plating, thereby putting the ship out of action if not actually sinking her. To be effective though, it had to be released at a height of above 3,500 feet.

Of the forty-two Barracudas in the strike force, nine would be armed with these weapons. Twenty-two would carry three 500lb semi-armour-piercing (SAP) bombs, which, if released above 2,000 feet, would smash through the upper deck and devastate the living spaces below. The other ten would be loaded with 500lb and 600lb high explosive and anti-submarine bombs intended to kill anyone not under cover if they hit the ship and to cause underwater damage if they missed.

Tungsten was originally timed for between 7 and 16 March. As the date approached, *Victorious* was still in Liverpool dockyard being fitted with new radar and the operation was postponed for two weeks. This turned out to be convenient. Convoy JW.58 was due to put to sea at the end of the month with a huge cargo of war materiel for an impatient Stalin. The escort required to cover the movement would provide excellent camouflage in which to conceal the carriers and the Tungsten strike force.

A huge armada assembled for the two operations. It was divided into two groups. Force One, led by Fraser flying his flag in *Duke of York*, would initially provide distant cover for the convoy. He would be accompanied by Henry Moore on the battleship *Anson*, together with *Victorious*, to provide air support if needed. Force Two was made up of Furious, three escort carriers, *Emperor*, *Pursuer* and *Searcher*, four cruisers and four destroyers. They were to sail directly to the rendezvous point where, once the convoy was out of danger, the operation would commence. Another carrier, *Fencer*, would also be at sea with twenty-eight aircraft to attack any lurking U-boats.

Convoy JW.58 left Loch Ewe on 27 March, followed three days later by Fraser and Force One from Scapa. On the mainland, spring was in the air but the northern seas were as vicious as ever. Spray and sleet froze solid as it hit the deck and upper works and on board *Victorious* Captain Denny ordered the engines of the Corsairs parked on deck to be run up every two hours to prevent them seizing in the cold. Denny had taken over the previous December and believed that 'the aroma of the ship's previously unrewarding efforts' against German battleships 'still remained in the nostrils of the Naval Air Arm'. A Swordfish from *Victorious* struck *Bismarck* with a torpedo in the chase of May 1941 but failed to inflict serious damage. The carrier had taken part in the bitterly disappointing air attacks on *Tirpitz* in March the following year and a few months later shared in the collective guilt of the PQ.17 catastrophe. An opportunity for revenge had now arisen but Denny worried that preparations had not been thorough enough to make the most of it. His ship's own squadrons were only recently formed and 'few of them had ever engaged in an offensive operation before'. At his reckoning, '85 per cent of them had never proceeded to sea in a ship other than in the smooth waters of the Clyde'.[11]

At this point it still seemed possible that, even though trials were not complete, *Tirpitz* might venture out against the convoy. The tanks and aircraft on board would add greatly to the burden of misery being borne by Hitler's armies, now falling back all along the Eastern Front. A short sharp foray, particularly if, as with the previous three sailings, the merchantmen had only a light escort, might be worth the gamble.

By the morning of 1 April, though, Fraser was coming to the conclusion that this would not happen. German air reconnaissance picked up the convoy and tried, unsuccessfully, to home U-boat packs onto it. But there had been no wider search to establish if JW.58 was being covered by a powerful force. 'This apparent lack of interest,' wrote Fraser later, 'suggested to me that *Tirpitz* was unlikely to threaten the convoy.' He decided to send off *Victorious* to join Force Two and advance Tungsten by twenty-four hours, while he withdrew westwards to await events.[12]

On the afternoon of 2 April, the two forces met up 250 miles north-west of Altafjord. None of the crews got any sleep that evening. They were called to a last briefing at 1.30 a.m., 'that hour,' wrote Denny, 'when man's stamina is at its lowest'. On board *Victorious* was a former naval officer, Anthony Kimmins, who had switched careers to become an actor and prolific film director. He was now back in the service and described the 'feverish activity' in the hangars as the fitters and riggers 'swarmed over their aircraft making final adjustments ... great yellow bombs were being wheeled down the narrow gangways, loaded up and fused', each with a chalked message for the *Tirpitz*. The Barracudas, with their wings folded back along their bodies seemed 'like enormous beetles'.

After the crews had eaten a hot breakfast he followed them up to the flight deck where, to their relief and surprise, they found 'perfect conditions – calm seas, clear skies with patches of cloud' and were assured by the met officer that the weather was even better inland. It seemed to everyone that 'providence was very much on our side. Even in the summer one would have been lucky to find such conditions, but at this time of year it was almost unbelievable.'

At 4 a.m. they boarded their machines. 'At exactly the pre-arranged minute, Commander, Flying, shouted the welcome order "Start up!" The words were hardly out of his mouth before there was a roar of engines. Gloves laid on the wings during the final adjustments went whisking over the side. Ice which had formed on the flight deck was sent scurrying in all directions.' As the ship swung into the wind for take-off 'lumps of ice shot up in the air and went slithering down the flying deck, got whirled up in the propeller slipstreams and went cracking against the flight deck crews, clinging to the wingtips and lying on the deck tending the chocks.'[13] Then the flight deck officer waved a green flag and the first Corsair went racing away over the bow. The fighters were followed by twelve Barracudas of 827 Squadron. A few minutes later nine Barracudas from 830 Squadron left *Furious*. They circled above the fleet forming up with their comrades from 8 Wing. It seemed to Denny, looking up at them, that 'they left the carriers' decks in the greatest of heart and brimful of determination … taking departure to the target exactly as if [in] a parade ground movement'.[14] The wing was led by Lieutenant Commander Roy Baker-Falkner, a twenty-seven-year-old professional naval officer who had taken part in the attack on the Italian navy at Taranto and whose action-filled war to date was a reproof to Churchill's suggestion that the FAA was slacking.

They set course to make landfall at the island of Loppa, cruising at fifty feet over the flat calm sea to slip in under the radar. Above them darted the blunt-nosed Wildcats and Hellcats, which would swoop to blast the onshore anti-aircraft batteries and strafe the decks of the *Tirpitz* while the Barracudas delivered their bombs. Visibility was perfect. Ahead, the crystal Nordic light bounced off the jagged snow-blanketed hills and silver inlets ahead. Twenty miles from land the strike force started to climb. At 5.08 they flashed over the coast at 7,000 feet, easing onto a course that would take them south of Altafjord and over the western end of Langfjord, before looping round to launch their attack from the south over the hills rising from Kaafjord.

Sub-Lieutenant John Herrold, a young New Zealand Barracuda pilot with 827 Squadron, looked down on 'a picture of incredible beauty'. The mountains 'were bathed on one side with the pink light of the sun'. The snow sweeping down the mountain sides to the fjords 'wasn't the white snow of a Christmas card. It was so brilliant it was more of a light blue colour.'

Alan Thomson, hunched over his guns several aircraft behind him, saw two small ships lying in Langfjord which opened fire. They were way out of range and the 'smoke puffs hanging there' did not disconcert him. About ten miles from the target, Baker-Falkner ordered the 830 Squadron aircraft to fall in behind the twelve Barracudas of 827 Squadron. By now Herrold could see the ridge beyond which lay Kaafjord. 'As I looked at this hill it seemed to come towards me so slowly, then suddenly, with a surge we were over the top and there beneath us lay the *Tirpitz*, and in exactly the place we'd been told to look for it.'[15]

She was lying in her berth, bows pointing north-east towards the entrance to the fjord. The first wisps of smoke were starting to curl from the artificial fog generators on ship and shore but far too late to spoil the bombers' aim. Surprise had been almost total. *Tirpitz* was due to set sail for high-speed trials in Stjern sound, at the entrance to the open sea at 5.30 that morning. Her five destroyers had already set off down the fjord, the net defences were open and the crew were casting off cables and weighing anchor when the radar warning came of approaching enemy aircraft. Kapitän Meyer ordered everyone to action stations but when the first aeroplanes appeared, flak crews were still scrambling to their posts and below decks watertight doors hung open.

As soon the ship came in sight, Baker-Falkner broke radio silence and Herrold heard him order 'all fighters anti-flak!'. The gun crews were still trying to bring their weapons to bear when they were set upon. The Wildcats of 882 Squadron 'whistled down over forested hills … [and] shot across the fjord in a straggling line abreast', their CO, Lieutenant Commander A. J. Cooper, reported later, 'shooting into the battleship … various missiles appeared to be whizzing in all directions … very exciting'.[16] Moments later, at 5.29, they were followed by the Barracudas, led by Baker-Falkner. Herrold watched him 'doing a half-roll and plunging towards the target. We peeled off and dived down behind him.' He could see the fighters 'strafing the anti-aircraft gun positions and the ship, spraying their machine gun fire … at incredibly close range.' The result of these attentions was 'a very slight and very ragged flak opposition during the whole operation'.

Herrold was fourth in line, swooping at an angle of fifty degrees. He 'had the nose of my aircraft pointing just below the funnel of the *Tirpitz* … and kept her nose glued to that point'. He could see the swastika painted on the forecastle and the 'white faces of the ack-ack crews looking up'. And then 'a great sight'. Two of Baker-Falkner's three 500lb high explosive bombs hit near the ship's two big forward turrets. Seconds later, with his altimeter showing 2,500 feet, Herrold let his three 500lb SAPs go, 'then pulled over and started weaving to dodge the flak'.

Bombs were bursting all over *Tirpitz*. Baker-Falkner was followed by Sub-Lieutenant H. R. Emerson, carrying a single 1,600lb AP, and it seemed to Sub-Lieutenant I. G. Robertson, hard behind him, that he had landed it 'aft of amidships'. This was dreamlike accuracy and as each subsequent pilot tilted onto the target they reported repeated huge red flashes and orange flames. It only took a few seconds for smoke from the explosions to roll over the ship. When the first 830 Squadron aircraft went into its dive the observer, Lieutenant J. Armitage, noted that 'amidships and forward parts of the ship were wreathed in smoke'. The result was that he was unable to follow his own 1,600lb bomb all the way down. Thereafter the aircraft were aiming into the smoke and flame. Alan Thomson's Barracuda was the last of the Barracudas to dive. As his pilot, Sub-Lieutenant Dickie Williams, put the nose down to sixty-five degrees he 'experienced negative G for the first time, I had a signal pad strapped to my knee and it floated as high as my eyes'. As they hurtled down he saw 'our bombs disappear into the smoke and fire … I don't know if we had hits or not. But the flashes suggested we did.'

As they turned to escape he noticed 'five columns of smoke on the shore'. He thought for a moment they might be the result of bombs that overshot. In fact they were produced by land-based fog generators starting up, 'but they'd left it too late and they had been caught with their trousers down'. Williams took the aircraft round, waiting for a chance to dart through a gap in the bowl of hills to the west that was their best route out. A 'gun battery ashore was concentrating fire on that point and it was a case of watching for the fire and trying to nip through before the next salvo came up'. When they passed safely through, the skies over Kaafjord were empty. The whole attack from first to last had taken, Baker-Falkner proudly reported later, 'sixty-seconds exactly'.

In the roiling smoke and flame below, the crew of *Tirpitz* were experiencing for the first time the real shock of war. The exposed upper decks had been crowded with men engaged in casting off when the attackers arrived. In seconds, the orderly drills were replaced by chaos, and the spotless decks were slippery with blood. Karl Rohwedder reached his action station commanding one of the light flak batteries and started to return fire at the blue-green bombers skidding down the sky towards him at 230mph. 'We kept on firing but could not get any more ammunition via the lift that usually brought it up and had to rely on our existing supplies,' he remembered. Flash from a blast scorched his face but he kept at his post until eventually persuaded to go below for treatment. 'The hospital area had taken a hit and we sat in the dark and waited. There were people who were a lot more seriously wounded than I was. It was terrible sitting there in the dark with all the shouting and screaming and in the end I couldn't stand it.' A nurse gave him a bandage and he tied it on himself before climbing back on deck to await a further attack.[17]

At 6.19 a.m. the first aircraft began landing on *Victorious*. By 6.38 the Barracudas were safely back on board their carriers. 'All aircraft returned in flight formation with a unanimous broad grin,' reported Captain Denny. Only one was missing. Aircraft 'M' from 830 Squadron, with Sub-Lieutenant Thomas Bell, Leading Airman George 'Paddy' Burns and Sub-Lieutenant Robert Drennan on board, had been seen by another aircraft 'going down in a controlled glide' over a lake on the return journey. Alan Thomson was friendly with Burns, who earlier in the year declined to fly with a pilot because he doubted his competence and was assigned to Bell instead. There was no time to reflect on the vagaries of fate. Thomson went below with the others for breakfast and a tot of rum. It felt like the start of a victory celebration.

By now the second wave of Barracudas was already over the target. The two squadrons of 52 Wing started taking off at 5.25. One developed engine trouble and there had been a fatal mishap when another, from 829 Squadron, crashed into the sea with a 1,600lb bomb on board, killing Sub-Lieutenant Francis Bowles, Lieutenant John Whittaker and Leading Airman Colin Colwill. Shortly after the remaining nineteen crossed the coast they could see, forty miles away, a dark cloud polluting the virgin blue of the sky, the product of the fog generators and the smoke from the onboard fires. As they approached Kaafjord the wing commander, Lieutenant Commander V. Rance, ordered them into two double columns, hoping this dispersal would make them a less concentrated target for the flak. Once again, the escorting Hellcats went in first to shoot up the onshore batteries while the Wildcats sprayed the ship.

Following the first attack, the ship had manoeuvred into a position where she was lying broadside across the fjord, with her bow facing west, apparently the better to bring her guns to bear in the direction of the next anticipated attack. It made little difference.

The close-range flak guns opened up as soon as they saw the approaching aircraft which, as Rance insouciantly reported, was 'much too early' to do any damage.[18] As they prepared to dive, a canopy of flak began bursting at about 3,000 feet. Undeterred, Rance led his men into the dive. It was 6.36 a.m. At intervals of a few seconds, the Barracudas slid towards the ship, showering two 1,600lb AP bombs and thirty-nine 500lb and 600lb bombs onto the still-visible shape below. A bare minute later the attack was over. Rance reported that '*Tirpitz* had ceased firing by the time the last aircraft dived'. Not, though, before its gunners claimed one of the attackers. An 829 Squadron Barracuda, with Sub-Lieutenants Hubert Richardson and Andrew Cannon and Leading Airman Ernest Carroll, was hit over the target but carried on the attack, only to be seen crashing into a hillside in flames.

The rest made their getaway over the mountains to the north and west. Forty minutes later they were landing on *Victorious* and *Furious* with reports of hits, explosions and fires. There was no doubt in Captain Denny's mind that the operation had been a success. At 6.28, while the first-wave aircraft were still landing on *Victorious*, he signalled Admiral Moore on *Anson*: 'It is certain that Tirpitz is badly hit by first strike.' He spent the rest of the day studying the crew debriefing notes and the photographs from the cameras of the bombers before delivering his preliminary assessment of the results. He judged that the first wave hit *Tirpitz* with three 1,600lb APs, four 500lb SAPs and three 500lb high explosive bombs. The second wave landed four SAPs, two 500lb and one 600lb anti-submarine bombs on target. One of the big armour-piercing bombs struck in the 'vicinity of the fore superstructure'. Other bombs landed on the forecastle, amidships, forward of the bridge, on the starboard side of the mainmast and close by two of the big gun turrets. At 5.37 p.m. he sent his report to Moore with the bold conclusion: 'I believe *Tirpitz* now to be useless as a warship.'

The emphatic tone was understandable. The great plumes of smoke visible in the photographs painted a dramatic picture of the destruction wrought. The superstructure of *Tirpitz* was a mass of twisted metal. The deck was rent with jagged holes and everywhere were spurting flames and billowing smoke. The ship's hospital was overwhelmed by the 316 men wounded in the attack and the passageways were lined with casualties awaiting treatment. Another 122 had been killed. Kapitän Meyer was badly wounded, and command of the ship passed to his second in command Kapitän zur See Wolfe Junge. Once she was back in her berth and no further attack arrived, a proper assessment of damage was possible. It soon emerged that the damage, though spectacular, was essentially superficial. Denny's tally of hits was not far from the findings of the ship's chief engineer, Fregattenkapitän Eichler, who counted twelve strikes and four near misses. None of them, though, did critical damage. Holes had been blasted in the port side of the deck, wrecking galleys and the officers' mess and reducing the grand piano on which Kapitän Assman once entertained the company to matchwood and wires.

One of the 1,600-pounders landed in the water, holing the hull below the armoured belt and causing extensive flooding and a list to starboard. But none of the other big armour-piercing bombs had done its job. One exploded on the port side of the upper deck. Two reached the armour deck but failed to penetrate it. One failed to explode at all. The vital parts of *Tirpitz* remained intact and the damage to its big guns was slight and easily reparable. Nonetheless, despite their escape, the mood on the ship was sombre. Among the casualties, the flak gunners had been particularly hard hit. Many of the guns had no armoured shields and the crews had no protection from the Wildcats' bullets. 'We missed the men who had sat down to eat with us, who had operated the turret gun with us,' wrote Adalbert Brünner. 'It was bitter to take down the photos of wife, parents, and children from their lockers and to send them home.'[19]

Subsequent analysis of the operation advanced the idea that the very zeal of the aircrews may have undermined the effectiveness of the 1,600lb bombs. They were supposed to be most efficient at heights over 3,500 feet, yet almost all the pilots carrying them dropped below 3,000 feet. The interpretation was that in their enthusiasm to hit the target they had gone in too low. Some doubted whether they would have pierced the armour deck at whatever height they were delivered. Among them was the civilian Director of Naval Construction, the astringent Sir Stanley Goodall. In the course of the post-operation evaluation, the Director of Naval Intelligence, Rear Admiral Edmund Rushbrook, queried the precise thickness of the armour over the *Tirpitz* magazines. Was it three and three-quarter inches as stated in one document or three and a quarter as in another? The reply came from the DNC's office that it made no difference. 'Whichever of the figures … is correct, the armour could not have been defeated by the bombs.'

The crews knew nothing of this as they toasted each other in Pusser's rum and endlessly replayed the morning's events. The day wore on and they began to wonder whether they would be called on to repeat the performance the following day. As they lay in their hammocks, catching up on lost sleep, Thomson heard some '831 personnel, [who] possibly had a stickier [time] than we had, [start] to grumble about the thought we were going back next morning. I just piped up and said, if you don't shut up and get some sleep you'll not be fit to go anywhere in the morning.' They did not have to worry long. During the afternoon, Admiral Moore had indeed planned to repeat the performance at first light. On receiving the first reports that *Tirpitz* had been seriously damaged and Denny's verdict that she was now 'useless', he reconsidered. He also took into account the 'fatigue of the crews and their natural reaction on completing a dangerous operation successfully'. Enough was enough. He 'decided against a repetition and ordered the forces to withdraw'.

At 4.40 p.m. on 6 April, the fleet arrived back in Scapa Flow. 'It was beautiful,' remembered Alan Thompson, aboard *Furious*. 'The carrier opened up to thirty knots and we were cheered around the fleet.' They took the applause standing on parade without greatcoats in a freezing Orkneys wind. There were letters of congratulation from King George VI and Churchill who praised a 'brilliant feat of arms'. But the Prime Minister, and the First Sea Lord, Admiral Cunningham, were unable to relax. *Tirpitz* was still afloat. Cunningham had doubted whether the Barracudas' bombs were heavy enough to put *Tirpitz* out of action and confined himself to hoping that 'her AA armament, controls and upper works are badly smashed up'.[20] He regretted Moore's decision not to launch a second assault the following the day. As serious analysis of the damage got under way, backed with agent reports and photographic reconnaissance, it became clear that the most that could be hoped for was that *Tirpitz* would be out of action for six months. The Germans had already demonstrated their ability to overcome huge logistical difficulties and work at a rate that confounded their enemies' optimistic estimates.

On 13 April, ten days after the attack, Cunningham called Moore in and asked him to repeat the operation. He appeared 'quite ready to do it'. When Cunningham rang Fraser to tell him of developments he found the Home Fleet's commander 'in a most obstinate and truculent mood'. Fraser had been sceptical about Tungsten's worth from the outset. He told Cunningham now that 'he had held a meeting with his admirals and captains and made the decision that "Tungsten" was not to be repeated'. Cunningham 'reasoned with him', arguing that the decision was not irrevocable and that the Admiralty must have a say in which operations were to be carried out. Fraser was adamant and said 'if we were not satisfied we must get another C-in-C and in fact indicated that he would haul down his flag (resign) if ordered to repeat "Tungsten"'.

Cunningham told him to sleep on it and to call him in the morning. When they spoke next day, Fraser seemed in a more acquiescent mood. Later on, though, Cunningham was told by the Vice-Chief of the Naval Staff, Neville Syfret, that Fraser was once again talking of resigning. Later in the day he seemed to have softened enough for Cunningham to risk sending a signal ordering the operation.

Fraser's subsequent version of events was less dramatic and he denied having threatened resignation. However, he remained

310 · PATRICK BISHOP

convinced that the favourable conditions of the first attack were unlikely to be replicated. The nights were shrinking and there was little hope of achieving the same surprise. As no convoys were scheduled for the next few months, there would be no sailing to divert the enemy's attention. There were also fears that *Tirpitz* now had fighter protection and the free run the bombers enjoyed to and from the ships would not be repeated.

Nonetheless he agreed – weather conditions permitting – to try again. As his destroyers were needed at the end of the month to take part in exercises for the Normandy invasion, he proposed that a new operation be mounted before then. Once again, he left his number two in charge. Moore sailed on 21 April with a similar force, planning to strike three days later. Fraser's pessimism was borne out. There was no recurrence of the freakishly fine conditions of Tungsten and the operation was called off, defeated by the weather. Intelligence from Alta suggested that the repair programme was progressing fast. On 9 May Torsten Raaby's clandestine wireless station at Alta sent a report that *Tirpitz* had her engines going and two hundred workmen had arrived from Germany to speed along the work.

On 14 May, another operation, Brawn, was launched, but the strike force was recalled before it reached the coast as the target was completely covered by cloud. A fortnight later, Operation Tiger Claw was also thwarted by bad weather. With the Normandy landings, attention was diverted away from *Tirpitz*, but not for long. On 14 June, the man who might have called a halt to the succession of expensive and fruitless missions departed. Bruce Fraser relinquished command of the Home Fleet to take over the Eastern Fleet and was replaced by Henry Moore. Moore was determined to carry on with carrier-borne attacks and plans were laid for Operation Mascot, scheduled for mid-July. The strike force took off on 17 July in the near daylight of an Arctic midnight. Improved radar cover picked up their approach. When they arrived in Kaafjord, *Tirpitz* was blanketed in smoke and none of the bombs dropped hit the target.

With each failed operation *Tirpitz* was returning to something like full health. Watching her progress from Stockholm, the energetic naval spy Captain Henry Denham reported she was making daily trips up and down Altafjord, reaching a speed of twenty knots, and her guns were in full working order. At the end of July she put to sea for an exercise with destroyers. The defences around Kaafjord were steadily growing stronger. More smoke generators had appeared along the shore. In the minds of the Admiralty, all this activity suggested that an aggressive sortie was imminent and that Kaafjord was being turned into a secure base for operations.

The summer of frustration only intensified the determination for another effort. This time, the biggest force the Fleet Air Arm had ever mustered was to be thrown at the ship. The operation was timed to coincide with the sailing of Convoy JW.59. On 20 August a huge fleet assembled off the Norwegian coast for the launch of Operation Goodwood. At its core were three fleet carriers, *Indefatigable*, *Formidable* and *Furious*, together with the smaller *Nabob* and *Trumpeter*, their hangars crammed with forty-eight Barracudas, twenty Avenger torpedo bombers and a hundred Corsair, Wildcat

Hellcats

and Seafire fighters. Moore oversaw events from his flagship, *Duke of York*, and the armada was attended by swarms of destroyers and corvettes.

Sub-Lieutenant Cyril Price, an observer in an 828 Squadron Barracuda embarked on *Formidable*, looked down while conducting an anti-submarine patrol at the sight of the ships and marvelled at the array of craft 'spread over a vast, vast distance ... unbelievable'. Even at this stage of the war, with Allied armies pushing out from the Normandy beachheads, the objective was still identified as of vital significance. Before leaving Scapa the crews were given a special briefing by civilian officials who 'told us how important it was that we did our very best ... [*Tirpitz*] was tying down the Home Fleet and was a terrific threat to the convoys.'[21]

Goodwood was due to start on 21 August but bad weather caused a day's postponement. The 22nd dawned cloudy and there were further delays until finally the first aircraft launched at 11 a.m., only for the Barracudas to be recalled when it became clear that thick cloud would make bombing pointless. Fog the next day ruled out another effort but on 24th the weather cleared sufficiently by the afternoon for another attempt. The strike force was made up of thirty-three Barracudas, each carrying a 1,600lb AP, as well as five Corsairs and ten Hellcats armed with armour-piercing bombs. By now it took only ten minutes for the smoke generators to blanket Kaafjord and by the time they arrived *Tirpitz* was invisible. From 12,000 feet all Cyril Price could see 'was smoke down below'. He and his pilot decided to aim at the flashes from the ship's guns and 'put the nose down and dived down through the smoke, hoping we were aiming in the right direction'. He found 'the scary part was pulling out of the dive at the bottom because you were in the smoke, surrounded by mountains, with all these aircraft dashing around'.

Out of the shower of bombs, two found the target. One 500-pounder hit the Bruno turret, doing minor damage. The other was a 1,600lb AP which for once achieved what it was designed to do, plunging through the ship at an angle to penetrate the armoured deck and ending up jammed lengthwise with its nose pointing at the bow in an electrical switch room below the water line. A detonation would, as the report later acknowledged, have done 'immeasurable' damage,[22] but the bomb failed to explode. The team given the delicate job of defusing it could find no obvious reason for the failure, noting only that the 'detonation device' was 'damaged'. The fuse was too awkwardly placed to remove immediately so they neutralized the bomb by sluicing out the explosive. The ship's log summed up: 'The hitherto greatest attack has not resulted in any lasting damage.'[23]

The fleet hung around for five more days, buffeted by gales and shrouded in fog, before launching a final attack on 29 August. Sixty aircraft took part, only to be frustrated again by the smoke generators. That evening the great armada began to disperse, with seventeen aircraft and forty airmen fewer than they had arrived with. The Fleet Air Arm's greatest operation of the war had ended in failure. It was now time for the RAF to take up the challenge.

18

The Third Man

One morning at the end of August 1944, a group of airman were playing football on their airfield at Woodhall Spa, Lincolnshire, when there was an interruption. 'Somebody arrived on the touch-line and asked for our CO, Willie Tait,' said Tony Iveson, a twenty-four-year-old flight lieutenant. Tait disappeared and came back later 'to say that we had a special job'. The game broke up and later that day the players were in the air on the first of a series of cross-country flights.

All the jobs the airmen did were special. They were members of 617 Squadron – the Dambusters – and they had spent the summer carrying out attacks requiring exceptional accuracy on vital targets in France. Tait did not tell his men the nature of their next mission and speculation bubbled. That afternoon the engines on Iveson's Lancaster were fitted with flow meters and he and his crew took off for seven and a half hours of tests at different heights and speeds to find the most economic rate of fuel consumption. Wherever they were going, 'we all knew it was going to be a long trip. It struck one or two people that *Tirpitz* was a possible target.'[1]

Even before the Fleet Air Arm's great effort had definitively failed, new plans were being hatched to dispose of *Tirpitz*. The repeated operations of the summer had revealed a simple truth: the Barracudas were simply not fast enough to get to Kaafjord in time to beat the smokescreen. At a meeting of the Chiefs of Staff Committee on 19 August – the day after the Goodwood force put to sea – Admiral Cunningham raised the possibility of using the RAF's faster Mosquito bombers, carrying 2,000lb armour-piercing bombs, to launch an attack from one of his carriers. The idea was passed up to the headquarters of General Eisenhower – who, in order to obtain the tightest coordination in preparations for the Normandy landings, had been given control of the strategic bombing force – and also to Bomber Command. The answer came back that the Supreme Allied Commander did 'not consider diversion of Mosquito bomber effort justifiable at this moment'. This rejection produced a sharp reaction from the Admiralty. It retorted that Eisenhower 'was not in a position to appreciate the significance which an attack on "Tirpitz" would have on the overall strategic plan' and dared to suggest that the direction of the bomber force should revert to the RAF.[2]

The admirals' indignation was stoked by their conviction that even in her diminished state *Tirpitz* still posed a serious threat to Allied shipping and a major obstacle to their plans. Cunningham had told his fellow chiefs that eliminating her would 'have an important effect ... on world wide dispositions of battleships and fleet carriers and on the early strengthening of the Eastern Fleet'.[3] The importance of finishing her off was emphasized in a report of the inter-service Joint Planning Staff of 23 August which claimed that *Tirpitz* was still 'capable of carrying out limited operations, or of returning to Germany [where] a period of a few months in a German dockyard would ... fully restore her fighting efficiency'. If left unmolested she might 'risk everything in a final effort' against a Russian or Atlantic convoy, or even attack a troopship bound for France. Her destruction would not only neutralize this menace; it would also remove the need to hold the minimum of 'one fast battleship and one fleet carrier' at the ready in case of a breakout.[4]

At this distance in time, these fears seem exaggerated. *Tirpitz* remained unsunk but she was battered and enfeebled. Despite the heroic efforts of the repair force she could only muster twenty knots, against the twenty-eight knots of her British equivalents. In this condition she was unfit for serious operations. If she did try to regain a German port she would be vulnerable to attack by Allied surface ships, submarines and aircraft on passage. If she survived the voyage, she would then be assured of the attentions of Bomber Command.

Admiral Dönitz had no intention of sending *Tirpitz* off on a last, death-or-glory sortie. The strength of the enemy, in the air and above and below the waves, meant the chance of success was minimal while catastrophe was virtually assured. He also recognized that it would have been 'impossible for her to undertake the long journey home through the North Sea without being detected by the enemy and subjected to attack by superior sea and air forces'. The ship had no role to play elsewhere. Her uses were therefore limited to 'protection against any enemy landing in the area' and '[tying] down the enemy heavy ships to the north European zone and [preventing] them being sent to some other theatre of war'.[5]

Of all the rationalizations for continuing the assaults, then, it was the argument that putting an end to *Tirpitz* would release heavy warships for duty in the Far East that had the most validity. The war in the central Pacific – a struggle in which aircraft carriers were of paramount importance – was moving towards a climax. The Americans were poised to close on the Philippines and the Royal Navy's Eastern Fleet needed reinforcements to play its part in the Allied plan and to assert its right to a continued presence in the area when peace came.

The solution to the Admiralty's problems now lay in the hands of a man who until recently had demonstrated little interest in *Tirpitz* or its destruction. Arthur Harris regarded battleships as pointless relics of a vanished age, whose survival owed more to the *amour propre* of admirals than to strategic necessity. Following the COS committee meeting of 19 August, Harris had also been asked for his opinion of Cunningham's proposal for an attack by Mosquito bombers. Nine days later, Sir Douglas Evill, the Vice Chief of the Air Staff, visited him at Bomber Command's High Wycombe HQ to hear the response. Harris rubbished the plan. He doubted 'very much' whether Mosquitoes were fast enough to get to the battleship before the smokescreen rolled in, and the capacity of the bombs to do serious damage. Nor did he want to divert his Mosquito force from its regular raids on Berlin.

Lurking in this disparaging assessment, though, was a possible solution to the navy's problems. According to Evill's report to his chief, Sir Charles Portal, Harris told him that Bomber Command 'had for some time been considering the problem of bombing the "Tirpitz" and the only reason they had not pressed on with it was because they did not realise the importance the Admiralty placed on this attack'.

The last part seems to have been an example of Harris's knockabout wit. No one could have been ignorant of the titanic efforts of the Fleet Air Arm throughout the summer. He appears to have realized that he may have overstepped the mark for when a copy of Evill's report reached him he protested that he had been misrepresented and the account was 'quite incorrect'. The true reason for holding back was that 'the only bomb suitable for an attack on "Tirpitz" is the "Tallboy," the supply of which has been barely sufficient to cover the Command's immediate commitments'. This version was duly inserted into the official record.[6]

In his 1947 memoirs Harris nonetheless presented a colourful account of how Bomber Command came to be engaged once more in the great campaign against *Tirpitz*:

> During all this period the Admiralty continued to worry about the German navy and in particular, in the autumn of 1944, about the *Tirpitz*. Our own battleships with their usual large complement of ancillary craft, were kept hanging about at home in case the Germans should decide to send the poor old lone *Tirpitz* to sea, and it was felt that some use might be found for these large units of the Royal Navy in the Pacific. I was accordingly asked to intervene in this fantastic 'war' between these dinosaurs … I was quite willing to do so, but only if this did not seriously interfere with more important operations; I gave an undertaking that we should sink the *Tirpitz* in our spare time.[7]

This interpretation, amusing though it was to Harris with its implication of a despairing Admiralty imploring Bomber Command for deliverance, is not quite in accordance with the record. At the meeting with Evill, Harris already had a fully-formed plan up his sleeve. He told him that he could have twenty-four aircraft available for an operation ready by 7 September – only ten days away. They would attempt to fly on a round trip from the far north of Scotland to Kaafjord and then back again to a base in the Shetlands. If the return journey looked risky, arrangements could be made for the bombers to carry on to north Russia, to land and refuel at Murmansk. Inquiries had already been made and it appeared suitable facilities were available.

Harris seems to have been in no doubt that the plan would be accepted and preparations were well under way by the time the final approval was received from Eisenhower's headquarters on 5 September. The operation was to be be carried out by his two Special Duties units, 617 and 9 Squadrons. They lived a few miles apart from each other in the rich, flat fields east of Lincoln. Of the two, 617 was by far the best known. It was 9 Squadron, though, that had the oldest pedigree. While 617 was only seventeen months old, having been formed specifically for the Dams raid, 9 Squadron dated back to 1914. After disbandment in 1919 it re-formed in 1924 as a night bomber squadron, later acquiring a bat as its badge symbol and the motto 'Per noctem volamus'. It started operations on the first day of the war, attacking shipping at Brunsbüttel at the mouth of the Kiel Canal, and losing two Wellingtons to ground fire or fighters. Since then it had been in the vanguard of the strategic bomber campaign, returning night after night to blast German cities and ports and suffering staggering casualties in the process. In 1943 it lost fifty-seven aircraft, nearly three times the squadron strength. In the spring and summer of 1944 it had been occupied with invasion targets, led by Wing Commander James Bazin, a former fighter pilot who flew Hurricanes with 607 in the Battle of Britain. Now it was to be switched away from the grind of 'main force' operations and join 617 on special operations, swapping its conventional bombs for the streamlined sophistication of the Tallboy.

The Tallboy was the latest invention of Barnes Wallis, 'our Number One Wizard' as Harris called him. Wallis was a creative engineer, and in the words of his friend and biographer J. E.

Morpurgo 'saw creative engineering as an art and himself as a sort of poet'.[8] In the forcing house of wartime, his prodigious talent and energy had produced some remarkable and valuable inventions.

The idea for the Tallboy dated back to 1940 but Wallis had only been put to work on developing it in the summer of 1943 when it was discovered that the Germans were close to deploying flying bombs and long-range ballistic missiles – the V1s and V2s. The only defence available was to bomb the sites where they were being developed or stored. A mass raid by nearly six hundred aircraft dropped 1,937 tons of bombs on the V2 missile research centre at Peenemünde on the Baltic coast on 17 August 1943. This was a huge attack but forty aircraft were lost and the programme was set

Number One Wizard

back by only two months. The blunt instruments that were all Bomber Command had available could not do the job. Something more precise and deadly was required.

Wallis had foreseen the need for a bomb for use against 'targets … of the most massive nature … practically invulnerable to attack by existing aerial methods'.[9] It was axiomatic that the bigger the bomb the greater its destructive potential but in the first years of the war aircraft lacked the lifting power to carry monster weapons. With the arrival of the Lancaster, capacity increased. Tallboy was not just a very big bomb: it was designed to bury itself in the ground and explode, producing an earthquake effect. Shockwaves ripple more powerfully through earth – and water – than they do through air. Thus, a Tallboy did not have to score a direct hit to destroy its target.

To achieve the penetration needed for the best results, the bomb had to be dropped from high altitudes. It needed to be tough and aerodynamically efficient to withstand the impact. Wallis's bomb was made of molybdenum steel, sufficiently strong and light to carry a high proportion of explosive – 5,000lb of Torpex in an all-up weight of 12,000lb. It was twenty-one feet long, tapering to a point that was as sharp as a pencil and fitted comfortably into the Lancaster's thirty-three-foot bomb bay. According to its inventor, 'previously bombs had just [been] made [of] thin steel casings which dropped from the sky. But I gave this bomb [a] perfect aero-dynamic shape and arranged the fins so they would impart to it an increasingly rapid spin. As the bomb attained a high velocity it actually passed through the speed of sound and penetrated the ground to a depth of about a hundred feet.'[10]

The loss of accuracy that grew with increased altitude was offset by the use of the Stabilized Automatic Bomb Sight (SABS). With conventional sights, the bomb aimer had to guide the pilot up to the moment of release. The delay between instruction and adjustment left an inevitable margin of error. The SABS was the most sophisticated aiming device to date. Shortly before arrival at the objective the navigator passed data to the bomb aimer, lying in the nose of the aircraft, on airspeed, altitude and wind direction to be fed into the instrument's computer. He then peered through the lens of the sight, speaking into the captain's earphones, calling 'left, right, steady' as needed until the target lay at the tip of a lit-up sword symbol reflected on a sheet of glass. As the target grew closer he held it in place, sliding down the blade of the sword, with two control wheels. These activated an instrument mounted in front of the pilot – the Bombing Direction Indicator. A needle on the face then told him the slight adjustments needed to keep the aircraft on track. Then, at the optimum moment, the bomb was released automatically. An experienced aimer could drop a bomb from 20,000 feet with an average margin of error of only eighty yards. To do so, of course, he needed to have clear sight of the target. Over cloud – or smokescreen – the SABS was useless.

Throughout the summer of 1944, 617 Squadron had been using both Tallboy and the SABS in specially modified Lancasters against V weapons sites buried deep under concrete in the Pas-de-Calais. In the month of August, prior to the summons to prepare for a 'special job' they had repeatedly and successfully bombed the previously invulnerable submarine pens at the Biscay ports of Brest, Lorient and La Pallice.

They were led into these attacks by a new commander, Wing Commander Tait, who for reasons never established was always known as 'Willie'. His arrival at 617 Squadron in July marked the opening of another remarkable passage in what was already an extraordinary wartime career. If there had never been a Second World War James Brian Tait's service career might have passed in obscurity. As it was, he emerged from it laden with decorations and bathed in the esteem of his comrades. Tony Iveson placed him in the highest rank of the aces of the war 'alongside Guy Gibson, Leonard Cheshire, Donald Bennett, Johnnie Johnson and Douglas Bader'. Unlike them, Tait would never become widely known in the world outside the RAF. That was exactly how he liked it. 'He had no interest in being the centre of attention,' said his son, Peter. 'Ever.'

There was, in his antecedents, some hint of what the demands of war might uncover. According to Iveson, 'bravery obviously ran in the Tait family' as James's father, Alexander, had been decorated for his exploits in mining operations under the German lines on the

Western Front.[11] Tait was born on 9 December 1916 in Manchester, where his mother had gone to stay with relatives while her husband was in France. At the age of twelve, he was taken by his father to watch the Schneider Trophy races off Portsmouth, and, like many others boys of his generation, was soon smitten by the world of flying. He was sent off to board at Wellingborough School in Northamptonshire, from where, in 1934, at seventeen, he won a prize scholarship to the RAF College at Cranwell.

Despite his love of flying 'the intention was that he was going to develop an engineering career in the RAF,' said Peter Tait. Throughout his service he maintained his knowledge and practical skills, to the extent of taking courses at the RAF apprentice school at Halton which qualified him to do some maintenance work on engines. This was unusual. Few officers had a detailed understanding of the functioning of the machines they flew in. Leslie White, the mechanic responsible for maintaining Tait's aircraft in 1942 told of him visiting the hangar on the morning of an operation to discover that his bomber was unserviceable due to a coolant leak in one of the engines. Tait asked how long the repair would take. White replied that he could not say, as the rest of the crew had been moved to another job and he was working alone. Reminding his old boss of the incident years later, White recalled: 'You said "I want that plane for tonight because I am leading the squadron on the raid … start getting the cowlings off and I will go for some assistance."' He returned half an hour later with several men. He then removed his cap and tunic, climbed into overalls, mounted a maintenance platform and got busy with spanners. The problem was fixed, and after an air test Tait led the squadron on that night's raid.[12]

At the start of the war he was with 10 Squadron, equipped with Heyford biplane bombers. 'I don't think he had the temperament for flying fighters,' said Peter. 'The Taits are not flamboyant.' He flew on his first operation in May 1940, and went on to do a hundred more. His emergence alive owed something to skill but also to what Iveson called 'that luck which was essential to survive in Bomber Command'.

As the boundaries of the bombing campaign advanced, he was always at the frontier. He took part in the first trip to Berlin – dropping leaflets – on the night of 1–2 October, and the first raid across the Alps to Turin. In February 1941, now commanding 51 Squadron, he led a small force of Whitleys from Malta to drop a team of parachutists tasked with blowing up an aqueduct near Tragino in southern Italy, the first British airborne operation of the war. The feat won him his first DSO.

He dodged death again and again. After joining 35 Squadron, the first to be equipped with the four-engined Halifax, he led a daylight raid on Kiel. When he landed at Linton-on-Ouse he was the only one of his crew who did not leave the aircraft on a stretcher. He flew on the first thousand-bomber raid, to Cologne in May 1942. One of his engines failed on the outward journey. He had every excuse to turn back but pressed on to the target.

In July 1942, he took over 78 Squadron and flew regularly alongside his men, disregarding the advice that squadron commanders should go on no more than one operation a month. In the spring of 1944 he was base operations officer at RAF Waddington. Again, he was discouraged from regular operational flying. Nonetheless, in his first six weeks he went on nine missions, joining inexperienced crews with two Australian Lancaster squadrons. The idea was to give them confidence. 'He insisted on first of all flying over the target to "acclimatize" them,' said Peter Tait. They then carried out the actual attack. Just as the novice crews thought their baptism of fire was complete, he 'insisted on flying low over the target to see what the damage was like'. Perhaps his intention was to inoculate them with his own contempt for death. It was, however, Peter reflected, 'an experience they never wanted to have again'.[13]

In May he returned to full-time operations and was appointed master bomber of No. 5 Group. On the eve of the Normandy landings he controlled a force of two hundred Lancasters tasked with smashing the coastal batteries covering the American landing beaches on the Cherbourg peninsula. The success of the mission earned him a second bar to his DSO. Once again, he took enormous risks, circling low, calmly floating around on what looked like a sea of flak while his cool, precise voice guided the bombers in.

What enabled Tait to remain so serene when all around him combat-hardened men were fighting panic? His comrades discussed it frequently. There were theories as to what drove him on when he had used up his fair share of luck long ago and in statistical terms should have been dead several times over. There was a theory that he was seeking revenge. Peter Tait recalled a rumour 'that father had a grudge because a German plane had succeeded in bombing the house that his fiancée had lived in. Totally untrue. I don't honestly think he felt the slightest enmity for the Germans.'

If anything, he had sympathy for them. His favourite composers were German and Austrian: Beethoven, and especially Schubert in whom he took an academic interest. 'He always used to say that the Germans were our traditional allies against the perfidious French,' said Peter, 'and that the First and Second World Wars were aberrations really, historically speaking.'

617 Squadron was founded in March 1943 under Guy Gibson. There were two brief appointments between Gibson's departure in August and the arrival of Leonard Cheshire in November. Squadron Leader George Holden was in command for six weeks before he was killed in a fruitless attempt to breech the banks of the Dortmund–Ems canal on the night of the 15/16 September. Flight Lieutenant Harold 'Mick' Martin, a brilliant Australian pilot, took temporary charge but the Bomber Command hierarchy decided against formalizing the appointment. Tait was thus the third man in a triumvirate of extraordinary figures to leave their mark on the Dambusters. The memory of Gibson was beginning to fade by the time he arrived on 12 July 1944. Cheshire, though, was still a palpable presence. In his time with the Dambusters, he had managed to inspire affection – even love – as well as awe in a group of men who were not easily impressed. He did it by a unique mixture of strength, humour and humility and an unusual concern for those under his command, aircrew and ground crew alike. 'It was very difficult to follow a man like Cheshire,' said one of his long-serving pilots, Bobby Knights. 'He [had] an aura that made everybody else rather small beside him. I hero-worshipped him.'[14]

There were obvious differences between the two. Cheshire was a would-be writer, playful and sophisticated, married to an American actress, Constance Binney, whom he whirled off to the Ritz for cocktails when in town. Tait was an RAF professional, with no interest in the high life. But there were similarities, too. Both had quick and questing minds. Above all they shared an uncanny interior calm. An old friend of Cheshire's noted that 'he did everything with an air, but that there was at the same time a withdrawn quality about him, a secret self-sufficiency.'[15] It was the same inviolable inner stillness that people sensed in Tait. There was another quality that united them – a flinty determination to achieve the objectives they had been set whatever the risk to themselves.

The two knew each other from Linton, when Tait had commanded 78 Squadron and Cheshire 76 Squadron. Tait liked Cheshire enough to make him godfather to his first child, Celia. 'As a fellow squadron commander there could be no finer person to work with,' he wrote in a private memoir. 'His clear, logical brain always picked out the essence of any problem.' The two worked harmoniously together 'free from the petty jealousy which was all too common between squadron commanders on the same station.'[16] Cheshire admired Tait sufficiently to try and convert him to Catholicism. It was never very probable. According to Peter, his father's religiosity extended only to being 'Church of England in an agnostic sort of way. He liked the ceremonial.'

He was unlikely to reproduce the warm relationship with his men that Cheshire had fostered. As Tait acknowledged, 'the charm of his personality was unique. It never broke down under stress, and in fact his endurance was remarkable. I have known nobody who could get more out of men than him, simply because they would do it for him. He was a leader and not a driver.'[17] Tait was himself an understanding boss, who, despite his own background as a pre-war professional, had little patience with attempts to impose service bull on men whose spirit was that of civilians in uniform. 'He certainly had a mind of his own,' said Peter Tait. 'On one station, there was a rather tedious group captain who wanted to put the airmen on parade. Of course bomber crews weren't much good at parades, so father said we're not going to [do it]. We're going to play football ... he was threatened with court martial for that.' The episode ended with him being sent to Harris for reprimand. 'Butch' delivered a rocket, then, as Tait was turning the door handle, spoiled the effect by saying, 'Well done, I'd have done the same thing myself.'

In the mess he 'looked like a hawk that had touched down for a drink beside a pool'.[18] He was a listener not a talker, standing quietly with pipe in hand, a modest half-pint tankard tucked under his arm. When he did speak it was with an intensity more appropriate to a university seminar than a bar-room chat. Lawrence 'Benny' Goodman, who arrived on the squadron in August, felt this reticence indicated diffidence rather than aloofness. 'He didn't keep himself to himself for any other reason than that he was, essentially, a shy person.'[19] Tait's social appearances were brief and Tony Iveson found he had to coax him to descend from his bedroom and join the squadron in the bar. While others roistered, he was 'more likely to be listening to Beethoven quartets on his gramophone,' said Peter.

Tait took over a squadron in flux. When Cheshire left, his three flight commanders, Dave Shannon, Les Munro and Joe McCarthy, moved on, too. They had been with 617 from the beginning and with their departure went the last of the original Dambusters. Those who remained were an individualistic and international bunch, all of them competent, experienced and self-confident. In the summer of 1944, Sir Ralph Cochrane, the commander of 5 Group to which both 617 and 9 Squadrons belonged, felt the unit was strong enough to be able to absorb new crews with less combat experience. In the case of Goodman and his comrades, they had none at all. They had been astonished to hear that as a 'sprog' crew they were being posted to the most famous squadron in the air force and arrived 'feeling very much like the underdogs, frightened to say boo to a goose'. The old hands, though, treated the new boys as equals 'and it soon became clear to us that we'd been accepted'.[20]

Despite his awesome record, Tait seems to have felt the need to demonstrate from the beginning that he would be leading from the front. His first operation with the squadron was on 17 July against the V2 rocket site at Wizernes, in the Pas-de-Calais. Tait flew as pathfinder in a Mustang fighter, as Cheshire had done, dropping red spot flares on the target for the Lancasters to aim their Tallboys at. 'When they got [to] the target [it] was covered in cloud,' said Peter Tait. 'So he dropped to a lower altitude and circled and said "Look for me".' Another version of the story had him waggling his wings to catch the sunlight providing those above with an aiming point. The result was that he 'got thoroughly shot up, and came back with a Mustang full of holes ... after that, no one was going to question his leadership.'

By the end of August, Tait and his men were adept at dropping Tallboys on land-based targets. The *Tirpitz* operation, though, would be the first time one had been used on a ship. It had soon become clear that with the distances involved, a round trip would not be feasible. The plan was changed so that after the attack the two squadrons would fly on to an airfield in north Russia. The initial choice of the Murmansk area was dropped as it was feared that the force would be vulnerable to attack by German fighters while on the ground. They settled on a base further east. A Soviet naval air station at Yagodnik, on an island in the Dvina river twenty miles south-east of Archangel, seemed suitable even though it had only a grass runway. After consultations with the Russians – who, now that victory was approaching, had adopted a more comradely attitude – Yagodnik was chosen.

The attack was codenamed Operation Paravane and all was due to be ready by 8 September. Good weather was crucial to success. Clear skies were essential if the 617 bomb aimers were to see the target. With preparations completed, the crews waited for a favourable forecast. Hanging about at Woodhall Spa was no hardship. The officers' mess was housed in Petwood, a mock-Tudor mansion built for an heiress of the Maples furniture family and the oak staircases, large rooms and sweeping lawns represented wild luxury in the monochrome austerity of wartime. By now, the crews knew the nature of their mission. On 8 September, 9 Squadron were driven the few miles over the flat Lincolnshire fields from their base at Bardney to join 617 at Woodhall for a secret briefing. The briefing room floor was covered with a large-scale model of Kaafjord complete with a miniature *Tirpitz*.

The mission was more complex and potentially dangerous than the short trips to the continent of the summer. Every aspect of the operation was problematical. The intention was to fly to Lossiemouth on the eastern tip of Scotland and refuel there before setting off for Russia. The Lancasters had been fitted with extra fuel tanks that took up much of the fuselage. Even with these, the 2,100-mile journey stretched the bombers' endurance to the limit. There were no radio beacons to guide them in until the last stage of the journey. For most of the way navigators would have to rely on dead reckoning and map reading to get to Yagodnik. On the actual attack they could expect to face fiercer flak than they encountered over France. There also remained the threat of fighters which, despite intelligence that they were present in the area, had mysteriously failed to come up to defend *Tirpitz* from the Fleet Air Arm.

Next day the forecast was bad again and there was a PT session to fill the time. There was one more day of standing by, then, on the 11th, the weather prospects brightened. Harris, who had taken a close interest in the operation, grasped the chance. At this last moment, he decided on a change of plan. Instead of bombing on the way to Russia, the aircraft would fly to Yagodnik first and launch their attack from there. The shorter distance involved meant a greater opportunity to catch the clear skies that were essential if the Tallboys were to be dropped with any accuracy. There was also the chance that the Germans would not be expecting an attack from Russia. An approach from the east might evade the radar and catch the ship's defences on the hop.

Harris called the Air Staff with the details of the new arrangements and the news that he intended to dispatch the bombers that evening. The announcement was received by the deputy chief, Sir Norman Bottomley, with some irritation. He complained that the plan should have been cleared with the Russians first. 'I pointed out that this was very short notice, especially in view of the possibilities of failures in recognition, if warning was not received in time, with consequent untoward incidents,' he huffed in a back-covering memo. Harris was unconcerned, telling him that there was 'no material change' to the situation and that he had, anyway, already given orders for the aircraft to proceed. As it was, the Russians accepted the new plan without fuss. The hurried departure, though, did cause problems which, but for luck, might well have proved catastrophic.

With no detour to Kaafjord on the outward journey, it was reckoned the Lancasters had the range to reach Yagodnik from their home bases. At 5 p.m on Monday, 11 September 1944, eighteen bombers from 9 Squadron left Bardney and twenty from 617 took off from Woodhall, each making their own way to their destination. The 9 Squadron force was preceded by two Liberators loaded with spares, stores and ground staff, who headed first to Lossiemouth to refuel. A Lancaster carrying three RAF cameramen, a BBC radio reporter and an Associated Press war correspondent went with the Bardney force to record the hoped-for triumph. It was piloted by Flight Lieutenant Bruce 'Buck' Buckham, a twenty-six-year-old Australian who had survived a tour with 426 Squadron, winning a DFC for struggling home on two engines after a raid on Essen and was on secondment with his aircraft 'Whoa Bessie' to the RAF film unit. A PRU Mosquito would join later to carry out weather reconnaissance. Twenty-six of the attacking force carried a single Tallboy. The others were loaded with JW 'Johnny Walker' anti-ship mines. No one had any confidence in their efficiency. They were 'supposed to fall into the fjord, reach the bottom and jump about in the hope that in one of their jumps they would strike the underside of the *Tirpitz*,' said Tony Iveson. 'I cannot think of anything more stupid than the JWs we carried that day.'[21] The weather forecast for the journey was good. The force was expected to land at Yagodnik at dawn and, if fine conditions persisted, to carry out the attack later the same day.

The crews took off as the early autumn afternoon was fading to dusk, climbing over the fens and flatlands, glancing back for a last look at the towers of Lincoln Cathedral lit by the setting sun, and turned over the limitless plain of grey water stretching north and east. The navigator was kept busy with his charts and calculations but for the others the time passed mostly in monotony and in their minds, apprehension changed places with boredom, then back again. When they reached the Gulf of Bothnia, things livened up. Tony Iveson looked down from the cockpit at lights glowing in the darkness below from neutral Sweden. To see a town illuminated after years of blackout was somehow shocking. Then there were other lights. As Flying Officer Bill Carey of 617 crossed into Finland, streams of flak rose towards him. He swung his aircraft off its straight and level course but there was a thud of impacts. The Lancaster was still flying and nobody was hurt but now a different danger was looming for everyone.

The good weather they had enjoyed for most of the journey was worsening. As dawn came up and they crossed the Finnish border into Russia, they were advancing into a wall of cloud, up to 6,000 feet thick and hovering only a few hundred feet above the ground. It was not what they had been told to expect. Travelling in one of the Liberators was Group Captain Colin McMullen, a thirty-six-year-old 5 Group staff officer, who left his home in Australia as a young man to join the RAF and was charged with controlling the operation from the ground. The appalling weather was 'hardly in keeping with the forecast anticipated', he wrote in his subsequent report. The speed of departure meant that no forecast had been sought from the Russians, who were much better placed to give an accurate prediction. At the last Met briefing, the crews had been told to expect a cloud base at 1,500 feet and visibility of six miles at Archangel.[22]

The aircraft were forced lower and lower. The bomb aimers looked down from their perches in the nose, hoping to identify some feature that would point them in the right direction. The landscape was a 'waste of marsh or endless pine forests and innumerable small lakes'.[23] The maps they had been given did not show towns and railways. Their best hope of help was from the Russians. During the final briefings the crews were given a radio call sign, which, when tapped out in morse, would raise Yagodnik. The letters were in English. The Russians worked in Russian. The signals meant nothing and the dots and dashes streamed out unanswered into the ether.

They rumbled on, through the murk and rain squalls, scouring the treetops below for some feature that might point the way. Tony

Iveson finally saw an expanse of water which he hoped was the White Sea. There was a town and an airfield on the shore and he made it the start point for his search for Yagdonik, reckoning he could always put down there if he didn't find it. They quartered the land to the east but eventually, with fuel running low, gave up and landed to be met by Russian soldiers, 'unshaven, wearing German greatcoats, carrying rifles and looking as if for two roubles they would do us'. Another Lancaster had also landed, piloted by Nick Knilans, a Wisconsin farmboy who, after being turned down by the US Army Air Force, joined the Royal Canadian Air Force and finally the RAF. They were all driven to the seaside town – Onega as it turned out – and taken to the office of the mayor who asked through a female interpreter where they had come from. 'They had a map on the wall,' remembered Iveson. 'I pointed to Lincolnshire and they couldn't believe it.'[24]

All over the area other crews were making their own unscheduled landings. Of the forty-two aircraft that left from Britain only twenty-one made it to Yagodnik. The rest roamed the skies as their tanks ran dry, eventually putting down in any airfield they could find or ditching with their wheels up in the least daunting looking stretch of tundra. Four Lancasters from 9 Squadron and two from 617 were written off in crash-landings. McMullen felt they had got off lightly. 'It is amazing that no one was injured in any of these crashes and it is even more extraordinary that so few crashes occurred,' he recorded. 'A loss of at least half the force might have happened in the circumstances.'

It was obvious that there would be no operation that day as the original orders had optimistically and unrealistically proposed. Throughout the rest of the day, Lancasters arrived at Yagodnik, and their crews went off in search of a bed leaving them to the attentions of the ground staff. Not all the aircraft that landed undamaged were serviceable and one Lancaster needed an engine change. It seemed that twenty-eight Lancasters, including the film unit aircraft, might be ready for operations the following day. Then came another unpleasant surprise. They had been told that three 5,000-gallon and five 2,000-gallon bowsers would be available at the base. In fact there were six with a capacity of a paltry few hundred gallons each, and refuelling all the aircraft for the attack would take eighteen hours.

All through Wednesday, 13 September the ground crews worked ceaselessly on the wet and windy airfield, servicing and pumping fuel and taking it in turns to grab a few hours' kip. The others hung around waiting on the weather reports. The base was bleak, a place of 'weather-beaten hutments, dun-coloured flat earth and grey winding river', in Tait's description.[25] The Soviets, though, were assiduous hosts. The surly resentment of the earlier stages of the war had given way to a keen desire to impress. They were playing host to 325 RAF personnel – seventy-five more than they had been told to expect – and they were determined to be hospitable. 'WELCOME THE GLORIOUS FLIERS OF THE ROYAL AIR FORCE' declared a banner stretched over a paddle steamer, *Ivan Kalyev*, moored on the Dvina, where some of the officers were billeted. The extra numbers meant the rest of the party were crammed into underground huts, where along with the overcrowding they had to contend with bed bugs. On the first night everyone, with the exception of Tait, was bitten, proving, it was said, that 'even communist bugs have respect for rank'.

Early on Thursday, the PRU Mosquito took off with Flight Lieutenant George Watson at the controls and Warrant Officer John MacArthur navigating to scout the weather in the Kaafjord area. They came back with bad news. Operations were officially scrubbed and the crews settled in for another day of inaction. In the afternoon, 617 took on an immaculately kitted Soviet side from the base at football and were beaten 4–0 – 'a diplomatic defeat which was fruitful', in McMullen's view.

The meals were good, served up on nice china with proper cutlery and napery. The largesse, McMullen was to discover later, was a touching deception. He and a few colleagues had to linger on for another ten days after the main party had departed for Britain and found that the quality of the food deteriorated to the point where they were forced to live off the tinned emergency rations they had brought with them from Britain. In addition, 'various amenities such as cutlery, table napkins, crockery etc were removed until there

Guy Byam (*right*) with fellow BBC war reporter Stanley Maxted

was insufficient for the small party that remained'. He speculated that his hosts had expected the RAF to stay only a week, after which time all the 'show items' had to be returned to some central store in Moscow. They were 'somewhat disconcerted that they did not possess the facilities to keep up the pretence for longer ... we were correspondingly sympathetic, even if somewhat uncomfortable'.[26]

While they waited, Tony Iveson killed some time playing bridge with the BBC reporter Guy Byam, a 'very impressive, tall good-looking man'. Byam-Corstiaens, to give him his full name, was twenty-seven years old, an intellectual forced by war into the life of a man of action. He was born in Buckinghamshire and went to school in Brighton and France, going on to study at the Sorbonne and Jesus College, Cambridge. He joined the RNVR and was a sub-lieutenant aboard the armed merchant cruiser *Jervis Bay* when it was sunk in a gallant action in November 1940. The ship was the sole escort of thirty-seven ships returning to Halifax, Nova Scotia, when the *Admiral Scheer* appeared. The commander of *Jervis Bay*, Captain Edward Fegen, told his charges to scatter while he took on the pocket battleship. There could be only one outcome and *Jervis Bay* was sunk, with the loss of 190 men including Fegen, who was later awarded the VC. Byam was one of the sixty-five survivors but he had been blinded in his right eye during the battle and invalided out of the navy.

He had hopes of being a writer before the war and written for the fashionable literary magazine *Lilliput*. He had given a talk on Canadian radio after the sinking, written a screenplay about the incident and submitted a script to the BBC. The Corporation seemed an obvious place for a man with literary ambitions and no hope of returning to active service. He was fluent in French and in October 1942 found a job as a sub-editor writing scripts for broadcasting to occupied France. A report a year later by his supervisor praised his 'bright and ingenious mind ... nice style and occasional flashes of brilliance'.[27] His reporting took him across the Atlantic and around Britain and as the invasion approached he was seconded to the BBC's War Reporting Unit. He underwent parachute training and won a place at the centre of the action in Normandy, dropping with airborne forces on D-Day and sending back vivid dispatches from the front line. He was about to produce another.

At 4.37 a.m. on Friday, 15 September, Watson and MacArthur set off for a weather recco. The crews were gathered in the open for a briefing when they returned at 8.50 a.m. They did not bother to land to report the good news, swooping low over the airfield and firing off a green Very cartridge, the signal that the skies over Kaafjord were clear. 'In no time the airscrew blades of the huge bombers commenced to whirr in aggressive chorus as they warmed up for take off,' recorded an RAF internal narrative of the action. 'The battle was on!'[28]

At 9.30 the first bomber took off, piloted by Flying Officer Frank Levy of 617, followed by twenty-six more Lancasters at one-minute intervals. Twenty-one of them were carrying Tallboys and the rest Johnny Walker mines. Tait's aircraft was fitted with two VHF radios to direct the other captains during the attack and its wings were painted with heavy white markings to identify his position in the order. They flew in a loose 'gaggle' formation, keeping low to avoid the radar, and Byam had a clear view of the lonely landscape below. 'It was a lovely day [he broadcast later] and soon we were flying over ice floes below us in the Gulf of Archangel. And then over Finland, over the Petsamo road, the famous motor road that goes into the Arctic Circle. We could see it below stretching northwards into the pine forests. And then on, over Finland and millions of lakes. And the Lancasters in the skies were all around us, and their camouflage hardly discernible against the greens and browns and the blues of the countryside. And on to the Norwegian frontier. And the country more hilly and undulating now.'[29]

At the Finnish border they climbed and set course for the rendez-vous point, a small lake about a hundred miles south of the target. *Tirpitz* lay moored in front of a spit of land projecting from the southern shore of the fjord, with her bows pointing towards the entrance. The approach would be from the south and west, bombing her from stem to stern. Before they again set off they got into battle order. They were grouped in ranks of five, roughly 500 yards apart and with the same distance between waves, stacked at varied heights. The loose formation made it difficult for the flak gunners to concentrate their fire. Each wave would follow immediately on the tails of the other. This, said Tait later, meant that 'the aircraft in the fourth wave could release their bombs before the bombs from the preceding attackers actually hit and by exploding perhaps obscured the target in smoke'.[30] Before they lined up, two aircraft from 9 Squadron took wind measurements to feed into their automatic Mark XIV bomb sights – regarded as less accurate than 617's SABS.

As they turned northwards, they had nothing to fear from the weather. The skies were clear. The one thing that could thwart the attack was the smokescreen. The film unit Lancaster was flying several thousand feet higher than the rest. From this vantage point, Guy Byam described what happened next.

'And now up to 16,000 feet, oxygen height. And far ahead of us, the white-capped hills and the sea. And then through the sparse cloud, the black granite, split by something. Yes! Water. A fjord. Altenfjord! [*sic*] And now it was touch and go because the Germans were known to have the biggest smokescreen in the world stretched around that fjord. We had to beat the smoke to enable our bombers to get a good sighting of the *Tirpitz* itself. We were coming in close now and the Lancs were flying steadily on, and scores of English and dominion airmen were around us, high in the sky over the cream of the German navy, high in the Norwegian sky, eighteen hundred miles from home ... and Buck our pilot checks his instruments momentarily with his eyes, and Doc the Scotch engineer checks the engine temperatures, and out there in the sun in the Arctic haze scores of crews are doing the same thing, doing it in that calm, imperturbable way, as they've done it over Berlin and Stuttgart. And then below us a fork of water and a ship.

'The *Tirpitz*! And like thin white streamers, the smoke is coming up from the hills around, covering the whole of the approaches to the fjord. But Wing Commander Tait, who is in the leading Lancaster, looks as if he will beat that smoke. He and another plane about two thousand feet below us are in on their bomb run. And they hold steady, steady as the flak comes up, and the flak comes up again all around the fjord and little spurts of light and there's flak all over the sky. And then the bombs go down. They go down from the two leading aircraft – two great five ton bombs. And leaping away from each Lancaster and going down and down. And then gathering speed and going down and down towards the ship to be lost out of sight. And the smoke is almost over the ship by now and we weave and turn away sharply. And there's lots of talk going on between the planes. English talk mixed with RAF slang going from plane to plane high over the Norwegian hills.

'And one voice says calmly: "Can I have another run in over the target please?" And the answer is "yes." And two others go in with him. And far below ... another party of bombers are swinging in. They almost seem to be flying on top of the smoke clouds and then for a moment in the middle of the vast billowing clouds of white smoke, a dull red glow hangs for a second and then dies down ... and we swing away now, towards the coast. The country below us is lovely. There are blues and browns in the white of the snow. And then a last look at the target where the black and brown smoke billows up from the clouds of the white smoke screen. We won't know for some time the exact results but they look very promising ...'[31] With that Buckham set course for Waddington, to carry back what seemed like very good news.

When Tait arrived, the tip of one mast was still poking out from the smoke and it was on this that his Canadian bomb aimer, Flying

Officer Danny Daniel, sighted his SABS. Alongside Tait was Flight
Lieutenant James Melrose of 9 Squadron who bombed simultaneously. At their bombing heights of above 14,000 feet the ship
already made a small target. As its narrow outlines disappeared,
there was nothing to aim at but the smoke. Jim Bazin, 9 Squadron's
leader, was seventh in line to bomb, but an inconvenient scrap of
cloud obscured his bomb aimer Pilot Officer Joe Gran's view of the
scene below, and they went round again. 'Huge mushrooms of
smoke and water rose up through the smokescreen,' he reported
later, 'and my bomb aimer was again unable to get the ship in his
sight. But at that moment the *Tirpitz* started to fire her ... light ack-
ack guns and the flashes below the smokescreen provided a perfect
marker so we bombed the centre of the flashes.'[32]

The combination of flak, fog and bomb smoke was impressive
but it was impossible to know how much damage had been done.
As they turned for home, Tait was 'cheered considerably' by 'a single
plume of thick black smoke emerging from the white'. The flight
back was uneventful with no sign of the enemy fighters which they
believed to be based somewhere along the return route. They landed
at Yagodnik at tea time after a 1,300-mile round trip to be met by a
brass band and a welcoming committee that included 'six local
belles'.[33] That night they drank vodka, steamed in the 'Russian baths'
laid on by their hosts and talked about the day's events. The PRU
Mosquito had carried out an afternoon recco. Cloud now covered
Kaafjord but Watson and MacArthur saw enough to confirm that
Tirpitz was still afloat. It seemed unlikely, though, that she had not
been harmed. A few of the aircraft, unable to get an aiming point,
had returned with their Tallboys and JWs. There were not enough
bombs to merit hanging around to wait for another opportunity.
Next day Tait and Bazin and their men climbed back on board their
Lancasters and set off for England where they would await full anal-
ysis of the results and learn whether they would have to return to
Tirpitz.

19

'My God Mac, they've had it today'

As the departing bombers vanished over the mountains the crew of the *Tirpitz* surveyed the destruction they had left behind. Georg Schlegel, the chief engine room officer, groped his way forward through smoke and twisted metal to see 'a huge gaping hole, like a barn door. The whole of the side had been ripped open and the bow started to sink … all the cabins and holds in the bow had disappeared … it was pretty much mayhem.'[1]

Despite the devastation, the ship's company had got off lightly. Five men were dead and fifteen wounded. It was clear at once to Kapitän Junge, who took command after Meyer was injured in the Tungsten attack of April, that severe structural damage had been done. The engines and guns were still working. The bow, though, was a wreck. One Tallboy had struck the foredeck and sliced through the ship, exiting via the hull and exploding on the starboard side, tearing a forty-foot hole. The front compartments were swamped with two thousand tons of seawater, dragging down the bow. Other bombs missed narrowly, but the shock waves rippling through the water had buckled plates and blown out bulkheads. *Tirpitz* was still afloat, but with the great hole in her bow she would sink if she tried to move. It was obvious, though, that she could not remain in Kaafjord. One of the Tallboys had landed on Straumsneset point just behind the anchorage. The hole it blasted in the rocky soil was unlike any bomb crater anyone had seen. When Adalbert Brünner, now manning a lookout post onshore, went to inspect it with his comrades 'it took our breath away'.[2] It was clear that the British had a new weapon, far more powerful than anything they had experienced before and, if they stayed where they were, it was certain they would be subjected to it again. The attack confirmed that the

Tallboy

smokescreen and flak batteries, the ship's main defences in the continued absence of fighter cover, provided insufficient protection. *Tirpitz* would have to move.

Admiral Dönitz sat down with his staff in Berlin on 23 September to discuss *Tirpitz*'s immediate future. The meeting heard that it would take nine months to make her seaworthy again and the work would have to be done on the spot. This was no time for a programme of lengthy repairs. Four days before the meeting Finland had switched from the losing to the winning side, abandoning an alliance of necessity with Germany to sign an armistice with Moscow. The northern front was crumbling. A big Soviet offensive was brewing. It seemed probable that German forces would soon be falling back and Kaafjord would have to be abandoned. Even if the repairs could be carried out, there seemed no realistic scenario in which *Tirpitz* might play the role for which she had been created. Dönitz now came to a crucial decision about the fate of Hitler's last battleship. It was no longer to be considered as a seagoing vessel. Instead, 'in future, *Tirpitz* would be used merely as a floating battery, in defence of northern Norway'.[3]

But where now should she go? Even though Allied armies were advancing on Germany's western borders, Hitler's belief that Norway was threatened by invasion remained firm. Tromsø, a major port, 120 miles to the west and south, seemed a likely enemy objective. If *Tirpitz* could be shifted there, her big guns might at last be put to some good use, opposing an Allied landing. As October progressed, it looked more likely that they would be employed to landward, part of the new defensive line drawn only forty miles to the east as German forces retreated in the face of the Russian push. There was another potential benefit. If the true extent of the damage to *Tirpitz* remained unclear, she might still serve as a fleet-in-being and, in Dönitz's words, 'continue to tie down enemy forces and by her presence ... confound the enemies' intentions'.[4]

Konteradmiral Rudolf Peters, who moved from command of the U-boat force in Norway to take over what remained of the northern task force in June, was told to find a suitable new anchorage in the Tromsø area. Dönitz specified that it must be shallow, so that if the ship was hit again she would stay above the surface and continue to serve as a gun platform. In the meantime *Tirpitz* was patched up for the move. A repair ship was brought in and new plates welded over the hole. By the middle of October, Junge reckoned she was fit to make the 170-mile voyage up Altafjord and south to Tromsø. Relieved of his onshore watch duties, Adalbert Brünner came aboard to 'notice a change on *Tirpitz*. The repairs looked rather makeshift and there was a more frantic atmosphere, not the nonchalance we were used to.'[5]

Konteradmiral Peters tried to rally spirits with an address to the company before the ship limped away. 'We are living in momentous but difficult times,' he said. 'I feel assured that in these changed circumstances, all the men ... under my command will, with undiminished vigour and determination, do their duty until victory is ours.' It was a hollow exhortation. By then he had been told that his – by now notional – task force was being disbanded. He recorded in his diary his chagrin that he had 'not been able to lead it in battle against the enemy', despite it being full of 'capable, well-trained men, eager to fight'.[6]

At midday on Sunday, 15 October, *Tirpitz* left Kaafjord for the last time, pushing through the water at a cautious seven to ten knots, escorted by tugs and every available destroyer in the area. At 3 p.m. the following day she dropped anchor at Haakøy, a low-lying island two and a half miles west of Tromsø. That afternoon, an agent, Egil Lindberg, mounted the stairs to the room on the top floor of the town's hospital where he hid his transmitter and radioed the news of her arrival to London. The significance of the move was not immediately clear. Reconnaissance flights over Kaafjord had failed to provide conclusive proof that she was *hors de combat* and incapable of mounting a last sortie.

Intercepted messages ordering U-boats to patrol at the entrance to Altafjord had given warning that *Tirpitz* might be departing and the fleet carrier *Implacable* had put to sea as a precaution. Early on 18 October, Firefly fighters flew off to try and get pictures of *Tirpitz* in her new berth. A reconnaissance Mosquito was also dispatched for a marathon eleven-hour round-trip flight from Dyce, near Aberdeen. The images they brought back showed the ship anchored on the southern side of Haakøy with her bow facing east towards the island on which Tromsø sat. She was already surrounded by nets. There was no sign of any smoke generators but flak batteries were in place on shore and demonstrated their efficiency by managing to put some holes in the Mosquito. Having shot up an aerodrome at Bardufoss, forty miles south of Tromsø, the Fireflies returned to *Implacable*. Her commander, Captain L. D. Mackintosh, requested permission from the Home Fleet to launch an attack on the battleship. The commander, Sir Henry Moore, wanted no more gallant efforts from the Fleet Air Arm, especially as *Implacable* did not have the aircraft on board to suppress the defences prior to dive-bombing. 'Return to Scapa,' he ordered. 'Do not, repetition not, try and bomb in the face of heavy flak with your inadequate anti-flak fighter strength', prefacing the signal with a cheery 'well done'.[7]

The photographs revealed little new about the state of the battleship. The evidence of agents, and the slow pace of the voyage to Tromsø, though, suggested that she was not in a seaworthy condition. On 1 October, the Alta resistance cell radioed that their agent in Kaafjord, 'a solid and reliable man', reported that she had received 'a direct hit on the starboard side which made a hole … so large that large motor boats could go in'.[8] Public confirmation that *Tirpitz* no longer posed a genuine threat seemed to have been given, obliquely, in a BBC radio talk by Wing Commander Bazin of 9 Squadron as early as 5 October. He concluded his broadcast with the words: 'It is understood from the Admiralty that she is now no longer a menace to our shipping.'[9] This was certainly how Arthur Harris later claimed to see it. In his post-war account he stated that after the 15 September attack 'we had very good reason to believe that the ship could never be made fit for operations before the probable end of the war and was therefore quite useless to the enemy'. This, however, 'did not seem to cut much ice with the Admiralty'. It came as no surprise when he was 'therefore pressed to attack the *Tirpitz* again'.[10]

Looked at from a distance of many years, the effort involved in another attempt, against what were known to be strong flak defences and the threat, mercifully unrealized as yet, of fighter attack, seems wasteful. The lives of brave men – some of whom had completed a hundred operations – were being risked against what was surely a spent force. It was reasonable now to conclude that the threat from *Tirpitz* had faded to insignificance. For her to venture out against the Arctic convoys, about to sail again after the summer lull, would be suicidal. Within the Kriegsmarine's pitifully depleted armoury, the U-boats still operating in northern waters were, anyway, potentially a far more efficient weapon. Passage to a German port was possible, but the journey would expose her to equal danger from ships, submarines and aircraft.

These, though, were peacetime considerations. Britain had been at war for five years now and was impatient for the end. Blood was up and the mood was for settling accounts and closing unfinished business. Even if the Admiralty and the Air Staff had wanted to leave *Tirpitz* in peace, it was unlikely that they would be allowed to do so. Churchill's eye was still fixed unwaveringly on the battleship. On 26 October, he informed Admiral Cunningham: 'I think it will be regarded as a very serious misfortune if the TIRPITZ succeeds in returning to Germany. I consider that every effort should be made to attack this ship, even if losses have to be incurred.'[11]

The First Sea Lord was quick to respond. 'I fully agree,' he replied the following day. By now intercepted messages had revealed Dönitz's intention to keep *Tirpitz* where she was and he concluded that 'it is most improbable that the long passage southward to Germany will be attempted at present'. He was able to tell the Prime Minister that 'Bomber Command has planned an attack on the ship in her present berth as soon as weather conditions are favourable'.[12]

It was fear of further air attacks that had prompted *Tirpitz*'s move to Tromsø, but, as everyone on board understood, there could be no hiding place. They were now in fact an easier target than before, for the shift south and westwards had edged them a fatal step closer to British air bases. The 5 Group planners calculated that modified aircraft, operating from forward airfields in northern Scotland would just have the range to carry out a direct attack on the battle-ship and return home.

Once again it was 617 Squadron and 9 Squadron that would carry it out. Both squadrons had been busy since their return from Russia. Satisfaction at a partial success, achieved without loss, was overshadowed by an accident on the homeward journey. Flying Officer Frank Levy, a Rhodesian with 617, flew into a mountaintop in Norway, killing himself, his six crew members and two additional aircrew travelling as passengers.

Now both squadrons were to experience more casualties. On the night of 23/24 September, 9 Squadron took part in a raid on a night-fighter base outside Münster. Two of their aircraft were shot down and all but one of the fourteen crew killed. Another crew was lost on the night of 19/20 October over Nuremberg. The luck of 617 Squadron, which had got through the summer with remarkably few losses, seemed to have changed. On 24 September the crews took part in a mass attack on the Dortmund–Ems Canal, a strategic waterway that linked the Ruhr with the North Sea. Their Tallboys smashed the banks, draining a seven-mile stretch and rendering it unnavigable for six months, but 10 per cent of the attacking force were shot down, including the Lancaster piloted by Flight Lieutenant Geoff Stout who was pounced on by night fighters as he left the target. Stout stayed at the controls while the crew bailed out and went down in flames with his aircraft. Two of those who escaped subsequently died of their wounds.

On Saturday, 7 October, a small force of thirteen Lancasters set off on a mission that would require particular sangfroid and skill. They were to bomb the Kembs barrage, on the Rhine just north of Basle. It held back a huge quantity of water which it was feared the Germans would unleash on American and French forces as they advanced from the south. The purpose was to pre-empt the move by triggering the flood before the Allies got into the danger area. Seven aircraft were to drop their bombs from 8,000 feet while the other six went in at 1,000 feet to lay delayed-fuse Tallboys alongside the lock gates of the dam. Tait, as always, led from the front. Despite intense light flak, he and the three aircraft following him dropped their bombs and emerged without serious damage. One of the last two, the Lancaster piloted by Squadron Leader Drew Wyness was hit on the approach and crashed into the Rhine, apparently with the loss of all on board. In the other, Flight Lieutenant Christopher Howard made one pass without dropping a bomb and despite being told by Tait, 'Kit, abandon, abandon', went round again. By this time the gunners had found their range and according to Tony Iveson, who was in the high level force, Howard's aircraft was 'shot to pieces'.

By now Iveson was used to the loss of comrades but, he said later, 'Drew's death affected me more than anybody else because we were very close'. He had taught Wyness while instructing in Rhodesia and felt a protective affinity for his amiable, blanket-hearted comrade. With others, 'although I knew them, it wasn't the same. The feeling was, well, hard luck, poor bugger. Like everyone else, I knew it might be me tomorrow.'*[13]

No one was untouchable. A few days after their return from Russia, the squadron had heard that 617's first leader was dead. On

* Iveson heard later that Wyness and his wireless operator Flying Officer Bruce Hosie had been shot in cold blood after capture.

19 September, returning from a raid in Germany, Guy Gibson's Mosquito had crashed in Holland. Only a few weeks before he had come over from Coningsby to have a drink in the mess at Petwood, even though none of the men he had flown with were still in the unit. The evening ended in the customary high jinks and Gibson was divested of his trousers.

The flamboyant personalities of Gibson and Cheshire coloured the squadron's own character. If Tait lacked their obvious charisma, what he had instead was an enigmatic quality that in its way was equally potent and inspirational. As preparations began for another attack on *Tirpitz*, this awkward, modest man was about to carve his niche in the 617 pantheon.

The new operation was called Obviate. The crews had long ago given up wondering how the names were chosen. The mission would test their endurance and the skill of the navigators to the maximum. It meant a round trip of 2,250 miles which, depending on conditions, could take nearly fourteen hours. For the Lancasters to make it there and back, they would have to carry every extra gallon of petrol they could cram on board and lose every pound of superfluous weight.

Each aircraft was fitted with two extra tanks in the fuselage to boost the fuel load to 2,400 gallons, a tedious job which required removing the rear gunner's turret. The mid-upper turrets were stripped out and the front guns and ammunition, spare oxygen bottles and even the armour plating behind the pilot's seat removed. This still left an all-up weight of aeroplane, bomb and fuel of nearly thirty-two tons, which was over the safety limit. To get the extra lift, Tait organized the replacement of the existing engines with more powerful Merlin T-24s and paddle-bladed airscrews, achieving the 'the stupendous task of scouring the whole of Bomber Command for the new equipment and installing it ... in five amazing days', according to an official RAF account of the operation.[14] To shrink the distance a little, the squadrons would take off from three bases in northern Scotland: Lossiemouth, Kinloss and Milltown. By mid-October everything was in place and the crews stood by to await the Met reports.

In Tromsø, *Tirpitz* was struggling to establish herself in her new home. For better or worse, it seemed that she would not be leaving it soon. On arrival, six hundred men – most of them engine-room hands – were moved ashore, leaving about 1,700 men on board. Dönitz had insisted on a shallow anchorage, but the best that could be found, off Haakøy, lay in open waters with no steep hills nearby to deter attacking aircraft like those which had protected her at Faettenfjord and Kaafjord. The water was still too deep. Nor was the sea bed beneath it stable, consisting of fifteen feet of mud topped with a layer of sand. Plans were made to use dredgers to raise the sea bed but to those on board it seemed that they had exchanged a dangerous situation for a fatal one. Smoke generators were brought from Kaafjord to set up on shore though it would be a while before they were installed and working. More were mounted on boats nearby but Hein Hellendoorn, second in command of the ship's flak batteries, worried that the fog they produced would be more likely to hinder his gunners than hide the ship. 'It was clear to us at that point that we were on borrowed time,' he said later. The crew began talking about their new duty as 'a mission to heaven'.[15] Kapitän Junge did not inspire the same confidence as Topp and Meyer, for 'he had little sea experience and we disliked him'. The feeling settled on the ship that the end, not just of *Tirpitz* but of Germany, could not be far off. 'Nobody believed in victory any more,' said Hellendoorn. There was continuous propaganda of new miracle weapons but 'no one really gave them any credence'. It was unwise to speak one's mind too openly. According to Klaus Rohwedder, a sailor who was arrested for drunkenness was found to have written 'defeatist' letters home and was court-martialled and sentenced to death. He was killed in the 15 September attack before the sentence could be carried out.[16]

The evidence of impending defeat, though, was all too visible, just across the water on Tromsø. The town was full of refugees, flooding back from the Soviet advance. The homes they left behind were now ashes, consumed in the fires of the scorched earth tactics of the retreating German forces. The citizens saw the anxiety on the faces of their conquerors and inwardly exulted. But the presence of the big grey ship across the bay was ominous. Their town had been dragged onto the front line. Whenever the skies cleared they braced themselves for the appearance of the bombers.

On the morning of Saturday, 28 October, Cochrane listened to the favourable reports of the weather over Tromsø and gave the signal for Obviate to begin. At Bardney and Woodhall Spa, the Lancasters of 9 and 617 Squadrons took off, one by one, and set course for north-east Scotland. They touched down at their allotted airfields for refuelling and a final briefing. By now it was officially conceded that the battleship was 'unfit for sea-going operations'. However, the 5 Group operation order claimed that 'it appears likely' that an attempt would be made to get it back to a base in Germany. 'So long as TIRPITZ remains afloat,' it concluded, 'it continues to be a threat to our sea communications with Russia.'[17]

The force was made up of eighteen aircraft from each squadron and a Lancaster from the RAF film unit. The Johnny Walker experiment had been abandoned. All the bombers would carry Tallboys. The first leg of the journey took them 237 miles north before turning due east to make landfall halfway between Bodø and Trondheim, where there was a gap in the German radar. They then crossed into neutral Sweden and swung north to rendezvous at a lake south of Tromsø for the final approach. In case of emergencies, aircraft were to press on to Yagodnik or Vaenga.

At 2.30 a.m., in gusting rain, they started to take off. There was a near catastrophe at Milltown when one of the engines on Tony Iveson's aircraft failed to develop sufficient power and he slewed off course on take-off, skimming over Benny Goodman on the perimeter track. 'All I could see was two massive main wheels and I thought "this is it",' Goodman remembered. 'It's a funny thing – there was no panic. I thought he was going to scrape along our canopy but he just got airborne. Thirty seconds later we'd all forgotten it.'[18]

They headed out over the sea, each aircraft making its own way, staying low at 1,500 feet to avoid radar. As they approached the Norwegian coast they saw daylight streaking the eastern sky. Once over, in Tait's account for the official RAF record, they began 'climbing steadily to get over the mountains … heading apparently for Russia. Soon they were … over the low country of northern Sweden and now they turned abruptly over lifeless wasteland for the rendezvous.' They met up over Torneträsk lake, 100 miles south of the target. It seemed extraordinary to Benny Goodman that they had all arrived at the right place at the right time, armed only with maps and dead reckoning. 'It was a navigators' trip not a pilots' trip,' he said long afterwards. 'I just flew the course I was given.'[19]

They circled around, getting into bombing formation, and then set off for Tromsø, climbing to their bombing heights of 13,000 to 16,000 feet. Visibility was excellent. It was all going suspiciously well. Then, according to Tait, 'the fliers' luck, which had held so well, now began to go against them as the nearer they got to Tromsø, the more obvious became a large sheet of low cloud with its tops at 6,000 feet almost completely shielding the … battleship from the bombers' view'. It had come up very quickly. Tait could see the target clearly on the approach but by the time he arrived it was disappearing. They carried on, showering strips of 'Window' to confuse the radar. Despite the conditions, Tait bombed anyway. The thought of flogging home with a 12,000lb bomb in the belly swamped pious injunctions issued at briefings that precious Tallboys should not be used unless there was a strong prospect of success, and all but four of the thirty-six Lancasters dropped their bombs. Then it was time to get out. The flak batteries below were now well tuned to air attack and smoke and flame blossomed around them as they closed. After several circuits looking for a hole in the grey blanket below, Easy Elsie, flown by Bill Carey, an Australian pilot with 617, had dropped its bomb and was heading south for home when it was hit. The flak knocked out an engine and damaged the hydraulics, leaving the bomb doors jammed open. Elsie would never make it back. Carey turned for Sweden and after an increasingly anxious search for a landing place amid the hills and forests, put her down in a field. He smashed his knee in the impact but all emerged alive to be interned and, shortly afterwards, sent back to England.

Everyone else returned safely after a record twelve-and-a-half-hour flight, 'tired out' according to Tait's report and 'despondent at the frustration of their skilled and strenuous effort'. Two 617 pilots claimed to have scored or seen a direct hit. It was obvious, though, that the job had not been done. The most persuasive testimony came from Bruce Buckham, once again flying the film unit Lancaster. He descended to 8,000 feet to try and get pictures and saw two bombs exploding about a hundred yards from the ship and two more hitting the net defences. As he left her guns were firing and she was still definitely afloat.

On board *Tirpitz*, satisfaction at the performance of the flak gunners soon evaporated. The first inspection showed that although they had suffered only three casualties and escaped any direct hits, a near miss had damaged the port engine shaft and rudder and caused more flooding. The gloomy certainty that the bombers would be back hung over the ship. Once again they had received no help from the Luftwaffe.

On 4 November *Tirpitz* got a new captain. Junge left to be replaced by the ship's executive officer, Kapitän zur See Robert Weber. Dredging had begun to reduce the depth of water under the keel but it would be a long, slow job before the bed of the fjord was raised to the required six and a half feet. Weber was desperate to get the protection of the aircraft now arriving at the airbase at Bardufoss, less than fifty miles to the south. An underground telephone cable was laid between the ship and the Luftwaffe's air warning centre in Tromsø. This received and broadcast reports of enemy air activity, collected from radar stations and observation posts, most of which looked out to sea in expectation of an Allied attack. The centre was controlled from the Bardufoss base.

On Friday, 10 November, Hein Hellendoorn visited the Tromsø office with the ship's first gunnery officer, Korvettenkapitän Willi Müller, where they were assured by the commander, Oberleutnant Walter Härer, that enough warning would be received to get fighters airborne in time to defend *Tirpitz* from another attack. Two days before, a squadron of aircraft from the Jagdeschwader 5 fighter wing had arrived in the area after being driven out of Finland by the Soviet advance. They were to be based in Bardufoss while they converted from their Messerschmitt 109s to new and superior

Focke-Wulf 190s. They were under the temporary command of Major Heinrich Ehrler, a twenty-seven-year-old former butcher and enthusiastic Nazi who had become one of the stars of the Arctic air war with 199 'kills' to his account. Härer told his visitors that 'the fighters would be informed of any expected attacks ... they were there only to support and defend us'. When Hellendoorn returned to *Tirpitz* and told his shipmates the good news they 'felt safe for the first time in years. Now nothing bad could happen to us. The fighters were there for us.'[20]

Nonetheless, as each new dawn broke the crew scanned the skies, praying for cloud and cursing the clear, windless weather that seemed treacherously prevalent in the first days of November. They longed for the end of the month to come, when the sun sank below the horizon, not to reappear until January.

In England, the 5 Group planners watched the approach of near-perpetual darkness with increasing alarm. From 26 November, *Tirpitz* would be safe from attack for several months, and repairs could go on unhindered. The experience of Obviate had underlined the lesson that success depended on the weather. Every day a Mosquito from the Met Flight took off from Sumburgh in the Shetlands and climbed high over the target area to gather temperature and humidity data. On its return, Cochrane and his staff gathered to read the runes and weigh the odds. On 4 November, the omens seemed good and the crews departed to the Scottish bases, only to return home when a gale warning was announced.[21] Tait noted that 'the combination of untoward weather, false starts, ill-luck and the depressing prospect of the descent on Northern Norway of its impenetrable winter blanket at any minute, reduced the spirit of the anxious crews'.[22]

As the winter deadline approached, caution dwindled and the temptation to take a chance mounted. On 11 November, with the weather prospects still uncertain, the squadrons were ordered north again, arriving at their forward bases that afternoon. Take-off was scheduled for early the following morning and empty hours of waiting lay ahead. At Milltown, the 617 crews were taken off and installed in cosy bedrooms with a coal fire burning in the grate where they lay down and tried to sleep. At midnight they were given the final briefing. The plan of attack had not been altered and the times and routes were identical to the Obviate operation. There was one ominous new development. The crews learned that there was now hard intelligence that a squadron of fighters was based in the target area tasked with protecting *Tirpitz*. This was very unwelcome news. They were going into battle with only a rear gunner to defend them, in an aeroplane laden with extra fuel. A single round through the fuselage could bring instant extinction. During the briefing there were more bad tidings. The Met Flight Mosquito had returned with reports of stratus cloud over Tromsø. Cochrane nonetheless decided to gamble. Operation Catechism, as it had been code-named, was on. The crews trooped off for a last meal of bacon, eggs and chips then climbed aboard the lorries to take them to their aircraft for a mission that seemed marked for likely failure and possible disaster.

The night was bitterly cold. As the temperature plunged, the ground crews had been busy spraying de-icer over the wings of the Lancasters. Six of the 9 Squadron aircraft were still weighed down with hoar frost when departure hour came. The force took off leaving Wing Commander Bazin and Flight Lieutenant Melrose, who had been credited with scoring the direct hit during Operation Paravane, grounded.

At 3.25 a.m., twenty-nine bombers and the faithful film unit Lancaster with 'Buck' Buckham at the controls were in the air and heading north, out over the Moray Firth, past the Orkneys and the Shetlands before turning east towards Norway, skimming along at a radar-dodging two thousand feet. Once again they were to make their own way to a meeting-up point south of the target to commence the attack. Just off the coast, looking out from the cockpit, Tony Iveson saw a 'tiny crack of daylight, like a silver thread on the horizon'. He noticed a Lancaster silhouetted against the dawn and pulled alongside it. It was Tait's aircraft. The rear gunner, Micky Vaughan, greeted him by 'making rude gestures towards me'.[23] They flew along companionably towards the rendezvous point over Torneträsk lake in the mountains of northern Sweden.

Tait and Iveson reached it first. As they did a circuit, Iveson saw the shapes of the other 617 Squadron Lancasters looming out of the black western sky. Two of 9 Squadron's aircraft failed to make the rendezvous. They could not hang around. Tait ordered a Very light fired to signal the advance to attack and they swung north. He remembered afterwards that 'the sun was resting on the horizon so that the snow-covered mountains were turned pink in its light. The sky was cloudless, the air calm and the aircraft rode easily without a bump to disturb the bomb-aimer.'[24] The visibility, as they were all to say afterwards, was 'gin clear'. Pleasure at the beauty of the new day and the knowledge that conditions were perfect for bombing were quickly overshadowed by alarm. 'We thought, Christ, if it's OK for us it is going to be equally OK for the fighters,' said Iveson.[25]

But as they flew steadily along at just over two hundred miles an hour there was no sign of them. When they were still twenty miles away Tait spotted *Tirpitz* 'lying squat and black among her torpedo nets like a spider in her web, silhouetted against the glittering blue and green waters of the fjord'. He was struck by the peacefulness of the scene. 'Everything was quite still,' he remembered. The whole

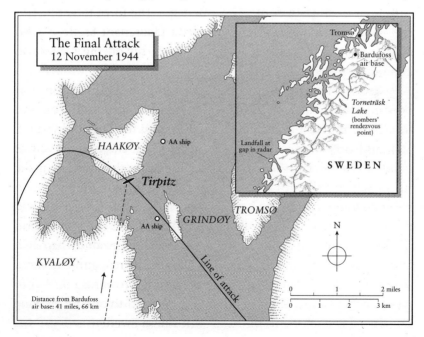

scene, water, mountains, sky blazed in the cold brilliance of the Arctic dawn.' There was no sign of a smokescreen. To Freddie Watts, following close behind, it seemed that they could not fail. Later he recalled 'saying to my bomb aimer, my God Mac, they've had it today'.[26] Then, when they were five miles away, the peace was shattered.

Tony Iveson was suddenly aware of a 'great unfolding golden cloud'. It was the explosion from the huge shells pumped out by the big, 15-inch guns in *Tirpitz*'s main turrets, fired at maximum elevation, bursting below. It was a measure of the alarm now gripping the ship. The monster guns had no hope of hitting the approaching Lancasters, which were still only specks in the sky at this range. Then the flak guns opened up. Tait saw the air ahead fill 'with smoke puffs as all the guns on the ship and those along the shore combined in a fusillade'. He noted that 'no aircraft deviated from the formation'. The men of 617 and 9 Squadrons were well used to flak by now and this did not seem too bad – certainly lighter than they had faced in the confined space of Kaafjord. So far there was no smokescreen and still no sign of fighters.

The eighteen aircraft of 617 Squadron came in from the southeast with the sun behind them, grouped together in a gaggle, layered at different heights with the lowest at 12,650 feet and the highest at 16,000. Tait was in the lead. He approached on his bombing run at 13,000 feet. The battleship lay straight ahead, starboard side-on, its bow pointing eastwards. The old asymmetric camouflage, designed to give the appearance of a much smaller ship, had been obliterated. Her hull now was a dark, uniform grey, with the upper works painted in a paler shade to help blend in with the snow dusting the low-humped hills of Haakøy, whose shore lay four hundred feet away on the port side. He kept on this course for five long minutes as the dirty bursts from the flak guns blossomed ahead and around them. Below, lying prone in the nose, his curly-headed Canadian bomb aimer, Flying Officer Danny Daniel, peered into the sight, speaking over the intercom into Tait's earphones, easing him onto a course that would put the ship on the blade of the sword glowing on the glass in front of him. Tait's eyes were fixed on his instruments, now and again making delicate banking turns to keep the needle of the bombing direction indicator glued to the vertical. Ten seconds before dropping, a red light went on. Then the automatic release mechanism tripped. The Tallboy slid away, and, suddenly freed from its five-ton burden, the Lancaster leaped thankfully upwards.

The bomb went into an aerodynamically perfect descent, spinning like a rifle bullet. Thirty seconds later it hit. The nose of Tait's Lancaster was over the target, obscuring the moment when the Tallboy struck but he 'turned and dived hard to port to see what was happening. The ship was almost hidden by smoke. A jet of white steam was gushing out and amidships she blazed fiercely.'

The sequence was captured by the film unit Lancaster's three cine cameras. When it first comes into view, *Tirpitz* looks tiny and exposed 'like a Dinky Toy', as some of the crews were to say later, lying broadside-on close to the flat shore of Haakøy. Bright lights flicker out of the monochrome as the flak teams frantically work their guns. Then, out of nowhere, a great white mushroom envelops the front of ship. There is a brief stutter of anti-aircraft fire from aft. A bomb splashes down close to the stern on the starboard side. Almost simultaneously an eruption three hundred yards away on the shore of Haakøy flings debris high and wide. It is followed by another white blossoming amidships. Two more bombs crash between ship and shore. After that it becomes impossible to follow the bombardment as the ship disappears under rolling banks of smoke, steam and fire.[27]

Tait's bomb went down at 8.41 a.m. He was followed by Bobby Knights, James Castagnola, Paddy Gingles, John Saunders and Bunny Lee, who came in, ranged in a loose gaggle and stacked up at between 12,650 and 14,400 feet. By 8.44, all 617's eighteen Tallboys were gone. The last was dropped by the Lancaster of Flight Lieutenant John Sayers of the Royal Australian Air Force, from 14,200 feet. 'We followed our bomb down nearly to the ship where it was lost in the smoke,' he told the debriefers on his return. 'It was either a hit on the bows or a near miss.'[28] Then, within seconds, the bombs from 9 Squadron's ten aircraft were falling into the inferno. Flight

Lieutenant Harry Watkins was the last to drop. He reported a 'glow seen amidships and a pillar of smoke both from bow and stern … own bomb fell in smoke at stern.'[29]

It was difficult for anyone to get an accurate view of what was happening. The speed of the bombs and the almost instant

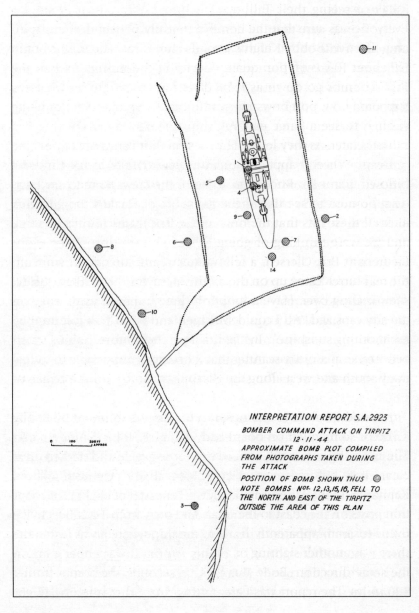

INTERPRETATION REPORT S.A. 2923
BOMBER COMMAND ATTACK ON TIRPITZ
12·11·44
APPROXIMATE BOMB PLOT COMPILED
FROM PHOTOGRAPHS TAKEN DURING
THE ATTACK
POSITION OF BOMB SHOWN THUS ⊘
NOTE BOMBS Nos. 12,13,15,16, FELL TO
THE NORTH AND EAST OF THE TIRPITZ
OUTSIDE THE AREA OF THIS PLAN

eruption of explosions made the reports the crews gave on their returns sketchy and generalized. Only three aircraft from 617 Squadron and one from 9 Squadron claimed to have scored direct hits. Tait himself reported that 'we did not see our bomb burst but the initial bombing was concentrated on the vessel'.[30] Most reports speak of seeing their Tallboys fall into the cauldron of smoke. Everyone was sure that the bombing was remarkably concentrated and effective. Bobby Knights gave the fullest account. 'Our bomb fell about 10 yds off port quarter,' he told the debriefer. 'We saw the first 4 bombs go down as follows: On or near starboard quarter, starboard bow, port bow and near funnel.' He stooged around long enough to see a 'large explosion' at 8.51 and a smaller one two minutes later. As they left 'we saw Tirpitz listing heavily to port'.

Despite several apparent bull's-eyes, the glow of fires and the billowing smoke, Buckham, flying the film unit machine, was disappointed to see that the ship was still afloat. 'I thought that after all these hits that the myth of the unsinkable Tirpitz was true and we were thinking of going home,' he said later. Then Flight Lieutenant Eric Giersch, a fellow Australian, looking down from the rear turret 'came up on the intercom, saying, "Hey, Skip, I think she's keeling over. Have a look."' When he turned again she had already capsized. 'All I could see was the red lead hull gleaming in the morning sunshine.'[31] By then most of the attackers were on their way home, anxiously scanning the skies for fighters as they hurried away south and west along the fjords that led to the sea and safety.

Tirpitz had awoken to the normal routines of shipboard life. The 1,700 or so men left on board had had breakfast and begun work. The morning was cold, minus eight degrees, and the skies were clear. Just before seven o'clock, the ship's first flak officer, Kapitänleutnant Alfred Fassbender, received a report that observation posts on the coast to the south had seen three Lancasters flying over Mosjøen, apparently heading east into Sweden. A little later there was another sighting of a lone Lancaster near Bodø, going in the same direction. Bodø was 220 miles away, Mosjøen a further 120 miles. The report was passed to him by Leutnant Leo Beniers,

from the air warning centre at Bardufoss. The base was unconcerned. The aircraft were probably on their way to Russia. Fassbender
was more cautious. The situation, and the weather, reminded him
uncomfortably of the Sunday a fortnight before when Lancasters
had appeared from the direction of Sweden. He 'immediately
grabbed the phone' to make sure that the recently arrived fighter
squadron was alerted.[32] Such were the complexities of the German
system of command and control that he had to contact the Tromsø
air warning centre to get the message through to the fighter
command post at Bardufoss, even though it was from the base that
the alert had emanated. He spoke first to Leutnant Ewald
Hamschmidt, a twenty-three-year-old junior officer whose dozy
reaction did not inspire confidence.

At 7.25 another report arrived saying four more Lancasters had
been seen over Mosjøen. Fassbender rang Tromsø again, this time
making sure he spoke to the chief, Oberleutnant Härer, with whom
he had held a reassuring meeting only two days before, and urged
him to 'make sure that fighter cover is prepared and because
Bardufoss is to provide it, keep them informed'.[32] At their subsequent court martial, both Härer and Hamschmidt denied receiving
the request.

By now the sighting of the bombers had been logged at Bardufoss.
By a stroke of fortune, the first of several for which 617 and 9
Squadrons would be forever grateful, the clerk noting the details
took down the wrong coordinates and plotted the incursion over
Hammerfest, 125 miles to the north.

Having taken these precautions, *Tirpitz*'s gunnery officers felt
reasonably secure. Then, at 7.54 a.m., another warning arrived. A
confused, and as it turned out erroneous, report from a coastal
battery suggested more aircraft were approaching from the north-
east. All over the ship alarm bells jangled and blue and yellow flags
were run up to warn that a raid was in the offing. At 8.02 the watertight doors slammed shut and the crew hurried to their action
stations. Seven minutes later, the first ominous blips began to show
up on the ship's Würzburg radar, showing aircraft seventy-five miles
to the south-east. They were succeeded by what seemed to be

another wave of bombers. Soon the lookouts could see the real thing, tiny specks against the flawless sky. Each new development was passed on to Tromsø and from there to Bardufoss. At 8.14 a.m. the alarm had finally been given at the base, setting in train another chapter of garbled orders, misunderstandings and coincidences that crippled the fighters' response.

As the crew prepared for battle, Kapitän Weber's voice echoed round the ship. 'We are expecting a heavy air attack,' he told his men over the loudspeakers, though by now that was hardly news. 'The ship's company will fulfil its duty again this time and prepare a hot reception for the bombers.' All the guns were trained towards the approaching aircraft. As they grew closer red light gleamed on the Perspex of the bombers' cockpits and some gunners believed the fighters had come to the rescue but it was only the rising sun glinting off the canopies and the Lancasters came on unmolested. There were no smoke generators to mask them from their attackers. Only their own guns could save them now. At 8.38 Weber gave the order to fire. The ship shook with the titanic jolt of the big guns and shells weighing nearly a ton each screamed out towards the uneven line of advancing bombers. It was no more than a gesture of defiance and they passed spectacularly but harmlessly underneath.

A minute later the secondary guns and the heavy 37mm flak artillery joined in. Hellendoorn and his team were stationed on the port side. They began firing their heavy guns, with the shells set to explode at different ranges to provide layered defence. Then they opened up with the 10.5cm flak. It made no impression on the attackers who came unwaveringly on. On the starboard side of the ship, Klaus Rohwedder was at his action station on the aircraft deck, manning one of the 10.5cm guns near the funnel. Through his headphones he could hear a stream of information about the distance and speed of the approaching bombers.

He did not need to be told. He had a perfect view of the attackers, streaming straight towards him. He watched a dark shape detach itself from one of the aircraft, but 'then we did not see it any more as it was travelling too fast'. He felt a 'quake' then saw a 'huge wall of water' rise from the sea and was suddenly drenched to the skin. Through the headphones the order at last came to fire. Before he engaged he felt 'a second quake and the ship almost immediately began to list'. The deck was tilting sickeningly to port. He clung to a gun mounting to stay upright, then his 'stomach was on the deck and I was hanging onto the railings'. He looked around. All his colleagues but one had disappeared. Together they pulled themselves over the railing and clung to the side of the ship.[34]

The transformation was astonishingly quick. In seven minutes the great ship had toppled onto her side. Hellendoorn remembered that during a brief lull between explosions 'there was a huge stillness'. People seemed bizarrely serene. 'Normally every sailor should have his life vest handy but I didn't see anyone with one on.' There was 'absolutely no panic.' He heard someone 'asking quite calmly if there was anyone there who couldn't swim and one chap answering, yes'. Hellendoorn was a strong swimmer and volunteered to help. 'I explained precisely that he mustn't hold on to me, I would hold on to him. But just as I was saying that the tower was hit and the chap I was talking to panicked and jumped into the water and I jumped in after him.'

When he surfaced he had to struggle through a thick blanket of oil and emerged blinded and choking. He flailed around in the freezing water, somehow locating his companion who was clinging to a piece of wood. There were others spluttering and gasping, grabbing the torpedo net to stay afloat. Hellendoorn clasped the non-swimmer to him and struck out for the shore, two hundred yards away. Eventually, streaked with oil and all but sightless, he and the man he had saved 'crawled ashore, completely exhausted'. It was a fortnight before he could see properly again.

That morning Adalbert Brünner was ashore on Haakøy with a work party building a jetty and watched the drama from the moment when the blue and yellow air raid warning flags began to flutter. 'Everything seemed to happen so quickly,' he recalled. 'The hellish roar of the flak set in but the detonations of the English bombs overwhelmed all other noise. Huge geysers of fire, water and debris covered everything and we had thrown ourselves on the beach to escape the shell splinters.' Then, 'suddenly, it was quiet – no guns, no detonations'. Out of the silence they heard a 'chorus of screams that reached all the way to the shore'. When the smoke cleared 'we could not believe our eyes. *Tirpitz* had gone. The hull stuck out of the water like a giant whale. There was nothing else.'[35] It had taken eleven minutes for the ship to turn turtle. The first bomb exploded amidships, on the port side, and the fourth, a few moments later, just abaft of it. The near misses that followed on the port side rent the hull, further increasing the list. As the ship leaned sideways, the mud and sand of the sea bed gave way beneath the keel. The climax came ten minutes after the first bomb struck. A huge explosion, probably the blast from the after magazines igniting, wrenched the Caesar turret from its mounting, flinging it through the air. *Tirpitz* toppled. Her mast and upper works slid below the surface digging into the unresisting mud and sand of the bottom, leaving her starboard side and keel naked above the water.

The flank of the ship now provided a haven for those like Klaus Rohwedder who had scrambled over the starboard rail as *Tirpitz* rolled. They slipped and skidded their way towards the rudder. Then, with no rescue boats in view and the plates heaving and lurching beneath his feet, there seemed nothing for it but to swim. Rohwedder flung off his jacket and jumped into the numbing waters, struggling through an oil slick towards a tree trunk and hauling himself onto it. 'I saw that there were many people in the water, screaming for help. There were others floating face down – the dead who were being kept afloat by the air trapped in their clothes.' He helped a comrade struggling in the water up onto the tree trunk. He could see that the torpedo nets were sagging below the water under the weight of desperate men. Rohwedder turned back for a last look at the ship. Then a trawler with German soldiers aboard was pulling him and his shipmate aboard and he was on his way to a nearby ship.[36]

The catastrophe had been so swift and violent that there was no time for an orderly evacuation. Above decks, many were killed in the storm of fire and blast. Below, the Arctic brine rushed through the great gashes torn by the near-misses, paralysing and overwhelming men as they scrabbled for ladder and hatch. Weber went down with his ship, trapped inside the armoured control room where he had gathered with his staff to direct the defence of *Tirpitz*.

Others found an at least temporary refuge in the many air pockets that formed in the upturned hull. The first rescue boat to arrive was requisitioned by Leutnant Walter Sommer who sent to Tromsø for oxyacetylene torches. Teams worked along the length of the hull, cutting through the steel wherever they detected any sign of life. In the first twenty-four hours, eighty-seven men were brought out alive, including Alfred Zuba with whose story this book begins. The work went on for two more days but no more survivors emerged. Of the 1,700 men or so on board, 971 had perished in the sinking.

From the shores of their hilly island, the people of Tromsø heard the explosions and watched the procession of dead and wounded arriving from Haakøy, with a mixture of hope and anxiety. Nine-year-old Aud Schreuder had been rushed to the cellar in her family's big white house on the heights of Tromsø, as the anti-aircraft gun the Germans had mounted in the garden began to fire. When she emerged and heard that *Tirpitz* was sunk she feared there would now be reprisals and the Germans would come for her father, who, along with her six brothers, was a member of the underground. Displays of joy were imprudent. Lars Thøring, Tromsø's town clerk, remembered that 'there was great enthusiasm ... over the successful attack and the joy manifested itself loudly which resulted in a number of arrests by the Gestapo during the day'.[37] Nonetheless, Aud could not help feeling a tremor of sympathy for the victims. 'It was a dreadful way to die,' she said.[38]

As the Germans surveyed the wreckage of their last battleship, and began burying their dead, the men who had destroyed it were heading home. One 9 Squadron Lancaster had been badly hit by flak. As it departed the target area it became clear that it would never make it home. For a few anxious minutes it was stalked by one of the Bardufoss fighters which had finally taken to the air, but it then unaccountably lost interest and they were able to make their way east to force-land in Sweden. The rest streamed towards Scotland, trying to keep themselves awake as the adrenalin ebbed and weariness flooded in. After twelve hours in the air they had a tiresome end to their journey, and winds and overcast skies meant many of them were diverted to land away from the forward base they had taken off from.

Just after three o' clock that afternoon they began to touch down. At 5 Group Headquarters, at Bomber Command, everyone was eager for news. As the details were flashed to Harris, he could not wait to pass it on to the man who would appreciate it most. That Sunday, Winston Churchill was in Paris, staying at the British Embassy. At 6.50 p.m., a member of his staff was handed a message telephoned from London asking him to relay a message to the Prime Minister. It read simply: 'Tirpitz sunk this morning'. It was signed 'Bert', the nickname by which Harris was known by his peers. Churchill instructed an assistant to telephone the Air Ministry offering 'heartiest congratulations to all'.

After years of proddings and interventions, urgings and suggestions, Churchill had finally got what he wanted. Before setting out that evening to visit the French and American headquarters he dashed off a telegram to Stalin. 'RAF bombers have sunk the Tirpitz', he informed him. 'Let us rejoice together.' The following day the Marshal replied that he was 'greatly delighted' and that 'the British airmen may legitimately pride themselves on this deed'. Roosevelt had listened frequently to Churchill's concerns about the battleship. On hearing the tidings he dispatched a message: 'The death of the Tirpitz is great news,' he said. Churchill's response carried the sound of genuine thankfulness. 'Thank you so much,' he replied. 'It is a great relief to us to get this brute where we have long wanted her.'[39]

Churchill's fascination for Tirpitz had seeped into the public consciousness. Since 1940 the ship had become steadily more notorious, a malign player among wartime's dramatis personae, symbolizing both the menace and the hubris of Hitler and the Germans. Official propaganda faithfully reported each attempt on her life. It had never been able to announce her death, and the victory was to be savoured and celebrated. On the 14th Willie Tait flew to London for a press conference and later described the attack in a broadcast on the BBC. Squadron Leader Bill Williams, who led 9 Squadron after Jim Bazin was forced to stay behind, went with him and that night was interviewed by Ed Murrow, whose radio dispatches for the CBS network reached millions in the United States and Canada. An interview with Bruce Buckham was relayed on the BBC World Service. By chance his wife Gwen was listening in Sydney when it was aired. It was the first time she had heard his voice in two years.[40] The news was splashed over that morning's papers and applauded in the editorials. 'The British people will rejoice at the valour of their airmen and at the final smashing of Hitler's sea ambitions,' exulted the *Daily Express*. In cinemas all over the free world, audiences watched the dramatic footage taken from the film unit Lancaster.

As soon as the sinking had been confirmed, telegrams started to pour into the headquarters of 617 and 9 Squadrons, beginning with the royal congratulations of King George VI who conveyed his 'hearty congratulations to all those who took part in the daring and successful attack'. He was joined by Crown Prince Olav, the heir to the Norwegian throne, exiled in Britain, who expressed the 'particular delight that we Norwegians hail the achievement of this deed'.[41] The Admiralty, who had been denied the prize themselves, praised a 'good job well done' and Barnes Wallis the 'tremendous courage and skill' with which the crews had deployed his bomb.

There were no lavish celebrations to match the enormity of the event. The first ten 617 crews who landed at Woodhall the day after the raid were greeted by a regimental band and a crowd of ground staff offering congratulations. That night, remembered Freddy Watts, they piled into the small bar at Petwood and all 'got very drunk'. It was clear now that they would not have to go back again. There was no doubt that *Tirpitz* was finished. A PRU Mosquito flight shortly after the raid showed the ship capsized to port with seven hundred feet of hull poking out of the oil-stained waters of the fjord. The RAF's interpretation unit at Medmenham compiled an approximate bomb plot from the film and photographs taken during the attack. It showed that Tait's Tallboy had been the first to hit the target. The obscuring smoke meant only sixteen bombs could be traced, and it was impossible to say with certainty who had dropped which. Though Tait's name would henceforth be linked to the operation, everyone could claim to have played a part in *Tirpitz*'s doom.

On 15 November the Air Minister, Sir Archibald Sinclair, visited Woodhall. After lunch in the officers' mess he spoke to the crews assembled in the briefing room. 'Gentlemen, we have sunk the toughest ship in the world and I'm sure in the war', he told them. 'You are now going on forty-eight hours' leave. Go home and tell your story. Your people have had a hard time in this war, a lot of troubles, losses, suffering. Thank you for all you have achieved in the sinking of *Tirpitz* and good luck to you in the hard fighting which ... lies ahead.'[42] The war was not yet won. Survival was distant and uncertain. It was the battles to come rather than recent victories that crowded their thoughts as they departed to their families, wives and girlfriends.

Epilogue

Wilhelmshaven, 12 November 2010

At eleven o'clock a small procession of old men and neat, white-haired women filed into the chapel of the Ehrenfrithof cemetery on the edge of town for a simple ceremony of readings, prayers and hymns. Afterwards they walked along a rain-soaked path, through an avenue of elm trees to lay a wreath at a granite slab set among the shrubbery. 'Schlachtschiff Tirpitz, 1.4.1939–12.11.1944' reads the legend, below an emblem of a Viking ship. Inscribed underneath are the words 'Unseren toten zum Gedanken' – in memory of our dead. It is a modest memorial to a ship that in its short life caused the world such trouble.

They stood for a while under the bare trees chatting quietly and taking photographs, before driving back to the hotel, through streets lined with the drab utilitarian shops and apartment blocks that rose in place of the old town after the RAF bombed it flat. Then the solemnity that hung over the morning's events dissolved and they sat down to a hearty lunch of meat, cabbage and potatoes, washed down with beer and schnapps. The veterans of the *Tirpitz* comrades association gather every year to meet old friends and tell old stories. For all present, their time on board seems to have been a precious experience, one to be preserved. Among them is Klaus Rohwedder, the young gunner who saw the fatal Tallboy fall. After the war he became a pacifist. 'That does not mean, though, that I have turned my back on the community we had on board or the memories that I still cherish today,' he said.

The *Tirpitz* survivors can remember their war with pride and without shame. They did their duty and defended their ship to the last. It is the Luftwaffe which gets the blame for its demise. Five weeks after the disaster, seven men went on trial at a military court in

Klaus Rohwedder at Ehrenfrithof

Oslo, accused of dereliction of duty. Major Heinrich Ehrler, the commander of Jagdegeschwader 5, was at the head of the list of defendants. He was sentenced to three years' imprisonment, but was released after a month. A loyal Nazi to the last, he died on 4 April 1945 over Berlin, reportedly ramming an American bomber after running out of ammunition.

His colleagues at Bardufoss believed Ehrler was a scapegoat in the affair. According to his adjutant, Oberleutnant Kurt Schulze, no specific orders had been issued to JW5 for the defence of *Tirpitz*, whose precise location was not even known to them. Their response had been crippled from the beginning by inaccurate plotting and poor communication.[1] The German defences were indeed chaotic. Had they been more effective, *Tirpitz* might have stood at the centre of a dramatic Allied defeat and 12 November 1944 remembered as the day when the Dambusters squadron and their comrades in 9 Squadron were annihilated.

As it was, she had already achieved much without having to fire her guns. After her move to Norway at the start of 1942 the Home Fleet was forced to manage the threat she posed to the Arctic and the Atlantic sea lanes, dedicating important resources to containing her that could have been put to much better use elsewhere. Her presence was directly responsible for one of the great failures of nerve of the Allied war – the decision to order PQ.17 to scatter. *Tirpitz* was, of course, to be feared. Had she ever got among a convoy the results would have been devastating. More appalling still was the prospect of her breaking into the Atlantic, perhaps sinking one of the transports laden with American troops which began arriving in 1942, bringing about both a military catastrophe and an Anglo-American political crisis.

The example of the *Bismarck*, though, showed that the chances of getting through to the North Atlantic undetected were slim, and the prospects of long-term survival small. Surface ships were, anyway, far less deadly to Allied shipping than aircraft and U-boats. From 1 June 1943 to 31 May 1944, warships and armed merchant raiders sank only five Allied ships. The overwhelming majority of the other 319 vessels lost to enemy action were destroyed by U-boats (216) and aircraft (64).[2] While achieving little, the big ships soaked up enormous resources. Vast quantities of scarce fuel were needed for a major operation, a consideration that weighed heavily in the question of whether or not to send them to sea. In this respect, *Tirpitz* perhaps placed almost as much of a burden on the German war effort as she did on British dispositions.

By the end of 1943, she had barely been put to aggressive use, with only an ineffective foray against PQ.12, a brief appearance during the PQ.17 disaster and the inglorious raid on Spitsbergen to her credit. After the midget submarine attacks of 22 September 1943 she was badly damaged, and put out of action for six months. A cool appreciation by her enemies might have concluded that, following the sinking of *Scharnhorst* in December 1943, *Tirpitz* was unlikely to be risked at sea again. Instead, throughout the summer of 1944 the Fleet Air Arm engaged in a series of full-scale operations against her, handing over in the autumn to the RAF. The zeal of the pursuit, whipped on by Churchill, seems excessive now, but wartime created its own dynamic. By the time of the last attack it was well understood that *Tirpitz* could no longer make any significant difference to the direction of the war. Willie Tait's characteristically cool judgement was that the feat had 'not contributed much to the Allied victory'.[3] Her death was still a cause for universal celebration. She had come to symbolize the hubris of a terrible regime. Her fate and that of Hitler seemed intertwined. Catharsis, deliverance, required that both should die.

The *Lincolnshire Echo*, whose circulation area included Woodhall Spa and Bardney, found a parable for 'the misguided German people' in 617 and 9 Squadrons' victory. 'They have been told that the *Tirpitz* was unsinkable – the RAF have proved that to be a fallacy; they have been told that Hitler was invincible, the reincarnation of the greatest virtues of the German spirit – and the [Allies] have proved that to be a fallacy also.'[4]

The conclusion of the war in Europe was still six months away. Some of those involved in the quest to destroy *Tirpitz* would make it to the end. Others would not. They included men for whom peace held bright promise. Guy Byam, the young BBC reporter who flew with the film unit Lancaster on 15 September was captured while reporting at Arnhem. He was ordered by the Germans to help collect casualties, but knocked out his guard and escaped back to the Allied lines. He was killed on a reporting mission when the American 8th Air Force bomber he was flying in was shot down during a daylight raid on Berlin on 3 February 1945, leaving behind a wife and a baby daughter.

The survivors of the X-Craft attack were released from PoW camp in May 1944. Godfrey Place returned to the navy, retraining as a pilot and flying with the Fleet Air Arm in the Korean War. He retired as a rear admiral in 1970. Don Cameron also stayed on and was about to take up an appointment at HMS *Dolphin* in Gosport, where his great adventure began, when he died suddenly in April 1961.

After the last *Tirpitz* raid, Willie Tait was taken off operations and spent the rest of the war training Canadian crews. He had flown 101 missions and earned four DSOs and two DFCs. Unlike Gibson and Cheshire he was not awarded the VC. He was recommended for one, nine days after the final attack, by Ralph Cochrane who praised 'a great leader who in danger is unperturbed and at all times pits a stubborn will against the enemy's heaviest defences.' His operational career, he went on, was 'one of prolonged and heroic endeavour continued at his own urgent request far beyond what is normal and reasonable.' The proposal was backed by Harris. According to the 617 Squadron veteran, Mick Martin, who, unbidden, delved into the matter, it was turned down by the 'political/inter-service committee for high awards'. Commenting on Tait's record, laid out in the recommendation, Martin, who was himself one of the best and bravest of Bomber Command's pilots, reckoned it 'quite magnificent – the very best of all in my opinion and the opinion of many others.'[5] No explanation emerged as to why the award was not granted. It was said in jest that the authorities did not want to give the impression that decoration came automatically with command of 617 Squadron. Tait stayed on after 1945, serving in the Middle and Far East, retiring as a group captain in 1964. He trained as a computer programmer and spent his leisure time studying the lieder of Schubert and tending his allotment. He retained his reserve to the end. Tony Iveson remembers a lunch at the RAF Club in Piccadilly to which Cochrane, Harris and the great figures of Bomber Command were invited. Tait was naturally included. Before the start Iveson received a telephone call from Tait's wife, Betty, who told him, 'he's left home but all I can say is wait outside for him'. It was, said Iveson, 'quite possible that he would get to the steps of the club and then turn back'.[6]

The exiled Norwegians returned home as heroes. Leif Larsen was showered with decorations and became the subject of several books and a film. He remained modest despite the exposure, dying aged eighty-four in 1990. Bjørn Rørholt went back to his engineering studies, before joining the Norwegian military, inventing in retirement a radar device for the blind. Torstein Raaby returned to his life as a telegrapher, sailed on the 1946 *Kon-Tiki* expedition as the raft's wireless operator and later went back to run the radio station on Jan Mayen Island. He died in 1964 on his way to join an expedition to the North Pole. Terje Jacobsen escaped to Sweden before the Gestapo closed in on him. After the war he married an Englishwoman and had a successful career as an architect. He still lives in Tromsø and now and then takes a visitor to Haakøy island. Once the war was over, a Norwegian salvage firm moved in to dismantle *Tirpitz*'s sad carcase. The work was dangerous, with unexploded ordnance everywhere, and often gruesome. Hundreds of corpses still lay trapped inside the hull. In September 1945, before they began work, Tait visited the wreck. It made a melancholy sight. 'From close-to' he wrote, it 'was huge, hideous and stank like a charnel house. There were nearly a thousand bodies still inside the flooded hull and the treacly black fuel oil still seeped out of the rents ... this rusty tomb was nothing to gloat over. It affronted the Arctic stillness of the unpolluted hills.'[7] When the salvors departed some debris remained, including the steel rings of the anti-torpedo nets, until they, too, were carted away. But even now you can still find, amid the rocks and seaweed of the peaceful shoreline, a hunk of steel, flaking and rusted through, a small memento of the folly and waste of war.

Notes

ONE

1 Taken from Alfred Zuba's account delivered to the 'Sink the *Tirpitz!*' Symposium organized by the Confederate Air Force Golden Gate Wing, 21 October 2001.

TWO

1 Letter to Ludovic Kennedy.
2 Shirer, William, *The Rise and Fall of the Third Reich*, Secker & Warburg, 1963, p. 467.
3 *The Times*, Monday, 3 April 1939.
4 Hassell, Ulrich von, *Die Hassell-Tagebücher 1938–1944: Aufzeichnungen vom Anderen Deutschland*, Siedler Verlag, pp. 87, 88–9.
5 *Daily Express*, Monday, 3 April 1939.
6 Raeder, Grand Admiral Erich, *Struggle for the Sea*, William Kimber, 1959, p. 95.
7 Evidence of Wilhelm Süchtig to Nuremberg War Tribunal, 16 May 1946.

THREE

1 Private Papers of C. T. Collett, IWM 3161.
2 Bercuson, David J., and Herwig, Holger H., *Bismarck*, Hutchinson, 2001, p. 50.
3 Ibid., p. 58.
4 Private Papers of C. T. Collett, IWM 3161.
5 Private Papers of Lieutenant G. P. Allen, IWM 1994.
6 Private Papers of Patrick Mullins, IWM 2432.
7 Harriman, W. Averell, and Abel, Elie, *Special Envoy to Churchill and Stalin*, Random House, pp. 33–4.

8 Bercuson and Herwig, op. cit., p. 241.
9 Ibid., p. 242.
10 Private Papers of Charles Friend, IWM 2751.
11 Private Papers of Lieutenant Commander J. A. Stewart-Moore, unpublished manuscript, IWM 91/291.
12 Interview with author and testimony from Moffat, John, and Rossiter, Mike, *I Sank the Bismarck*, Corgi, 2009.
13 Private Papers of A. E. Franklin, IWM 11581.
14 Bercuson and Herwig, op. cit., p. 298.

FOUR

1 Private Papers of A. F. P. Fane, IWM 7685.
2 Churchill, Winston, *The Second World War*, vol. IV, Cassell, 1951, p. 98.
3 Gilbert, Martin, *The Churchill War Papers*, vol. III, Heinemann, p. 1037.
4 Ibid., p. 1134.
5 Ibid.
6 Ibid., p. 1344.
7 Briefe von der 'Königin des Nordens', September 1941– Oktober 1942, ed. Jürgen Voigt – unpublished letters of Kurt Voigt (hereafter Voigt Letters).
8 Interview, *Schlachtschiff Tirpitz: Die Einsame Königin des Nordens*, History Films, 2006.
9 Raeder, op. cit., p. 214.
10 *Fuehrer Conferences on Naval Affairs, 1939–1945*, Greenhill Books, p. 234.
11 Roskill, Stephen, *The War at Sea*, vol. I, HMSO, 1954, p. 116.

12 Sweetman, John, *Hunting the Beast*, Sutton, 2000, p. 15.
13 Brünner, Adalbert, *Schlachtschiff Tirpitz im Einsatz. Ein Seeoffizier berichtet*, Podzun-Pallas, 1993.
14 Sweetman, op. cit., p. 16.
15 Interview with Georg Schlegel, *Schlachtschiff Tirpitz*.
16 Brünner, op. cit.
17 Interview with Georg Schlegel, *Schlachtschiff Tirpitz*.
18 Middlebrook, Martin, and Everitt, Chris, *The Bomber Command War Diaries*, Penguin, 1985, p. 165.
19 Peillard, Léonce, *Sink the Tirpitz!*, Jonathan Cape, 1968, p. 40.
20 Roskill, op. cit., vol. I, p. 159.

FIVE

1 See Woodman, Richard, *Arctic Convoys 1941–1945*, Pen and Sword, 2007, for the best account of these operations.
2 Memoir of Able Seaman William Smith DSM, The Second World War Experience Centre.
3 Quoted in Roskill, Stephen, *Churchill and the Admirals*, William Collins, 1977, p. 124.
4 *The Cunningham Papers*, ed. Michael Simpson, Publications of the Navy Records Society, 1999, vol. I, p. 169.
5 Roskill, op. cit., vol. I, p. 188.
6 PRO PREM 3/191/1.
7 PRO CAB 69.
8 Private Papers of R. P. Raikes, IWM 6349.
9 Private Papers of C. Friend, IWM 2751.
10 Wikipedia, Harrison, W. A., Fairey Albacore (Warpaint Series No. 52).
11 Roskill, *The War at Sea*, vol. II, HMSO, pp. 119–23.
12 Sweetman, op. cit., p. 28; Kennedy, Ludovic, *Menace*, Sidgwick & Jackson, 1979, p. 43.
13 IWM 2751, p. 122.
14 IWM 2751, p. 125.
15 Kennedy, op. cit., pp. 43–4.
16 Sweetman, op. cit., p. 31.
17 Kennedy, op. cit., pp. 44–5.

18 IWM 2751, p. 126.
19 Sweetman, op. cit., p. 31.
20 Roskill, *The War at Sea*, vol. II, p. 123.
21 Ibid., vol. II, p. 124.
22 Kennedy, op. cit., p. 45.
23 PRO PREM 3/191/1.

SIX

1 Webster, Sir Charles, and Frankland, Noble, *The Strategic Air Offensive Against Germany*, vol. IV, HMSO, 1961, pp. 133–4.
2 Ryder, Robert, *The Attack on St. Nazaire*, John Murray, 1947, p. 3.
3 Lt Bill Watson, quoted in Dorrian, James G., *Storming St Nazaire*, Pen and Sword, 1998, p. 37.
4 www.commandoveterans.org/history
5 Ashcroft, Michael, *Special Forces Heroes*, Headline Review, 2008, p. 56.
6 www.history of war.org
7 Ryder, op. cit., p. 80.
8 *The Daily Telegraph Book of Naval Obituaries*, Grub Street, 2005, p. 23.
9 Private Papers of W. L. Stephens, IWM 1927.
10 Private Papers of Philip Dark, IWM 3028.

SEVEN

1 Bennett, Air Vice-Marshal D. C. T., *Pathfinder*, Goodall Publications, 1988, p. 116.
2 IWM Sound Archive Recording 10310.
3 Private Papers of A. F. P. Fane, IWM 7685.
4 PRO ADM 223/87.
5 Sweetman, op. cit., p. 43.
6 Ibid.
7 PRO PREM 3/191/1.
8 Quoted in Sweetman, op. cit., p. 44.
9 IWM Sound Archive Recording 9378.
10 Interview on BBC TV, *Target Tirpitz*, director Edward Mirzoeff, presenter Ludovic Kennedy, 1973.

11 IWM Sound Archive Recording 10310.
12 IWM Sound Archive Recording 9378.
13 Interview with author.
14 IWM Sound Archive Recording 9378.

EIGHT

1 Roskill, *The War at Sea*, vol. II, p. 130.
2 Churchill, op. cit., vol. IV, p. 233.
3 Private Papers of R. P. Raikes, IWM 6349.
4 Ibid.
5 Roskill, op. cit., vol. II, p. 130.
6 Ibid.
7 Connell, Brian, *Knight Errant: A Biography of Douglas Fairbanks, Jnr*, Hodder & Stoughton, 1955, p. 106.
8 Ibid., p. 112.
9 Kennedy, op. cit., p. 71.
10 Denham, Henry, *Inside the Nazi Ring: A Naval Attaché in Sweden, 1940–1945*, John Murray, 1984, p. 90.
11 Roskill, op. cit., vol. II, p. 136.
12 Kennedy, op. cit., p. 65.
13 PRO KV2/1137.
14 Kennedy, op. cit., p. 64.
15 Kennedy, op. cit., p. 71.
16 Winn, Godfrey, *PQ.17*, Hutchinson, 1946, p. 67.
17 Ibid., p. 74.
18 Roskill, op. cit., vol. II, p. 138.

NINE

1 Interview, *Target Tirpitz*, BBC, 1973.
2 Roskill, op. cit., vol. II, p. 140.
3 Interview, *Target Tirpitz*, BBC, 1973.
4 Connell, op. cit., p. 173.
5 Merchant Navy in Second World War website.
6 Interview with author.
7 Churchill, op. cit., vol. IV, p. 236.
8 Roskill, op. cit., vol. II, p. 140.
9 Kennedy, op. cit., p. 84.
10 Winn, op. cit., p. 96.
11 Irving, David, *The Destruction of Convoy PQ.17*, St Martin's Press, New York, 1987, p. 157.

12 Interview, *Target Tirpitz*, BBC, 1973.
13 Irving, op. cit., p. 153.
14 Quoted in Kemble, Mike, The Merchant Navy in World War 2, www.secondworldwar.org
15 Churchill, op. cit., vol. IV, pp. 235–6.
16 PRO ADM 119/913.
17 Roskill, op. cit., vol. II, p. 144.
18 Kemble, op. cit.

TEN

1 PRO PREM 3/191/1.
2 Warren, C. E. T., and Benson, James, *Above Us the Waves: The Story of Midget Submarines and Human Torpedoes*, Pen and Sword, 2006, Appendix 1.
3 Davies, Robert H., *Deep Diving and Submarine Operations*, Siebe, Gorman, 1955, p. 291.
4 www.underwaterheritagetrust.org.uk
5 Peillard, op. cit., p. 119.
6 Howarth, David, *The Shetland Bus*, Shetland Times Ltd, 1998.
7 Ibid.
8 Quoted in Warren and Benson, op. cit., p. 51.
9 Ibid., p. 54.
10 Ibid., p. 56.
11 Ibid., p. 58.
12 Ibid., p. 63.
13 Ibid., p. 64.
14 Ibid., p. 68.
15 *Nuremberg Trial Proceedings*, vol. 13, 14 May 1946.
16 Peillard, op. cit., p. 166.

ELEVEN

1 Voigt Letters, 8/01/42.
2 Interview with author.
3 Herbert Ludwig, unpublished memoir.
4 Brünner, op. cit.
5 Peillard, op. cit., p. 95.
6 Voigt Letters, 8/01/42.
7 Kennedy, op. cit., p. 70.
8 Voigt Letters, 8/01/42, p. 102.
9 Ludwig, op. cit.
10 Interview with author.

11 Kennedy, op. cit., pp. 92–3.
12 PRO ADM 223/87.
13 Raeder, op. cit., p. 226.

TWELVE

1 Raeder, op. cit., pp. 226–31.
2 Peillard, op. cit., p. 174.
3 Roskill, op. cit., vol. II, p. 354.
4 Ibid., p. 299.
5 Dönitz, Karl, *Memoirs*, Weidenfeld & Nicolson, 1959, p. 300.
6 Ibid., p. 310.
7 Roskill, op. cit., vol. II, p. 354.
8 Sweetman, op. cit., p. 72.
9 Dönitz, op. cit., p. 371.
10 Ibid., pp. 310–11.
11 Ibid., p. 372.
12 Peillard, op. cit., p.180.
13 Dönitz, op. cit., p. 373.
14 Peillard, op. cit., p. 242.
15 Brünner, op. cit.
16 Roskill, op. cit., vol. II, p. 399.
17 Ibid., vol. II, pp. 397–8.
18 Ibid., vol. II, pp. 400–401.
19 Quoted in Jacobsen, Alf R., *X-Craft Versus Tirpitz: The Mystery of the Missing X5*, Sutton Publishing, 2006, p. 113.
20 Dönitz, op. cit., p. 374.
21 Private Papers of E. C. Dabner, IWM 3886.
22 Brünner, op. cit., p. 6.

THIRTEEN

1 PRO PR PREM 3/19/1.
2 PRO PREM 3/191/1, Pound to Churchill, 15.4.43.
3 PRO PREM 3/191/1, Churchill to Cherwell, 1.5.43.
4 PRO PREM 3/191/1, Churchill to Pound, 5.5.43.
5 IWM Sound Archive 28642.
6 Interview with author.
7 IWM Sound Archive 13422.
8 Interview with author.
9 Interview with author.
10 Interview with author.
11 Interview with author.
12 Warren and Benson, op. cit., p. 47.
13 Interview with author.

14 Shean, Max, *Corvette and Submarine*, Claremont, WA, 1994, p. 126.
15 Peillard, op. cit., p. 85.
16 Shean, op. cit., p. 134.
17 Interview with author.
18 IWM Sound Archive 28642.
19 Shean, op. cit., p. 136.
20 Gallagher, Thomas, *Against All Odds*, Macdonald, 1971, p. 50.
21 IWM Sound Archive 28642.
22 Shean, op. cit., p. 154.
23 IWM Sound Archive 28642.
24 Interview with author.
25 IWM Sound Archive 13422.
26 Shean, op. cit., p. 157.
27 Gallagher, op. cit., p. 51.
28 Interview with author.
29 Gallagher, op. cit., pp. 33–5.
30 Quoted in Jacobsen, op. cit., p. 108.
31 www.yorkshiredivers.com
32 IWM Sound Archive 13422.
33 Shean, op. cit., p.169.
34 Quoted in Peillard, op. cit., p. 193. Authenticated by Eve Compton-Hall (Cameron's widow).

FOURTEEN

1 IWM Sound Archive 02440.
2 Shean, op. cit., p. 170.
3 Quoted in Gallagher, op. cit., p. 79.
4 Quoted in Jacobsen, op. cit., p. 127.
5 Gallagher, op. cit., p. 81, authenticated by Eve Compton-Hall.
6 Peillard, op. cit., p. 217.
7 Interview with author.
8 Quoted in Gallagher, op. cit., p. 83.

FIFTEEN

1 Peillard, op. cit., p. 224.
2 PRO ADM 1/20026.
3 PRO ADM 1/20026.
4 IWM Sound Archive 2441.
5 *Tirpitz: Kriegstagebuch* [hereafter *KTB*], p. 233.
6 Peillard, op. cit., p. 251.
7 *KTB*, p. 204.
8 Gallagher, op. cit., p. 125.

9 Interview with author.
10 Quoted in Jacobsen, op. cit., p. 161.
11 Obituary, *The Times*, 9 February 2006.
12 Interview with author.
13 Gallagher, op. cit., p. 141.
14 Interview with author.
15 *KTB*, p. 205.
16 Interview with author.
17 Until long after the war Henty-Creer's family clung to the belief that he had suceeded in dropping *X-5*'s mines under *Tirpitz* and campaigned for the award of a VC. In 2011 a Royal Norwegian Navy ordnance disposal team working in Kaafjord destroyed a device which may have been one of *X-5*'s side charges.
18 Quoted in Peillard, op. cit., p. 255.
19 Interview with author.
20 *KTB*, p. 99.
21 Ibid., p. 237.
22 *Fuehrer Conferences on Naval Affairs, 1939–1945*, p. 381.

SIXTEEN

1 Churchill, op. cit., vol. V, p. 233.
2 Quoted in Brodhurst, Robin, *Churchill's Anchor*, Leo Cooper, 2000, p. 1.
3 Quoted in Churchill, op cit., vol. V, p. 118.
4 Ibid., p. 237.
5 Loewenheim, Francis L., Langley Harold D., and Jonas, Manfred, eds, *Roosevelt and Churchill: Their Secret Wartime Correspondence*, Barrie & Jenkins, 1975, p. 380.
6 Churchill, op. cit., vol. V, p. 239.
7 Ibid., p. 244.
8 Jacobsen, op. cit., p. 182.
9 Golovko, Admiral Arseni, *With the Red Fleet*, trans. Peter Broomfield, Putnam, 1965, pp. 180–81.
10 Roskill, op. cit., vol. III, p. 78.
11 www.admirals.org.uk
12 Interview with author.
13 Quoted in Woodman, op. cit., p. 256.
14 Interview with author.

15 Dönitz, op. cit., pp. 375–6.
16 PRO ADM 1/20026.
17 Dönitz, op. cit., pp. 381–5.
18 Woodman, op. cit., p. 372.
19 Interview with author.
20 Roskill, *The War at Sea*, vol. III, part 1, p. 88.
21 Dönitz, op. cit., pp. 383–4.

SEVENTEEN

1 Brünner, op. cit.
2 Interview with author.
3 Sweetman, op. cit., p. 83.
4 Woodman, op. cit., p. 385.
5 PRO PREM 3/191/1.
6 AIR 2/8394.
7 PRO ADM 205/56.
8 PRO ADM 205/43.
9 *Cunningham Papers*, vol. II, p. 234.
10 IWM Sound Archive 31043.
11 PRO ADM 199/941.
12 Ibid.
13 IWM Sound Recording 2507.
14 PRO ADM 199/941.
15 IWM Sound Recording 2508.
16 Quoted in Sweetman, op. cit., p. 92.
17 Interview with author.
18 All details drawn from reports in PRO ADM 199/941, the Admiralty report on the operation, unless otherwise stated.
19 Brünner, op. cit.
20 *Cunningham Papers*, vol. II, p. 233.
21 IWM Sound Recording 28775.
22 Quoted in Sweetman, op. cit., p. 122.
23 *KTB*, 25/08/44.

EIGHTEEN

1 Interview with author.
2 AIR 14/1971.
3 Quoted in Sweetman, op. cit., p. 128.
4 Ibid.
5 Dönitz, op. cit., pp. 385–6.
6 AIR 14/1971.
7 Harris, Sir Arthur, *Bomber Offensive*, Pen and Sword, 2005, p. 255.
8 Morpurgo, J. E., *Barnes Wallis*, Longman, 1972, p. xv.

9   Quoted in ibid., p. 283.
10 Interview, *Target Tirpitz*, 1973.
11 Address at memorial service, St Clement Danes, London, 21 November 2007.
12 Private Papers of J. B. Tait.
13 Interview with author.
14 IWM Sound Recording 9208.
15 Edith Stowe, quoted in Morris, Richard, *Cheshire: The Biography of Leonard Cheshire VC*, Viking, 2000.
16 Private Papers of J. B. Tait.
17 Ibid.
18 Quoted in Morris, op. cit., p. 99.
19 Interview with author.
20 Interview with author.
21 Iveson DFC, Squadron Leader Tony, and Milton, Brian, *Lancaster: The Biography*, André Deutsch, 2009, p. 189.
22 AIR 14/1971.
23 Ibid.
24 Iveson and Milton, op. cit., p. 187.
25 AIR 20/6187.
26 AIR 14/1971.
27 BBC Archives, Caversham.
28 AIR 20/617.
29 IWM Sound Recording 2509.
30 AIR 20/6187.
31 IWM Sound Recording 2509.
32 IWM Sound Recording 2510.
33 AIR 20/6187.

NINETEEN

1   Interview with Georg Schlegel, *Schlachtschiff Tirpitz*.
2   Brünner, op. cit.
3   Dönitz, op. cit., p 386.
4   Quoted in Sweetman, op. cit., p.181.
5   Brünner, op. cit.
6   Quoted in Jacobsen, op. cit., p. 228.
7   PRO ADM 223/87.
8   Ibid.
9   IWM Sound Recording 11592.
10 Harris, op. cit., p. 256.
11 PRO PREM 3/191/1.
12 Ibid.
13 Iveson and Milton, op. cit., p. 193.

14 AIR 20/6187.
15 Interview with author.
16 Ibid.
17 AIR 14/1903.
18 Interview with author.
19 Ibid.
20 Ibid.
21 AIR 27/2129.
22 AIR 20/6187.
23 Interview with author.
24 IWM Sound Archive 2519.
25 Interview with author.
26 IWM Sound Archive 21029.
27 See www.liveleak.com, 'RAF Bombers sink the *Tirpitz*'.
28 AIR 27/2129.
29 AIR 27/128.
30 Ibid.
31 IWM Sound Archive 2518.
32 Quoted in Jacobsen, op. cit., p. 240.
33 Military Court Proceedings of 17, 18 and 20 December 1944 Arising out of the Loss of the Battleship *Tirpitz*.
34 Interview with author.
35 Brünner, op. cit.
36 Interview with author.
37 The Sinking of the Tirpitz, Report of an Eye Witness.
38 Interview with author.
39 PRO PREM 191/1.
40 Bruce Buckham obituary, *Sydney Morning Herald*, 17 August 2011.
41 AIR 27/2129.
42 Quoted in Cooper, Alan W., *Beyond the Dams to the Tirpitz*, Goodall Publications, 1991, p. 123.

EPILOGUE

1   Iveson and Milton, op. cit., pp. 198–202.
2   Roskill, *The War at Sea*, vol. III, part 1, p. 388.
3   Private Papers of J. B. Tait.
4   *Lincolnshire Echo*, 14 November 1944.
5   Private Papers of J. B. Tait.
6   Interview with author.
7   Private Papers of J. B. Tait.

Acknowledgements

The *Tirpitz* story took me into new territory historically and geographically and I am grateful to those who helped me to explore it. As the years pass, the number of participants dwindles. It has been a great pleasure to meet some of those who remain and to hear their extraordinary stories. To them, a heartfelt thank you for the privilege. In Norway I would also like to thank Karen Sofie Aanjesen, Einar Ianssen, Terje Jacobsen and Aud Schreuder. My friend Nina Watts was the perfect guide and companion. In Germany I am particularly grateful to Kurt-Jürgen Voigt for allowing me access to his father's letters and to Hein Hellendoorn and Klaus Rohwedder and the members of the *Tirpitz* comrades association for making me so welcome at their annual gathering. In Britain I was given every assistance by the Imperial War Museum – especially Edgar Aromin of the sound archive – the Public Records Office, with special thanks to William Spencer, all the staff at the Churchill Centre in Cambridge and Jeff Walden at the BBC Written Archives Centre in Caversham. I must also record the debt I owe to earlier historians of the *Tirpitz* saga, notably James Benson, Alan Cooper, James G. Dorrian, Thomas Gallagher, Alf R. Jacobsen, Ludovic Kennedy, Léonce Peillard, John Sweetman, C.E.T. Warren and Richard Woodman.

The official historian of 617 Squadron Rob Owen was generous with his time and a source of much food for thought. Ian Weatherhead kindly lent me documents relating to the service of his father Wing Commander Trenham Weatherhead at RAF Medmenham and Ken Lowden provided valuable material on the war in Norway. Thanks too for the hospitality and help of Ian Cameron, Vernon Coles and his daughter Jane, Eve Compton-Hall, Dave Graham, Bridget Lorimer and Squadron Leader Ian Smith. I was greatly assisted with the research on the German aspect of the story by my former colleague and fellow foreign correspondent Robin Gedye, and Geli von Hase. Arnt Sundstol read the manuscript with a Norwegian eye and saved me from many *bêtises*. Rear Admiral Nick Wilkinson kindly did the same from a nautical perspective and corrected a crop of landlubberly errors. For those that remain, *mea culpa* …

I owe a particular debt to Peter Tait and Irene Bridgmont for their help in my researches into the career of their remarkable father. I would like to pay tribute to the superb professionalism of the HarperCollins team in producing a handsome book, and in particular the editing of Arabella Pike and Kerry Enzor. As always, Helen Ellis was a source of cheer and encouragement. To Henrietta and Honor, once again, a thousand thanks for your patience, support and fortitude.

Index